FAMILIA CAESARIS

A SOCIAL STUDY
OF THE EMPEROR'S FREEDMEN
AND SLAVES

FAMILIA CAESARIS

A SOCIAL STUDY OF
THE EMPEROR'S FREEDMEN
AND SLAVES

P. R. C. WEAVER

Professor of Classics
University of Tasmania

CAMBRIDGE
AT THE UNIVERSITY PRESS
1972

CAMBRIDGE UNIVERSITY PRESS
Cambridge, New York, Melbourne, Madrid, Cape Town, Singapore, São Paulo

Cambridge University Press
The Edinburgh Building, Cambridge CB2 8RU, UK

Published in the United States of America by Cambridge University Press, New York

www.cambridge.org
Information on this title: www.cambridge.org/9780521083409

© Cambridge University Press 1972

This publication is in copyright. Subject to statutory exception
and to the provisions of relevant collective licensing agreements,
no reproduction of any part may take place without the written
permission of Cambridge University Press.

First published 1972
This digitally printed version 2008

A catalogue record for this publication is available from the British Library

Library of Congress Catalogue Card Number: 76-171686

ISBN 978-0-521-08340-9 hardback
ISBN 978-0-521-07016-4 paperback

MEMORIAE
A.H.M.JONES

CONTENTS

Preface	page	ix
Abbreviations		xi
INTRODUCTION		1
PART I: NOMENCLATURE AND CHRONOLOGY		15
1 Dated inscriptions		20
2 Nomina and praenomina		24
Earlier chronological limits		24
Later chronological limits		30
Irregular *nomina* of Imperial freedmen		35
Omission of *nomen*		37
Abbreviation of *nomen*		40
3 Status indication		42
Extended form of status nomenclature		43
'Caesaris' and 'Augusti' in the status indication		48
'N(ostri)' in the status indication		54
'Augustorum libertus/servus'. Slaves and freedmen of the Augustae		58
Abbreviation of the status indication		72
Position of the status indication		76
Regional variation in status nomenclature		78
Omission of status indication		80
4 Cognomina and agnomina		87
Cognomina		87
Agnomina		90
PART II: THE FAMILY CIRCLE		93
5 Age at manumission		97
6 Age at marriage		105
7 Status of wives		112
Wives of Imperial slaves		112
Wives of Imperial freedmen		122

Contents

8	Status of children	page 137
	Children of *Caesaris servi*	137
	Children of *Augusti liberti*	148
9	The Senatusconsultum Claudianum and the Familia Caesaris	162
10	Women in the Familia Caesaris	170
11	The marriage pattern of slaves and freedmen outside the Familia Caesaris	179

PART III: THE EMPEROR'S SERVICE — 197

12	Vicarii	200
13	Liberti servus and liberti libertus	207
14	'Vicariani'	212
15	The occupational hierarchy: some points of method	224
16	Sub-clerical grades	227
17	Adiutores: junior clerical grades	231
18	Intermediate clerical grades	241
19	Senior clerical grades	244
20	Senior administrative grades: *a rationibus, ab epistulis*, etc.	259
21	Freedman procurators	267
22	Imperial freedmen and equestrian status: the father of Claudius Etruscus	282

CONCLUSION — 295

APPENDIXES — 297

I	'Familia Caesaris'	299
II	Inscriptions of Imperial freedmen and slaves dated to a particular year or reign	301
III	Wives of Imperial freedmen and slaves	307

Bibliography — 313

Index — 319

PREFACE

The origin of this work was a footnote in an article by Professor A. H. M. Jones on the Roman Civil Service. Since 1955 the footnote has grown into a book and beyond, largely because neither he, as I suspect, nor I certainly, envisaged that the evidence would present itself in quite such formidable quantities or pose such challenging problems of interpretation and presentation. These factors also made necessary a long series of preliminary studies, which in turn have contributed to the long delay in putting this book into definitive form. The nature of the material and of the writing is intractable, and it has become increasingly clear to me that time and effort will not bring much improvement. Hence I have thought it better to present the subject all together as it appears to me now rather than to pursue an unattainable perfection at the cost of an indefinite delay.

This is also an appropriate moment for stocktaking. Until quite recently the Familia Caesaris was an almost totally neglected field, despite its obvious importance for early Imperial social and administrative history, as well as for onomastics. But in the last few years two major studies in particular have appeared by G. Boulvert and H. Chantraine. I have taken this opportunity to point out the areas where progress and agreement can be recorded and where the main problems still lie.

I have deferred to advice consistently offered by those best qualified to judge and have given the concordances to *CIL* with Dessau's *ILS* and the other main epigraphical collections. In many instances, however, the current epigraphical conventions produce unnecessary complications, e.g. III 431 = 7116 = 13674 = D 1449 or VI 8655 a = XIV 4120.3 = XV 7142 = D 1702 or even X 6638 = I^2 pp. 247 f. No. xvii = *I. It.* XIII 1, pp. 320 f. No. 31; not to mention the Greek inscriptions from the eastern provinces. I remain to be fully convinced that this practice is justified in terms of practical value when measured against the potential source of error it introduces, the increased costs of publication and the considerable expenditure of time and mental energy that it entails in a work of this sort. A standard, readily accessible, complete set of epigraphical concordances to which reference could easily be made, e.g. for *ILS*, by a simple symbol added to the basic *CIL* reference, would seem to be a modest desideratum.

Preface

My grateful acknowledgements are due to King's College, Cambridge, for the award of the Augustus Austen Leigh Studentship which enabled me to begin, and for much subsequent hospitality; to the University of Western Australia for an extended period of leave in 1962-4 which enabled me to continue; to the Australian Research Grants Committee and to the University of Tasmania for generous research grants and a period of study-leave in 1970 which enabled me at last to finish. To the Council of the Society for the Promotion of Roman Studies and to the editors of *Classical Quarterly*, *Historia*, and *Proceedings of the Cambridge Philological Society* I am indebted for permission to incorporate in Parts I and III of this book revised versions of articles which originally appeared in their journals. My thanks are also due to many friends and colleagues, especially in the Universities of Cambridge, Western Australia and Tasmania, for much helpful discussion. In particular I should mention Dr A. H. McDonald and the late Sir Frank Adcock for help in the choice of a topic, Miss J. M. Reynolds and J. A. Crook for expert advice unfailingly given, and Professor Moses Finley, who took an unusually keen and stimulating interest in *Familia Caesaris* from the beginning, for making my several returns to Cambridge so pleasant and profitable. My greatest debt, however, is due to the late Professor A. H. M. Jones for his guidance, criticism, deep scholarship and warm friendship. His sudden death has meant the loss of one of the greatest of ancient historians. It is as a personal token of piety and appreciation that I dedicate this volume to his memory.

P.R.C.W.

University of Tasmania
Hobart, Tasmania
December 1971

ABBREVIATIONS

For periodicals, the system of abbreviations used in *L'Année Philologique* is generally followed, with some slight modifications (e.g. *Class. Phil.* for *CPh*) for reasons of clarity. Where short titles are used in footnotes, the Bibliography should be consulted for full details. For inscriptions, Roman capital numerals (I, II, III, IV, V, VI, etc.) refer to volumes of the *Corpus Inscriptionum Latinarum*.

AE	*Année épigraphique.*
BGU	*Aegyptische Urkunden aus den staatlichen Museen zu Berlin. Griechische Urkunden.* 1895–1937.
Bömer	F. Bömer, *Untersuchungen über die Religion der Sklaven in Griechenland und Rom*, Vol. I. Mainz, 1957.
Boulvert, *EAI*	G. Boulvert, *Esclaves et Affranchis Impériaux sous le Haut-Empire romain.* Naples, 1970.
Boulvert, II	Volume II of the original polycopied edition (not included in *EAI* above). Aix-en-Provence, 1965.
Bruzza	L. Bruzza, 'Iscrizioni dei Marmi Grezzi', *Ann. dell'Instituto di Corrisp. Archeol.* 42 (1870), 160–204.
Bull. Com.	*Bullettino della commissione archeologica comunale di Roma.*
CAH	*Cambridge Ancient History.*
Chantraine	H. Chantraine, *Freigelassene und Sklaven im Dienst der römischen Kaiser: Studien zu ihrer Nomenklatur.* Wiesbaden, 1967.
Chrest.	L. Mitteis and U. Wilcken, *Grundzüge und Chrestomathie der Papyruskunde*, Vol. I. 2. Leipzig, 1912; repr. 1963.
CIG	*Corpus Inscriptionum Graecarum.* 1825–77.
CIL	*Corpus Inscriptionum Latinarum.* 1863–.
D	H. Dessau, *Inscriptiones Latinae Selectae.* 1892–1916.
Diz. Epig.	E. de Ruggiero, *Dizionario epigrafico di Antichità romane.* 1895–.
D–S	C. Daremberg and E. Saglio, *Dictionnaire des antiquités grecques et romaines.* 1877–1912.
EE	*Ephemeris epigraphica.* 1872–1913.
Epigr.	*Epigraphica.* Rivista italiana di epigrafia. Milan.
FIRA	*Fontes Iuris Romani Anteiustiniani*, ed. S. Riccobono, etc. 1941–3.
Gordon, *Alb.*	A. E. and J. S. Gordon, *Album of Dated Latin Inscriptions, Rome and the Neighborhood.* 1958–65.
Hirschfeld, *Verwalt.*	O. Hirschfeld, *Die kaiserlichen Verwaltungsbeamten bis auf Diocletian* (2nd ed.). Berlin, 1905.
Hoffiller–Saria	V. Hoffiller and B. Saria, *Antike Inschriften aus Jugoslavien.* 1938.

Abbreviations

IG	*Inscriptiones Graecae.* 1873–.
IGR	*Inscriptiones Graecae ad res Romanas pertinentes*, ed. R. Cagnat, etc. 1911–27.
I. It.	*Inscriptiones Italiae.* 1936–.
ILAlg.	*Inscriptions latines de l'Algérie*, ed. S. Gsell and H.-G. Pflaum. 1922 and 1957.
ILGall.	*Inscriptions latines de la Gaule Narbonnaise*, ed. E. Espérandieu. 1929.
ILS	*Inscriptiones Latinae Selectae*, ed. H. Dessau. 1892–1916.
ILTun.	*Inscriptions latines de la Tunisie*, ed. A. Merlin. 1944.
IPO	*Inscriptions du Port d'Ostie*, ed. H. Thylander. 1951–2.
IRT	*Inscriptions of Roman Tripolitania*, ed. J. M. Reynolds and J. B. Ward Perkins. 1952.
IRT Suppl.	'Inscriptions of Roman Tripolitania: a Supplement', J. Reynolds, *PBSR* 23 (1955), 124–47.
Jones, LRE	A. H. M. Jones, *The Later Roman Empire 284–602.* Oxford, 1964.
Jones, Studies	A. H. M. Jones, *Studies in Roman Government and Law.* Oxford, 1960.
LBW	P. Le Bas and W. H. Waddington, *Voyage archéologique en Grèce et en Asie Mineure*, III: *Inscriptions grecques et latines.* Paris, 1870.
MAMA	*Monumenta Asiae Minoris Antiqua.* 1928–62.
NS	*Notizie degli Scavi di Antichità.*
OCD	*Oxford Classical Dictionary.*
OGI	*Orientis Graeci inscriptiones selectae*, ed. W. Dittenberger. 1903–5.
Pflaum, CP	H.-G. Pflaum, *Les Carrières procuratoriennes équestres sous le Haut-Empire romain.* Paris, 1960–1.
Pflaum, Proc. Equest.	H.-G. Pflaum, *Les Procurateurs équestres sous le Haut-Empire romain.* Paris, 1950.
PIR[1]	*Prosopographia Imperii Romani saec. I, II, III*, ed. E. Klebs, H. Dessau, P. von Rohden. 1896–8.
PIR[2]	*Prosopographia Imperii Romani saec. I, II, III*, ed. E. Groag, A. Stein. 1933–.
P-W	Pauly–Wissowa, *Real-Encyclopädie der classischen Altertumswissenschaft.* 1893–.
Ramsay, RP	W. M. Ramsay, *The Social Basis of Roman Power in Asia Minor.* Aberdeen, 1941.
RIB	*Roman Inscriptions of Britain*, I: *Inscriptions on Stone*, ed. R. G. Collingwood and R. P. Wright, 1965.
Rostovtzeff, SEHRE[2]	M. Rostovtzeff, *The Social and Economic History of the Roman Empire.* Oxford, 1957.
SEG	*Supplementum Epigraphicum Graecum.* 1923–.
TAM	*Tituli Asiae Minoris.* 1901–.
Taylor	L. R. Taylor, 'Freedmen and Freeborn in the Epitaphs of Imperial Rome', *AJPh* 82 (1961), 113–32.
Thylander, Étude	H. Thylander, *Étude sur l'Épigraphie latine.* Lund, 1952.
TLL	*Thesaurus Linguae Latinae.* 1900–.
Vermas.	M. J. Vermaseren, *Corpus Inscriptionum et Monumentorum religionis Mithriacae.* The Hague, 1956–60.

INTRODUCTION

In the study of social structure in the Roman world of the first and second centuries AD nothing is more important or more complex than the slave and freed slave classes. Their numbers, although not absolutely determinable, were large and even predominant in many urban and some rural areas. Most urban slaves of average intelligence and application had a reasonable expectation of early manumission and often of continued association with their patron. They enjoyed a high rate of social advancement, which was often much greater than that of the freeborn proletariate. The fundamental social legislation of Augustus attempted to provide a stable social hierarchy based on legal status. But, at the same time, there was in the early Imperial period a degree of social mobility sufficient to prevent the structure breaking down in violence and social discontent. Among the mobile sections of society the slave-born classes played a significant role.

But the status ladder within these classes themselves is both long and complex. From the point of view of juridical status, there is not only the fundamental distinction between slaves (*servi*) who are without rights, and freed slaves or freedmen (*liberti*) who are citizens, but there are also further distinctions within each of these classes – formally manumitted freedmen with full citizenship, informally manumitted freedmen (*Latini Iuniani*) who did not acquire Roman citizenship, but only Latin status without full political rights, and *dediticii* who could never become Roman citizens. Among the slaves there were those whose masters were free and those whose masters were themselves slaves (*servi vicarii*). From the point of view of social or occupational status the differences are even greater, depending on the status of the master or patron. They range from the freedmen and slaves of the emperor himself and of other wealthy *nobiles*, all the way to the penal slaves in the mines. The owners of slaves were typically not only freeborn citizens, especially the members of the senatorial and equestrian orders, but also many freedmen and slaves themselves. It is important, therefore, for any deeper analysis of the social structure of the early Empire to distinguish between the different status-groups of the slave-born classes in general, in order to isolate, if possible, those elements of exceptionally high status and mobility which were an example and incentive to the rest. The most important of these in

Introduction

the early Empire were the slaves and freedmen of the emperor, the Familia Caesaris.

The Familia Caesaris was intrinsically important because the master and patron of its members was the emperor himself. This alone was sufficient to accord them high status in slave-born society. The Familia Caesaris is also important to us because of its continuity – its development can be studied in detail over a long period extending from the time of Augustus to the early third century, when the epigraphical evidence ceases. Each succeeding emperor inherited the ownership and patronal rights over the slaves and freedmen of his predecessor. As a general rule, a continuity was maintained between one reign and the next in the personnel of the domestic Palace service and especially in the Imperial administration properly so-called. The careers of individual freedmen can frequently be traced without interruption through the reign, or even several reigns, following that of the manumitting emperor. The longest career was that of the father of Claudius Etruscus[1] which began under Tiberius and ended under Domitian, but there were many like Graptus who in AD 58 had been familiar with the Palace since the days of Tiberius,[2] and C. Iulius Aug. l. Samius, freed by Gaius, who held a procuratorial post under both Claudius and Nero.[3] The bulk of the Imperial civil service was made up of those who were below equestrian rank and who were almost entirely the emperor's freedmen and slaves. The administrative and social history of these levels of the civil service is of particular interest and importance, but has nevertheless been grievously neglected.

From the methodological point of view also, the Familia Caesaris is a particularly suitable group for such a study. By contrast with most other groups in the sub-equestrian levels of society, the individual slaves and freedmen who comprised the emperor's *familia* can be positively identified. Equally important, they can mostly be readily dated. In the chronological and status wilderness of the sepulchral inscriptions these two advantages together are almost unique; and the scale on which they occur is certainly unparalleled.

To the single personal name, which was the only name a slave possessed in normal circumstances, the emperor's slaves added the distinctive mark of status 'Caes(aris) ser(vus)' or 'Aug(usti) vern(a)', or simply 'Aug(usti)' or 'Caes(aris)'. The emperor's freedmen, in addition to the usual *tria nomina* of a Roman citizen (*praenomen, nomen* (*gentilicium*) and *cognomen*), took the status indication 'Aug(usti) lib(ertus)' or 'Aug(usti) l(ibertus)'. This they displayed with pride as a status symbol even in the period beginning with the first century AD when the freedmen of private citizens were ceasing to use any

[1] PIR^2, C 763: and especially Statius, *Silvae* iii. 3. See Part III, below, pp. 284 f.
[2] Tacitus, *Ann.* xiii. 47; PIR^1, G 140.   [3] XIV 3644 = D 1942.

2

Introduction

form of freedman indication at all.[1] Imperial freedmen would thus appear as, e.g., Ti. Claudius Aug. l. Onesimus, T. Flavius Aug. lib. Onesimus, M. Ulpius Aug. lib. Onesimus, etc., in each case deriving their *praenomen* and *nomen* from the emperor who manumitted them: e.g. 'Ti. Claudius' from Claudius or Nero, 'T. Flavius' from Vespasian, Titus or Domitian, 'M. Ulpius' from Trajan, and so on. In many cases they omitted their *praenomen* and *nomen* and would appear with *cognomen* (personal name) and status indication only, e.g. Onesimus Aug. lib., still positively identified as a freedman of an emperor.

The criteria for dating the inscriptions of these Imperial freedmen and slaves are more complex and, indeed, have advanced considerably in sophistication as a result of recent studies.[2] But the basic chronological framework is derived from the *nomina gentilicia* of the freedmen which occur in the majority of their inscriptions: Iulius, Claudius, Flavius, Ulpius, Aelius, Aurelius, Septimius, and some associated with other non-reigning members of the Imperial family. These Imperial *nomina* when used in conjunction with the Imperial freedman status indication establish positive chronological limits for a very large number of inscriptions, and can be used in turn to establish secondary chronological criteria based, for example, on the form of the status indication for both Imperial freedmen and slaves.

Thirdly, the Imperial slaves and freedmen who can be thus identified and dated are sufficiently numerous to permit a quasi-statistical treatment of the wealth of data which their inscriptions afford – over four thousand individuals in all are recorded.[3]

From the social point of view, however, the Familia Caesaris was far from homogeneous. It comprised in the first instance the slaves that belonged to or came into the possession of successive emperors either as personal property by family inheritance, private bequest, gift or by purchase, or as part of the

[1] L. R. Taylor, 'Freedmen and Freeborn in the Epitaphs of Imperial Rome', *AJPh* 82 (1961), 113 f.
[2] Cf. H. Chantraine, *Freigelassene und Sklaven im Dienst der römischen Kaiser* (Wiesbaden, 1967); and see Part 1 below.
[3] Statistics in the full sense that will satisfy the mathematical purist are not to be looked for in ancient studies. We have no means of determining the *proportion* of Imperial freedmen and slaves of the Familia Caesaris whose names have survived in any given period, nor can we even be sure that the proportion is the same for different periods, e.g. for the Julian (early first century), Flavian (late first century) or Aurelian (late second century–early third century) periods. The results will depend mainly on the nature of the question under consideration. Despite the pessimistic warnings of F. G. Maier, 'Römische Bevölkerungsgeschichte und Inschriftenstatistik', *Historia* 2 (1954), 318–51, about the use of statistics in ancient demographic and social studies, the attempt should be made where feasible, as with the Familia Caesaris, and not abandoned on *a priori* grounds. For some of the kinds of problems involved in this area and the results to be expected, see M. K. Hopkins, 'The Age of Roman Girls at Marriage', *Population Studies* 18 (1965), 309–27; and 'On the Probable Age Structure of the Roman Population', *Population Studies* 20 (1966), 245–64 (with numerous further references); and for freedmen, Taylor, 113–32.

Introduction

patrimonium which passed from each emperor to his successor by virtue of his official position, irrespective of family connections. The basic relationship between the ordinary *Caesaris servus* and the emperor, while it was essentially the legal one between master and slave,[1] was complicated by the great size and geographical diffusion of the Familia Caesaris throughout the empire. Hence the multiplicity of opportunities for professional and social advancement, and corresponding differentiation between the successful and the unsuccessful.

In the second place, the Familia Caesaris included those ex-slaves who had been manumitted by an emperor either during his lifetime or after his death by testament. The relationship here between *Augusti libertus* and emperor was that of *clientela*, in its formal obligatory aspect, with the rights and obligations which this would confer on both *libertus* and *patronus*.[2] Among the Imperial freedmen there are marked differences of social status, which largely depend, as with the slaves, on the particular branch of the emperor's service to which they belonged and on the professional grade and rate of advancement achieved within that service. Hence in addition to the legal categories it is necessary to describe the Familia Caesaris from the point of view of the functions of the slaves and freedmen who comprised its services.

The traditional division of any large *familia* into the *familia urbana* (slaves attached to the household of their master in the city), and *familia rustica* (slaves working on the rural estates of their master) is not appropriate for the Familia Caesaris.[3] On the domestic side, one might equate the Palace management and staff in Rome with the *familia urbana*. On the other hand, the management and staff of the patrimonial estates and other property throughout the empire, in so far as freedmen and slaves with Imperial status

---

[1] For all legal aspects of Roman slavery see the full treatment of W. W. Buckland, *The Roman Law of Slavery* (Cambridge, 1908), and M. Kaser, *Das Römische Privatrecht*, 2 vols. (Munich, 1955). See also the useful *Encyclopedic Dictionary of Roman Law* (Philadelphia, 1953) by A. Berger. The bibliography of Roman slavery in general is very extensive: cf. R. H. Barrow, *Slavery in the Roman Empire* (London, 1928), W. L. Westermann, *The Slave Systems of Greek and Roman Antiquity* (Philadelphia, 1955) and the works there cited. Also see the Bibliographical Essay in *Slavery in Classical Antiquity: Views and Controversies*, ed. M. I. Finley (Cambridge, 1960), pp. 229–35.

[2] On *liberti* the best general treatments are: Vitucci, *Diz. Epig.* IV (1958), 905 f., and A. M. Duff, *Freedmen in the Early Roman Empire* (Oxford, 1928, repr. Heffer 1958); Lécrivain in D–S III, 1200 f. is sometimes useful. I have not seen C. Cosentini, *Studi sui liberti* (Catania, I 1948; II 1950). On legal relations between patron and freedmen: *Dig.* xxxvii. 14 (de iure patronatus); ib. 15 (de obsequiis parentibus et patronis praestandis); xxxviii. 1 (de operis libertorum). Kaser, *ZSS* 58 (1938), 88 f., *Röm. Privatrecht*, I, 103 f., 256 f. Duff, *Freedmen*, pp. 36 f. On *clientes*: A. von Premerstein, P–W IV, 23 f. Th. Mommsen, *Römische Forschungen*, I (Berlin, 1864), 255 f.; *Römische Staatsrecht*, III (3rd ed. Leipzig, 1887–8, repr. Basle, 1952), 54 f.

[3] *Dig.* l. 16.166 (Pomponius): 'urbana familia et rustica non loco sed genere distinguitur'; cf. *CIL* VI 1747; VIII 5704; IX 825, 3028 = D 7367; XII 1025; and Bömer, I, 440 f. For a full list of occupations illustrating the division of labour, see Marquardt, *Privatleben der Römer*, I (2nd ed. Leipzig, 1879), 137 f. – *familia rustica*: 137 f.; *familia urbana*: 142 f.

Introduction

indication were involved, can scarcely be said to belong to a *familia rustica*. Their affinities are much more with the domestic and in some cases with the administrative service. This applies even to those who call themselves *vilici* (estate managers), an occupational term traditionally associated with the *familia rustica*. The slave workers in the Imperial mines and quarries and on the estates, with rare exceptions, did not carry the Imperial status indication; they were of very low status, inferior to the *aquarii* for example, who only occasionally had the Imperial status indication, *Caesaris servus* or its variants. Although they could be said to make up a *familia rustica*, they do not belong to the Familia Caesaris status group we are considering. Even more clearly, the freedman heads of departments and the subordinate officials, both clerical and sub-clerical, of many administrative departments in Rome and the provinces do not easily fit into the category of *familia urbana*. The fact is that the Familia Caesaris, consisting essentially of the private staff of the emperor who came to perform public or semi-public functions, broke through all the traditional categories belonging to the *familia* of a *privatus*, and came to form what was virtually an *ordo libertorum et servorum principis*, a new 'estate' or status-group in the hierarchy of Roman Imperial society.[1]

The most important functional division within the Familia Caesaris is between the staff engaged in the personal service of the emperor as the greatest of the noble Roman magnates, an extension of the domestic household of any wealthy Roman, on the one hand, and on the other, the staff assisting the emperor in his duties as magistrate, albeit one with a vast and ill-defined sphere of competence. Not that any clear-cut separation of these functions into domestic on the one hand, and administrative on the other is possible. The very nature of the Imperial position in the context of social and political change ruled this out. The emperor's *patrimonium*,[2] for example, held an ambivalent position as more than personal and less than state property attached to the Imperial title. It was not to be disposed of by will as if

---

[1] The suggestion that the Imperial slaves and freedmen, as an élite status-group in Roman Imperial society, may well be described in terms of an *ordo* is due to Boulvert. For discussion on this, as on much else, I am grateful to him.

[2] On the private fortune of Augustus, its growth from gifts, legacies and inheritances, and the expenditure from this source for public purposes: Augustus, *Res Gest.* 15, 18; Suetonius, *Aug.* 101; Dio, liii. 28. Cf. M. Rostovtzeff, *SEHRE*², pp. 55 f., 561 f. (nn. 16-17). On the *patrimonium*: O. Hirschfeld, 'Der Grundbesitz der römischen Kaiser in den ersten drei Jahrhunderten', *Klio* 2 (1902), 46 f. = *Kleine Schriften*, 516 f.; R. S. Rogers, 'The Roman Emperors as Heirs and Legatees', *TAPA* 78 (1947), 140 f.; F. Millar, 'The Fiscus in the First Two Centuries', *JRS* 53 (1963), 29 f.; and esp. P. A. Brunt, 'The "Fiscus" and its Development', *JRS* 56 (1966), 75 f. (The last four articles mentioned give full references to the evidence.) See now also: G. Boulvert, 'Tacite et le Fiscus', *Rev. Hist. de Droit franç. et étrang.* (1970), 430-8. Rostovtzeff (*SEHRE*², p. 562 n. 17) observed that the evidence on the fortunes and property of Augustus' family, his friends and associates had never been collected and investigated; this gap has at least been partly filled by the recent studies cited above.

Introduction

belonging to a private estate.[1] And what of the disputed meaning of the term *fiscus* and the part that it played in the financial structure of the empire?[2] Even the private property of a new *princeps* and of a new Imperial dynasty could not be insulated from the rest of the Imperial *patrimonium*; it was simply added to it and passed *en bloc* to the next succeeding *princeps*, whether he was a relative or not. Thus, the *figlinae Domitianae*, the property of Domitia Lucilla, inherited by her son Marcus Aurelius, passed into the Imperial *patrimonium* and completed the Imperial monopoly of the brick industry in the mid-second century.[3]

The broad distinction is between (*A*) the staff employed in the daily maintenance, provisioning and supervision of residences and properties for the emperor's personal upkeep, enjoyment and consumption, and (*B*) the staff engaged in supervising the revenue-producing Imperial properties or in the basically financial and administrative functions of the civil service proper. Careers of individual freedmen and slaves could embrace both types of service, but rarely, and usually only at the topmost levels open to them.

A. The domestic group includes the staff of the Imperial Palace on the Palatine, the *domus Augustiana*, and of the villas and residences at Tibur, Tusculum, Alsium, Antium, Caieta, Tarracina, Pausilypum and elsewhere in Italy, the Imperial gardens in Rome, such as the *horti Sallustiani, Serviliani, Maiani et Lamiani*, and others at Puteoli, Surrentum and elsewhere.

Their duties ranged from the menial, such as *custos* and *aedituus* (guard and keeper), *lecticarius* (litter-bearer), through those with some degree of responsibility or skill, *topiarius* (ornamental gardener), *tricliniarchus* (who was in charge of the dining-room), *praegustator* (Imperial taster), *archimagirus* (head chef), and the almost absurdly minute differentiation of duties that seems to have been characteristic of the Palatine establishment, to the managerial posts of *procurator* and *subprocurator domus Augustianae*. The head of the domestic organisation, with overall financial responsibility for its budget, was the *procurator castrensis*. The latter post formed part of the normal freedman procuratorial career which could include posts in both the domestic and administrative services, particularly in those posts where financial experience and ability was at a premium. Even more influential,

---

[1] The same applies to the *res privata* in view of the evidence that its establishment as a separate branch of the administration dates back to the Antonine period at least to Antoninus Pius. See: H. Nesselhauf, 'Patrimonium und res privata des römischen Kaisers', *Historia Augusta Colloquium* 1963 (= *Antiquitas* 4, 1964), 73 f.; Boulvert, *EAI*, pp. 300 f.

[2] Cf. *Dig.* xliii. 8.2.4: 'res enim fiscales quasi propriae et privatae principis sunt'. For a good collection of material on the *fiscus* and discussion see the articles of Millar, Brunt and Boulvert referred to above (p. 5 n. 2).

[3] On the *figlinae Domitianae* see H. Bloch, *I bolli laterizi e la storia edilizia romana* (Rome, 1947), p. 339. Further examples in Millar, 'The Fiscus in the First Two Centuries', at pp. 41 f. and n. 176.

Introduction

especially under particularly susceptible emperors, were the *cubicularii* who, together with the freedmen *ab admissione*, controlled access to the emperor, and because of their close and confidential contact with the emperor exercised a potent but unofficial (hence uncontrolled) influence on matters of policy outside their strictly domestic sphere.[1]

B. The administrative staff were employed in a wide variety of departments including all aspects of the receipt and payment of funds under the emperor's control, as well as many concerned with public services such as aqueducts, libraries, the post, roads, public works and buildings, and Imperial enterprises such as mines, marble quarries, and the mint. Here too the range in status is wide, extending from the sub-clerical functionaries, of whom the *pedisequi, custodes, nomenclatores* and *tabellarii* are typical, through the junior and intermediate clerical grades of *adiutor, vicarius, dispensator, a commentariis* and *tabularius*, and those of senior clerical rank, the *tabularii a rationibus* and the *proximi*, to the senior administrative positions of *procurator, a rationibus, ab epistulis, a libellis* and others of undisputed eminence. Again, there is a wide variation in the status attached to a post of the same rank in different departments, for example the numerous departments in Rome concerned principally with finance, ranging from the central finance bureaux of the *a rationibus* and the *ratio patrimonii*, down to the department responsible for the most minor tax. There is also the status dimension which is linked with the location of different sections of the same department; the head office in Rome naturally took precedence over the branch offices in the provincial centres, and even here the differences between, for example, Carthage, Ephesus, Lugdunum, Virunum, Sarmizegetusa and Apulum have to be taken into account in presenting the full status picture.

Lastly, there are the Imperial slaves and freedmen found in private commercial and industrial enterprises on their own account or otherwise engaged in activities not connected with the emperor's service. Many members of the Familia Caesaris had occupational titles which indicate that they practised a skilled trade, *vestifex* or *vestifica* (tailor, dressmaker), for instance, or *caelator* (engraver), *argentarius* (silver-smith), *speclariarius* (mirror-maker) and many others.[2] These, however, were engaged in domestic production for the Imperial household, and by so doing contributed to its economic self-

---

[1] Under the absolutist regime of the later empire, the ex-slave eunuchs held the highest positions in the Palace domestic service and were, indeed, among the most important in the empire. Two of the chief posts were the *praepositus sacri cubiculi* and the *primicerius sacri cubiculi*; these represent a formal recognition of, and a formidable increase in, the power of the officials of the Imperial Bedchamber. See Jones, *LRE*, II, 566 f.; III, 162 f. (references). Also M. K. Hopkins, 'Eunuchs in Politics in the Later Roman Empire', *Proc. Camb. Phil. Soc.* 9 (1963), 62 f.

[2] Boulvert, *EAI*, pp. 27 f.

Introduction

sufficiency. While it is possible that some of their products were sold on the open market or even to other members of the Familia, this was not the primary purpose of these activities.

Similarly, the emperor's building activities required a work force of skilled craftsmen and unskilled labour; these activities also had as a necessary consequence the acquisition of control by the emperor over the sources of supply for building materials. Craftsmen who worked outside the household, such as *lapidarii* (stonemasons), *marmorarii* (marble-cutters), *structores* (carpenters), *architecti* (master-builders), were engaged on projects under Imperial direction and not working, except incidentally, on their own account. The Imperial freedmen *officinatores* (workshop supervisors) whose names appear on the lead *fistulae* produced in the Imperial factories were Imperial employees, as were those found in the brick industry, where the Imperial monopoly was more complete.

Apart from their participation as workers or managers in Imperial enterprises, the main contribution of Imperial freedmen and slaves to the general commercial and industrial life of the empire was not active working competition in private enterprise. Their contribution lay rather in the capital which they could supply. Many of the freedmen became modestly or even exceedingly wealthy. Like other Roman capitalists they invested if possible in land, but also in industry. Evidence is not plentiful. The estates of Pallas in Egypt, the ownership of the *figlinae Ocianae* by Ti. Iulius (Aug. lib.) Optatus *praefectus classis Misenensis*, and of the *praedia Quintanensia* by Agathyrsus, freedman of Trajan or Plotina, are examples of investment in property by members of the Familia Caesaris, a practice that can be assumed to have been fairly common.[1] But on the inscriptions, which are mostly sepulchral, the Imperial status indication together with an occupational title reveal a post in the emperor's service, not independent private activity on their own account.

THE SOURCES

The primary material for the study of the Familia Caesaris is predominantly inscriptional. A great mass of inscriptions directly relevant to the subject is to be found in the volumes of the *Corpus Inscriptionum Latinarum* and in the supplementary epigraphical publications embracing all parts of the Roman empire. These are mainly sepulchral, but also include many dedications and public documentary inscriptions. From them no fewer than four thousand

---

[1] On Imperial slaves and freedmen in industry see esp. H. Gummerus, art. 'Industrie und Handel', P-W IX (1916), 1455 f.; H. Bloch, *I bolli laterizi*, pp. 14 f., 90, 209 f. For Pallas: *P. Ryl.* II 255; *P. Bour.* 42.4.

Introduction

individual slaves and freedmen of the emperor can be identified. The very magnitude of the list, and the fact that, in particular, *CIL* Volume VI is deficient in indexes of any kind, except the *Index nominum*, has inspired in scholars a despair as complete as it has been justified.[1] A systematic collection of this material was an essential preliminary to a detailed study of the Familia Caesaris. As the indexes of the *CIL* are not consistently reliable for information on status indication, I have made an independent search of all volumes. Most of the inscriptions are brief, but nearly all give some information, however exiguous, about wives, family relationships, ages, etc. and nearly half of them mention occupations and official posts held and membership of *collegia*, benefactions and municipal honours received, if any. The treatment of this material is basically statistical rather than prosopographical, except for freedmen in the senior ranks. One of the limitations of this material is the restricted range of the information given. Another is the uneven distribution of it throughout the various regions of the empire, partly because of the haphazard chance of archaeological discovery. Nearly three-quarters of all the inscriptions come from Rome, and over four-fifths from Rome and Italy together. The provinces, with the notable exception of Africa and some administrative centres such as Ephesus and Lugdunum, are under-represented, in particular the Greek-speaking region of the empire, except Asia Minor. There are barely two hundred Greek inscriptions, or only five per cent of the whole. This makes any statistical comparison of one province or group of provinces with another very hazardous and subject to caution.

Complementary to the inscriptions, but less important for this subject, is the literary evidence. This is abundant for the first century in Tacitus, Suetonius and Cassius Dio, but less satisfactory both in quality and quantity for the second and early third centuries with the *Historia Augusta*, Herodian and the fragments of Cassius Dio. There are discussions and remarks of varying value in Strabo, Philo, Pliny the Elder, Seneca, Josephus, Pliny the Younger, Epictetus, Frontinus, Plutarch, Martial, Statius, Juvenal, Fronto and others. But on the Familia Caesaris the literary sources as a whole are prejudiced, sensational, repetitive and depressing. Casual references, for example, in Pliny, Tacitus and Martial reveal a common attitude towards the emperor's freedmen and slaves. The degree of control exercised over his 'famuli' was one of the criteria for distinguishing an emperor's worth in the

[1] Mention should be made here of the project, now completed, under the direction of Dr E. J. Jory at the University of Western Australia and to be published under the auspices of *CIL* at the Deutsche Akademie der Wissenschaften zu Berlin, to produce a complete word-index, *index cognominum*, *index fragmentorum*, etc. to *CIL* Vol. VI using advanced computer methods. Such an index should greatly assist studies in this and other fields where the primary evidence is predominantly epigraphic, voluminous, and heavily concentrated in Volume VI of *CIL*.

Introduction

eyes of his class-conscious contemporaries.[1] Their range of interest is largely confined to the few freedmen at the top whose careers impinged on politics. Among the literary authorities, it would perhaps be naive to expect the consular historians, such as Tacitus and Cassius Dio, to admit slaves and freedmen regularly into their pages, unless to provide spectacular examples of non-virtue. But Pallas, Narcissus, Callistus and other notorious top freedmen are so untypical of the ordinary freedman personnel in the administration, both in their influence and affluence, that their cases must be used with caution. Their careers, however, do raise the questions of how and from what beginnings they rose to eminence. Tacitus is of no special value to us here. He is consistently indignant about freedmen and his main indignation is reserved for the *potentia* exercised by Imperial freedmen. The key words in the discussion of the occupational aspect of the Familia Caesaris, such as *tabularius*, *dispensator*, *vicarius*, with a single exception (*Hist.* i. 49), simply do not occur in Tacitus, nor does he ever seem to use the word 'procurator' of freedmen.[2] It is mostly from writers such as the senatorial Frontinus and Pliny, and the equestrians Suetonius and the elder Pliny, working inside the administration and writing technical or anecdotal works, that we get the valuable but meagre literary information relevant to this subject.[3]

The papyrological evidence concerns almost entirely the administration of Egypt. Because of the nature of the documents and a tendency by Imperial freedmen and slaves to omit the formal status indication in them, or have it omitted by others, this material presents problems of its own and needs separate treatment as, indeed, does the place of Egypt in the provincial administrative system.

The legal sources, which are very voluminous on Roman slavery in general, contain a large number of references to the Familia Caesaris, although the majority of the relevant legal texts themselves belong to the period after the early third century and concern the fiscal slaves of a later period than that with which we are here concerned. The difficulty here is to decide with any

---

[1] Pliny, *Panegyr.* 88: 'plerique principes cum essent civium domini, libertorum erant servi; horum consiliis, horum nutu regebantur...'; Martial, ix. 79.1: 'oderat ante ducum famulos turbamque priorem et Palatinum Roma supercilium...'; Tacitus, *Hist.* i. 49: '(Galba) amicorum libertorumque, ubi in bonos incidisset, sine reprehensione patiens, si mali forent, usque ad culpam ignarus'.

[2] See D. Stockton, *Historia* 10 (1961), 116 f. esp. at 119 n. 11.

[3] Suetonius, more successfully than Tacitus, writes 'sine studio et ira' on the subject of the Imperial freedmen and slaves and is often more rewarding for his factual attitudes; e.g. *Calig.* 56: 'non sine conscientia potentissimorum libertorum praefectorumque praetorii'; in discussing the preparations for Gaius' assassination, Suetonius juxtaposes Imperial freedmen and the praetorian prefects, qualifying both groups with the epithet *potentissimi*, but refraining from further comment on the role of the freedmen, except perhaps by implication in mentioning them first. One cannot see Tacitus being so restrained.

Introduction

helpful degree of precision how far back into the first and second centuries AD did the rules apply which are characterised in the Theodosian Code and the Justinian *Corpus* simply as 'ius vetus'.[1] Of great interest for the Familia Caesaris, but of greater difficulty in dating and interpretation, are the excerpts from the treatise on the rights of the Fiscus, found with the *Institutiones* of Gaius, and known as the *Fragmenta de Iure Fisci*.[2] Despite these difficulties of interpretation, however, the legal background is of vital importance in this kind of social study where questions of precise legal status are constantly arising, and especially with the Imperial freedmen and slaves where dissonance between the legal and the other status criteria cannot be ignored.[3]

Lastly, archaeological data are very important for dating inscriptions studied *in situ*. But this has rarely been possible; few such data are available and in many cases the earlier inscriptions themselves have disappeared. The dating of inscriptions from the letter-forms and other palaeographical criteria, at least for the first to third centuries AD, is very subjective and unreliable and should either be used with considerable caution or, preferably, abandoned.[4] However, it is sometimes possible to make safe deductions about the social standing and other aspects of individual freedmen or slaves from the external aspect and surroundings of their monuments.

OBJECT AND PLAN OF THIS STUDY

The first requirement is to establish the principles by which membership of the Familia Caesaris can be determined. In the epigraphic sources the use of the Imperial status indication, *Augusti libertus* or *Caesaris servus*, in the customary abbreviated forms or variants, is the usual criterion. The mere possession of an Imperial *nomen* (e.g. *Iulius*, *Claudius*), in the absence of other positive evidence, does not constitute a reason for inclusion. Instances where the Imperial status indication is omitted must be dealt with on their merits, on the basis of other evidence, and generally in a conservative fashion.

It is necessary to go further. Given the nature of the main evidence – sepulchral inscriptions with all their difficulties of dating – it is essential to make the best possible use of the resources of nomenclature preserved therein. In the last resort, we have massive quantities of names to exploit but not a great deal else. An exhaustive analysis of all aspects of nomenclature is the

[1] E.g. *Cod. Theod.* iv. 12.3 (AD 320). For a full discussion of this passage see pp. 165 f.
[2] *FIRA*² II, 627 f.
[3] Weaver, *Past and Present* 37 (1967), 4 f.
[4] H. Thylander, *Étude*, 40 f.; cf. J. S. & A. E. Gordon, *Contributions to the Palaeography of Latin Inscriptions* (Berkeley and Los Angeles, 1957), esp. p. 217.

Introduction

best hope of establishing a sound chronological framework embracing the period from Augustus to Severus Alexander. This in turn is required to support the whole structure of a study in which we are concerned with social and administrative change.

Hence the subject matter of Part I, which presents, in a form which represents a compromise between extended argumentation and bare summary, the results obtained by recent fundamental work in the closely related fields of nomenclature and chronology.

Using this chronological dimension wherever possible the members of the Familia Caesaris – who are considered primarily from their personal standpoint and not from that of the administration – are treated in relation to the social groups to which they belong, in order of increasing size and complexity; in Part II, their intimate family circle, with a detailed consideration of their wives, marriage pattern, children and the light these throw on social status; and in Part III, their occupational environment, the administrative and domestic services of the Familia Caesaris itself, where the questions of recruitment, promotion and careers are in the forefront. Throughout, the influence of the Familia Caesaris as an element of high social mobility, and in particular the social differentiation within the Familia Caesaris, are considered in relation to social structure in the early Empire. The social aspects of the Familia Caesaris can only be profitably studied on the basis of an exhaustive collection of the evidence, particularly in inscriptions, and this is what is, perhaps rashly, attempted here.

The patent neglect of this subject hitherto is evident from the fact that prior to 1963 very few articles had been published in the specific field of the Familia Caesaris. Most notable were those by C. Hülsen,[1] E. Fairon,[2] J. Michiels,[3] and M. Bang,[4] published in 1888, 1900, 1902 and 1919 respectively. Prior to 1965 no single monograph devoted to the subject had been published. O. Hirschfeld's *Die Kaiserlichen Verwaltungsbeamten bis auf Diocletian* (2nd ed. Berlin, 1905) and more recently H. G. Pflaum's works on the equestrian procurators, *Les Procurateurs équestres sous le Haut-Empire romain* (Paris, 1950) and *Les Carrières procuratoriennes équestres sous le Haut-Empire romain* (Paris, 1960–1), have been of great value in providing a framework for the study of the freedman–slave careers. Then, by a remarkable coincidence, in 1964 three theses on the Imperial freedmen and slaves were presented almost simultaneously without any of the authors being aware

---

[1] C. Hülsen, 'Sopra i nomi doppi di servi e liberti della casa imperiale', *Röm. Mitt.* 3 (1888), 222 f.
[2] E. Fairon, 'L'organisation du palais impérial à Rome', *Musée Belge* 4 (1900), 5 f.
[3] J. Michiels, 'Les Cubicularii des empereurs romains d'Auguste à Dioclétien', *Musée Belge* 6 (1902), 364–87.
[4] M. Bang, 'Caesaris servus', *Hermes* 54 (1919), 174 f.

Introduction

of the work of the others: G. Boulvert: *Les Esclaves et les Affranchis impériaux sous le Haut-Empire romain* (Aix-en-Provence); H. Chantraine: *Freigelassene und Sklaven im Dienst der römischen Kaiser; Studien zu ihrer Nomenklatur* (Mainz); and my own entitled *Familia Caesaris: A Social Study of the Slaves and Freedmen of the Roman Imperial Administration* (Cambridge).[1]

In order to make the results of my work available as soon as possible and to provoke discussion in what I considered to be virtually a new field, between 1963 and 1968 I published a fairly long series of articles, mostly concerned with aspects of nomenclature and administrative careers.[2] In 1967 Chantraine published (with Steiner, Wiesbaden) a revised version of his work, taking into consideration that of Boulvert and those of my articles published prior to 1965. Boulvert's thesis was first published in polycopied form in two volumes (numbered consecutively) by the Centre régional de Documentation pédagogique, Aix-en-Provence. The first volume, thoroughly revised and corrected in detail, has now appeared (1970) published by Jovene, Naples.[3]

Chantraine has covered the vast epigraphic material with exemplary thoroughness, both in compilation and in interpretation. His primary and almost exclusive concern is an exhaustive examination of all questions of nomenclature. His studies confirm most of my own published conclusions on the basic questions of nomenclature and chronology, except on the special problem of the *Augustorum liberti* (on which see Part I, pp. 58 f. below). It is now possible to affirm with some confidence that much of the methodological foundation for the systematic study of the Familia Caesaris has been laid. This can replace the process of conjecture and subjective impression that has prevailed hitherto, whereby the familiar but usually atypical example often acquired the status of a paradigm. Chantraine's work, however, has only a limited application to other aspects of this study, for instance the chronology of the occupational titles and the use of family nomenclature.

Boulvert, on the other hand, is concerned with the whole range of questions involved in the study of the Familia Caesaris. His interests are primarily administrative, juridical and sociological; he is less concerned with detailed problems of nomenclature and chronology. On the major areas of careers and family life of the Imperial slaves and freedmen, here too it is possible to

---

[1] A *fourth*, also finished in 1964 (!), has recently come to my notice but unfortunately too late to be taken into account in this study: M. Wolf: *Untersuchungen zur Stellung der kaiserlichen Freigelassenen und Sklaven in Italien und den Westprovinzen* (Diss. Münster, 1965).

[2] For the list, see the Bibliography, p. 318. They relate especially to Parts I and III of this book.

[3] The second volume presently awaits publication. References to this second volume are to the original polycopied edition of 1965, provided to me through the kindness of the author.

Introduction

measure a substantial amount of agreement and progress through approaches which tend to be complementary.[1]

[1] Chantraine's criticisms of Boulvert (cf. Chantraine, p. 12 with n. 15) are based on the unrevised, polycopied edition of 1965. Volume I (pp. 1–455 of that edition) has now been superseded by the edition of 1970 (*Esclaves et Affranchis Impériaux sous le Haut-Empire romain: rôle politique et administratif* (Jovene, Naples) – abbreviated as *EAI*) which incorporates substantial corrections in detail. Volume II (pp. 457–832 of the polycopied edition) is also to appear separately in a new, revised edition. Page references to Vol. II are to the original polycopied edition.

PART 1

NOMENCLATURE AND CHRONOLOGY

It is not possible to establish precisely defined periods within the overall span of two and a half centuries of the Familia Caesaris' effective existence. The dating criteria applied to the inscriptions are most fruitfully based on aspects of personal nomenclature which are not susceptible of rigid demarcation, especially the Imperial *nomina gentilicia*. We usually have to be content with a chronological tolerance of twenty years or even more. This means that not only does the possible date of a particular inscription overlap the reigns of two successive emperors, but not infrequently of three or even four.

For this reason a reign-by-reign account of the development of the Familia Caesaris is to be generally avoided as being methodologically dangerous and misleading. Unless, of course, it is somehow based on the literary sources – a procedure which, although partly satisfying the desire for precision, is even more detrimental to truth. Uncomfortably often we have to be content with sensing general trends, not with seizing on dramatic reversals of policy traceable to a single decision. The influence of individual emperors on the general development of the Familia Caesaris, both in its administrative and in its domestic services, can only be felt within quite narrowly defined limits. On special issues or for particular appointments the workings of the system of patronage give the emperor a decisive voice. By virtue of his position in the state he was required to deal personally with an incredible amount of detailed, day-to-day business. But, with the exception perhaps of Augustus, even the emperors who were most important in the history of the administration, Vespasian, Hadrian, M. Aurelius and Septimius Severus, mostly responded to the major pressures inseparable from the administration of a world-wide empire and sought, vainly, to control them. They could not attempt to reshape them after their heart's desire. The Familia Caesaris was an essential part of the power structure of the empire until the increasing militarisation of the third century swept its power away.

Chronology and nomenclature are here closely intertwined. But first, what can be said of dating criteria independent of nomenclature?

The main source of information on the Familia Caesaris, it must be emphasised, is the inscriptions – over four thousand of them, mostly sepulchral, brief, stereotyped and undated. The material is intractable. To extract and use effectively the information they contain, the first essential is to establish a chronological framework that is based on objective criteria. It is clearly not possible to date any but a small minority of these inscriptions to

Nomenclature and chronology

within a year, and few of those that can be so dated are sepulchral. On the other hand, such comforting expressions as 'litteris bonis saeculi I medii vel exeuntis' or 'litteris saeculi II', although freely used by editors, for instance throughout much of *CIL*, are based on largely subjective palaeographic dating criteria. These are very unreliable and should be used with great caution.[1] In any case, without further archaeological data they cannot provide us with the degree of precision we require.[2]

One positive contribution to the notoriously difficult problem of dating sepulchral inscriptions has been that of H. Thylander,[3] who rightly stresses the importance of archaeological criteria for inscriptions studied *in situ*. In a careful examination of the group of inscriptions in the necropolis of the Isola Sacra between ancient Portus and Ostia, and by a detailed comparison of one tomb with another, he succeeded in establishing relative but reasonably precise dates for many of the sepulchral inscriptions in a way that would have been quite impossible if he had had to rely only on the internal evidence, especially the nomenclature, of the inscriptions themselves. This method is valuable for a given site and a limited group of inscriptions or even sometimes for a whole area. Occasionally such sites are of considerable importance for the Familia Caesaris, for example the two *sepulcreta domus Augustae* discovered at Carthage in 1880-1,[4] and several *columbaria* in and around Rome, such as the *monumenta Liviae, filiorum Drusi, Marcellae*, the *monumenta in vinea Codiniorum effossa* and others.[5] But to be successful this method requires a detailed, if not exhaustive, archaeological context; nor has it always been applied with such precision as distinguishes the work of Calza and Thylander himself at Ostia. For most of the inscriptions edited in *CIL*, and especially for those found in or originating from Rome, edited in Volume VI, so little relevant archaeological data was available or is given that Thylander's ideal is quite impossible to attain or even approach in practice. In some cases there is even a risk of circular argument when nomenclature is used as an archaeological dating criterion.

Although most of the inscriptions relevant to the Familia Caesaris are found in Rome, the important remainder is scattered throughout every region of Italy and every province outside Italy. The unevenness of their distribution, however, is only matched by that of the editorial conventions

---

[1] See J. S. & A. E. Gordon, *Contributions to the Palaeography of Latin Inscriptions*, esp. p. 217.

[2] H. Thylander, *Étude*, pp. 40 f.

[3] Op. cit. and *Inscriptions du Port d'Ostie*, 2 vols. (Lund, 1951-2) (abbrev. *IPO*); G. Galza, *La Necropoli del Porto di Roma dell'Isola Sacra* (Rome, 1940).

[4] *CIL* VIII 12590-13186; 24681-24861. Even in these *sepulcreta* all the inscriptions found do not form a homogeneous group. Several are clearly late intruders; cf. Mommsen ad loc.

[5] VI 3926-4307; 4327-4413; 4418-4708; 4881-5168; 5179-5538; 5539-5678; 5679-5886.

Nomenclature and chronology

adopted by those who published them. But there are distinguished recent advances to record, particularly the painstaking and exacting standards of the editors of the *Inscriptiones Italiae* and of the Gordons in their invaluable *Album of Dated Latin Inscriptions*.[1]

[1] A. E. & J. S. Gordon, *Album of Dated Latin Inscriptions; Rome and its Neighborhood*, 4 vols. (Berkeley and Los Angeles, 1958–67).

CHAPTER I

DATED INSCRIPTIONS

Two kinds of dated inscriptions are important for the Familia Caesaris: (*a*) those that can be dated to within a particular year; (*b*) those that can be dated to within a particular reign. The value of both kinds is that they provide fixed points of reference for the use of particular formulae in nomenclature. They help to establish the chronological range of usages which in suitable circumstances, either individually or in combination, can then become secondary dating criteria. This applies to the *nomen gentilicium*, status indication, *agnomina*, occupational titles and abbreviations.

(*a*) Precise dating of the inscriptions to *within a particular year* is comparatively rare for the Familia Caesaris. The commonest form is by the names of consuls, less frequently by the tribunician year of the emperor.[1] But these inscriptions are usually official or quasi-official, including *fasti* of various kinds, municipal honours, records of *collegia* especially burial colleges, quarry-marks, brick-stamps and even a military diploma. There are also administrative and private records, including a group of papyrus documents from Egypt in the reign of Augustus.[2] In a few cases the emperor's regnal year in Egypt provides a date.[3] Less than half of these dated inscriptions are private dedications, of which many are those of the form 'pro salute imp(p).' in vogue after 161. These do not often contain details of family interest. The other key group, the *sepulcrales*, is the smallest – only seventeen are precisely dated for both freedmen and slaves.[4] Less than one sepulchral inscription in a hundred for Imperial freedmen can be dated to within a year,

---

[1] Examples: 13/12 BC: XI 3200; AD 37: *AE* 1935, 47; AD 52: X 769 = XVI 1 = D 1986; AD 80: *AE* 1930, 86; AD 101/2: VI 2184 = 32445 = D 4971; AD 136: VI 975 = D 6073; AD 147: VIII 2339.

[2] *BGU* 1137 = *Chrest.* 112; *P. Oxy.* 743; and from the Protarchus Archive from Alexandria, covering various private business transactions during the period 24–4 BC: *BGU* 1110, 1118, 1129, 1130, 1152, 1166, 1171, 1175, 1177. In this study papyri may be conveniently grouped with inscriptions for most purposes and will not be treated separately unless special reasons are indicated.

[3] AD 49: *IGR* I 1262 = *SEG* VIII 794; AD 118: *IGR* I 1255–6. In the papyri this form of dating is regular for the Imperial slaves and freedmen; cf. the Protarchus archive (*BGU* 1110 f.), *P. Oxy.* 735, *P. Tebt.* II 296; *Chrest.* 79, 175: *BGU* 102.1.

[4] *Freedmen*: AD 11: XIV 2302; AD 18/26: VI 1963 = 5180; AD 41: 20141; AD 80/120: 9100; AD 110: 8821; AD 126: 4228; AD 117/30: 1884, 8550; AD 149: 10235; AD 183: 8420; AD 187: 8775; AD 199: 2270; AD 207: III 4035; AD 211: VI 10233; AD 217: 8498. *Slaves*: AD 13: VI 9050; AD 110/11: *IGR* IV 1738.

Dated inscriptions

and for Imperial slaves less than one in 300. Also the chronological distribution is uneven, with one group concentrated in the early first century and almost half the total belonging to the period after 161. These factors limit the usefulness of the inscriptions in this category.

(b) *Inscriptions dated to within a particular reign.* This group is much more numerous. It includes, firstly, the *fistulae plumbeae*, the sections of lead piping used in the water supply and stamped with the name of the emperor during whose reign they were fabricated. This indicates that the pipes were produced in the Imperial factories. The pipes were also stamped with the name of the *procurator aquarum*, who was an Imperial freedman till the time of Trajan, and later also in association with an equestrian *rationalis*. In most cases is added the name of the *officinator* responsible for the actual fabrication (usually signified by 'f(ecit)' following the name). The *officinator* was normally an Imperial slave before M. Aurelius and an Imperial freedman afterwards.[1] The great majority of these stamps come from Rome and Ostia and from the period beginning with Vespasian. The compressed nature of these stamps makes them unsafe guides for nomenclature, not so much because of violent or unusual abbreviation as for omissions, e.g. 'lib.' (for 'Aug. lib.'), 'ser.' (for 'Caes. ser.'), etc. This applies also to the quarry-marks which are, if anything, even more elliptic in form.

Secondly, a more numerous and more useful group, the dedicatory inscriptions without precise dating which mention the reigning emperor or Imperial family by name. The usual formula: 'I(ovi) O(ptimo) M(aximo) pro salute Imp. Caes. (Traiani...)' is varied by the beginning of the third century with such additions as 'pro salute et reditu', 'pro salute et victoria', 'fortunae Augg.', or the omission of the initial 'I. O. M.' In this group there is an even heavier concentration of inscriptions in the last seventy-five years of our period – I have been able to find only five out of eighty-four not precisely dated from before the second century[2] – whereas the previous 190 years, particularly the first century, are comparatively bare.

Thirdly, the most numerous group, comprising nearly three hundred instances, are those freedmen and slaves who include the name of an emperor as part of their own name – of their status indication in fact – on their inscriptions. An Imperial slave normally on the death of his original master passed into the ownership of the next emperor so that *slave* inscriptions mentioning a particular emperor as part of the name can, in the absence of

---

[1] Cf. Hirschfeld, *Verwalt.* pp. 280–2; Dressel, *CIL* xv 907 f.

[2] XI 3083 = D 5373 (Augustus); V 6641 = D 191 (Gaius); *IGR* III 578 = *TAM* II 178, cf. *IGR* III 579 = *TAM* II 1842 (Claudius); VI 927 = D 236 (Nero); *IGR* IV 228 (Vespasian, Titus, Domitian).

Nomenclature and chronology

evidence to the contrary, be taken as dating from that reign.[1] Representative examples are: *Tiberius*: VI 5358 = D 1772: Pinytus Ti. Caesaris Aug. ser.; 5200: Dascylus Ti. Aug. *Gaius*: 21162: Melior C. Caesaris Aug. Germanici ser.; 3991: Felix C. Caesaris. *Claudius*: 8822 = D 1655: Cinnamus Ti. Claudi Caesaris Aug. Germanici disp. Drusillianus; IX 321: Adiutor Ti. Claudi Caesaris Aug. ser. *Nero*: VI 8864: Epaphroditus Neronis Caesaris Augusti; 8889: Primigenius Neronis Aug. *Vespasian*: XI 1315: Stephanus Imp. Vespasiani Caesaris Aug. *Titus*: VI 276: Daphnus Imp. T. Caes. Aug. Vespasiani ser. *Domitian*: 8831 = D 1657: Eutychus Imp. Domitiani Caesaris Augusti Germanici servus dispensator Montanianus; 9052 = D 1703: Placidus Imp. Domitiani Aug. *Trajan*: 18456: Onesimus Imp. Caesaris Nervae Traiani Aug. Germ. ser. Phoebianus. After Trajan there are only isolated instances of this kind of nomenclature among the Imperial slaves.[2] Inscriptions of this type are numerous among the slave *sepulcrales* of the first century, particularly among the *columbaria* in and near Rome. The chronological balance of the dated inscriptions is thus redressed in favour of the first century.

The fact that over three-quarters of the examples are of slaves confirms the slave origin of this nomenclature. It was also used on *freedman* inscriptions, but much less commonly. Isolated examples are found from Augustus[3] to as late as Gordian III.[4] The point of freedmen using this form of nomenclature is evidently the same as for slaves – pride in the connection with a particular emperor as master or patron. These inscriptions too are to be dated to the reign of the emperor in question,[5] with the obvious proviso that the *liberti divi Augusti* and *divi Claudii* cannot be earlier than the date of deification of the emperor concerned.

A fourth group of Imperial freedman and slave inscriptions is to be in-

[1] The only exception is the use of 'Divi Aug.' by a slave of Augustus: VI 8887 = 14399 = 33754, Hyblaeus divi Augusti a ma(nu); and possibly VI 26608, Sitalces divi Augusti opses Thracum, and VI 8764, [....]ion divi [Aug. ?] a cubiculo. This usage parallels that of the 'liberti Divi Augusti/ Claudi'. After Augustus the use of 'Divi' in the slave indication ceases.

[2] For a full list of the variant forms according to reign, but all given under the one rubric 'Onesimus' as slave name, consult Chantraine, pp. 15 f.

[3] The earliest instance, that of a freedman of Augustus belonging most probably to the period 42–30 BC, has turned up recently among the unpublished material from Aphrodisias in Caria. He is Γάιος Ἰούλιος Ζώιλος θεοῦ Ἰουλίου υ[ἱ]οῦ Καίσαρος ἀπελεύθερος, and reveals the origin of the use of 'Divus' in the status indication of the Imperial freedmen. I owe this reference to Miss Joyce Reynolds who has kindly allowed me to use it.

[4] In *IGR* I 623 = D 8851 (Tomi, Moes. Inf.): Κατυλλεῖνος ἀπελεύθερος τοῦ κυρίου Αὐτοκράτορος Μ.'Ἀντ(ωνίου) Γορδιανοῦ Σε(βαστοῦ) λιβράριος, Chantraine (p. 27) expresses doubt as to whether the emperor's name forms part of Catullinus' status indication (so that he was manumitted by Gordian) or is to be taken with the occupational title (so that he could have been manumitted by an earlier emperor). Unnecessarily, I think. The order of words makes the second alternative very unlikely.

[5] Cf. Chantraine, p. 34; but on ib. n. 67 see above, n. 4.

Dated inscriptions

cluded here. The dating of these depends on the naming of senatorial or equestrian officials – in association with Imperial freedmen or slaves – whose years of holding the office mentioned are known from other sources or can be inferred from the internal evidence of the inscription itself.[1] In almost all these cases the dating can be reduced to a narrow range of years rather than a precise year, or at least to within the reign of a particular emperor.

The total number of inscriptions and papyri dated according to these criteria is 607. The list is given in Appendix II, with the distribution reign by reign, and the numbers of items dated according to each of the categories discussed above, with full individual references. These figures do not take into account the frequent use of *agnomina* (or second *cognomen* in *-ianus*) by Imperial slaves and freedmen in the period up to Hadrian. There are over 300 examples of these *agnomina*, which often derive from the name of a well-known person of senatorial, equestrian or freedman rank, e.g. Agrippianus, Maecenatianus, Pallantianus, etc., and thus provide a further dating criterion. These names, however, do not necessarily provide a dating to *within* a particular reign as some are found among the dated inscriptions belonging to more than one reign, e.g. Agrippianus, Antonianus, Drusillianus, Germanicianus, Vedianus, etc.[2]

For Imperial freedmen, and for Imperial slaves occurring in the same inscriptions with *Augusti liberti*, the important question to decide is how long after the death of their patron do they normally survive, and thus establish the *terminus ad quem* for their inscriptions. The great bulk of these are sepulchral and relatively seldom dateable by the methods discussed above. For this purpose the *nomina* of the Imperial freedmen are particularly important.[3]

---

[1] Chantraine includes three instances in his list of dated freedman inscriptions, but the list is considerably longer, viz.: VI 8470 = D 1535 (54/68); *IGR* I 781 (88/90); III 14195.2 = D 4046 (103/4); III 7130 = *AE* 1966, p. 134 (98/117); VIII 25902.1.2 = *ILAlg*. I 440 = *FIRA*² I pp. 484 f. no. 100 (114/17); *AE* 1922, 19 = *ILAlg*. I 3992 (*c*. 122); VIII 25943.4.5 f. = *FIRA*² I pp. 491 f. no. 101 (117/38); *AE* 1928, 18 = *ILAlg*. I 3991 (117/38); LBW II 1076 = D 8849 (117/38); III 431 = 7116 = 13674 = D 1449 (*c*. 137); XIII 1808 = D 1454 (*c*. 135/45); XIV 2008a = XV 7740 = D 8686 (*c*. 144); *OGI* 707 = *IGR* III 1103 = D 8846 (159/60); VIII 7039, cf. p. 1848 = *ILAlg*. II 665 = D 1437 (138/61); IX 2438, cf. VI 455 (168/9-172); *AE* 1956, 123 = *Libyca* 3 (1955), pp. 123 f. (*c*. 170); III 6574 = 7126 = D 1344 (176/80); *AE* 1965, 1-2 = *Act. Ant.* 13 (1965), 207-11 (184/5); III 8042 (*c*. 183); VI 632 = D 5094a (185/92); III 6575 = 7127 = D 1421 (*c*. 196); 249 = 6753 = D 1396 (*c*. 198); 6075 = D 1366 (*c*. 204); II 1085 = D 1406 (*c*. 208); X 7584 = D 1359 (198/209); III 4024 (198/211); VIII 7053 = *ILAlg*. II 668 = D 1438 (198/211); *IGR* III 168 (198/211); III 251 = D 1373 (198/211); VI 36935 (212/17); VIII 11175 (*post* 217); *IGR* I 623 = D 8851 (238/44); *AE* 1908, 30 (*c*. 246/9). For detailed comments on this list with prosopographical details, in connection with corrections and additions to Chantraine's list of dated inscriptions of Imperial freedmen and slaves (Chantraine, pp. 56-8), see *Epigr. Studien* (1972).

[2] For detailed references see Chantraine's list, pp. 295 f., and for discussion Part III below, pp. 212 f.

[3] Cf. Thylander, *Étude*, pp. 12 f.; Chantraine, pp. 60 f.

CHAPTER 2

NOMINA AND PRAENOMINA

EARLIER CHRONOLOGICAL LIMITS

An Imperial *nomen* in itself only gives a fixed *earlier* chronological limit, or *terminus post quem*, for an *Augusti libertus*. Thus, when used in conjunction with the Imperial *praenomina*, the earliest dates possible for the following are: C. Iulius Aug. l. 27 BC; M. Iulius Aug(ustae) l. AD 14;[1] Ti. Iulius Aug. l. AD 14; Ti. Claudius Aug. lib. 41; Ser. Sulpicius Aug. lib. 68; T. Flavius Aug. lib. 69; M. Cocceius Aug. lib. 96; M. Ulpius Aug. lib. 98; P. Aelius Aug. lib. 117; T. Aelius. Aug. lib. 138; M. Aurelius Aug(g). lib., L. Aurelius Aug(g). lib. 161; L. Septimius Aug. lib. 193, Augg. lib. 197, Auggg. lib. 198.[2] The freedmen of the *Aurelii Augusti*: M. Aurelius (161–80), Commodus (177–92), Caracalla (197–217), Elagabalus (218–22), Severus Alexander (222–35), all have the same *nomen* and *praenomen*, except some with the

[1] Freedmen of Livia before her adoption by Augustus in AD 14 called themselves 'M. Livius (Liviae/Aug(ustae) l.)', deriving their *praenomen* from Livia's real father, M. Livius Drusus. After her adoption Livia's freedmen did not take the *praenomen* 'C. (Iulius Aug(ustae) l.)', as was strictly possible, but retained the original *praenomen* 'M.' There is only one example of the *praenomen* 'C.' with a freedman of Livia, VI 20237 = D 8052: C. Iulius Augustae l. Prosopas. In VI 4448: C. Iulius Eutyches, Fausti Iuliae Augustae a manu filius, the *praenomen* cannot be derived from the father, who is still a slave of Livia, but probably is from the mother, who is not recorded, whether or not she was a freedwoman of Augustus. The freedmen of Livia after 14 can, and could, thus be distinguished. Cf. the well-known case of M. Pomponius Dionysius (Cicero, *ad Att.* iv. 15.1), the freedman of T. Pomponius Atticus, who took Cicero's *praenomen* as an honour to the latter. After Livia became Iulia Augusta her freedmen regularly used the *nomen* 'Iulius', e.g. VI 3945–6, 3980, 5243, 20130, etc. Cf. Chantraine, p. 74.

[2] VI 8825b = 26277 reads: 'd. m./Septimiae Philadelphiae b. m./f. C. (c.?) Septimius Philadelphus/ Aug. lib. et Septimia Helice fecerunt/l. lib. pos. eorum/C. S. Heliconi filio piissimo bene merenti/ vixit an. XVIII menses X'. No member of Septimius Severus' immediate family had the *praenomen* 'C.' Chantraine argues (p. 80 with n. 84) that in line 3 the *nomen* also of C. Septimius Philadelphus need not derive from the Imperial Septimii. He considers C. Septimius Vegetus, *praefectus Aegypti c.* 80–85, as a possible patron. The inscription would then date from the late first century. I am disinclined to accept this solution. The abbreviated *nomen* of the son, C. S(eptimius) Helicon, the postponed position of the status indication 'Aug. lib.', and the *nomen* of the wife, Septimia Helice, while singly not decisive, taken together do tell against a first-century date. The only other wife in the Familia Caesaris material with *nomen* 'Septimia' occurs in VI 10246 which is evidently third-century in date. The fact that the son died aged only 18 makes it not unlikely that he was freeborn, rather than manumitted very early. He derives his *cognomen* from his mother, similarly freeborn, and his *praenomen* from *her* father who was perhaps in turn connected with the C. Septimii, the Italian branch of the family. In lines 2–3, therefore, I would propose reading: 'Septimiae Philadelphiae b(ene) m(erenti)/f(iliae) c(arissimae), Septimius Philadelphus Aug. lib. ...'. Cf. in line 6: 'filio piissimo bene merenti'.

Nomina and praenomina

praenomen 'L.' manumitted either by L. Verus or by Commodus at certain periods,[1] probably 177–80 and 190–2. The separate freedmen of these emperors cannot be distinguished by nomenclature alone, except the cases of M. Aurelius Auggg. lib.[2] which are *post* 198 when Geta became Caesar. It is sometimes possible to distinguish between the freedmen of Augustus and Gaius by means of the forms of the status indication characteristic of the former, e.g. Caesaris l., Caesaris Augusti l. But separation of the freedmen of Claudius and Nero, and those of Vespasian, Titus and Domitian is very difficult in the absence of other dating criteria.

Where Imperial freedmen with *different nomina* appear in the same inscription, as often happens, or with the slave of a particular emperor, the earliest possible date is that of the *latest nomen* or reign concerned, e.g. VI 18456: Flavia Aug. lib. Tyche and Onesimus Imp. Caes. Nervae Traiani ser. Phoebianus, cannot be earlier than 98 (nor later than 117); VI 15235: Ti. Claudius Aug. lib. Protas and his wife Flavia Aug. lib. Helias, cannot be earlier than 69. In conjunction with the latest date probable for the *earliest nomen* in an inscription, narrower limits can be established for some of these inscriptions, e.g. VI 29396: Ulpia Aug. lib. Saturnina and T. Aelius Aug. lib. Felix, must be later than 138 and earlier than *c*. 160.[3]

Only one freedman of Otho is found in the inscriptions.[4] Not surprisingly, freedmen of the following are not represented at all: Vitellius, Pertinax,[5] Didius Iulianus, Clodius Albinus,[6] Pescennius Niger and Macrinus. The identification of Imperial freedmen after Severus Alexander becomes difficult because of the brevity of the reigns, the dearth of inscriptions from the period, and especially the difficulty of distinguishing the Imperial *nomina* from those of the early Principate: C. Iulius Maximinus (235–8), M. Antonius Gordianus (Gordian III, 238–44), and M. Iulius Philippus (244–9).[7] The only certain instance of a freedman of any of these emperors is the freedman of Gordian III in *IGR* I 623 = D 8851[8] which dates from his

---

[1] E.g. *EE* VIII 369 = D 5186: L. Aurelius Aug. lib. Pylades 'ex indulgentia imperatoris Commodi', cf. V 7753 = D 1585; and XIV 4254 = D 5191; VI 10117 = D 5190; XIV 5735: L. Aurelius Augg. lib. Apolaustus Memphius.

[2] VI 816 = D 1928 (dated to May 238); III 1328; *AE* 1928, 199.

[3] For difficulties with VI 8634 = D 1697: Ti. Claudius Aug. lib. Avitus with T. Aelius Aug. lib. Theodotus; and VI 15317: Ti. Claudius Aug. l. Censorinus with P. Aelius Aug. lib. Ianuarius; and *NS* 1917, p. 291, nos. 6–7, see below, pp. 35 f.

[4] VI 25833: M. Salvius Romanus Aug. lib.

[5] There is one slave of Pertinax in XIII 4323 = D 410, a dedication to Pertinax and Fl(avia) Titiana August(a).

[6] Unless Adrastus Augg. nn. lib. in 193 (VI 1585b = D 5290) refers in his status indication to Septimius Severus *and* Clodius Albinus.

[7] All the (theoretical) possibilities are given in detail by Chantraine, pp. 61 f.

[8] See above, p. 22 n. 4.

Nomenclature and chronology

reign (238–44).[1] The latest dated inscription of an Imperial freedman with *nomen* is VI 816 = D 1928: M. Aurelius Auggg. lib. December, May 238.[2] The literary and legal sources continue to refer to 'Caesariani' long after this date but, while the status of these as officials of the Imperial administration is certain, it is not at all clear that they are freedmen as many scholars have thought. They are in fact probably of freeborn status.[3]

Some special groups of freedmen need to be discussed here. The group of seven freedmen, 'T. Aurelius Aug. lib.',[4] are to be assigned to Antoninus Pius, who before his adoption by Hadrian in 138 was T. Aurelius Fulvius Boionius Arrius Antoninus. This is shown by XIV 250: T. Aurelius Aug. lib. Strenion, which is dated to 152, nine years before the accession of M. Aurelius. Another, T. Aurelius Egatheus (VI 8440 = D 1529), was called 'Imp. Antonini Aug. lib. a codicillis' (cf. Fronto, *Epist.* ii. 16) and was also certainly a freedman of Pius. Another, XIV 2104: T. Aurelius Aug. lib. Aphrodisius, was 'proc. Aug. a rationibus' and received a dedication from the Senate and People of Lanuvium under aediles whose year of office is not known. It is to be noted that three of the seven held positions of importance and influence, most likely all under Antoninus Pius, and that none of the seven has the status indication 'Augg. lib.' They would have been manumitted by him before his adoption but their inscriptions were put up after his accession.

A further group of freedmen, 'L. Aelius Aug. lib.',[5] belong either to L. Aurelius Aug. Verus, who from 138 to 161 was L. Aelius Aurelius Commodus (before his adoption he was L. Ceionius Commodus), or to

---

[1] Another possible instance is *SEG* XIII 623 = Sadurska, *Inscr. lat. et Monum. funer. rom.* (Warsaw, 1953), No. 40: 'Iulia Syntyche M. Iulio Aug. l. Sisto viro suo' where the Greek version has Σεβαστοῦ ἀπελευθέρῳ. This inscription, of uncertain origin, is firmly assigned to the middle of the third century by *SEG* and Sadurska on internal evidence (Σεβαστοῦ), and on the lettering, especially the Greek, which it is said, cannot be earlier than late second-century. In this case Sistus would have to be a freedman of M. Iulius Philippus (Philip the Arabian, 244–9). But it should be noted that the style of the inscription is unusual for the third century (cf. the status indication 'Aug. l.'). VIII 7075 = *ILAlg.* II 783: 'M. Antonius Ianuarius Aug. lib. adiutor tabularii', is to be assigned to the first century despite the fact that freedmen of Antonia Minor are not otherwise found outside Italy and that in all very few freedmen of the Julio-Claudian emperors are found in Africa. In XV 7327, a *fistula* from the joint reign of Septimius Severus and Caracalla, read: 'M. AV(relio) FEL(ice) AVGG. LIB.' for 'M. AN(tonio)...'.

[2] On his status indication and probable patrons see below, p. 58 n. 4.

[3] For the literary evidence on *Caesariani*, e.g. Cyprian, *Epist.* 80.2 (AD 258), see Mommsen, *Hermes* 34 (1899), 151–5; Jones, *JRS* 39 (1949), 46 f. = *Studies in Rom. Govt. and Law*, 164 f.; *LRE*, 564 f., who attribute the change from Imperial freedmen to military organisation in the administration to Diocletian or later. But the date is earlier, the reign of Gallienus at the latest, see Boulvert, II, 807 f. (ed. polyc.); Chantraine, pp. 69 f.

[4] VI 5, 8440 = *IGR* I 113 = D 1529, 13219, 13331 = 34063; *AE* 1953, 64; XIV 250 = D 6174 (Ostia), 2104 = D 1475 (Lanuvium); cf. *IGR* IV 544: Τ. [Α]ἴλιος Αὐρήλιος Σε[β]αστο[ῦ] ἀπελεύθερος Ν[ίγε]ρ.

[5] VI 8778, 10644, 10762, 18457, 25085; IX 344 = D 5188; and possibly a seventh, XIII 5244 = D 1562.

Nomina and praenomina

L. Aurelius Commodus, son of M. Aurelius and Augustus with his father from 177 to 180. After the death of his father he took the name of M. Aurelius Commodus Antoninus Aug. and in the period 190–92 that of L. Aelius Aurelius Commodus Aug.[1] In five cases 'L. Aelius Aug. lib.' probably indicates that these were freedmen of L. Verus and were manumitted between 138 and 161 but their inscriptions date from after 161, in a similar way to the 'T. Aurelii Aug. liberti' mentioned above. It is to be noticed that in this case none of these freedmen of L. Verus Antoninus held official posts in the administration, by contrast with the previous group. Here also is to be placed '[L. Aurelius (Aug. lib.) Nicomedes qui et] Ceionius et Aelius vocitatus est'.[2] Originally a slave of L. Aelius Caesar (father of L. Verus), who manumitted him, and the 'educator' of his son Verus (mentioned in SHA *Verus* 2.8), his alternative *nomina* reflect the changing names of his patrons, L. Ceionius Commodus later L. Aelius Caesar, and then his son, L. Aelius Verus later L. Aurelius Aug. Verus. This was exceptional (for an exceptional freedman-equestrian), as may be seen by contrast with VI 34805: L. Ceionius Aug. lib. Hermes, also a freedman of L. Ceionius Commodus before his adoption by Hadrian. These two were manumitted before 138 but their inscriptions date from 161 or later.

The remaining case (IX 344 = D 5188) is more difficult. The name is given as '[L. A]elius Aug. lib. [Aur]elius Apolaustus', with double *gentilicia*. The *praenomen* 'L.' is restored.[3] This Apolaustus is referred to in a letter to Fronto which is most probably to be dated to 161/2, i.e. *before* Verus' departure for the East; and, according to SHA *Comm.* 7.2, he was put to death along with other palace freedmen by Commodus in 189. He would have been freed by L. Verus before the latter became emperor in 161, and would have acquired his second *gentilicium* in the same fashion as Nicomedes above. He is, however, to be distinguished from another well known *pantomimus*, L. Aurelius Augg. lib. Apolaustus Memphius who, according to the SHA again (*Verus* 8.10), was brought back from Syria by Verus after the Parthian war. He was distinguished by the second *cognomen* 'Memphius' and was the

---

[1] Cf. D 378, 400, 401, 405. I find it difficult to agree with Chantraine (p. 63 with n. 12) that L. Aelius Caesar, father of L. Verus, is a candidate as the original patron of these freedmen. The parallel with the 'T. Aurelii Aug. lib.' rather points to L. Verus, who did later become an 'Augustus'. All these inscriptions must be dated to 161 or later. For the one example of a 'L. Ceionius Aug. lib.' (VI 34805) see below.

[2] VI 1598 = D 1740; Pflaum, *CP* No. 163, pp. 393 f.; Chantraine, p. 92. His *nomina*, especially the restoration 'Aurelius', could imply manumission by L. Verus rather than by his father L. Aelius Caesar; but the age of L. Verus at the time is against this (he would have been less than six years old), and the position 'a cubiculo' held under Aelius Caesar presupposes freedman status already.

[3] In the other inscription referring to this Apolaustus the *praenomen* is similarly restored, X 3716 = D 5189: [L.] Aurel[ius] Apolaustus. Cf. Fronto, *ad Ver.* i. 2 (p. 115 Nab.); SHA *Commod.* 7.2: 'cum etiam Apolaustus aliique liberti aulici pariter interempti sunt'.

Nomenclature and chronology

recipient of an honorific inscription in 199 (i.e. ten years *after* the death of the first Apolaustus mentioned above).[1]

Another case of twin *gentilicia* occurs in *IRT* 606 = *AE* 1953, 188 (Lepcis Magna): M. Septimius Aurelius Agrippa M. Aureli Antonini Pii Felicis Aug. lib. This is another *pantomimus*. He was clearly not jointly manumitted by Septimius Severus and Caracalla but by the latter alone; the inscription is to be dated after 211 (cf. 'Felix' among Caracalla's titles).[2] Such double *nomina* are exceptional.[3] So, indeed, is the nomenclature of star actors.

Alongside the freedmen and slaves of the emperors (*Augusti*) should be considered the freedmen and slaves of the *Augustae*, in whatever relationship the latter stood to the emperor, whether 'mater Augusti', e.g. Livia, Antonia Minor (also grandmother of Gaius), or 'uxor Augusti', e.g. Poppaea Sabina, Domitia Domitiani, Plotina, or 'soror Augusti' (Marciana) and even 'neptis Augusti' (Matidia Maior). The *Augustae* were wealthy owners of property, including many slaves. Their freedmen provide a distinctive series of secondary Imperial *gentilicia* which are useful for dating. Joint manumissions by an *Augustus* and an *Augusta*, frequent intermarriage between members of their respective *familiae* and the general closeness of social intercourse between them qualify them for associate membership of the Familia Caesaris. Thus inscriptions referring to a 'Liviae l(ib.)' are to be

---

[1] XIV 4254 = D 5191 (AD 199). Cf. XIV 5375; X 6219 = D 5187; VI 10117 = D 5190; XI 3822 = D 5192 (frag.); SHA *Verus* 8.10. The distinction between these two *pantomimi* has been convincingly argued by Boulvert in an unpublished article entitled 'Le Gentilice de L. Aurelius Augg. lib. Apolaustus Memphius', which the author has kindly made available to me; cf. T. D. Barnes, 'Hadrian and Lucius Verus', *JRS* 57 (1967), 72; against Chantraine, pp. 380 f., cf. 255 n. 85a; Stein, *PIR*², A 148; Dessau, ad loc., and others. According to Boulvert, Apolaustus Memphius, after having been acquired by Verus, was manumitted by Commodus. He kept his original *praenomen* 'L.', but under Septimius Severus and Caracalla he took the status indication 'Augg. lib.' in place of 'Aug. lib.'

[2] Chantraine (p. 97) thinks that the *nomen* 'Septimius' placed first indicates that he was manumitted during Septimius Severus' lifetime. If this was during the period of joint rule by Septimius and Caracalla, the form is exceptional. The inscription comes from Severus' birthplace.

[3] Other examples of Imperial freedmen are all late second or early third century: *IGR* IV 544 (p. 26 n. 4, above), the earliest, manumitted by Antoninus Pius *before* his adoption by Hadrian; VI 13209: M. Aur(elius) Rutilius Eutyche[s] Aug. lib.; 17920: Aurelius Aug. lib. Fidicinius Maximus; 26261: L. Septimius Vibius Trophimus Augg. lib.; *Ant. Class.* 24 (1955), p. 74 no. 26: M. Aurelius Allidius [Ia]nuarius August[...?]. On this group, see Chantraine, pp. 96 f.

Equally exceptional, but different, are the alternative *nomina* in VI 8432 = D 1526: 'd. m. Ulpiae sive Aeliae Aug. lib. Apate et Ulpio Felici fil(io)...fecit P. Aelius Aug. lib. Florus....coniugi piissimae'. Chantraine derives 'sive Aeliae Aug. lib.' not from Hadrian directly, but from the *nomen* of her husband. Apate's son, Ulpius Felix, who died aged 10, would be freeborn and born after the mother's manumission by Trajan. The couple were married for forty-four years, so that Florus must have been at least 60 at the date of the inscription which would date from well into the reign of Antoninus Pius. Florus, who became a *procurator*, may have previously been a *dispensator*, which involved delayed manumission, i.e. till a reign later than his wife's.

Nomina and praenomina

dated before AD 14, 'M. Livius Aug(ustae) l(ib.)' after 14, although manumission presumably took place before that date; 'Iuliae Aug(ustae) l(ib.)', 'M. Iulius Aug(ustae) l(ib.)', both manumission and inscription after 14; 'M. Livius Divae Aug(ustae) l(ib.)', manumission before 14, inscription after 41, the date of Livia's deification by Claudius;[1] 'M. Iulius Divae Aug(ustae) lib.', manumission between 14 and 29, inscription after 41; 'M. Antonius Aug(ustae) l(ib.)', manumission before summer 37, inscription after spring 37;[2] 'Iulia Agrippinae Aug(ustae) lib.', after 51; 'C. Poppaeus Aug(ustae) lib.' or 'Poppaeae Augustae lib.', after 63; 'Divae Iuliae Aug(ustae) lib.' (daughter of Titus), after 87; 'Domitiae Aug(ustae) lib.', after 81;[3] 'L. Pompeius Aug(ustae) lib.', after c. 105;[4] 'Divae Plotinae lib.', after 122; 'L. Vibius Aug(ustae) lib.'[5] or 'Sabinae Aug(ustae) lib.', after 128; 'Galerius Aug(ustae) lib.'[6] or 'Faustinae Aug(ustae) lib.', after 138; 'M. Annius Aug(ustae) lib.'[7] or 'Lucillae Aug(ustae) (lib.)', after 169. Freedmen of Iulia Domna, Fulvia Plautilla, Iulia Maesa, Iulia Soemias and Iulia Mamaea do not appear.

Around the *Augusti* and *Augustae* were other personages of the Imperial family each with their number of freedmen and slaves whose nomenclature was designed to draw attention to their attachment to the Imperial household. These again are useful for dating and cross-checking with freedmen and slaves of the emperor with whom they frequently intermarried. I have noted freedmen and slaves of the following: Scribonia Caesaris (Augusti uxor), Octavia Augusti soror, Marcella Minor, M. Agrippa, M. Antonius (triumvir), Germanicus Caesar, Agrippina Germanici (uxor), Iulia Germanici filia, Drusus Caesar Tiberii filius, Claudia Livia Drusi Caesaris (uxor), Ti. Germanicus (Claudius before he became emperor), Messalina Aug(usti uxor) and Ti. Claudi Caesaris (uxor), Ti. Claudius Caesaris f. (Britannicus),

---

[1] VI 1815 = D 1926, 4159.

[2] For inscriptions before 37 the status indication was 'Antoniae Drusi l.'

[3] It is stated that 'there are no recorded instances of freedmen of Domitia' (B. Wilkinson, *Names of Children in Roman Imperial Epitaphs* (Diss. Bryn Mawr, 1961), p. 33 n. 11; cf. Chantraine, p. 65). This is strictly true only of the formula 'Cn. Domitius Aug(ustae) lib.' In XIV 2795 = D 272, a dedication 'in honorem memoriae domus Domitiae Augustae Cn. Domiti Corbulonis fil.' dated to 140, Cn. Domitius Polycarpus and his wife Domitia Europe are most probably a freedman and freedwoman of Domitia. Domitia survived into the reign of Hadrian, as brick-stamps dated 123-9 attest (XV 552-4) (cf. Syme, *Tacitus* (Oxford, 1968), p. 300). Cn. Domitius Chrysanthus (X 1738) is also a freedman of Domitia (cf. P-W V, 1513). On the large and important *familia* of Domitia, see below, pp. 65 f. Domitius Lemnus of VI 8500 = XI 1753 = D 1490 is to be assigned to Nero before his adoption by Claudius in 50 (Weaver, *Historia* 14 (1965), 509 f.; Chantraine, p. 65 n. 15; cf. Smallwood, *Documents...of Gaius, Claudius and Nero* (Cambridge, 1967), No. 179 (= McCrum and Woodhead, No. 201).

[4] VI 1878 = D 1912; *AE* 1958, 184.

[5] VI 28804; XI 4657 (?).

[6] VI 8866 = D 1793.

[7] But (M.) Annius Phlegon Aug. lib. (XV 7740 = XIV 2008a = D 8686; 7743 = XIV 1980; XIV 5309.19; cf. *PIR*², A 675), dated to the reign of Antoninus Pius, was probably manumitted by M. Aurelius before his adoption by Pius in 138. For the other possibilities, see Chantraine, p. 64.

Nomenclature and chronology

Octavia Caesaris Augusti f(ilia, Neronis uxor), Claudia Antonia (Claudi) Aug(usti) filia, Vibia Aurelia Sabina Marci Aug(usti) filia, (Commodi) Aug(usti) soror.[1]

LATER CHRONOLOGICAL LIMITS

The *terminus ad quem* for inscriptions of freedmen with Imperial *nomina* is of great importance as on it depends the possibility of establishing useful dating criteria for some 1,500 out of more than 2,500 known freedmen of an *Augustus* or an *Augusta*. Many factors are involved, some rarely determinable, such as the point in the reign of an emperor at which manumission took place; there is no reason to suppose that manumissions did not occur fairly regularly throughout an emperor's reign but only in the case of a few freedmen can one assert that they were definitely *not* manumitted in the last years of the reign. This factor, however, does tend to reduce the *average* figure for the number of years freedmen of an emperor survived after his death. Another important factor is the age at which manumission took place. The legal minimum for freedmen in general was thirty years, but there were numerous exceptions.[2] One should also consider whether a freedman's tombstone was erected in his lifetime or, if after his death, by how long. But most important is the age at death. For freedmen this is known in some 200 cases. Thus, for example, a 'Ti. Claudius Aug. lib.' or a 'M. Ulpius Aug. lib.' who died aged forty years, if the other factors mentioned above are taken into account, is unlikely to have lived more than ten years after the death of Nero or Trajan respectively, i.e. their inscriptions are not likely to be later than 78 or 127.

The limits of survival can be established from the dated inscriptions.[3] The latest dated inscriptions are: 'Divi Augusti l(ib.)' AD 44 (VI 10399 = XI 3806, cf. XI 3805, AD 26); 'Ti. Iulius Aug. l(ib.)' 52 (X 769 = XVI 1 = D 1986);[4] 'Ti. Claudius Aug. lib.' 108 (VI 630 = D 1699 = 3541); 'T. Flavius Aug. lib.' 136 (VI 975 = D 6073); 'M. Ulpius Aug. lib.' 153 (VI 10234 = D 7213); 'P. Aelius Aug. lib.' 153 (VI 10234 = D 7213) – that is 30, 15, 40, 40, 36 and 15 years respectively after the death of the last possible manumitting emperor. In four instances out of six freedmen were alive 30–40 years after the death of the emperor who was their patron. While these cases cannot be character-

---
[1] For full details on the *familiae* of the Imperial princes, see Chantraine, pp. 35 f.
[2] See below, pp. 97 f.
[3] Cf. Thylander, *Étude*, pp. 12 f. and above, pp. 20 f.
[4] The latest dated 'C. Iulius Aug. lib.' is in VI 376 = D 3670, on an altar with the date 157 'in latere'. There appears to be no distinction between the lettering in different parts of the inscription, which must be assumed to have been put up all at the one time. If C. Iulius Aug. lib. Satyrus was living at the dedication date, he would have had to be 116 years old even if *born* at the death of Gaius. A possible solution to this problem may be in the application of the SC Claudianum, on which see below, pp. 162 f. See also Chantraine, pp. 77 f.

Nomina and praenomina

istic there is nothing in the inscriptions themselves to suggest that they are notable examples of longevity and it is interesting that four such figures should be found among the few surviving dated inscriptions before the Aurelii.

In fact these figures can easily be paralleled among the other categories of dated inscriptions. Coetus Herodianus, *praegustator* under Augustus (VI 9005 = D 1795) lived till AD 39/42. Freedmen of Tiberius and Gaius lived on into the reign of Nero: Ti. Iulius Aug. lib. Xanthus (VI 32775 = 33131 = D 2816), subprefect of the fleet at Alexandria; Ti. Iulius Aug. l. Secundus (VI 37752), an ear specialist; C. Iulius Aug. l. Samius (XIV 3644 = D 1942), *procurator* and *accensus* to both the emperors Claudius and Nero; and the most notable case on record, the father of Claudius Etruscus, who survived the death of his manumittor Tiberius by fifty-five years, dying in AD 92 under Domitian. In several of these cases the senior appointments held testify to their senior age and status. But the fact that both Xanthus and Etruscus' father among them lived to the age of ninety points to the importance of the age factor in determining the period of survival after the death of the manumittor.[1]

Among the dated inscriptions of Imperial freedmen from Vespasian to Antoninus Pius those freedmen with Imperial *nomen* provide useful confirmation. Compared with the dated freedmen who have a *nomen* and *praenomen* which indicate manumission during the same reign as the date of the inscription, we find twice as many with a *nomen* indicating manumission in an earlier reign and half of these at least two reigns earlier. For example, under Domitian only one 'T. Flavius Aug. lib.' appears amongst the dated inscriptions as against five 'Ti. Claudii Aug. lib.'[2] Several of the latter have senior appointments, e.g. Ti. Claudius Aug. lib. Bucolas who was *procurator*

---

[1] This use of Imperial *nomina* does not hold for a *libertus liberti* who could equally survive *his* patron by as long again; e.g. *AE* 1953, 24 = Gordon, *Alb.* I 90: M. Livius Augustae liberti libertus Tanais (AD 45?); VI 644 = D 3537: Cassianus T. Flavi Aug. lib. Celadi libertus (AD 149). But this is scarcely a solution to the problem of C. Iulius Aug. lib. Satyrus who died in 157.

[2] *Domitian*: Ti. Claudius Aug. lib.: XV 7279 = D 8679, 7280, cf. XI 3612 = D 1567; *IGR* I 781 (AD 88); III 14192.10 = *IGR* IV 847 = *MAMA* VI 2; VI 31295a; X 6640 = D 3338 (AD 85). T. Flavius Aug. lib.: *AE* 1959, 42.

Trajan: Ti. Claudius Aug. lib.: VI 32429 (frag. AD 98/100); VI 630 = D 1699 = 3541 (AD 108). T. Flavius Aug. lib.: III 14195.2 = D 4046 (AD 103/4); VI 18456. M. Ulpius Aug. lib.: XI 3614 = D 5918a (AD 113/14); *SEG* XI 1124 (AD 102/14); VI 8821 (AD 110); cf. III 7130.

Hadrian: T. Flavius Aug. lib.: VI 975 = D 6073 (AD 136); 30901 = D 1622, cf. 682 = D 1623 (AD 128). M. Ulpius Aug. lib.: VI 975 = D 6073 (AD 136); 1884 = D 1792 (AD 130) twice; 4228 (AD 126); *SEG* XIII 601 = *IGR* I 1255 = *OGI* II 678 (AD 118). P. Aelius Aug. lib.: VI 975 = D 6073 (AD 136); 4228 (AD 126); III 6998 = D 7196; *SEG* I 441, cf. IV 417, II 529 = *AE* 1924, 103.

Antoninus Pius: C. Iulius Aug. lib.: VI 376 = D 3670 (AD 157; see p. 30 n. 4 above). T. Flavius Aug. lib.: X 4747. M. Ulpius Aug. lib.: VI 10234 = D 7213 (AD 153). P. Aelius Aug. lib.: VI 10234 = D 7213, twice; VI 10235 = D 8364 (AD 149). T. Aurelius Aug. lib.: XIV 250 = D 6174 (AD 152); VI 8440 = *IGR* I 113 = D 1529; *AE* 1956, 19. (T?.) Aelius Aug. lib.: VIII 2339 (AD 147).

Nomenclature and chronology

aquarum under Domitian and subsequently *procurator castrensis* in charge of the Palatine domestic establishment; Ti. Claudius Aug. lib. Zena who was trierarch in the fleet at Perinthus; (Ti. Claudius) Atticus Aug. lib. who was *a rationibus* under Domitian subsequent to Etruscus' father, himself a 'Ti. Iulius Aug. lib.' Under Trajan the dated inscriptions record two 'Claudii Aug. lib.' and two 'T. Flavii Aug. lib.' to three 'M. Ulpii Aug. lib.' Under Hadrian there are two 'Flavii Aug. lib.' and five 'M. Ulpii Aug. lib.' to four 'P. Aelii Aug. lib.', while under Antoninus Pius there is only one (doubtful) case, out of as many as ten examples of dated freedmen with *nomen*, who was manumitted during the actual reign.

The evidence of the dated inscriptions, together with the large number of inscriptions in which freedmen of *different* Imperial *nomina* appear together and were therefore manumitted by different emperors, suggest that more, perhaps many more, freedmen outlived the emperor who manumitted them than those who did not, and that more of their inscriptions probably date from the decade after than the decade before the emperor died. For freedmen holding relatively senior posts not normally held till some years after manumission it would be almost regular for their inscriptions to date from a later reign than that of the manumitting emperor, particularly in the case of the M. Ulpii, P. Aelii and T. Aelii whose manumission can be pinpointed to a single reign of not very long duration. To a lesser extent this applies to the Ti. Claudii and the T. Flavii.

The length of reigns of successive emperors becomes an important factor in attempting to establish a chronology for the Familia Caesaris. Augustus reigned for over forty years. This was nearly twice as long as the next longest reign in the history of the early Empire. By contrast, only two of his successors held power for as long as twenty-three years, and the first of these was Tiberius (14–37) his immediate successor. From the point of view of freedman nomenclature, as in many other respects, the reign of Tiberius is to be viewed as a continuation of that of Augustus rather than as providing a contrast with it. Even allowing for the *columbaria* of the first century, which in any case contain more inscriptions of slaves than of freedmen, the number of Imperial freedman inscriptions from the whole period of Augustus and Tiberius is much smaller than for any subsequent period of comparable length. This is partly accounted for by the smaller size of the Familia at that stage of its development. But the two longest reigns in the early Empire and the thinnest concentration of freedman inscriptions coincide with the earliest phase of the Principate.

The next reign as long as that of Tiberius was not till over a century later, that of Antoninus Pius (138–61). In between came reigns of four years

Nomina and praenomina

(Gaius), thirteen (Claudius), fourteen (Nero), the year of the four emperors, then reigns of ten (Vespasian), two (Titus), fifteen (Domitian), two (Nerva), nineteen (Trajan), and twenty-one years (Hadrian). After Antoninus there was no reign of even twenty years' duration till Diocletian, and after Septimius Severus scarcely any that lasted ten years. Exclusive of the periods of civil war (68–9, 193–7) and Macrinus (217), the average length of reign by all emperors during the flourishing period of the early Empire from Tiberius to Severus Alexander inclusive was a bare thirteen years each.

A general working rule would be that, on average, a freedman survived as many years after the death of his manumittor as he himself lived after the age of 35–40 years. A limit of survival of 40 years after the death of the manumitting emperor would imply an age-at-death limit of about 75–80. This limit is suggested by the dated inscriptions. Thus, reasonable limits of survival for freedmen would be: 'Ti. Iulius Aug. l.' *c.* AD 77, 'Iulius Aug. l.' *c.* 80, 'Ti. Claudius Aug. lib.' *c.* 110, 'T. Flavius Aug. lib.' *c.* 140, 'M. Ulpius Aug. lib.' *c.* 160, 'P. Aelius Aug. lib.' *c.* 180, 'T. Aelius Aug. lib.' *c.* 200. In practice, however, the great majority of freedman inscriptions would be at least twenty years earlier, implying death no later than the age of 55–60. These limits, which are inferred solely from the *nomen* (and *praenomen*), both in cases where this is formally stated and where it can be safely inferred (e.g. from the *nomen* of a freedman's own freedman), apply to some 1,500, or just under 60%, of the known *Augusti liberti*.

The limits may be reduced by additional information. Thus for a 'Iulius Aug. lib.' known to have been manumitted by Augustus the *terminus* would be *c.* AD 55, for a 'Ti. Claudius Divi Claudi lib.' *c.* 95, a freedman of Vespasian *c.* 120, and so on. Where the age at death of a freedman is known to be 60 years or less, if we assume that early manumission before the age of 20 was exceptional in the Familia Caesaris,[1] the limit can be reduced by as many years as the age falls short of 60. By the same token, where ages of 80 or over are recorded the limit may have to be correspondingly extended. For example, Ti. Claudius Aug. l. Abascantus (VI 8411 = D 1473), *a rationibus* who died aged 45, would have a limit of AD 95 for his death (i.e. fifteen years less than the limit for a 'Ti. Claudius Aug. lib.' (*c.* 110) because his age at death falls thus far short of 60). If, however, we assume that *normally* manumission did not take place till the age of 30, we can establish a more probable limit which is ten years earlier than the extreme limit, i.e. Abascantus *probably* died before AD 85. For Flavius Alexander Aug. lib. (VI 8610), *ab epistulis Latinis* who died aged 40, the possible and probable limits would thus be AD 120 and

---

[1] It cannot be assumed, as by Taylor (113 f.) and by Wilkinson (*Names of Children*, pp. 21, 104), that manumission *regularly* took place at *any* age.

Nomenclature and chronology

110 respectively; for T. Flavius Aug. l. Ianuarius (VI 8449 = D 1552) who died aged 26, the limits would be 106 or more probably 96; for M. Ulpius Aug. l. Thallus (VI 29272) who died aged 35, AD 135 and 125; for P. Aelius Aug. lib. Secundus (VI 8997), who died aged 46, AD 165 and 155; for T. Aelius Aug. lib. Titianus (VI 8878 = D 1685) who died aged 42, AD 180 and 170; and so on.

On this basis Ti. Iulius Aug. l...., the father of Claudius Etruscus, who died aged 90, could not have died later than *c.* AD 105 and would probably not have survived AD 95. He died in fact in AD 92. From the list of dated inscriptions, Ti. Iulius Aug. lib. Xanthus (VI 32775 = 33131 = D 2816) who similarly lived to the age of 90, survived at least into the reign of Nero when he held the post of *subpraefectus classis Alexandriae*, but he probably lived on some thirty years after retirement into the reign of Domitian. M. Ulpius Aug. lib. Phaedimus, *Divi Traiani a potione*, etc. (VI 1884 = D 1792) would have his possible and probable limits set at AD 128 and 118; he died in fact in AD 117. M. Ulpius Aug. lib. Menophilus (VI 4228) *adiutor proc(uratoris) ab ornamentis*, died aged 35, with limits AD 135 and 125. He died in fact in 126.

In some cases where children are recorded as *Caesaris servi* or *Augusti liberti*, and therefore born before the manumission of the father, and where the years of married life of the father and mother are recorded as having been 40 or less, the limits of survival can similarly be reduced from the maximum by the number of years of married life less than 40 on the assumption that marriage and the birth of the first child took place about the age of 20 for the father. Thus Ti. Claudius Aug. l. Diomedes (VI 22423) who was married for 36 years with Meroe Felix and had a son Ti. Claudius Strenuus, *l(ibertus) et f(ilius)*, is unlikely to have died before the age of about 56 years, with possible and probable limits of AD 105 and 95. T. Flavius Aug. lib. Chrysogonus Lesbianus (VI 8438), who was married for 45 years with Flavia Nice and had a son T. Flavius Aug. lib. Urbanus, is likely to have lived to about the age of 65, with limits of *c.* AD 145 and 135.[1] M. Ulpius Aug. lib. Cerdo (*AE* 1946, 140), married 25 years with Ulpia Nice with a son Antiochianus Caes. n. ser. (i.e. born before the father's manumission), would have limits of *c.* AD 145 and 135.

In a similar way the limits can be reduced in a substantial number of cases, especially for freedmen with different Imperial *nomina* appearing in the same inscription, when the earlier chronological limit will depend on the latest *nomen* and the later limit can be worked out from the survival range of the earliest *nomen*.

---

[1] In this case, for the son to have been manumitted at the regular age of 30 under a Flavian emperor, he would have to have been born *c.* AD 65 or earlier. The father's manumission, if about ten years later, would have been under Vespasian, *c.* 75, rather than later under Domitian.

Nomina and praenomina

IRREGULAR NOMINA OF IMPERIAL FREEDMEN

Problems of two kinds arise: (*a*) where Imperial *nomina* of *Augusti liberti* cannot be reconciled with the dating criteria proposed in the previous section, and (*b*) where non-Imperial *nomina* occur which are used by *Augusti liberti* in an anomalous fashion.

(A) IRREGULAR IMPERIAL NOMINA

One case, (i) C. Iulius Aug. lib. Satyrus (VI 376 = D 3670) with the consular date 157, has already been mentioned. It is over 75 years later than the latest date normally possible for a 'C. Iulius Aug. lib.'

Less extreme, but equally difficult to explain under the normal rules, are (ii) Ti. Claudius Aug. lib. Avitus (VI 8634 = D 1697), *i(n)(v)itator*, who appears in the same inscription with his brother T. Aelius Aug. lib. Theodotus, *adiutor a cognit(ionibus)*; and (iii) Ti. Claudius Aug. l. Censorinus (VI 15317) whose father is P. Aelius Aug. lib. Ianuarius. Somewhat different, but also difficult, is (iv) T. Aelius Aug. lib. Paris (*NS* 1917, p. 291, no. 7) whose father is Ti. Claudius Aug. lib. Eutrapelus. It is almost as hard to imagine the circumstances in which a son could receive manumission at least 70 years after his father (i.e. the son not before 138, the father not after 68) as it is to explain how in (ii) one brother could be manumitted at least 60 years later than another, or how in (iii) a son could be manumitted at least 50 years *before* his father.

In each of these cases it is clear that there are irregularities in the use either of the Imperial *nomen* or of the Imperial freedman status indication. Not only (i) but also (ii) and (iv) should be dated to the reign of Antoninus Pius or later, and (iii) to that of Hadrian or later. There are no real grounds for the suggestions made by several scholars that freedmen can change their *nomen* almost arbitrarily and take that of someone other than their manumittor and patron.[1]

A possible solution to (iv) is provided by a companion inscription *NS* 1917, p. 291, no. 6, which indicates that Ti. Claudius (Aug. lib.) Eutrapelus, the father of T. Aelius Aug. lib. Paris, was himself the freedman of a Ti. Cl(audius) Aug. l. Paris, whom he could have survived by some years. But it has still to be explained why, if the father then became a direct freedman of a Flavian emperor or of Trajan but retained the *nomen* Claudius of his

---

[1] For other views see my discussion of (ii) and (iii) in *CQ* 15 (1965), 323 f., and Chantraine's exhaustive treatment of (i) to (iv), pp. 77 f. For a different view see Boulvert, *EAI*, pp. 95 f. n. 29.

Nomenclature and chronology

original freedman patron, he is such an isolated instance of what must have been a common phenomenon.

A probable solution to (iii) is also indicated by the names of Ti. Claudius Aug. l. Censorinus' mother, Claudia Successa, and of his other brother, Ti. Claudius Vitalio, who died aged 11 years. Both children derived their *nomen* from their mother. The irregularity lies in Censorinus' use of the status indication 'Aug. l.' as does that of Eutrapelus in (iv). Similarly it can be assumed that the use of the status indication in (i) and (ii) is also the source of the problem. The solution I have suggested for these problems requires the application of the SC Claudianum of AD 52, which in turn involves a change of status to that of *serva* on the part of a freeborn mother who cohabited with a slave under certain conditions.[1]

(B) NON-IMPERIAL NOMINA

Three anomalous cases need to be mentioned:[2] (i) C. Asinius Aug. lib. Paramythius Festianus (VI 12533 = 34057 = X 2112); (ii) C. Plotius Aug. lib. Gemellus (VI 24316);[3] (iii) M. Macrius Trophimus Aug. lib. (VIII 12922).

On the grounds alone of the rarity of non-Imperial *nomina* among Imperial freedmen, and because of the problems involved in assuming an arbitrary change of *nomen* back to that of the original owner after manumission by an emperor, we cannot satisfactorily explain these cases as either slaves of private persons bequeathed or otherwise given to the emperor, or as freedmen of *privati* who somehow entered the Imperial service. Unauthorised attempts by the latter to gain entry are recorded – the freedman of M. Claudius Marcellus Aeserninus (Pliny, *NH* xii. 12) during the reign of Tiberius, and freedmen of the exiles recalled by Vitellius (Tacitus, *Hist.* ii. 92). In both cases the 'potentia' which their assumed status as *Augusti liberti* would bring was their motive for the attempted change.

The *nomina* 'Asinius' and 'Plotius' both appear in the family relationships of the Familia Caesaris; e.g. VI 15041: C. Asinius Eulalus son of Ti. Claudius Aug. l. Eulalus. The son died aged 19 years and was therefore probably

---

[1] See below, pp. 162 f. for a full discussion. Chantraine (pp. 86 f.) also has recourse to the SC Claudianum, but sees the explanation of the present second-century cases to lie in the modifications made by Hadrian to the *senatusconsultum* to bring it into accord with the *ius gentium*. Hadrian required the status of the children to follow that of the mother, whatever her status was under the *senatusconsultum*.

[2] Chantraine (p. 79 with n. 81) would add VI 33731: 'T. Siverus Aug. lib. tab. rat. aquariorum', without noting that it is the same inscription as the extant X 1743, cf. p. 971 = D 1608: 'T. Fl(avius) Verus Aug. lib. tab. rat. aquariorum'. The wife's name is Octavia Thetis. See further Weaver, *CQ* 14 (1964), 313 n. 4.

[3] Chantraine twice (pp. 79, 80) misprints VI 21346 for 24316.

Nomina and praenomina

freeborn, deriving his *nomen* from his freeborn mother Asinia. In VI 6189, a Plotia Venusta is found married to Ti. Claudius Aug. l. Phoebus. This shows that the *nomen* 'Plotius' in the Familia Caesaris goes back to about the mid-first century and need not involve the family of Plotina, wife of Trajan.[1]

Once it is possible to demonstrate the applicability of the SC Claudianum to the irregular nomenclature of the Familia Caesaris,[2] the simplest explanation of the present non-Imperial *nomina* is to invoke the *senatusconsultum*, as in the cases considered in (A) above, and to consider these as sons of freeborn women, reduced to the status of *servi/liberti Claudiani* under the SC, but anomalously retaining their original *nomen* derived from their mother.[3]

OMISSION OF NOMEN

The value of the Imperial *nomina* in conjunction with status indication for establishing the chronological basis for the study of the Familia Caesaris can scarcely be overestimated. It is therefore of some importance that over one in three of the Imperial freedmen of whom we have record do not in fact use their *nomen* or have it recorded on their inscriptions as part of their name. To what extent can we infer with certainty the *nomina* of these 800 or so *Augusti liberti*? In general one must use caution.

The fact of omission can be amply illustrated from the dated inscriptions. Philippus Augusti libert(us) (XI 3200 = D 89) dated to 12 BC must be a 'C. Iulius', as with Gratus Caesar(is) l. in AD 3 (*EE* VIII 316 = D 6387). Fourteen of the thirty 'Divi Augusti liberti' do not have *nomen* and *praenomen* (VI 5289, 8012 = D 8436, 11377, 11381, 12595, 16586, 19060, 24223, 38419 b, Gordon, *Alb.* I p. 60, no. 51; XIV 3539 = *I. It.* IV 1.41; V 236 = *I. It.* X 1.53; 1251, 1319). Among the freedmen of Tiberius dated to his reign only two have *nomen* (VI 10449 = D 7909 (liberta); *AE* 1923, 72 (libertus liberti? cf. Chantraine, p. 18 n. 13)), against eight without (VI 4312 = D 1733, 8409, 12652 = *IG* XIV 1892; *AE* 1930, 66; VI 20497, 10383, 17900, 33130), and so on. On documentary and public inscriptions officials tend *not* to use their full name with *nomen* and *praenomen*. At least 125 of 210 recorded freedman

---

[1] For other views on this problem: Mommsen, *CIL* VIII p. 1335 n. 10; Hirschfeld, *Verwalt.* p. 458 n. 1; Vitucci, *Diz. Epig.* IV, 912; Chantraine, pp. 79 f.; Boulvert, II, 499 f. Chantraine suggests that the *nomen* 'Plotius' in (ii) is connected with the *cognomen* of Plotina, Trajan's wife. It is derived from the conjectured *nomen* of Plotina's mother 'Plotia' (otherwise not known). With less plausibility Chantraine (p. 80 n. 3) also suggests that the *nomen* 'Macrius' in (iii) is wrongly inscribed instead of 'Marcius', and could then be derived from either Marcia, wife of Titus, or from the *nomen* 'Marcius' which is said to be implied in the *cognomen* of Trajan's sister, Marciana.

[2] On the names and status of children, see Part II below, pp. 137 f.

[3] In the case of (i), C. Asinius Aug. lib. Paramythius Festianus could then derive his second *cognomen* either from his mother, an Asinia Festa, or from her father, C. Asinius Festus.

Nomenclature and chronology

procurators, i.e. nearly 60%, do not have *nomen*. These include many well known from the *fistulae* (e.g. XV 7282 f.), the patrimonial auxiliary procurators in Africa (VIII 25902, 25943, 26416, 14464 = *FIRA*² I p. 485 f.), the freedman Metrobius (X 6785) who was for a long period in charge of the island of Pandateria, but at a time we cannot determine with any precision because of the absence of *nomen*; and in Rome and Italy, Bassus Aug. lib. (VI 8608), Martialis A[ug. lib.] (VI 8515), Acastus Aug. lib. (X 6081), Paean Aug. lib. (XIV 2932), and many others who raise chronological problems that are important because of the importance of their careers in tracing the history of the senior administrative service. Omission of the *nomen* occurs frequently among Imperial freedmen of all periods and no particular trend is discernible.[1]

The reasons for the omission of the *nomen* are not so clear, nor do they matter very much. Avoidance of unnecessary duplication plays some part, for instance with the freedmen of *Augusti liberti*; the *nomen* must be the same in both cases and is usually omitted from the name of the patron, e.g. III 2097: C. Iulius Sceptus Admeti Aug. lib. [l]ib.; XIV 2780: Ti. Claudius Oniri Aug. l. l. Domesticus; 51: P. Aelius Trophimi Aug. l. lib...; and the group of *lib. liberti* from the early first century who omit the *cognomen* as well as the *nomen* of their patron: VI 5909: C. Iulius Augusti l(iberti) l(ibertus) Priamus; VI 5294, 20002, 32450; XIV 2302; *AE* 1953, 24.

Another reason for omission of *nomen*, as Chantraine has shown, is the naming of the emperor in extended form whether as part of the nomenclature of the freedman himself or in another part of the inscription. The *nomen* of the Imperial freedman is usually given in such cases only when it differs from that of the emperor in question.[2]

In both of the groups already mentioned it is possible to infer the *nomen* of the freedman with confidence. A third group of names falls into this category when the same person is referred to more than once in the same inscription or group of inscriptions, at least once with *nomen* but on other occasions without. The motive is simply economy. Examples: (Ti. Claudius) Bucolas Aug. lib.: XV 7279 = D 8679; cf. XV 7280; XI 3612 = D 1567. (Ulpius) Vesbinus Aug. lib.: XI 3614 = D 5918a. (M. Ulpius) Valens Aug. lib. Phaedimianus: VI 1884 = D 1792; 8550 = D 1756. (Ti. Claudius) Fortunatus Aug. lib.: VI 604, 630 = D 1699 = 3541.[3] In some cases a *nomen* may have been dropped because it was no longer felt to be appropriate, e.g. the procurator of Nero who appears as Domitius Lemnus before Nero's adoption

---

[1] Thylander, *Étude*, p. 84, but cf. pp. 98, 132; Taylor, p. 122; Chantraine, pp. 101 f.
[2] Chantraine, pp. 29 f., 53 f., 103.
[3] On Valens, see Chantraine, p. 106.

Nomina and praenomina

by Claudius (VI 8500 = XI 1753 = D 1490), and after Nero's accession simply as Lemnus Aug. l. (VI 8499 = D 1489).[1]

But once we pass outside the comparatively restricted number of cases in these three groups we encounter much greater difficulties in attempting to infer the *nomina*, and hence the dates, of Imperial freedmen. Internal criteria are frequently used for this purpose, for want of anything better. In particular, the *nomina* of wives and children of *Augusti liberti*. When these coincide with the Imperial *nomina*, e.g. for wives and daughters, Iulia, Claudia, Flavia, Ulpia, Aelia, Aurelia, even though they are accompanied by no status indication whatever, they are often assumed to be as valid for dating purposes as if they were the *nomina* of the *Augusti liberti* themselves. In an earlier article[2] I considered in detail two conspicuously misleading examples of this method, VI 8574 and X 6092 = D 1500; cf. VI 8608. Others will be considered below. The dangers are patent, particularly when this approach actually serves to obscure rather than clarify the chronological significance of other aspects of nomenclature. These are especially the titles of official posts held in the administration, which can themselves be used for dating purposes.

The status of the wives and children of members of the Familia Caesaris is a crucial social and legal question which must be reserved for detailed treatment in Part II. Here it is sufficient to point out that even among those wives with Imperial *nomen* who are *not* 'Augusti libertae' there are almost as many examples where the *nomina* of wife and Imperial freedman husband differ as where they are the same, at least from the Flavian period onwards. In this period there are 128 couples with different Imperial *nomina* compared with 135 couples with the same Imperial *nomen*. As for the wives with non-Imperial *nomina*, these considerably outnumber either of the two Imperial groups with 178 couples in this period. Thus it is possible to find in any period from Augustus to the third-century emperors many examples of wives with the *nomen* 'Iulia' or 'Claudia'. There are several examples of 'Flaviae' married to 'Claudii Aug. lib.' (VI 1859–60, 10089 = D 1766, 15110, 15235) and to Imperial freedmen in all later periods. There is even an example of an 'Ulpia' married to a 'Claudius Aug. lib.' (VI 8898). The earliest 'Aeliae' appear married with 'Flavii Aug. lib.' (VI 8467, 18094). The earliest 'Aureliae' in the dateable material are found married with 'T. Aelii Aug. lib.' (VI 10728, 13339, cf. 13394). *Augusti liberti* without *nomen* are found with wives of every Imperial *nomen* from Iulia to Aurelia. It is possible to argue for an approximate *terminus post quem* for the 'Flaviae', 'Ulpiae', 'Aeliae' and 'Aureliae', but these all begin to appear with freedmen manu-

---

[1] See Weaver, *Historia* 14 (1965), 509 f.   [2] *JRS* 58 (1968), 110 f.

Nomenclature and chronology

mitted at least one reign earlier than that of the emperor whose *nomen* they share, and in some cases two Imperial *nomina* earlier. So the chronological value even of these *nomina* of wives is very limited In addition, wives bearing every Imperial *nomen* are found married with *Caesaris servi* in Rome, Italy and the provinces.

With the names of children it is even more difficult to find any satisfactory chronological criterion. There are very many examples in the Familia Caesaris of children of *Augusti liberti* deriving their *nomen* from their mother and not their father. In fact where the *nomen* of the mother differs from that of the father, the children take the father's *nomen* in less than half of the extant examples. Indeed there are so many examples of children in the Familia whose *nomen* differs from that of both father and mother, even where these differ, that the *nomen* of a child, without other evidence, is practically useless as a safe dating criterion. For example, Claudia Voluptas (VI 10648) has as 'parentes' T. Aelius Aug. lib. Astius and Flavia Deutera.[1] Some examples from the dated inscriptions: XIII 1820 = D 1639: Iulia Adepta, wife of Nobilis Tib. Caesaris Aug. ser., has a son *L.* Iulius Cupitus. The *praenomen* shows that the mother does not belong to the Imperial Iulii. VI 8849: Cinnamus Ti. Caesaris (ser.) has a son C. Sulpi(c)ius Nymphalis. XI 3612 = D 1567: Ti. Claudius Aug. lib. Bucolas has a son *Q.* Claudius Flavianus and a mother Sulpicia Cantabra. VI 15368: Daphnus Imp. Domitiani Aug. Germanici ser. has a daughter Claudia Bassilla. VI 4228 (AD 126): M. Ulpius Aug. lib. Menophilus had as parents P. *Aelius* Aug. lib. Menophilus and Caminia Fortunata, and as wife Iulia Passerilla. One other well-known example may suffice here. The father of Claudius Etruscus was manumitted by Tiberius and would therefore have been called 'Ti. Iulius Aug. l....' To add further to the mysteries of nomenclature which envelop this famous family, it is not even known for certain whether Claudius Etruscus derived his *nomen* from his mother.[2]

ABBREVIATION OF NOMEN

Abbreviation of the *nomen* is not uncommon for Imperial freedmen from the Claudii onwards and provides no chronological clues. The practice is comparatively frequent for the Flavii and Aurelii, and infrequent for the Ulpii. The number of instances I have noted of all kinds of abbreviation is: Ti. Claudii 16, T. Flavii 24, M. Ulpii 8, P. Aelii 17, T. Aelii 15, M. Aurelii

---

[1] For further examples involving the nomenclature of children, see Part II below, pp. 151 f.; also *Proc. Camb. Phil. Soc.* 10 (1964), 86 f.

[2] See Weaver, *CQ* 15 (1965), 150 f.; Chantraine, pp. 89 f.

Nomina and praenomina

50, L. Aurelii 3, Aurelii (without *praenomen*) 30.[1] Single letter abbreviations of the Imperial *nomina*, however, are rare, with five out of seven instances occurring with Flavii: 'T. F(lavius) Aug. lib.': VI 602, 8954 = D 1782, 8973b = D 1830, 18166; X 2433; the others are 'M. U(lpius)': *AE* 1922, 9; 'T. A(elius)': VI 22789.

The one point of interest is that the *praenomen* always precedes the abbreviated form of the *nomen*, until we reach the 'Aurelii Aug. lib.'[2] I have found no example of abbreviated *nomen* without *praenomen* among the 'Aelii Aug. lib.', despite the fact that this group frequently omits the *praenomen* with the unabbreviated form of *nomen*. Then under the Aurelii there are no fewer than thirty examples of abbreviated *nomen* without *praenomen*, compared with fifty examples of abbreviation with *praenomen*.

[1] See Thylander, *Étude*, pp. 97 f.; Weaver, *CQ* 13 (1963), 278.
[2] There is one exceptional form under the Iulii (XIV 3565, the only example of abbreviation for the Iulii), and a brick-stamp under the Claudii (XV 814). On *IPO* A 7, see Weaver, *CQ* 13 (1963), 278 n. 4.

CHAPTER 3

STATUS INDICATION

In the foregoing discussion on dating certain assumptions have been made about the membership of the Familia Caesaris which must now be examined. How can we identify Imperial freedmen and slaves and what limits are to be set to the range of persons included in this study? This is of basic importance, not least because of the frequently made assumption that many persons, especially in the eastern provinces, who possess Imperial *nomina* are by that fact alone Imperial freedmen, particularly if their place of residence or their occupation can be in any way connected with the emperor or the emperor's property.[1] In some cases this is undoubtedly true, but in most cases we cannot be sure. They may be enfranchised provincials or not even Roman citizens at all. If in Rome all persons with an Imperial *nomen* and a Greek-derived *cognomen* were Imperial freedmen, there would scarcely be standing room for anyone else in the Flavian amphitheatre. Some more positive means of identification is required. This is provided by what may conveniently be called the 'status indication'.[2]

In Roman nomenclature generally status is commonly indicated for *ingenui* by filiation – the word 'f(ilius)' or 'f(ilia)' preceded by the father's *praenomen* which is usually abbreviated. This filiation is included in the full nomenclature after the *nomen* and before the tribal indication and *cognomen*, e.g. M. Tullius M. f. Cicero. This filiation indicates his freeborn status. For freedmen (*libertini*) the patron's *potestas* is generally indicated, at least till the mid-first century AD, by 'l(ibertus)' following the patron's *praenomen*, similarly abbreviated (e.g. VI 35612: C. Aufidius C. l. Davus), or less commonly following the patron's *cognomen* (e.g. VI 19060: Iulia Thyrsi l. Iole), or even his full name (VI 9050 = D 1787: Secunda C. Corneli Elenchi liberta). Freeborn status for two generations back can be indicated by 'n(epos)', e.g. M. Tullius M. f. M. n. Cicero, a formula not available to the freeborn son of a freedman, who would be simply, e.g., M. Tullius M. f. Felix as his father, M. Tullius M. l. Felix, had no filiation. The form with 'n(epos)' is an emphatic form of the freeborn status indication but its absence does not necessarily imply freeborn descent for only one generation. Absence of both

---

[1] E.g. among many others, the works of Sir W. M. Ramsay. See further in the section on omission of status indication below, pp. 80 f.   [2] See Mommsen, *Staatsr.* III, 427 f.

Status indication

filiation and the freedman status indication for a person with the *tria nomina* can indicate either an enfranchised *peregrinus* who took the *praenomen* and *nomen* of his benefactor but who, not being subject to his *patria potestas*, has no equivalent for filiation; or it can indicate a *libertus* or an *ingenuus* who has omitted his status indication. Freedmen, with the exception of the *Augusti liberti*, from the mid-first century AD increasingly omitted their status indication. One contributing factor in this decline of the traditional nomenclature is precisely the use of the status indication 'Aug. lib.' by the Imperial freedmen who thus identified themselves as an élite group of higher status than those bearing other forms of the freedman indication.[1] But the study of Roman names which lack status indication is difficult and elusive. It cannot be proved and should not simply be assumed that most of these are freedmen. For slaves status is indicated by the name of their *dominus* in the genitive case, sometimes followed by 'ser(vus)' or 'vern(a)' variously abbreviated, sometimes not.[2]

In the Familia Caesaris the status indication both of freedmen and slaves assumed a variety of forms, all of which had in common some form of reference to the emperor. This is the basic means of identifying its members. Using the inscriptions and the dating methods outlined above, it is possible to trace the general chronological development of these forms and thus discover further dating criteria for the sepulchral inscriptions.[3] In what follows, under each heading the freedman status nomenclature is discussed first, using the basic dating criteria of the dated inscriptions and the Imperial *nomina*. This nomenclature is then compared with that of the Imperial slaves for the same period where this is possible, if not, over the broader divisions of first, second and third centuries. Regional and provincial variations are considered where they are significant, and also the interaction of the slave and freedman status nomenclature on each other. Lastly, where it is relevant, the nomenclature of the freedmen and slaves of the *Augustae* and of other members of the Imperial family is considered.

EXTENDED FORM OF STATUS NOMENCLATURE

From the dated inscriptions we have already seen the general chronological distribution of this form referring to individual emperors. It extends from the

---

[1] Cf. Taylor, pp. 113 f.

[2] On slave nomenclature in general, see A. Oxé, *Rh. Mus.* 59 (1904), 108 f., which deals fully with the Republican nomenclature, with a summary (p. 140) of the normal forms under the Empire. See also now Chantraine, pp. 170 f.

[3] All aspects of the status nomenclature of the Imperial freedmen and slaves have now been treated in massive detail by Chantraine, pp. 140–292. While warmly acknowledging the great value of his study, I cannot refrain from commenting that the detail is frequently overdone, to the point where it is confusing and difficult to see the wood for the leaves. See esp. his chapters VIII and X.

Nomenclature and chronology

'Divi Augusti liberti' (e.g. VI 5870 = 33081: C. Iulius Divi Aug. l. Dionysius) and freedmen of Tiberius (e.g. VI 8409: Antemus Ti. Caesaris Aug. l.) to those of Claudius (e.g. V 2931: Claudia Ti. Augusti l. Toreuma; VI 4305 = D 1732: Ti. Claudius Divi Claudi lib. Actius) and Nero (e.g. XIV 2780: Ti. Claudius Neronis Aug. l. Daphnus; VI 194 = XIV 2861: Nomaeus Neronis Aug. l.). Thereafter the instances are very isolated. Of five clear cases after Nero three are Greek inscriptions – *AE* 1905, 188 = *IG* V 1.1431.40 f. (Vespasian, AD 78); *SEG* II 529 = *AE* 1924, 103 (Hadrian); *IGR* I 623 = D 8851 (Gordian III); one is bilingual – VI 8440 = *IG* XIV 1039 = *IGR* I 1113 = D 1529 (Antoninus Pius; T. Aurelius Egatheus Imp. Antonini Aug. lib.); and the other, from Lepcis Magna, is a rarity in that it also exhibits twin *nomina* – *IRT* 606 = *AE* 1953, 188 (Caracalla).[1] These instances occur in the provinces or under the influence of the less rigid Greek forms of Imperial nomenclature. The use of this extended form by freedmen is thus almost entirely confined to the Julio-Claudian period.

Occasionally useful distinctions were introduced:

(*a*) between freedmen of Augustus and those of Tiberius, by including the emperor's *praenomen* in the status indication when the freedman's *nomen* and *praenomen* were omitted (e.g. VI 4312 = D 7909: Carnius Ti. Caesaris Aug. l.; cf. 8409, 12652 = *IG* XIV 1892; VI 10383: Pin(i)us Ti. Caesaris l.; cf. 17900, 33130), and especially with *libertae* who otherwise lacked the distinguishing *praenomen* (e.g. VI 10449 = D 7909: Iulia Ti. Caesar. Aug. l. Iconio; 20497: Ti. Caesaris l. Iulia Hellas); also with joint freedmen of Tiberius and Livia (e.g. VI 4173: Merops Ti. et Aug(ustae) l. Demosth(enianus); 5223: Castor Ti. Caesa(ris) et August(ae) l. Agrippi(anus); cf. 4776, 5226, 8989 = D 1827, 9066).

(*b*) Between freedmen of Claudius and Nero, who themselves always had the same *praenomen*, by the use in their status indication of the *praenomen* 'Ti.' for Claudius, and 'Neronis' for Nero; e.g. Claudius: V 2931: Claudia Ti. Augusti l. Toreuma; VI 15455: Claudia Ge(r)manici Caesaris Ti. l. Hedone (both these *libertae*); Nero: VI 8783: Ti. Claudius Neronis Augusti l. Hicelus; XIV 2780: Ti. Claudius Neronis Aug. l. Daphnus; cf. (without *nomen*) VI 14647, 194 = XIV 2861; and the *corporis custos*, VI 8803 = D 1730: Ti. Claudius Chloreus Neronis Claudi Caesaris Aug. corporis custos. 'Neronis' was never used as a personal *praenomen* by Nero's freedmen.[2]

(*c*) The use of 'Divus' ('Divi Augusti l.', 'Divi Claudi lib.') in their status indication by freedmen of Augustus and Claudius respectively after the deaths

---

[1] See above, p. 28.
[2] One fragmentary inscription indicates that this distinguishing *praenomen* was used by freedmen of Gaius also – VI 19785: [C. Iul]ius C. Caesaris [lib.].

Status indication

of these emperors. This can distinguish between freedmen of Augustus and of Tiberius without *nomen*, and between those of Claudius and of Nero; e.g. Divi Augusti: VI 8012 = D 8436: Philager Divi Aug. l. Agrippianus; 12595: Athamas Divi Augusti libertus; and twelve further examples, including eight in the inscriptions of their own *liberti* or *servi*.[1] There are perhaps a further sixteen examples with *nomen*; e.g. VI 5870 = 33081: C. Iulius Divi Aug. l. Dionysius.[2] These freedmen can scarcely be using this form of status indication consciously to distinguish themselves from freedmen of Gaius, although they do provide such a criterion. At this early stage in the development of the Familia Caesaris the freedmen manumitted by Augustus were exploiting his posthumous deification as a matter of pride in their previous association with the great founder of the Principate and of the Familia Caesaris.[3]

The freedmen of Claudius were noticeably less inclined to use the title 'Divi Claudi' after his death than were the freedmen of Augustus, at least in the surviving examples. Among the 'C. Iulii Aug. l.' the proportion showing 'Divi Aug. l.' to those showing simply 'Aug. l.' is 1:1·3 (30:40 examples), whereas for the 'Ti. Claudii Aug. lib.' there are only nine instances of 'Divi Claudi Augusti'[4] against over 210 examples of 'Aug. l(ib.)', i.e. 1:24. While one can understand less enthusiasm amongst freedmen in the reign that saw the publication of the *Apocolocyntosis* to advertise their manumission by Claudius, the main reason for this change is the general movement of freedmen away from considering themselves as associated with a particular emperor. The Familia Caesaris had by now passed under the control of its fifth master and patron. The length of reigns became noticeably shorter after the initial exceptionally long rule of Augustus and the comparatively long one of Tiberius. Among freedmen there grew a sense of belonging not to a particular emperor but to an increasingly institutionalised Familia Caesaris. From being *an* emperor's freedmen they became 'Imperial' freedmen. The change is clearly marked by the accession of Vespasian after the Civil War, when the rights of patronage over the emperor's freedmen for the first time passed out of the one family of the Julio-Claudians into that of the Flavii, who had no strictly legal claim thereto. This is paralleled by the passage from the patrimonial to the more distinctly bureaucratic phase of the administration's

---

[1] For references, see Chantraine, p. 17 n. 8, with the addition of V 1319 (Aquileia): Nymphodotus Plocami Divi Aug. l. ser.

[2] See Appendix II, list of dated inscriptions, under 'Divus Augustus' (included in those of Tiberius' reign).

[3] Occupational data are mostly lacking for this group and do not favour the assumption that there was any particular personal association; e.g. VI 8980, 5747 = D 1743, 5202 = D 1778; *EE* VIII p. 164, no. 671. For slaves there is one with the function 'a ma(nu)', VI 8887 = 14399 = 33754.

[4] Including one 'Ti. Claudius Divi l.', X 527 = D 1671. The others are: VI 1921, 4305 = D 1732, 8554 = D 1765, 8636 = D 1682, 9060 = D 1641, 15314, 34909; *AE* 1946, 99.

Nomenclature and chronology

development. In terms of status nomenclature this is marked by the dominance of the now regular form 'Aug. lib.' Hence neither the title 'Divus' nor the other forms of reference to individual emperors are used (or only very exceptionally) by freedmen of the Flavian emperors and their successors, whether deified or not.

With slaves the position is somewhat different. An Imperial slave was always owned by the reigning emperor as the inheritor of the *patrimonium* of his predecessor. In his nomenclature, with very few exceptions, a slave looked to his present circumstances. A freedman looked to the past – to the time of his manumission, which would often have been in the previous reign or the one before that. The institutionalisation of the Familia Caesaris is not reflected to the same extent in the slave nomenclature. 'Divi Augusti' is used once by a slave under Tiberius, VI 8887 = 14399 = 33754: Hyblaeus Divi Augusti a ma(nu).[1] Thereafter, as was to be expected, the use of 'Divi' in the slave indication ceases, as indeed does reference to any previously reigning emperor. The naming of individual reigning emperors lasts in the slave nomenclature till Trajan. It is very common under Tiberius (60 examples), to some extent due to the frequency of finds in the early first-century *columbaria*. But thereafter the practice is found with diminishing frequency in relation to the length of reign – Gaius: 18 examples; Claudius: 38, including *corporis custodes*; Nero: 22, including *corporis custodes*; Vespasian, Titus and Domitian: 34; Trajan: 13.[2]

With the Flavians the *praenomen* 'Imp(eratoris)' appears in the slave indication for the first time and indeed becomes regular in the extended form of status indication.[3] The *praenomen* 'Imp.' continues to occur in this form under Trajan – in fact nine times out of ten for his slaves. For the undated slave inscriptions the form 'Imp. (ser.)' occurs rarely and indicates the period Vespasian to Trajan.[4] The form 'Imp(eratoris) lib(ertus)' does not appear. The reason is not far to seek. The *praenomen* 'Imperator' taken early by Augustus, but not used thereafter by the Julio-Claudian emperors,[5]

---

[1] There is possibly another instance lurking in VI 21748: 'Diony[....] Divi Augusti [....]'; cf. the almost identical fragment, VI 30556.146 (also in the Lateran Museum); also 26608: 'Sitalces Divi Augusti opses Thracum'.

[2] For the commoner forms, see the section above (pp. 21 f.) on dated inscriptions, and for references Appendix II.

[3] For the various forms, see Chantraine, pp. 22 f.; and for references, see Appendix II below. The *praenomen* 'Imp.' does not occur for slaves of the Julio-Claudian emperors, except perhaps in VI 25556: 'Epaphra Imperatoris', named in conjunction with slaves of Messalina.

[4] VI 15492, 20564, 33737 (Agrippinianus); V 96 = *I. It.* X 1. 59, 8386; VIII 12652 ('Imp. n. ser.'); cf. *P. Ryl.* IV 608.

[5] There are isolated instances of its use by Nero from late in his reign (Chantraine, pp. 3, 267); cf. the *corporis custos*, Nobilis miles Impera(toris) Neronis Aug. (VI 8806 = D 1729), but this is not otherwise used by the *corporis custodes*, despite their military associations.

Status indication

became a regular part of the Imperial titulature from the time of Vespasian. The military connotation of the title was not felt suitable for the Familia Caesaris, which was concerned with domestic and civil administration. The *Augusti liberti* and *Caesaris servi* were in any case, like other freedmen and slaves, excluded from directly serving in the army, though they were sometimes given special financial assignments involving the military. The military title 'praefectus' was not used in the Familia either, and 'praepositus' in the administrative service had only a very restricted use before the third century. The use of the *praenomen* 'Imp.' in the extended status indication of Imperial slaves corresponds with its use by the emperors themselves from Vespasian to Trajan. It is also worth noting that the time from Augustus to Nero, during which the *praenomen* 'Imp.' was dropped from the Imperial title, coincided with the formative period of Imperial freedman nomenclature from which 'Aug. lib.' emerged as the regular freedman indication.[1] After Trajan *praenomina* of any sort disappear from the Imperial slave indication, with very rare exceptions.[2] The slave indication in this respect, at a distance of half a century, follows the same pattern as the freedman indication. This may be taken as a sign that by Hadrian's reign a greater degree of bureaucratisation had been reached in the Familia Caesaris than hitherto and now embraced the slave occupational levels as well as those of the freedmen.

The status nomenclature of freedmen and slaves of the *Augustae* tended to be less formalised than that of the Familia Caesaris proper. Where they do not use their distinctive *nomina* and *praenomina*, e.g. 'M. Iulius Aug(ustae) l.', 'M. Antonius Aug(ustae) l.', 'L. Pompeius Aug(ustae) lib.', etc., they continue to use the personal *cognomen* of their patron in their status indication, as do freedmen of other non-reigning members of the Imperial family. Indeed, this full nomenclature was the regular way of distinguishing them from freedmen of the emperor.[3] They also continue to record the deification of their patron after the Imperial freedmen had ceased to do so; for example, the freedmen of Livia after 41, despite the interval of twelve years between her death in 29 and her deification by Claudius in 41. Other isolated examples reach well into the second century.[4] This continued use of the extended form

---

[1] Cf. Chantraine, pp. 264 f., and esp. 267 f.

[2] VI 619: 'Speratus Imp. Caesaris Hadriani Aug. ser.', restored under Caracalla; 19365: 'Chelys Severi Imp. Aug.'

[3] E.g. Octavia Aug. soror: VI 8881 = D 1877, 33378. Germanicus: VI 4328 = D 7694a, 4372, 4401, 4487 = D 7882c, 14909, 34107. Antonia Drusi: VI 4148, 33794 = D 1696, 37451. Agrippina Germanici: 5772. Messalina: 5537. Agrippina Augusta: 20384, 37591. Claudia Antonia: 2329 = D 4992, 9802 = D 7466, 15517. Poppaea Augusta: X 6787 = D 3873. Domitia Augusta: VI 8850 = D 1545. Marciana Augusta: *AE* 1906, 81. Sabina Augusta: VI 11221; *AE* 1915, 9.

[4] VI 18038: Artemis Divae Aug. lib. (Iulia, daughter of Titus); *AE* 1958, 184: L. Pompeius Venustus Divae Plotinae lib.; *AE* 1956, 19: Divae Faustinae Antonini Strenion lib.

Nomenclature and chronology

of status indication by the *Augustae liberti* emphasises by contrast its discontinuance within the Familia Caesaris proper. Slaves of the *Augustae* and of other non-reigning members of the Imperial family also continue to use the personal *cognomen* of their *domina* or *dominus* in their status indication as the regular way of distinguishing themselves from the emperor's slaves.[1]

'CAESARIS' AND 'AUGUSTI' IN THE STATUS INDICATION

There is an obvious distinction between slaves and freedmen in their use of 'Caesaris' and 'Augusti' in the normal status nomenclature of the first and second centuries. 'Caesaris' is favoured for slaves, and 'Augusti' for freedmen – 'Caesaris servus' but 'Augusti libertus'.[2] In all cases of this simple, unextended form of status indication the emperor or the Imperial position in general is referred to, in contrast with the extended form where reference is to a particular emperor. There is no implied distinction between an 'Augustus' and a 'Caesar' among members of the Imperial family. 'Caesar', the family name, in general characterises the position of the *dominus*, the *paterfamilias* *vis-à-vis* his personal property, e.g. 'patrimonium Caesaris', 'praedia, villae, figlinae, horrea, metalla Caesaris'; it is thus used for the emperor's slaves. 'Augustus', on the other hand, according to Bang, is the publicly conferred honorific title expressing the official power and position of the emperor, e.g. 'numen Augusti', 'milites Augusti n(ostri)', 'evocati, castra Augusti', etc. Freedmen, by the act of manumission, have become members of the citizen community, and it is the title 'Augustus', conferred by the citizen community, that best expresses the relationship between the emperor as patron and his freedmen.[3]

Chantraine (esp. pp. 399 f.) prefers to see 'Augustus' as the *cognomen* of the emperor expressing the individual relationship between a freedman and his manumittor to whom he is obligated. By contrast 'Caesar' the family name is more suitable for expressing the more general relationship of ownership which passes from one master to another in the family without personal obligation. There are difficulties in this view. For instance in the longer persistence of the extended, more personal form of status indication among slaves than among freedmen. I think there is more force in Bang's argument than Chantraine allows; the progressive dominance of 'Augustus' in both the slave and the freedman nomenclature reflects the gradual institutionalisa-

[1] For examples see Bang, *Hermes* 54 (1919), 178 n. 1; Chantraine, pp. 35 f. (Imperial princes only).

[2] M. Bang, 'Caesaris Servus', *Hermes* 54 (1919), 174–86 first made this distinction clear. Cf. Weaver, *CQ* 13 (1963), 272 f.; 14 (1964), 134 f.; Chantraine, pp. 140 f.

[3] Bang, *Hermes* 54 (1919), 185 f.

Status indication

tion of the Familia as an element of the bureaucracy and is in fact an acknowledgement of its public function.

However this may be, the distinction between 'Caesar' and 'Augustus' is in general valid but not absolutely, and not equally for all periods. It does not date from the earliest Principate nor does it last into the third century. Finally, it should not be pressed too hard in the case of slaves, and not at all for *vernae*. The distinction is most apparent in the numerous inscriptions naming Imperial freedmen and slaves together, e.g. VI 9051: T. Flavius Aug. lib. Aihi and Montanus Caesaris tabell(arius); 682 = D 1623: Maior et Diadumenus Caes. n. ser. and Crescens Aug. l.[1] The distinction established itself in the first century as the freedman forms which included 'Caesaris' in the status indication dropped out of use. It is scarcely possible to speak of their elimination as if by Imperial order or enactment. Rather the nomenclature reflected the changing character of the administration or of the freedman–slave role in it.

The form 'Caesaris l.' is an indication of early date. I have found eighteen instances of 'Caesaris l.' under the Iulii, of whom sixteen are certainly or probably freedmen of Augustus, one of Tiberius, and one freedwoman of either.[2] There are six more who probably belong to the Julian emperors, including five from the *monumentum Marcellae* and *monumentum Liviae*.[3] There are only three 'Ti. Claudii Caesaris l.'[4] The latest dated 'Caesaris l.' is X 4734: Amemptus Caes. l. (AD 71) who is probably a freedman of Nero or Claudius. There is no clear indication of the form having been used by the freedmen of the Flavian or later emperors. The decline in this usage after Augustus is most marked, to the point where, in the absence of other data, the simple form 'Caesaris l.' is practically an indication of Augustan date.

---

[1] VI 7973, 14452, 22789, 22937, 30553.7, 32429, 37748, 37958, 38351, *AE* 1946, 140; XV 941, 1147; *IGR* I 1255–6. For further examples, which come from all periods, see Bang, *Hermes* 54 (1919), 184 n. 1. 'Aug. lib.' and 'Aug. ser.' in the same inscription is rare: VI 8957; VIII 12656.

[2] VI 4479, 4771, 5871, 7793, 11320, 19968, 20002, 20335, 26254; X 3357 = D 2817; XI 3083, 7802; XII 3625; *EE* VIII 316 = D 6387; *Epigr.* 16 (1954), 31; VI 20259: Ti. Iulius Caesar. l. Scymnus; 20432: Iulia Egloge Caesaris l. Chantraine (pp. 143 f.) incorporates in his figures instances of the extended forms, e.g. 'Ti. Caesaris l.', already considered above, pp. 44 f. These have been excluded here.

[3] VI 2368 = 4690, 4058, 4199, 4589, 4793, 8730. Bang, *Hermes* 54 (1919), 183 n. 2 includes VI 1261, but this is better completed 'C. Iuli Caesa[ris Aug. l.]', as variation between 'Caes. l.' and 'Aug. l.' in the same inscription is not found. '(C. Iulius) Aesc(h)inus Caes. l.' who appears as *duumvir* on a local bronze issue of Cnossos (F. Imhoof-Blumer, *Monnaies Grecques* (Paris, 1883), p. 214 n. 10) deserves to be given a special place. There is no doubting the reading of the legend from several specimens. Aesc(h)inus is unique as the only member of the Familia Caesaris to appear on a coin legend. Cf. Vitucci, *Diz. Epig.* IV, 926.

[4] III 2022; VI 8711 = D 7803, 25028. Perhaps a fourth, V 1167 (cf. VI 29045 = *IGR* I 287). There are no grounds for assuming that 'Caesaris l.' indicates manumission before 27 BC, as does Starr, *Roman Imperial Navy* (New York, 1941), chap. 2, n. 10.

Nomenclature and chronology

Not relevant to the question of dating this formula are the literary authorities, especially Tacitus, who regularly and characteristically use 'libertus Caesaris', thus differing from the normal nomenclature used by the freedman officials; e.g. Tacitus, *Hist.* ii. 65; iii. 12; *Ann.* v. 10; vi. 38; xiii. 12, 47; xvi. 23; Pliny, *NH* xiii. 29; Pliny the Younger, *Epist.* vi. 31.4.

The other early form of the freedman indication, 'Caesaris Augusti l.', arises from the personal nomenclature of Augustus. The dateable instances fall less markedly within the period of Augustus but are nevertheless heavily concentrated in the period of the Julian emperors.[1] There is one example that is definitely Claudian (xv 814); but thereafter nothing, unless one accepts Chantraine's restorations and forceful arguments for the *Trajanic* date of the fragmentary inscription vi 8633, at least thirty or forty years later than any other example of the form.[2]

The form 'Aug(usti) Caesaris l.' does not occur. The exceptional forms 'Caesaris n(ostri) lib.' and 'Aug(usti) n(ostri) lib.' are discussed in the following section.

For slaves 'Caesaris Aug(usti) (ser.)', as with other early forms of the status indication, survives longer than for freedmen, certainly into the Flavian period and perhaps later.[3] Most examples are from the period Augustus–

---

[1] vi 1261 (?), 20375, 38494; v 3404; *AE* 1913, 216 – all before AD 14. Three others bear *agnomina* which indicate the period Augustus–Tiberius: vi 5849 (Agrippianus), 16658 (Cornificianus – from L. Cornificius, *cos.* 35 BC; cf. Chantraine, p. 309), 27686 (Sallustianus – from Sallustius, grand-nephew of the historian). Four others are undated but are probably from the same period: vi 8918, 10356 = D 7874, 12797, 17323.

[2] Chantraine's date (p. 300 no. 44; 316 nos. 169–70; 340 no. 333) is based on the identity of (1 a) 'Ascanius [Ca]esaris Au[g. l. Ant]iochianus a co[mmentariis]', in the restorations proposed for vi 8633, with (1 b) 'Ascanius Aug. l. a comment(ariis) rat(ionis) hereditat(ium)' who appears in vi 8933 = D 1689. In the latter inscription Ascanius is co-dedicator with (2a) 'Patiens Aug. l. tabul(arius) me(n)sor(um) aedificior(um)' to their friend (3a) 'Ti. Claudius Ianuarius Gratianus nomenclat(or) Aug(usti)'. The Trajanic date is founded on the further identity of (2a) 'Patiens Aug. l.' with (2b) 'M. Ulpius Aug. l. Patiens Victorianus tabularius menso(rum) aedificiorum' of vi 37759, and a further twist is added by the identification of (3a) 'Ti. Claudius Ianuarius Gratianus' with (3b) 'Ianuarius Aug. l. Gratianus nomenclator' of vi 8934a.

Apart from the vital restorations which make (1a) Ascanius a *libertus* and his job that of *a co[mmentariis]*, there are a number of inconcinnities here that might make one hesitate. All of the three pairs of names differ within themselves: (1b) differs in status indication from (1a) and has no *agnomen*; similarly (2a) differs from (2b) in the absence of *agnomen* (and also *praenomen* and *nomen*); (3a) differs from (3b) in having no status indication at all, but does have a *nomen* (Claudius) which gives rise to the further problem of a 'Ti. Claudius (Aug. l.)' in the reign of Trajan. Although such a *nomen* is not excluded for an Imperial freedman in that period, it is approaching the limit of the possible. Throughout, the abbreviation 'l(ibertus)' is used in four different inscriptions from the early second century, despite the normally first-century date for this abbreviation. Finally, there is the status indication '[Ca]esaris Au[gusti l.]' long after the virtual standardisation of the freedman indication as 'Aug. lib.' under the early Flavians. Despite the attractiveness of these identifications, I would prefer to suspend judgement on the identification of (1a) and (1b).

[3] Chantraine argues for one case even after Hadrian (viii 13130) on the grounds that it is from the second *columbarium* at Carthage, first opened under Antoninus Pius. This seems hardly conclusive on its own.

Status indication

Tiberius,[1] but there are some which are later.[2] 'N(ostri)', which appears from the Flavian period, does not occur with the form 'Caesaris Aug. (ser.)'. This suggests a pre-Flavian date for the latter. The order 'Aug. Caes(aris)' is very unusual; it occurs only twice (VI 4884, 26732), in the latter case with the addition of 'n(ostri)' – 'Stachys Aug. Caesaris n.'

The period from the accession of Vespasian to that of M. Aurelius saw 'Aug(usti) lib(ertus)' established as the dominant and almost exclusive status indication for the Imperial freedmen. For slaves in the same period the forms with 'Caesaris', variously abbreviated, by contrast do not dominate the status indication to nearly the same extent. Examples of 'Aug. (ser.)' and 'Aug. vern(a)' appearing in the same inscription with 'Aug. lib.' are frequent.[3]

Apart from 'Aug(usti) et Aug(ustae)' for the joint slaves of Tiberius and Livia,[4] 'Augusti' variously abbreviated, with or without 'ser./vern(a)', occurs for slaves as early as Tiberius and continues thereafter.[5] Thus while forms with 'Augusti' in the slave indication were much less common than forms with 'Caesaris' before the middle of the second century, they nevertheless appear too frequently in all periods to provide any accurate dating criterion. The form 'Aug(usti) ser(vus)' has special features which are discussed below in connection with the African inscriptions.

'Verna' is rare in the Familia before Hadrian.[6] I have found only five examples of 'Caes. vern.' or 'Aug. vern.'[7] There is one instance among slaves with *agnomen* in *-ianus*[8] who are all pre-Hadrianic. In the same period 'Caes. n. vern.' occurs three times and 'Caes. n. ser. vern.' once – all of these

---

[1] E.g. VI 3975, 4032 (Maecenatianus), 4086, 4213, 9050 = D 1787. See further Chantraine, p. 190.

[2] For references, see Chantraine, pp. 189 f. He includes, however, inscriptions such as VI 8835 and III 333 = *IGR* III 25 = D 1539, on the basis of the wives' *nomina* – Flavia Macaria, Flavia Sophene, both without status indication. But *Flaviae* as wives of Imperial freedmen do appear as early as the 'Ti. Claudii Aug. lib.' (VI 1859–60, 10089 = D 1766). On the value of wives' *nomina*, including 'Flavia' and 'Ulpia', as a dating criterion, see above, pp. 39 f.

[3] E.g. VI 8409, 8542, 9042, 9045, 10734, 10860, 10872, 11552, 16811, etc. Cf. above, p. 49 n. 1.

[4] E. g. VI 5181 = D 1676, 5215, 5745 = D 5001. The fragmentary VI 24079 is the same inscription as VI 8989 = D 1827 (recognised by Chantraine, p. 218 n. 8).

[5] VI 34005 (AD 24), 8409a (Gaius). Also early are: VI 5355 (Aemilianus), 5872 (Arc(h)elianus), 22970 (Maecenatianus). Claudian or later: VI 8829, 8957, 9042, 15350; III 12289; XI 3173 (Vestinianus); *AE* 1953, 24 (Iulianus, AD 45?). Other *Iuliani*: VI 5837, 22679. Flavian or later: VI 8404 (Atticianus); VIII 12656. For full local and chronological details of all the variant forms, see Chantraine, pp. 180 f.

[6] On the derivation and meaning of 'verna', and for the modern literature, see Chantraine, pp. 170 and esp. 171 n. 137.

[7] VI 5822 (Gaius), 8823–4 (Gaius–Claudius), 20042 (Augustus–Gaius), 34005 (Tiberius); cf. 5745 = D 5001 (Iuliae Augustae verna).

[8] VI 8824: Cinnamis Caes. Aug. verna Drusilliana.

Nomenclature and chronology

in inscriptions with 'T. Flavii Aug. lib.', which does not exclude the possibility of a late Trajanic or early Hadrianic date.[1]

Another question is the omission of 'ser.' or 'vern.' from the slave indication. This is of some importance because of its bearing on the membership of the Familia Caesaris and because of the attempt by some scholars[2] to connect this form of the status indication of Imperial slaves syntactically with a following title or occupation rather than with the preceding personal name, and thus to argue that the persons in question were of freedman status. Thus, for example, in IX 41 = D 2819: 'Malchio Caesaris trierarchus', according to Starr,[3] the genitive 'Caesaris' depends on the title 'trierarchus' and is considered as an equivalent of 'quei militant Caesari' in X 3341. In fact, as Bang pointed out,[4] 'Caesaris' is the characteristic form of the Imperial slave indication in the Julio-Claudian period and is particularly common in the *columbaria* of the early Principate. Both the dated and the undated inscriptions show that 'Caes(aris)', 'Aug(usti)', 'Caes(aris) n(ostri)', and 'Aug(usti) n(ostri)' are more often not followed by a title or occupation and are thus in the majority of inscriptions syntactically complete.[5] In many cases where the occupation follows it cannot be connected with the preceding status indication.[6] This shows even more clearly from the more numerous inscriptions where the slave indication is followed by the occupation and where the *agnomen* in *-ianus* intervenes between the status indication and the occupation, e.g. VI 5197 = D 1514: Musicus Ti. Caesaris Augusti Scurranus disp(ensator) ad fiscum Gallicum.[7] It follows that in all the above cases we have to do with slave members of the Familia. This is also probably true of those relatively few cases where the occupation immediately follows the name, e.g. VI 8965 = D 1825: Halotus ex paedagogio Caesaris.[8] Common usage at all periods makes 'Caesaris' following a personal name, especially one such as Malchio, necessarily a slave indication.[9] Only with a *praenomen* and *nomen* present

---

[1] VI 8870, twice; XI 4462; VI 35308. Chantraine (pp. 203 f.) includes in his references examples based on family dating criteria, e.g. VI 4412: foster-parent T. Flavius Eutychus; 18348: mother Flavia Haline (both without status indication). See above, p. 51 n. 2.

[2] Starr, *Roman Imperial Navy*, pp. 44, 69 f.; C. Cichorius, *Römische Studien* (Leipzig-Berlin, 1922), pp. 257 f.; D. Kienast, *Kriegsflotten der röm. Kaiserzeit* (Bonn, 1966), pp. 12 f. Cichorius (p. 258), followed by Starr (p. 44 with n. 65), assigns IX 41 = D 2819 to before 27 BC on grounds of nomenclature and argues that Malchio's *nomen* was omitted because his wife's name came first. Neither assertion is justified. See further L. Wickert, *Würzb. Jahrb. f. Altertum.* 4 (1949/50), 100 f., esp. 107 f.   [3] *Roman Imperial Navy*, p. 44; cf. ed. 2, p. 229.   [4] *Hermes* 54 (1919), 176.

[5] For the details, see now Chantraine, pp. 187 f.

[6] Note: VI 9058: 'Threpte Aug(usti)' and 'Communis Aug(usti) tabul(arius)'; III 4712: 'Aquilinus Caes(aris) n.', cf. V 706: 'Aquilinus vilicus Augg.' – the same person?

[7] Cf. VI 8575 = D 1502, 8723.   [8] Cf. VIII 12640; X 1751.

[9] But see now the arguments for these *trierarchi* being *peregrini* given by S. Panciera in *Atti del Convegn. intern. di studi sulle antichità di Classe* (1967), pp. 313 f. See, however, no the *corporis custodes*, p. 83 below.

Status indication

could it be otherwise. Where it mattered a Roman citizen would avoid ambiguity by giving his *nomen* or a periphrasis.

Omission of 'ser./vern.' continued well after the Julio-Claudian period, as the numerous instances of 'Caes. n.' and 'Aug. n.' suggest.[1] Under the Aurelian emperors 'Augg. nn.' for joint slaves is not infrequent. But this form of the slave indication becomes the exception rather than the rule.

In the slave indication the balance between the forms of the 'Caesaris' group and those of the 'Augusti' group gradually changes from the massive dominance of the former in the early Julio-Claudian period to something nearer parity by the middle of the second century. The forms in 'Augusti' first appear in significant numbers in the period beginning with the Flavians (it cannot be determined with any greater precision within that period). The forms with 'verna' become common by the reign of Hadrian. The respective use of 'Caesaris' and 'Augusti' with 'verna' thus should give a fair picture of the balance between these two forms for the middle of the second century in the period from Hadrian to 161. According to Chantraine's overall figures,[2] the proportion is 110:102 in favour of forms with 'Caesaris', i.e. almost parity within the margin of error allowable for this kind of data. If one excludes the forms in which 'verna' occurs with 'servus', the proportion for the pure forms in 'verna' is 85:98 in favour of those with 'Augusti'.

From 161 and the co-regency of M. Aurelius with L. Verus their jointly owned slaves use almost exclusively the forms with 'Augg.' There are only six examples of forms with 'Caess.', 'Caesarum' in the slave indication.[3] Forms with 'Caes(aris)' are found less and less; the last dated case of 'Caes. n. ser.' is from 182, and 'Caes. ser.' is found only once in this period.[4]

The decline in the use of 'Caesaris' in the slave nomenclature coincides with the distinction between the titles 'Augustus' and 'Caesar' in the Imperial family itself from the end of Hadrian's reign.[5] The virtual disuse of 'Caesaris' coincides with the co-regency of 161–9 (M. Aurelius and L. Verus) and of 177–80 (M. Aurelius and Commodus), when the successor to the throne now also had the title 'Augustus'. The form 'Auggg. nnn. (ser./vern.)'

---

[1] On the chronological significance of 'n(ostri)' in the status indication, see below, pp. 54 f.
[2] Pp. 175, 181, 200, 206, cf. 209 f.
[3] Two in the one inscription, X 7653; the others: VIII 24756; XI 534: '[...Ca]ess. nn. [ver]na' – all no doubt Aurelian in date. The others (VIII 12758, 22924) may be earlier (cf. *Historia* 13 (1964), 198 Addendum) but I now think this unlikely in view of the triple iteration 'nnn.' which implies a Severan date. On these see Bang, *Hermes* 54 (1919), 177 n. 1, 180 n. 3; Chantraine, pp. 259 f. VI 8494 = D 1613 has 'Caesarum n.' The Greek inscriptions and the papyri tend to preserve the earlier nomenclature: *SEG* VI 380: Καισάρων δοῦλοι; *BGU* I 156: Καισάρων οἰκονόμος (AD 201); *P. Oxy.* 735.5.
[4] III 7435 (AD 182), cf. 349 = *MAMA* V 197: Craterus Caes. n. ser. ver. (Commodus); *P. Oxy.* 735.5 (AD 205); *AE* 1954, 64 (*fistula*, Caracalla).
[5] Mommsen, *Staatsr.* II, 1139 f.

Nomenclature and chronology

dates from the Severan period and signifies joint ownership by the two *Augusti* Septimius Severus and Caracalla, and Geta as *Caesar* or *Augustus* (197–211); e.g. *AE* 1952, 192: Philoxenus Auggg. nnn. ser. (AD 206).

The Greek inscriptions in general conform to the above pattern. The distinction between Σεβαστοῦ ἀπελεύθερος and Καίσαρος δοῦλος is maintained. The unabbreviated forms are regular.[1]

'N(OSTRI)' IN THE STATUS INDICATION

The term *noster*, as Chantraine well points out,[2] belongs to the emotional sphere. It has no legal implications. In this respect it differs from *verna* which, though optional in the status indication, does reflect the legal fact of slave birth, and the social if not legal fact of birth within the slave *familia*. The use of *noster* is widespread outside the status indication both in literature and inscriptions. It gives expression to a more than strictly formal relationship between the recipient and the speaker or writer. Thus it is commonly found, apart from the Familia Caesaris, in references, dedications and addresses of all kinds to the emperor to the point where it forms part of informal Imperial nomenclature. Thus in dedications, e.g. 'numini Imperatoris n(ostri)', 'pro salute Imp(eratoris) n(ostri)'; in occupational titles in the administration and in many forms of address, e.g., from the dated material, VI 8826 = D 7276 (AD 102): 'collegio Liberi Patris et Mercuri negotiantium cellarum vinariarum novae et Arruntianae Caesaris n.'; 8978 = D 1834: 'Pierus Aug. l. praec. puerr. Caesaris n.' with 'Herma Aug. l. a cub. Domitiae Aug.'; 2120 = D 8380, cf. 32398a: 'Arrius Alphius Arriae Fadillae Domini n. Imp. Antonini Aug. matris libertus' (AD 155). An early example from the present material is III 7380 = D 5682 (AD 55) recording the gift of baths 'populo et familiai Caesaris n.'

'N(ostri)' was common enough also in the status nomenclature of slaves of *privati* by the first century AD.[3] Another early example connected with the Familia Caesaris is VI 11242–3: 'Agathopus Actes n. ser.' Once the term was introduced into the Familia proper it rapidly became a common but optional part of the standard slave indication. As its use here begins in the slave indication, it is convenient to take this first.

'N(ostri)' provides another dating criterion in the slave nomenclature. It does not appear in the numerous inscriptions of Imperial slaves from

---

[1] Καίσαρος ἀπελεύθερος occurs for the Claudian period: *IGR* I 287, 1262 (AD 49); from the second century: *AE* 1949, 194; *IGR* III 1056 (AD 137); undated: *IGR* I 1101; III 728; IV 245. See also Chantraine, pp. 169 f.

[2] See Chantraine, pp. 193 f., 216 ('dominus noster').

[3] For references, see Bang, *Hermes* 54 (1919), 175 n. 4, and Chantraine, p. 193 n. 1.

Status indication

Augustus to Nero. The first dated example of 'Caes(aris) n(ostri) ser(vus)' is on a lead pipe from the reign of Vespasian,[1] and then two more under Domitian.[2] 'Caes. n.' and 'Caes. n. ver(n).' occur in the inscription of a *collegium familiae domus Palatinae* dated to 98/100.[3] By then 'n(ostri)' occurs regularly – on several brick stamps dated to 101/113,[4] eight times out of twelve in inscriptions of Imperial slaves where they occur with 'T. Flavii Aug. lib.', and ten out of fourteen times with 'M. Ulpii Aug. lib.' Forms with 'Caes. n. (ser.)' continue till the early Aurelian period when they gradually disappear. The forms with 'Aug(usti) n.' begin later and continue longer than those with 'Caes. n.' There is one doubtful case under Trajan,[5] and one with *agnomen* in *-ianus* holding the post of *ark(arius) provinciae Africae*. Thereafter not till Hadrian or even Antoninus or later. Examples of 'Aug. n. (ser.)' continue well into the third century.[6]

It is clear that from soon after its introduction 'n(ostri)' became something of a fashion in the slave indication. There are approximately three times as many surviving examples of 'Caes. n. ser.' in the century beginning with the Flavians as there are of 'Caes. ser.' in the whole period from Augustus on (*Caes. n. ser.*: 270; *Caes. ser.*: 93). For the simple forms 'Caes.' and 'Aug.' the proportions are reversed, with nearly three times as many instances without 'n(ostri)' as with it.[7] This no doubt reflects the fact that the form 'Caes.' was predominant in the first century before 'n(ostri)' came into fashion. For the 'Augustorum (servi/vernae)', who belong to the period from 161 onwards, if we exclude the African inscriptions, all forms with 'n(ostrorum)' are almost exactly equal in numbers with all forms without it. The geographical distribution of forms with 'Caes. n.' and 'Aug. n.' also differs. 'Caes. n.' is predominantly found in Rome, whereas for forms in 'Aug. n.' a much higher proportion is from Italy and especially the provinces.[8]

The form 'Caes. n. ser.' was thus the dominant form of the slave indication at least during the first half of the second century and probably earlier.

[1] *AE* 1951, 198 = *NS* 1949, 71.
[2] xv 7285, 7286; cf. vi 5405: Euhodus et Evander Imp. Domitiani n. ser.
[3] vi 32429.
[4] Bruzza, Nos. 200-1, 205, 209, 294; also under Trajan: vi 252 = D 1824.
[5] viii 14560 (AD 107) where the reading 'Aug. n. s.' is uncertain. vi 8575 = D 1502: Antiochus Aug. n. Lucconianus, if Trajanic, is an early example of other usages as well – 'provinciae' in the occupational title of *arcarii*, and the form 'ar*k*arius'.
[6] vi 5304, 9042, 9045. Cf. *AE* 1915, 9 = D 3563: dedic. to Hadrian and 'Sabina Aug. n.' by 'Autarches Sabina(e) Aug. n. lib.' Chantraine (pp. 207 f.) allows this form a somewhat earlier possible dating, e.g. 'Aug. n.': Flavian–Hadrian: vi 8575 = D 1502 (see above, n. 5); Flavian or later: vi 17015; ix 3721; v 475 = *I. It.* x 3.50. 'Aug. n. ser.': Flavian or later: vi 14663. But this depends on Imperial *nomina* unsupported by status indication in family dating criteria, which have little if any independent chronological value.
[7] See *CQ* 14 (1964), 138 (Table c); cf. Chantraine, pp. 181, 206.
[8] Cf. Chantraine, pp. 198, 210 f.

Nomenclature and chronology

But with the introduction of forms with 'verna' and the increasing use of forms with 'Aug.', the relative frequency of forms with 'n(ostri)' declined to about only half or less of all examples. For the forms with 'verna', both those with 'Caes(aris)' and those with 'Aug(usti)', the surviving examples are about equally divided between those with 'n(ostri)' and those without. For 'Aug. ser.'/'Aug. n. ser.', by contrast, the figures are 153:12 in favour of the former.[1] But this is a special case, heavily influenced by the Carthage inscriptions which must be considered separately below.

The forms in 'n(ostri)' are not paralleled in the Greek inscriptions. Even in bilingual inscriptions 'n(ostri)' appears in the Latin but not in the Greek: e.g. III 6574 = 7126 = D 1344: Spectatus Augg. n. lib. = Σπεκτατὸς Σεββ. ἀπελεύθερος; *Hesperia* 10 (1941), 243 f. = 32 (1963), 87: Antiochus Caes. n. s. vern. = ᾽Αντίοχος Καίσ(αρος) δοῦλ(ος).[2]

For the freedmen, on the other hand, the position is quite different. 'N(ostri)' is scarcely used at all. This is surprising in view of the supposed 'individualising' significance of 'Augusti' in the freedman indication and the same kind of role attributed to 'n(ostri)'.[3]

'Caes(aris) n(ostri) lib.' occurs in only six inscriptions, four of which are certainly or probably Trajanic or later;[4] the other two[5] have the abbreviation 'lib.' (not 'l.') as do all the others except one with 'libert.' On the other hand, the abbreviation 'l(ibertus)' is almost universal for the form 'Caesaris l(ibertus)' without 'n(ostri)', occurring in 27 out of 29 examples.[6] We must conclude that these are two separate groups. 'Caesaris l.' disappeared from the status indication of Imperial freedmen along with other alternative formulae from the time of Vespasian or shortly after. 'Aug(usti) lib(ertus)' then became the standard and almost exclusive form. It had always predominated, except for the freedmen of Augustus where it is still the largest group although occurring in less than half of the cases.

The occurrence of 'n(ostri)' in the freedman indication demands further investigation. For Imperial slaves in the second century, as we have seen, the

[1] See above, p. 55 n. 7.
[2] Cf. Chantraine, p. 214.
[3] Chantraine's explanation is given p. 400 ('widerspricht nur scheinbar').
[4] VIII 12857: M. Ulpius Clarus Caesaris n. lib.; VI 8463: Secundus Caes. n. lib. off(icinator) mon(etae), cf. 8463b: M. Ulp. Secundus nummularius offic. monetae; 24806: Oceanus sen(ior) Caesaris n. lib. (his sister was Aelia Galatia, but scarcely 'wohl frühestens hadrianisch', as Chantraine, p. 195; two 'T. Flavii Aug. lib.' were already married with 'Aeliae' – VI 8467, 18094); 29299: Lamyrus Caesaris n. libert(us) (his wife was Ulpia Amabilis; 'Ulpia' was a rare *nomen* before Trajan (cf. Taylor, p. 119), but caution needs to be exercised in this case as the earliest instance of an 'Ulpia' as a wife in the Familia Caesaris is with a 'Ti. Claudius Aug. l.' – VI 8898).
[5] VI 151 = 30704, 7502 (not certainly first century, as Bang, *Hermes* 54 (1919), 183 n. 5).
[6] On the significance of this abbreviation, see below, pp. 73 f.

Status indication

form 'Caes. n. ser.' constitutes the largest group. But in the nomenclature of Imperial freedmen 'n(ostri)' was late in making its appearance. The earliest example is VIII 12857: M. Ulpius Clarus Caesaris n. lib., from Carthage, followed by another who was certainly a freedman of Trajan, VI 8463, cf. 8463 b: (M. Ulpius) Secundus Caes. n. lib., and then possibly another, VI 29299: Lamyrus Caesaris n. libert.

The form 'Augg. nn. lib.' occurs in only a small minority of inscriptions of *Augustorum liberti* – 16/200 – the earliest of which are Hadrianic or later.[1] The form 'Aug. n. lib.' is even rarer.[2] I can find only thirteen examples, the only three with *nomen* being VI 18428: Aelia Severa Aug. n. l.,[3] 10860: Aurelius Alexander Aug. n. lib., and V 3510: M. Aurelius Euporus Aug. n. lib. Another, *AE* 1940, 177: Genialis Aug. n. lib., has a son L. Septimius Gratianus; a fifth, III 249 = 6753 = D 1396: Marianus Aug. n. lib., is from the third century;[4] and a sixth, XV 1531 = V 8110.166, is dated in *CIL ad loc.* 'saec. II fere exeuntis'.[5] None of the examples can be definitely dated before 161 and most are probably considerably later. Among the freedmen of the *Augustae* there is only one example, from the time of Hadrian or later.[6] Also noteworthy is the high proportion of examples from outside Rome and Italy.

It is clear that 'n(ostri)' never became common in the freedman status nomenclature of the Familia. It appears first in the earlier half of the second century under the influence of the slave nomenclature where it was regular by the time of Trajan. 'Caes. n. lib.' is analogous to 'Caes. n. ser.' 'N(ostri)' later appeared in the forms 'Augg. nn. lib.' and 'Aug. n. lib.', but rarely and mostly in the provinces. 'N(ostri)' is thus characteristic of the relationship of master and slave, not of patron and freedman, and is paralleled by the increasing use of 'dominus noster', 'procurator Aug. n.', etc. in the late second century, perhaps a sign of increasing absolutism. In slave nomenclature, moreover, 'n(ostri)' is particularly associated with the form 'Caes-(aris)', and much less with the form 'Aug(usti)'.

---

[1] VI 27807; VII 232 (?); VIII 9434 (P. Aelius). The others are: VI 29807 (T. Aelius); 8480, cf. 33728 = D 1601; V 27 = *I. It.* X 1.41 (AD 198); VIII 10630; XIII 1816 (M. Aurelius); VI 1585 a–b = D 5920 (AD 193), 410, cf. 30760 = D 1707; *AE* 1930, 152 (L. Septimius); V 5090 = D 1561 (AD 217/46). Undated, but probably late second or third century: II 4519; III 3964, 6574 = 7126 = D 1344.

[2] Despite Vitucci, *Diz. Epig.* IV, 919. See now also Chantraine, p. 198 n. 18.

[3] Cf. Chantraine, p. 195 n. 10.

[4] Cf. Pflaum, *CP*, pp. 765 f.

[5] The others are: III 4063; VI 15424, 29116; VIII 7665, 9362; X 1737; *AE* 1925, 73. Doubtful: III 1313 (but cf. 1297; Chantraine, p. 196); X 2799.

[6] *AE* 1915, 9 = *EE* VIII 305 = D 3563: Autarches Sabina(e) Aug. n. lib. (misprinted by Chantraine, pp. 45, 195).

Nomenclature and chronology

'AUGUSTORUM LIBERTUS/SERVUS'. SLAVES AND FREEDMEN OF THE AUGUSTAE

We must now consider the numerous cases of Imperial freedmen and slaves whose nomenclature indicates more than one *Augustus/Caesar* as patrons or masters. There are some 200 of these among the freedmen and over 100 slaves; e.g., from the dated inscriptions, II 2552 = D 9125: Hermes Augustor. lib., AD 163; cf. II 2556 = D 9129, AD 165/6; II 2553 = D 9127, AD 167; VI 2270 = D 4331: Eutyches Augg. lib., AD 199; VI 552 = D 3861: Earinus Augustor. n. ser., AD 164; *AE* 1967, 444 (Samothrace): Felix Augustor. verna, AD 165; *EE* VIII 307-8 (Spain): Reginus verna Augustorum, in a dedication to M. Aurelius and L. Verus.[1] Among the abbreviated forms 'Augustor(um)' is common, and especially 'Augg.' and 'Auggg.' Forms in 'Caess.' and 'Caesarum' are exceptional and restricted to slaves.[2] The question arises as to the dating of these inscriptions, and a problem also, when it becomes clear that many of the freedmen at least are to be dated *before* 161, the beginning of the reign of the first joint-ruling Augusti, M. Aurelius and L. Verus.

To begin with those dated to 161 and later. This automatically includes all *Augustorum liberti* with 'Aurelius' or 'Septimius' for *nomen*, i.e. some 75 freedmen out of 200. A high proportion of the 95 without *nomen* are also to be dated to this period on other grounds, probably at least two-thirds of them.[3] With all these there is no problem. The 'Augg. (nn.) liberti' were manumitted jointly by two co-ruling *Augusti*, i.e. M. Aurelius and L. Verus (161-9), M. Aurelius and Commodus (177-80), L. Septimius Severus and Caracalla (197-209). With the 'Auggg. liberti' there is a problem if we assume that all such manumissions date from the joint rule of *three Augusti*, i.e. Septimius, Caracalla and Geta (209-11), as one of the two dated examples is from 207 (III 4034 = D 1499), and the other, M. Aurelius Auggg. lib. December (VI 816 = D 1928) dates from 238.[4] Further, a slave inscription, *AE* 1952, 192 (Moesia): Philoxenus Auggg. nnn. ser., is dated to 206, also *before* Geta became an *Augustus*. With the proviso that 'Auggg.' can include Geta as *Caesar*, we can date the 'Auggg. liberti' and 'Auggg. servi' (of which

---

[1] For complete lists with chronological details see Chantraine, pp. 225 f.
[2] There are only six examples: X 7653 (Tantilia C(a)esarum; Cornelianus Caess.); VIII 24756 (Carthage), 22924; XI 534 (frag.); VI 8494 = D 1613.
[3] See Chantraine, pp. 225 f. for details, esp. p. 227 n. 13 (eight lines from bottom: for *AE* 1922 read 1932).
[4] It is perfectly possible for December to have survived nearly thirty years after the date of manumission. The *nomen* 'Aurelius' instead of 'Septimius' still needs to be explained in that case. The *nomen Aurelius* must come from either Caracalla, Elagabalus or Severus Alexander. Dessau (ad *ILS* 1928), Chantraine (p. 73), Boulvert (II, 520 n. 377) consider him to have been manumitted by Severus Alexander.

Status indication

there are only thirteen and eleven examples respectively) to the period 198–211 for the slaves and from that period or later for the freedmen.[1]

In the absence of firm indications of an earlier date in individual cases we can also date the 'Augg. (servi/vernae)' to these periods of co-rule by two *Augusti* who were thus joint masters, as in the examples of Earinus, 164; Felix, 165; and Reginus, 161–9, given above. This can be checked from the list of dated inscriptions. In these there is no example of an 'Augg. (ser./vern.)' before 161. Of Imperial slaves dated after 161, all those with plural indication are dated to periods of joint rule,[2] and of nine dated slaves with single indication only one, Maximianus Aug. n. verna (XIV 4570 = *AE* 1922, 92; cf. 'Callistus Aug. lib. proc.' in the same inscription) is dated to a period of joint rule, AD 205.[3] This is because the slave indication reflects the status situation of a slave *vis-à-vis* his master/masters at the actual time or period in question. This situation can change, e.g. with the death of one of the joint masters (L. Verus in 169), or with the accession of a new co-emperor (Commodus in 177, Caracalla in 197). The same need not hold good for the Imperial freedmen. In the case of jointly-manumitted freedmen of *privati* their status indication is taken to represent the patronal facts *at the time of manumission*, or at least the status indication does not *necessarily* change with any changes in the patronal situation. But I must agree that just this solution, advanced now for the Imperial freedmen by Boulvert, is the best for those

[1] The use of the title 'Caesar Augustus' for Geta, and the formula 'Auggg.' to include Geta as Caesar, is found in dated inscriptions of the period before 209, especially in the provinces, e.g. *IRT* 913–16; D 427, 1152–3, 9155. Whether the distinction between the titles 'Caesar' and 'Augustus' was as freely ignored in the Severan period as Gilliam (*Class. Phil.* 58 (1963), 28) implies, and whether a single Caesar was accorded the straight title 'Augustus' deserves full investigation based on a collection of all the evidence. (Cf. A. Stein, *Reichsbeamten von Dazien* (Budapest, 1944), p. 61 n. 2; also Mommsen, *Staatsr.* II, 1164, n. 5.2: 'Diese Verwendung des Augustusnamens findet sich in keiner massgebenden Urkunde und ist sicher abusiv.') The formula 'Augg. et Caes.' does occur in the Fam. Caes. material: VI 776: 'Constantius Augg. et Caes. tabul(arius) s(ummi) c(horagii)'. It is referred (*CIL* ad loc.) to Severus and his two sons.

[2] In addition to the examples Earinus, Felix and Reginus (see above): XIV 4322 = *AE* 1921, 78: Ammonius Augg. nn. ser., 199; *BGU* 156 = *Chrest.* 175: Σατουρνεῖνος Καισάρων οἰκονόμος, 201; *P. Oxy.* 735, 205; *AE* 1952, 192: Philoxenus Augg. nn. ser., 206; VIII 27550: Victoris (!), Gaetulicus, Ianuarius vernae Augg., dedication to Sept. Sever. and family; *AE* 1932, 15 = *ILTun.* 1534: [...] Augg. vern., dedication to Sept. Sever. and family. Earinus Augustor. n. ser. ped(isequus) (VI 552 = D 3861, dated to 164) also appears in the undated inscription VI 8992 as 'Earinus Caes. ser. pedisequus'. If the identification is accepted as probable, the change in status indication reflects the single ownership after the death of L. Verus and before Commodus became joint owner. VI 8992 should therefore be dated to 169–77, or possibly 180–92 when Commodus was sole emperor.

[3] III 752 = 7435 = D 1856: Maceio Caes. n. serv., 182; V 2155 = D 1574: Chaeron Aug. n., c. 180–90; III 349, cf. p. 1265 = *MAMA* V 197: Craterus Caes. n. ser. ver., dedication to Commodus; III 6575 = 7127 = D 1421: Salvianus Aug. n. vern., c. 196; *Chrest.* 81: Μητίοχος οἰκονόμος τοῦ κυρίου...Σεου[ή]ρου, 197; VI 15 and 1071 = 36883: Eutychus Aug. n. ver., dedication to Caracalla and Iulia Domna; *AE* 1959, 308: [S]uriacus Aug. n., 215; *AE* 1934, 234: Eutyches Aug. n. ser., dedication to Caracalla.

59

Nomenclature and chronology

cases where the status indication of particular individuals varies between 'Aug. lib.' and 'Augg. lib.' in different inscriptions or even different sections of an inscription that have been erected at different times, e.g. *EE* VIII 369 = D 5186; V 7753 = D 1585: L. Aurelius Aug. (Augg.) lib. Pylades, under Commodus; XIV 2113 = D 5193; XIV 2977 = D 5194: M. Aurelius Aug. (Augg.) lib. Agilius Septentrio, under Commodus, AD 187, and Septimius Severus and Caracalla;[1] VI 1585b = D 5920: (H)adrastus Aug. (Augg. nn.) lib. AD 193; and IX 2438, XV 7443 = D 1476; VI 455: Cosmus Aug. lib. a rationibus (a rationibus Augg.), AD 168–72, a period which bridges the death of L. Verus in 169.[2]

Therefore, in the absence of positive evidence to the contrary,[3] we can assume that all instances of 'Augg. (nn.) (ser./vern.)' are to be dated to actual periods of double rule from 161, and all of 'Auggg. (nnn.) (ser./vern.)' to the Severan period of triple rule, 209–11 or 198–211 (where there is evidence of a date earlier than 209. We can also observe a tendency for the freedman nomenclature to follow the pattern of the slave indication, and change according to whether or not there was single, joint or triple rule at the date of any particular inscription.

But for those examples of the formula 'Augustorum libertus' ('Augg. lib.') which are certainly or probably to be dated to the period *before* 161, the problems of interpretation are more acute. Some forty-two inscriptions, naming freedmen with *nomina* from 'Claudius' to 'Aelius', come into this category. We can add up to another ten without *nomen* but with the status indication of the form 'Augustorum lib.' or abbreviated 'Augustor. lib.' (but not 'Augg. lib.' which is preferred in the period after 161).[4] We shall also consider the freedmen and slaves of the various *Augustae*, the *familiae Augustarum*, and the instances of slaves and freedmen jointly owned or jointly manumitted by an *Augustus* and an *Augusta*.[5]

Among the 'Augustorum liberti' from the period before 161 we have three Claudii, two Flavii, nine Ulpii, ten P. Aelii, seven T. Aelii and eleven Aelii without *praenomen*. These represent only a very small proportion of all surviving examples of Imperial freedmen with the same *nomina* – less than 2% for the Claudii and Flavii, less than 4% for the Ulpii, and 9% for the Aelii as a whole; for the Aurelii the corresponding figure is 26%. The pre-

---

[1] On L. Aurelius Augg. lib. Apolaustus Memphius (XIV 4254 = D 5191, dated to 199 under Sept. Sever. and Caracalla; cf. XIV 5375, etc.) and the distinction between him and [L. A]elius Aug. lib. [Aur]elius Apolaustus (IX 344 = D 5188, dated to the reign of Commodus), see Boulvert, art. cit. (above, p. 28 n. 1).

[2] Cf. Chantraine, pp. 255 f.

[3] Chantraine, pp. 237 f., dismisses some possible candidates.

[4] See Chantraine, pp. 235 f., who well illustrates the point.

[5] See Weaver, *Historia* 13 (1964), 188 f., and Chantraine's criticisms (Chantr. pp. 243 f.)

Status indication

Aurelian figures are too small to justify any conclusions about significant changes in the frequency of these cases before 161, or at least before 138. If we were to consider most of the examples of Aelii without *praenomen* to be late and to belong to the reign of Antoninus or later, the proportion of T. Aelii would be not far behind the figure for the Aurelii, i.e. 20% or more.

In view of the dating criteria for *nomina* established above[1] a 'Ti. Claudius Augg. lib.', if manumitted under Claudius or Nero, could not have erected a tombstone much later than AD 100–10, and a 'Flavius Augg. lib.' much later than 130–40.

One desperate solution would be to date all these cases to the period after 161 by invoking the SC Claudianum for the Claudian, Flavian and Ulpian examples and allowing the rest to have survived into the joint reign of M. Aurelius and L. Verus. This is patently unsatisfactory in view of the number of cases involved, especially of the Ulpii, and also because the age data would involve several of the P. Aelii as well. One Claudius and the two Flavii (both in the same inscription, XIV 3935) might be considered candidates under the SC because of the abbreviation 'Augg. lib.'[2] But this does not help with the other Claudii. Ti. Cl(audius) Augustor(um) l. Domnio (VI 9047 = D 1810) who died at the age of 23 years, and whose sister was Antonia Asia, is to be presumed to be first-century in date.

Boulvert's solution[3] is that 'Augustorum' in the status indication of the Claudii and Flavii, and in some cases of the Ulpii and Aelii, indicates that they served as freedmen under *successive* emperors beginning with an emperor bearing the same *nomen*, who originally manumitted them. The rest belong after 161. Chantraine, following most recently E. Meyer[4], sees all these pre-Aurelian cases as examples of successive patrons, the formula 'Augg. lib.' representing one form of a generalised status indication, in the sense of 'Imperial' freedman rather than a particular emperor's freedman. In these instances, according to Chantraine, the freedmen take pride in having served under more than one emperor; the freedman indication has little to do with the facts appertaining to the actual time of manumission. He repeatedly illustrates this thesis with parallels drawn from the occupational nomenclature of the procurators where 'proc. Augustorum' with equestrians before 161 clearly implies successive emperors. Thus the status indication of these freedmen, and by implication of Imperial freedmen in general, is not

---
[1] Chapter 2, pp. 30 f.
[2] XIV 821, 3935; cf. 176 (all from Ostia).
[3] Boulvert, II, 516 f., esp. 517 n. 365.
[4] E. Meyer, *Basler Zeitschr. f. Geschichte u. Altertumskunde* 42 (1943), 59 f.; *AJA* 63 (1959), 384; *Mus. Hel.* 16 (1959), 273 f.; 17 (1960), 118; H. U. Instinsky, *Jahrb. d. röm.-germanischen Zentralmuseums Mainz* 5 (1958), 249 f.; H. Petersen, *Class. Phil.* 57 (1962), 33 n. 4; Gilliam, *Class. Phil.* 58 (1963), 28; Chantraine, pp. 250 f.

Nomenclature and chronology

to be compared with that of other freedmen outside the Familia Caesaris or with the formula used for filiation, which represent the legal facts of manumission and of parentage, but with the *occupational* nomenclature especially of equestrians, as 'Augusti' and 'Augustorum' are little used in this position by freedmen. Chantraine argues at considerable length against my view (expressed in *Historia* 13 (1964), 188f.) that the freedman indication must reflect the legal facts of manumission, and that, therefore, an 'Augustorum libertus' must have been jointly manumitted in some sense.[1]

My own solution to this problem was that the pre-Aurelian cases should be considered as examples of joint manumission by an *Augustus* and an *Augusta*. It might be appropriate, therefore, to begin with the uncontested examples of joint manumission of this kind – the jointly-held *familia* of Tiberius and Livia after the death of Augustus; then consider the *familiae* of other *Augustae*; and finally the normal nomenclature of freedmen who passed under the *ius patronatus* of a second patron in succession to the first.

Joint ownership of slaves was permissible in Roman law; indeed if the multitude of legal questions concerning *servi communes* is any indication, this form of ownership of slaves was common, and the whole subject legally complex.[2] Manumission of a *servus communis* had to be performed jointly by all the owners to be valid, as a man cannot be partly free and partly slave.[3] The nomenclature of a freedman with joint patrons involved no problem if they all had the same *nomen*. If their *praenomina* were different one was chosen, e.g. N. Bovius N. et M. l. Hilarus. Similarly, if the *nomina* were different, the *libertus* took only one of them, e.g. L. Cocceius L. C. Postumi l. Auctus.[4] In view of the frequency of common ownership of slaves and joint manumission of them and the large number of extant inscriptions of slaves and freedmen of the Familia Caesaris, it would indeed be surprising if no trace of joint ownership could be found among them.

In fact jointly-manumitted Imperial freedmen with this form of status indication are to be found, but only of the emperor Tiberius and his mother Iulia Augusta after the death of Augustus, e.g. VI 4770: Ti. Iulius Aug. et Augustae l. [D]iomedes; 14843: Iulia Pasti Augusti et Augustae l. l. Rhodine; 8913: Ti. Iulius Aug. et Aug. l. Pelagius.[5] The *praenomen*, where one of the joint patrons is a woman, is normally that of the male patron, not that of the woman's father. In the above cases the male patron is also the emperor. The

---

[1] See Chantraine, pp. 238 f., for further references to the modern literature.
[2] Buckland, *Roman Law of Slavery*, pp. 372–96.
[3] Ib. p. 575.
[4] D 5879, 7731a; cf. *ILS Index Nominum* for numerous examples of joint manumission. For Republican examples see Chantraine, pp. 216 f.
[5] See list of dated inscriptions (Appendix II); also Chantraine, pp. 217 f.

Status indication

formula 'Aug(usti) et Aug(ustae) l.' was not possible before AD 14, when Augustus in his will adopted Livia as his daughter and had the title 'Augusta' conferred on her. If the sources of joint ownership are sought a hint is contained in VI 5248: Ti. Iulius Aug. et Aug. l. Nereus paternus..., where the epithet 'paternus' probably indicates that Nereus had formerly been a slave of Augustus and had been bequeathed jointly to Tiberius and Livia who manumitted him. Joint freedmen without *nomen* are also clearly joint freedmen of Tiberius and Livia. Joint slaves of Tiberius and Livia are also attested;[1] and a procurator of their joint property, X 7489: Cornelius Mansuetus, procurat(or) Ti. Caesar(is) Aug(usti) et Iuliae August(ae).

Livia also owned many slaves in her own right and was sole patron of many freedmen, both before and after AD 14. The *monumentum Liviae* and other early first-century *columbaria* are prolific in examples.[2] Whatever the legal effects were of her adoption by Augustus, it seems to have made little difference to her personal property. Her freedmen continue to use her father's *praenomen* and not that of her new adoptive father Augustus. And clearly her property was not all distributed by Augustus' will as property jointly held with the new *Augustus*, Tiberius. I find somewhat unconvincing Chantraine's argument that Livia, by virtue of her adoption by Augustus, was in a unique position among the *Augustae* whereby she was the only *Augusta* who could own property jointly with a reigning *Augustus*. There seems to be no objection to an *Augusta* owning property jointly with a *Caesar*, as in the case of Faustina II Augusta and M. Aurelius Caesar. It is hard to see what difference Augustus' adoption of Livia made in practice to her ownership of property.[3] If no other emperor actually adopted an *Augusta*, were all emperors prevented thereby from making distribution of property, as they did to others on many occasions, whether land, money or slaves, by gift or will to any *Augusta*? If not, why could an *Augusta* not legally hold such property jointly with the reigning emperor as with the person who was to become the next emperor? The onus of proof, it seems to me, is really on Chantraine to show why such joint ownership is impossible rather than to deny that examples of such ownership exist and then to argue vigorously from silence.

The problem is that no example yet exists of a 'Ti. Claudius Aug. et Aug. lib.' or of a 'T. Flavius Aug. et Aug. lib.' etc. or of slaves other than of Tiberius and Livia calling themselves 'Aug. et Aug. (ser.)'. In the Claudian period there was no lack of *Augustae*. Antonia Minor, the mother of Claudius

---
[1] VI 4358, 4776, 5181 = D 1676, 5215, 5226, 5316, 5745 = D 5001, 8989 = 24079 = D 1827, 9066, 33275, 37661.
[2] See above, p. 18.
[3] Chantraine, p. 221; cf. Mommsen, *Staatsr.* II, 773.

Nomenclature and chronology

and of Germanicus, had the title conferred on her in 37 by her grandson Gaius. Messalina appears not to have been so rewarded by her husband Claudius, but Agrippina, wife of one *Augustus*, Claudius, and mother of another, Nero, was made *Augusta* in 50. Poppaea Sabina and her newly-born child Claudia received the title 'Augusta' in 63. All of these *Augustae* were owners of substantial property and large numbers of slaves in their own right, especially Antonia Minor and Agrippina. Even Messalina's slaves are extant.[1] Antonia died late in the year 37. For the 'Ti. Claudii Augustorum lib.' joint manumission with Claudius Augustus is therefore improbable. It is possible that slaves of Claudius and his mother were jointly manumitted before the death of Antonia but the tombstone not erected till 41 or later.[2] This is the case with the freedmen and freedwomen of Livia, some manumitted before AD 14, some between 14 and 29, all of whose monuments were erected in 41 or later, after her deification by Claudius.[3]

There is, however, another possibility: joint manumission by Nero Augustus and Agrippina Augusta. There is some evidence for the existence of joint property of Nero before his accession and Agrippina: *AE* 1927, 2: 'C. Iulius Spartiaticus procurator Caesaris et Augustae Agrippinae, trib(unus) mil(itum) equo p(ublico) exornatus a divo Claudio'. Nero is known to have possessed property of his own requiring a procurator, Domitius Lemnus, in the period immediately before his accession.[4] If it was possible for Nero to own property jointly with his mother both after as well as before his accession – and I think that the burden of proof here rests with those who would deny it – then Ti. Claudius Aug. lib. Eutychus proc(urator) Augustorum (VI 9015 = 29847 a = D 8120) is as likely to have been a procurator of this joint property as of the property of Claudius and then of Nero in succession. If the latter is the case, the failure of Eutychus to call himself 'Augustorum lib.' is not helpful to those who would argue that in the status indication 'Augustorum' means 'successive Augusti', as Eutychus had every reason to use it in that case. In 50 Agrippina acquired the title 'Augusta'. Freedmen of Agrippina alone bore the *nomen* of their patron, e.g. VI 20384: Iulia Aventina Agrippinae Augustae lib.; 37591: Iulia Agrippinae Augustae l. Zosime. But joint freedmen of Claudius and Agrippina or of Nero and Agrippina would in both cases prefer the emperor's *nomen* 'Claudius'. The small numbers of their joint freedmen would then be due to the relatively brief period of

---

[1] Messalina's slaves: VI 5537, 35700; XV 7148. Her title reads 'Messalina Aug(usti uxor)'.

[2] E.g. VI 9047 = D 1810: Ti. Claudius Augustor. l. Domnio whose sister was Antonia Asia. A connection with the *familia* of Antonia Minor is at least plausible.

[3] VI 4159: M. Livius Divae Aug. l. Astio; 1815: Livia Divae Aug. lib. Culicina; 3945: M. Iulius Divae Aug. l. Agathopus; cf. 8949, 8955, 11541, 23338.

[4] For Nero's property in this period, and on Domitius Lemnus, see Weaver, *Historia* 14 (1965), 509 f., esp. 511 n. 15.

Status indication

Agrippina's sway, between 51 and 55, the circumstances of her death and the official attitude towards it afterwards.[1] Agrippina's property, including slaves, passed into the hands of Nero. Conditions in the last decade of Nero's reign clearly would have had some effect on the readiness of Imperial freedmen to claim Agrippina as joint patron, had they been entitled to, or of others to make that claim for them after their death. The other *Augusta* of the period is Poppaea Sabina. Inscriptions of her freedmen and slaves exist,[2] but in the absence of definite evidence one way or the other it is preferable to place joint manumissions early in Nero's reign in conjunction with his mother Agrippina rather than later with his wife Poppaea. In my view this is still the preferable explanation of the formula: 'Ti. Claudius Augustorum lib.' in the three inscriptions cited above.[3]

Freedman of the Flavian emperors also occur calling themselves 'Augustorum (Augg.) lib.'[4] The reigns of Vespasian and Titus afford no example of an Imperial consort who had the title 'Augusta'. Their matrimonial circumstances made this either impossible or inexpedient. The wife of Domitian, however, Domitia the daughter of Cn. Domitius Corbulo, received the title in 81. She was disgraced and divorced probably in 83. Domitian then lived with his niece Iulia, the daughter of Titus, and widow of his cousin T. Flavius Sabinus, apparently without marriage although she was an 'Augusta' while she lived and 'Diva Iulia' after she died in 87. Domitia in any case returned to the palace before that time and remained to participate in Domitian's murder. She undoubtedly wielded important influence under Domitian, as is shown by the fact of her reinstatement and her part in the assassination. Her own property and *familia* was large and important. Brick stamps exist bearing her name.[5] One of her slaves, Rhodon Domitiae Aug. ser. (VI 8434 = D 1523), bore the title 'exactor hered(itatium) legat(orum)

---

[1] Tacitus, *Ann.* xiv. 10 f.; Dio, lxi. 13.

[2] x 6787: Argenne Poppaeae Augustae Augusti liberta; xi 5610: Polytimus Poppaeae Aug(ustae) Neronis Caesaris Aug(usti uxoris) dispensator; cf. xi 5609; vi 8946.

[3] Note vi 9015 = 29847a: 'Claudia, Octaviae Divi Claudi f. lib., Peloris et Ti. Claudius Aug. lib. Eutychus proc. Augustor(um) sororibus...' If this inscription is taken to refer to service under successive Augusti, the difference between 'Aug(usti) lib.' and 'proc. Augustor(um)' needs to be accounted for. If it refers to joint property of an *Augustus* and *Augusta*, these are unlikely to be Nero and Poppaea, because of the full reference to Octavia – who did not have the title 'Augusta'. The reference is rather to Nero and Agrippina and would date from the early years of Nero's reign (cf. Divi Claudi f.); cf. Hirschfeld, *Verwalt.* p. 28 n. 1. Chantraine argues (p. 223) that this interpretation would postulate an unwarranted change in occupational nomenclature from 'proc. Augustorum' referring to successive *Augusti* to meaning 'Augusti et Augustae'. This is gratuitous, unless it is possible to prove the disappearance of such joint property. In any case a change of nomenclature in the same direction has to be postulated by Chantraine himself, at a later date, i.e. by 161, when 'Augustorum' has to change from meaning successive *Augusti* to mean 'Augusti et Augusti'. See further below. [4] xiv 3935 (two examples); a third is possible in xiv 2807 = D 6220.

[5] Cf. Dressel, *CIL* xv p. 157 and Nos. 548-58.

Nomenclature and chronology

peculior(um)'. If this title applies to Domitia's private property, as it probably does, the title used in imitation of the official nomenclature implies that her property and *familia* were fairly extensive. Another freedman was *sevir Augustalis* in Peltinum (IX 3432). There are *tabularii* (VI 7886, 7887) and a *procurator* (X 1738). In fact the *familia* of Domitia is very widespread, being found in Rome, in Italy and as far abroad as Galatia.[1] Domitia emerges as a wealthy property owner and business woman, an economic as well as political force, and no doubt the head of a faction.[2]

There were three *Augustae* during Trajan's reign: Pompeia Plotina his wife, Marciana his sister, and Matidia his niece. The first two were given the title 'Augusta' together with the right of placing their effigy on coins from at least 105.[3] Marciana died in 112, and in the same year her daughter Matidia was made *Augusta*. She lived till 119. All three had their own *familia*, of which Plotina's appears to have been the most important. Brick stamps name a slave of Plotina and perhaps also a freedman. One of her freedmen held the title 'numiclator a censibus' and 'lictor Aug. III decuriarum'. A freedman 'Divae Plotinae' is found, and slaves.[4] Freedmen of Marciana are known, including a *procurator*, and slaves of Matidia.[5]

In the next reign Hadrian's wife Sabina became *Augusta* in 128. Her *familia* is found not only in Rome and Italy[6] but also in Spain.[7] And in the next reign the *familia* of Antoninus' wife Faustina, in so far as it can be separated out from that of her daughter, Faustina II, also appears in Rome and Italy.[8]

In considering the *Augustorum liberti* of the period from Claudius to Antoninus Pius it is convenient again to begin at the later end. No fewer than twenty-eight out of forty-two examples with *nomen* which we are discussing, i.e. two-thirds, fall under the Aelii. Chantraine's interpretation of 'Augg. lib.' as 'liberti of successive Augusti' requires that all the 'T. Aelii

---

[1] *MAMA* IV 293 (Dionysopolis); cf. *IGR* IV 228, also from Asia Minor, belonging to the Flavian period. Other freedmen and slaves of Domitia: VI 8667, 8850, 8959, 9082, 11569, 20492, 24655, 35337; *AE* 1945, 111; IX 3419, 3469, cf. 3432.

[2] Note also XIV 2795 (Gabii), a dedication dated to 140 'in honorem memoriae domus Domitiae Augustae Cn. Domitii Corbulonis fil.'; and two inscriptions (VI 8570 = D 1517, 8978 = D 1834) recording a freedman, Herma Aug(ustae?) lib. a cubiculo Domitiae Aug.

[3] XI 1333 = D 288; cf. A. Garzetti, *L'Impero da Tiberio agli Antonini* (Bologna, 1960), p. 369.

[4] XV 921; 464-5 (AD 123), 461 (AD 135); cf. XIV 2161: Agathyrsus Aug(ustae?) lib., in a dedication to Plotina. VI 1878 = D 1912 (freedman 'numiclator a censibus', etc.); *AE* 1958, 184: L. Pompeius Venustus Divae Plotinae lib.; VI 8557, 8559, 8696 (slaves).

[5] Freedmen of Marciana: X 106 (a procurator), *AE* 1906, 81 (from Latium). Slaves of Matidia: VI 25417; XI 6727.1 = D 8632.

[6] VI 11221, 28804, 33802; *AE* 1916, 53; XI 4657.

[7] *AE* 1915, 9; cf. *AE* 1954, 86: P. Aelius Ianuarius Augustor. libertus.

[8] VI 8866 = D 1793; *AE* 1956, 19 (Naples); cf. VI 8896, 8941, 9062; XV 7358; X 4242; XI 3732 = VI 585.

Status indication

Augg. lib.' and a proportion of the 'Aelii Augg. lib.' without *praenomen* are to be dated to the next reign, i.e. *after* 161. This is in any case highly probable for those holding senior posts which they would not be expected to reach until some years after manumission. Thus, T. Ael(ius) Augg. lib. Restitutus *proc(urator) Syriae Palaest(inae)* (VI 8568 = D 1482; P-W IA, Aelius 122), and T. Ael(ius) Augg. lib. Saturnin(us) (VI 8450 = D 1521) who after a distinguished freedman career as *tabularius* in the offices of the corn supply at Ostia and *tabularius a rationibus* in Rome (both freedman posts, the latter the most senior of its grade and one which opened the way to the procuratorial career) became *procurator fisci libertatis et peculiorum* and finally *procurator provinciae Belgicae* (a senior freedman post at procuratorial level, assistant to the equestrian procurator of the province).

Two inconsistencies in Chantraine's interpretation follow from this: (1) he has to allow a change in the system of nomenclature, whereby 'Augustorum' = *successive* Augusti *till* 161, and 'Augustorum' = *jointly-reigning* Augusti *after* 161, a change of nomenclature analogous to the kind he will *not* allow for the first century, i.e. 'Augusti et Augustae' > 'Augustorum'; and (2) he allows, even requires, these two different meanings of 'Augustorum' to coexist and be consciously employed by different individuals at the same time – by the 'T. Aelii Augg. liberti' and by the 'M. Aurelii Augg. liberti'. Apart from other difficulties mentioned below, I find this hard to accept in the terms of Chantraine's own arguments, for these 'T. Aelii Augg. liberti' would *first* use the term 'Augustorum' in their status indication *after* 161, when, at least when not accompanied by the *nomen* 'Aelius' as is supposed often to be the case, it would lose its meaning; in that period 'Augg. lib.' meant something else, i.e. joint manumission, and so the motive of pride in their length of service disappears along with the lack of ambiguity.

On the other hand, as 'T. Aelii Augg. liberti' undoubtedly survived after 161, I find attractive, if not compelling, Boulvert's view (II, 516 f.) that the status indication of this group must derive from the period of joint rule by M. Aurelius and L. Verus. The same could well be true of many or most of the 'Aelii Augg. lib.' and some of the 'P. Aelii Augg. lib.', e.g. XIV 2504 = D 1491: P. Aelius Hilarus Augg. lib. *qui proc(uravit) Alexandriae ad rat(iones) patrimonii*; and even of M. Ulp(ius) Augg. lib. Probus *proc. provinc(iae) Pannoniae Super(ioris) et Africae reg(ionis) Thevest(inae)* (XIV 176 = D 1484) who lived to the age of 71 years 5 months, and so could have been manumitted at the age of 27 by Trajan and still have lived into the year 161. Cf. VIII 12667 (Carthage): P. Aelius Augustorum lib. Felix who died aged 77, and who if manumitted by Hadrian at the age of 30 in 120 would have

Nomenclature and chronology

lived till 167. In these examples the form 'Augg.' (not 'Augustorum') is most often used, which is predominantly *post* 161, according to Chantraine; cf. the frequent abbreviation of the *nomen* without *praenomen*. This objection would also apply to my own assumption that these *Augustorum liberti* with pre-Aurelian *nomina* who lived after 161 were jointly manumitted by an *Augustus* and an *Augusta*. There is a further objection: it is more appropriate that freedmen who reached the senior grades open to them should belong to the Familia Caesaris proper, that is belong wholly to the reigning *Augusti*, than that the *familia* of an *Augusta* should be involved, even partly, in the official administration at this level. The increase in the proportion of *Augustorum liberti* under Antoninus also does not accord well with the short period during which Faustina I was *Augusta* – 138 till her death in 141 – as Chantraine points out (p. 247 with n. 50). I am now inclined to think that most of the 'T. Aelii Augg. lib.' and other 'Aelii Augg. lib.' and 'Ulpii Augg. lib.' who lived on into the joint reign of M. Aurelius and L. Verus, particularly those in senior official positions, must derive their status indication from the same source as the 'M. Aurelii Augg. liberti'. This does involve a change in the system of freedman nomenclature whereby status indication for freedmen is assimilated to that for slaves; but, as we have seen earlier, we are forced to this conclusion on other grounds, i.e. those freedmen from the Aurelian period whose status indication varies between 'Aug. lib.' and 'Augg. lib. at different dates.

We thus have jointly-manumitted freedmen ('Augusti et Augustae') under Tiberius at one end of the period, and jointly-manumitted freedmen ('Augusti et Augusti') at the other end, after 161. The remaining question is the meaning of 'Augustorum libertus' in the period from Claudius–Nero to Hadrian. It is to be remarked that there are relatively few cases involved – five (or perhaps six) from the first century, and about twenty from the first half of the second century.

A surprising number of these cases died at a very early age for freedmen and were therefore manumitted at an even earlier age. To suppose that 'Augustorum libertus' refers to *successive* emperors means that these freedmen must have been manumitted even earlier still, in a *reign* earlier than would otherwise be the case, in fact. Chantraine does not attempt to deal with this point. No fewer than five of our group (at least a fifth) certainly come into this category:

VI 9047 = D 1810: Ti. Cl. Augustor. l. et structor Domnio, who died aged 23 (sister Antonia Asia);

VI 29133: M. Ulpius Augg. lib. Agilis, died aged 15;

Status indication

VIII 9434: P. Ael. Augustor. n. lib. Processianus, died aged 16 (father P. Aelius Pecuarius);
VI 10778: T. Ael. Augg. lib. Probus, died aged 19 years (father T. Ael. Augg. lib. Felicianus);
VI 29152: M. Ulpius Augg. lib. Chariton, who died aged 35, but as P. Aelius Augg. lib. Africanus appears in the same inscription, according to Chantraine's explanation (pp. 254 f.) the inscription must be dated to after 138 (to accommodate Africanus' status indication), and so Chariton could not have been manumitted by Trajan less than 21 years earlier, i.e. at the age of 14 or earlier.

Two others who might be noted here are: *AE* 1954, 86: P. Aelius Ianuarius Augustor. libertus, who died aged 30 (wife Ti. Claudia Cale, son P. Aelius Ephesius); and *AE* 1927, 136: Proclus Augg. lib., who died aged 24 years (he could date from the Aurelian period).

In defence of the difficulty with M. Ulpius Chariton it is not sufficient for Chantraine simply to point to the high frequency of early manumissions found in the same group. His argument is dangerously circular. He would do better to comment on the exceptional nature of early manumission, at least before the age of 20 or even 25, in the inscriptions of the Imperial freedmen as a whole. For those holding posts in the administrative service the proportion is very low. We have at best only three clear parallels to a clerical official of freedman status under the age of 25: VI 8417: T. Aelius Crispinus Aug. lib. a(d)*iutor a rationibus*, died aged 22; 8613; Faustus Aug. lib. *adiutor ab epistulis Lat.*, aged 19; XIV 4062 = D 1673: Artemidorus Aug. lib. *adlectus* (?) *a memoria*, aged 17.[1] For all *Augusti liberti* with *nomina* from 'Iulius' to 'Aelius' (excluding these *Augustorum liberti*), i.e. in the whole period before 161, there are found only another six freedmen who died (and were therefore manumitted) under the age of 25: VI 8656: C. Iulius Aug. l. Eutychus, aged 24; 33966 = D 5182: C. Iulius Aug. lib. Actius, 19; 18142: T. Flavius Natalis Aug. lib., 19; X 654: M. Ulpius Aug. lib. Euphoru(u)s, 3 years (!); VI 10666: P. Aelius Aug. lib. Mariensis, 20; 10685: T. Aelius Eros Aug. lib., 19. (After 161 there are five 'M. Aurelii Aug. lib.' and one 'L. Septimius Aug. lib.' who died under 25.) If we consider only the *nomina* 'Claudius'–'Aelius' (with which we are concerned for the *Augg. liberti*) there are only five manumissions under 25 for *Augusti liberti* with *nomen* compared with five also for the *Augustorum liberti*. But when expressed as a proportion of the total surviving inscriptions in these categories the result is quite different. Compared with 5/40 for the *Augg. liberti* we have only 5/880 for the *Aug.*

---
[1] In X 1729, Gregorius, who died aged 18 years, is not a freedman but son of M. Ulpius Nicephorus Aug. lib., as I have argued in *Antichthon* 5 (1971).

Nomenclature and chronology

liberti. A rough calculation shows that an 'Augg. lib.' in the period from Claudius to Antoninus Pius had at least twenty times more chance of being manumitted early (under 25) than an 'Aug. lib.' Only a minority of all inscriptions record the age-at-death figure for Imperial freedmen, but it is reasonable to suppose that exceptionally early manumission followed by early death would be just the occasion for recording this figure.

The comparable figure for *Augusti libertae* manumitted early (in this case 26 years, for the sake of comparison) in the period Claudius to Antoninus is also five, this time out of a total of 80 (VI 15579: Claudia Aug. l. Sabina, 19; XIV 2690: Claudia Primigenia lib. Aug., 15; V 2931: Claudia Ti. Augusti l. Toreuma, 19; X 1311: (Flavia) Lasciva Aug. lib., 25; VI 8502: Cocceia Aug. l. Restituta, 25). Women in general had a decisive advantage over men as slaves in gaining early manumission; manumission 'matrimonii causa' worked in their favour. In the Familia Caesaris they also, for whatever reason, have a much higher rate of early manumission than male slaves. Yet, on the above estimates, *Augustorum liberti* would seem to have a chance of early manumission at least the equal of the women, and probably a much greater chance.

The *Augustorum liberti*, therefore, appear to have very early manumission as a special characteristic of the group. This is not helpfully explained by asserting that their deaths are in fact to be dated to a reign *later* than would be otherwise necessary. Chantraine's solution to the problem of their status nomenclature should reasonably be expected to show, if anything, *less* likelihood of early manumission, not more, as they would have had much less chance of dying early if they had to live into the reign following their manumission.

In the Familia Caesaris as a whole, much the highest proportion of early manumissions are found among the 'lib. libert*ae*', the female slaves of Imperial freedmen who are manumitted early 'matrimonii causa'. Next come the *libertae* and *liberti* of the *Augustae*. And this is where the manumission pattern places the *Augustorum liberti* – somewhere between the freedmen and freedwomen of the *Augustae*, on the one hand, and the freedwomen of the emperor, the *Augusti libertae*, on the other. Small though the number of instances is in each group, they have to be explained; we may reasonably conclude that an *Augusta* was involved in the manumission of the *Augustorum liberti* in the period before 161.

There are further objections to Chantraine's argument. If 'Augustorum (Augg.)' represents *successive Augusti*, why did so few of the freedmen during the period who would undoubtedly have qualified for such a status indication use it as the matter of pride or 'act of devotion' that Chantraine assumes it

Status indication

to have been? They would have been as many in proportion as those who would have been qualified to use the status term 'verna' among slaves also as a matter of pride. The number of examples of *Augustorum liberti* is very small indeed in the period up to Hadrian – too small, one would think, to support the far-reaching thesis raised upon them. Rather the smallness of the number involved is in favour of the interpretation 'Augusti et Augustae', relevant to only a restricted category of freedmen, rather than 'successive Augusti', for which vast numbers of Imperial freedmen would have qualified. In many cases we know that the contrary practice was the case: e.g. XIV 3644 = D 1942 = *I. It.* IV 1.179: C. Iulius *Aug. l.* Sam(ius), proc(urator) accensus Divi Claudii et Neronis Augusti *patronorum*, who, despite his occupational title and the date of his inscription under Nero, does not use the status indication 'Augustor(um) lib.'; cf. VI 32775 = 33131 = D 2816: Ti. Iulius *Aug. lib.* Xanthus, tractator Ti. Caesaris et Divi Claudi et subpraef(ectus) classis Alexandriae; *AE* 1946, 99; etc. The reigns from Claudius to Hadrian were relatively short, only those of Trajan and Hadrian lasting longer than fifteen years. Many, or even a majority of freedmen manumitted by all emperors during this period would have been entitled to show their piety and pride by using this more 'honorific' status indication. They decisively do not do so.

The final point worth making is that Chantraine's view here of the nature and function of the status indication of Imperial freedmen cannot be right. He argues that there is no legal constraint on a freedman to conform to the precise facts of his manumission. He cites the use of 'n(ostri)' and 'vern(a)' by slaves in their status indication, and the use of *agnomina* by slaves and freedmen alike in the period till Hadrian. There is no doubt that in these instances the Imperial slaves and freedmen exercised their own personal choice. But slaves do not call themselves 'Caess. ser.' at will even though they may have lived and served under two successive emperors. If slaves were restricted in their use of the Imperial name in their status indication to representing the legal facts of their relationship to their actual master, it is not unreasonable to suppose that freedmen would be under a similar constraint. That part of their status indication which contained the Imperial title or reference should be taken to represent the legal facts of manumission – that is till the joint rule of M. Aurelius and L. Verus changed the meaning of the indication 'Augustorum libertus'.

The parallels adduced with the nomenclature of the procurators, *legati* and others are not valid, quite apart from the difference in status of these, who are either equestrian or senatorial. We are there in the sphere of occupational titles which regularly follow *outside* the personal nomenclature. We are in

Nomenclature and chronology

danger of overlooking the basic difference between personal and occupational nomenclature. The status indication is a regular part of the name proper and in the full name is usually placed *inside* the name before the *cognomen*. Usage and position are important, if not crucial, in the interpretation of nomenclature. The status indication, whether 'Aug. lib.', 'Augg. lib.' or any other form, is in no way to be assimilated with occupational nomenclature, which it is not. The real parallel is with other forms of the patronal name in status nomenclature. And in this regard, if we follow Chantraine, we might also feel obliged to consider the possibility that *all* freedmen who mention two or more *patroni* in their status indication have not been jointly manumitted, but have conceivably named *successive* patrons. Mommsen's remark is worth quoting still: 'si in principe per exceptionem eiusmodi patronatus admissus est, exempla similia abundarent'.[1]

I would maintain, therefore, my previous contention that 'Augustorum (Augg.) libertus' in the period from Claudius to Antoninus is best explained as signifying joint manumission by an *Augustus* and an *Augusta*. Thereafter, for freedmen manumitted after 161 in periods of joint rule it signifies joint manumission by two *Augusti*. It is also used for some freedmen of Trajan, Hadrian or Antoninus Pius who lived into the period of joint rule. It also appears to have become the practice in this period, at least in the cases of some notable freedmen, *pantomimi*, procurators and the like, for the freedman indication to be varied according to whether the inscription was erected in a period of single, double or triple rule.

ABBREVIATION OF THE STATUS INDICATION

The status indication was very rarely written out in full in the Latin inscriptions, although frequently in the Greek; e.g. *EE* VIII p. 164, no. 671: Iulia Divi Augusti liberta Aphrodisia veneria; VI 632 = D 5084a: Marcus Aurelius Augusti libertus Euporas; Greek examples: *IGR* IV 333, 1297, etc.; and the unpublished first-century BC inscription from Aphrodisias in Caria (see p. 22 n. 3 above). Even such a form as 'Pthongus Ti. Claudii Caesaris Augusti ser.' (VI 5011) is comparatively rare. The forms of 'Augusti' are usually abbreviated as 'Aug.' But those of 'Caesaris' are much less regularly abbreviated to 'Caes.', except in the standard slave indication. Cf. most forms of the

---

[1] Mommsen, ad *CIL* VIII p. 1335 n. 10. Chantraine also argues from the Greek nomenclature. He asserts (p. 245 n. 68) that Σεβαστῶν is never ('niemals') used in the sense of Σεβαστοῦ καὶ Σεβαστῆς. I cannot follow his assertion that in *OGI* 606 = *IGR* III 1086: ὑπὲρ [τ]ῆ[ς] τῶν κυρίων Σε[βαστῶν] σωτηρίας καὶ τοῦ σύμ[παντος] αὐτῶν οἴκου (referring to Tiberius and Livia in the period 14–29), Σεβαστός is used *adjectivally* (presumably κυρίων is used substantivally; but cf. ὁ τοῦ κυρίου Καίσαρος οἰκονόμος and similar phrases).

Status indication

extended freedman and slave indication where the usual combination is 'Caesaris Aug.'[1]

In the freedman indication the standard form 'Aug. lib.' had established itself by the end of the Flavian period. A chronological analysis of the main abbreviations 'l(ibertus)' and 'lib(ertus)' gives the following result:[2]

	(%) Aug. l.	(%) Aug. lib.
Livii	80	20
Iulii	68	32
Claudii	61	39
Flavii	32	68
Ulpii	13	87
Aelii	5	95
Aurelii	2.5	97.5
Septimii	—	100

These figures show a 4:1 predominance of 'l.' over 'lib.' for the freedmen of Livia manumitted before AD 14, reducing to 2:1 for the Julio-Claudian period as a whole. The proportions are almost exactly reversed for the Flavii, and the proportion of 'l.' to 'lib.' drops rapidly from the early second century, being at least halved for each subsequent *nomen* from the Claudii to the Aurelii, vanishing entirely with the Septimii.

Perhaps more striking still is the contrast between the proportions for those forms of the freedman indication which have been identified above as pre-Flavian, and those found to be post-Flavian (percentages first, absolute figures in parentheses):

A. Pre-Flavian

	l.	lib.
Caesaris	96 (27)	4 (1)
Liviae[3]	93 (42)	7 (3)
Divi Aug.	92 (24)	8 (2)
Caesaris Aug.	91 (10)	9 (1)
(Praenomen) Aug.	90 (16)	10 (2)[4]

---

[1] See the examples in Appendix II, Category D.

[2] See Weaver, *CQ* 13 (1963), 276; Chantraine, p. 150. The variation in the absolute figures there given, especially for the Aelii and Aurelii, depends on the proportion of those without *nomen* allocated to these groups on the basis of internal criteria. For the Aurelii family dating criteria are more reliable than for earlier Imperial *nomina*. However, the overall result expressed in percentage terms does not vary significantly. Chantraine includes the joint freedmen of Tiberius and Livia with the 'Iulii Aug. l.' The 'Livii Aug. l.' represent a basically Augustan situation, the 'Iulii Aug. l.' the whole period of the Julian emperors up to and including Gaius. The 'Aelii Aug. lib.' also include the 'T. Aurelii Aug. lib.' and other related Imperial *nomina* of the period, 'Vibius Aug. lib.' and one 'Ceionius Aug. lib.'

[3] There are occasional examples of 'lib.' among the freedmen of Antonia Minor and Agrippina the Younger; but thereafter hardly a single instance of 'l.' among freedmen of the *Augustae*.

[4] Chantraine's figures for these distribute the '(praenomen) Aug.' forms over the other groups.

Nomenclature and chronology

B. Post-Flavian

	l.	lib.
Caesaris n.	—(—)	100 (6)
Aug. n.	—(—)	100 (11)
Augg. nn.	—(—)	100 (12)

Outside the Familia Caesaris the freedmen of *privati* use the form 'l.' The abbreviation 'lib.' was not common amongst this group or else it disappeared along with the status indication in general of these freedmen from the beginning of the second century.[1]

Thus at the very time when the designation 'l.' and status indication in general was on the decline outside the Familia, inside it the form 'l.' was also being abandoned, but in favour of 'lib.', and the freedman nomenclature became much more uniform than before.

It is worth noting here that the abbreviation for 'filius' in the Familia Caesaris also shows a chronological development from 'f(ilius)' to 'fil(ius)' similar to that of 'libertus' from 'l(ibertus)' to 'lib(ertus)'. In the early first century 'f.' is commonest; but it rapidly gives place to 'fil.' which predominates by the end of the Claudian period and excludes 'f.' altogether in the course of the second century. The freedman inscriptions which are dated by the Imperial *nomina* show this as follows (percentages first, absolute figures in parentheses):

	f.	fil.
Iulius	65 (13)	35 (7)
Claudius	30 (12)	70 (28)
Flavius	15 (5)	85 (28)
Ulpius	21 (7)	79 (26)
Aelius	9 (4)	91 (41)
Aurelius	5 (2)	95 (40)
Septimius	—(—)	100 (3)

This use of 'lib.' in the status indication and 'fil.' in the naming of family relationships in the Familia Caesaris, it should also be noted, runs counter to the prevailing contemporary tendency towards abbreviation in other respects, particularly in sepulchral inscriptions; e.g. 'd(is) m(anibus)' and 'd(is) m(anibus) s(acrum)' from the late Claudian or early Flavian period onwards, 'v(ixit) a(nnos)'; cf. the increasing tendency towards abbreviation of the Imperial *nomen* in the freedman nomenclature in the second century.[2]

The question arises from the findings in relation to the use of 'l.' and 'lib.' above whether these abbreviations provide a further secondary dating

---

[1] Cf. the examples of freedman indication in Dessau, *ILS Index Nominum*. See also Taylor, 118 f.; Vitucci, *Diz. Epig.* IV, 917; Chantraine, pp. 70, 154.
[2] See above, pp. 40 f.

Status indication

criterion. 'Aug. lib.' occurs too frequently in the early periods to be of much use. But after Hadrian 'l.' is exceptional. Chantraine has listed 27 instances of 'l.' in the freedman indication in this period and has considered in detail special reasons, such as position, space, etc., for its use. His aim is to establish a *terminus ante quem* for the use of 'l.' as a dating criterion for Imperial freedmen without *nomen*.[1] From the dated inscriptions listed in Appendix II a similar result emerges.

Under Trajan, 'l.' occurs several times, e.g. VI 32429 (twice); *AE* 1940, 40 (*fistula*); XV 7295 (*fistula*). A certain overlap of the forms is still apparent, e.g. VI 42 (cf. 43 = D 1634): Felix Aug. lib.; 44 = D 1635: Felix Aug. l. (AD 115). XI 3614 = D 5918a: Vesbinus Aug. l., Vesbinus Aug. lib., Ulpius Vesbinus (113/14). VI 1884 = D 1792: M. Ulpius Aug. lib. Phaedimus (who died 117, but inscription dates from 130); cf. III 575; but X 6773: 'M. Ulpius Phaedimus Aug. l.' alongside 'Phaedimus Aug. lib.'

Under Hadrian, three examples of 'l.' occur in one inscription (VI 975 = D 6073) of 136 recording the *magistri vicorum urbis*, including a 'T. Flavius Aug. l.', a 'M. Ulpius Aug. l.' and a 'P. Aelius Aug. l.' VI 682 = D 1623: Crescens Aug. l., who is the same as T. Flavius Crescens in VI 30901 = D 1622 of 128. XIV 51 (dated to 124): (P. Aelius) Trophimus Aug. l. proc. prov. Cretae, in the inscription of his own freedman who is simply 'P. Aelius Trophimi Aug. l....lib.' VI 9100 = D 1850 (AD 120): Diadumenus Aug. l., 'ordinatus ultro a Divo Tito' AD 80, died 120.

The instances of 'l.' then become quite scarce – only two under Antoninus Pius, VI 10234 = D 7213 (AD 153): Capito Aug. l., who appears elsewhere in the inscription as 'M. Ulpius Aug. lib. Capito' with two 'P. Aelii Aug. lib.'; and XV 467 (AD 151): Agat(h)yrsus Aug. l., on one out of half-a-dozen brick stamps of the same person between 123 and 152 where the indication is otherwise 'Aug. lib.' (XV 466, 468–70). There is one 'Aug. l.' on a *fistula* under Commodus (XV 7744), and one instance under Septimius Severus, VI 724 = D 4204 (AD 194): M. Aurelius Aug. l. Euprepes, who appears on an adjacent inscription under Commodus, VI 723 = D 4203 (AD 184), as 'M. Aurelius Aug. lib. Euprepes'.

From this we may reasonably conclude that 'l.' in the freedman indication is a very probable indication of a date before Antoninus, and a probable one also of a date before Hadrian. The *terminus ante quem* cannot with any confidence be taken back any earlier than Hadrian.

In the slave indication the normal abbreviations are 'Caes.'/'Aug.', 'n.', 'ser.'/'vern.' No dating criteria can be extracted here from changes in abbreviations; a pattern does not exist. The single letter abbreviation 's(ervus)'

---

[1] Chantraine, pp. 155 f., 157 f.

Nomenclature and chronology

is rare,[1] and 'v(erna)' perhaps does not occur at all for Imperial slaves.[2] The single letter abbreviation 'C(aesaris)' is also rare in the slave indication and when it does appear is almost invariably used in association with 'n(ostri)'.[3] The earliest instance is from the reign of Domitian (XV 7286); the others are all probably second century.[4] 'A(ugusti) n.' is very rare and only in *signacula*.[5]

POSITION OF THE STATUS INDICATION

For slaves there is no problem: the status indication follows the personal name. Where an occupational title exists, as we have seen above, it does not form part of the slave nomenclature, but directly follows it. It is exceptional to find an occupational title intruding between the personal name and status indication. The only influence on nomenclature which the occupational title does appear to exert, at least in the first century, is on the omission of 'ser.' in the slave indication, the simple forms 'Caes.'/'Aug.' being somewhat preferred when followed by such a title.

For freedmen without *nomen* and *praenomen* the status indication must also necessarily follow the *cognomen*. Where the full nomenclature with *praenomen* and *nomen* is used, however, it is usual for the status indication to be placed between the *nomen* and the *cognomen*, as with filiation, tribal indication, and in the nomenclature of freedmen belonging to *privati*. But with the Imperial freedmen it is not unusual for the status indication to be placed *after* the *cognomen*.[6] The chronological pattern of this usage has some interest.[7] Its relation to the omission of *praenomen* by Imperial freedmen is also noteworthy.

In terms of percentage as well as absolute numbers of all examples of Imperial freedmen in each group, those with postponed indication and omitted *praenomen* are (absolute numbers in parentheses):

---

[1] 'Caes. n.s.': VI 8495 = D 1612 (twice), 8523 = D 1823; *Hesperia* 10 (1941), 243 = 32 (1963), 87. 'Aug. s.': III 12301; VIII 12810, 13084; in VIII 14560 (AD 107) the reading is doubtful (see above, p. 55 n. 5). 'C. n. s.': VI 598, 24578.

[2] Unique would be VI 19015: 'Genesius C. n. v(erna)', where the reading 'U(lpia)' is more likely.

[3] The one exception I can find is from the period of Antoninus Pius – VI 27289: 'Myrine C./T. A. Alexandro Aug. l.', which has more than one unusual abbreviation.

[4] 'C. n. (ser./vern.)': VI 8467, 8524 (Chantr. p. 201 misprints 8528), 12053, 16868, 17413, 18428, 22960, 30901 = D 1622, 37748; V 237 = *I. It.* X 1.62; VIII 12819, 13131; XI 5807; XIV 1636 = *IPO* B 152 = D 7926.

[5] XI 6712.7–8; *AE* 1908, 194 (?); cf. VIII 9362: 'Alexander A. n. lib.'

[6] Contrary to the assertions of most writers on the subject, e.g. Thylander, *Étude*, p. 64; Vitucci, *Diz. Epig.* IV, 917. But see now Chantraine, p. 282, who gives earlier references.

[7] See Weaver, *CQ* 13 (1963), 277; and the full-scale treatment of Chantraine, pp. 281 f.

Status indication

Aug. lib.	Postponed indication	Praenomen omitted
Iulii	6 (7)	4 (4)
Claudii	11 (25)	2 (4)
Flavii	12 (25)	3 (6)
Cocceii	21 (3)	— (—)
Ulpii	19 (36)	5 (9)
P. Aelii	21 (30)	. .
T. Aelii	17 (16)	. .
Aelii	44 (24)	. .
all Aelii	24 (70)	10 (30)
M. Aurelii	29 (39)	. .
Aurelii	64 (58)	. .
all Aurelii	43 (100)	27 (61)

In chronological terms there is no significant change towards the postponing of the status indication or the omission of *praenomen* till we come to the Aelii.[1] With the Aelii the rate of omission of *praenomen* suddenly doubles, with for the first time a significant absolute number of examples.[2] It is precisely among the Aelii *without praenomen* that the rate of postponed indication also suddenly doubles from the rate shown by the P. Aelii, T. Aelii and earlier *nomina*. Similarly under the Aurelii the rate of postponed indication for those *without praenomen* is more than twice that for the M. Aurelii (i.e. with *praenomen*). The M. Aurelii themselves show an increase in postponed indication, no doubt under the influence of the by now common practice of omitting the *praenomen*. Abbreviation of the *nomen* is also much commoner with the Aurelii than with earlier *nomina*. Chantraine (p. 288) also well points to the preference for postponed indication amongst the *Augusti libertae* of all periods who, of course, never had a regular *praenomen*. On the other hand, the shift in the position of the status indication is not to be connected with the following official title or occupation.[3] Where the status indication is postponed, occupational titles occur in only about one instance out of three at the same rate throughout the whole period from the Claudii to the Aurelii.

Another modification of status nomenclature under the Aurelii is the omission of 'Augg.'/'Aug.' and the simple use of 'lib.' by Imperial freedmen in dedications to the emperors and their families. There also appears in dedications of this period the use of 'eorum'/'eorundem' in place of 'Augg.' in the status indication of both slaves and freedmen.[4]

---

[1] See now the detailed figures of Chantraine, pp. 283 f. The change in the position of the freedman indication is thus not to be dated from the Flavian period, as by Taylor, p. 122 with n. 25.
[2] Thylander, *Étude*, pp. 77 f., 131, dates the omission of the *praenomen* among the plebeian and freedman classes simply to the second century AD.
[3] As by Taylor, p. 122 with n. 25.
[4] See esp. Chantraine, pp. 234 (list), 245 f. (discussion).

Nomenclature and chronology

It is clear that by the end of the second century the well-defined system of nomenclature for Imperial freedmen first established under the Flavians, probably under Vespasian, had now begun to alter rapidly as it entered the last phase of its existence. This nomenclature thus falls into three phases: first, that of the Iulii and Claudii, when considerable variety is evident, particularly in the indication of status. Second, the period from the freedmen of Vespasian to those of Antoninus Pius, when 'Aug. lib.' became the standard title of the Imperial freedmen and in formal nomenclature the order: *praenomen – nomen* – status indication – *cognomen* was fairly strictly adhered to. Third, the period beginning with M. Aurelius and the co-regency with L. Verus when 'Augg. lib.' became very common, the traditional order was increasingly changed, the *praenomen* omitted, and the *nomen* abbreviated. Often all these changes occurred together.

In the Imperial slave status nomenclature, on the other hand, distinct phases are less easily discerned. In the Julio-Claudian period the simple genitive form 'Caes(aris)' is more frequent than the forms with 'ser.' From the Flavian period the forms 'Caes. ser.' and later 'Caes. n. ser.' become dominant. Forms in 'Aug.' also appear in the first century, although 'Aug. ser.' was never very common outside the African inscriptions. 'Aug. n.' was later in making its appearance, not till the Hadrianic period, and thereafter increasingly in association with 'vern(a)' which also becomes frequent from the time of Hadrian. From the time of M. Aurelius the forms in 'Aug(g).' and 'Aug(g). n(n).' with or without 'vern(a)' come to exclude all other forms.

REGIONAL VARIATION IN STATUS NOMENCLATURE

Regional variations are not uncommon in most aspects of Latin inscriptions and nomenclature is no exception. For example, in personal nomenclature, a number of peculiarities occurring in the inscriptions from North Africa have been pointed out by Kajanto, arising from his study of Latin *cognomina*.[1] The same phenomenon can also be observed for status nomenclature in the Familia Caesaris, especially in relation to North Africa.

Chantraine's detailed geographical analyses of all forms of this nomenclature from all parts of the empire make it unnecessary to go over this ground in detail again.[2] I shall content myself with presenting a conspectus of the main forms of the slave indication where the most significant variations occur, and with making some general comments on what emerges from this.

---

[1] I. Kajanto, *Philologus* 108 (1964), 310 f.; see also the same author's *The Latin Cognomina* (Helsinki, 1965).

[2] Chantraine, pp. 140 f., 150 f., 175 f., 181 f., 200 f., 206 f., 225 f., 231 f., 283 f., 289 f.

Status indication

For this purpose I have divided the material into four groups, for the sake of simplicity and convenience: (1) Rome and environs, including Ostia; (2) the rest of Italy; (3) North Africa; (4) all other provinces. I have revised the absolute figures previously given in *CQ* 14 (1964), 138, and present them in percentage form as well for purposes of comparison.

	Rome (%)	No.	Italy (%)	No.	North Africa (%)	No.	Other provinces (%)	No.	Total (%)	No.
Caes.	**83**	(164)	11	(22)	2	(4)	4	(7)	100	(197)
Caes. n.	**75**	(45)	13	(8)	9	(5)	3	(2)	100	(60)
Caes. ser.	**72**	(66)	8	(8)	16	(14)	4	(4)	100	(92)
Caes. n. ser.	**50**	(117)	13	(30)	33	(77)	4	(8)	100	(232)
Caes. vern.	**74**	(29)	21	(8)	—	—	5	(2)	100	(39)
Caes. n. vern.	**70**	(28)	15	(6)	10	(4)	5	(2)	100	(40)
Aug.	37	(70)	17	(32)	36	(69)	10	(20)	100	(191)
Aug. n.	27	(22)	22	(18)	16	(13)	**35**	(28)	100	(81)
Aug. vern.	39	(22)	19	(11)	35	(20)	7	(4)	100	(57)
Aug. n. vern.	41	(26)	3	(2)	15	(10)	**41**	(26)	100	(64)
Aug. ser.	15	(24)	7.5	(12)	**75**	(120)	2.5	(4)	100	(160)
Aug. n. ser.	37.5	(9)	21	(5)	29	(7)	12.5	(3)	100	(24)
Total	50	(622)	13	(162)	28	(343)	9	(110)	100	(1237)

Bold figures indicate points raised in the following discussion.

The most striking general feature is the extent to which *all* forms with 'Caes.' are predominant in Rome. On the figures under consideration, an overall average proportion for Rome would be 50% in each case. But except for 'Caes. n. ser.' which is 50% exactly, the figure is above 70% for 'Caes.', 'Caes. n.', 'Caes. ser.', 'Caes. vern.', 'Caes. n. vern.', and even over 80% for 'Caes.' Only for 'Caes. n. ser.' is the distribution nearly what one might call normal. This no doubt partly reflects the large *columbaria* in and near Rome giving a high concentration of the first-century forms in Rome. But this cannot be the whole explanation; considering the total number of inscriptions involved, Rome would also be fairly represented in the distribution of second-century forms, as the figure for 'Caes. n. ser.' shows.

For some forms in 'Aug.', on the other hand, the provinces show a striking preference. Outside Africa 'Aug. n.' and 'Aug. n. vern.' occur four times as often as one would expect on a strict percentage distribution of these inscriptions, but not the corresponding forms *without* 'n.', viz. 'Aug.' and 'Aug. vern.', which have about the normal proportion for this group of

Nomenclature and chronology

provinces, i.e. about 9% of the total. The African inscriptions, however, are surprisingly under-represented in these otherwise favoured provincial forms 'Aug. n. vern.' and 'Aug. n.' But they show a remarkably high proportion of the form 'Aug. ser.' – as high as 75% of all cases everywhere. Moreover, 'Aug. ser.' scarcely occurs at all elsewhere in the provinces. Even Rome shows only 24 examples of 'Aug. ser.' compared with 120 from Africa. These latter come mainly from the second-century *columbaria* in Carthage, but the pattern in the rest of North Africa is not significantly different from that of Carthage in this respect. The form 'Aug. n. ser.', on the other hand, is rare, there being only 24 examples from all areas of the empire, i.e. about 2% of the total number of inscriptions here considered.

We might be tempted to explain the variations between different areas by largely accidental factors, e.g. that inscriptions from Rome reflect a basically first-century situation, that the provincial forms are largely mid-second century and later, and that the figures for the African forms are heavily influenced by the *columbaria* in Carthage. This is no doubt partly true. But the distribution of the characteristic early to mid-second-century form 'Caes. n. ser.' is perfectly normal, and the characteristically late second-century forms with 'Augg. (nn.)' are not included, so that the overall bias is unlikely to be in favour of the second century rather than the first. The above factors also do not adequately explain the African preference for some forms above others; besides 'Aug. ser.', the following forms are all over the average proportion for Africa: 'Aug. vern.', 'Aug.', 'Caes. n. ser.' Nor do they explain the lack of provincial interest in the dominant early to mid-second-century form 'Caes. n. ser.'

There are other features of the African status nomenclature that point to strong regional peculiarities there: the frequent use of the status indication, both the slave and the freedman indication, for wives and young children, groups for whom it is not used elsewhere to anything like the same extent. This, of course, may reflect a difference between Africa and the rest of the empire in respect of the status of wives and children of Imperial slaves and freedmen. But this does not necessarily follow for children, and if these wives in Africa have a status pattern significantly different from that of wives in other provinces, it still has to be explained why this is so.[1]

OMISSION OF STATUS INDICATION

In the case of the freedman and slave groups discussed above their membership of the Familia Caesaris is formally expressed in their status indication.

---

[1] On the status of wives and children, see Part II below.

Status indication

There are, however, numerous cases where there is no clear status indication but where, with varying degrees of certainty, we have to do with Imperial freedmen and slaves. It is particularly necessary to decide where the line must be drawn in the case of freedmen as there are countless thousands of inscriptions in Rome, Italy and the provinces where the Imperial *nomina*, especially 'Iulius', 'Claudius' and 'Flavius', appear without status indication or filiation. They do not certainly belong to Imperial freedmen or even to freedmen at all, but they are often confidently assumed to do so.[1] But while most often it cannot be definitely proved that these and similar cases are not Imperial freedmen and slaves – although the conjecture is sometimes legitimate – it also cannot be proved that they did belong to the Familia Caesaris. In fact it is more probable that they did not, as the tendency, if not temptation, to proclaim association with the Imperial Familia was very strong in most parts of the empire at most times for reasons of social prestige. As seen above, non-Imperial freedmen tended to drop their status indication at the same time as, and perhaps because, the indication 'Aug. lib.' became a freedman status symbol.

On the other hand, omission of the status indication of Imperial freedmen and slaves does occur, as is shown most clearly where the same name appears both with and without the indication in the same inscription or group of inscriptions; e.g. VI 8499 = D 1489, 8500 = XI 1753 = D 1490: Lemnus Aug. l. = Domitius Lemnus; XI 3614 = D 5918a: Vesbinus Aug. l. (lib.) = Ulpius Vesbinus; VI 682 = D 1623, 30901 = D 1622: Crescens Aug. l. = T. Flavius Crescens; VI 634 = 30804 = D 1540a, 544 = D 1540: Crescens Alypianus, etc. Partial omission occurs regularly for Imperial slaves, not always obviously for reasons of space, on the *fistulae*, brick-stamps, etc.[2] There is also the tendency in the third century to use simply 'lib.' and 'ser.' in dedications to the emperor.[3] Omission can sometimes be proved for well-known freedmen from the naming of their official post on an inscription when

---

[1] Two examples: *IGR* IV 754, on which W. M. Ramsay (*Cities of Phrygia* I, 157) conjectures that Claudius Clemens was a freedman of Claudius the emperor; and 755 where T. Fla(v)i(u)s Epaphroditus is considered to be a freedman of Titus (cf. Cagnat, *IGR* ad locc.). Cf. *AE* 1923, 70–1; 1941, 65; 1948, 225; *ILAlg.* I 759; W. M. Ramsay, *Social Basis of Roman Power in Asia Minor* (Aberdeen, 1941), Nos. 136, 139, 140, 157, 280, etc. Throughout his works Ramsay proceeds as if such assumptions were proven. See also Taylor, 113 f.; Wilkinson, *Names of Children*, passim; and numerous conjectures in footnotes by scholars, e.g. S. J. De Laet, *Portorium* (Brugge, 1949), pp. 373 n. 3 (a plain misreading of the inscription, VIII 12655), 390 n. 3, 398 n. 1 (a misinterpretation of the nomenclature – *agnomina* were not used by Imperial slaves or freedmen from the time of Hadrian; see below, pp. 91, 217).

[2] E.g. under Domitian: XV 7279 = D 8697 and 7280; 7818 = XIV 2657 = D 8681 and XV 7819 = XIV 2304 = D 8680. Trajan: XV 7770–1 = XI 3548a–b and XV 7893; *AE* 1940, 40 and XV 7296, 7297. M. Aurelius and L. Verus: XV 7741–2, etc.

[3] E.g. XIV 2856 = D 376: Aurelia Restituta lib. (AD 179); *AE* 1933, 282: Aurelius Takitus lib. (dedic. Iulia Domna).

Nomenclature and chronology

taken in conjunction with the literary evidence; e.g. P. Aelius Alcibiades, *a cubiculo* to Hadrian;[1] M. Aurelius Cleander, under Commodus;[2] Aelius Cladeus, *a memoria et cubiculo Aug.*[3] The use of 'conlibertus' and 'conservus' sometimes suffices when there is a definite connection with the Imperial household.[4] On the other hand, several who have a clearly expressed occupational connection with the Imperial household, but no status indication, are classed as freedmen by Dessau and others presumably on the grounds of occupation and absence of filiation. But in the absence of more definite criteria, especially dating, it is by no means certain that they are not descendants of Imperial freedmen.[5]

In these and similar cases there is sufficient doubt about the freedman or servile status of the occupants of these posts to exclude them from the statistics given above. They will be considered later in connection with the careers and social status of the children and other descendants of the Imperial freedmen and slaves.

Sometimes connection with the Imperial household is claimed by freedmen (and freeborn) not belonging to the Familia Caesaris, though in some cases their *nomina* are those of relatives of the emperor.[6] This is especially the case with the *medici Augusti*, many of whom are not Imperial freedmen at all.[7]

---

[1] P. Aelius Alcibiades, *a cubiculo* to Hadrian: *CIG* 2947 = D 8857; cf. *SEG* I 441, II 529; *PIR*², A 134; P-W I (Aelius 19).

[2] M. Aurelius Cleander, *a cubiculo* to Commodus: xv 8021 = D 1737; SHA *Commodus* 6.3; see Moretti, *Riv. fil. class.* 38 (1960), 68 f.; Pflaum, *CP* No. 180 bis, p. 1007.

[3] Aelius Cladeus, *a memoria et cubiculo Aug.*: VI 8618 = D 1672; *PIR*², A 160.

[4] E.g. VI 4566 (Monumentum Marcellae): '...C. Iuli T(h)repti et collibertorum eius et ex donatione Ti. Claudi Homeri et collibertorum eius'. *Colliberti* with Imperial *nomina* but no definite connection with the Familia Caesaris have been excluded, e.g. VI 7543 = D 8195a, 18100 = D 8295, 27365 = D 8201a, 35594; X 2289 = D 8201, etc.

[5] *C. Iulii*: VI 3919 = D 1847: praeceptor Caesarum; 8724 = D 7733: C. Iulius Luciferi filius Posphorus architect. Aug. (freeborn).
Ti. Claudii: VI 4887: Ti. Claudius Caesaris numunclator Amaranthus (perhaps a freedman, cf. order of the names); 8501 = D 1487: Ti. Claudius Marcellinus [proc. A]ug. a patrimonio (taken as *Aug. lib.* by Dessau, followed by Duff, Vitucci, and others; he is probably an equestrian – see Weaver, *Historia* 14 (1965), 511 n. 21; Boulvert, *EAI*, p. 105 n. 70; Pflaum, *CP*, p. 1025).
M. Cocceius: X 3356: 'tr(ierarchus) Aug(usti) C(aesaris)' (?) (taken as *Aug. lib.* by Mommsen, *CIL* ad loc.)
M. Ulpius: VI 746 = D 4202: praepositus tabellariorum (AD 183 – cannot be *Aug. lib.*).
L. Aelius: VI 9995 = D 7417: L. Aelius Protus scrib. unctorum (cf. Dessau ad loc.).
Aurelius: VI 8932: nomenclator Caesaris n.

[6] E.g. VI 1944 = D 1934: M. Falcidius Cupitus praeco et apparitor Aug.; 4649: L. Scribonius (Eros) archimimus Caesaris (lib. ?); 4871: Domitius Philetus interpretes Aug. n.; 8846: C. Verres Eros obstipator Caesaris Augusti; *AE* 1953, 57: C. Octavius Fructus archit. Aug.; IX 4057: L. Aninius L. l. Eros lictor Augusti Caesaris.

[7] E.g. VI 8895 = D 1842: L. Arruntius Sempronianus Asclepias; *IGR* IV 1444: M. Artorius Asclepias (early first century; cf. Mommsen, *CIL* VI, p. 3157; *PIR*², A 1183; P-W II, 1461); IX 740; *SEG* VI 554; *IGR* III 1061; and four Claudii, none of whom is clearly an Imperial freedman: *IGR* I 283: Ti. Claudius Alcimus; 286: Ti. Claudius Quir. Menecrates; *AE* 1941, 64: Ti. Claudius Athenodorus; XIV 3641: Ti. Claudius Aelius Sabinianus.

Status indication

Lastly, there are the *corporis custodes*, sometimes called *Germani*, who were the emperor's personal bodyguard under the Julio-Claudians. Recruited from the German tribes subject to Rome, especially the Batavi, Frisii and Veii, they were dismissed and sent home by Galba, as they had been previously by Augustus at the time of the Varian disaster.[1] Though a military body the *corporis custodes* were Imperial slaves and occasionally freedmen, at least under Nero and probably under Claudius also.[2] This anomaly is to be explained by the use of slaves for bodyguards and is paralleled by their use as gladiators. Their organisation as a *collegium Germanorum* with *curatores* and so on is similar to that found elsewhere in the Familia Caesaris. 'Miles' occurs once (VI 8806 = D 1727), a usage which Mommsen says: 'sicher abusiv ist';[3] cf. in the same inscription: 'Imperatoris Neronis Aug.', 'militavit'. As for the slave indication, this is regularly the simple genitive followed by 'corpore (corporis) custos' or 'Germanus'.[4] Omission of 'corp. cust.' is rare.[5] The indication 'ser(vus)' does not occur at all. The nomenclature of the *corporis custodes* is closely parallel to that of the *trierarchi* and conforms to the dominant pattern for Imperial slaves in the Julio-Claudian period.

This brings us to the more general question of the omission of parts of the Roman name by persons outside the Familia Caesaris. Often this is quite arbitrary, and arguments for the status of individuals on the basis of what parts of a name appear in a given inscription and what do not are particularly hazardous. For instance, a single personal name often, perhaps usually, points to slave status especially if the name is of Greek derivation, but not always and certainly not by rule. A single name is not an indisputable proof of slave status. The *nomen* can be omitted as well as the *praenomen*, and *both* were often omitted by the freed as well as the freeborn. Particularly interesting is the omission of the status indication. Determination of status is at the heart of most problems that arise in the study of the sub-equestrian classes of Roman society under the Empire. Unfortunately, along with chronology, it is also the most intractable problem for these social levels.

Lily Ross Taylor in her stimulating article 'Freedmen and Freeborn in the

---

[1] Suetonius, *Galba* 12; *Aug.* 49; Cassius Dio, lvi. 23.
[2] E.g. VI 8803 = D 1730: Ti. Claudius Chloreus, cf. Ti. Claudius Diadumenus. The one exception is XI 3526: C. Lucilius Valens. See Mommsen, *Staatsr.* II, 808–9; Chantraine, p. 20 n. 23; above, p. 46.
[3] *Staatsr.* II, 808 n. 4.
[4] VI 4340: 'Macer Ti. Germanici Germanus corpore custos' has both, although the reverse order is sometimes found especially with 'Germanus', e.g. VI 4337 = D 1718, 4341 = D 1717, 4345 = D 1723, 8810 = D 1724.
[5] VI 4344 = D 1722: Peucennus Germanicianus Neronis Caesaris.

Nomenclature and chronology

Epitaphs of Imperial Rome'[1] reopened the question of race mixture, or rather status mixture, in urban areas of the early Empire and strongly reinforced the famous but startling conclusions of Tenney Frank[2] that at least 90% of the inhabitants of the city of Rome in the first and second centuries AD were either slaves or freedmen or of freedman descent within two or at most three generations. H. Thylander came to similar conclusions.[3]

I. Kajanto, on the other hand, concludes from his massive study of over one hundred thousand examples of Latin names[4] that only 7% of these belong to persons from the slave or freedman classes. It is scarcely possible to have a greater variation in results. Even those scholars who have tried to estimate the population of the city of Rome in the early Empire – another important question – have not varied by a quarter as much.

The explanation of this variation is quite simple. It lies in the method of analysing the names in the epitaphs. Kajanto adheres rigidly and mechanically to status indication as the only true criterion of status, and as fewer and fewer slaves or freedmen in this period in fact used status indication at all outside the emperor's Familia, as Taylor amply shows, he not unnaturally finds little evidence of slaves and freedmen in the epitaphs. But neither do the freeborn classes of the population at sub-equestrian level outside of the army use their status indication, i.e. filiation, or tribal indication to any great extent. Those who omit their status indication – the *incerti*, as Professor Taylor calls them – amount in fact to no less than 67% of the persons from Rome. Kajanto appears simply to assume that all these are freeborn. Taylor argues with some success that most of these are freedmen. Kajanto is certainly wrong, but Taylor is not certainly right, and some consideration of her method of analysing the names is necessary.

Her basic criteria are (i) the inter-generational change in the proportion of names of Greek and Latin derivation, (ii) the steady growth in the number of *incerti* accompanied by an increase in the number of epitaphs in which freedman status is indicated only by internal evidence such as reference to a patron, *collibertus* or *contubernalis*, and (iii) the association in the epitaphs of men and women with the same *nomen*, which in Taylor's view implies origin from the same slave *familia*, especially if in addition the *cognomina* are of Greek derivation. None of these criteria can by themselves be regarded as conclusive.

The most important argument has centred on the derivation of *cognomina*. When both parents had Greek names, 40% of their children were given Latin names. When the father had a Greek name and the mother a Latin one,

[1] *AJPh* 82 (1961), 113–32. [2] *AHR* 21 (1916), 689–708.
[3] *Étude*, pp. 143 f., esp. 178 f. [4] *The Latin Cognomina*.

Status indication

56% of their children had Latin names. When the father had a Latin name and the mother a Greek one, 72.5% of their children had Latin names. And when both parents had Latin names, 83.5% of their children had Latin names.[1] The argument is that the proportion of Greek *cognomina* diminished from generation to generation, and the predominance of Greek *cognomina* in the inscriptions is to be explained by new manumissions, particularly in the sepulchral inscriptions of the common people.

Greek names were common in the Senate of the second century. Tacitus, indeed, has one of his speakers say that many (*plerique*) senators were of servile descent (*Ann.* xiii. 27). But what of the freeborn *peregrini* and their descendants? And above all, what chronological pattern, if any, did the preference for Latin *cognomina* follow in children's names? The pattern may have varied as between the first and second centuries as, we can assume, did the proportion of *vernae*, the rate of manumissions, and other factors. Control groups which can be fairly strictly dated are needed to test these assumptions. The control group that is most readily to hand, the Familia Caesaris, shows if anything a mid- to late second-century preference for Latin *cognomina* among children of Imperial slaves.[2] But this corroboration is of doubtful value because, as will be suggested later, the mothers in most cases – about two-thirds of them at the least – were themselves of free birth, whereas this was rare in the slave population in general.

Nor can we accept without qualification the assumption[3] that persons in the epitaphs with names of the form 'T. Flavius T. f.', 'M. Ulpius M. f.', 'P. Aelius P. f.', are simply freeborn sons or grandsons of the emperor's freedmen. The habit of assuming that persons with Imperial *nomina* 'Iulius', 'Claudius', and especially 'Flavius', 'Ulpius', 'Aelius' and 'Aurelius', who are not of attested senatorial or equestrian status will probably be Imperial freedmen or their descendants or the descendants of their descendants neglects three important facts about the emperor's freedmen and slaves: (1) The size of the emperor's Familia, especially in the status-carrying administrative posts, was at any given time economically small, or at least much smaller than is often supposed, too small at any rate to have peopled the Roman world with the host of persons bearing the Imperial *nomina*. The number of *peregrini* enfranchised in a given emperor's reign and bearing his *nomen* was probably at least several times the number of his own slaves who bought or were given their freedom. (2) The average size of family of Imperial freedmen, as in most élite social groups, seems to have been small, perhaps not more

---
[1] I take these figures from Beryl Rawson's important review of Kajanto's *Latin Cognomina* in *Class. Phil.* 63 (1968), 157 f. at n. 4.
[2] See below, chapter 4, pp. 89 f.
[3] Taylor, p. 123.

Nomenclature and chronology

than two children. This would not be much more than replacement rate for their parents, given their expectation of life. (3) The average age of the parents in the Familia Caesaris at the time of marriage was so much less than their average age at manumission that most children would have been born to them while they were still slaves and so the children would have been born either as slaves themselves or would have taken the *nomen* of the mother if she was freeborn. A large and increasing proportion of wives of Imperial slaves and freedmen had non-Imperial *nomina*. In fact, where the proliferating freeborn generation descended from Imperial freedman parents could have come from in the numbers required by this assumption is something of a mystery. A further weakness of this thesis is the need virtually to ignore the law regarding the minimum age for manumission as it stood from the lex Aelia Sentia (AD 4) to Ulpian.[1]

Professor Taylor's methods of treating the epitaphs of Volume VI of *CIL* merely point up the problems and areas of disagreement. But her *general* conclusions may now be regarded as firmly enough established: (1) that the names in the epitaphs do not give us a cross-section of the population; (2) that there is, nevertheless, a very large freedman or freedman-descended element in the population of the city of Rome and other important urban areas.[2] But what her article has *not* established is any rule for the interpretation of the status of individual persons belonging to the category of the *incerti* in the sepulchral inscriptions.

[1] See Part II below.
[2] Cf. for Ostia the comparable conclusions reached by R. Meiggs, *Roman Ostia* (Oxford, 1960), pp. 217 f., cf. 196 f.

CHAPTER 4

COGNOMINA AND AGNOMINA

COGNOMINA

From the middle of the first century AD the *cognomen* had replaced the *praenomen* as the personal name for both freedmen and freeborn. This was true even in the equestrian and senatorial classes, as the nomenclature of Vespasian's family illustrates. This change occurred much earlier with the freedmen, who retained their slave name as their personal name or *cognomen*.[1]

The social significance of *cognomina*, particularly those of Greek derivation, as has been mentioned above, is a matter of controversy. The high proportion of Greek-derived *cognomina* in the sepulchral inscriptions of Rome and elsewhere in the empire, together with the inter-generational change in the relative proportions of Greek and Latin *cognomina*, has led to the conclusion that a Greek *cognomen* is likely to indicate slave origin or freedman descent within two or three generations.[2] The general weaknesses of this conclusion have been discussed above.[3] But the high proportion of Greek personal names in the Familia Caesaris does nothing to disprove it.

Besides the controversy over whether some *cognomina* can be specified as servile in origin, there is the corresponding question whether some *cognomina* can be considered to have a distinctively freeborn or even upper-class connotation – the so-called 'cognomina ingenua' and 'cognomina equestria'.[4] The Familia Caesaris might be thought to have an illustrative role here, especially with those rare freedman members who were elevated to equestrian status. The test case is the *cognomen* 'Marcianus' taken by the freedman

[1] On *cognomina* and personal nomenclature in general, see W. Schulze, *Zur Geschichte lateinischer Eigennamen* (1904, repr. 1966), 487 f.; Thylander, *Étude*, pp. 99 f. On slave names: J. Baumgart, *Die römischen Sklavennamen* (Diss. Breslau, 1936); M. Lambertz, *Die griechischen Sklavennamen* (Vienna, 1907–8). For the basic bibliography, both on epigraphic and literary sources, see esp. Thylander, *Étude*, pp. 54 f.; Chantraine, pp. 128, 131.
[2] See above, p. 84 nn. 1–3.
[3] Cf. M. L. Gordon, *JRS* 14 (1924), 93 f.; Westermann, *Slave Systems*, pp. 96 f.; Thylander, *Étude*, pp. 143 f.; F. G. Maier, *Historia* 2 (1953/4), 343. See now the additional arguments adduced against Thylander and others by Chantraine, pp. 134 f., who also considers the relevance for this question of the work of H. J. Leon (*The Jews in Ancient Rome* (Philadelphia, 1960); *TAPA* 59 (1928), 205 f.) on the personal names in Jewish inscriptions in Rome.
[4] *Staatsr.* III, 426 n. 2; cf. 209, 425 n. 2; Dessau, *Hermes* 45 (1910), 25: '...das für die Freigelassenen selbst ziemlich streng festgehaltene *Verbot* der *nomina equestria*'.

Nomenclature and chronology

Icelus on his gaining equestrian rank under Galba. The sources are three passages: Tacitus, *Hist.* i. 13, Plutarch, *Galba* 7, and Suetonius, *Galba* 14.[1] Of these Tacitus and Plutarch agree that the name 'Marcianus' was freely chosen by Icelus and not conferred in any formal sense (*vocitabant*, καλούμενος), whereas Suetonius implies the latter (*cognomine ornatus*). The priority and weight of authority are in this case with Tacitus and Plutarch, deriving from their unknown common source, and not with Suetonius.[2] Icelus of his own choice adopted a name which in the first century still had upper class associations and in taking this new personal name 'Marcianus' he presumably intended to drop his former one with its servile associations.

But Icelus was a degenerate who later paid heavily for his pretensions. The earlier cases of Pallas, Narcissus, Callistus, Epaphroditus and others, and the eloquent silence on the personal name of Claudius Etruscus' father, when similarly but more justifiably elevated to equestrian rank, show that Icelus was an isolated case and was not following or setting a fashion. We hear little of such changes of personal name in the Familia Caesaris even in cases where they might be expected, if not condoned.[3] When freedmen of *privati* tried to claim illegally equestrian status, presumably by methods involving a change of name, Claudius checked the practice with some sternness.[4]

Much writing on the lower classes also has been based on the same assumption of a discernible difference between distinctively 'freeborn' personal names (*cognomina ingenua*) and those that are distinctively 'servile' (*cognomina servilia*). These latter Duff[5] goes so far as to describe as 'the most tell-tale evidence of a man's servile extraction'.

The evidence of the personal nomenclature of the Imperial slaves and freedmen is particularly valuable here. In the Familia few problems of status determination arise. The distinctive status nomenclature is quite explicit. Also the fact that a large proportion of these inscriptions can be dated, at least approximately, in the ways considered in a previous chapter, makes it possible to trace the chronological development, if any, from the first to the early third century in the use of *cognomina* by one élite group of servile origin.[6]

The results of such an investigation, however, are largely negative. *Cognomina* of Greek origin abound for Imperial freedmen and slaves of all

[1] For a discussion of these passages, see *CQ* 14 (1964), 311 f.
[2] On the question of sources, see Syme, *Tacitus*, pp. 180 f., and for the relevant literature, esp. Appendix 29, pp. 674 f.
[3] The circumstances of the case of Aurelius Zoticus (*PIR*², A 1641), the athlete from Smyrna and favourite of Elagabalus, were, to say the least, unusual. But this case of whimsy does not imply that such changes of name were commonplace, only that they were possible. Cf. Chantraine, p. 138.
[4] Suetonius, *Claud.* 25.1.
[5] *Freedmen*, pp. 55 f., cf. 110 f.
[6] See Weaver, *CQ* 14 (1964), 311 f.

Cognomina and agnomina

periods and also for their freeborn wives and children. No pattern of chronological value can be traced nor can useful dating criteria be extracted from individual names. The first-century case of Cerulus, freedman of Vespasian, is significant as stated by Suetonius, *Vesp.* 23: 'de Cerulo liberto, qui dives admodum ob subterfugiendum quandoque ius fisci *ingenuum* se et *Lachetem* mutato nomine coeperat ferre'. Cerulus was wealthy but his guilt lay in attempting to defraud the *fiscus* by secretly pretending to be of different status, not in his taking a different name. In any case, what was to be his new '*cognomen ingenuum*' was in fact a pure Greek one – hardly convincing support for the idea of *Latin cognomina ingenua*, even in the first century.[1]

For Latin *cognomina* a slightly clearer picture emerges. The last of the names claimed as 'cognomina ingenua', *Marcellus, Marcella, Rufus, Verus*, as well as others often cited as such, e.g. *Celer, Capito, Florus, Fronto, Probus*, etc., can all be illustrated by more than one example from the Familia Caesaris, in most cases dating from the end of the first century AD and later.[2] Similarly, *cognomina* either identical with or derived from the names of *emperors* themselves or the Imperial family are constantly appearing, e.g. Titus, Domitianus, Traianus, Geta; Domitia, Faustina, Agrippina; Iulianus, Claudianus, Flavianus, Ulpianus, Antonius, Agrippa, Pertinax, etc.[3] These names at best provide vague *termini post quem*, but of no specific chronological value, e.g. Ulpianus, Flavianus, Aurelianus.

More significant is the general chronological distribution of personal names ending in *-ianus* (to be distinguished from *second cognomina* (*agnomina*) in *-ianus*), e.g. Cornelianus, Iustianus, Licinianus, Maecianus, Marcianus, Maximianus, Priscianus, etc. Few *cognomina* of this type can be securely dated to the first century. But they become increasingly common throughout the second century and by the early third century actual *nomina* are being used as personal *cognomina* by Imperial slaves and freedmen alike, e.g. Antonius, Cassius, Domitius, Flavius, Sempronius, etc.

The personal *cognomina* of the equestrian procurators in the mid- and late second century are closely similar to those of many of the Imperial slaves and freedmen, and almost all the commonest equestrian names are also among the commonest Imperial slave and freedman names, e.g. *Celer, Clemens, Felix, Maximus, Priscus, Proculus, Sabinus, Saturninus, Victor*, etc. In the second century the equestrian procurators show the same preference

---
[1] Different is the case of Milichus, freedman of Flavius Scaevinus, who took the Greek name 'Soter' (Tacitus, *Ann.* xv. 71: 'Conservatoris sibi nomen Graeco eius rei vocabulo adsumpsit' – Tacitus cannot bring himself to give the actual Greek name). But this was in the aftermath of the Pisonian conspiracy under Nero, when a *Greek cognomen* might be positively recommended.
[2] For references, see *CQ* 14 (1964), 313 f.
[3] For references, see *CQ* 14 (1964), 313 f.; and Chantraine, pp. 128 f.

Nomenclature and chronology

for names in *-ianus*, e.g. *Clementianus, Clodianus, Flavianus, Priscillianus, Volusianus,* etc., which by the late second century had become common in the Familia Caesaris also, but which are rarely found there in the first century.[1]

Any gesture by social upstarts to change their personal name to something more socially acceptable would have thus become practically meaningless by the late second century. It follows from this also that personal names on their own cannot be used as significant evidence for the status of wives and children of Imperial freedmen and slaves. The barriers between the personal nomenclature of the upper classes and the slave and freedman classes, which were still felt to some extent in the early and mid-first century, broke down in the course of the second century. This is a symptom of the interpenetration of classes in Roman Imperial society and if it is revealed more clearly in the personal nomenclature of the Familia Caesaris than in that of other slave and freedman groups, this demonstrates from one more point of view the important role of the Imperial slaves and freedmen as an element of high status and exceptionally high mobility in the changing social structure of the early Empire.[2]

AGNOMINA

Of much greater importance for nomenclature and chronology in the Familia are the *agnomina* (or second *cognomina*) ending in *-ianus* (sometimes *-anus* or *-inus*). These names are derived from the *nomen* or *cognomen* of a former master from whose *familia* the slaves have passed, either by gift, purchase, legacy or inheritance, into the Familia Caesaris. In the latter there are over three hundred examples.[3]

Though most numerous in slave-born society among the emperor's freedmen and slaves, these *agnomina* occur in only a distinct minority of cases in the groups and periods of the Familia to which they belong. But the names of previous masters recorded in these *agnomina* provide a valuable record of at least one important source of recruitment for the emperor's Familia. For this reason a full discussion of these inscriptions is reserved for Part III below.[4] Here we should note that for dating purposes many of these names are derived from well-known members of the Imperial family, e.g.

---

[1] For references, *CQ* 14 (1964), 314.

[2] On slave names as evidence for place of origin, and on the supposed methods of naming slaves, little enlightenment is to be gained from the Fam. Caes. material. See the discussion of Chantraine, pp. 130 f.

[3] Hülsen, *Röm. Mitt.* 3 (1888), 222 f.; Weaver, *JRS* 54 (1964), 123 f.; Boulvert, II, 464 f.; and most recently Chantraine, pp. 293 f., who has drawn up the most complete list of these inscriptions, with detailed comments and discussion; cf. ib. p. 295 for bibliography.

[4] Below, pp. 212 f.

Cognomina and agnomina

Agrippianus, Antonianus, Drusianus, Germanicianus, etc., or from dateable senators and equestrians, e.g. Cornificianus, Crispinillianus, Fabianus, Scapulanus, Vinicianus,[1] or from client kings and princes, e.g. Amyntianus, Archelaianus, Herodianus, Iubatianus, Pylaemenianus, or even from the names of emperors themselves, e.g. Galbianus, Neronianus, Domitianianus.[2] All of these provide valuable dating points.

As *agnomina* derive from a previous master, they can provide only a *terminus post quem*. Such a *terminus* would be earlier than the date of the inscription for both slaves and freedmen, but for freedmen it would as a rule be further back in time than for slaves, as it would have to relate to the period before manumission. We cannot look for any high degree of precision, but the *agnomina* do provide a supplementary dating criterion more precise than that of the Imperial *nomina* alone. Many of them derive from the names of Imperial freedmen and slaves themselves, e.g. Acteanus, Atticianus, Epaphroditianus, Gamianus, Thamyrianus, etc. Some of these also can be identified with freedmen and slaves well-known from other sources, but many of them cannot be pinned down with confidence or precision. Nevertheless, the overall value of this group for dating purposes is considerable.

The *agnomina* are found in abundance from the beginning of the Familia. Perhaps a third of all examples are from the period Augustus to Gaius. There is still a steady stream of them during the reign of Trajan.[3] But by early in the reign of Hadrian this dwindles to a trickle, then stops completely.[4] The reasons for this cessation will be considered in Part III below. Though only a minority of slaves and freedmen in any given period before Hadrian used *agnomina*, it is clear that this was far from including all slaves who entered the Familia Caesaris from outside *familiae*. It is also clear that slaves did not cease entering the Familia from these sources from the reign of Hadrian onwards. The fact that, without exception, these did not use *agnomina* after

---

[1] Cornificianus: VI 5245, 8753, 16658 – L. Cornificius, *cos.* 35 BC; *PIR*², C 1503. Crispinillianus: VI 8726 = D 7733a – Calvia Crispinilla, Nero's former 'magistra libidinum' (Tacitus, *Hist.* i. 73); *PIR*², C 363. Fabianus: VI 23569; XIV 3920 – equestrian Fabius put to death by Claudius (Tac. *Ann.* xi. 35 f.; Seneca, *Apocol.* 13); *PIR*², F 13. Scapulanus, Scaplianus: VI 4358, 4402, 5226, 9061, 10302 = D 7352 – Q. Ostorius Scapula, *praef. praet.* 2 BC, *praef. Aegy.* AD 3–11; cf. Chantraine, pp. 333 f. Vinicianus: VI 8938 = D 1690 – M. Vinicius, *cos.* 30, *cos.* II 45; *PIR*¹, V 445. (Or perhaps the equestrian Vinicius Rufinus, *PIR*¹, V 448; cf. Chantraine, p. 340 No. 334.)

[2] For references, Chantraine, pp. 299 f., 302 f., 317, 319 f., 331; and see Part III below, pp. 213 f.

[3] E.g. from the list of dated inscriptions (Appendix II), Aegilianus: VI 31099; Alypianus: 634, cf. 544 = D 1540a, 1540; Cosmianus: VI 9090; Domitianianus: VI 8532 = D 1747; *AE* 1922, 122; etc.

[4] See Part III below, p. 217. To the examples discussed there should perhaps be added the brick-stamps XV 811a–c: 'Anteros Severi(anus) Caesaris n.'; cf. 810: 'Anteros Caes. n. ser.' (without *agnomen*), which is dated AD 123 (cf. Chantraine, p. 335 No. 300, and p. 366). Also VI 29194: M. Ulpius Aug. lib. Felix Crispianus, who is married to a Vibia Fortunata (cf. Chantraine, p. 309 No. 105).

Nomenclature and chronology

Hadrian cannot be accidental. For purposes of chronology it is sufficient here that, in the absence of data pointing to Hadrian's reign, *agnomina* in the Familia Caesaris date from Trajan's reign or earlier. Within the period Augustus to Hadrian the date of these inscriptions is determined by the date of death of the previous master and the limits of survival afterwards of the slave or freedman in question. For freedmen these limits would be earlier in most cases than the possible or probable limits for freedmen with the same Imperial *nomen* only.

PART II

THE FAMILY CIRCLE

In Roman society of all periods the nuclear family constituted the basic social unit whether in freeborn, freed or slave society, whether the members were citizen or non-citizen. We are not here concerned with *familia* in the sense of household or that slave–freedman unit under the control of the *paterfamilias*. It is evident that in the exercise of his *potestas* the *dominus* had originally a complete authority over his own slave household that could have profound effects on the intimate family life of his own slaves and freedmen. He could break up these units by selling children to other masters, forbid marriages with slaves of other masters, and in general act out his absolute legal powers to the point of inflicting the death penalty. But there came increasing legal restraints on arbitrary conduct by masters, and also an increasing obligation on the part of the master, in his own economic self-interest, to conform to the domestic law of his own *familia*. This meant the recognition of his slave's right to his *peculium* or savings, with the primary purpose of buying his manumission, and no doubt the recognition of the existence of family ties as well among his slave family units, including their marriages and children. The fact that so many slaves themselves were owners of slaves would help to give a humanitarian balance to the way the system worked. These aspects as they concern the Familia Caesaris have been discussed in the Introduction. Here we shall be concerned with the normal social life of the family-unit and its functioning inside the Imperial *familia* as a whole.

The basic family relationships are those between husband and wife and between parents and children. In discussing the intimate family circle of members of the Familia Caesaris we can start from the known status of the freedmen and slaves with status indication who are for the most part males and husbands. The central questions then become the legal and social status of their wives and children. The status of the wives is especially important as it determines the status of the children. The position of female Imperial slaves and freedwomen and the role of women in the Familia Caesaris in general will be dealt with in a separate section at the end. Before grappling with the status of the wives, however, it is necessary to consider two preliminary questions, the age at manumission and the age at marriage of both men and women in the Familia. Manumission and marriage were the two most important events in the life of a slave. Without speculating on the relative importance of each to the slave, it is important to decide at what age either event was likely to happen to slaves of the emperor. If manumission or

The family circle

marriage normally took place some years prior to the other, this is important for determining the status of the children, whether they were normally born to slave or manumitted parents. For comparison with the situation in the Familia Caesaris a separate study along the same lines has been made of a group of slave and freed married couples not belonging to the Familia Caesaris, drawn from the inscriptions from the city of Rome.

CHAPTER 5

AGE AT MANUMISSION

It is generally assumed that manumission was not difficult for an intelligent, energetic and thrifty slave in the early Empire. Apart from other evidence,[1] the legislation of Augustus to regulate manumission – the lex Iunia, the lex Fufia Caninia and the lex Aelia Sentia – points to the prevailing ease of manumission and did little to restrict any reasonably justifiable manumission.[2] For the Familia Caesaris the question really is what is the average expectation of slavery for the various groups of slaves, and whether this varied according to occupation, area or period in the early Empire.

According to the lex Aelia Sentia of AD 4, the minimum age for formal manumission was 30 years for the slave, while the manumittor had to be 20 or older. Slaves under 30 did not acquire full citizenship on manumission but became *Latini Iuniani* unless, after due cause having been shown ('causae probatio'), approval was given by a special *consilium* followed by manumission 'vindicta' or formal manumission.[3]

As to what constituted a 'iusta causa manumissionis' for slaves under 30, Gaius (i. 19; cf. 31) includes in the list blood relationship ('si quis filium filiamve aut fratrem sororemve naturalem...apud consilium manumittat'), foster relationship ('...aut alumnum aut paedagogum'), future services ('aut servum procuratoris habendi gratia') – provided the slave was over 18 years[4] – and intended marriage ('aut ancillam matrimonii causa'); to which Marcianus adds past services ('si periculo vitae infamiaeve dominum servus liberavit').[5] There were thus substantial provisions whereby a slave could be manumitted as a full citizen while still in his twenties or even earlier. Under Augustus even those manumitted before 30 who became *Latini Iuniani* could on the first birthday of their first child acquire full citizenship for both themselves and child by 'anniculi probatio'.[6] Under subsequent

---

[1] Cf. Cicero, *Phil.* viii. 11: 'cum in spem libertatis sexennio post simus ingressi diutiusque servitutem perpessi quam captivi servi frugi et diligentes solent'. On the Republic, see now S. Treggiari, *Freedmen in the Roman Republic* (Oxford, 1969); also her article 'The Freedmen of Cicero', *Greece & Rome* 16 (1969), 195–204.
[2] For discussion of the Augustan legislation, see Duff, *Freedmen*, pp. 72 f.; Last, *CAH* x, 425 f.
[3] Gaius, i. 18; Ulpian, i. 12. The passage in Ulpian continues: 'ideo sine consilio manumissum Caesaris servum manere putat', where 'Caesaris' makes no sense and 'servum manere' cannot be right. Cf. id. iii. 3, where Latin status is assumed for those manumitted under 30.
[4] *Dig.* xl. 2.13.   [5] Ib. 9 pr.   [6] Gaius, i. 29; Ulpian, iii. 3.

The family circle

emperors additional paths to full citizenship were opened to the *Latini Iuniani*, including those under 30. These are listed in Ulpian, iii. 1 as follows (with, in brackets, the name of the first emperor to apply a given provision): 'ius Quiritium consequitur his modis: beneficio principali, liberis (Augustus), iteratione, militia (Tiberius), nave (Claudius), aedificio (Nero), pistrino (Trajan)'. They include, especially, services to the state in time of need or shortage, such as military service (exceptional), providing shipping for transport of corn, supply of bread, and the construction of buildings (in connection with the rebuilding of Rome after the fire).[1] Modifications were also made to the lex Aelia Sentia under Vespasian, AD 75,[2] and Hadrian.[3] It remained in force till Justinian abolished the classes of *Latini* and *dediticii*. The path to full citizenship, which was not in any case difficult for a Latin, was made progressively easier during the first and early second centuries. Hence the 'ius Latinorum', the patronage and right to the estate of a *Latinus Iunianus*, which Pliny found so acceptable (*Ep.* x. 104), was of diminishing value and no serious motive for a master deliberately to manumit his slaves either informally or under the age of 30 'sine consilio'. Rather the effect of the law must have been to tend to delay manumission till the age of 30, when slaves could buy their freedom with their *peculium*, than to prevent any reasonably justified manumission under that age. Under Justinian there was no age limit at all on manumission of a slave.[4]

The evidence of the inscriptions shows that many slaves were manumitted before the age of 30. For example, in an early first-century inscription, VI 4951, seven *liberti* and *libertae* are mentioned of whom four died in infancy or childhood at the ages of 4, 5, 9, 13. The other three were regular manumissions all at the age of 30. The children may have been informal death-bed, or 'pathetic', manumissions such as that of Martial's 19-year old slave, Demetrius (*Epigr.* i. 101); but we simply do not know how far this kind of manumission was practised and what were the legal technicalities involved.

In the Familia Caesaris informal manumission, apart perhaps from some cases of 'pathetic' manumission, and the concept of *Latinitas* which went with it would seem to have little place – if it meant anything like the 'failure of the patron to give an implicit testimonial of the freedman's fitness for the full franchise'.[5] The one mention of *Latini* is late and outside the period under consideration.[6] Nor is there any evidence that the lower legal status of *Latinitas* was used as a step in the hierarchy of the Familia Caesaris as a matter of policy. It was in the emperor's interest to extract good service from his slaves

[1] Cf. Gaius, i. 33–4.   [2] Gaius, i. 31.   [3] Ib. 30.
[4] *Cod. Iust.* vii. 15.2.   [5] Duff, *Freedmen*, p. 78.   [6] *Cod. Theod.* iv. 12.3 (AD 320).

Age at manumission

in their early working life, and in the interest of the *fiscus libertatis et peculiorum* to have manumission purchased by Imperial slaves from their *peculium*, which presumably, barring special favour, could not be done before the legal age. Even free manumission, with exemption from payment, did not imply early manumission, as the case of Claudius Etruscus' father shows. Also the 'iustae causae manumissionis' for slaves under 30 'apud consilium', such as blood or foster relationship to the master or patron, or intention to marry him, could scarcely apply to Imperial slaves, despite some emperors' propensity to indulge in concubinage. And one does not imagine manumission to procurators under age for *future* services finding much favour in the administrative code. But these causes, especially marriage with a patron, do account for the high rate of early manumission found among the freedmen and especially freedwomen of Imperial freedmen (the *lib. liberti* and *lib. libertae*). The 'beneficium principis', so readily exercised by Trajan in response to Pliny's requests,[1] was not likely to have been extended beyond granting the *ius Quiritium* to those who were already *Latini*. For *Caesaris servi* early manumission as a reward for good service may not have been impossible – although it seems to have been very uncommon in the administrative service – but in such circumstances it would have been formal and complete.

Let us look first at a small group of inscriptions of the *lib. liberti* and *lib. libertae*, former personal slaves of Imperial freedmen. Where the age at death is stated, these show a very high rate of manumission before the age of 30. From nineteen examples the ages are: 5, 7, 10, 10, 13, 14, 16, 17, 22, 23, 25, 25, 30, 40, 41, 44, marr. 23 y., marr. 24 y., 72 (marr. 46 y.).[2] Manumission preceded death by a longer or shorter period which cannot be determined. The above number of cases is too small to be taken as *proof* of regular early manumission but the proportion under 30 – 63% – is very high by comparison with any other group. The distribution by age and sex gives us a glimpse at the reason. The first three, children aged 10 or under, are all males; we don't really know why children were manumitted under the age of puberty or the legal age for marriage but let us suppose that these are cases of 'pathetic' manumission on their death-bed. Their *peculium* would perhaps have been negligible and of no interest to their freedman patron; but the gesture was probably a simple expression of affection, however it fared with the law. But the next group, who died between the ages of 10 and 30, are all

[1] Pliny, *Epist.* x. 104, 105; cf. Gaius, iii. 72; Ulpian, iii. 1.
[2] In order of age: VI 14990, X 6144, VI 8485 (children all male); VI 15580, *AE* 1903, 338 (*verna*); VI 25033, XIV 524, VI 8866, 20173, 16586, 29378, 36186, VIII 8996 (all women, ages 10 to 30); VI 13659, 10547, 18112, XIII 2308, VI 6191, 15598 (a woman married for twenty-four years can be considered to be about 40 or older; a man married for twenty-three years would be slightly older).

The family circle

female – over half of all the examples of all ages. The reason is clear in most cases – early manumission 'matrimonii causa'. This is specifically stated in three cases: VI 29378: 'Ulpiae Paezusae (25 y.) fecit M. Ulpius Aug. lib. Rufio lib(ertae) et coniugi'; XIV 524: 'Aeliae Helpidi (16 y.) P. Aelius Aug. lib. Symphorus patronus et contubernalis'; VI 8866: 'Galeriae Claudiae (17 y.) Galerius Anthophorus Aug. lib. lib(ertae) et coniugi'. The early age at which women normally married in the early Empire (it was later in Christian times) would account for many early manumissions.

Turning to the *Augusti liberti* themselves, the first conclusion to be drawn is that, although the emperor's slaves have a high expectation of manumission in due course, they nevertheless have less chance of *early* manumission, i.e. before 30, than other slave groups that we can identify. (Compare the group studied in Chapter 11 below.) Before the age of 25 their chance is very much less, particularly if they are males and holding official posts. The proportion of those who died as freedmen under the age of 30 is much smaller than with other groups. 173 ages at death are recorded, distributed as follows:

Ages	Number
1–10	4
11–19	12
20–29	26
30–39	33
40–49	25
50–59	21
60–69	18
70–79	14
80–99	20
Total	173

24% (42/173) were definitely manumitted before 30. As the patron is the emperor, the main reason for early manumission in the *lib. libertae*, intent to marry the patron, cannot apply. The close ties of familiarity and affection which often linked personal slaves to their masters, and so increased the likelihood of early manumission for personal services rendered, is relatively less important in the Familia Caesaris because of the greater number of slaves. Ties of sentiment were likely to give place to the need for rules and regulations in running an organisation as complex as the Imperial household, not to mention the administration itself. The more impersonal spirit is symbolised most strikingly by the existence of a special branch of the *fiscus* (*libertatis et peculiorum*) to deal with their claims, and in hard fact by the small number of holders of official posts who gained early manumission – only three holders of clerical posts (including one with the peculiar title 'adlectus a memoria'), and only eight officials of any kind under the age of 25 (in-

Age at manumission

cluding one *pantomimus*).[1] The power of the emperor's procurators in the provinces to recommend, let alone grant, early manumission must have been very limited. If Pliny's correspondence with Trajan on such matters, or Suetonius' administrative anecdotes on Vespasian (e.g. *Vesp.* 23) are any indication, such matters would inevitably have been referred back to the emperor, or at least the central administration in Rome, for decision at what would seem to us an astonishingly high level. Manumission of those who were 30 and over would be a more routine matter, again probably handled by a department of the central administration, according to more standardised procedures, perhaps on an annual basis, and in the financial interests of the *fiscus*.

A closer look at the way early manumission worked in practice is worthwhile. Manumission of children under 11 years of age is very rare – there are only four cases that I can find in the whole Familia Caesaris, all males and three of them 'M. Aurelii Aug. liberti'. Conjecture here is fruitless. But a warning is in place: these examples should be treated as the exceptions they are, and not quoted as if they established on their own a pattern of childhood manumission in the Familia Caesaris.[2] The teenage manumissions also have characteristics that do not belong to any other group. Between the ages of 11 and 19 there are thirteen examples; three are girls, including the youngest in the group who died aged 15; three are *Augustorum liberti* (on whom see Part I above, pp. 68 f.); four are youths without occupations specified; the remaining three are the officials already mentioned.[3]

---

[1] *Clerical administrative:* XIV 4062 = D 1673: Artem(i)dorus Aug. lib. adlectus (!) a memoria, aged 17; VI 8613: Faustus Aug. lib. adiutor ab epistulis Lat., aged 19; VI 8417: T. Aelius Crispinus a(d)iutor a rationibus, aged 22.

Domestic: VI 33966 = D 5182: C. Iulius Aug. lib. Actius prior pantomimus Cucuma (?), aged 19; VI 9047 = D 1810: Ti. Cl. Augustor. l. et structor Domnio, aged 23; VI 8656: C. Iulius Aug. l. Eutychus medic. dom. Pal., aged 24; 8931: M. Aurelius Reginus Aug. lib. nomenclator ab ammissione, aged 24 y. 11 m.; *AE* 1927, 136: Proclus Augg. lib. diaetarius, aged 24.

Excluded are: X 1729 (Gregorius is not an Imperial freedman – see above, p. 69 n. 1); and the fragmentary *AE* 1933, 28; and 1935, 56; also XIV 3718, where the reading is uncertain and the ages wrong, unless T. Aelius Ianuarius Aug. lib. married at the age of 6 (!).

[2] Some features of these four should be noted: X 654: M. Ulpius Aug. lib. Euphoruus (!) died aged 3 (conjecture a stonemason's error in the number?). VI 7778: Aurelius Felix Aug. lib., aged 5; his father is M. Aur. Caricus Aug. lib. (status indication inserted in error?). VI 13151: M. Aurelius Aug. lib. Marcianus, aged 4 years 8 months; parents M. Aur. Aug. lib. Eutyches and Valeria Eutychia. How did Marcianus acquire his *nomen* or his status indication? If he were of slave birth he should follow the *nomen* of his mother, not of his father. If his *nomen* is derived from his father after the latter's manumission, he should not have a freedman status indication. III 8914: M. Aur. Aug. lib. Hermeros, aged 10; his parents, Germanio and Stephane, from their single names both appear to be slaves.

[3] *Girls:* XIV 2690: Claudia Primigenia lib. Aug., aged 15; mother Mamilia Albana. Again, how did this girl get her *nomen* and status indication? Together or separately they cannot come from mother or father. VI 15579: Claudia Aug. l. Sabina, aged 19; V 2931: Claudia Ti. Augusti l. Toreuma, aged 19, about whom the detail 'condor humo multis nota Toreuma iocis'.

Augustorum lib.: VI 29133: M. Ulpius Augg. lib. Agilis, aged 15; VIII 9434: P. Ael. Augustor. n.

The family circle

A greater number of slaves were naturally manumitted in their twenties, with proportionately more as the legal age of 30 is approached.[1] Quite a number of these (6/26) were freed near the limit, at the age of 29 in fact: two *tabularii* actually being particular about the number of months as well: 29 years 10 months. Officials of junior and intermediate rank are also found in the years penultimate to the legal limit. Women are represented out of proportion to their surviving numbers in the Familia Caesaris as a whole: seven of the twenty-six are women; and two more *Augustorum liberti* who died at the age of 23 and 24. Again this is not typical of the whole Familia. The most notable feature is the proportion of women, 27% (7/26), about the same as in the teenage group. In all the early manumissions from the age of puberty, women account for 26% (10/38). This is *twice* the proportion of women found in normal manumissions in the Familia at the age of 30 or over, where it is 13% (17/131), more than *three* times as much as the overall percentage of women found in the Familia Caesaris as a whole, slave and freed (excluding those of the *Augustae*): 8% (291/3,616), and more than *four* times the proproportion of females to males among all the Imperial *libertae* and *liberti*: 6% (130/2,112).

Women are thus distinctly favoured for early manumission. So too appear to be the *Augustorum liberti*, although their numbers are not large.[2] Holders of official posts are not; they must conform to the service rules governing length of service, grades of promotion and what might be called quality of career. It is noticeable that those administrative

lib. Processianus, aged 16; father P. Ael. Pecuarius. VI 10778: T. Ael. Augg. lib. Probus, aged 19; father T. Ael. Augg. lib. Felicianus (early manumission of the son in conjunction with normal manumission of the father?).

Youths: VI 18142: T. Flavius Natalis Aug. lib., aged 19; sister Flavia Helpis. VI 10685: T. Aelius Eros Aug. lib., aged 19; mother Aelia Piaeris. VI 25721: Sabinus Aug. lib., aged 17 y. 10 m. His brother, Augustalis Aug. n. vern., died at a later age (20 y.) but still a slave. VI 8077: M. Aurelius Aug. lib. Miccalus, aged 17, whose *nomen* cannot possibly derive from either of his parents, L. Flavius Miccalus and Fabia Zone.

Officials: see above, p. 101 n. 1.

[1] VI 1884 = D 1792, 8417, 8449 = D 1552, 8488 = D 1607, 8502, 8656, 8931, 8951 = D 1783, 8957, 9047 = D 1810, 10666, 10988, 13252, 17474, 20432, 26242, 27285 = D 8067 = IG XIV 2036, 29069, 29175, 29658; V 7759; X 1311; XI 4698; XIV 4482 = *IPO* B 68; *AE* 1927, 136; 1956, 73.
Included is VI 29069 which reads: '[d]is ma./[......]v(i) Aug. l. Vitali/[.....]ixit ann. XXV/ [....]us Symmachus et/[.....] Elegans fecerunt fil./[......]mae et sibi' etc.
CIL restores line 2: [Iulio di]v(i) Aug. l...., which ignores the adjectival ending '[...]mae' in line 6. If we restore here '[carissi]mae' the daughter's name is required in line 2. I would suggest the following restoration: '[d]is ma./[Iuliae di]v(i) Aug. l. Vitali/[quae v]ixit ann. XXV/[C. Iuli]us Symmachus et/[?Iulia] Elegans fecerunt fil(iae)/[carissi]mae et sibi...'
The following in the group above are of interest: VI 8957: Claudia Aug. l. Parata ornatrix, aged 27, who was commemorated jointly by her three husbands, Ti. Iulius Romanus, Ti. Claudius Priscus and Nedimus Aug. ser. VI 10988: Aelia Aug. lib. Thallusa, aged 29, whose husband was Eutychus Aug. (ser.). *Augusti libertae* rarely married outside the Imperial Familia.

[2] The *Augustorum liberti* are discussed above, pp. 68 f.

Age at manumission

careers that differ least from the norm date from the Flavian period and later.[1]

What is known of the ages at death of Imperial slaves confirms that their normal manumission age was 30 or over. Of 187 examples, not including those from Africa,[2] one-half reached the age of 28; of 253 from Africa, again one-half reached the age of 28. The figures are as follows:[3]

Age	Outside Africa	Africa only	Total
1–9	20	41	61
10–19	26	31	57
20–24	26	24	50 ⎫ 114
25–29	24	40	64 ⎭
30–34	33	22	55 ⎫ 91
35–39	19	17	36 ⎭
40–49	21	29	50
50–59	9	8	17
60–69	4	14	18
70–79	2	10	12
80–100	3	17	20
Total	187	253	440

These figures cannot be used, of course, to indicate life-expectancy among the Imperial slaves; but they are useful for giving a general picture of the expectation of manumission. One-half of these slaves whose age at death is known were 28 or older, one-third were 35 or older, and only one-fifth were 41 or older. The rapid decrease after 40 is not to be attributed entirely or even mainly to the low expectation of life at these ages for Imperial slaves, but more to the high expectation of manumission by the age of 40. This is shown by the table of ages at death for Imperial freedmen (see above, p. 100), of whom one-half reached the age of 42 or older, one-third 55 or older, and

---

[1] *Intermediate clerical posts:* XIV 4482 = *IPO* B 68; cf. XIV 4483 = *IPO* B 67: (T. Flavius) Ingenuus Aug. lib. tabularius portus Aug., aged 29 y. 10 m. VI 1884 = D 1792: M. Ulpius Aug. lib. Phaedimus...a comment(ariis) beneficiorum, aged 28. A career favourite of Trajan. VI 8488 = D 1607: Salvius Aug. lib. tabul(arius) aquarum, aged 29 y. 10 m. Undated, but scarcely early first century.

Junior clerical posts: VI 8449 = D 1552: T. Flavius Aug. l. Ianuarius adiutor tabular. XX hereditatium, aged 26. VI 8951 = D 1783: Chrysaor Aug. lib. adiutor a commentaris ornamentorum, aged 27 y. 9 m.; parents Cl(audius) Apelles and Cl(audia) Primitiva.

But: VI 8417: T. Aelius Crispinus Aug. lib. a(d)iutor a rationibus, aged 22, who is much younger than the other freedmen, but the normal age for a *slave adiutor*; and the most difficult of all – VI 8613: Faustus Aug. lib. adiutor ab epistulis Lat(inis), aged 19 y. 4 m.

[2] Africa has a special role because of the number of slave inscriptions found in the Imperial *sepulcreta* at Carthage. Burn and others have claimed an especially low life expectancy for the population of the African provinces. This is not borne out by the data on the Imperial slaves.

[3] The figures show the familiar preference for stating ages in multiples of 5 or 10 (cf. A. R. Burn, *Past & Present* 4 (1953), 7, 19). With Imperial slaves, in all cases from 25 years onwards the number of ages given in multiples of 5 exceeds that for all the remaining years combined.

The family circle

one-fifth 65 or older.[1] The figures for the *Augusti liberti* whose ages at death are known cannot be used to determine more precisely the average age at manumission in the Familia Caesaris as the length of the period between manumission and death cannot be determined.[2]

To conclude this section: the average age at manumission for Imperial slaves was certainly between the ages of 30 and 40, and probably between 30 and 35. Normally manumission took place as soon as it was possible for the slave to purchase his manumission after the age of 30, which was the normal minimum prescribed by the lex Aelia Sentia. In cases of unskilled jobs and slow accumulation of *peculium* the age at manumission could be considerably later than 40 – 20% of slaves (89/440) are over the age of 40; 15% (66/440) are over 50. It is at this point that there is a significant divergence in the figures for Africa as compared with the rest; 19% (49/253) of slaves from Africa are over 50, but less than 10% (17/187) of the others. The African inscriptions, as has been noted, have a number of divergent features of this kind that cumulatively outweigh the argument that we have only an unrepresentative selection of African inscriptions for the Familia Caesaris from Carthage. Care should be exercised, however, in drawing conclusions from these last figures. The difference between freedmen and slaves should be noted, but there is no substantial reason for their life expectancy to differ to the extent implied. The slaves who had not been manumitted by the age of 40 did not find their chances substantially improved the longer they lived. In some special cases, such as financial officials like *dispensatores* and 'vicariani',[3] manumission was delayed for a number of years, till about 40 or later, as a matter of administrative policy. This was not because slaves in these lucrative posts lacked the money in their *peculium* to buy their manumission at the regular time but precisely because their special and remunerative financial responsibilities required them to remain slaves until they were promoted. For them manumission must have seemed less important than for other slaves. Lastly, manumission not infrequently took place before the age of 30, more commonly for women than for men, and more commonly for those in the fringe groups of the Familia, the *lib. liberti* and the slaves of the *Augustae*. In most cases the reasons for early manumission are not apparent. For children, however, and possibly for some others, 'pathetic' manumission at the point of early death may be the reason. It is clear that the slaves of the emperor were not more privileged than other slaves in regard to early manumission. Indeed they were at a disadvantage. But the status that accompanied membership of the Familia Caesaris would be held to be more than adequate compensation.

---

[1] Among the freedmen also the bunching of ages in multiples of five is very pronounced.

[2] For the use of the age-at-death figures in determining the occupational hierarchy in the Familia Caesaris, see Part III below, pp. 225 f.   [3] See Part III below.

CHAPTER 6

AGE AT MARRIAGE

The next question to consider is the age at marriage of the slaves and freedmen of the Familia, and whether this occurred in general before or after manumission. It is important also to compare, if possible, the age of female slaves at marriage with that of male slaves and to estimate, if the evidence permits, the average differential in age between slave-born husband and wife.

In the strict sense of *iustum matrimonium* between partners with *conubium*, which alone was recognised as legally valid in Roman law with all the legal consequences (e.g. law of succession) that were involved therein, it is not possible to speak of slave marriage at all, but only of *contubernium* or concubinage. This applied when one or both parties were of slave status.[1] But the terminology of legal marriage (e.g. 'uxor', 'maritus', 'coniunx', etc.) is so constantly used of *contubernium* in the inscriptions and even in the legal texts themselves[2] that it is convenient to speak normally of slave marriage and to use such terms as 'contubernium' and 'matrimonium' only when the distinction is relevant to the argument.[3]

The direct evidence for age at marriage in the Familia Caesaris is small and is derived from inscriptions mentioning both the age at death of one of the partners and the number of years of married life they enjoyed. The difference between the two figures represents the age at marriage.

HUSBANDS

To take first the age of men at marriage. There are only eight such figures. All date from the second century or later.

(a) Freedmen

(1) VI 8737: M. Ulpius Aug. lib. Dionysius (married at 20, died at 45) = Ulpia Aug. lib. Herois.

(2) XIII 2308: Quartus(?) Ulpius libert. Augg. patronus (married at 23, died at 46) = Quartia Secundilla liberta et coniunx.

---

[1] E.g. Ulpian, v. 5: 'cum servis nullum est conubium'; *Pauli Sent.* ii. 19.6: 'inter servos et liberos matrimonium contrahi non potest, contubernium potest'.
[2] Cf. Buckland, *Roman Law of Slavery*, p. 76 n. 15; Kaser, *Privatrecht*, I, 269.
[3] Cf. *TLL* IV, 790 s.v. 'contubernalis' II. A; ib. 792 s.v. 'contubernium' I. B.I.

The family circle

(3) *Arch. Class.* (1953), p. 264 (Rome): P. Aelius Aug. lib. Fortunatus (married at 18, died at 50) = Aelia Chrysogone.

(4) VI 8878 = D 1685: T. Aelius Aug. lib. Titianus marit. virgin. (married at 30, died at 42) = Fl(avia) Ampelis.

(5) 13060: Aurelius Cyrenus Aug. lib. (married at 24, died at 40) = Asinia Spes.

(6) II 6085 = D 1560: [Aur. Fa]ustinus Augustorum lib. (married at 21, died at 42) = Statia Felicissima.

(b) Slaves

(7) VI 19172: Hedistus Aug. n. vern. (married at 20, died at 30) = Licinia Kale.

(8) 29116: Ulpianus Aug. n. vern. (married at 20, died at 35) = Ianuaria Aug. n. vern.[1]

These marriage ages range from 18 to 30, with an average and halfway point of 22 (freedmen: 22 years 8 months; slaves 20 years). Macdonell's figures,[2] from twenty-nine examples of marriage ages of men from the empire as a whole, ranged from 15 to 63, with eleven marrying between the ages of 17 and 20, and one-half by the age of 21. Harkness,[3] from a list of ninety-nine examples of the age at marriage of men, calculates an average of 26 but remarks that there is not the same tendency to record early marriages as in the case of women. Hopkins[4] considers these figures too high.

WIVES

For women there are fifteen marriage ages arranged chronologically as follows:

(a) Marriage with freedmen

(9) VI 15598: Ti. Claudius Aug. l. Nymphodotus, patronus et contubernalis = Claudia Steptenis (married at 26, died at 72).

(10) VIII 12951: P. Aelius Euhodus Aug. lib. = Antonia Haline (married at 32, died at 72).

(11) XIII 2068: T. Ael. Aug. lib. Eutychus = Attia Successa (married at 12, died at 43).

(12) VI 13017: L. Aurelius Aphradas = Aurelia Vitalis Aug. lib. (married at 13, died at 32).

(13) XIII 2189: Aurelius Aga(th)opus libertus Aug. = Iuventia Felicissima domina (married at 15 or 20?, died at 38 or 43?).[5]

(14) *AE* 1949, 68: Aurel. Augg. lib. Hermes = Fannia Redempta (married at 13, died at 46).

(15) VI 9072: Catervarius Augg. lib. = Lucida Augg. vern. marita (married at 18, died at 33).

---

[1] In XIV 3718 the reading is uncertain and the marriage age (6 years) for T. Aelius Ianuarius Aug. lib. is unlikely.

[2] W. R. Macdonell, 'On the Expectation of Life in Ancient Rome, and in the Provinces of Hispania and Lusitania, and Africa', *Biometrika* 9 (1913), 366 f.

[3] A. G. Harkness, 'Age at Marriage and at Death in the Roman Empire', *TAPA* 27 (1896), 35 f. esp. 45 f., 49.

[4] M. K. Hopkins, *Population Studies* 18 (1965), 309 f.; 20 (1966), 245 f.

[5] The reading for age at death is 'XXX[.]/III' which gives either 'XXX[V]/III' or 'XXX[X]/III' as possibilities; I have preferred the former.

Age at marriage

(16) *AE* 1930, 152: L. Sep(timius) Augg. nn. lib. Polybius = Ceionia Maxima quae et Achorista lib. Plautiae divi Veri sororis (married at 23, died at 30).

(17) VI 25444: Rogatus Augg. lib. = Ama(?) Eutychia qu(a)e et Gatis (married at 18, died at 25).

(18) 34320: Salutaris Aug. lib. = Aemilia Myri(ne) (married at 21, died at 25?).

(b) Marriage with slaves

(19) VI 8740: Onesimus Ti. Claudi Germanici atriensis = Vinia (married at 18, died at 26).

(20) 15615: Epaphroditus Caes. ser. Agnianus = Claudia Thelge (married at 23, died at 45).

(21) 24337: Epiterpes Caes. = Plotia Fortunata (married at 21, died at 55).

(22) 23044 = 37881: Victorinus Caes. n. ser. = Nonia Hieronis (married at 24, died at 37).

(23) *IPO* A 261: Olympus Matidiae Aug. f. ser. = Urbica (married at 13, died at 15).

These ages at marriage range from 12 to 32, with an average of 19 years 4 months (19 y. 1 m. for wives of freedmen; 19 y. 10 m. for wives of slaves). The age of 19 is higher than the average of known marriage ages for women outside the Familia Caesaris during the early Empire. The legal age for marriage in Rome was 12 years, and early marriage for women was often taken for granted.[1] From a much larger number of examples Macdonell's figure[2] was 15 years, and Bang's[3] was 14. Harkness,[4] who is sceptical of early marriage for women in the Empire, gives a list of 171 examples which show an average age of 18. Hopkins[5] concludes that 14 was the average age for girls and earlier for girls of aristocratic birth, one-half of whom married by the age of 12. The figures relating to the Familia Caesaris are too small for useful comparison by percentage, but at least do not conflict with this pattern.

Some provisional results and comment on this group. First, the age at marriage does not vary according to *status*; it does not matter whether the

---

[1] Cf. Epictetus, *Enchiridion* 40: αἱ γυναῖκες εὐθὺς ἀπὸ τεσσαρεσκαίδεκα ἐτῶν ὑπὸ τῶν ἀνδρῶν κύριαι καλοῦνται. See also the section on the marriage pattern outside the Familia Caesaris (chapter 11 below).

[2] *Biometrika* 9 (1913), 380. Macdonell's figures for the age of 59 Roman women at the date of marriage are:

Age at Marriage	No.	%
under 12	4	7
12–19	39	66
20–29	12	20
30 and over	4	7
Total	59	100

[3] M. Bang, 'Das gewöhnliche Alter der Mädchen bei der Verlobung und Verheiratung', in Friedländer, *Sittengeschichte*[10], IV, 133 f., esp. 136.

[4] *TAPA* 27 (1896), 40 f.

[5] *Population Studies* 18 (1965), 316 f., 326.

The family circle

husbands are slaves or freedmen, or whether the wives are slaves, freedwomen or freeborn; there is no significant difference in the age at which they married. The important point here is that Imperial freedmen, as regards their family life, are best considered as Imperial slaves at a later stage in life; it is while they are still slaves that they marry for the first time. To the question what difference does manumission make to the marriage pattern of Imperial slaves, the provisional answer is little or none at all. This is in quite striking contrast to the pattern for slaves and freedmen outside the Familia Caesaris, where the the proportion of wives who are freeborn increases significantly after the manumission of the husbands.

It is much more important to discover the age *difference* between husbands and wives at the time of the first marriage of both, and especially the *status* of the wives at that time, i.e. whether they are slaves, freedwomen, or freeborn women. The importance of determining the age and status of the wife at marriage is paramount for determining the status of the children, as in marriage outside *conubium*, that is *contubernium* or concubinage, the status of the illegitimate children born of such a union follows the status of the mother and not that of the father. This would apply to all unions involving male slaves before manumission, that is most probably the great majority of all unions in the Familia. The marriage and manumission ages of the wives thus determine the status of most children born in the Familia Caesaris.

Secondly, the age differential can be illustrated from the above group. More important than the difference in the *average* age between these groups – 22 years for husbands and 19 years for wives[1] – is the distribution. Only one husband out of eight is married under 20, and none under 18; whereas more than half the wives (8/15) married under 20 and five under 16. Only two wives out of fifteen married over the age of 23, one at 26 to her patron, and we are left to conjecture a second marriage for the other, marrying at 32 and living through forty years of marriage to the age of 72. Three years is probably too small for the difference between the average age of husbands and wives at marriage. Men probably married in their twenties, but women anywhere in their teens. We would not be far wrong in assuming an age difference of about five years or even longer on average.

Thirdly, the status pattern of the wives. We have seven wives who are slave-born:[2] Nos. 9, 12, 15, 16, 17 (?), 19, 23. These well illustrate the

---

[1] The samples are not large enough for meaningful comparison in this way and are unduly affected by single examples, e.g. one wife at 32 is six years later than any other in the group, and one husband at 30 is also six years the oldest at marriage.

[2] Note that a single name, in the absence of other data, is taken to imply slave status. This will weight the figures, if anything, in favour of a higher proportion of wives of slave-born status. This is justifiable if we are seeking to determine the *minimum* proportion of wives of *freeborn* status.

Age at marriage

relation between ages at marriage and at manumission for women in the Familia. Claudia Steptenis (No. 9) was manumitted early, by the age of 26, 'matrimonii causa', but all the others probably married well before manumission. Thus, Lucida Augg. vern. (No. 15), who was married at the age of 18, was still a slave when she died aged 33; Aurelia Vitalis Aug. lib. (No. 12), on the other hand, who married at the age of 13, had been manumitted by her death at the age of 32; Ceionia Maxima (No. 16) married at 23 and died a *liberta* aged 30; Vinia (No. 19) married at 18 and died a slave aged 26; Urbica (No. 23) married at 13 and died a slave at the age of nearly 15; and Eutychia (No. 17) married at 18 and died a slave (?) at 25. These figures, though few, are consistent enough to justify the assumption that for *servae* there was a delay of about ten years or more between marriage and manumission. A further point of interest is the chronological distribution: among the husbands of these slave-born wives are the only two we can positively date to the first century (Nos. 9 and 19). Among the wives without status indication the only one with an *Imperial nomen*, Claudia Thelge (No. 20) who died aged 45, is married to the only husband in this group with *agnomen*, (H)agnianus, who is thus also likely to be first-century in date. All the other wives (second-century or later, or undated) have *non-Imperial nomina*: Antonia (No. 10), Attia (No. 11), Iuventia (No. 13), Fannia (No. 14), Aemilia (No. 18), Plotia (No. 21), and Nonia (No. 22). The implications of this pattern will be considered in the next chapter.

Indirect confirmation of the early marriage of women can be gained from the figures for age at death of wives of Imperial freedmen and slaves. These are given in two groups according to the status of the husband. (Wives who are themselves *Augusti libertae* are included in Group A.)

Age at death	A. Wives of Aug. liberti %	No.	B. Wives of Caes. servi %	No.
Under 20	11	8	15	16
20–29	41	31	39	41
30–39	21	16	28	29
40 and over	27	20	18	19
Total	100	75	100	105

The pattern for both groups is essentially the same up till the age of 30; in Group A, 52% of the wives of *Aug. liberti* died under the age of 30, the biggest concentration being between the ages of 20 and 25. In Group B, 54% of the wives of *Caesaris servi* died under 30, with the same point of concentration. Once again there is close agreement between the data for wives of

The family circle

freedmen and of slaves. This is in harmony with marriage before manumission with wives of the usual age-group at marriage, i.e. between 12 and 18.

These figures should be linked with those for the number of years of married life recorded in the sepulchral inscriptions for Imperial freedmen and slaves. (Figures in brackets are those also mentioning age at death.)

Years of married life	Aug. liberti	Caes. servi
Under 10	5 [3]	4 [2]
10–19	8 [4]	6 [3]
20–29	18 [4]	5 [1]
30–39	19 [3]	5 [1]
40 and over	9 [2]	3
Total	59 [16]	23 [7]

With freedmen (who may be regarded as long-lived slaves for this purpose) nearly half of the marriages whose length is recorded lasted *30 years* or longer; with slaves (who did not live long enough to see the day of manumission), from a smaller sample, half lasted *20 years* or longer. For slave marriages this is significant. There might have been a tendency to mention only long marriages and not those of short duration which were terminated by the death of one of the partners, but pathos also is common enough in the *sepulcrales*. The implication of these figures, however, is best seen when taken in conjunction with the data on the age at which wives most commonly died, i.e. more than half under 30, with 20–5 the most dangerous years. In most cases, assuming that unusual longevity would also have been mentioned if possible, marriage must have taken place well before the age of 30 or indeed before 20.

It can be concluded, then, that the majority of Imperial freedmen married while they were still slaves, probably on average some eight to ten years before manumission. Imperial slaves and freedmen in general married at a later age than their wives. How much older the average husband was than the average wife the meagre evidence does not permit us to say exactly. It may not have been very much, i.e. not more than about five years. A certain proportion of wives older than their husbands must always be allowed for but, except in the case of wives marrying for the second time with husbands marrying for the first time, they would not have been very common. Direct evidence for the number of second and third marriages is not great. In society at large, particularly in aristocratic society where the age difference between husbands and wives was so much greater, widowhood must have been a more serious problem than would appear from the inscriptions. In the Familia Caesaris

Age at marriage

the remarrying widow is not conspicuous, indeed she is scarcely identifiable. Nor is it easy to trace second wives or husbands where divorce has taken place, at least in the reticent world of the sepulchral inscriptions. It follows that in the great majority of marriages in the Familia the status of most of the children is determined, unless legitimisation by the father after his manumission takes place, by the status of the mother. If the mother was of slave origin or status, it is likely that several of her children would have been born before her own manumission.

The proportion of slaves in the Imperial Familia who married even once is also difficult to assess. The evidence again is largely the sepulchral inscriptions which are mostly expressly concerned with recording family relationships. There is no evidence for assuming that Imperial slaves were not encouraged to marry or that they did not normally, or even overwhelmingly, do so.[1] The notorious cases of Narcissus and Pallas, who appear not to have married (or not to have been inhibited thereby from adultery), do not amount, in this respect as in any other of their activities, to a rule of conduct for Imperial freedmen and slaves. They must be set against that equally notorious example of domestic bliss, the father of Claudius Etruscus and his spouse Etrusca, and we might add Pallas' aptly named brother Felix who was as uxorious as his famous brother was not; in marrying three wives of foreign royal blood he achieved a social success far above that of any other member of the Familia Caesaris.[2]

[1] Cf. T. Frank, *AHR* 21 (1916), 697; Boulvert, II, 722 f.
[2] On the eunuchs Posides, Halotus, Sporus, etc. see Boulvert, II, 722 f.

CHAPTER 7

STATUS OF WIVES

The next question is to determine, if possible, the status of wives in the Familia Caesaris. What proportion at the time of marriage were freeborn (*ingenuae*) and how many of servile origin (*servae* or *libertae*)? And of the latter, how many were slaves from within the Imperial Familia, and how many belonged to masters other than the emperor and his relatives? These are matters of the greatest importance for the social history of the Familia, and must be studied in at least three dimensions: (1) *Chronologically:* did the pattern change from the early first to the early third century, and if so why? (2) *Geographically:* does the pattern vary significantly between the central departments and services in Rome (including Ostia) and Italy, Africa and the other provinces? (3) *Seniority:* do we find senior freedmen, such as procurators, and slave–freedman officials in favoured careers, favoured also in their family life by marrying more successfully and being more socially mobile than others? The status of the children from these marriages will be considered in the following chapter.

The problem is complicated: only 13% of wives of *Caesaris servi* give a status indication of any kind, and for wives of *Augusti liberti* the figure is only 11%. The overall status picture for wives is given in Tables I and III, where the figures are expressed as percentages of *all* examples of the group in question. Absolute figures are given in parentheses. It will be most convenient in what follows to use percentage rather than absolute figures to facilitate comparisons between the various groups. The real problem is how to analyse the names of the remaining 87% of wives of slaves, and 89% of wives of freedmen without status indication.

WIVES OF IMPERIAL SLAVES

It is best to begin with the wives of the Imperial slaves. As most marriages in the Familia must have taken place *before* the manumission of the husband, the slave marriage pattern should be basic for the freedmen as well, as the husband and wife couples remain the same couples in most instances; barring separation or death followed by remarriage, the only change of status that can affect the general pattern is the change of one or both partners from

Status of wives

slave to freed status at manumission. The nomenclature of *freeborn* women who marry slaves will not be affected by the change in their husband's status at manumission; any juridical effects they may suffer under the SC Claudianum (see chapter 9 below) will occur at the time of marriage.

In analysing the names of wives both of Imperial slaves and freedmen one preliminary assumption is made: that wives who give a single personal name only, i.e. without *nomen* or status indication, are assumed to be of slave status and origin; e.g.

VI 12603: Adiutor Caes. n. ser. = Athenais amica.

16572: Crescens Aug. ser. = Romana coniunx.

The effect of this assumption will be to increase, if anything, the proportion of wives of slave status in the figures and possibly reduce the numbers of those who might be freeborn. But this is justifiable on the grounds that we are concerned to establish a *minimum* figure for freeborn wives. In some cases there is doubt, when the sole name given could be a *nomen*; e.g. III 1085 = 1301 = D 3014: Cornelia eius; *IGR* IV 1297: Antonia. These cases are discussed where relevant.

The omission of the *nomen gentilicium* was frequent in the Familia in all periods[1] both in the principal and subsidiary positions in the funerary inscriptions, but the status indication 'Aug. lib.' is used in the majority of such cases; in others, especially with names in subsidiary positions, the freedman status can be inferred from the use of terms such as 'collibertus', 'colliberta', 'patronus', etc. In other cases the *nomen* is omitted for reasons of space when there is no doubt as to status.[2] The proportion of wives of freedmen who use personal name only is very small, averaging only 4% for all wives, and in no group rising above 6%. But for wives of slaves the figure is naturally higher, accounting for 16% of all wives of *Caesaris servi*. These would be much more likely to be still of slave status at the time of their inscription. The lowest proportion is 13% from Rome; and from the provinces, where manumission tended to be later than at Rome, the figure is 26%. For wives of *Augustarum servi*, who are more typical of the slave classes in general, the proportion is as high as 48%. The great majority of names of wives in the Familia Caesaris of all periods and classes, except wives of the *servi Augustarum*, have both *nomen* and *cognomen*; this indicates freed or freeborn status at the time the inscription was put up. The natural interpretation of the very small proportion of cases where the *nomen* is not used is that it *could* not be used.

Again, the names and status of the children born of such unions in the great majority of cases confirm the slave status of the mother; e.g. *AE* 1930, 64

[1] See Part I, pp. 37 f.   [2] Cf. Thylander, *Étude*, pp. 98 f., and see Part I, p. 38.

The family circle

(Rome): Priscus Caesaris servos = Heuresis + Prisca (daughter). Children with the slave indication (apart from some notable exceptions discussed below) invariably have mothers with slave indication or single name; e.g. VI 22960: Primigenius C. n. ser. = Voluptas C. n. ser. + Nicephorus C. n. ver. (son); VIII 24792: Optatus Aug. ser. = Salvia + Faustus Aug. ser. (son).

Table I gives the distribution of 462 wives of Imperial slaves into the status categories: slave, freed, freeborn, and *incertae*, according to the main geographical divisions of the empire.

TABLE I

Wife	Slave indic. %	Slave Cogn. %	Freed Indic. %	Freeborn Filiat. %	Incertae Nomen + Cogn. %	Total %
Rome	4 (14)	13 (43)	6·5 (21)	2.5 (8)	74 (247)	100 (333)
Italy	10.5 (4)	23.5 (9)	— —	— —	66 (25)	100 (38)
Africa	20 (9)	26 (12)	— —	2 (1)	52 (24)	100 (46)
West	— —	23 (3)	— —	— —	77 (10)	100 (13)
Danube	6 (1)	22 (4)	— —	— —	72 (13)	100 (18)
Asia	14 (2)	29 (4)	— —	7 (1)	50 (7)	100 (14)
Total	7 (30)	16 (75)	4 (21)	2 (10)	71 (326)	100 (462)

Excluded have been twelve cases where the wife's name is too fragmentary to be determined.

From this table a startling and important fact emerges – that only 23% of the wives of Imperial slaves from all areas can possibly have been slaves at the time their inscription was erected: and from Rome, whence come over three-quarters of all these inscriptions, the proportion is as low as 17%. This means that over four out of five of all wives of Imperial slaves from Rome already have a *nomen before* the manumission of their partners. The significance of this is increased when we compare this with the pattern of other slave groups. Among the slaves of the empresses (*servi Augustarum*) 14/29 (48%) of wives are presumed slaves on the basis of their single name. In the control group from the *sepulcrales* in Rome outside the Familia the proportion of wives of slaves who are still slaves themselves is 50%, while as many as 68% of husbands of *servae* are still slaves. Allowing for the fact that female slaves tended to be manumitted earlier than their slave husbands, some explanation of this difference between the groups is required. There are also the regional differences within the Imperial slaves themselves. From Italy the slave figure rises to 34%, and for the slave wives from Africa, mostly in

Status of wives

the *columbaria* from Carthage, a quite different picture is gained: 21/46 or 46% of these wives must be presumed to be of slave status. Carthage and indeed Africa is thus very similar to the non-Imperial group from Rome in this respect.

Let us begin with these African inscriptions as they show the closest resemblance to the normal situation in Roman society at large and are least favourable towards a special status for the Familia Caesaris. The ages of the slave-wives range from 18 to 68 (18, 23, 24, 24, 28, 30, 35, 35, 40, 68) with 6/10 aged 30 or under. In two cases where the ages of husband *and* wife are known the husband is older:

VIII 12630: Gallus Caes. n. ser. tab(ellarius)? aged 28 = Eugenia Caes. n. ser., aged 18.
VIII 24815: Secundus Aug. ser. (72) = Satura (68).

More interesting are the twenty-four wives with *nomen*. Twelve have Imperial *nomina* and thus could possibly be Imperial freedwomen, but *none* uses status indication. The possibility that some are *not* Imperial freedwomen is made clear by the thirteenth example, VIII 12657 = D 1744: Valentinus ex numero cubicular. Augg. = Claudia Ti. f. Euresis (17). Here is a freeborn Claudia who died at the age of 17. Other wives with *nomina* also died under 30, VIII 13189: Caecilia Felicitas, aged 21; 12792: Minucia Prima, aged 26; 24688: Terentia Successa, aged 28; and possibly 18327: (Aelia) Polychron[...], aged 22. (The others are 12836: Tullia Tertulla, aged 32; 24740: Erucia Vitalis, aged 34; 13090: Rabiria Spes, aged 37; 24717: Caecilia Nia[...], aged 40; 12785: Iulia Fortunata, aged 65.) There would seem to be a good prospect of some more freeborn wives in this group with non-Imperial *nomina*. How many we cannot tell from these data.

On the other hand some Imperial freedwomen might easily lurk among the wives with Imperial *nomina*. If we consider the ages of the slave husbands, a whole bunch died at a much later age than 30–35, the normal age range for manumission, several having wives with Imperial *nomina*:

(1) VIII 12620: Alexander Caes. n. ser. notarius (40) = Flavia Atalante.
(2) VIII 12641: Anteros Aug. ser. pediseq. (40) = Flavia Tyche.
(3) VIII 12642: Campanus Caes. n. ser. pedisec. (55) = Flavia.
(4) VIII 12637: Didymus Aug. ser. mensor agrarius (46) = Iulia Primig[e]nia.
(5) VIII 12892 = D 1510: Epictetus Augustorum ver. disp. reg. Thug. (37) = Aelia Satyra.
(6) VIII 12918: Felix Caesaris nost. ser. custos Lar(um) (76) = Aelia Ianuar(ia) cons(erva?).
(7) VIII 24695: Felix Caesaris n. ser. pediseq. (48) = Aelia Melpomene.

These examples raise immediately the question of dating by slave indication. We clearly cannot make any assumptions on the basis of their wives'

The family circle

nomina, which are if anything a distraction from helpful chronology. No. 5 is dated to after 161; there is nothing improbable in assuming Aelia Satyra and Epictetus to have been slaves together under Antoninus, the wife being manumitted at the normal age, the husband having his manumission delayed because of his post as *dispensator*, so that the inscription would belong to the period 161–9. A similar status and origin is likely in No. 6 for Aelia Ianuaria, if 'cons(erva)' is correct. The husband Felix, whose post of *custos* is not a career one in the sense of involving expected promotion up a regular scale or 'cursus', was never manumitted. A similar case would be No. 7 where the husband's post of *pedisequus* is too lowly to cause surprise at his not gaining manumission in a centre like Carthage by the age of 48. But if these inscriptions are mid-second-century in date we are in difficulties if we accept a similar explanation for No. 4. A *mensor agrarius* was perhaps a cut above a *pedisequus* in occupational status, although he did not gain manumission by the age of 46; in any case his wife Iulia cannot be an Imperial freedwoman in the period required. She could be a freedwoman of a non-Imperial Iulius, but is more likely to be a freeborn Iulia (whether a descendant of Imperial freedmen Iulii is socially irrelevant after two or three generations). Perhaps she was from a local family not otherwise distinguished than that their daughter married an Imperial slave. The same would also hold good for Nos. 1, 2 and 3, although with less conviction; Nos. 2 and 3 are *pedisequi* (attendants in the same category as *custodes* in terms of occupational status), hence late manumission need not surprise, whereas it might for No. 1, a *notarius* unmanumitted at 40. In this small group of seven wives it is not unreasonable to see four who are probable candidates for freeborn status and three who are freedwomen. This proportion has no relevance to any general division of such names. But what the data from this group does point to is that the status of the wife and the occupational status of the husband have no clear relationship. If *custodes* can marry freeborn Iuliae and *dispensatores* marry Aeliae who are former Imperial slaves themselves, the picture is complicated and we need to look further afield.

To test this conclusion let us now look at the other provincial groups, smaller in number but with a higher degree of occupational reference. In the western provinces we have ten couples where the occupation of the husband is mentioned. These are in general chronological order:

(1) XIII 1820 = D 1639: Nobilis Tib. Caesaris Aug. ser. aeq(uator) monetae = Iulia Adepta, with daughter Perpetua and son L. Iulius Cupitus (cf. XIII 2177).
(2) II 1197: Pius Aug. n. verna dispensator = Aelia Italia.
(3) XIII 5697: Lucrio Aug. n. (?) disp. = Aelia Dati(v)a; son Lucrio.
(4) XIII 3089: Agathocles Aug. [...] disp. = Aelia Epicarpia.
(5) II 2644–5: Lupianus Aug. dispensator = Aelia Myrsine.

Status of wives

(6) XII 4471: Erasinus dis(pensator) Au[g]. = Aur(elia) Secundina.
(7) XIII 1824: Felicianus Aug. n. verna ex dispensatoribus = Satria Lucilla, son Sex. Terentius *Lucillus* (13).
(8) XII 1926: Rufinus Caes. n. vil. XX her. = Taminia Severina.
(9) *AE* 1897, 4 = D 9035: Amaranthus Aug. n. ver. vil. XL Galliar. = Chelidon, daughter Acaunensia.
(10) XII 717 = D 1565: Apronianus Auggg. nnn. vern. vilicus XL Gall. = Baedia Politice.

In No. 1, the earliest in this group, Nobilis, an official at the mint in the reign of Tiberius, might be thought to have clearly married *within* the Imperial Familia from his wife's *nomen* Iulia; but this cannot be so if the son's *praenomen* is L. This is a warning against the over-ready assumption that wives with Imperial *nomina* must come from the Familia Caesaris, even in the early first century. Four *dispensatores* (Nos. 2, 3, 4, 5) all marry Aeliae, and another (No. 6) an Aurelia. At least some of these (Nos. 2, 3) come from the mid-second century. These wives could all be former Imperial slaves. A hint of this is in No. 3, the single (slave) name for the son Lucrio born before the mother's manumission. The propensity of such high-status slave officials as *dispensatores* to marry wives with Imperial *nomina*, who could also be actual Imperial freedwomen, would be as noteworthy as the delay in their manumission. But this is unlikely to be so if the wives of the *vicarii*, their own subordinates who later replace them, themselves frequently were freeborn women from outside the Familia.[1] This pattern needs to be examined further.

In No. 7 a *former dispensator* has a wife with non-Imperial *nomen*, Satria; the son Sex. Terentius Lucillus, aged 13, is most probably a step-son, despite the use of the term 'parentes'. Slave *vilici*, officials at various customs posts in the provinces, are not quite of such high status as *dispensatores*, yet in two cases here (Nos. 8, 10) their wives have non-Imperial *nomina* and must be considered most probably as freeborn. A third (No. 9) has both wife and daughter with single (slave) name. By contrast with the African inscriptions we do not have age figures for any of these couples.

From the Danube provinces 13/18 wives have *nomina* (i.e. are either freed or freeborn) although their husbands are still slaves.[2] There are five wives of *dispensatores*, all with *nomina*, but only three of these are Imperial: III 754 = 7436: Aelia [...]; 1839: Aelia Nice; 4828: Claudia Domna; 1085 =

[1] See Part III, p. 204 below.
[2] *Nomina*: III 754 = 7436 (Aelia), 1085 = 1301 = D 3014 (Cornelia), 1303 = D 3382 (Aur(elia)), 1468 (Aurelia), 1470 = 7974 = D 1513 (Cassia), 1554 = 7998 (Iulia), 1839 (Aelia), 1995 (Iulia, aged 30), 1996 = D 1557 (Iulia), 2082 (Orchivia), 4828 (Claudia), 4894 (Flavia), *Hesperia* 1941, p. 243 n. 43 = 1963, p. 78 (Valeria).
Single name: III 1532 (Imp(p. nn.), aged 47), 2128, 2336, 4065 (Venuleia?), 4526 = 11099.
To these may be added: *AE* 1959, 307 (Aelia, wife of a *vicarius*); III 1222 = 7802 (vik(aria?), aged 18); *EE* VIII 265 (uncertain).

The family circle

1301 = D 3014: Cornelia eius (? *cognomen* only); 2082: Orchivia Phoebe. The last should be freeborn as she has a son, C. Orchivius *Amemptus*, aged 18 (father Amemptus Caesaris Aug. disp.). And of those with Imperial *nomina* there is one that cannot be an Imperial freedwoman: III 4828: Eutyches Aug. n. disp. p(atrimoni) r(egni) N(orici) (?) = Claudia Domna, because of the date (mid-second century or later), but who is not certainly freeborn because of the curious formula for the children: 'Faustina et Romulus fili et *vikari eius* (i.e. Claudiae Domnae)'. Among the slaves with lesser occupations there are some whose wives cannot be Imperial freedwomen despite their Imperial *nomina*: III 1995: Phrygius A[u]gg. nn. ab instrumentis, aged 38 = Iulia Valeria, aged 30; III 1996 = D 1557: Quintianus verna Aug. vilicus et arcarius XX her. = Iulia Helpis; and others with non-Imperial *nomina*: III 1470 = 7974 = D 1513: Valentinus qui et Potinianus Aug. n. vern. libr(arius) ab instrumentis = Cassia Rogata (whose daughter's status, Valentina Aug. n. vern., aged 10, presents a problem, as it cannot derive from the mother's and is irrelevant to the father's); and III 4065: Proculus Aug[g]. nn. vern. vi[l]. XX hered. = (Venuleia) (?) Valentina (they had a son, Venuleius Proculus, who died aged 1 year).

The position is similar for the Imperial slave inscriptions from the Asian provinces: 7/14 have wives with *nomina* (including one with filiation, indicating free birth), 5/14 have a single name, indicating slave birth; and the remaining two have single names Antonia and Plotia, which could be *nomina*.[1] Where the husband's occupation is mentioned, only one out of six has a wife of slave status – he is a *notarius* and she is specifically an Imperial slave (*IGR* IV 235). The two *dispensatores* have wives who are Flaviae (III 12143; 333 = *IGR* III 25 = D 1539); one of these has a son, T. Fl(avius) Diomedianus, and may not be an Imperial freedwoman: III 12143: Diomedes Aug. dis[p.] = Fl. Camilla. The two *arcarii* have wives with non-Imperial *nomina*; one, the wife of a slave of Domitian, is simply called Antonia (*IGR* IV 1297), and the other, much later in date, Acilia: III 6077 = D 1505: Apollonius Aug. n. verna arcarius provinc(iae) Asiae = Acilia Lamyra. A *tab(ularius?)* under Nero (III 704 = *IGR* IV 710 = *MAMA* IV 53) is married to the freeborn Arruntia L. f. Attica, with a son Q. Arruntius Iustus.

The same pattern with the same problems of interpretation in specific instances thus arises in all the main provincial areas. It also applies without

---

[1] *Nomina*: III 333 = *IGR* III 25 = D 1539 (Flavia), 704 = *IGR* IV 710 = *MAMA* IV 53 (Arruntia L. f. Attica), 6077 = D 1505 (Acilia), 12143 (Fl(avia)); *IGR* IV 529 (Aur(elia)), 1477 (Cl(audia)), *MAMA* I 25 (Aur(elia)).
Single name: *IGR* III 265; IV 235 (Caes. ser.), 531, 538 (Plotia), 753 = *MAMA* IV 114 (Caes. ser.), 1297 (Antonia); *SEG* VI 380 = *MAMA* I 29.
Doubtful: *MAMA* I 28 (Caes. ser.).

Status of wives

significant change to Italy outside Rome. Africa is notable only in the fact that a higher proportion of Imperial slaves there are married to women who are still of slave status themselves (nearly 50%) compared with just over 30% for all the other provincial slaves. In Rome and Ostia, however, the proportion is nearly half that again; from a much larger sample only 57/333 (17%) of wives can be of slave status.[1] Yet in terms of the occupational status of the husband, we find in Rome substantially the same picture as in the provinces outside Africa. It makes very little difference whether the husband is of clerical or sub-clerical status, whether he is in the administrative or domestic service, whether he is a *dispensator* or *arcarius* over the age of 30, or a junior clerical *adiutor* under the age of 30; or whether he is a *pedisequus* with few prospects of becoming anything else or even of gaining manumission; or a *paedagogus, vilicus, ministrator, diaetarchus*, or fills any of the innumerable domestic occupations. There appears to be very little difference in the overall marriage pattern of any of these; and, more significant, the age of the husband makes no difference – whether he is over the normal age for manumission or under it. If marriage with slave-born women were an important factor the age of the husband ought to make a difference: there should be more slave wives of husbands who die before 30, and more freed wives of older husbands who are still slaves.

It is salutary to look at the overall status distribution of wives by occupational categories taken from the whole range of inscriptions including those from Rome. Table II sets out the main categories; it includes only those instances where the status of the wife is certain and where the *nomen* can be clearly attributed to one or other of the categories Imperial/non-Imperial.

TABLE II

Husband ...	Dispensator[2]	Arcarius[3]	Adiutor[4]	Pedi-sequus[5]	Domestic[6] Rome	Italy and provs.	Africa
Wife							
Serva	4	—	5	3	13	5	5
Imperial *nomen*	29	2	8	6	19	6	5
Non-Imperial *nomen*	12	5	5	3	27	5	1
Total	45	7	18	12	59	16	11

[1] For refs. see Appendix III, section 13.
[2] *Serva:* VI 8472 = XIV 2834 = D 1537 (cf. XIV 2833 = D 1538), VI 8822/4, 37546; VIII 17051 = ILAlg. I 758.
  Imperial nomen: Iulia: VI 6639, 8687, 8839, XIV 3920. Claudia: VI 4426 (wife?), XIV 2431 = D 1586, III 4828. Flavia: VI 8835, 8853 = D 1536, X 3346 = D 2906, III 333 = IGR III 25 = D 1539,

The family circle

These occupations can be classed according to career seniority (and age of husband):

(1) intermediate clerical (i.e. usu. over 30): *dispensator, arcarius*.
(2) junior clerical (i.e. usu. under 30): *adiutor*.
(3) sub-clerical (all ages from *c.* 18): *pedisequus*.
(4) domestic (all ages from *c.* 18): *ministrator, a manu, diaetarchus, paedagogus*, etc.

There are some surprises in this table. While the highest proportion of slave-wives is found among the domestic posts from Africa, in Rome only 13/59 (22%) of wives of all *domestic* slaves are themselves slaves, and about

12143. Ulpia: XI 2706. Aelia: VI 8828, 10166 = D 5154, X 1730, II 1197, 2644-5, III 754 = 7436, 1839, VIII 12892 = D 1510, XIII 3089, 5697. Aurelia: VI 8841, *EE* VIII 720, V 7752 = D 1658, X 1731, XII 4471.
Non-Imperial: Atilia: V 2385 = D 1509. Cornelia: III 1085 = 1301 = D 3014 (?). Geminia: VI 8819 = D 1656. Herennia: X 529 = D 1605. Lucilia: XIV 2259 (Lucilia C. f. Pira). Orchivia: III 2082. Pomponia: XI 3738. Quintilia: VI 33775-6. Sallustia: VI 8454. Satria: XIII 1824. Statia: VI 8837 = 33752. Valeria: VI 5349+5486 = 33077.

[3] *Arcarius: Imperial nomen:* Iulia: VI 8575 = D 1502. Ulpia: VI 8865. *Non-Imperial:* Acilia: III 6077 = D 1505. Antonia: *IGR* IV 1297 (single name?). Caninia: VI 8574 = D 1501. Maia: VI 8444. Plautia: VI 8723.

[4] *Adiutor: Single name:* VI 8717 = D 1686; V 369; VIII 10628, 16561 (?), 24704. *Imperial nomen:* Iulia: VI 8596. Claudia: VI 5062 = 9092 = D 1794, 8419 = D 1479. Flavia: VI 8539, 33798. Aelia: IX 4782. Aurelia: III 1468; V 368. *Non-Imperial:* Caecilia: VIII 13189. Lucretia: VI 9077. Numisia: VIII 12611. Papiria: VI 33724. Sulpicia: VI 5884. *Doubtful:* VIII 18327.

[5] *Pedisequus: Single name:* VI 4354, 8524, 8657. *Imperial nomen:* Flavia: VIII 12641, 12642 (single name?). Ulpia: VI 8658. Aelia: VI 8521, 8522; VIII 24695. *Non-Imperial:* Lucilia: VI 37762. Malia: VI 8996. Novia: VI 8994 = 37749.

[6] *Domestic (Rome): Single name:* VI 1876, 3951, 8548, 8558, 8645, 8740 (Vinia), 8864, 8926 (?), 9040, 9099, 33235; XIV 196 = D 1590; *AE* 1959, 299.
Imperial nomen: Iulia: VI 5200 (Augustae pedis(equa)), 5359 (Iulia C. l. Phoebe), 8497 = D 1614 (Iulia C. l. Zosime), 8669 = D 1617, 8785, 8790; XIV 2420 = XI 2916; *AE* 1925, 20. Claudia: VI 8494 = D 1613, 8495 = D 1612, 8560, 8668 (?), 8921 = D 1804, 8924 = D 1808, 37769; XIV 2832 = D 1760. Flavia: VI 8473 = D 1705 (aged 17). Ulpia: VI 8897. Aelia: VI 8984.
Non-Imperial: Aemilia: VI 8984. Alidia: 8818 (C. l. Myrtale, aged 28). Allenia: 8465 (single name?). Annia: 8973a = D 1830. Caesetia: XIV 198. Caesia: VI 33781. Cariana: 8887 = 14399 = 33754 (L. l.). Catia: 8655 = D 1629. Cornelia: 9050 = D 1787 (Secunda C. Corneli Elenchi liberta, aged 20; AD 13). Domitia: 8923. Fabia: 8495 = D 1612. Fenia: 30855 = D 1621. Octavia: XIV 2465. Pedia: VI 8592-3 = D 1566. Pompeia: 8939. Pontia: 8793 (L. l. Tertulla). Rustia: VI 33780 = D 1806. Scandilia: 33789. Sextia: 8436a. Sextilia: 8674. Sutoria: 8963 (wife?). Titinia: 33746. Trebonia: 8644. Turia: 9052 = D 1703 (Saturnina Soranae lib.). Venuleia: 8552 = D 1759. Vestoria: 33733 = D 1611. Volumnia: *AE* 1928, 7.
Domestic (including vilici) (Italy and Provinces): Single name: III 2128; VIII 12597, 12629 (conserva), 12630 (Caes. n. ser., aged 18), 12635, 12903 (Caes. ser., aged 36); X 713 (conserva), 1749; *IGR* IV 235 (Caes. ser.); *AE* 1897, 4 = D 9035.
Imperial nomen: Iulia: III 1995 (aged 30), 1996 = D 1557; V 706; VIII 12637; X 1750 = D 7368; XIII 1820 = D 1639. Claudia: VIII 12657 = D 1744 (T. f. Euresis, aged 17); XI 1358. Flavia: VIII 1027 = D 1710 (cf. VIII 12468), 12620. Aelia: 12918.
Non-Imperial: Baedia: XII 717 = D 1565. Cassia: III 1470 = 7974 = D 1513. Circenia: X 1751. Taminia: XII 1926. Terentia: VIII 24688. (Venuleia): III 4065 (Valentina, single name?).

Status of wives

the same for the sub-clerical *pedisequi*. In both cases the proportion is *less* than for the *career* slaves, the *adiutores*. We are pressed to the conclusion that the basic division as far as marriage pattern is concerned is between the Familia Caesaris as a whole and those outside, and *not within* the Familia between the administrative and domestic services. Selection for the élite administrative services took place at a relatively early age, even as early as admission to one or other of the Imperial training establishments, such as the *Ad Caput Africae* on the Caelian in Rome. Marriage would take place at about the same time as the husband entered on his career, but his career prospects would be known, if anything, before rather than after marriage. Yet it seems to have made little difference to his marriage prospects what his career prospects were within the Familia, as long as his status was secure by his being an Imperial slave in the first place. Surprises are also the high proportion of *domestic* officials in Rome who, while still slaves, marry wives with *non-Imperial* nomina (27/59 in fact) who, for reasons considered below, must be considered strong candidates for freeborn status; and the high proportion of élite *dispensatores* who have wives with *Imperial nomina* (29/45), and who are thus more likely to be freedwomen from the Imperial Familia itself.

Two qualifications need to be made to this broad lack of differentiation within the Familia, one geographical, the other chronological, and both associated with *columbaria*. The African inscriptions, besides showing in their age figures a later age for manumission than elsewhere, also show many more wives of slave status despite the greater age of the husbands, and very few wives with non-Imperial *nomina*. Secondly, the inscriptions from the earlier half of the first century from Rome account for a good number of wives with slave or freed indication, including freedwomen with non-Imperial *nomina*; e.g.

    VI 9050 = D 1787: Epigonus Caesaris Aug. sutor = Secunda C. Corneli Elenchi liberta (AD 13).
    VI 8887 = 14399 = 33754: Hyblaeus Divi Augusti a ma[nu...] = Cariana L. l. [...].
    VI 8963: Eros [...] Augusti [...] ostiarius = Sutoria Ↄ. liberta Lepida (wife?).
    VI 8793: Tholus Caesar. cubicl. = Pontia L. l. Tertulla (wife?).
    VI 5200: Dascylus Ti. Aug. ministrat(or) = Iulia Nebris Augustae pedis(equa).
    VI 5359: Hebemus Caesaris tabellarius = Iulia C. l. Phoebe.
    VI 3951: Stephanus Ti. Caesaris aurifex = Philete.
    VI 8497 = D 1614: Suavis Caesaris supra formas = Iulia C. l. Zosime.
    VI 8740: Onesimus Ti. Claudi Germanici atriensis = Vinia.
(But: VI 9052 = D 1703: Placidus Imp. Domitiani Aug. tabellarius = Turia Saturnina Soranae lib.
    VI 8818: Phyrrus (!) Caesaris n. servos dietarcha (!) = Alidia C. l. Myrtale, aged 28.)

The family circle

On the other hand, among these occupational inscriptions there are the usual fair number of wives with Imperial *nomina* who cannot be Imperial freedwomen without status indication; e.g. (in addition to examples already discussed above):

VI 8494 = D 1613: Cleme(n)s Caesarum n. servus castellarius aquae Claudiae = Claudia Sabbathis;

cf. 8495 = D 1612, where two 'vilici aquae Claudiae' with indication 'Caes. n. s.' (i.e. early second century or later) marry a Claudia and a Fabia respectively. For the mingling of Imperial and non-Imperial among wives' *nomina*, cf. VI 8984: Niceratus Augustorum n. ser. paedagogus a caput Africae, whose two wives were first Aelia Quinta, and second Aemilia Anthusa. (Were either or both freeborn or slave-born?)

VI 8921 = D 1804: Paris Imp. Domitiani Aug. Germanici ser. ministrator = Claudia Agathetyche, aged 21. (If she survived till AD 83, when Domitian took the title 'Germanicus', she would have had to be manumitted by Nero at the age of 7 years at the latest, scarcely 'matrimonii causa'.)

cf. 8790: Thallus N(eronis) Caesaris Aug. cubicl. = Iulia Arne, son Ti. Iulius Thallus, who died aged 4. (Wife possibly, but not probably, a freedwoman of Tiberius.)

XI 1358: Abascantus Imperatorum horrearius = Claudia Benedicta (late second-century date?).

V 706: Aquilinus vilic. Augg., aged 46 = Iulia Stratonic(e), son T(itus) Iulius *Aquilinus* (*post* 161).

VI 5884: Antiochus Ti. Claudi Caesaris a bybliotheca Latina Apollinis = Sulpicia Thallusa. (She cannot be a freedwoman of Galba as emperor at this date.)

VI 8687: Sabinus Caesaris verna dispensat(or) Capitoli, aged 30 = Iulia Artemisia.

VI 6639: Menophilus Aug. n. d[i]spensator Ciliciae = Iulia Eleutheris.

VI 8575 = D 1502: Antiochus Aug. n. Lucconianus ark(arius) provinc(iae) Africae = Iulia Iusta.

The major question is: What was the status of these 83% of wives in Rome with *nomina*? Are they freedwomen or freeborn? The discussion of the marriage pattern of Imperial slaves so far provides little hope of a solution by means of a case-by-case or even reign-by-reign study of the examples, although the evidence of the *columbaria* from early first-century Rome and second-century Carthage can be seen as distinguishable from the rest.

WIVES OF IMPERIAL FREEDMEN

At this point we must change ground to the wives of the Imperial freedmen to see if a comparison between the two groups of freedmen and slaves is fruitful. We can here make use of the massive chronological data provided by the Imperial *nomina* of the husbands which is, of course, not available when considering the slaves. It is also necessary to change the method of investigation, to take the figures for each main group *en bloc*, and to try to distinguish trends on a statistical or percentage basis rather than taking a close-up view

Status of wives

of individual cases. Thirdly, in order to proceed, we must make a further assumption. This is based on the average age of manumission for both female and male slaves within the Familia (which, as has been shown, is not normally early, and unlikely to be as early as the slave population outside the Familia) and on the age-at-marriage estimates (which have been shown to be about the same for the Familia as for the non-aristocratic population in general). The effect of these two factors is to widen the normal age difference between marriage and manumission for Imperial slaves of both sexes, as compared with, in particular, slave women outside the Familia. The assumption we make, therefore, is that of wives not otherwise accounted for, who already have a *nomen gentilicium*, and are married to husbands who are still slaves, a maximum of only one-third can themselves be *libertae*. If a higher proportion were allowed, that would imply that marriage between a *servus* and a *liberta* would be *normal* in the Familia, which the discussion on age figures has shown to be highly unlikely. While a figure of one-third is an arbitrary one, some assumption of the kind is required. If the proportion allowed for freedwoman wives is thought too low, it is to some extent offset by the initial assumption made above that, unless other evidence points to the contrary, all wives with single name are counted as slaves. Among these wives there are no doubt freed and freeborn women, but we have no way of even estimating what proportion.

Table III shows the distribution of all wives of Imperial freedmen into two main categories: (*a*) wives of *slave* status; (*b*) wives who are *not* slaves, i.e. they each have a *nomen*. Group (*a*) is made up of those with the actual slave indication (= *Indic.*) and those with single name only (= *Cognom.*) who are assumed to be slaves. (See above, p. 113.) Group (*b*) comprises all those with *nomen* and is subdivided into those with freed indication (= *Freed*), those with filiation (= *Freeborn*), and those with *nomen* and *cognomen* but without status indication (= *Incertae*). Percentage figures are given on the basis of the total in each horizontal group = 100%, e.g. Iulii, Claudii, etc. The detailed references to the inscriptions are given in Appendix II, where they are arranged in the chronological groups corresponding to Tables III, IV and V (see below).

Table III shows that the proportion of wives with *nomina* is as high as 95% for freedmen, as compared with 83% for slaves from Rome, and that the proportion of wives with *nomen* but without status indication (*incertae*) is as high as 85% of all wives of freedmen. It is important to trace any chronological variation or development in the marriage pattern of the Imperial slaves and freedmen. This is possible in practice only for the wives of the *Augusti liberti*, using the dating criteria afforded by the Imperial *nomina* in conjunction with the Imperial status indication.

The family circle

TABLE III
Wives of freedmen: all groups

Wife	Slave Indic. %	Slave Cognom. %	Freed Indic. %	Freeborn Filiat. %	Incertae Nomen+cognom. %	Total %
Augusti liberti						
Iulii	—	—	30 (11)	8 (3)	62 (23)	100 (37)
Claudii	1 (1)	2 (2)	9 (8)	—	88 (78)	100 (89)
Sulpicii	—	—	—	—	(3)	100 (3)
Flavii	—	3 (3)	2 (2)	10 (9)	85 (79)	100 (93)
Cocceii	—	—	—	(1)	(4)	100 (5)
Ulpii	1 (1)	2 (2)	3 (3)	4 (4)	90 (83)	100 (93)
P. Aelii	1 (1)	3 (2)	3 (2)	—	93 (68)	100 (73)
T. Aelii	2 (1)	2 (1)	6 (3)	—	90 (48)	100 (53)
Aelii	5 (1)	—	5 (1)	11 (2)	79 (15)	100 (19)
Aurelii	—	6 (7)	4 (4)	2 (2)	88 (98)	100 (111)
Septimii	—	—	(1)	—	(10)	100 (11)
Incerti	1 (2)	6 (11)	6 (13)	5 (9)	82 (172)	100 (207)
Total	1 (7)	4 (28)	6 (48)	4 (30)	85 (681)	100 (794)
Augustarum						
Liberti	—	4 (1)	38 (10)	—	58 (15)	100 (26)
Servi	—	48 (14)	—	4 (1)	48 (14)	100 (29)
Total	—	27 (15)	18 (10)	2 (1)	53 (29)	100 (55)

A distinction is apparent between the wives of the 'Iulii Aug. lib.', dated to the early and mid-first century AD, and those of later freedmen. While the proportion of slave and freeborn wives is fairly constant and unimportant for all periods, the *freed* wives with status indication account for as many as 30% of all wives of the 'Iulii Aug. lib.', but the next highest figure is only 9% for the Claudii, and the average for all *Augusti liberti* 6%. Conversely, the figure for the *incertae* (*nomen* and *cognomen* only) is lowest for the Iulii (62%) and contrasts with the overall average for *Augusti liberti* of 85%. The figures for the *Augustarum liberti* are useful for comparison, as they mostly belong to the first half of the first century. Although the sample is small, these show 38% for wives who are freed with status indication and only 58% for the *incertae* – in both respects significantly close to the 'Iulii Aug. lib.', and in contrast with all other groups of Imperial freedmen. This could be interpreted simply as a reflection of the tendency of freedmen (and freedwomen) other than *Augusti liberti* from the mid-first century AD to drop their status indication.[1] But in conjunction with the analysis of the *nomina*, particularly the Imperial *nomina*,

[1] See Part I, p. 74.

Status of wives

of the wives given below, these figures indicate a significant change in the marriage pattern of the Familia Caesaris – a sharp decrease in the proportion of wives of slave origin and an increase in the proportion of wives who are freeborn.

Of basic importance for this study is the question of the status of wives classed as *incertae*, whether they are freedwomen or freeborn or, if a mixture of both, whether a closer analysis can determine the approximate proportions of each class. They cannot simply be assumed to be predominantly *libertae*[1] for several reasons. Apart from the certainty that, as with wives of *servi publici*, some wives of *Augusti liberti* were freeborn, there is the evidence contained in the names of their children, many of whom die very young, too early for regular manumission, but who have every appearance of freeborn status. Many take their mother's *nomen*. There is also the general improbability of Imperial slaves marrying in massive numbers female slaves of masters outside the Familia. These wives would undoubtedly have carried less social status than women from within the Familia itself. If Imperial slaves must marry slave women, let them be Imperial slaves. It is difficult to accept the argument that non-Imperial slave women would have been manumitted in large numbers *before* marriage with Imperial slaves. Where would be the economic incentive for their masters to manumit them early without slave children to remain as compensation in the usual way? Or does one suppose that these women are widows or divorcees whom the Imperial slaves are taking to wife – women who are in one way and another older than women usually were at marriage? If non-Imperial masters for status reasons manumitted their female slaves early to gain prestige marriages with Imperial slaves, these same reasons would tell even more strongly in favour of the wives being freeborn in the first place. There is the further consideration involved in the assumption outlined above that Imperial slaves cannot marry *regularly* for the first time with Imperial ex-slaves in more than a minority of cases, if the age figures from the Familia are to have any meaning. And, as we shall see from the Imperial *nomina*, only some of these wives can possibly have been *Imperial* slaves or freedwomen at the time of marriage.

Table IV gives the figures for all *nomina* of wives, including those whose status is certain (Table III, 'Freed' and 'Freeborn'). The percentage figures are expressed in terms of *all* wives of 'Iulii Aug. lib.', 'Claudii Aug. lib.', etc. The wives' *nomina* are divided into two groups:

A. Imperial nomina: Iulia, Claudia, Sulpicia, Flavia, Cocceia, Ulpia, Aelia, Aurelia, Septimia.

[1] See Part I, pp. 83 f.

The family circle

B. *Non-Imperial nomina:* including the *nomina* of the *Augustae* and of other families related to the Imperial family (Livia, Octavia, Scribonia, Vipsania, Antonia, Silia, Valeria, Domitia, Pompeia, Vibia, Annia, Ceionia, Plautia), as well as over 240 other *nomina* having no connection with the Imperial family (e.g. Abuccia, Accia, Acilia, etc.)[1]

TABLE IV

Wives of freedmen: all nomina

Wife	Same nomen %	A All Imperial nomina %	B Non-Imperial nomina %	Total %
Augusti liberti				
Iulii	62 (23)	68 (25)	32 (12)	100 (37)
Claudii	31 (28)	52 (46)	45 (40)	97 (86)
Sulpicii	(1)	(1)	(2)	(3)
Flavii	33 (31)	56 (52)	41 (38)	97 (90)
Cocceii	(3)	(4)	(1)	(5)
Ulpii	32 (30)	62 (57)	35 (33)	97 (90)
P. Aelii	29 (21)	60 (44)	36 (26)	96 (70)
T. Aelii	34 (18)	62 (33)	34 (18)	96 (51)
Aelii	42 (8)	63 (12)	32 (6)	95 (18)
Aurelii	21 (23)	51 (55)	43 (48)	94 (103)
Septimii	(2)	(4)	(7)	(11)
Incerti		43 (89)	50 (105)	93 (194)
Total		53 (422)	42 (336)	95 (758)
Caesaris Servi				
Rome		41 (137)	42 (139)	83 (276)
Outside Rome		41 (55)	20 (26)	61 (81)
Total		41 (192)	35 (165)	76 (357)

[1] A separate category for *nomina* connected with the *Augustae* and other families related to the emperors might be thought desirable, but is singularly unhelpful in practice. Few of these *nomina* show more than five examples for wives of Imperial freedmen over the whole period: Valeria (15), Antonia (10), Domitia (7), Annia (7) – and even these appear in unexpected combinations; there are no particularly fruitful points of concentration; e.g. Valeria: 3 with Claudii Aug. lib., where we would expect them to occur if they are connected with Messalina's *familia*; but no more till the P. Aelii Aug. lib. (3), T. Aelius Aug. lib. (1), with Aurelii Aug. lib. (5) and *incerti* (3). The ten Antoniae are similarly well spread: Claudius (2), Flavius (2), Ulpius (1), P. Aelius (1), Aurelius (1), *incerti* (3). Domitia: Iulius (1), Flavius (1), P. Aelius (3), *incertus* (1). And perhaps most revealing of the non-usefulness of these *nomina* for dating purposes: Annia: Claudius (2), Flavius (1), P. Aelius (1), T. Aelius (1), Aurelius (1), *incertus* (1). Amongst Imperial slave husbands the frequency of these *nomina* for wives is in exactly the same order: Valeria (8), Antonia (6), Domitia (4), Annia (3).

It cannot be maintained, on the basis of chronological distribution, that these *nomina* have any significant connection with the *familiae* of the *Augustae* or of related members of the Imperial family. After examining the chronological distribution of all the other wives with non-Imperial

Status of wives

The chronological arrangement shows that the Iulii have the highest percentage of wives with Imperial *nomina*,[1] and especially of wives with the same *nomen* as themselves – 62% of *all* their marriages. This might appear perfectly natural, as there was at this period no other Imperial *nomen* for their wife to have, *if* she were an Imperial freedwoman. But there is only one example of a freedwoman of Livia.[2] And although we might expect the same to hold good for the 'Claudii Aug. lib.' if they married Imperial freedwomen as a matter of course, what we do find is a drop by half in the proportion of freedmen marrying wives with same *nomen*. Furthermore, this proportion remains remarkably constant thereafter. Thus, Claudius = Claudia 31%, Flavius = Flavia 33%, Ulpius = Ulpia 32%, Aelius = Aelia 32%, dropping to 21% for Aurelius = Aurelia. Marriages between Imperial freedmen and women with *subsequent* Imperial *nomina* are surprisingly rare, i.e. Iulius Aug. lib. = Claudia; Claudius Aug. lib. = Flavia, Ulpia, etc.[3] The bulk of marriages involving Imperial *nomina* which are not the same are between Imperial freedmen and wives with *earlier* Imperial *nomina*, i.e. Claudius Aug. lib. = Iulia; Flavius Aug. lib. = Claudia, Iulia; Ulpius Aug. lib. = Flavia, Claudia, Iulia, etc.[4] This again suggests that marriage with freedwomen is more likely for the 'Iulii Aug. lib.' than for other Imperial freedmen. During the early first century, in the first two generations of Imperial slaves, the normal marriage pattern found in the slave classes in general, of slave with slave from the same *familia*, followed after a period by manumission of both partners, was the commonest type of marriage in the Familia Caesaris.

nomina, I have reluctantly come to the conclusion that worthwhile results cannot be obtained from Lily Ross Taylor's interesting suggestion (*AJPh* 82 (1961), 125 n. 30) that these *nomina* might provide insights into the social and political connections of the Imperial family through the intermarriage of members of their *familiae*. Not counting all the examples of wives of freedmen and slaves with 14 quasi-Imperial *nomina*, yielding 87 examples in all, there are some 244 other non-Imperial *nomina* (excluding fragmentary *nomina*) yielding a total number of 401 examples, i.e. *less* than two examples each on average. This distribution is extraordinarily widespread and does not encourage the supposition that there are significant connections with non-Imperial *familiae* or indeed that there are large numbers of non-Imperial freedwomen lurking among these *nomina* at all.

[1] Not considering the Sulpicii, Cocceii or Septimii, where the absolute figures are too small for percentage treatment.

[2] VI 5436: Ti. Iulius Aug. l. Tertius = Irena Liviae l. (wife?). 'Liviae' are surprisingly absent from the wives of both the Iulii Aug. lib. and the Claudii Aug. lib., and only appear with any frequency, as is to be expected, among the *familia* of Livia herself.   [3] See Table V, p. 129.

[4] See Table V, p. 129. As the Julian period of 68 years (27 BC–AD 41) was much longer than that of any subsequent period except that of the Aurelii (Claudii 27 years, Flavii 28 years, Ulpii 21 years, Aelii 44 years), it might be thought that marriages of Iulius Aug. lib. = Iulia could have taken place over a longer period than with other *nomina* except the Aurelii and thus lead to a distortion of the pattern. However, there is no significant increase above the average for the other longer periods, e.g. Aelius Aug. lib. = Aelia, Aurelius Aug. lib. = Aurelia. In fact, in the last case the figure is well below the average, so that length of period does not appear to distort this pattern in favour of marriage with a partner of the same Imperial *nomen*. Such distortion might imply frequent marriage with Imperial freedwomen, lack of it the opposite.

The family circle

The problem of the proportion of freeborn to slave-born (including freed) among the wives of Imperial freedmen and slaves may be approached first through a comparison of the slave and freedman patterns, and secondly through the chronological distribution of the wives with Imperial *nomina* and the extent to which these correspond with the *nomina* of their freedmen husbands.

As most marriages in the Familia Caesaris took place before the manumission of the husband, the marriage pattern of *Caesaris servi* should not differ radically from that of *Augusti liberti*, but merely represent, with certain reservations concerning the area from which the slave sample is taken, the marriage pattern of the *liberti* at an earlier age, i.e. before manumission. The proportion of *ingenuae* (freeborn women) among the wives should be more or less the same for both *liberti* and *servi*, as it would make no difference to their name and status whatever age they married at. On the other hand, the proportion of *libertae* among the wives will be higher for *liberti* than for *servi*, as the freedman inscriptions would naturally have been erected at a later stage in life than those of the slaves, and by this time the wives of slave origin would normally have been manumitted also. In these terms we can explain the differences in the percentage figures for Imperial and non-Imperial *nomina* of wives found with the various husband groups. Thus in Table IV, Column A, 53% of all wives of *liberti* have an Imperial *nomen* (i.e. Iulia, Claudia, Flavia, etc.), but only 41% of all wives of *Caesaris servi*; and in the latter case it makes no difference whether they are from Rome or the provinces. This difference of 12% most plausibly represents slave wives who gained an Imperial *nomen* on manumission, and were thus most probably Imperial slaves themselves. This group, accounting for 12% of all wives of *Augusti liberti*, will be of Imperial slave origin. On the other hand, from Table IV, Column B it emerges that, while 42% of all wives of *liberti* have a *non*-Imperial nomen, 42% of wives of *servi* from Rome also have a non-Imperial *nomen*; but only 20% of wives of *servi* from outside Rome. Given the lack of wives with non-Imperial *nomina* especially from Africa, and the fact that no significant manumissions took place in Rome among wives with these *nomina* (at least none that are reflected in the overall freedman figures in Column B), then we can conclude that the difference of 22%, which is common to both *servi* from Rome and *liberti*, must be made up almost entirely of wives who are *ingenuae*. This means that a minimum of about 22% of all wives of *Augusti liberti* and of *Caesaris servi* from Rome are of freeborn origin. The corresponding fraction of wives of *servi* outside Rome will consequently be of slave status. Thus, while only 17% of wives of *servi* from *Rome* show that they are still *servae*, there are 39% in this category outside Rome.

Status of wives

1. WIVES WITH IMPERIAL NOMINA

Let us turn now to the chronological distribution of wives with *Imperial nomina*. The figures are given in Table V in terms of the correspondence of these *nomina* with those of their husbands. Again the percentage figures are expressed in terms of *all* marriages of the group of freedmen concerned.

TABLE V
Status of wives: Imperial nomina

Wives	Iuliae %	Claudiae %	Flaviae %	Ulpiae %	Aeliae %	Aureliae %	Total %
Liberti Augusti							
Iulii	**62 (23)**	6 (2)	—	—	—	—	68 (25)
Claudii	14 (12)	**31 (28)**	5 (4)	1 (1)	—	—	52 (45)
Flavii	9 (8)	10 (9)	**33 (31)**	2 (2)	2 (2)	—	56 (52)
Ulpii	4 (4)	8 (7)	12 (11)	**32 (30)**	1 (1)	—	62 (53)
P. Aelii	5.5(4)	5.5(4)	8 (6)	12 (9)	**29 (21)**	—	60 (44)
T. Aelii	6 (3)	4 (2)	11 (6)	4 (2)	**33 (18)**	4 (2)	62 (33)
Aelii	5 (1)	5 (1)	5 (1)	—	**43 (8)**	5 (1)	63 (12)
Aurelii	2 (2)	5 (5)	4 (4)	8 (9)	10 (11)	**21 (23)**	51 (54)
Incerti	5 (11)	5 (10)	7 (15)	6 (13)	10 (21)	8 (16)	43 (86)
Sulpicii, Cocceii, Septimii							(18)
Total	9 (68)	9 (68)	10 (78)	8 (66)	11 (82)	6 (42)	53 (422)

The Sulpicii, Cocceii and Septimii, who have not been included in the body of the table, total 2% of all marriages.[1]

Figures for husband and wives with the *same nomen* are given for each Imperial *nomen* shown in heavy type which appears diagonally across the table from Iulius = Iulia at the top left to Aurelius = Aurelia at the bottom right. The percentage and absolute figures for wives with *preceding* Imperial *nomen* can thus be easily seen to the *left* of the heavy type for each group of husbands, and the figures for wives with *subsequent* Imperial *nomen* appear to the right.

Among *liberti* the commonest marriage pattern is with wives bearing the same *nomen*.[2] Apart from 62% for the Iulii, this accounts for one-third of all marriages of Imperial freedmen from the Claudii to the Aelii, and one-fifth

---

[1] Details are as follows: Sulpicius (Aug. lib.) = Sulpicia (1); Cocceius = Coccia (3), = Aelia (1); Septimius = Septimia (2), = Ulpia (1), = Aurelia (1); Claudius = Sulpicia (1); Ulpius = Sulpicia (1); Aurelius = Sulpicia (1); T. Aelius = Sulpicia (1); Ulpius = Cocceia (3); Aurelius = Cocceia (1); Aurelius = Septimia (1). These have been included in the overall percentage figures for each group. The detailed references for these marriages are given under the appropriate headings in Appendix III.

[2] In the light of these figures, Chantraine's assertion (p. 111) that in the majority of cases wives of Imperial freedmen have a *nomen* of an *earlier* dynasty (my italics), can be seen to have no foundation, and would indeed be most surprising.

The family circle

of all marriages of Aurelii. Apart from the Iuliae, less than one in fifteen of these wives indicates status, and all but two of those that do are *Augusti libertae*. Deceased wives occupy about half the principal positions in these sepulchral dedications, so that the omission of the status indication is regular and not due to space exigencies in the inscriptions. Whether wives in this group are predominantly *libertae* or not can be checked by the nomenclature and status of the children.[1] Such wives as are *libertae* would normally have married while both partners were still slaves. Hence, if the mothers were slaves of the emperor, the children would be born slaves (*vernae*), and themselves members of the Familia Caesaris. But if the mothers were slaves of a master other than the emperor, the children would be born slaves of that master.

Further, because *servae* in the Familia Caesaris tended to marry at an earlier age than *servi* but without correspondingly early manumission, if the wives were of predominantly servile origin, one would expect the next most numerous group of wives' *nomina* to be the *subsequent* important Imperial *nomina*[2] in each case. But from the Iulii (Iulius = Claudia 6%) and Claudii (Claudius = Flavia 5%) the proportion dwindles even further to an insignificant 2% or 1% of all marriages for a given group of freedmen (Flavius = Ulpia 2%; Ulpius = Aelia 1%; Aelius = Aurelia 2%).[3]

By contrast, the proportion of wives from the *immediately preceding* important *nomina* is much larger, varying from 14% to 10%; the average is 12% (Claudius = Iulia 14%, Flavius = Claudia 10%, Ulpius = Flavia 12%, P. Aelius = Ulpia 12%,[4] Aurelius = Aelia 10%). This poses the following questions: if these wives with preceding Imperial *nomina* are *libertae*, were they manumitted early or were their slave husbands manumitted late, or did the wives marry unusually late, after manumission, or as a second marriage? Or are most of them not *libertae* at all but *ingenuae*, for example, freeborn descendants of Imperial freedmen with an earlier *nomen*, or of enfranchised provincials or other citizens?

An indication that some at least of these wives with preceding *nomen* are *libertae* is to be found in the inscriptions where both husband and wife use a status indication showing membership of the Familia Caesaris.[5] Delayed

---

[1] See pp. 148 f.   [2] I.e. excluding Sulpicia, Cocceia, Septimia in each case.

[3] VI 37752: Ti. Iulius Aug. l. = Claudia Aug. l. (second husband Ti. Claudius Aug. l.); 15110: Ti. Claudius Aug. lib. Hermes Caenidianus = Flavia Aug. lib., son Ti. Claud. Iustus (cf. 18358); 15235: Ti. Claud. Aug. lib., aged 60 = Flavia Aug. lib.

[4] The increasing proportion of Aelii = Aeliae, from 29% to 43%, is due to the later Aelii under Antoninus Pius marrying Aeliae rather than Ulpiae.

[5] *Wife with preceding nomen:* V 7209 (Flavius = Claudia Aug. l.); VI 8542 (Ulpius Aug. lib. = Flavia Aug. lib., sons Satyrus (19), Crescens (13) vernae Aug., M. Ulpius Aug. lib. Saturninus); 18358 (M. Ulpius Aug. lib. = Flavia Aug. lib., married 50 years, daughter Ulpia Calliste); 8502

Status of wives

manumission of the husband is a probable explanation in several cases, especially those of *dispensatores* and 'vicariani' who were not normally manumitted till the age of 40 or thereabouts; e.g. VI 18358: (M. Ulpius) Callistus Aug. lib. Hyginianus = Flavia Aug. lib. Helpis Caenidiana; 15350: Actius Aug. lib. Gamianus = Claudia Aug. lib. Amanda; 18456: Onesimus Imp. Caes. Traiani Aug. ser. Phoebianus = Flavia Aug. lib. Tyche; 8821: Callistus Aug. lib. dispensator = Ulpia Aug. lib. Acte (AD 110); XIV 2856: Fortunatus (Augg.) vern. disp. = Aurelia Restituta (Augg.) lib.; and perhaps VIII 12656: Princeps Aug. ser. = Flavia Aug. lib. Successa.

Whatever the explanation of the *nomina* of wives in the groups mentioned above who were *Augusti libertae* – and it must be borne in mind that wives and, to a lesser extent, children with status indication are in any case very much the exception in the Familia Caesaris – the general conclusion regarding wives with *immediately preceding* Imperial *nomina* but without status indication is that only a minority can be Imperial slaves, or indeed slaves of other masters, by origin. We can assume a maximum of one-third. Freeborn status, therefore, is to be postulated for at least two-thirds of wives with immediately preceding *nomina*, i.e. 8% of *all* marriages; and freed status for the remainder, i.e. 4% of *all* marriages.

In the case of wives with Imperial *nomina* of *two reigns or dynasties preceding*, there is no doubt that these, with very rare exceptions, cannot be Imperial ex-slaves at all. They must be nearly all *ingenuae*, whether first or second generation descendants of Imperial freedmen or otherwise. The shortest possible period between Imperial manumissions of a Flavius and a Iulia is 28 years, of an Ulpius and Claudia 30 years, a P. Aelius and Flavia 19 years, a T. Aelius and Ulpia 21 years, an Aurelius and Ulpia 44 years. The

(M. Ulpius Aug. l. = Cocceia Aug. l., aged 25); XI 1222 (P. Aelius Aug. l. = Ulpia Aug. lib., sons Aeli Similis et Prothymus); VI 8432 (P. Aelius Aug. lib. = Ulpia sive Aelia Aug. lib., married 44 years, son Ulpius Felix, aged 10); 29396 (T. Aelius Aug. lib. = Ulpia Aug. lib., daughters Ulpiae Attica et Atticilla).

The only instance of a freedwoman wife with a *nomen* belonging to an emperor of *two* reigns previously (apart from instances of Ulpius Aug. lib. = Flavia Aug. lib., where the two-year reign of Nerva is too short to count for this purpose) is VI 29396: T. Aelius Aug. lib. Felix = Ulpia Aug. lib. Saturnina. The shortest possible interval between the manumission of wife and husband is AD 117-38, i.e. 21 years. This would presuppose a considerably older wife or very late manumission for the husband or both. The daughters, Ulpia Attica and Ulpia Atticilla, were born before the manumission of the father (unless born to a previous husband). If the husband was manumitted *before* 138, we must assume a change of *nomen* from T. Aurelius to T. Aelius, in accordance with the changed *nomen* of Antoninus himself, but this would be exceptional. Cf. the examples of 'T. Aurelius Aug. lib.' (p. 26).

Second marriage, paradoxically, appears only in the case of a wife with subsequent *nomen*: VI 37752: Ti. Iulius Aug. l. Secundus = Claudia Aug. l. Cedne, whose other husband was Ti. Claudius Aug. l. Eunus; and perhaps also in the case of Claudia Aug. l. Parata (VI 8957), who died aged 27 having had three husbands, Ti. Iulius Romanus, Ti. Claudius Priscus, Nedimus Aug. ser.

The family circle

average difference would have to be greater, about 30 to 40 years, which is too great to be seriously considered. The proportion of marriages in this category is quite considerable, rising steadily from the Flavii to the Aurelii, and averaging 9% of all marriages.

Although wives with these *nomina* cannot be Imperial freedwomen, it is just possible that some of them could be freedwomen of patrons other than emperors having Imperial *nomina* themselves. At most one can allow a third of this group for these, i.e. 3% of all marriages. The remaining 6% of all marriages will be the minimum for *ingenuae*.

The wives with *same nomen* and those with *subsequent* Imperial *nomen* may be taken together, as there is not likely to be any significant difference in their marriage pattern. Together these groups total 32% of all marriages. It has already been shown above that 12% of all marriages must come from wives with Imperial *nomina* who were slaves. If we recall the marriage patterns for freedmen and the slaves from Rome (Table IV), the figure of 12% represents the difference between the two groups both in the Imperial *nomina* (53–41) and, conversely, in the wives of slave status (5% and 17%) who appear as manumitted wives with Imperial *nomina* on the freedman table. These wives of slave origin must come almost exclusively from the group with same *nomen* as their husbands or with subsequent Imperial *nomina*. This leaves a further 20% out of the 32% of all marriages found in this group as yet unaccounted for. Of those wives who already possessed a *nomen* before the manumission of their husbands, if we allow a maximum of one-third to be *libertae*, we get a further 14% *ingenuae* and 6% *libertae* of all wives of freedmen.

To sum up this section of the argument: the 53% of all wives of freedmen with Imperial *nomina* is made up as follows:

Wives	*Ingenuae* (%)	*Libertae* (%)	Total (%)
Immediately preceding *nomen*	8	4	12
Earlier preceding *nomen*	6	3	9
Same or subsequent *nomen*	14	6 / 12	32
Total	28	25	53

Thus, 28% of all freedman marriages is the minimum figure for wives who are freeborn from this group alone. Taken chronologically, the proportion of freeborn wives rises for those with an earlier Imperial *nomen* than their husbands—from 10% for the 'Claudii Aug. lib.' to 20% already for the 'P. Aelii Aug. lib.', i.e. from one-fifth (10/52) to one-third (20/60) of all wives with

Status of wives

Imperial *nomina*. The explanation is to be found in the increasing prestige of the Familia Caesaris, both in its administrative and its domestic services. In the first two or three generations of the Familia's existence the normal slave marriage pattern continued, though no doubt already changing by the time of Gaius or even earlier, when many of the important freedmen under Claudius, e.g. Callistus, Polybius and Pallas, were establishing their careers.[1] The administrative service first achieved under Claudius its high status that was to last till the third century. Under Claudius the marriage pattern for the first time departs from that of the typical large *familia*. Not unexpectedly. The slaves of the emperor's service had assumed the status if not the functions of the *servi publici*. They had even improved upon this. Why not then also assume or improve upon their social status? This is revealed in their marriage pattern and is just what we might expect. Marriages with freeborn women, including daughters and granddaughters of successful Imperial freedmen or of influential provincial or Italian municipal families increase markedly and continue to increase till the early third century.

2. WIVES WITH NON-IMPERIAL NOMINA

It remains to consider the large group of wives both of Imperial freedmen and slaves who have non-Imperial *nomina*. Here again we must begin with the wives of slaves. This time there is *no* difference between the freedmen and the slaves from Rome in regard to the proportion of their wives who fall into this category. The figures in both cases are based on a reasonably large sample – 139 wives of slaves from Rome and 336 wives of freedmen. They comprise in both cases 42% of all marriages in that group. This constant figure indicates that manumissions of wives with non-Imperial *nomina* are an insignificant factor in the marriage pattern of these groups, as otherwise *some* difference would have been shown. On the other hand, there is a marked discrepancy between the figures for the *slaves* from Rome (42% of all marriages) and those from Italy and the provinces (20% of all marriages). This contrasts with the uniform 41% for the wives with *Imperial nomina* from *both* these groups of slaves. The reason appears to be that the Imperial slaves away from the capital in the provinces, especially Africa, when they married freeborn women, married for the most part those with Imperial *nomina*, presumably daughters and granddaughters of Imperial freedmen. Also when they married slaves, these were from the Familia Caesaris rather than slaves

[1] I do not know on what grounds Chantraine bases his assertion (p. 110) that the Imperial freedmen and slaves 'in grösseren Masse als es sonst üblich war, Frauen geheiratet haben, die selbst Augusti libertae waren oder doch von solchen stammten...'.

The family circle

of other masters with Imperial *nomina*. Slave-wives in the last category must have had the lowest status of all as their children would belong not to the emperor but to their own non-Imperial master.

But neither could the Imperial slaves from Rome have married to any significant extent slave women of masters with non-Imperial *nomina*, as the percentage of wives in this category is the same as for freedmen. The slaves in the central administration and the Palace service in Rome were certainly of higher status and received manumission earlier than slaves in the provinces, or at least in Africa and perhaps elsewhere The age figures from Carthage show this conclusively. It follows that the difference in the figures for non-Imperial wives of *Caesaris servi* from Rome and those from outside Rome – 42% and 20% respectively of all marriages – i.e. 22% of all marriages in the group from Rome is made up almost entirely of *ingenuae* wives. Conversely this figure of 22% represents the difference between the percentage of wives of *slave* status recorded for the two groups of slaves – 17% for Rome and 39% outside Rome. Thus, while Imperial slaves in the provinces tend to marry a much higher proportion of *servae* than do the slaves in Rome, and these wives predominantly from the Familia Caesaris itself, the slaves in Rome on the other hand marry a much higher proportion of freeborn women with non-Imperial *nomina* than do the slaves elsewhere.

This proportion of *ingenuae* (22%) passes into the table of wives of *liberti* without change on the manumission of the husbands. If we take the remaining 20% (i.e. 42%–22%) of wives with non-Imperial *nomina* common to Imperial slaves both in Rome and outside and allow the maximum proportion of these who could be of slave origin but are manumitted already at the time of marriage to their slave husbands to be one-third according to the formula adopted above, we get a further 14% of all marriages to be with *ingenuae* and 6% with *libertae*.

Thus, the 42% of all wives of freedmen and of slaves from Rome who have non-Imperial *nomina* are made up as follows:

	Ingenuae (%)	Libertae (%)	Total (%)
Wives of freedmen and of slaves from Rome	22 14	— ⎫ 6 ⎭	42
	36	6	42
Wives of slaves from outside Rome	14	6	20

To complete the picture we must add to the total of wives of slave origin the 5% of all wives of freedmen who are still *servae* (i.e. with slave indi-

Status of wives

cation or single name). This gives an overall estimate for the wives of *freedmen* and *slaves from Rome* as follows:[1]

Wives	Ingenuae (%)	Libertae et servae (%)	Total (%)
Imperial *nomina*	28	25	53
Non-Imperial *nomina*	36	6	42
Servae	—	5	5
Total	64%	36%	100%

The great majority of inscriptions relating to the Familia Caesaris come from Rome – at least two-thirds for the *Caesaris servi* and four-fifths for the *Augusti liberti*. Outside Rome the numbers and concentrations of *Augusti liberti* are insufficient for useful comparison. But for Imperial slaves outside Rome, especially in Carthage where large numbers have been found, the pattern is significantly different. Marriages with partners of slave origin are much more frequent and account for perhaps one-half of all slave marriages there. However, it must be remembered that the following figures for marriages of *Caesaris servi outside* Rome represent a *minimum* for wives who are *ingenuae* and therefore a *maximum* for wives of slave origin. For wives of *slaves outside Rome* the overall estimate is as follows:

Wives	Ingenuae (%)	Libertae et servae (%)	Total (%)
Imperial *nomina*	28	13	41
Non-Imperial *nomina*	14	6	20
Servae	—	39	39
Total	42%	58%	100%

The preceding analysis should not be pressed too hard in points of detail, but it gives what I believe is a reasonably reliable overall picture of the marriage pattern of the Familia Caesaris from the Claudii to the Aurelii. It is based on the assumptions stated above, namely that the pattern of marriage for slaves is essentially the same as that for freedmen, representing an earlier

---

[1] In the foregoing discussion a chronological grouping rather than a geographical one has been used for the marriage pattern of freedmen, partly because of the valuable dating criteria offered by the *nomina* of the husbands, and partly because the number of *freedman* marriages found in the provincial areas and Italy is relatively so small when compared with those from Rome. To have imposed a geographical pattern on the discussion of freedman marriages would have considerably complicated the discussion without, I think, adding much of compensating value to the overall result.

The family circle

age level than that of freedmen; the *Caesaris servi* from Rome, the great majority of whom became *Augusti liberti* before their fortieth year, are more truly representative of this pattern than the slaves from Italy and the provinces, where manumission sometimes came late or not at all. It is also based on the assumption, which derives from the average age-at-marriage and age-at-manumission figures, that a maximum of one-third of wives not otherwise accounted for who already have a *nomen gentilicium* and are married to husbands who are still slaves can be themselves freedwomen. The validity of the conclusions reached, especially that a minimum of nearly two-thirds of the wives in the Familia Caesaris in Rome are freeborn, can be tested by an examination of the nomenclature and status of the children of such marriages.

CHAPTER 8

STATUS OF CHILDREN

The terms used to refer to children and to express parental relationships are the same for children of all classes and status. It makes no difference whether they or their parents are slave, freed, or freeborn; *filius, filia, pater, mater, parens*, etc., and their Greek equivalents, are basic. More rarely used are: *liberi, infans, delicium, mama*, or even a periphrasis, e.g. 'duo incrementa' (VI 8984). The one point of nomenclature with any chronological significance is the form of abbreviation for 'filius' which shows a development from 'f(ilius)' to 'fil(ius)' similar to that for 'libertus' from 'l(ibertus)' to 'lib(ertus)'.[1] As with the status of wives, it is best to approach the naming and status of children in two sections according to the status of the father.[2]

CHILDREN OF CAESARIS SERVI

It is convenient to begin with the children of the Imperial slaves because in these cases the status of the father at the time of the birth of the children is positively known. All these unions are strictly *contubernium* and hence the status of the children should in all normal cases be determined by that of the mother at the time of birth of the child, in accordance with the principle of the *ius gentium*. Using the same groups of Imperial slave fathers as we used in the previous discussion for slave husbands (i.e. Rome, Italy and the provinces), we may proceed within these groups on the basis of the mother's status. We can include with these those children from whose names the status of the mother can be inferred with some degree of certainty. We shall consider in turn children whose mothers are slaves, and children whose mothers have *nomen gentilicium*.

[1] See Part I, p. 74 for details.
[2] On children in the Familia Caesaris see esp. Boulvert, II, 726 f., and 752 f. (concerned primarily with the juridical nature of marriage unions within the Familia, but also dealing with the nomenclature and status of the children); Chantraine, pp. 108 f. (dealing with the use of family nomenclature as possible dating criteria, especially in cases of omission of *nomen* by *Augusti liberti*); Thylander, *Étude*, pp. 88 f.; and B. Rawson, *Class. Phil.* 61 (1966), 71 f. (who deals with family nomenclature found in the *sepulcrales* in general in Rome – including many from the Familia Caesaris – and its social implications. See Part II below, pp. 194 f.).

The family circle

CHILDREN OF SLAVE MOTHERS

Children of mothers with slave indication or with personal name only (who have been assumed to be *servae* in the discussion above) present few problems: these children must be slaves at birth, and at the time of the inscription either still slaves or (exceptionally, if manumitted before their parents) freed slaves; e.g.

> VI 22960: Primigenius C. n. ser. = Voluptas C. n. ser. + Nicephorus C. n. ver., aged 18.
> VIII 13146: Faustus = Secunda Aug. + Tertia Aug., aged 7.

The children in both these cases died too early for manumission; it would be unusual if it were otherwise, as both parents are themselves still slaves at the time. It is not regularly that children have the Imperial slave indication as well as both parents; usually a single name suffices to indicate slave status; e.g.

> VI 11244: Agathopus Caes. n. ser. = Macedonia Caes. n. + Victorinus.
> VI 17328: Eudorus Caesaris ser. = Festa Caes. + Euhans, aged 2.
> VI 19365: Philotechnus = Chelys Severi Imp. Aug. + Herma, aged 1.

Frequently both mother and child do not have status indication; e.g.

> VI 8472 = XIV 2834 = D 1537: Abascantus Caes. n. ser. vern. = Carpime + Laurus.
> *AE* 1930, 64 (Rome): Priscus Caesaris servos = Heuresis + *Prisca*, aged 1.
> VIII 12629: Felix Caesaris n. ser., died aged 30 = Victoria conserva + Donata.

Sometimes both father and mother are without indication; e.g.

> VI 22330: Maximus = Helena + *Maximus* Caes. n. vern., aged 11.
> *AE* 1936, 27 = *ILTun.* 213: Quintus = Optata + Sedatus Aug., aged 10.

In these examples the status of father, mother and children is clear – in all cases they are slaves, and presumably also Imperial slaves. Before drawing conclusions we should look at the total picture of children in this category with personal name only. There is a total of thirty-eight slave mothers of children whose fathers are Imperial slaves. Nearly half (17/38) are stated to be *Caesaris servae*.[1] There is no hint whose slaves the remaining twenty-one are, but they must be presumed to be also slaves of the emperor rather than of masters outside the Familia. The children of such unions would by law belong not to the emperor but to the master of the *serva*; again there is no

---

[1] VI 8822–4, 11244, 12464, 14100, 17328, 19365, 22014, 22960, 27361, 27674; VIII 5384 = 17500 = *ILAlg.* I 323, 12802, 13146, 24744, 24782; X 7653; *IGR* IV 235. There is also an instance of an *Aug. serva* who married outside the Familia – IX 888: Ti. Statorius Geminus = Numisia Aug. n. ser. + Capriolus (filius naturalis patri). Cf. VI 14452: Cartorius Horaeus = Cartoria Elpis + Martialis Aug. l., *Elpistus* Caesaris. Boulvert (II, 779) considers that the mother of Martialis Aug. l. and Elpistus Caesaris (ser.) was herself originally an Imperial slave, then sold or transferred to her (original?) husband, Cartorius Horaeus, who manumitted her.

Status of children

hint of this. The children all have single names (we are not considering here those with Imperial status indication) and must all be slaves, again presumably Imperial slaves without the Imperial slave indication.[1] There are a further twenty children with single name whose mothers are not known but are also probably of slave origin.

From this pattern of nomenclature it is obvious that the status indication is used for slave wives of the Familia in only about half the possible cases, and even less by the children of such *contubernales*. The children are about evenly divided between the sexes. Their ages are mostly those of infants or young children – there are thirty-one aged 9 years or under, three aged 11, and only seven aged 12 or over. Such a neglect of the slave indication by wives and children occurs irrespective of whether they are the dedicants or the person to whom the inscription is dedicated. The use of the status indication by mothers and children in fact appears to be haphazard.

The complementary case is where children with the status indication 'Caes. ser.', 'Aug.', etc. use the single name to refer to mother or father or both. There are sixty-three Imperial slave children, including some girls, whose parents are named in this fashion and must therefore be presumed to be slaves. For this group of children (with status indication), their ages where given are in general higher than for the previous group (without indication), nearly half being aged 17 or over; e.g.

VI 4951: Ichmas = **** + Expectatus verna Caesaris, aged 25.
XIV 487: Ilus = Prisca + Restituta verna Caesaris, aged 19.
EE VIII 266 (Italy): Sabinus = Aucta + *Sabina* Caes. n. ser., aged 13.

But not those from Africa, where the average age is considerably lower and comparable with the group of children above without slave indication; e.g.

VIII 12926: Adiutor = Cale + *Adiutor* Caes. n. ser., aged 5.
VIII 12721: Dassius = Nymphe + Felix Caes. n. ser., aged 2.

The single name without status indication is thus, in the absence of other data, a sign of slave status. Other points emerge on the use of the status indication in the Familia Caesaris in general. It is *sometimes* not used by slave fathers of slave children. It is *regularly* not used for wives who are slaves; and even less for young children who are slaves, except in Africa. For children over the age of 12 it is more common.

To complete the picture we should include brothers and sisters of Imperial

[1] There is an exception to this pattern of nomenclature – III 4065: Proculus Aug(g). nn. vern. = Valentina + Venuleius *Proculus*, who died aged 1 year. The son should be freeborn in view of his age and *nomen*; we must suppose inadvertent omission of the mother's *nomen* Venuleia. In VI 14047: Hatenio Caes. = Successa + L. Caietius Ianuarius, the son, who died aged 17, and is presumably freeborn, is specifically 'filiaster' (of Successa).

The family circle

slaves in inscriptions where neither parent is mentioned. Not including brothers or sisters who are *Augusti liberti* (*-ae*) and are considered below, I have listed forty-five of these, of whom ten are Imperial slaves with indication, twenty-four have single name without indication (i.e. are slaves), and eleven have *nomen* (i.e. are either freed or freeborn);[1] e.g.

VI 8795 = D 1809: Alcimus Caes. n. ser. structor – Ingenu(u)s Caes. n. ser. a cura amicorum.

AE 1945, 112: Successus verna Caesaris, mulio, died aged 16 – Antigonus Domitiae Aug. ser. tabul.

VIII 12896: Primigenius Aug. adiutor a comment(ariis), aged 37 – Priscus.

VIII 12599: Eminens Aug. adiut. tabul., aged 30 – Phaenippus.

VI 4636: Alexio Caesaris ser. – Philia Iulia.

VI 10480 = 34267: Liberalis Cae(s). vern. – Aelia Trophime, aged 11.

The following table summarises the use of status indication by slave children in the Familia. (It does not include children with *nomina*, nor a small number of children of Imperial freedmen who are slaves.)

	Without indication %	With indication %	Total %
Rome	65 (50)	35 (27)	100 (77)
Italy	44 (35)	56 (49)	100 (84)
Provinces	52 (85)	48 (76)	100 (161)
Total	53 (170)	47 (152)	100 (322)

Thus in Rome the status indication is used by only about one in three of slave children of slave parents in the Familia Caesaris, whereas in the provinces the proportion is higher. In Africa, in fact, two out of three such children use the slave indication. In all areas the status indication is regularly used in conjunction with an occupational title in the Familia, but otherwise only sporadically, except in Africa.

CHILDREN OF MOTHERS WITH NOMEN (I.E. FREED OR FREEBORN)

Next to be considered are the children of fathers who are still *Caesaris servi* but of mothers with *nomina gentilicia*, and the children with *nomina* whose

---

[1] *Caes. ser.*: VI 8421, 8527, 8663, 8795 = D 1809, 8838, 24163, AE 1945, 112; VIII 24697, 24698; XI 3435.

Single name: VI 5305, 8531, 8562, 8792, 8868–9, 8967, 8992, 15988, 16741 = XIV 2343, 17264, 17924, 25921, 30676, 33687, 33739 = D 1648, *Bull. Com.* 1941, p. 187 n. 132; *IPO* A 101; III 1610 = AE 1956, 209, 2320; VIII 12599, 12622, 12686, 12896, 24797.

Nomen: VI 4636, 4775, 5768, 8754, 8784, 9857, 10480 = 34267, 16741 = XIV 2343, 23549, 25731, 26608.

Status of children

mothers are not named. In all there are seventy-eight examples from Rome, and thirty-three from Italy and the provinces. The fact that the great bulk of examples comes from Rome – 78/111 (70%) compared with 77/322 (24%) from Rome in the case of children in the previous section – reflects the much higher proportion of marriages between Imperial slaves and freeborn women in Rome, both those with Imperial and non-Imperial *nomina*, as compared with women who are slaves; whereas in the provinces there was a higher proportion of marriages with *servae*, mostly belonging to the emperor.

(*a*) In the first place, we can separate off those cases where *both mother and children have the same nomen*; e.g.

(1) VI 18290 = 34114: Apollonius Imp. Domitiani Aug. Germ. ser. pecul. = Flavia Pallas + Flavia Athenais, aged 8 months.

(2) *IPO* A 251: Trophimus Caes. n. ser. = Claudia Tyche + Claudia Saturnina, aged 15.

(3) IX 4782: Daphnis Caes. n. ser. adiutor tabul. = Aelia Melitene + P. Aelius Karissimus, aged 4.

(4) *AE* 1959, 307 (Dacia): Piper(as) Timostrati disp. vik(arius) = Ael(ia) Epicte(sis) + P. Ael(ius) Aelian(us), aged 3.

(5) VI 8444: Andragathus Caes. ser. arcar. XX her. = Maia Procla + M. Maius M. f. Orat. Fabianus, aged 9.

(6) VI 33781: [...]s Caesaris [ser]vos ministrator = Caesia Tertia + Caesia C[...] = Genialis Caesaris servos victimarius (gener).

Nos. 1, 2, 3, and 4 all show children and mothers with Imperial *nomina*. But it can by no means be assumed that these mothers are therefore Imperial freedwomen and their children ex-slaves also. The very young ages of several of the children (8 months, 3 years, 4 years), together with their lack of status indication, make it probable that they are not of freed status at all, but freeborn; e.g. Nos. 3 and 4, and probably also Nos. 2 and 1, even though in this last case the *nomen* of the wife (Flavia) happens to correspond with the Domitianic date implied by her husband's indication ('Imp. Domitiani Aug. Germ. ser.'). No. 4 shows the freeborn son of a *vicarius dispensatoris*. The age of the son P. Aelius Aelianus (3 years) makes it most probable that the wife is freeborn. Similarly other wives with Imperial *nomina* are freeborn because of the name and age of the children.[1]

When the mothers have non-Imperial *nomina* they and their children are even more likely to be freeborn. This is specifically indicated in No. 5. Especially interesting is No. 6, which shows the freeborn daughter of an Imperial slave and a freeborn woman (Caesia Tertia) marrying again an Imperial slave (Genialis) in the second generation. It is not unlikely that

---

[1] Other examples of mother and children with same *nomen* are: Rome: VI 74, 8631, 8785, 8790, 8792, 8819, 8835, 8892, 9077, 11931, 13850, 15114, 15396, 18424, 27274, 28593, 29513, 34901, 37749; XIV 2465. Italy: V 368; XI 6379a. Provinces: III 2082, 4894, 12143; VIII 18327.

The family circle

freeborn daughters of Imperial slaves married back into the Familia Caesaris by themselves marrying Imperial slaves. This may have happened much more frequently than we can document and could be important as the source of a substantial number of wives of Imperial slaves and freedmen who are classed as freeborn. Some of these may possibly be traced in the recurrence of wives with unusual non-Imperial *nomina* in the same or successive reigns; e.g.

    VI 8811: Ti. Claudius Aug. lib. Ductus = Luria Paezusa.
    VI 18211: T. Fla(b)ius Aug. lib. Soterichus = Luria Faustina.
    VI 23398: Ti. Claudius Aug. lib. Primus = Ofillia Methe.
    VI 26955: Ser. Sulpicius Aug. liber. Erotillus = Ofillia Phlegusa.[1]

(*b*) *Mother has Imperial nomen without status indication, children are Caesaris servi:* e.g.

    VI 5189: **** = Iulia Acca, aged 48+Callisth(e)nes Ti. Caesar. Aug. a bybliothece Latina Apollinis, Diopithes a byblioth. Lat. Apoll.
    VI 18348: **** = Flavia Haline+Hermes...verna Caesaris nostri, aged 21.
    VI 37746: T. Fl(avius) Thesmus = Fl(avia) Eudosia+Hedistus Caes. n. ser. a vest. mund.
    VI 29266: M. Ulpius Successus = Ulpia Veneria+Modestus Caesar. n. ser. vern.
    VI 19405: Hermias = Aelia Victoria+Hermes Caesar. n. verna, aged 2.

In all these examples the mother must be an Imperial freedwoman but without status indication, as the children – in all cases sons here – are Imperial slaves. In two examples the father also is an Imperial freedman without indication, while in the last he is presumably an Imperial slave without indication. The fluidity in the use of the status indication is well illustrated by the first example where the mother, to whom the inscription is primarily dedicated, is an Imperial freedwoman without indication, and the brothers are both Imperial slaves employed in the *bybliotheca Latina Apollinis*, but one has the slave indication while the other does not. Cf. VI 9857: two brothers, Ti. Claudius Trophimus and Apolaustus Caesaris n. ser., where Trophimus must be an *Augusti libertus*.[2]

Similar to these is a group where the father is an Imperial slave, the mother has an Imperial *nomen* without status indication, and the children have a single name without indication; e.g.

    VI 8668: Successus Caesaris n. tabellarius, aged 40 = Cl(audia) Fortunata+Vitalio, aged 2.
    VI 11186: Epictetus Caes. n. vern., aged 45 = Aelia Aestiva+*Aestiva* aged 6, *Epictetiana* aged 5.

---

[1] Baebia: VI 18305–6, 29124. Coelia: 9035a, 8550 = D 1756. Larcia: 29224, *AE* 1908, 250. Lucceia: VI 29128, 10660. Statia: 13070, II 6085 = D 1560. Tettia: VI 8426 = D 1642, 15153. Vettia: X 1739, VI 8673, 28700, 9042.

[2] Other examples in this group are: VI 8424, 8831, 8889, 8993, 10166, 10839, 19015, 25722. Italy: *AE* 1919, 69. Carthage: VIII 13145.

Status of children

XI 2706: Securus Aug. disp. = Ulpia Terpsis+Hilarus.
XIII 5697: Lucrio Aug. n. disp. = Aelia Dati(va)+*Lucrio*.
Cf. VI 10898, 29645.

These are clear cases of mother and children without status indication. The mother is in each case a former Imperial slave manumitted before her husband – in the first two cases the husband died a slave at the age of 40 and 45 respectively; in the last two the husband's position as *dispensator* is sufficient to explain his late manumission. The children were all born while the mother was still of slave status.

In three further cases the mother is a Iulia of freed status but not belonging to the Familia Caesaris or at least not with the regular nomenclature:

VI 4776: Dardanus Ti. Caesaris Aug. et Augustae ser. Archelaianus = Iulia Bolae l. Glycera+Vitalis.
XIII 1820: Nobilis Tib. Caesaris Aug. ser. aeq(uator) monet(ae) = Iulia Adepta +Perpetua;
cf. 2177: **** = Iulia Adepta+L. Iulius Cupitus et Perpetua. (In this case Iulia Adepta is a freedwoman as her first child, Perpetua, is of slave status, but not an Imperial freedwoman as the *praenomen* of her second child, born after manumission, is non-Imperial.)
V 8386: **** = Iulia C. l. Iucunda+Firmus Imp. (This is unusual both in the slave indication 'Imp.' and in the status indication of the mother, if she is in fact an Imperial freedwoman. 'C(aesaris) l(iberta)' is scarcely feasible.)

(*c*) *Children freeborn with nomen omitted.* In some cases the simplest account of children with single name without indication is that they are not of slave status at all but freeborn with *nomen* omitted – an explanation always to be used with caution, but seemingly required in:

VI 9077: Viator Aug. n. vern. adiut. tabul. = Lucretia Hilara+Lucretia Alexandria et Purpurio et Viator et Lucretia Saturnina (where the two daughters have the *nomen* of the mother, but the two sons from some reason have not).
III 4065: Proculus Augg. nn. vern. vil. XX hered. utramq. Pann. = (Venuleia?) Valentina +Venuleius *Proculus*, aged 1. (Proculus the father, with a good position in the administration in Pannonia, is likely to have married an *ingenua*. The son derives his name from his father. Omission of the *nomen* of the mother is preferable to assuming adoption of their one-year son into another family.)[1]

[1] Cf. VI 8644, 8792, 17159, where omission of either *nomen* or status indication has to be postulated. A curious case arises in comparing VI 18398 and 8580 = D 1497:
(*a*) VI 18398: Fl(aviae) Phronime, Phoenix Caes. n. ser. coniugi et Fl. Cerialis et *Phronimus* et Celerina matri.
(*b*) VI 8580 = D 1497: T. Flavio Aug. lib. Ceriali tabul. reg. Picen., Phoenix Caes. n. ser. filio, P. Iunius *Frontinus* fratri, Celerina soror.
The same family is evidently involved in both inscriptions but the names differ in details. The earlier inscription is (*a*), which is dedicated to the mother Fl(avia) Phronime by her husband (Phoenix Caes. n. ser.) and their three children (Fl. Cerialis, Phronimus and Celerina). The later inscription (*b*) shows that one son is a freedman, now called T. Flavius Aug. lib. Cerialis, with the

The family circle

(*d*) *Nomen of children different from that of mother.* In another group where the father is an Imperial slave but the *nomen* of the children differs from that of the mother, second marriage of the mother or adoption must be invoked as the explanation. Step-children are usually explicitly indicated by 'privignus', 'filiaster', or 'filius *eius*' where 'eius' indicates that only one of the parents is the natural mother or father.[1] But where the word 'parentes' occurs, or both parents put up an inscription to a child, or where a lengthy marriage is implied, it is better to explain the different *nomen* of the child as due to adoption into another family rather than due to a previous marriage of the father or mother.[2] *Alumni* adopted *into* the family of Imperial freedmen take the *nomen* of their adoptive parents, usually of the adoptive father.[3]

Children born 'in contubernio', if of a freeborn or freed mother, would be *sui iuris* and capable of being legally adopted. Moreover, as illegitimate children could not simply be legitimised in the classical law by the subsequent marriage of the parents ('per subsequens matrimonium'), or 'per rescriptum principis', as in the law of Justinian,[4] adoption of an illegitimate child by his father was the only method of legitimisation open to the father. If the father died or remained a slave, or on manumission did not or could not through any cause adopt his illegitimate children, then adoption and legitimisation of children of Imperial slaves and *ingenuae* by the maternal grandparents or by someone else would no doubt often be an attractive prospect for both adopting and adopted. Adoption was common enough in other classes of Roman society so that it would be surprising if no trace of it could be found in the Familia Caesaris. A further possibility is that children sometimes took the *nomen* of one of their grandparents, particularly that of their maternal grandfather, when this differed from that of their mother for reasons other than adoption. This is attested in the senatorial class for Poppaea Sabina

post of *tabul(arius) reg(ionis) Picen(ensium)*, hence his use of full status indication. The daughter Celerina remains a slave, as does the father, Phoenix Caes. n. ser. But Phronimus, the second son, named after his mother, appears now as P. Iunius Frontinus. This cannot be an error of transmission. The stone is extant in Paris, and the name is spread over two whole lines (7–8): 'ET P IUNIUS/ FRONTINUS/...', whereas (*a*) survives in manuscript form. So despite the obvious naming of the slave son Phronimus after the slave-born mother Phronime, we must in this case suppose manumission for Phronimus followed both by adoption by a 'P. Iunius', and by a change of personal name from Phronimus to Frontinus; or sale as a slave and subsequent manumission by a 'P. Iunius'. This would be almost unique evidence for change of name in the Familia Caesaris after manumission. Wallon (*Esclavage*, III, 53 n. 2) took this as evidence for separation of slave families even within the Imperial Familia.

[1] VI 8627, 10925, 29154; cf. the Greek *IGR* IV 1477: τέκνοις αὐτῆς, also VI 8456, and 8495: 'Sabbio Caes. n. s. vilic. aquae Claudiae...sibi et Fabiae Verecundae coniugi...et libertis libertabusque *eius* et vicariis *suis*' for the contrast between the wife's freedmen (Sabbio being still a slave cannot have freedmen of his own) and Sabbio's own slave *vicarii*.
[2] On 'parens' see B. Rawson (Wilkinson) in *Class. Journ.* 59 (1964), 358–61.
[3] E.g. VI 8409, 18094, 29191, 29198, etc.
[4] Cf. Schulz, *Classical Roman Law* (Oxford, 1951), pp. 143 f.

Status of children

(Tacitus, *Ann.* xiii. 45) where the 'illustris memoria' of the grandfather is given as the reason, and for Faustina II, daughter of Antoninus Pius.[1]

The following examples come within this general group, whatever the precise explanation of the *nomen* of the children:

(i) WITH FATHER'S COGNOMEN

VI 8655 = D 1629: Iucundus vilic. d(omus) Tib(erianae) = Catia Sympherusa + P. Hellenius *Iucundus*, aged 2.

VI 11002: Urbicus Aug. = Mulvia Iucunda + Aelia *Urbica*, aged 18.

(ii) WITH MOTHER'S COGNOMEN

VI 8865: Epaphroditus Imp. Caes. Traiani ser. (H)ygianus arcarius a iuvencis = Ulpia Bassa, married 24 years + Sex. Atilius *Bassus* (unlikely to be a son of an earlier marriage although this is possible).

VI 18315: Felix Aug. = Aemilia Chrysauris + Flavia *Chrysophorus*.

XIII 1824: Felicianus Aug. n. verna ex dispensatorib. = Satria Lucilla + Sex. Terentius *Lucillus*, aged 13.

(iii) WITH COGNOMEN OF NEITHER PARENT

XIV 662: Gratus Caes. = Sulpicia Lasci(b)a + Aurelius Lucanus.

III 1995: Phrygius Augg. nn. ab instrumentis, aged 38 = Iulia Valeria, aged 30 + L. Aurel(ius) Castus, C. Iulius Honoratus. (Iulia Valeria is probably a second wife of Phrygius. Both she and his first wife, an Aurelia, would have been freeborn, as the sons can scarcely be of an age for manumission, given the age of the parents at death.)

VI 35188: Eutrapelus Caesaris ser. = Ammaea Synerusa; Statilia T(h)yche = C. Marcius Felix 'parentes *eius*'. (It is simplest to assume that Ammaea is the adoptive *nomen* of the wife of Eutrapelus, and that the parents mentioned here are *hers*, not his.)

(*e*) *Children who are Imperial slaves with status indication from mothers with non-Imperial nomina.* Lastly, we come to the most intractable group of inscriptions. The mothers, who have non-Imperial *nomina*, are thus mostly freeborn, and yet the children are Imperial slaves with slave indication. The fathers, where mentioned, are also Imperial slaves with indication. With these may be included cases where the brother or sister of an Imperial slave has a non-Imperial *nomen*:

(1) VI 25033: **** = Egnatia L. l. Antiochis + Princeps Caesaris ser. Anterotianus, Egnatia L. l. Protogenis, aged 33.

(2) VI 8885: **** = Amatia L. l. Calliste + Bathyllus Caesaris ser. qui proxime manum Caes. est.

(3) VI 8816: **** = Herria Verecunda + Doryphorus Caesaris a cyato, aged 20.

(4) VI 13328: **** = Aemilia Primitiva + Numida Aug. n. ser., Catulus, aged 26.

(5) VI 16823: **** = Flavia Cara + Deuter Caesaris verna, M. Flavius Eudaemon. (Flavia Cara will not be an Imperial freedwoman; cf. the non-Imperial *praenomen* of her son M. Flavius Eudaemon.)

(6) VI 22284: Ursulus Augg. ser. = Publicia Helpis + Maternus Caes. n. vern., aged 24.

(7) III 1470 = 7974: Valentinus qui et Potinianus Aug. n. vern. = Cassia Rogata + *Valentina* Aug. n. vern., aged 10.

[1] Cf. Thylander, *Étude*, pp. 92 f.; Chantraine, pp. 94 n. 136, 109.

The family circle

(8) IX 3640: **** = Pompeia Verecunda + Secunda Caesaris n. ser.
(9) X 7819: **** = Victoria Caesilla + (?) *Victorianus* [Caes. n.].
(10) VI 36507: Philetianus Augustorum (b)erna = (B)ehilia Horestina + *Philetus* Aug. n.
(11) *IGR* IV 1699: Φοῖβος = 'Ακυνέα Εὐ(τ)ελεῖα + 'Ατείμητος Κέσαρος (!) δοῦλος οἰκονόμος.
(12) VI 4636: Alexio Caesaris ser. – Philia Iulia.
(13) VI 8754: Photius Caesaris n. servus cocus Sestianus – Fabia Iulia.
(14) VI 16741 = XIV 2343: Daphnus Caes. – Iunia Veneria – H(i)aero.
(15) VI 23549: Optatus Aug. ser. – Pompeia Syntyche.

The mother in each case is freeborn or at least a freedwoman. Definitely *libertae* are only No. 1: Egnatia L. l. Antiochis, and No. 2: Amatia L. l. Calliste. In all these cases is there a connection between the status of the *father* and that of the children, and not between that of mother and children? This is legally impossible, although there are exceptional cases where illegitimate children have the *nomen* of their father and not of their mother.[1] A clear explanation is forthcoming in only one case, No. 1; Princeps Caesaris ser. Anterotianus has a sister Egnatia L. l. Protogenis, who died aged 33, and (a later addition to the inscription) a freedwoman Iulia Principis l. Amaryllis, who died aged 14. The mother of Princeps and Protogenis is a former slave, Antiochis, of one L. Egnatius. Both mother and elder child, Protogenis, were manumitted, but Princeps became the *vicarius* of an Anteros Caes. ser. (who was perhaps a *dispensator*) and subsequently replaced him or otherwise entered the emperor's service. After the inscription was originally erected Princeps was manumitted by Tiberius or Gaius and as Iulius Aug. l. Princeps Anterotianus then manumitted a slave of his own who died at the age of 14 as Iulia Principis (Aug. l.) l(iberta) Amaryllis.[2]

Princeps is the only slave with *agnomen* in this group and is probably the earliest. In No. 2, Bathyllus Caes. ser., 'qui proxime manum Caes(aris) est', whose mother was Amatia L. l. Calliste, may have been born the slave of a L. Amatius and later been sold or given to the emperor as a personal slave with special skills. In another case – *AE* 1945, 112: Successus verna Caesaris mulio, aged 36; brother Antigonus Domitiae Aug. ser. tabul(arius) – Successus, one of two slave brothers from the *familia* of Domitia Augusta, appears to have been transferred to the emperor's Familia and died as a *mulio* at the age of 36; his brother Antigonus remained as *tabularius* of Domitia. In the remaining cases where the mother (or sister or brother) has no status indication we are faced with difficulties or at best improbabilities, if we are to stick to this line of interpretation. We have to assume[3] that the mother is a freedwoman whose children were born before her manumission and the

---
[1] See Thylander, *Étude*, p. 89 n. 2.   [2] Cf. Chantraine, p. 300, No. 43.
[3] Boulvert (II, 779) argues in favour of this explanation.

Status of children

family then broken up so that a slave son (or daughter) passed into the Familia Caesaris by gift, legacy or sale. This is conceivable in No. 14 as Hiaero the brother could well be a slave, and in No. 4, where the brother Catulus also could be a slave, and in No. 13, where Photius Caesaris n. servus Sestianus would have been the former slave of a Sestius, although the sister is a Fabia Iulia.[1] In Nos. 8 and 15 the *nomen* 'Pompeia' would have to signify freedwomen of Pompeia Plotina without status indication, preferably before 105 when she became *Augusta*.

A similar, but in my view improbable, explanation could also apply to Nos. 3 and 5 (although Flavia Cara would not be an Imperial freedwoman), and No. 9, although the relationships here are doubtful.[2] But when we come to Nos. 6, 7 and 10 (cf. No. 11), an already improbable explanation (i.e. mother a freedwoman and family separated) becomes most improbable when the *father* as well as the child is stated to be an Imperial slave. One would have to assume in these cases not only that the wives are *libertae* without indication but also that the children of such marriages between Imperial slaves and *servae* outside the Familia were presented back to the emperor or that this was made a condition of allowing the union to take place. There are so many hypotheses and improbabilities here that the explanation should be sought elsewhere – in the provisions of the SC Claudianum.[3] The same problem arises in a much larger number of cases (discussed in the next section) where Imperial freedmen marry women with non-Imperial *nomina*, but the children somehow have the status of *Augusti liberti* or *Caesaris servi*, or have a single name without status indication, often named after one parent.

Thus a detailed consideration of the nomenclature of the children of Imperial slaves in general confirms the analysis of the status of wives, and in particular the slave status of persons with single name in these inscriptions. The number of examples where it is necessary to assume omission of the *nomen* is very small. Moreover, when considering separately the children from Rome and those outside Rome, a much smaller proportion of those with single name comes from Rome, and a much larger proportion of those with *nomen* also comes from Rome. But an anomaly occurs in the not insignificant number of wives with *nomina*, especially non-Imperial *nomina*, whose children are Imperial slaves. Even if it is assumed that these wives are not *ingenuae* but *libertae* (i.e. belong to the very small proportion of marriages of Imperial slaves with non-Imperial *libertae* or *servae*) the status of the children is not convincingly explained. On the other hand, there are many instances of children with non-Imperial *nomina* derived from their mother,

---

[1] Cf. Chantraine, pp. 334 f., No. 299.
[2] x 7819: '*Victoriae* Caesillae *Victorianus* [Caes. n.] f.' where 'f(iliae)' or 'f(ilius)' is possible.
[3] Cf. Weaver, *CQ* 15 (1965), 324 f.; Boulvert, II, 780 f.; and see below, chapter 9.

The family circle

representing Imperial slave marriages with non-Imperial *ingenuae*, especially in Rome. There is evidence for second marriage and for the practice of adopting children out of the Familia – but without any reliable criterion for distinguishing between the two.

CHILDREN OF AUGUSTI LIBERTI

The nomenclature of the children of Imperial freedmen should follow the same principles as those for children of Imperial slaves, with the additional factor that while children born before the manumission of the father will take their *nomen*, if any, from their mother, children born after the manumission of the father will take their *nomen* from their father Thus it should be possible in cases where the mother and father have different *nomina* to determine the proportion of children born after the manumission of the father. In general, the average age of marriage and manumission discussed above would lead us to expect that most children would be born *before* manumission of the father, i.e. in the first ten years or so of married life. But, as we have seen in chapter 6 above, the number of examples available for the age of husbands at marriage is too small to provide statistics comparable even with those for wives.

1. CHILDREN WITH NOMEN BUT WITHOUT STATUS INDICATION

As we found in the previous section, problems over the status of children and mother arise, ironically enough, mostly when the status of the children is positively indicated. Before considering these, therefore, there is advantage in disposing of those children with *nomen* but *without* status indication. They must be either freed or freeborn. Several possibilities arise depending on whether the child's *nomen* coincides with that of either or both parents.

(*a*) *Child's nomen same as that of both parents:* e.g.

VI 38489: C. Iulius Aug. l. Clonius = Iulia Nothis + Iulia Magna, aged 30.

VI 9003 = D 1796: Ti. Claudius Aug. lib. Zosimus = Claudia Entole + Claudia Eustachys.

VI 18254: T. Flavius Aug. lib. Chrysogonus = Flavia Primitiva + T. Flavius Urbicus, aged 4.

VI 8642: M. Ulpius Augusti lib. Graphicus = Ulpia Fortunata + M. Ulpius Felix, aged 4.

VI 10849: P. Aelius Aug. lib. Inachus = Aelia Maximilla + Aelia Artemidora, aged 2.

There are many examples of this type. When it cannot be determined whether the child follows the *nomen* of the father or the mother, it does not follow in all cases that the mother is *necessarily* an Imperial freedwoman without indication. This is probable in only a majority of cases. Additional data often point to the probability of the mother being freeborn. Thus the

Status of children

age-at-death figures in the last three examples given above are too low for the children to have been born when the mother was still a slave, unless one accepts massive disregard of the lex Aelia Sentia on the minimum age for manumission. The ages are also somewhat too low for legitimisation by the father after his manumission; children in that category might be expected to be older, say in their teens. Instead of insisting that the children above, who appear to be only children, were born after the mother's manumission, it is simplest to assume that the mother was freeborn in the first place, as many wives with Imperial *nomina* were in any case.

(*b*) *Child's nomen same as father's but different from mother's:* e.g.

(1) VI 14913: Ti. Claudius Aug. lib. Alexsander = Pinnia Septima + Claudia Successa, Claudia Olympias.

(2) VI 1859/60: Ti. Claudius Aug. lib. Secundus Philippianus = Flavia Irene + Ti. Claudius *Secundinus*, Claudia *Secundina*.

(3) VI 17992: T. Flavius Aug. l. Alexander = Iulia Coetonis + T. Flavius Epagathus.

(4) VI 18305/6: T. Flavius Aug. lib. Clymenus = Baebia Ianuaria + Flavia Cara qu(a)e et *Ianuaria*, aged 13.

(5) VI 15592/5 = D 8063a-c: M. Ulpius Aug. lib. Crotonensis = Claudia Semne + M. Ulpius (M. fil. Pal.) *Crotonensis*, aged 18.

(6) VI 29244: M. Ulpius Aug. lib. Nec[tareus] = Voconia C. f. Nymph[...] + M. Ulpius M. f. *Necta[reus]*, aged 4 months.

(7) VI 10935: P. Aelius Aug. lib. Romanus = Feridia Marciana + Aelia *Marcia*, aged 16.

(8) XIV 3637: T. Aelius Aug. lib. Ampliatus = Flavia Aphrodisia + Aelia T. f. Perpetua, aged 3.

In cases of this kind we must assume the legitimacy of the children (and thus their freeborn status) either because of their birth or legitimisation *after* the manumission of their father (where the mother was freeborn or freed at the time of their birth). Legitimisation is specifically indicated by the use of filiation, sometimes accompanied by tribal indication, as in Nos. 5, 6 and 8 above.[1] The low ages of the children in Nos. 6 and 8 suggest legitimate birth rather than legitimisation.

An extension of this category is where the father's *nomen* is not given, but the *nomina* of mother and children are different; e.g.

(9) VI 15131: Atimetus Aug. l. = Iulia Cypare + Ti. Claudius Ti. f. Pal. *Iulianus*, aged 19.

(10) VI 8451: Epaphra Aug. l. Atticianus = Herennia Secunda + Ti. Claudius Ti. f. Priscus, Ti. Claudius Ti. f. *Secundus*, aged 7, Ti. Claudius Ti. f. Priscianus, aged 3, Herennia A. f. Nome.

(11) VI 29234: Onesimus Aug. lib. = Iulia Marcellina + Ulpius *Marcellinus*, aged 4.

(12) VI 8608: Bassus Aug. lib. = Fabia Q. f. Priscilla + Claudius Comon.

Can we deduce the *nomen* of the father from that of the children in these cases? Here we must be careful, particularly if the assumed *nomen* of the

---

[1] Cf. Boulvert, II, 755 f.

The family circle

father is then to be used for dating purposes in other contexts. In the examples above there is a gradation of certainty. The legitimate birth of the children in Nos. 9 and 10 argues strongly for the father's *nomen* being 'Claudius' in both cases. In No. 11 the father is probably but not certainly M. Ulpius Aug. lib. Onesimus, because the age of the child argues for its free birth, and the *cognomen* Marcellinus makes it clear that it was born to Iulia Marcellina. We either assume a previous marriage of Marcellina or, more likely, that Onesimus is the legitimate father. In No. 12 the case is somewhat different. There is no filiation or derivation of *cognomen* from either mother or father. There is also the evidence from the occupational title of the father – *proximus ab epistulis Graecis, procurator tractus Carthaginiensis* – which (as suggested in Part III below) argues for a later date than that of a 'Claudius Aug. lib.' In such cases we need some extra evidence from personal nomenclature to outweigh that of the occupational nomenclature. This would be provided by similarity between *cognomina* of father and son, as was common (cf. Nos. 2, 5, and 6), or between mother and son (Nos. 4, 7, 9 (?), 10 and 11), or by filiation.[1]

(c) *Child's nomen same as mother's but different from father's:* e.g.

(1) VI 16663: Ti. Iulius Aug. l. Glycon = Curtia C. l. Prapis + P. Curtius Sp. f. Col. Maximus.

(2) VI 8506/7: Ti. Claudius Aug. l. Primigenius = Iulia Prima + Iulia Septimina, aged 22, Iul(ia) Palatina, C. Iulius Felix.

(3) VI 14945: Ti. Claudius Aug. l. Ater = Trebonia Oeanthe + L. Trebonius Fundandus.

(4) III 2483: T. Flavius Aug. l. Suavis = Pontien(a) Cale + Q. Pontienus *Suavis*, aged 15.

(5) VI 23716: M. Ulpius Aug. lib. Argaeus = Pacuvia Sperata + Pacuvia Hygia et Proculus.

(6) VI 8648: P. Aelius Aug. lib. Orestes = Licinia Primilla + Licinius Processus, aged 5. Cf. VI 8451, 18122.[2]

In these cases the child's status is either freed or freeborn, depending on whether the mother was a slave or not at the time of the child's birth. In No. 1 the child is freeborn, though illegitimate, from a freedwoman mother. Freed status is more likely where the *nomina* of mother and child are Imperial (as in No. 2) rather than non-Imperial. But the Imperial *nomen* in that case must not be out of step with that of the husband by more than one Imperial dynasty. In a number of cases the mother's *nomen* is not given but can be inferred from that of the child which differs from that of the father, especially when the *cognomina* of child and father are connected; e.g.

VI 15041: Ti. Claudius Aug. l. Eulalus = **** + C. Asinius *Eulalus*, aged 19.

But as with the *nomina* of fathers in the same circumstances, caution is required in deducing the *nomen* of a mother from that of a child as there are a

---

[1] Cf. Chantraine, p. 116.   [2] Cf. Boulvert, II, 767 f.

Status of children

number of instances where the child's *nomen* differs from that of both parents, even when these differ from one another; e.g.

VI 10648: T. Aelius Aug. lib. Astius = Flavia Deutera + Claudia Voluptas.
Cf. XI 3612 = D 1567: Ti. Claudius Aug. lib. Bucolas = Sulpicia Cantabra + Q. Claudius Flavianus.
VI 8077: L. Fl(avius) Miccalus = Fabia Zone + M. Aur(elius) Aug. lib. *Miccalus*.

However, as the mother's *nomen* rarely has any chronological significance, we need not pursue this in further detail.

(*d*) *Children with different nomina in same family:* lastly, there are a number of cases of children from the same family with *nomina* different from each other and, in some instances, different from one or other parent; e.g.

(1) VI 9041: P. Aelius Aug. lib. Telesphor(us) = Naevia Tyche + P. Aelius *Telesphorus*, Naevius *Telesphorus*, Naevius Successus (filiaster).
(2) XIV 508 = *IPO* A 1: T. Aelius Aug. lib. Demetrius = Claudia Marina + T. Aelius *Demetrius*, aged 4, C. Cornelius *Marinus*.
(3) VI 18122 a–b: T. Flavius Aug. lib. Lucrio = Vitellia Grata, aged 35 + Ti. Claudius Flavianus, T. Flavius Augustianus, Vitellia Vitalis.
(4) VI 10089 = D 1766: Ti. Cl(audius) Aug. lib. Philetus = Flavia Procula + Claudia Faustina, aged 16, Flavius Daphnus, Cl(audius) Martialis.
Cf. VI 8451, 38366 = XI 3835, etc.

In cases where the names are the same as those of the mother and father, the mother's name is taken by children born *before* manumission of the father, and the father's name is taken *after* his manumission, either by birth or by legitimisation. Where a third *nomen* appears, it can be derived from a previous husband/wife (the children are thus step-children of one or other parent), or if Imperial *nomina* are involved, the child can be of slave birth, manumitted by a later emperor than either husband or wife. Thus in No. 1 above Naevius Successus is specifically named as step-son (to P. Aelius Aug. lib. Telesphorus), Naevius Telesphorus is the son of Naevia Tyche and Telesphorus before the latter's manumission, and P. Aelius Telesphorus was born last, presumably after his father's manumission. (If he was legitimised, why was not his elder brother similarly treated?)

In No. 2 Demetrius, who died aged 4 years, would be a legitimate son of T. Aelius Aug. lib. Demetrius; C. Cornelius Marinus would be son of Claudia Marina and a previous husband, a 'C. Cornelius'. Similarly, in No. 3 Vitellia Vitalis will be the illegitimate daughter of Flavius Lucrio and Vitellia Grata, and T. Flavius Augustianus their legitimate son born later. The remaining child, whose name Flavianus is connected with his father's rather than his mother's name, would have been born earlier to a 'Claudia', first wife of Flavius Lucrio. In all these cases the mother is very probably freeborn.

The family circle

In No. 4 Flavia Procula with Imperial *nomen* subsequent to that of her husband would more probably be a freedwoman of the emperor. Claudia Faustina because of her age is not so likely to have been of slave birth and would have been born last after the manumission of both parents; the remaining two children, on the other hand, could be Imperial freedmen without status indication, the eldest, Claudius Martialis, freed before his mother, the other, Flavius Daphnus, after his mother. But this is difficult. Procula the wife could easily be freeborn and Martialis and Faustina both legitimate.

The question remains – what proportion of children were born after the manumission of the father? Some data on this can be obtained when the children take their *nomen* from their father and not their mother, when father and mother have different *nomina*. The following table summarises the position from all the available marriages from this category in the Familia Caesaris:

TABLE VI

Names of children whose parents have differing nomina

Children with ...	Father's nomen	Mother's nomen	Other nomen	Aug. lib./ Caes. ser.	Single name	Total
Wife with Imperial *nomen* different from husband's	28	14	6	12	6	66
Wife with non-Imperial *nomen*	32	19	5	9	6	71
Total	60	33	11	21	12	137

Only children with the father's *nomen* can have been born after his manumission. These figures, although not large, do show that 28/66 (or 42%) of children born to Imperial freedmen and a wife with a different *Imperial nomen* take the father's *nomen*, and 32/71 or 45% of children born to Imperial freedmen and a wife with a *non-Imperial nomen*. That about two children out of five should be born after the father's manumission seems too high a proportion, particularly as this includes many only children. Legitimisation, involving the possibility of a change of *nomen* on the part of the children after the father's manumission, cannot be excluded. In fact, this seems the likely explanation. No change of status would be involved. The children born 'in contubernio' to a slave father and a mother who was freeborn were often legitimised through adoption by their father following his manumission.

It is also clear from the foregoing discussion on the nomenclature of children how unreliable a criterion the *nomen* of a child is for inferring the

Status of children

nomen of the father, particularly when the father is an *Augusti libertus*, and even for inferring the *nomen* of the mother. In most of the marriages of Imperial freedmen with freeborn women the *nomen* of the wife differs from that of the husband. In these cases the *nomen* of the children born before manumission of the father would be different from that of the father. If two children in three were born before the manumission of the father, we might expect (other things being the same) about two-thirds of the children born to freeborn women to follow the *nomen* of the mother, or at least not to follow that of the father, i.e. about 40-45% of all children born in the Familia Caesaris. But in the group above, where the *nomina* of father and mother can be clearly distinguished, we find the reverse of what we might expect, i.e. 60/137 (44%) of children taking the *nomen* of the father, and only 33/137 (24%) taking that of the mother, while another 8% (11/137) take neither. This points to the existence of important disturbing factors, especially legitimisation by the father, adoption, second marriage, and even change of status. Before proceeding further with this question we must consider the evidence for the children of Imperial freedmen who have been, or are still, of slave status.

2. CHILDREN OF FREED OR SLAVE STATUS

These fall into three groups: (i) those with Imperial *slave indication*, i.e. 'Caes. ser.', 'Aug.', etc.; (ii) those with *single name* without indication; and (iii) those with Imperial *freed indication*. The status of the father is irrelevant to the status of the children as they are all slaves or have been slaves. They have been born 'in contubernio' and must follow the *mother's* status. The mother, in all cases in each of these groups, we would expect to be of freed or slave status.

The following are some examples:

Group (i)

(1) VI 8546 = D 1763: M. Cocceius Aug. lib. Ambrosius praepositus vestis albae triumphalis, married 45 years = Cocceia Nice + Rufinus Caes. n. vern. adiutor tabul.

(2) VI 8476 = D 1544: P. Aelius Aug. lib. Donatus = Aelia Caenis + *Donatus* Augustorum, aged 29, tabul. ration. fisci frumenti.

(3) VI 8542: M. Ulpius Aug. lib. Crescens ab vehiculis = Flavia Aug. lib. Salvia + Satyrus, aged 19, Crescens, aged 13, vernae Aug.

(Cf. 16811: Felix Aug. ver. = Pacata Aug. lib. + Demetrius Aug. ver. aged 3.)

(4) VI 22937: Secundinus Aug. lib. = Iulia (H)ieratice + Nicanor Caes. n. ser.

These present no difficulty: the mother is either an Imperial freedwoman with indication or has an Imperial *nomen* that matches chronologically with that of her husband. The ages of these children are all under 30. In No. 1

The family circle

both father and son have official posts, the father in charge of a section of the domestic service, the son a junior in the clerical service – which represents a probable upward mobility in career opportunities between the two generations. In No. 2 Donatus Augustorum died aged 29, presumably between 161 and 169, having reached the intermediate clerical level before manumission. His father was freed under Hadrian; if Donatus died *c.* 161, his birth can be placed at *c.* 132, and thus can be before his father's manumission.

Group (ii)

(5) VI 19870: Ti. Iulius Aug. l. Augustianus = Iulia Hieria + Dynamis.

(6) VI 8981: P. Aelius Aug. lib. Epaphroditus = Nicopolis Caesaris. n. + Soter.

(7) *AE* 1937, 111: P. Aelius Aug. li[b]. Fortunatus = Kyri[l]la + Paulina, aged 10 months.

(8) VI 10728: T. Aelius Aug. lib. Longus = Aurelia Martha + Aelia Antigona, *Longinus* (daughter freed before mother?).

(9) VI 8745: Aur(elius) Germanicus Augg. libertus = Marcia + Ingenua, Mercurius = Musica (coniunx eius).

(10) VI 11373: Alcibiades Aug. lib., married 15 years = Iucunda + *Alcibiades*, aged 20.

(11) VI 8445 = D 1553: M. Aur(elius) Aug. lib. Alexander = Claudia Macaria + Donatus.

Cf. 18325: Idaeus Caesaris n. ser. = Flavia Aug. l. Doris + Epaphroditus.

These examples are spread from the early first to the early third century. In all cases except No. 11 the slave status of the children is confirmed by the name of the mother who is or can be of freed or slave status herself (freed or slave indication: No. 6; Imperial *nomen* matching husband's: Nos. 5 and 8; single (slave) name: Nos. 7, 9 and 10). But in No. 11 the *nomen* of the wife (Claudia) does not match that of the husband (Aurelius); hence a problem, unless we make the (unlikely) assumption that she is simply an ex-slave of a master outside the Imperial Familia, as the son Donatus would appear to be of slave status.[1]

Group (iii)

(12) VI 15648: Ti. Cl(audius) Aug. l. Euhelpistus = Claudia Victoria + Ti. Cl(audius) Aug. lib. Petronius.

(13) VI 8438: T. Flavius Aug. lib. Chrysogonus Lesbianus, married 45 years = Flavia Nice + T. Flavius Aug. lib. Urbanus.

(14) X 1311: Ti. Claudius Pri[mige]nius = Flavia Aug. l. Carinia + Lasciva Aug. lib., aged 25, T. Flavius Aug. l[....].

(15) VI 8732 = D 1811: Gamus Aug. l. praepositus auri escari = Flavia Tyche + P. Aelius Aug. l. Constans.

(16) VI 8931: M. Aurelius Afrodisius Aug. lib. nomenclator = Aurelia Hedones + M. Aurelius Reginus Aug. lib., nomenclat. ab ammissione, aged 24.

---

[1] No. 8 shows a son, Longinus, who is still a slave and derives his *cognomen* from his father, and a daughter, Aelia Antigona, who has either been manumitted before her mother Aurelia Martha, or legitimised by the father after his manumission. Either alternative presents some difficulty but is not impossible.

Status of children

These children with Imperial freed indication have *nomina* that match with both those of mother and father where these have them. There is no difficulty in No. 15 where the mother would have been freed under the Flavians and the son not till Hadrian, at least about twenty years later. This would have been quite normal. In No. 16 there is another example of father and son as officials, this time both *nomenclatores*; the son is *nomenclator ab a(d)missione* and freed at the age of 24.

If we take all the children in the Familia who are of slave or freed status – i.e. born before the manumission of either or both parents – the same pattern should be observable whether the father or children are freed or slave, as manumission of neither will make any difference to the original facts of marriage or birth. This is best seen if arranged according to the forms of the *mother's* name: (1) single name (mother a slave); (2) Imperial *nomen*; (3) non-Imperial *nomen* (Table VII).

TABLE VII
Status of children according to name of mother

Father's status ...	Aug. lib.		Caes. ser.
	A	B	C
Children's status ...	Aug. lib.	Caes. ser./ser.	Caes. ser./ser.
Mother's name	(%)	(%)	(%)
Single name	14 (8)	18 (13)	50 (31)
Imperial *nomen*	63 (38)	60 (45)	35 (22)
Non-Imperial *nomen*	20 (12)	17 (13)	15 (9)
Incertae	3 (2)	5 (3)	— (—)
Total	100 (60)	100 (74)	100 (62)

This table shows that of Imperial freedmen's children who are still slaves (Column B) 58/74 (78%) have mothers with single name or Imperial *nomen*. In these cases there is no difficulty in assuming that the mother was a *Caesaris serva* at the time the children were born. For the children who are stated to be Imperial freedmen (Column A) the same points emerge, with a slightly higher proportion of mothers having Imperial *nomina* – 38/60, and slightly less with single name – 8/60. As the children have been manumitted, it is natural to expect a somewhat higher proportion of mothers to have been manumitted – in fact the difference in the figures (63% as compared with 60% for mothers of slave children) is rather small, as mothers would normally be manumitted well before their children. However, the total proportion of mothers of Imperial slave origin is practically the same for both groups of

The family circle

children: 77% for children who are *Aug. liberti* (Column A), 78% for children who are slaves (Column B). The two groups merely represent the same set of facts at different ages of the children.

For comparison are included the figures – from Rome only – for mothers of slave children whose fathers are *Caesaris servi* (discussed above). If the assumption made above that the slaves from Rome, due to their very high expectation of manumission, represent fairly closely the *Augusti liberti* in general at an earlier stage in their career, the proportions for the two groups should be similar. They show, as is natural, a much higher proportion of mothers who are still slaves: 50% (as against 18% and 14% in Columns B and A), and a much lower proportion of mothers who have Imperial *nomina*. But this is merely a reflection of the younger age of the wives corresponding to the younger age of the husbands who are still slaves. The total proportion of mothers of Imperial slave origin is, however, not much different: 85% compared with 77% and 78%. So far there is no problem.

A problem does arise, however, with the group of mothers with non-Imperial *nomina*. How can *their* children have been, or become, Imperial slaves? These wives total 20%, 17% and 15% respectively (Columns A, B and C) of all mothers in each of the groups above. As we have seen, a single name indicates a slave and only in exceptional circumstances where the context of the inscription makes the status clear can it be assumed that a *nomen* is omitted by a child who is freeborn or a freedman. The majority of the children of mothers in this group (Table VII, Group 3: non-Imperial *nomina*) in any case have the status indication 'Aug. lib.' or 'Caes. ser.' The list for children of freedmen is as follows (for children of Imperial slaves see the previous section, pp. 145 f.):

Group (i): Children are Imperial slaves

(1) VI 38351: M. Ulpius Aug. lib. Pacatus = Caelia Venusina + Felix Caes. n. ser. vern., aged 14.

(2) VI 8518: T. Aelius Aug. lib. Aelianus = Folia Chresime, married 20 years +*Chresimus* Aug. lib. adiut. offici commentar. kastr., Aphrodisius Caes. n. vern. adiut. offici tabulari kastr.

(3) VI 9042: T. Aelius Theon Aug. lib. = Vetia Verylla + *Theon* verna Aug. nostr., aged 5.

(4) VI 18824: Vesbinus Aug. l[ib.] = Furnia Lucifera + Exsochus Aug[...].

(5) *AE* 1959, 303: Herculanus Aug. lib. adiut. tab. = C. (?) Turpilia + Caed.(?) Caes. n. v[...].

Group (ii): Children have single name

(6) VI 6189: Ti. Claudius Aug. l. Phoebus = Plotia Venusta + Nice, aged 7, *Phoebe*.

(7) VI 10518: T. Flavius Aug. l. Epaphroditus = Acilia Eleutheris + *Epaphroditus*, Tuccia Athenais, Acilia Prepontis.

Status of children

(8) VI 10712 = XIV 4019: [P.] Aelius Aug. lib. Fronto = [Gr]ania Dia + Feliciss[ima et Act]e.
(9) VI 13226: M. Aurelius Augg. lib. Secundus = Caelia Marcellina + *Secundus*, aged 9.
(10) X 2799: Marcellus Aug. lib. = Octavia Dia, married 27 years + Uxulamus.
(11) X 2810: Amandus Aug. l. = Oppia T. fil. Bassilla + *Bassus*.
(12) XI 466: Felicissimus Aug. lib. = Furfulana Irene + *Irene*, aged 10.
(13) XI 3553: Symphorus Aug. lib. = Antistia Tecusa, aged 40 + *Symphorus*.

Group (iii): Children are Imperial freedmen

(14) VI 28699: **** = Vettia Helpis + Ti. Claudius Aug. l. Amianthus.
(15) XIV 2690: **** = Mamilia Albana + Claudia Primigenia lib. Aug.
(16) XIV 3393: **** = Acilia Eut[y]chia + M. Ulpius Aug. lib. (H)esych[us], Acilia Vic[tor]ia.
(17) VI 4228: P. Aelius Aug. lib. Menophilus = Caminia Fortunata + M. Ulpius Aug. lib. *Menophilus* proc. ab ornamentis, aged 35.
(18) VI 10666: P. Aelius Aug. lib. Cladus = Lucilla Chrysopolis + P. Aelius Aug. lib. Mariensis, aged 20.
(19) VI 10682: P. Aelius Aug. lib. Erasinus = Aemilia Helene + P. P. Aelii Aug. lib. Musicus et *Helenus*.
(20) VI 8634 = D 1697: **** = Antonia Rhodine + Ti. Claudius Aug. lib. Avitus im(b)itator, T. Aelius Aug. lib. Theodotus adiutor a cognit., Scetasia Octavia.
(21) VI 13084: **** = Valeria Capitolina, aged 60 + Aur(elius) Augg. lib. Epictetus.
(22) VI 13151: M.¦ Aur(elius) Aug. lib. Eutyches = Valeria Eutychia + M. Aurelius Aug. lib. Marcianus, aged 4.
(23) VI 19710: **** = [Vale]ria Irene + [A]urel(ia) Aug. lib. Hi[...].
(24) VI 8796: **** = Pomponia Victorina + M. Aurelius Successus Aug. lib. a cura amicor. q. q.
(25) VI 27749: **** = Tullia Apollonia + Faustinus Aug. lib.
(26) XIV 4062 = D 1673: **** = Valeria Philocene + Arte[mi]dorus Aug. lib. adlectus a memoria, aged 17.

As a child who is a *servus* or a *libertus* cannot be born of a mother who is freeborn, are we to suppose that these mothers are freedwomen of non-Imperial patrons? The proportion of marriages of this type in the Familia

TABLE VIII
Status of children: brothers and sisters

Brother/sister	Aug. lib. (%)	Caes. ser. (%)	Total (%)
Single name	39 (37)	72 (39)	88 (76)
Imperial *nomen*	48 (45)	17 (9)	(54)
Non-Imperial *nomen*	13 (12)	11 (6)	12 (18)
Total	100 (94)	100 (54)	100 (148)

The family circle

Caesaris has been estimated above at not more than 7% of all marriages. However, the children would be either freeborn if born after the manumission of the mother, or slaves of the non-Imperial master if born before the manumission of the mother. But in *neither* case slaves of the emperor.

The same situation arises from the figures for the names of brothers and sisters of Imperial freedmen and slaves (see Table VIII, p. 157).

Between 87% and 89% of brothers and sisters of Imperial freedmen and slaves are or can be of Imperial slave origin themselves (i.e. have single name or Imperial *nomen*, with or without indication). But 13% of brothers/sisters of *Augusti liberti*, and 11% of brothers/sisters of *Caesaris servi* have non-Imperial *nomina*. The examples not already included above are:

(27) VI 10449 = D 7909: Iulia Ti. Caesar. Aug. l. Iconio – A. Turranius Synethus.

(28) VI 8580 = D 1497: T. Flavius Aug. lib. Cerialis tabul. reg. Picen. – P. Iunius Frontinus – Celerina.

(29) VI 22044: M. Ulpius Aug. lib. Harmonianus – A. Marcius Alexander A. fil., aged 18.

(30) VI 12348: M. Ulpius Aug. lib. Philetus Arminianus – C. Arminius Hermes.

(31) VI 2997: Aelius Aug. lib. Argantho – Athenaeus Firmus.

(32) *AE* 1937, 159: M. Aurelius Aug. lib. Hermes archimagirus – Aurelius Ianuarius – Cn. Octavius Martialis.

(33) VI 4049: Epaphroditus Aug. l. – P. Caetennius Heraclides.

(34) VI 16658: Photius Caesar. Aug. l. Cornificianus – T. Magius T. l. Hilario.

(35) VI 17301: Euaristus Augg. lib. – [....] Augg. lib. – Plautius Ianuarius.

(36) VI 24108: Crescens Aug. lib. – [...]nia Philetenis.

In the cases of brothers/sisters of different *nomina* when the mother is not known, it is possible to conjecture adoption or different parents, i.e. stepbrother/step-sister, or even separation of slave families, unlikely as this would appear to be for the Familia Caesaris, at least from the middle of the first century.[1] The clearest case of transference between families is No. 30 – Philetus, a slave of a C. Arminius, was transferred to the emperor and manumitted as M. Ulpius Aug. lib. Philetus Arminianus; his brother, C. Arminius Hermes remained to be manumitted by C. Arminius. Another case (not included in the list), this time of *two* brothers both transferred from a non-Imperial *familia* to the Familia Caesaris, is XIV 1386 where the parents are L. Nae(b)ius Chrysogonus and Clodia Victoria, while the sons are M. Aurelius Augg. lib. Vitalio and M. Aurelius Augg. lib. Peculiaris. The mother may be of slave origin; this is suggested by another inscription, XIV 331, where the father of a Clodia Victoria, who died aged 19, is Clodius Lucrio

[1] For the interesting case of the children of Phoenix Caes. n. ser. (VI 18398 and 8580 = D 1497) see above, p. 143 n. 1.

Status of children

sevir Aug(ustalis) and thus most probably himself a freedman. Cf. VI 14452. Adoption or an earlier marriage is indicated in VI 15406: M. Ulpius Aug. lib. Nicanor = Cl(audia) Euphrosine + L. Baebius Onesiphorus, where the son dedicates the inscription 'matri'.

The only *Aug. liberta* in this group of brothers/sisters is in No. 27: Iulia Ti. Caesar. Aug. l. Iconio, whose brother is A. Turranius Synethus. *Libert*ae of Augustus show a further peculiarity in two further cases (not listed above) in using 'C. l.' as their status indication: X 3357 = D 2817: C. Iulius Caesaris l. Automatus whose sister is Iulia C. l. Plusia; and VI 35612: C. Iulius Divi Aug. l. Halys whose sister is Iulia C. l. Tryphera. The abbreviation 'C. l.' is not likely to stand for 'C(aesaris) l(iberta)'. In the early first century there are in fact several cases of brother and sister having patrons from different branches of the Imperial family; e.g. VI 4053: Altes Liviae lib. - sister Livia Eleutheris - brother C. Iulius Augusti l. Thoas; 9047 = D 1810: Ti. Claudius Augustorum l. Domnio - sister Antonia Asia; 14897: Ti. Claudius Aug. l. Abascantus - *colliberta* Antonia Stratonice. In all these five cases it is the brother who has the regular status indication of the Familia Caesaris, but not the sister. This reveals what was a likely source of recruitment for the Familia during its early period of expansion, namely *servi* who were no doubt qualified for particular positions because of special skills or training and then transferred from the *familiae* of other members of the Imperial family, e.g. Livia, Antonia.

In the inscriptions discussed above there is an irreducible minimum of about twenty cases, and perhaps a dozen more, where the status, and especially the use of the slave and freedman indication, is inexplicable according to any normal rules. Their status cannot be derived from the mother whether she is *ingenua* or *liberta* as her *nomen* is non-Imperial. Nor from the father as children born before his manumission would take their status from the mother and those born after his manumission could not be *servi* or *liberti*. It is possible to add further to the hard core of examples from the marriages of Imperial freedmen to women with *preceding* Imperial *nomina*, especially *nomina two preceding*:

(37) VI 15317: P. Aelius Aug. lib. Ianuarius = Claudia Successa, married 31 years + Ti. Claudius Vitalio, aged 11, Ti. Claudius Aug. l. Censorinus.

(38) *AE* 1923, 76: Aelius Aug. lib. Hermes = Claudia Methe, aged 45 + Chrysanthus, Claudia Eucharis.

(39) VI 15860 = D 8304: Aurelius Aug. lib. Agapetus = Ulpia Festa + Aurelius Aug. lib. Hermetianus.

(40) VI 8445 = D 1553: M. Aurelius Aug. lib. Alexander = Claudia Macaria + Donatus.

(41) VI 13200: M. Aurelius Aug. [lib.] Regulus = Flavia Aphrodisia + M. Aurelius Aug. [lib.] *Aphro*[*disius*] (?).

The family circle

Of the several examples where the wife has an immediately preceding *nomen* and thus could be of Imperial slave origin, one case is of interest:

(42) VI 38366 = XI 3835: T. Flavius Aug. lib. Demosthenes = Claudia Danae + Ti. Claudius Mucro, M. Ulpius Aug. l. Romanus.

Here probability as well as the absence of status indication would make Claudia Danae (clearly stated to be the mother of both sons) freeborn, and also Ti. Claudius Mucro, the first son. But how can the second son then be a freedman of Trajan?

It is to be noted that the cases under discussion range in time from the Iulii to the Aurelii, although the majority are from the second century. Of the children with status indication only one in over thirty cases is a woman (No. 27). She is also the only case from the Julian period when, as has been explained above, the nomenclature of *libertae* in the Familia Caesaris exhibits some peculiarities. Her status can be explained on the grounds that she was a gift to the emperor, as was common particularly in the early period of the Principate. Her brother was A. Turranius, a freedman without indication who was not given to the emperor. But from an otherwise undated inscription, VI 5873, it can be concluded that another slave of A. Turranius,[1] Amaranthus Augusti ministrator Turranianus, was transferred to the Familia Caesaris; as was often the case, the *agnomen* in *-ianus* was taken by the *servus* in conjunction with his occupational title (*ministrator*), but not by the female *serva* who was manumitted as Iulia Ti. Caesar. Aug. l. Iconio. Whenever both brothers and sisters are mentioned in these inscriptions, it is always the brother who carries the status indication of the Familia Caesaris and not the sister (Nos. 16, 28 and 36). Thus the irregular use of the status indication in these cases is to be connected not with any legal category nor is it due to any personal idiosyncrasy, but with the causes for which women in general in the Familia do not use status indication.[2] Young children with status indication are also infrequent in these inscriptions – only two under ten years (Nos. 3 and 22; the latter case, M. Aurelius Aug. lib. Marcianus, aged 4, shows an unusually early manumission age as well, if the age figure is to be relied on).

It is no solution to the problem of the nomenclature of the children in these inscriptions to suppose that the mothers in all these cases are *not ingenuae*. The same solution is unlikely for the children of Imperial slaves and freeborn women who call themselves *Caesaris servi* (discussed above, pp. 145 f.). The number of cases involved is too large for them all to be classed simply as

---

[1] Not to be identified with C. Turranius, *praefectus annonae* under Augustus; *PIR*¹, T 295 f. Cf. Chantraine, p. 339, No. 323.   [2] See chapter 10 below.

Status of children

irregularities. Their nomenclature errs not on the side of claiming higher status but lower legal status than that to which they are entitled. As children of *ingenuae* they should be legally *ingenui*. Further elucidation of the status of these children, and indeed of all children and wives in the Familia, requires an examination of the Senatusconsultum Claudianum and its application to the Familia Caesaris.

CHAPTER 9

THE SENATUSCONSULTUM CLAUDIANUM AND THE FAMILIA CAESARIS

The legal implications of a marriage pattern for Imperial slaves and freedmen where at least two-thirds of the wives were freeborn (*ingenuae*) must now be examined. There are two main questions; first, the legal status of the wives of Imperial slaves and freedmen who were *ingenuae*; and second, the status of the children who were the issue of such unions.

The general principle of the law regarding the status of children born to parents without *conubium* is clear – the status of the child follows that of the mother in accordance with the *ius gentium* (Gaius, i. 80: 'semper conubium efficit ut qui nascitur patris condicioni accedat; aliter vero contracto matrimonio eum qui nascitur iure gentium matris condicionem sequi'. Cf. ib. 82; Ulpian, *Reg.* v. 9). But according to Gaius (i. 84) the rule of the *ius gentium* was modified by the SC Claudianum of AD 52, whereby, *inter alia*, the child of an *ingenua* could be a *servus*. This would seem to account for the status of the wives in the Familia Caesaris who were *ingenuae* and the group of children discussed above, who were *Caesaris servi* or *Augusti liberti*. Hadrian, however, according to Gaius (loc. cit.) restored the rule of the *ius gentium*. As most of the children with whose status we are concerned are dated to the period *after* Hadrian, we must therefore look elsewhere for an explanation.

The SC Claudianum itself requires closer examination. The two main sources are Gaius, i. 84, and Tacitus, *Ann.* xii. 53.1.

The important passage of Gaius, i. 84, is as follows: 'Ecce enim ex senatusconsulto Claudiano poterat civis Romana, quae alieno servo volente domino eius coiit, ipsa ex pactione libera permanere, sed servum procreare; nam quod inter eam et dominum istius servi convenerit ex senatusconsulto ratum esse iubetur. sed postea divus Hadrianus, iniquitate rei et inelegantia iuris motus, restituit iuris gentium regulam, ut, cum ipsa mulier libera permaneat, liberum pariat.'

In this passage Gaius is giving an example of how the *ius gentium* in regard to the *status of children* was modified by statute. Cf. i. 83: 'animadvertere tamen debemus, ne iuris gentium regulam vel lex aliqua vel quod legis vicem optinet, aliquo casu commutaverit'. Hadrian restored this rule. (Cf. i. 85 for

The SC Claudianum and the Familia Caesaris

a second case where the *ius gentium* on the status of children was modified by statute – possibly the lex Aelia Sentia – whereby slave women could bear free children. The rule of the *ius gentium* was again restored, this time by Vespasian 'inelegantia iuris motus'.)[1] A question arises as to the content of the SC Claudianum in 52.[2] Was the *pactio* between the master of the *servus* and the 'mulier libera', by which she remained free but her child was born a *servus*, provided for in the original *senatusconsultum*? This was condemned by Hadrian on the grounds of 'iniquitas rei et inelegantia iuris', whereas the SC itself was moved in the senate by Claudius himself. Claudius' inelegancies in other fields are more readily conceded than an untidy compromise with the law, even if we know that it was Pallas' hand on the pen. But the words of Gaius 'nam quod inter eam et dominum istius servi convenerit *ex senatusconsulto ratum esse iubetur*' leave little room for doubt.

If the SC was designed as social legislation to discourage marriage between slave and freeborn, it seems singularly late and ill-conceived – especially if, as Crook points out,[3] it left out the cases of an *ingenua* marrying her own slave (or *libertus*), and if a nullifying *pactio* was incorporated in it from the start. But whatever its original purpose was, the SC instituted a penalty (*poena*) whereby a freeborn woman who cohabited with a slave belonging to another owner was reduced to the status of *ancilla* (*serva*) or *liberta*. The idea of '*poena*' is common to all the other legal and literary sources: Gaius, i. 91, 160; Ulpian, *Reg.* xi. 11; *Pauli Sent.* ii. 21.1; iv. 10.2; Tacitus, *Ann.* xii. 53.1; Suetonius, *Vesp.* 11; Tertullian, *ad ux.* ii. 8. Important and earliest among these is Tacitus, *Ann.* xii. 53.1, referring to the year 52: 'Inter quae refert ad patres de poena feminarum quae servis coniungerentur; statuiturque ut ignaro domino ad id prolapsae in servitute, sin consensisset, pro libertis haberentur.' The alternatives for women cohabiting with slaves were either enslavement or the status of *libertae*. No mention is made of the *pactio*. The women suffer a penalty by being reduced in status from being freeborn (*ingenuae*) to being freed (*libertae*), which also involved the loss or transfer of certain rights, e.g. over inheritance, to the patron. This need not differ from Gaius' 'libera permanere', which would mean *not* 'remain freeborn' *but* 'not become a slave along with the children, but be reduced to the status of *liberta*'. As Crook points out, 'libera' can mean either 'ingenua' or 'liberta', and is conveniently used by Gaius to cover both meanings. For the child, 'liberum pariat' can only mean that it is freeborn, so there would be no

---
[1] See J. A. Crook, *CR* 17 (1967), 7 f.
[2] On the SC Claudianum see: Mommsen, *Strafrecht*, pp. 854 f.; Buckland, *Roman Law of Slavery*, pp. 412 f.; Castello, *Studi Solazzi* (1955), 232 f., esp. 249 f.; Hoetink in *Mélanges Henri Lévy-Bruhl* (1959), pp. 153 f.; Weaver, *CR* 14 (1964), 137 f.; Crook, *CR* 17 (1967), 7 f.
[3] Crook, art. cit. p. 7.

The family circle

confusion. The notion of penalty for the mother is implied, but not for the child who must take his status from his mother in the usual way. Hadrian did not intend to abolish the SC as its continued operation afterwards shows. The idea of penalty for the woman always remains – so that the effect of Hadrian's change would have been to give masters of *servi* cohabiting with *ingenuae* the choice of either (*a*) gaining rights of ownership both over mother and child as his own slaves, or (*b*) gaining patronal rights over the mother only. His object was to eliminate discrimination against the children, not to eliminate the penalty against the mother. This is the essential point so economically expressed by Tacitus in the words beginning 'de poena feminarum...' and omitting any reference to the children. Gaius, on the other hand, is concerned primarily with the status of children, not of the mother, and so does not stress the notion of penalty.

About the same time as Hadrian's modification or slightly later, application of the *senatusconsultum* was softened in practice. The enslavement of the woman became hedged about with conditions – the master must forbid and the woman persist. Tacitus had mentioned enslavement if cohabitation had taken place without the master's knowledge ('ignaro domino'). Gaius (i. 91, 160) states that the woman can only be enslaved if the master forbids and warns her ('invito et denuntiante domino') and the woman persists. Later still, after Gaius, three *denuntiationes* were required and then enslavement was only by due process of law. The penalty of the *senatusconsultum* continued in operation until finally abolished by Justinian.

Several texts mention women enslaved, and at least one text mentions women made *libertae* under the SC Claudianum – *Pauli Sent.* iv. 10.2: 'ad filiam ancillam vel libertam ex senatusconsulto Claudiano effectam...'. This last text, though it could mean that a woman was reduced to slavery and then manumitted in due course, implies more probably that there were two levels at which the penalty on the woman could be enforced – one, enslavement, whereby the children also became slaves, and the other whereby she became a freedwoman of her partner's master but the children had freeborn status.

What then was the original and continuing purpose of the SC Claudianum? It has much more to do with property rights over wives and children of slaves than with preventing mixed marriages, which surely must have been irrelevant by the second century AD, if not long before. This purpose becomes clearer if we consider its application to the wives and children of the Familia Caesaris. This must have become an important issue if from the time of Claudius, as has been argued in chapter 7, at least two-thirds of the wives and their children came within the scope of its provisions. Moreover, the deviser of the *senatusconsultum*, according to Claudius, was Pallas, himself an

The SC Claudianum and the Familia Caesaris

Imperial freedman. His name is placed prominently and ironically by Tacitus at the beginning of the next sentence in *Ann.* xii. 53: 'Pallanti quem repertorem eius relationis ediderat Caesar...'. The motives and timing of Pallas require explanation. Whatever Pallas 'devised' in the field of status, and the rights of property involved in status, this was unlikely to be contrary to the best interests of the Imperial financial administration. Whether he was also incapable of acting against the best interests of the Imperial slave and freedman 'estate' from which he had so brilliantly emerged himself is more debateable.

Important here is the fact that the marriage and family pattern of the *Caesaris servi*, especially those from Rome, is in significant contrast with that of the slave and freedman classes outside the Familia. The results of an analysis of 700 slave and freedman marriages from Rome, outside the Familia, are given in chapter 11 below. These show that for *liberti* in this group a *maximum* of only 15% of wives can be *ingenuae*, and for wives of *servi* the figure is 5%. This can be taken to represent the normal slave and freedman marriage pattern. These marry to an overwhelming extent with partners of their own status and origin. By contrast, the upward mobility of the Imperial slaves in respect of the status of their wives is very marked, if not astonishing.

It is certain that *servi publici* frequently married *ingenuae*.[1] Nothing is known of the application of the SC Claudianum to *servi publici*. But the notion of 'poena' was applied in classical law to *ingenuae* cohabiting with *municipal* slaves; in fact *enslavement* was possible for such women *without denuntiatio*: *Pauli Sent.* ii. 21.14: 'mulier ingenua quae se sciens servo municipum iunxerit *etiam citra denuntiationem ancilla* efficitur; non item si nesciat. Nescisse autem videtur quae comperta condicione contubernio se abstinuit aut libertum putavit.' The position of *ingenuae* cohabiting with *Caesaris servi* was different in two respects, as we learn from *Cod. Theod.* iv. 12.3.

This passage reads: 'Cum ius vetus ingenuas fiscalium servorum contubernio coniunctas ad decoctionem natalium cogat, nulla vel ignorantiae venia tributa vel aetati, placet coniunctionum quidem talium vincula vitari; sin vero mulier ingenua vel ignara vel etiam volens cum servo fiscali convenerit, *nullum eam ingenui status damnum sustinere*, subolem vero, quae patre servo fiscali, matre nascetur ingenua, mediam tenere fortunam, ut servorum liberi et liberarum spurii Latini sint, qui, licet servitutis necessitate solvantur, patroni tamen privilegio tenebuntur.' (*Servi fiscales* are for practical purposes under the later Empire the same as *servi Caesaris* in the domestic services.) Thus under the previous rule ('ius vetus') *ingenuae* can become *libertae* and

---
[1] See Halkin, *Les esclaves publics*, pp. 117 f.

The family circle

not *servae*, but they must *necessarily* ('ius...cogat') *lose their freeborn status* ('ad decoctionem natalium'). And in their case neither age nor ignorance of the status of their partner made any difference. This earlier rule ('ius vetus') is assumed by Buckland[1] to go back to classical law and perhaps even to the first century, to the SC Claudianum itself. The element of *poena* is still present – freeborn women became *libertae*, and freedwomen, if their patrons consented to the union, became presumably *libertae Caesaris* (cf. *Pauli Sent.* ii. 21.6). The rights of patronage would in both cases pass to the emperor. Cf. *Cod. Theod.* x. 20.10 (AD 380). Not till AD 320 (*Cod. Theod.* iv. 12.3) was the new rule laid down that *ingenuae* cohabiting with *servi Caesaris* should retain their *freeborn* status ('nullum eam ingenui status damnum sustinere'), but even then the children were of Latin status and classed as *spurii* ('mediam tenere fortunam ut servorum liberi et liberarum spurii Latini sint'), with rights of patronage belonging to the emperor.

Another passage referring to *libertae Caesaris*, apparently in connection with the SC Claudianum, is *Frag. de iure fisci* 12: 'libertae Caesaris tam manumissione quam beneficio coniunctionis effectae...'. This distinguishes between two groups within the one legal category of *libertae Caesaris*, according to the manner in which that status had been acquired – one, *Caesaris servae*, from whatever source they came, who had been regularly manumitted (*manumissione*); the other, those *ingenuae* who became *libertae* under the SC Claudianum. That the status of these latter was viewed as a concession seems to be implied by the phrase 'beneficio coniunctionis', with which should be compared 'beneficio principali' used of the concession of early manumission (Ulpian, iii. 2; cf. *Frag. de iure fisci* 16: 'hoc principali beneficio'). Buckland[2] says that the rule that they were to be *libertae* is no doubt due to the superior dignity of fiscal slaves who frequently, if not usually, 'married' free women.

If a distinction was made in the SC Claudianum between *servi Caesaris* and other slaves to the advantage of the former, this would have been the first formal juridical recognition of their superior status. But there is some reason to doubt Buckland's assumption that the preferential treatment under the 'ius vetus' mentioned in the Theodosian Code goes back to the classical law of the first and second centuries at all. The evidence is the whole group of inscriptions discussed above, where the children of fathers who are Imperial slaves or freedmen and of mothers with non-Imperial *nomina* who are almost certainly freeborn are themselves Imperial slaves or freedmen, with status indication to prove it, i.e. *Caesaris servi* or *Augusti liberti*. As the mother is in most cases fairly certainly an *ingenua*, the children should have been freeborn

---

[1] *Roman Law of Slavery*, p. 417.   [2] Loc. cit.

The SC Claudianum and the Familia Caesaris

even if the mother had been reduced to the status of *liberta Caesaris* under the SC Claudianum or by modifications of it under the early Empire. The most probable, and perhaps the only way of accounting for the status of these children is to assume that the mother was an *ingenua* who suffered the full 'poena' of the SC Claudianum and had been reduced to the status of *Caesaris serva* for cohabiting with a slave of the emperor. The woman, however, does not appear to have changed her name or given any indication in her nomenclature of such a change in status.

The chronological development in the marriage pattern of the Familia Caesaris is important in this regard. The high proportion of *ingenuae* mentioned above is found with comparatively little variation from the Claudian period onwards at least till the end of the second century.[1] In the Julian period, however, the proportion of *ingenuae* among wives is, on average, much lower, in fact barely half the later figure. During the early first century in the first two or three generations of Imperial slaves under the Principate the normal slave marriage pattern of slave with slave, mostly within the same *familia*, represented the commonest type of marriage in the Familia Caesaris. By the date of the passing of the SC Claudianum in 52, midway through the Claudian period, this marriage pattern must have already altered substantially in the direction of increasing marriage with *ingenuae*. In view of the very low proportion of slave unions with *ingenuae* outside the Familia and the increasingly high proportion within the Imperial Familia, and the fact that, according to Tacitus, Pallas, the Imperial freedman *a rationibus*, was himself the instigator of the SC Claudianum, a close connection between the SC Claudianum and the Familia Caesaris is probable. In fact, even though it was officially presented as having a different object, one can go so far as to assert that one of its main purposes was to regulate the status of wives and children in the Familia.

This was necessary for two reasons. Firstly, the interest of the *fiscus* in the rights of inheritance accruing from the wives and children of Imperial slaves. If the wives were predominantly *ingenuae*, the *fiscus* would lose its interest in both the wives and the children who would be freeborn. The *fiscus* did not remain indifferent to its share in these rights of inheritance. The *Frag. de iure fisci* 12 lays it down that if a *liberta Caesaris* dies intestate everything goes to the *fiscus* ('totum fisco vindicatur'), but if she makes a valid will only half her estate is claimed. This appears to be exacting the full amount the patron could claim under the law of testamentary succession and makes no allowance for the normal exceptions which diminished the patron's share, for instance if there were more than three children or direct

[1] See above, pp. 124 f.

The family circle

descendants.[1] Nor is it fortuitous that when the law was changed in 320 (*Cod. Theod.* iv. 12.3) the mother retained her share as *ingenua* but the children became *Latini*, which meant that the whole of their estate went to the *fiscus* in practically all circumstances. Cf. the phrase also in *Frag. de iure fisci* 6: 'nisi cum in fraudem portionis Caesaris fiat'.

In the second place, the recruitment of the Familia Caesaris was ultimately involved. If more and more of the children of Imperial slaves were born as *ingenui* and not as *vernae*, where were the ablest recruits for the administrative élite to come from? At the same time as these freeborn wives steadily increase in number, recruitment into the various services of the administration from the end of the first century, and certainly from the time of Hadrian, was increasingly from within the Familia. Not exclusively, but predominantly, as is indicated by the arrival of the term 'verna' in large numbers as a status symbol in the indication of Imperial slaves in the period of the early second century.[2] Son tended to follow father into the domestic or administrative service, which became more and more a closed circle. The problem arises, however, how these *vernae* could be increasingly recruited from the children of *Caesaris servi* and *Caesaris servae* if the total proportion of such marriages was not more than about 30% of all marriages of *Caes. servi* and possibly less, and was, if anything, probably decreasing still further throughout the second century. This would imply increasing recruitments precisely from the least socially mobile and therefore, in one important sense, least successful section of the Familia. We can scarcely contemplate the Imperial service admission committees being forced to go out to the provinces where a higher proportion of Imperial slaves married *servae* in order to get recruits of suitable *status* for the administrative élite.

The solution lies, I think, in the SC Claudianum which, to safeguard the interests of the *fiscus*, reduced all freeborn wives of *servi Caesaris* to the legal status of *Caesaris servae* and all children of such wives to the status of *Caesaris vernae*. The wives and children, especially daughters, for the most part appear to have retained their original *nomen* and not to have used any status indication. But among wives and daughters this was a normal practice, in Rome at least, even for those with Imperial *nomina* or single name who can be shown on other grounds to be freedwomen and slaves. Even among the male children only a small proportion of the children are *Caes. servi/vernae* or *Aug. liberti*. This is to be explained, at least in part, by the tendency for the prestigious Imperial status indication to be used more by adult males as a

---

[1] *Frag. de iure fisci* 13: 'ancilla Caesaris quae quinque liberos habuerit...', which is fragmentary, does mention *five* children, but this may refer to manumission.

[2] See Part I, p. 53.

The SC Claudianum and the Familia Caesaris

badge of office. There are very many cases of father or son being the only members of a family to have status indication. And status indication almost invariably accompanies the use of occupational title in the Imperial service. Recruitment for the Imperial service was selective and only a minority of children of Imperial slaves and freedmen could be successful in obtaining a post.

We must take into account also the problems of nomenclature over the use of status indication with irregular *nomina* and the status of children already referred to. With adequate support from the legal sources, this interpretation is offered as the best way of explaining these considerable difficulties and of accounting for the facts as we have them both about the SC Claudianum and the Familia Caesaris.

CHAPTER 10

WOMEN IN THE FAMILIA CAESARIS

What was the role of women – the *Augusti libertae* and *Caesaris servae* – in the Familia Caesaris and how does their status compare both with that of the *Augusti liberti* and *Caesaris servi* on the one hand, and with that of women of the slave and freed classes outside the Familia on the other?

Libertae in general in Roman society show a much more marked upward mobility in status than *servi* or *liberti*.[1] One important aspect of this mobility, marriage with one's patron, needless to say was denied to the *Aug. libertae*, but not to the *Aug. lib(erti) libertae*, the freedwomen of Imperial freedmen, who very frequently marry their freedman patron. The well-known case of Acte, the freedwoman concubine of Nero, belongs to the exceptional personal history of that emperor. But Vespasian also had a famous concubine, Caenis the freedwoman of Antonia Minor. He lived with her after the death of his wife Flavia Domitilla, and he maintained her without embarrassment as a *de facto* wife till her death (Suetonius, *Vesp.* 3: 'paene iustae uxoris loco'; cf. ib. 21). Another freedwoman, Lysistrata, was concubine of no less revered an emperor than Antoninus Pius after the death of his wife Faustina. Lysistrata, a freedwoman of Faustina no less, indeed appears in an inscription after Pius' death with the actual title 'concubina divi Pii' (VI 8972 = D 1836: Galeria [Aug(ustae) liber]tae Lysistrate concubina Divi Pii). These three Imperial cases do reveal something of the nature, extent and acceptance of concubinage in Imperial society.

Concubinage thus existed at the highest level. It is found in the household of Vespasian 'l'empereur de bon sens', and of Antoninus called Pius. Other emperors had concubines, but only as temporary liaisons, and not with their own freedwomen, and not with quasi-official approval of their status. Neither the fact of taking a concubine nor the fact that she was of servile origin constituted conduct sufficiently scandalous to cause these emperors to desist. Caenis was an *Augusta* in all but title. Lysistrata had a title but not that of *Augusta*.

Concubinage was prevalent among all ranks of society from the emperor and his family downwards. It was frequent when both partners were free-born. It was perhaps even more frequent when one partner, usually the

[1] See chapter 11 below.

Women in the Familia Caesaris

woman, was of freed status.[1] Concubinage can be detected on inscriptions sometimes by such terms as 'concubina', 'amica', etc. (e.g. VI 29242, X 2857) but much more frequently by the illegitimate status of the children, which is indicated when they take the *nomen* of the mother when it is different from that of the father. The terms 'vir', 'uxor', 'maritus', etc. are of no use to distinguish between *matrimonium* and *contubernium*.[2] They are normal for all groups in the Familia Caesaris. Nor even does 'contubernalis' always indicate that one or both partners are of slave status or origin.[3]

To be distinguished from the voluntary cases of concubinage, where the partners are free, are those cases where *contubernium* was necessary. From the reign of Augustus, under the lex Iulia of 18 BC[4] *matrimonium* (as opposed to *contubernium*) was illegal between one of freed status and a member of the senatorial order. There are few exceptions even in the Familia Caesaris. If Claudius Etruscus' mother was really Tettia Etrusca from a senatorial *gens*, then Statius discreetly refrained from saying so. *Silvae* iii. 3.114: 'nec vulgare genus' is not convincingly senatorial and 'si quicquid patrio cessatum a sanguine, mater reddidit' is engagingly unspecific.[5] Lacking in specificity also is Statius on the status of Priscilla, wife of Abascantus who was *ab epistulis* under Domitian. *Silvae* v. 1.53: 'quamquam et origo niteret et felix species' does not clinch her *senatorial* origin; she could be of equestrian family. Cf. under Commodus the probably no less equestrian wives of the favourites Cleander and Eclectus, including Marcia, a former concubine of the emperor himself.[6]

When either or both of the partners were of slave status, *contubernium* was the necessary, and not legally recognised, status of their union even though, as was very often the case, such unions were intended to be permanent. For *contubernium*, as for *matrimonium*, the normal terminology of family relationships is used. The children born while the parents were still 'in contubernio' were illegitimate and would follow the status of the mother and take her *nomen* if she was a *liberta* or *ingenua*. But legitimisation of the children following the manumission of the father could be achieved by the father adopting his children born 'in contubernio', in which case they would change their *nomen* to that of the father. This must have happened quite often and is

---

[1] Cf. J. Plassard, *Le Concubinat romain*; P. Meyer, *Konkubinat*, pp. 82 f.
[2] Despite Starr, *Roman Imperial Navy*, ch. III, n. 49.
[3] Cf. *TLL* IV, 790 s.v. 'contubernalis' II. A.
[4] *Dig.* xxiii. 2.44.
[5] Claudius Etruscus' parents had married when his father was still of freedman status and only moderately advanced in the freedman career under Claudius (see Weaver, *CQ* 15 (1965), 150 f.). Hence the later equestrian status of the father cannot be relevant to the status of the mother at marriage, as Boulvert (II, 750) suggests.
[6] Herodian, i. 17; Cassius Dio, lxxii. 4; cf. Boulvert, II, 750 with notes 125 and 126.

The family circle

indicated in the Familia Caesaris by the quite high proportion of children with the *nomen* of the father when this differs from that of the mother.

Before examining the marriage pattern of the *servae* and *libertae* of the Familia it is necessary to consider the distribution between the sexes of those with status indication.

Under normal circumstances in any given homogeneous social group one expects to find a rough balance between the sexes, if the data considered are sufficiently representative of the whole. In Roman society one sometimes finds a moderate preponderance of males over females, especially when the evidence is derived from sepulchral inscriptions which frequently exhibit a preoccupation with the male line of succession. Exposure of baby girls, whatever the extent of this practice may have been, would also tend to give a preponderance of males in the population.[1]

We can test this for the Familia Caesaris by considering various groups in turn.[2] Of all children with or without status indication born to parents at least one of whom was an Imperial freedman or freedwoman, there are recorded 332 sons and 210 daughters. Where the highest status of one or both parents is that of Imperial slave, there are 108 sons, compared with 80 daughters. This gives a total of 440 male children and 290 female children in the Familia, a proportion of 60% sons to 40% daughters. This distribution is also found in two other groups which closely resemble the normal slave *familia* – the freedmen and freedwomen of the *Aug. liberti* themselves, and in the *familiae* of the *Augustae*. In the former group there are found 123 *lib. liberti* to 82 *lib. libertae*, again 60% males to 40% females. Among the slaves and freedmen of the *Augustae*, 113/318 are *servae* or *libertae*, i.e. 64% males to 36% females. The figures are consistent and these three groups can be taken to represent the normal distribution between the sexes found in the lower social strata.

But in the Familia Caesaris proper, i.e. those with the formal status indication of Imperial freedmen, freedwomen or slaves, the nearest approach to this proportion of women is to be found amongst the Imperial slaves in Africa, particularly in Carthage where *children* of Imperial slaves and freedmen regularly bear the Imperial status indication (as they do *not* elsewhere), and where the Imperial *sepulcreta* were used almost as family *columbaria* by the emperor's slaves and freedmen stationed in Carthage. Here the proportion of males to females is 76% to 24%. The figures for groups from other parts of the empire show a steady decline in the proportion of women from 17%

---

[1] On the distribution between the sexes of the Roman population in general see Hopkins, *Population Studies* 20 (1966), 260 f.

[2] These figures include *alumni* and *alumnae*, but do not take into account brothers and sisters whose parents are not known.

Women in the Familia Caesaris

for Imperial slaves from all the provinces, i.e. outside Rome and Italy, to barely 3% or 4% for the *Augusti libertae* in Rome, especially in those groups dated to the second century. Table IX summarises the position for the Familia Caesaris proper. The total figures in each group include all cases with status indication, counting separately those where more than one name appears on the same inscription.

TABLE IX
Distribution of females/males in the Familia Caesaris[1]

	Rome and Italy	Provinces	Total
Libertae			
Iulia	13/146 8%	–/5 —	13/151 8%
Claudia	28/225 12%	4/24 17%	32/249 13%
Flavia	17/202 8%	4/23 17%	21/225 9%
Cocceia	4/15	–/2	4/17
Ulpia	6/168 4%	–/22 —	6/190 3%
Aelia	13/270 5%	5/50 10%	18/320 6%
Aurelia	6/210 3%	1/50 2%	7/260 3%
(Without *nomen*)	20/562 4%	9/138 7%	29/700 4%
Servae	63/938 7%	98/566 17%	161/1504 11%
Total	170/2736 6%	121/880 14%	291/3616 8%

Apart from the 'Cocceiae Aug. libertae' where the numbers are small and can be disregarded, the highest proportion of women (17%) is found in the provinces, both for *servae* as a whole and for *libertae* of the first century. The percentage figures for Rome and Italy are consistently well below those for the provinces,[2] and here again the highest figures are from the first century, especially the 'Claudiae Aug. lib.' where the figure is 12%. In the second century the figures are consistently 5% or even lower, i.e. the distribution between the sexes for this group is ninety-five males to every five females. The proportion of women in all these groups is therefore not that of the normal *familia*. This points to special factors operating in the use of the Imperial status indication.

Both in place and period the figures are highest where, as appears from the discussion on the status of wives, the proportion of wives who are *ingenuae* is found to be lowest, i.e., geographically, in the provinces, especially Africa, and for slaves there rather than for freedmen; and chronologically, the early and mid-first century. The variation in the proportion of women with the Imperial

[1] The totals appearing under several *nomina* are approximate only to the nearest ten. There are numerous fragmentary and doubtful inscriptions which make a precise count of all inscriptions of Imperial freedmen unrewardingly difficult.
[2] Apart from a solitary instance of an 'Aurelia Aug. lib.' from Africa (VIII 8938).

The family circle

status indication is not exactly in inverse proportion to the percentage of wives who are *ingenuae*, but the relationship is nevertheless striking. This is what might have been expected, except that a far lower proportion of wives use the status indication than would seem entitled to do so. The use of the status indication by Imperial freedwomen, and probably by female Imperial slaves also, declined from the Flavian period. This was the same period at which the status nomenclature first of the Imperial freedmen and then of the Imperial slaves became more and more formalised – a development connected with the institutionalisation of the Familia Caesaris in the bureaucracy. Women in the Familia, who did not share in this recognition of official status, tended to drop the use of the status indication at the same time as other variants in nomenclature were dropped by the *liberti*. The Familia of the first century is displayed in its *columbaria*, but by the second century it reveals a basically bureaucratic face. Where we do have a surviving record of the *familia* community in the second century, as in the Carthage *columbaria*, the women and children re-emerge in their numbers using their status indication, in a way reminiscent of the early first century. We must always allow for considerable variations in social practice in regard to, e.g., marriage pattern and nomenclature depending on such factors as geographical isolation and lack of opportunities for mobility, on community cohesiveness, and so on. Carthage happens to be our best and only fully documented second-century example of this to set against the inscriptions from Rome.

The next step is to consider the marriage pattern of the *Aug. libertae* and the *Caesaris servae*. The figures for the marriages recorded are given in Table x.

Columns (1) and (2) show the husbands who have been or are Imperial slaves with indication, i.e. the *minimum* of husbands in this category, as others without indication could lurk in Columns (3) and (5). This minimum figure is for *Aug. libertae*: 52/74 (70%), for *Caes. servae* from Rome: 19/24 (79%), and from Italy and the provinces: 19/45 (42%). These minimum figures can be raised both for *libertae* and *servae* as several husbands without formal indication who are included under Column (5) are very probably *Caes. servi*: e.g.

vi 19181: Edychrys = Medusa Aug. lib.+Taurus.
x 6775: Amycus atr(iensis?) = Uranie Aug. [lib.].
viii 23336: Helenus = Aquilina [Au]g. lib.+Maxima, aged 24.

This is particularly true of the high proportion of husbands of *Caes. servae* in Africa who are *servi* without indication: 12/25.[1] Only in one case where the

---

[1] In most cases their status indication may have been dropped when they appeared in a secondary position on a small epitaph; e.g. viii 1898, 12685, 12780, 12825, 12863, 12903 (praeco), 12909 (tabellarius), 13026, 13145, *AE* 1914, 228; *AE* 1957, 181; *ILAlg.* I 476.

Women in the Familia Caesaris

TABLE X

Marriages of Augusti libertae and Caesaris servae

	(1) Aug. lib.	(2) Caes. ser.	(3) Imperial nomen	(4) Non-Imp. nomen	(5) ser.	Total
Aug. liberta =						
Iulia	2	—	—	1	1	4
Claudia	7	6	3	1	2	19
Flavia	6	4	1	—	—	11
Cocceia	1	—	—	—	—	1
Ulpia	4	1	—	—	1	6
Aelia	5	1	3	—	1	10
Aurelia	2	1	1	—	1	5
(Without *nomen*)	8	4	—	2	4	18
Total	35 (47%)	17 (23%)	8 (11%)	4 (5%)	10 (14%)	74 (100%)
Caes. serva =						
Rome	7 (29%)	12 (50%)	—	—	5	24
Italy	—	5	1	4	3	13
Africa	1	9	2	—	13	25
Other provinces	—	4	2	—	1	7
Total	8 (12%)	30 (43%)	5 (7%)	4 (6%)	22 (32%)	69 (100%)

husband is a slave is he indicated as being a slave *outside* the Familia Caesaris –

AE 1959, 300: Saturninus Servil(iae?) Abibelae (ser.) = Verecundia Neronis Caesar. ancill(a) veneria de hort(is) Servil(ianis);

and this instance is not certain.

Several of the husbands with Imperial *nomen* but without indication (Column 3) also probably belong to the Familia as the children in almost all cases have the Imperial indication or are slaves.

Thus one can assume that at least 80% of all marriages of *Aug. libertae* and *Caes. servae*, whether formed before or after manumission, were with *Caes. servi* or *Aug. liberti* (with the latter presumably mostly before *their* manumission). Outside Rome marriages with *servi* outside the Familia may have been commoner but the absence of indication does not constitute definite proof of this.

Marriage of Imperial *libertae* and *servae* with *freeborn* husbands is at a maximum of 16% for the *libertae* (Columns 3 and 4), and 13% for *servae*. But in fact some of the husbands in these two groups can be, and probably are, freedmen. The proportion of husbands who are freeborn cannot be more than about 10% at most.

This marriage pattern is in striking contrast not only with that of the male members of the Familia, whether freed or still slave, but also – and this may

The family circle

seem paradoxical – with that of women of the slave and freed classes in general. In both of these latter groups upward mobility through marriage is very marked. *Caes. servi* from Rome marry at *least* 64% *ingenuae*, but *Caes. servae* and *Aug. libertae* from Rome marry at *most* 16% *ingenui*. The paradox is because both of these groups have advantages for mobility which are denied to freedwomen and female slaves of the emperor. These latter do not have access to the administrative posts and most of the domestic posts which give male Imperial slaves and freedmen their power and social status. On the other side, they do not have the advantage which other female slaves and freedwomen possess, who can gain early manumission and marry their patron. Even the female slaves and freedwomen of the Imperial freedmen have this advantage. But comparison of rates of mobility expressed in this way is misleading. The *Aug. libertae* and *Caes. servae* do have access to husbands of the status of the Imperial freedmen and slaves themselves. The overwhelming proportion of *Caes. servae* marrying within the Familia represents a considerable social achievement compared with other slaves and women. The *Caes. servi* – at least those in Rome – increasingly marry *ingenuae*, and it is the social status of these freeborn women to which the *Caes. servae* are assimilated by their marriages.

The children of Imperial slave and freed women follow the status of the mother at the time of birth or take the *nomen* of the mother in seventy-eight cases, and that of the father (which can be traced only when it differs from that of the mother) in only six or seven cases. These latter are accounted for as having been born after the manumission of both parents, or by adoption by the father for the purpose of legitimisation after their manumission. In only two cases do children have a non-Imperial *nomen* and both of these are mid-first century:

VI 4923: ****** = Claudia Aug. lib. Nereis + M. Valerius Futianus.
VI 15489: ****** = Cl(audia) Latens Aug. l. + Fabius Sabinianus.

The only case where the brother of an Imperial freedwoman has a non-Imperial *nomen* (VI 10449 = D 7909, discussed above) is also from the early first century.[1] Although the great majority of the children must be of slave or freed status, in only about a dozen inscriptions out of over eighty do they use the Imperial status indication.[2] Sometimes the brother has the Imperial indication but the sister does not; e.g.

VI 35308: **** = Flavia Aug. lib. Regilla + Cosmus Caesaris n. ser. verna, Laudice (soror).

[1] See p. 160 above. There is also a sister of a *Caes. serva* named Salonria Felicula (VI 5768).
[2] VI 7528, 8542 (bis), 16811, 17440, 18428 (?), 22960, 29116, 35308; VIII 13112, 13146, 16564, 24701; X 1311 (bis).

Women in the Familia Caesaris

Of all children of *Caes. servae* and *Aug. libertae* there are fifty-seven sons and twenty-eight (i.e. 33%) daughters. Thus we find, as in other groups of the Familia, a marked absence of the use of status indication by women.

The social position of women in the Familia, notable exceptions apart, cannot have been as high as that of the men. What gave the members of the Familia their status and influence was their proximity to the emperor or their administrative posts in the Imperial service or both. In the administration the procuratorial, clerical and even sub-clerical posts were all designed for and held by men. There was no equality of opportunity or pay for women in the Imperial administration, except in the domestic Palace service where women slaves and freedwomen were required for those occupations which were common to all large households with a slave *familia*. The heavy imbalance in the Familia Caesaris between men and women who are found with status indication must, in general terms, from the Flavian period reflect the relative proportions of men and women employed in the emperor's service. The uniqueness of the Familia Caesaris lies in the extensive public and administrative duties of the master and patron of the *familia*. For the efficient performance of these he required large numbers of personal assistants of all grades and status from *servi vicarii* to equestrian procurators and prefects. Women had no part in this just as they had no part in the duties of the *servi publici*.

Further, many women who had the legal status of *Aug. libertae* did not bear the Imperial status indication. This is obvious from the abnormally low proportion who do have the indication, and the instances of mothers without indication whose children are *Caesaris vernae*. This raises the question, where did the *Caesaris vernae* come from? If a maximum of only one *Caes. servus* in three marries a *Caes. serva*, and if we assume that the average number of children in each family who survive infancy is as high as three, divided roughly equally between boys and girls, then the numbers and proportion of children of both sexes born *as slaves* into the Familia Caesaris must have declined. And the proportion of children born as *ingenui* or *ingenuae*, legitimate or illegitimate, must have increased. If freeborn women became the main source of wives for Imperial slaves, then the idea of large numbers of slave-born children (*vernae*), or even of sufficient replacement numbers, being produced in the emperor's Familia must be abandoned – unless the legal status of the wives who are *ingenuae* be accepted as having been reduced to that of 'servae Claudianae' under the SC Claudianum. The emperor would then select as *Caes. vernae* those children of his slaves whom he wished to recruit into the administration, regardless of the original status of the mother.

The family circle

The alternative, that there was large-scale recruitment of Imperial slaves from outside, is difficult to accept. Such recruitment would have to be on a large scale as the administration's needs for such slaves would be increasing at the very time that the supply of *vernae* to fill the new posts was declining. Merely on grounds of economy in the running of the administration it would be very improbable that the emperors had to resort to large-scale purchase or other forms of acquisition of slaves while – and because of – permitting their own slaves at the same time to continue marrying *ingenuae*. All this to the increasing financial disadvantage of the emperor and *fiscus*. One is forced to the conclusion that the emperor was able to recruit into the Familia *as servi* from *all* the children born to Imperial slaves before manumission, whatever the nomenclature or original status of their wives. He would not voluntarily and arbitrarily be restricted as to the choice and quality of recruits vital to administrative needs because of the fashion prevalent among his slaves for marrying freeborn women. Nor did he simply refuse to allow them to continue doing so. As *dominus* he had the power, but in practice he had best avoid using it. There must have been some accommodation between the needs of the emperor and the social status of his slaves. Moreover, the status attaching to these slave posts in the administration made them so desirable and rewarding that the exclusion of freeborn children of slave officials would raise a problem with these children themselves. The evidence is strong that by the second century these slave posts in the emperor's service became something of a closed shop. But the fact that female children of Imperial slaves whose wives were originally freeborn would not be thus recruited into the Familia Caesaris, together with the use of the Imperial status indication as a prestige symbol more and more connected with employment in the emperor's service, would then help to explain the low proportion of female slaves and freedwomen found in the Familia.

CHAPTER 11

THE MARRIAGE PATTERN OF SLAVES AND FREEDMEN OUTSIDE THE FAMILIA CAESARIS

If the Familia Caesaris is indeed an élite in the slave and freedman classes of society, we would expect its marriage pattern to be significantly different from that of the slaves and freedmen outside the Familia. These slaves and freedmen themselves need not be considered as economically underprivileged; the only material available for such a study is their tombstones or funerary inscriptions – and the mere fact of being able to afford a tombstone, with or without decoration, as many of them conspicuously had, or of having access to a burial monument of a patron, implies security of a kind somewhat removed from the poverty of the ghetto.

A detailed study of the marriage pattern of these classes has yet to be made. The following discussion aims merely to supply material for such a study and to examine a control group as a basis of comparison between the Familia Caesaris and the slaves and freedmen outside it. To obtain a sufficiently large and homogeneous sample the *sepulcrales* of *CIL* VI, Parts 1–4, have been used. From these have been extracted the cases of marriages where the slave or freedman status of one of the partners is specifically stated or can be inferred with certainty (e.g. from the occurrence of 'collibertus', 'patronus', etc.), and where both partners are named and the relationship between them is specifically that of man and wife. All the relevant examples in these parts of *CIL* VI have been included but not cases where there is a reasonable doubt as to the status or relationship of the persons mentioned, e.g. where they could be brother and sister, or father and daughter, mother and son.

As on pp. 105 f. above, the usual terms for family relationships are used, e.g. *maritus*, *coniunx*, *uxor*, etc., although the union in most cases is from the juridical point of view strictly concubinage (*contubernium*). When both partners have been manumitted in due form they are juridically capable of *conubium* or *iustum matrimonium*. But this is a legal distinction which did not conform to the social facts. At least it has little bearing on the status pattern of marriages where slaves and freedmen are recorded, as most marriages in this category took place *before* the manumission of both partners, who thus

The family circle

had the status of *contubernales*. The partners themselves are not affected by their juridical status at the time of marriage, although this did, of course, determine the status of the children. I am not here concerned with the status of children outside the Familia Caesaris.[1]

The examples come from all types of sepulchral inscriptions, including those from the *columbaria*, those where occupations are mentioned (*officiales et artifices*), and religious dedications (*sacrae*), as well as the alphabetised collection of *sepulcrales*. It is characteristic of the *sepulcrales*, apart from those of the Familia Caesaris, that in the great majority of cases even approximate relative dating criteria are lacking. Many examples from the *columbaria*, however, are certainly of first-century date and fewer are certainly from the second or third centuries. Many of the *officiales* can be assigned to either the first or second century. The majority of undated *sepulcrales* used here are probably first century or from the first half of the second century, when the use of status indication outside the Familia Caesaris dwindled. So that while no attempt can be made to trace a chronological pattern, it is reasonable to assume that the examples are well spread over both first and early second centuries.

A total of 700 marriage couples from Rome, meeting the criteria described above, has been taken in successive order through *CIL* VI without further selection. They are made up as follows:

Group I: Both partners with same *nomen*	336
Group II: Partners with different *nomina*	217
Group III: One partner with slave indication or single name	87
Group IV: Both partners with slave indication or single name	60
Total	700

(It is assumed that a single name, in conjunction with a partner who has the slave or freedman status indication, indicates slave status; cf. the discussion on wives and children in the Familia Caesaris where they have single name without indication.)

Before discussing the implications of these figures, some comments on Group I are needed:

(i) Of 143 patron-husbands only one has filiation and 8 have freedman indication. Of 15 patron-wives only one again has filiation and one has the freed indication.

(iii) (*a*) Where both partners have the same freed indication they are probably *colliberti*, e.g. VI 10884: T. Aelius T. l. Hermias = Aelia T. l. Eutychia coni.

(*b*) Where the wife's freed indication corresponds with the husband's *praenomen* (without status indication), the husband's status is uncertain; the

[1] On this see Beryl Rawson (Wilkinson), *Names of Children*, and 'Family Life among the Lower Classes at Rome in the First Two Centuries of the Empire', *Class. Phil.* 61 (1966), 71 f.

Marriage pattern outside the Familia Caesaris

husband could be *collibertus*, an *ingenuus*, or even *patronus* of the wife, e.g. 15811: M. Clodius Trophimus = Clodia M. l. Fortunata coni.

(*c*) Husband and wife have *different* freed indication, e.g. 23681: L. Pacilius L. l. Septumus = Posilla(?) Pacilia C. l. Varda ux.

(*d*) Wife's freed indication does not correspond with the husband's *praenomen* (without status indication), e.g. 13716: Q. Caecilius Bargates = Caecilia A. l. Ru[...] ux.

(*e*) Where the husband has freed indication but the wife has not, no opinion is possible as to whether they are *colliberti* or not, e.g. 20794: M. Iunius M. l. Hamillus = Iunia Pieris coni.

(*f*) Where neither partner has the freed indication, but it is certain that one or both partners are of freed status, it is not possible to decide which, e.g. 25198: N. Publilius Felix = Publilia Transtiberina coni., Onesima conlib.

These groups break down according to formal criteria as follows:

GROUP I: SAME NOMEN

(i) *Patronus* marries *liberta*   143
    Patrona marries *libertus*   15
                                                    158
(ii) *Collibertus* marries *colliberta*   59
(iii) Other combinations:
    (a) both have *same* freed indication   35
    (b) wife's freed indication corresponds with husband's *praenomen*   19
    (c) husband and wife have *different* freed indication   8
    (d) wife's freed indication does not correspond with husband's *praenomen*   5
    (e) husband has freed indication, wife has not   29
    (f) neither partner has freed indication   23
                                                    119
                                                 Total   336

GROUP II: DIFFERENT NOMINA

(i) Both husband and wife have freed indication   67
(ii) Husband has freed indication, wife without indication (or has filiation – 7 exx.)   74
(iii) Wife has freed indication, husband without indication (or has filiation – 6 exx.)   76
                                                 Total   217

GROUP III: ONE PARTNER WITH SLAVE INDICATION OR SINGLE NAME

(Other partner with *nomen* and *cognomen*, i.e. freed or freeborn)
(i) Husband of slave status   59
    (wife has freed indication in 37 cases;
    wife has no indication in 22 cases)
(ii) Wife of slave status   28
    (husband has freed indication in 23 cases;
    husband has no indication in 5 cases)   Total   87

GROUP IV: BOTH PARTNERS WITH SLAVE INDICATION OR SINGLE NAME

                                                 Total   60

The family circle

While these categories, which are based on the formal criteria of nomenclature, are useful for purposes of classification, the basic division in the marriage pattern is not between slave and freed but rather between slave or freed on the one hand, and freeborn (*ingenui* or *ingenuae*) on the other; also basic is the difference in the marriage patterns for males and females. It is crucial, both for its own sake and for purposes of comparison with the marriage pattern of the Familia Caesaris, to decide the *maximum* proportion of wives of freedmen and slaves who can be *ingenuae*. The proportion of husbands of freedwomen and slaves who can be *ingenui* is also important but less vital.

In marriage the slave–freed division is not basic for social structure. The age at which a slave was manumitted did not, or very rarely, determine the age at which he married. Rather the other way round; manumission was more likely to follow marriage and the birth of children. This was particularly so for women who could rarely accumulate a *peculium* from earnings, at least in the normal way, but could earn manumission at the price of bearing up to four children. These children would remain as slaves belonging to the master's *familia*. Thus, apart from marriages that took place after manumission, especially in the case of the wife, the marriage pattern expresses the same set of facts for slave and freed, at different stages in the life of the persons concerned. We must look at the evidence for the age of both partners at marriage and at manumission. The fact that both husband and wife are slaves in only 9% (60/700) of the examples above, and that one partner is a slave in only a further 12% (87/700), does not of course mean that marriage in the other 79% of cases took place after manumission. Rather the opposite is the case.

AGE AT MARRIAGE

The legal age at which Roman boys and girls could marry was 14 and 12 years respectively. This is not necessarily related to the age at puberty which was not decisive in fixing the age at marriage. The normal age at which Roman girls married for the first time was very early by modern western standards, 14 or earlier. But there are class differences and for girls of aristocratic families marriage could take place earlier still, even before *menarche*, according to recent studies.[1] Octavia, daughter of Claudius, married at eleven, Agrippina the Younger first married at twelve, Julia the Elder at 14; Agricola's daughter married Tacitus at the age of 13, and perhaps Pliny the Younger's third wife was equally young. After 15 an

---

[1] See M. K. Hopkins, *Population Studies* 18 (1965), 309–27; 20 (1966), 245–64; and the articles of M. Durry, *CRAI* (1955), 84–91; *RIDA* 2 (1955), 263–73; 3 (1956), 227–43.

Marriage pattern outside the Familia Caesaris

aristocratic girl who was still unmarried began to become an object of concern to her family. Thus, Tullia, Cicero's daughter, who did not marry till 16, and Julia and Drusilla, the daughters of Germanicus, who were married off at the 'late' age of 15 and 17 respectively, 'after the age of the girls began to press' according to Tacitus (*Ann.* vi. 15).[1] Girls at this early age would most often marry husbands considerably older than themselves, with the consequently greater expectation of early widowhood the greater the age difference between themselves and their husbands.

Among the slave classes the age of girls is also a matter of concern to masters who saw the main function of their female slaves as an economic one – the breeding of slave children (*vernae*) to swell their own *familia* or for sale. Specially important is the gap between the average age at marriage and at manumission both for male and for female slaves. The extent of this gap has a vital bearing on the question of what proportion of children of *freed* parents was likely to have been born *before* manumission. If the average gap was as much as ten to fifteen years, we can assume with some confidence that most of their children would be born as slaves before the manumission of their parents, especially of their mother.

The data on age at marriage in the examples above are not extensive, but are basically in accord with the results gained from studies on the population in general. There are only six figures for women and none for men. These ages are: two *libertae* married to *patroni* at the age of 13 and 10, one wife without status indication married to a freedman at the age of 21; two *libertae* married to husbands without status indication at the age of 20 and 15 respectively; and one *serva* married to a *servus* at the age of 28. ('Without status indication' in this discussion means that the person in question has a *nomen* and *cognomen*, i.e. is either freed or freeborn but not of slave status. Slave status is implied by a single personal name.) These figures are not sufficient on their own. But the early age of marriage is confirmed, for *libertae* marrying their patrons, by the proportion of such wives who died as *libertae* under the age of 30 (5/14, of whom 3/14 died under 20). It is likely that early manumission accompanied early marriage in this group. In fact manumission of an 'ancilla apud consilium matrimonii causa' was one of the causes of manumission of a slave under the age of 30 expressly provided for under the lex Aelia Sentia (Gaius, i. 18).

The other groups in which early marriage can be deduced from the figures for age at death are, naturally enough, those where one or both partners are of slave status (Groups III and IV), i.e. death occurred before the age of manumission was reached. Thus in Group IV (both partners slaves) 11/16 slave-

---

[1] Cf. Hopkins, *Population Studies* 18 (1965), 316 f., where the examples are collected.

The family circle

wives for whom ages are given died under 30, and 4/16 under 21. In Group III, 10/17 wives (including 2 *servae* and 5 *libertae*) died under 30, and 4/8 husbands (including 3 *servi* and 1 *libertus*). In the other freed groups (I and II) wives who died as *libertae* under the age of 30 are less common (8/21). In all these cases it is impossible to estimate by how many years marriage preceded death.

There is no reason to doubt that women of the slave or freed classes married early. It is possible that freeborn women may have married slightly earlier than *servae*, but there is little indication of any significant difference, except for the nobility.

The age at marriage of slave or freedman-husbands in our group is more difficult to gauge. Of slave-husbands 5/10 for whom there are figures died under 30. There is only one freedman-husband under 30, which tends to support the idea that the lex Aelia Sentia did have some validity. Even for *ingenui* evidence is scarce. Macdonell (art. cit. p. 371) collected only twenty-nine examples from inscriptions of all classes. The ages range between 15 and 63, but the highest concentration (11/29 examples) was between the ages of 17 and 20. All that can be stated is that it is highly unlikely that *servi* delayed their first marriage, particularly marriage within the same *familia* or where the slave lived away from the house of the master, till manumission if this did not come till the age of 30 or later. On the other hand, it is possible that a higher proportion of marriages between partners of different *nomina*, i.e. not between members of the same *familia*, were made *after* the manumission of the husband than between those of the same *nomen*. In Group IV, in those cases where it is possible to tell the *nomina* of the masters of *both* partners – only in 18/60 examples – marriage within the same *familia* accounts for sixteen of these instances, and marriage unions outside the *familia* for only two instances.

AGE AT MANUMISSION

As for the age at manumission, the statutory limit established by the lex Aelia Sentia of AD 4 was 30 for formal manumission, and there is little indication that this was not the regular age of manumission for men. Of eighteen figures for age at death of *liberti* in the examples above, only one died under 30.

As for the 'iustae causae manumissionis' for slaves under 30 mentioned by Gaius (i. 19; 39) and in the *Digest* (xl. 2.9; 13), the only important ones appropriate to males outside the Familia Caesaris are blood relationship and foster relationship. Such expressions as 'patronus et frater', 'frater et libertus', 'filius et libertus' reveal the occasional application of these *causae*. In general, however, it seems that early manumission for *servi* was not particularly common.

Marriage pattern outside the Familia Caesaris

With *servae* on the other hand the case is different. In the examples above, 43% (18/42) of those whose age at death is stated died under the age of 30. One substantial advantage which *servae* had over *servi* in this regard is that the law provided for the early manumission of an 'ancilla matrimonii causa', whether the *patronus* was himself *ingenuus* or *libertus*, but not for the reverse case of a freeborn *patrona* and *libertus*. But a *patrona* who was herself a freedwoman might marry a former fellow slave who had been left to her 'matrimonii causa' (*Dig.* xl. 2.14.1: 'sunt qui putant etiam feminas posse matrimonii causa manumittere, sed ita si forte conservus suus in hoc ei legatus est'). In fact there was a definite prejudice against this type of union, especially a freeborn *patrona* marrying her own freed slave. Such unions did occur, however, and were prohibited by Septimius Severus in a high moral tone reminiscent of the author of the Senatusconsultum Claudianum – *Cod. Iust.* v. 4.3: 'libertum, qui patronam seu patroni filiam vel coniugem... uxorem ducere ausus est, apud competentem iudicem accusare poteris moribus temporum meorum congruentem sententiam daturum, quae huiusmodi coniunctiones odiosas esse merito duxerunt'. This is confirmed by the fact that in the examples above, of 158 cases of marriage between patron and freedman or freedwoman in no fewer than 143 cases, or just over 90%, the woman is the partner of freed status and the husband the patron, and in only 15 cases (less than 10%) is the wife the patron and the husband her freedman. The prejudice against an *ingenua* 'marrying' or cohabiting with a *servus* is well known and is exemplified in the penalties provided for under the SC Claudianum, and thereafter retained with modifications till Justinian. The extent of the prejudice is admirably revealed by the pattern of the present group.

Another substantial group of *libertae* manumitted under the age of 30 are those who marry a *collibertus*, and when a *liberta* marries a former *conservus*. Together these account for no fewer than 10/18 instances of early manumission of *libertae*. The patron of these *conservi* may have either manumitted both partners together at the regular age of manumission for the husband, i.e. normally some years after the union began, and the wife being normally several years younger than her husband was thus manumitted earlier, perhaps informally if there were no children. (If such early manumission was informal the Latin status of one or both of the partners could always have been converted into full citizenship on the first birthday of their first child by the simple procedure of 'anniculi probatio'.) Or, in the case of *liberta* and *conservus*, the master may have occasionally consented to the early manumission of the wife in the interests of the status of the children whom he did not wish to claim as his slaves. It is worth recalling here that the very high

The family circle

rate of manumission under the age of 30 which is found among the *liberti* and *libertae* of the Imperial freedmen applies in the cases of those who died between the ages of 11 and 29, that is within the ages at which marriage was possible before manumission at the legal limit. In as many as 9/11 of these cases the Imperial freedmen manumit their own female slaves, mostly to marry them.

To conclude this section: in the group under discussion *servae* normally married in their teens, perhaps by the age of 16, and *servi* later by about five years, although precise evidence for this is lacking. This is approximately what one finds from the known age figures for the population as a whole, and is little different from what one finds in the Familia Caesaris as well. On the other hand, the age of manumission for males is normally 30, with few exceptions and these mostly provided for under the lex Aelia Sentia. But women were often manumitted earlier than their husbands. Such early manumission may sometimes have been informal. Informal manumission of either *servi* or *servae* is considered unlikely to be of any account in the Familia Caesaris. Most *servi* and *servae*, therefore, married and would have had at least their first child and possibly most of their children born before manumission. That the expectation of manumission was high for both *servi* and *servae* is suggested by the fact that of nineteen figures for *servae* only one died over the age of 40 and only another four aged between 30 and 40; 14/19 are aged 30 or under. Of ten *servi* one died aged 55, three aged 34 and 35, and the rest (6/10) aged 30 or under. This is comparable with the rate of manumission for Imperial slaves in Rome, and higher than that for Imperial slaves in the provinces, especially Africa.

STATUS OF WIVES/HUSBANDS

The next question is to determine the proportion of *servi* and *liberti* marrying (*a*) *servae/libertae* from the same *familia*, or (*b*) *servae/libertae* from a different *familia*; or (*c*) *ingenuae*. And similarly for the marriage pattern of *servae* and *libertae*.

The following table gives the distribution of the 700 husbands and 700 wives into status groups according to status indication, filiation, or other indication: (*a*) *servi* (*-ae*); (*b*) *liberti* (*-ae*); (*c*) *ingenui* (*-ae*); and (*d*) *incerti* (*-ae*), i.e. *liberti* (*-ae*) or *ingenui* (*-ae*), with *nomen* but without status or other indication.

Marriage pattern outside the Familia Caesaris

	Husband					Wife				
	(a) Ser.	(b) Lib.	(c) Ingen.	(d) Incert.	Total	(a) Ser.	(b) Lib.	(c) Ingen.	(d) Incert.	Total
Group										
I. Same *nomen*										
(i) Patron et conj.	—	23	1	134	158	—	144	1	13	158
(ii) Collib.	—	59	—	—	59	—	59	—	—	59
(iii) Others	—	87	—	32	119	—	82	—	37	119
	—	169	1	166	336	—	285	1	50	336
II. Different *nomen*										
(i) Both lib.	—	67	—	—	67	—	67	—	—	67
(ii) M. lib.	—	74	—	—	74	—	—	7	67	74
(iii) F. lib.	—	—	6	70	76	—	76	—	—	76
	—	141	6	70	217	—	143	7	67	217
III. One slave	59	23	—	5	87	28	37	—	22	87
IV. Both slaves	60	—	—	—	60	60	—	—	—	60
	119	23	—	5	147	88	37	—	22	147
Total	119	333	7	241	700	88	465	8	139	700

Note: A total of 23 couples with same *nomen* of whom it was certain that at least one partner was of freed status, but which one was not specified, have been assigned as follows: *colliberti*: 7; husband *lib.*, wife *incerta*: 8; wife *lib.*, husband *incertus*: 8.

The next table gives the overall relation of husband/wife in terms of the status-groups used above:

Wife ...	Serva	Liberta	Ingenua	Incerta	Total
Husband					
Servus	60	37	—	22	119
Libertus	23	185	8	117	333
Ingenuus	—	7	—	—	7
Incertus	5	236	—	—	241
Total	88	465	8	139	700

Expressed in terms of percentages the table is as follows:

Wife ...	Serva	Liberta	Ingenua	Incerta	Total
Husband					
Servus	50	31	—	19	100
Libertus	7	56	2	35	100

Husband ...	Servus	Libertus	Ingenuus	Incertus	Total
Wife					
Serva	68	26	—	6	100
Liberta	8	40	1	51	100

The family circle

SERVI AND LIBERTI

The wives of *servi* are 81% of slave origin (i.e. *servae* or *libertae*). The remaining 19% is made up of wives without status indication who are either *libertae* or *ingenuae*. This gives a maximum of 19% *ingenuae*. It is important to determine what proportion of these are *probably libertae*.

The proportion of *ingenuae* can be reduced with great probability in those cases where the *nomen* of the master of the husband is known and is the same as the *nomen* of the wife. Specifying the *nomen* of the master would be a suitable way of indicating membership of the same *familia* where the terms 'conservi' or 'colliberti' for partners of different status might be thought inappropriate, and where the wife did not wish to use the formal freed indication (the common practice from the second century). This accounts for no fewer than 13/22 instances of *servus* = *incerta*, as follows: VI 454: Annia Euresis; 27387: Arun(n)culeia Sabina, died aged 25; 9902 = D 7415: Asinia Prepusa; 9120: Aurelia Sabina; 17152: Iulia Hygia; 9328: Iulia Tyche; 9334: Licinia Helpis; 11873: Ofillia Tigris; 9344: Paccia Secunda; 26036: Scribonia Helpis; 26338: Sergia Nice, died aged 19; 9346: Valeria Successa; 7300: Volusia Aucta. The *cognomina* of the wives do not suggest *ingenuae*, but this is a largely valueless criterion for status from the early first century. In two cases the age figures (25, 19) would require the wife, if a *liberta*, to have been manumitted early. If we allow the probability that most of these wives are *libertae*, say up to 10/13, the maximum possible percentage of *ingenuae* marrying *servi* is reduced to below 10%. Of the other nine wives who are *incertae* in this class, in only four cases do they have a different *nomen* from that of the master of their husband. These are more likely to be, but are not certainly, *ingenuae*. In one further case, 14242-4: Calpurnia Pia, died aged 20, the age figure would suggest an *ingenua*. Thus we are left with a maximum of less than 10%, and possibly less than 5%, of wives of *servi* who could be *ingenuae*.

If this is the case, the SC Claudianum either successfully discouraged unions between *servi* and *ingenuae* or, indeed, never had any wide application outside the Familia Caesaris itself. The proportion of *servi Caesaris* in Rome marrying *ingenuae* has been estimated above at a *minimum* of 64%. This illustrates in the most striking way the most significant difference between the marriage pattern of Imperial slaves and that of other *servi* outside this élite.

One of the assumptions on which the estimate of wives in the Familia Caesaris is based is the substantial identity of the patterns for *servi* and for *liberti* in Rome. Does the same hold good for the *servi* and *liberti* in Rome

Marriage pattern outside the Familia Caesaris

outside the Familia Caesaris? We expect that wives of *liberti* will also have gained manumission after marriage in the same way as their husbands, and thus appear as *libertae* rather than *servae*. This in fact happens: *servae* are found in only 7% of cases as wives of *liberti*, compared with 50% as wives of *servi*. This merely reflects the later age of the couples at the time of their inscription. But there is a complication. This sharp decrease in wives who are *servae* is not reflected fully in the increase in the proportion of wives of *liberti* who are *libertae* with status indication. It rises from 31% to only 56% (only a 25% rise to compensate for a 43% drop). Only 2% of wives of *liberti* are specifically *ingenuae* with filiation; the rest, 35%, are *incertae*. Thus there are 16% more *incertae* among wives of *liberti* than among wives of *servi*. Can this increase of *incertae* be fully accounted for by wives who are *libertae* without status indication? Or do freedmen marry *freeborn* wives (*ingenuae*) in significant numbers *after* their own manumission, i.e. does the marriage pattern of freedmen differ from that of slaves at this point?

Of the 117 wives of *liberti* who are classed as *incertae* 50 have the same *nomen* as their husbands and 67 have a different *nomen*. *Patronae* marrying their own *liberti* account for 13/50 with same *nomen*. As early manumission of a *libertus* was only permitted for a *patrona* when both were former *conservi*, such marriages either took place after the normal age of manumission for the husband, i.e. 30, or else the *patrona* is herself a freedwoman. Unions of *ingenuae* with their own *servi* without manumission of the latter are much less likely. As late first marriages were not normal, and because of the prejudice against *ingenuae* marrying their own *liberti* (or *servi*), in most of these instances the *patrona* is probably a *liberta*. In the other 37/50 instances with *same nomen*, where the husband has the freed indication but the wife has not, it is also likely that many if not most wives are *libertae*, corresponding to the high proportion of *incertae* who are probably *libertae* when they marry *servi* apparently from the same *familia*.

Most of the increase in the proportion of *ingenuae* marrying *liberti* as compared with *servi* is in fact likely to be found among the wives with *different nomen* from their husbands who are *liberti*. These amount to 67/117, a somewhat high proportion. No guidance is to be found in the *cognomina* of the wives as these can almost without exception be found frequently as names of *servae* or *libertae*. Marriages that took place after the manumission of the husband are more likely to be between *ingenua* and *libertus*, and the *ingenua* is more likely to have a different *nomen* from her husband than for any other group of freedman marriages. However, it is difficult to assess the proportion of such marriages in which the freedman pattern would differ from that for *servi*, as the marriage-age figures for men are so few. Macdonell's

The family circle

figures show that 7% of women married at the age of 30 or over – including second marriages. As women tended to marry earlier than men, we can allow a higher proportion of men to have married, or married for a second time, after the age of 30. The few age-at-death figures in the examples above are not inconsistent with late marriages for this group of *liberti*: 65, 63, 38, 32; whereas the figures for wives are rather too low for *libertae*: 23, 17, 16. It is also to be noted that for those wives with filiation, who are definitely freeborn, 7/8 marry *liberti* with *different nomen*, and for husbands with filiation 6/7 marry *libertae* with *different nomen*. This strongly suggests that most of the *ingenui* or *ingenuae* in our examples are to be found among partners with different *nomen*. On the other hand, of all marriages between partners with different *nomina* a further 67, or nearly one-third of marriages in Group II, have the freed indication for *both* partners. So that in a substantial proportion of marriages in the group we are considering, i.e. *libertus = incerta* of different *nomen*, the wife is probably a *liberta* without status indication. Allowing as many as half, 33/67, of these wives to be *ingenuae*, we get a possible increase in the proportion of wives who are *ingenuae* of the order of 33/333, or 10%, for *liberti* compared with *servi*.

A general estimate, therefore, of the proportion of wives who could be *ingenuae* (and the *general* nature of this conclusion has to be stressed) gives about 5% for *servi* and about 15% for *liberti*. These are the probable *maximum* ranges; the minimum figures, which may well be nearer the truth, could be a negligible 1% or 2% for *servi*, and 5%–10% for *liberti*. This compares with a *minimum* figure of 64% for wives of *both Caesaris servi and Augusti liberti* from Rome who are *ingenuae*. The reason for assuming a rise in the proportion of wives who are *ingenuae* between *servi* and *liberti outside* the Familia Caesaris but not for those *inside* the Imperial Familia is that *Caesaris servi* in Rome already before manumission marry such a high proportion of *ingenuae* that, as the figure given is the minimum level, any increase to be possibly found among *Aug. liberti* marrying after manumission or for a second time would be quite small. The real level for *Aug. liberti* as well as for *Caes. servi* marrying *ingenuae* may in fact have been nearer 75% in Rome by the second century. There would not be much greater incentive for *Aug. liberti* to marry *ingenuae* after manumission that there was while they were still *Caes. servi*. But for the ordinary middle-class freedmen outside the Imperial Familia, who had won their manumission by their own talents and economic effort and who had lost their first wife during her childbearing years or had been too busy to marry earlier, there was considerable incentive to indulge in social mobility by marrying a freeborn wife who would bear freeborn children. At an age perhaps considerably younger than *libertae* after

Marriage pattern outside the Familia Caesaris

manumission, she would have the advantage of youth also, as well as conferring the benefit of status on husband and children.

The next question is how often a slave or freedman married a wife of slave origin within the *same familia* or in a *different familia*. This has importance because of the notion that a master would favour marriage within his own *familia* for economic reasons as well as sentiment. Children of female slaves belonged as property to the master of the slave-mother not of the father according to the rule of the *ius gentium*. True, slave marriage was only *contubernium*, not a true marriage, but the creation of a slave family could not be ignored as a social fact by masters with any degree of feeling. Better then to keep the slave families within his own household. For aristocratic owners of large *familiae* this could well have been the common practice. But for the smaller scale ordinary slave owners, whose numbers of slaves in total were nevertheless very considerable, and many of whom were slaves and freedmen themselves, marriage within the *familia* must have broken down in practice, even if tried out, if only because of the difficulty of finding wives from a small group and because of the dangers of inbreeding.

The data from unions where both partners are slaves (Group IV) are not very helpful. Out of 60 cases the same *familia* is attested only 16 times, and a different *familia* in only two cases. In Group III, where only one partner is still a slave, out of 87 cases the same *familia* is attested in 20 instances and a different *familia* in 8. These figures may be weighted in favour of the same *familia*, but it is interesting that in Group III where the *familia* of both parties is known, one partner still being a slave, nearly 30% (8/28) of slave marriages are outside the *familia* of the husband. Allowing for some of these to be with *ingenuae*, we still have as a rough estimate 25% or more of *servi* marrying *servae* from another *familia*. (Note that in this Group there are twice as many male slaves (59) as female slaves (28), suggesting again earlier manumission for female slaves.)

Along these lines we can take a step further the socially important question of how many freedmen outside the Imperial Familia married freeborn wives, i.e. altered their marriage pattern after emerging from slavery. Of 185 instances of *libertus = liberta*, 67 or 36% have different *nomina*. This figure on its own establishes the relatively high frequency of marriages between *liberti* (or *servi*) and *libertae* (or *servae*) from different *familiae*. This in turn bears on how many wives of *liberti* are *ingenuae*. If marriages between those of slave origin from *different familiae* were so common in proportion to slave marriages within the *same familia*, then many of the cases of *libertus = incerta* with *different nomen* must involve *libertae*. Of 117 instances of *libertus = incerta*, 67 or 57% have different *nomen*. If half these *incertae* with

The family circle

different *nomina* are in fact *ingenuae* (as we allowed above to be the likely maximum), then the proportion of *libertus* = *liberta* in this group would be reduced to 34/117 or 29%. In the fully attested cases of *libertus* = *liberta* there are different *nomina* in 36% of all instances. This is some confirmation that the maximum figure set for *ingenuae* above is not too low and may even be a little high. There remain the instances of *libertus* = *incerta* of same *nomen*; these amount to 50 cases, i.e. 117 less 67 of different *nomen*. If all 50 *incertae* in this group were *libertae*, the proportion of slave marriages within the same *familia* to those between different *familiae* would be 50:34 or 60% to 40%, which is close to that for the fully attested cases, 64% to 36%. This may be taken as justification for two assumptions made above, namely, that there are few if any *ingenuae* among the *incertae* of same *nomen* as their freedman husbands; and secondly, that as many as half of the *incertae* with different *nomen* from that of their freedman husbands may be *ingenuae*.

Thus we get the following approximate distribution of wives between those of servile origin and *ingenuae*. For comparison the figures for the Familia Caesaris in Rome from the Claudian period onwards are given in brackets. Note that under the *ingenuae* the figure given is the *maximum* for this control group, but the *minimum* for the Familia Caesaris.

Husband marries	*serva/liberta* %	*ingenua* %
Servus	95 (36)	5 (64)
Libertus	85 (36)	15 (64)

With these figures may be compared those for the *liberti* and *servi Augustarum*, where at least 50%, and perhaps 60% or more, of wives are of servile origin. (See Table III (p. 124): Wives of freedmen: all groups.) They are thus intermediate between the slaves and freedmen of the Familia Caesaris and those outside, although as most of the instances are from the first half of the first century, they are to be compared with the Familia Caesaris of the Julian period when marriages with partners of servile origin were much commoner than from the time of Claudius onwards. The *familiae* of other prominent noble houses may have similarly married a higher proportion of *ingenuae* than was the average outside the Familia Caesaris.

It thus appears that whereas the *servi Caesaris* show a very marked upward mobility in respect of the status of their wives, slaves and freedmen in general marry to an overwhelming extent with partners of their own status and origin. Here it must be repeated that the slaves of other noble houses

Marriage pattern outside the Familia Caesaris

which were also socially mobile are merged in the figures with those of the humbler families where opportunities for mobility through marriage must have been very limited. Marriage with *ingenuae* was more common for freedmen after manumission, but even here the proportion of total marriages involved cannot have been large. Even of these marriages after manumission the proportion which involved *ingenuae* was not very significant – only up to 15%. The *servi Caesaris* who married *ingenuae*, whether freeborn daughters of freedmen or not, in very large numbers at the normal age for marriage and long before manumission, were clearly very exceptional among the slave and freedmen classes in general and constituted from this point of view a social élite among them.

SERVAE AND LIBERTAE

The marriage pattern of *servae* and *libertae*, on the other hand, differs from that of *servi* and *liberti* in important respects – earlier manumission and strong upward mobility through marriage on the part of *libertae*. In the following table, for convenience, the corresponding percentage figures for *husbands* are given in parentheses (see table, p. 187 above).

Wife marries ...	servus	libertus	ingenuus	incertus	Total
Serva	68 (50)	26 (31)	– (–)	6 (19)	100 (100)
Liberta	8 (7)	40 (56)	1 (2)	51 (35)	100 (100)

The percentage table shows that *servae* married *servi* or *liberti* with indication to the overwhelming extent of 94%. Of the remaining 6% (*incerti*), over half have the same *nomen* as the masters of the *servae* and are thus probably *liberti* from the same *familia*. But for *libertae*, as we would expect, the proportion of husbands with slave indication drops, in fact from 68% to 8%. This drop of 60% is not nearly compensated for by the corresponding rise of only 14% in the percentage of their husbands who are now freedmen with freed indication. There is an insignificant 1% of *ingenui*, 6/7 of them husbands with different *nomen* from their wives. The remainder, 236/465 or 51%, are *incerti*. Of these, 134/465 or 29% of the total marriages of *libertae* are with their own patrons. Many of these *libertae* will have been manumitted early 'matrimonii causa'. As there was not the same prejudice against an *ingenuus* marrying his *liberta* as there was for an *ingenua* marrying her *libertus*, it is likely that a high proportion of these 134 husbands are *ingenui*. The *cognomina* of these husbands cannot be relied upon to provide proof of their freeborn status, but such names as Coruscus, Firmus, Martialis, Proculus,

The family circle

Stephanus, Vibianus, etc., occur often. In a further seventy cases *libertae* marry husbands who have a different *nomen* and do not have status indication. Allowing up to one-half of these to have been *ingenui*, we have a further thirty-five (8% of the total) who were not of servile origin. Thus we get approximately an additional 35% of marriages of *libertae* with *ingenui* which did not occur for *servae*. Add 3% for marriages of *servae* with *ingenui* derived from the *incerti*, and the total is 38% of *libertae* who married *ingenui*. This is at least *twice* the proportion of *liberti* marrying *ingenuae*. Thus outside the Familia Caesaris women of servile origin married upwards much faster than men of the same status, whereas inside the Familia Caesaris the reverse is the case.

The important topic of the children of slaves and freedmen outside the Familia Caesaris has been discussed by Beryl Rawson in her Bryn Mawr thesis already referred to (p. 180 n. 1). She analyses the names of children where the names of both parents are known in 1,500 inscriptions drawn from *CIL* VI.[1] Her conclusions on concubinage, illegitimacy and sale of slave children, among other topics, are well summarised in her article in *Class. Phil.* 61 (1966), 71 f.

In the 700 *sepulcrales* used above I have not found sufficient examples of children's names to make it worthwhile making a detailed analysis. One group of children, however, may be mentioned briefly, as their names suggest that it was common for children to be legitimised after the father gained his manumission and became a Roman citizen. Group II above includes parents who have different *nomina* but of whom only the father has the freedman status indication. The mother has been estimated above to be possibly an *ingenua* in a maximum of half of the total instances in this group. There are 14 children recorded. If born before the father's manumission as we would expect most of them to have been, the children should take the *nomen* of the mother, whether she were freed or freeborn. But this occurs in only 4/14 cases. The *father's* name is found in 9/14 cases, more than twice as often as the mother's, including one example where the mother has filiation and the husband is a freedman: VI 20268: Domitia Q. f. Luperca, C. Iulius C. l. Socrates, Iulia C. f. Agele patri; so that Iulia Agele was either born or legitimised *after* her father's manumission. In one other case, 11801, the children have no *nomen* and are still slaves – Onesime, Euhemerianus, and Nice, born before the manumission of the mother, Annia Nice, and of the

[1] The analysis is vitiated, however, by the assumptions that absence of status indication together with Greek-derived *cognomen* indicates slave status or origin, and that manumission regularly took place at any age before or after 30. See Part I, pp. 83 f. for a discussion of these questions.

Marriage pattern outside the Familia Caesaris

father, Clodius Euhemerus. In four of these nine cases where the children follow the father's *nomen* they have filiation: Iulia C. f. Agele (above), P. Postumius P. f. Flaccus, L. Tarquitius L. f. Fab. Severianus (father's *cognomen* Severus), M. Antonius Antoni Pothini f. Claud. Iustus. Are we to conclude from this sample that nine of these children were born after the father's manumission and only four before? This would be contrary to the facts about age at marriage and age at manumission; the proportion of children born after the father's manumission should be much less, no more than, say, a third. Perhaps this is just too small a sample to base any conclusions on. But a preferable explanation of the nomenclature of these children is that many of them were born illegitimate, i.e. while the father was still a slave, but that after he gained his manumission he adopted his children born in concubinage with a freeborn woman in order to legitimise them.

One last general point needs to be made. No claim of exactness is made for the precise figures given above. This essay may be regarded as primarily an exercise in method. The figures are merely meant to illustrate the main features of the marriage pattern of a particular group in order to examine the truth or falsehood of some common assumptions about slave and freedman marriage, as well as to provide a basis of comparison with the Familia Caesaris. This control group is arbitrarily selected, but at least it has the merit of being homogeneous in status and place, and reasonably also in time. Statistical precision in these matters is a desideratum that is perhaps always unattainable in ancient studies. But, as the study of the Familia Caesaris itself repeatedly shows, assumptions must be tested in the best way that is to hand and not allowed to gain currency by default if we are to advance beyond the realm of myth.

PART 3
THE EMPEROR'S SERVICE

From the end of the first century, and certainly from the time of Hadrian, recruitment into the various services of the Familia Caesaris was predominantly from within the Familia, from the children, and especially the sons, of the *Caesaris servi* and *Augusti liberti* themselves. This is indicated especially by the increasing use of the term *verna* in the status indication of Imperial slaves in the second century. Recruitment from within, it has been argued in a previous chapter, is compatible with the predominance of *ingenuae* among the wives of the *Caesaris servi* only because of the application of the SC Claudianum.[1]

In the first century, however, slaves entered the Familia Caesaris in considerable numbers from outside. This inflow can be directly traced in all periods up to the time of Hadrian by the *agnomina* in *-ianus* derived from the previous owners. They are particularly apparent in the period of Augustus and Tiberius. The methods of acquisition were the same as those by which the emperor's *patrimonium* in general was increased – gift, bequest and legacy, and, no doubt exceptionally in the case of slaves, even purchase and confiscation.

A further source of recruitment was through the slaves of Imperial slaves themselves, *vicarii*, who were in law strictly always the property of the emperor – and thence, as what may be called 'vicariani', into the Familia Caesaris itself. These status levels begin with the lowest legal category, that of the slave of a slave (*servus vicarius*), and lead upward after the manumission of one or both parties to the slave and freedman of a freedman (*liberti servus*, *liberti libertus*), and lastly to a special group in the Familia Caesaris, those *vicarii* who passed from the *de facto* ownership of their Imperial slave-master to the direct ownership of the emperor himself. The *vicarii* in this group became *Caesaris servi* and those who reached the appropriate age and were subsequently manumitted by the emperor directly, became *Augusti liberti*. It is to this group that the term 'vicarianus' is applied in this study. These groups need to be examined one by one in order to determine whether the legal lines of demarcation correspond with social status within the Familia Caesaris, and in particular to see what light their occupational status can throw on the slave hierarchy in the Imperial administration of the first and second centuries AD.

[1] See Chapter 9 above, esp. pp. 168 f.

CHAPTER 12

VICARII

From the point of view of legal status or legal capacity the most notable differentiation within the slave section of society is between the slave who forms part of another slave's *peculium*, i.e. is his de facto property, the *servus vicarius*,[1] and other slaves. Slave-owned slaves were fairly numerous in Roman society. Such wide differences of wealth and position existed among different kinds of slaves that inevitably the wealthier and more important slaves, with their master's consent, acquired slaves of their own whether for their personal use or to aid them as deputies in their master's service.[2]

The Roman terminology for the slaves of slaves is not without significance.[3] 'Servus servi', on the Greek model of δοῦλος δούλου, is very rare in the literary, legal and epigraphical sources, as is 'servus peculiaris'. The usual term is '(servus) vicarius' which is derived, as is much of the domestic terminology of Roman slavery, from military usage and organisation. It originally meant 'substitute' or 'replacement' (*vices agens*).[4] The owner-slave is called 'ordinarius', regularly in the legal texts but only occasionally elsewhere.[5] In the inscriptions his status is usually obvious from the nomenclature of the *vicarius* and needs no special definition; e.g. VI 64 = D 3502:

[1] The subject of *servus vicarius*, although of considerable interest, has seldom been discussed, and then usually from the purely legal point of view. See Buckland, *The Roman Law of Slavery*, 239–49; Lécrivain, D–S v, 823–5. The social position of *servi vicarii* has been seriously discussed only once, in 1896, by H. Erman in a monograph which is still basic for all aspects of the subject, *Servus Vicarius, l'esclave de l'esclave romain*, to be found in *Recueil publié par la Faculté de Droit de l'Université de Lausanne*. The most recent treatment is by K. Schneider, P–W VIII A, 2046–53. See also remarks by R. Düll, *ZSS* 57 (1950), 173 f. and A. Berger, *Iura* 8 (1957), 122 f. On nomenclature, see now Chantraine, pp. 389 f.

[2] For references to *vicarii* outside the Familia Caesaris see P–W VIII A, 2047; Chantraine, p. 389 n. 3.

[3] Erman, *Servus Vicarius*, pp. 399 f.

[4] 'Agens vices' perhaps occurs once in the abbreviation 'a(gens) v(ices) v(ilici)', *AE* 1945, 123 (Acaunum, Alp. Poen.): 'Montanus Augg. nn. vern(a), a(gens) v(ices) v(ilici) stat(ionis) Acaun(ensis) XXXX Gal(liarum)', an Imperial slave acting as temporary replacement for the *vilicus* in charge.

[5] Suetonius, *Galba* 12. Cf. Seneca, *de Benef.* iii. 28; *CIL* VI 33469. The evidence for the use of 'peculiaris' in the sense of 'ordinarius' in the Familia Caesaris (as P–W VIII A, 2046) and for the use of 'servus peculiaris' referring to Imperial slaves in contrast with *servi publici* (as P–W XIX, 13) is very meagre if not non-existent – VI 14428 where the juxtaposition of 'verna peculiaris' and 'vicarius' is probably fortuitous. Suetonius, *Iul.* 76, is scarcely relevant as the alternative to Caesar putting his *servi peculiares* in charge of the mint and the *vectigalia publica* is not the *servi publici*. For the use of 'peculiaris' see Chantraine, p. 29.

Vicarii

Venustus Philoxeni Ti. Claudi Caesaris servi dispensatoris vicarius. The slave *vicarius* could be:

(i) a replacement, deputy or auxiliary of a slave official;
(ii) a personal slave of another slave irrespective of function or skill.

In both cases the *vicarius* would form part of the *peculium* of the *ordinarius*.[1] The use of 'vicarius' in this last sense is not found in Plautus but is well established by the time of Cicero and is the normal sense in later writers and in the jurists [2]

In the Familia Caesaris it is natural to suppose that important slave officials such as *dispensatores* and others devoted some portion of their wealth to the easing of their personal lot through personal slaves of their own. There is inscriptional evidence to prove it, especially in the much quoted case of Musicus Scurranus *dispensator ad fiscum Gallicum* at Lugdunum, who was attended on his journey to Rome, where he died, by no fewer than sixteen personal slaves, including cooks, footmen, butlers, secretaries, and so on. None of them held any official post in the administration although some were employed to manage Musicus' personal property.[3] But a closer examination of all the published inscriptions of the Imperial slave *vicarii* shows this instance to be curiously isolated. Multiple slaves, especially more than two, belonging to the one *ordinarius*, as in the case of Musicus, are certainly personal slaves, not deputies or occupational replacements. But out of sixty-five instances where the actual term 'vicarius' is found in the Familia Caesaris the only other comparable examples of *ordinarii* with multiple *vicarii* are those of Felix, *dispensator arcae patrimonii* at Hispalis, who has five, and Heracla Aug. *dispensator*, who has only two.[4] In 59/65 cases the *ordinarius* has a single *vicarius*.

More significant is the occupation of the *ordinarius* where this is stated. There are 45 instances as follows:[5] *dispensator* 30, *arcarius* 4, *vilicus* 5,

---

[1] Erman (pp. 405, 413) considered that most *vicarii* who were replacements of slave officials (Category I) belonged to the master, in these cases the emperor, and not to the *peculium* of the *ordinarius*. But this double meaning of 'vicarius' is difficult from the juridical as well as the epigraphical point of view (cf. Erman's explanation of VI 8950 = D 1771 at p. 413) and is to be rejected. See also Boulvert, *EAI*, p. 199 n. 736.

[2] Cicero, *Verr.* i. 91, 93; iii. 86; *pro Rosc. Com.* 27. Cf. Horace, *Sat.* ii. 7.79; Martial, ii. 18.7 ('esse sat est servum, iam nolo vicarius esse'); *Dig.* ix. 4.19, etc.

[3] VI 5197 = D 1514. For freedman officials examples of personal assistants as *tabularii, dispensatores, vilici*, etc. are not numerous: e.g. VI 70, 586, 8410; X 1732; cf. Hirschfeld, *Verwalt.* p. 463 n. 2.

[4] II 1198 (Felix is without status indication); VI 8832. For a *vic(arii) vicarius*, cf. *Bull. Com.* (1925), p. 218. On the other general instances of 'vicarii' in the plural, see Weaver *JRS* 54 (1964), 118 n. 9.

[5] *Dispensator:* VI 64 = D 3502, 5197 = D 1514, 8478 = D 1604, 8719, 8832, 8845, 8863, 8950 = D 1771, 31012 = D 3554; XIV 202, 1876, 4485; II 1198 = D 1659; III 1222 = 7802, 3269, 4828, 7938 = D 4261, 8112, 12379 = 14207.39; *AE* 1914, 114 = *Dacia* I, 249–50; *AE* 1959, 307; *Bull. Com.*

The emperor's service

exactor 3, *contrascriptor* 1; *qui praefuit pedisequis* 1; *tab(ellarius?)* 1.[1] This is no ordinary cross-section of Imperial slave occupations, and even less so of those jobs which personal slaves would be required to perform, as were the cooks, footmen, butlers, etc. of Musicus Scurranus above. Only one (VI 33788 = D 1821) might fit into this category. The term 'vicarius' cannot stand for the masses of personal domestic slaves which must have been owned and employed by the emperor's slaves.

The key to its use is to be found in the functions of the *dispensatores, arcarii, vilici, exactores*, and the *contrascriptor*, who together make up 43/45 (96%) of all occupations here. They have in common responsibility for the handling of Imperial funds. In the case of *dispensatores* and *vilici* this was considerable. A *dispensator* was an important official in the Imperial financial administration. He was in charge of the funds in a particular department or *ratio*, most of which were in the provinces, or at least not under the direct supervision of the emperor or the administration in Rome.[2] *Vilici* who are found in charge of particular *stationes* of the *portorium* (customs) and of the exploitation of particular estates, mines, etc. belonging to the *patrimonium*, had similar financial responsibilities, but these could often only be part of their more general managerial functions, though the most important part.[3] *Vilici, exactores* and *contrascriptores* were all particularly connected with the collection of customs revenue in the provinces. The *vicarius* of one *vilicus*, indeed, was engaged in Africa in rebuilding at his own expense the local customs office (*teloneum*).[4] Thus in the cases where occupational data are available, the use of the term 'vicarius' in the Familia Caesaris is so closely associated with a restricted category of financial official that it must have administrative significance itself, and be a technical term for the deputy or auxiliary of these slave officials. In the cases where the occupation of the *ordinarius* is not stated, it is probable from the single *vicarius* together with other indications, e.g. second name in *-ianus*, that the *vicarius* is also to be considered in the technical sense as a replacement for the *ordinarius* and not

---

1925, p. 218; VIII 17335; XII 117; XIII 1054, 1818, 3461, 5194; *BGU* 102.1; *P. Oxy.* 735.7. *Arcarius:* III 556 = D 1504 (cf. 7268 = V 8818 = D 1503); V 1801 = *AE* 1956, 265; *AE* 1895, 10 = D 3580 (cf. *AE* 1937, p. 15); *AE* 1937, 29. *Vilicus:* II 8495 (bis); III 3937 = 10821; VIII 8488, 12314 = D 1654. *Exactor:* III 11549; VIII 2228 = D 4258; XIII 178 = 5092 = D 15192. *Contrascriptor:* VI 8950 = D 1771. *Qui praefuit pedisequis:* VI 33788 = D 1821. *Tab(ellarius?):* VIII 12631.

[1] In VIII 12631 (Carthage), 'tab(ellarius)' is preferable to 'tab(ularius)', as *tabellarii* were mostly of slave status but *tabularii* from the later first century almost always freedmen. Moreover, in this case the *vicarius* was only 4 years old, hence the term here cannot mean 'occupational replacement', but rather 'slave-born child' (*verna*). Cf. below, p. 203.

[2] On *dispensatores*, see now Boulvert, *EAI*, pp. 429 f.

[3] On *vilici*, see Boulvert, *EAI*, pp. 433 f., who points out that the Greek οἰκονόμος is used as the equivalent of both *dispensator* and *vilicus*.

[4] VIII 12314 (not 12134 as in Dessau) = D 1654.

Vicarii

as his personal servant or attendant.[1] The inscriptions of the *vicarii* are spread over the whole period from the Iulii to the Aurelii and Septimii, and over the whole empire. The instances that can be definitely dated to the late second or early third centuries all conform exactly to the same pattern.[2] Clear support for this use of the term 'vicarius' to denote a substitute deputising for the *ordinarius* in his professional capacity comes from a legal source, the *Fragmenta de iure fisci* 7: 'qui mutuam pecuniam contra interdictum dispensatori *vicariove eius* crediderit...', where loans are officially forbidden to a *dispensator* in his official capacity, and similarly to his official *vicarius*.[3]

On the other hand, it can be shown that the term was positively avoided, as a rule, in referring to personal slaves of Imperial slaves. First, the evidence of the age-figures. There is only one instance of a *vicarius* who died in childhood, in an African inscription which has other unusual features.[4] The regular term for Imperial slaves who died under about 18 years of age is 'verna'. This applies also to the personal slaves/children of Imperial slaves, among whom the ages at death of *vernae*, where recorded, are 22, 14, 10, 9, and 6 years, and another six infants who died at the age of 3 years and under.[5] The oldest, a woman, who is also the earliest in date, is from the reign of Gaius (VI 5822). These *vernae*, children including girls, are distinct from the *vicarii*, who were, almost without exception, adult males, and thus suitable for administrative employment.

Even more significant, therefore, is the absence of women from the lists of *vicarii*. In any representative sample of a normal social group, unless special restrictions apply, some reasonable balance between the sexes might be expected. But in this case there is only one uncertain example of a *vicaria* to

---

[1] VI 138 = D 3969, 4409, 9061, 13850, 14428, 15492, 16787, 18296, 26065; *Bull. Com.* 1941, p. 173 n. 81a; *AE* 1964, 96; XIV 50; *AE* 1939, 145–6; II 6091; III 256, 4808; V 7239; VIII 12727, 24710; IX 321. *Vicarii* of the *Augustae* and some doubtful cases have been excluded, as follows: VI 4332, 7467 = D 7429, 9991 = D 7374 ('Lupercus subvillicus hortorum Antonianorum', without status indication), 35700; XI 5418 = 5459; *AE* 1945, 123; *AE* 1958, 278.

[2] III 3269: Marcus Sperati disp. vi(k). (Carcacalla and Iulia Domna); III 8112: Myrism[us] Felicis d[isp.] vil. (AD 228); VIII 2228 = D 4258: vik. Augg. n. vernae exac(toris); XIII 1818 = D 1662: vikarius quond(am) Augustor. ex dispensatoribus; *AE* 1914, 114 = *Dacia* I, 249–50: vik. Augg(g). nn(n). disp. It is to be observed that the form 'vikarius' appears in all these cases where the reading is preserved, perhaps influenced by the Greek οὐικάριος; cf. *BGU* 102.1 dated to 161. This form does not occur in the Julio-Claudian period nor indeed certainly in the first century. It may be taken as provisionally indicating a second-century date. The form 'servus vicarius' does not appear.

[3] Text of the *Frag. de iure fisci* in *FIRA²* II, pp. 627–30. 'Vicarius' in this sense may also be inferred from the use of the term 'ordinarius dispensator' in Suetonius, *Galba* 12. Cf. *Dig.* xlvii. 10. 15.44 (Ulpian).

[4] VIII 12631, aged 4 (see above, p. 202 n. 1). Curiously in *AE* 1939, 145–6 two different *vikarii* of the Imperial slave Thaumastus both appear to have died at the age of 14 years.

[5] VI 5822, 8516, 8578 = D 1511, 18369, 19018, 21604, 26091, 38178; IX 5481; XIV 202; Thylander, *IPO* A 102; *AE* 1929, 154; *NS* 1928, 209 n. 11.

The emperor's service

be found compared with up to sixty-four male *vicarii*.[1] This requires explanation, as we know from the inscriptions that female slaves of Imperial slaves, as we might expect, existed in large numbers. They are to be found both before and after manumission among the *servae* and *libertae* of *Augusti liberti*. In fact there are as many *libertae* as *liberti* in this group. Amongst the 'vernae' of Imperial slaves, girls are well represented.[2] Outside the Familia the term *vicaria* is common enough.[3] The absence of *vicariae* from the Familia is not a normal social phenomenon, but the consequence of the administrative use of the term 'vicarius'. Women would have no place as officials in the financial administration.

Furthermore, from the social point of view it does not appear that *vicarii* in the Familia Caesaris were in that underprivileged condition that the legal sources would lead us to expect of slaves of slaves in general. The Imperial slave *vicarii* tend to marry upwards into the freed and freeborn classes.[4] From a small sample, in the five cases where the husband–wife relationship is expressly indicated, one wife is freeborn, one is a freedwoman, and three are either freed or freeborn. In four cases the *nomina* of the wives are from outside the circle of Imperial *nomina*, and in the remaining case, Flavia Heuresis, the wife of a *vikarius*, perhaps from the third century, is not likely to be an Imperial freedwoman. Most of the wives without status indication are thus likely to be freeborn. This is a pattern which is typical of the most favoured ranks of the Imperial slaves and corresponds closely with the marriage pattern of the 'vicariani' which is based on a much larger sample. Not surprisingly if, as is suggested below,[5] many of the 'vicariani' are merely *vicarii* at a later stage of their careers.

It is also worth considering the geographical distribution of the *vicarii*. Careers in the financial services of the administration frequently took the *ordinarius* and his *vicarius* outside Rome. As the case of Musicus Scurranus shows, a certain amount of travelling to and from Rome must have been

---

[1] III 1222 = 7802: 'd. m. Isidorae domo Asiae (aged 18), Primus Aug. disp. vik. b. m.' The interpretation 'vik(ariae)' is not entirely certain. It could be used in the sense of 'vernae', as for a child; cf. above, p. 203 n. 4 and n. 5. It is possible, however, that the name of the *dispensator* has been omitted (cf. the earlier reading in III 1222). For a comparable omission in the formula 'Augusti l(iberti) l(ibertus)' see p. 208.

[2] E.g., from Rome alone: VI 5822, 18369, 21604, 26091, 38178.

[3] E.g. VI 6392: Felicia Hipparchi vicaria; XII 4451 (Narbo): Myrine Fausti col. Narbonesium servi vicaria; cf. VI 6393–6, 6398–401. 'Ancilla' occurs once for the female slave of an Imperial slave (*NS* 1939, 86–7).

[4] VI 13850, Caecilia Primigenia; their daughter is Caecilia Sp. f. Saturnina; 15492, Claudia Laurina; 16787, Aemilia Secunda coniunx; *AE* 1964, 96 (Rome): Flavia Heuresis coniunx (3rd c.?); VIII 17335, Pompeia Chelia (viro); V 1801 = *AE* 1956, 265: Sallustia Minnidis l. Ionis contubernalis; 7239: Iulia Prima; IX 321, Zosimenis conserva.

[5] See chapter 14 below.

Vicarii

necessary, and one can infer from this the existence of personal slaves. But for the *vicarii* the proportion of inscriptions from Rome is remarkably small, while the majority are well spread throughout the provincial centres of administration and customs posts.[1] These date from the Flavian period and especially the second and third century. Such a distribution is significant and illustrates the occupational or career aspect of these *vicarii*.

Thus, in the Imperial household *vicarius* is a term which is not used for personal slaves of slaves in the general sense common in the literary and legal texts. The term is kept fairly strictly for occupational replacements in the literal sense of 'vicarius'. On the other hand, such *vicarii* are to be considered as part of the *peculium* of the Imperial slave *ordinarii* and not as having been assigned by the emperor from his own *familia* as a replacement for a particular post. This is shown by the fact that when the *ordinarius*, who was normally only in the middle order of the occupational hierarchy, was promoted, manumitted or retired, his *vicarius*, if he succeeded him in this post, as was common, was transferred to the direct ownership of the emperor but nevertheless retained the name of the *ordinarius* as a second name with the suffix *-ianus*. There is evidence in the legal sources that one of the special conditions of manumission could be the transfer of the *vicarius* to the master of the *ordinarius* – a form known as manumission 'vicario relicto'.[2] Certain financial posts in the administration were always held by slaves despite or rather because of the important responsibilities involved.[3] Boulvert has well pointed out that this was precisely because the slave's lack of separate legal personality enabled him to handle funds directly on behalf of his master, whereas free persons not *in potestate*, at least in the time of the jurist Gaius (ii. 95), could not act as representatives on behalf of another with the same direct effects.[4] The same considerations would explain in turn the use of a slave *vicarius* by *dispensatores*, *vilici*, etc. This is preferable to the alternative explanation offered that the emperor, by being able to put suspected slaves to the torture if need be, could thus better guard against peculation. These *dispensatores* in their turn needed to exercise a similar control over their

---

[1] Spain: Hispalis (II 1198 = D 1659), Tarraco (II 6091); Gaul: Lugdunum (XIII 1818 = D 1662), Mediolanum Santonum (XIII 1054), Suessiones (XIII 3461 = D 4376a), Aventicum (XIII 5092 = D 1519a), Vindonissa (XIII 5194); Noricum: Virunum (III 4808, 4828, 11549); Moesia: Viminacium (III 8112); Dacia: Sarmizegetusa (III 7938 = D 4261), Apulum (III 1222 = 7802); Achaia: Athens (III 556 = D 1504), Corinth (III 6268 = V 8818 = D 1503); Galatia: Ancyra (III 256); Africa: Carthage (VIII 12631, 12727, 24710), Thabraca (VIII 17335, *AE* 1895, 10 = D 3580, cf. *AE* 1937, p. 15); Numidia: Tebessa (*AE* 1937, 29), Mascula (VIII 2228 = D 4258); Mauretania: Sitifis (VIII 8488).

[2] *Cod. Theod.* iv. 8.7; *Cod. Iust.* vi. 46.6; vii. 9.1; see Erman, *Servus Vicarius*, p. 432 and n. 3.

[3] *Cod. Iust.* xi. 37.1: 'praesertim cum servi eiusmodi officia administrare debeant'. Cf. Mommsen ad *CIL* v 83.

[4] Boulvert, *EAI*, p. 430 with n. 328. Cf. Kaser, I, 226 f.; Buckland, *Textbook*, pp. 200 f.

The emperor's service

deputies for whom they were in the last resort answerable to the emperor. The legal status of these deputies (*vicarii*) also explains a notable omission from the ranking nomenclature of the junior clerical grades in the administration – there is no grade of 'adiutor dispensatoris' (assistant *dispensator*) corresponding to that of *adiutor a commentariis* or *adiutor tabulariorum*, although assistants were needed for *dispensatores* as much as for the corresponding grades of *a commentariis* and *tabularius*. In the Familia Caesaris the 'assistant *dispensatores*' are in fact called *vicarii*.

Successful *dispensatores*, however, were not confined to slave status till the end of their careers. They were usually manumitted about the age of forty or soon after and promoted to senior clerical status, or indeed became freedman *procuratores* in both financial and non-financial departments. Continuity was maintained for the slave financial posts by the *vicarius* taking over – as 'vicarianus' – with, in his turn, a *vicarius* of his own.

CHAPTER 13

LIBERTI SERVUS AND LIBERTI LIBERTUS

It is clear that personal slaves of Imperial slaves must have existed in considerable numbers. What was their social status and how does it compare with that of the *vicarii* above? To find out this we must examine the inscriptions of the slaves and freedmen of the *Augusti liberti*, as both personal slave and slave-master, and particularly the latter, had often gained manumission by the time of life at which their inscriptions were put up.

The nomenclature of the *Aug(usti) lib(erti) libertus* presents few problems.[1] Normally in inscriptions the *lib. libertus* takes the *nomen gentilicium* while the freedman-patron is referred to by his *cognomen* only – no doubt to save space as both have the same *nomen*; e.g. VI 4281: Ti. Iulius Demetrius Anthi Aug. l. lib., Ti. Iulius Anthi Aug. l. lib. Hilario, where the status indication is exhibited in different positions within the same inscription.[2] The terms 'patronus', 'libertus', etc. are used as normal. But 'verna' is frequently not an indication of slave status at all, being in fact used for *lib. liberti* who died early, or for slaves who may have been manumitted at the point of an early death, or indeed for freeborn children of *liberti*.[3] As for the slaves of Imperial freedmen, not only are their inscriptions much fewer in number than those of the *lib. liberti*, but also they mention the *nomen* of their freedman-master much less frequently – in fact in less than a third of the examples (12/40), including several *vernae* who are presumably, but not certainly, slaves. The reason for this is that most of the inscriptions are not primarily dedicated to the freedman-patrons but to the individual *lib. servi* and *lib. liberti*. The *lib. servi* have no *nomen* to boast of in their inscription, and thus frequently do not even mention that of their freedman-master. The *lib. liberti*, on the other hand, do have a *nomen* and are usually anxious to display it.[4]

There are many more *lib. liberti* than *lib. servi* – over 200 freedmen mostly

[1] On this nomenclature see now Chantraine, pp. 389 f.
[2] But there are numerous exceptions, e.g. VI 10547: Acratus Ti. Iuli Aug. liberti Himeri lib., which also exhibits the full spelling of 'libertus' common in inscriptions of *lib. liberti* but not elsewhere.
[3] E.g. VI 14990: 'l(iberto) et vernae' (5 years old); *AE* 1903, 338: 'Flaviae Sozusae Flavia Aug. lib. Oeogonomia vernae suae' (13 years); VI 12948: 'Sex. Avonio Primigenio Euzelus Aug. lib. fecit vernae suo' (12 years).
[4] E.g. VI 8441: 'd. m. Aegypto servo Barbari Aug. lib. a codicillis'; cf. VI 5264: 'Iulia Restituta Acuti Aug. lib. liber.'

The emperor's service

from Rome, compared with only 40 slaves. This preponderance was partly due no doubt to the fact that a slave would always tend to put up his inscription after manumission if his hope of early manumission was reasonably high. The age-at-death figures of the *lib. liberti* show that one-half reached the age of only 22 years. The ages of the *lib. servi*, on the other hand, are even lower still, the halfway point being under ten years.[1] The explanation of the small number of personal slaves of Imperial slaves in the inscriptions lies, as these age figures suggest, in the high expectation of early manumission, one of the highest rates of early manumission for any group in the Familia Caesaris.[2] Imperial slaves, of course, who were sufficiently wealthy to own personal slaves, would have no difficulty in gaining their own manumission, by purchase if necessary, but they would normally have to wait till the regular age of 30.[3]

One curious group of *lib. liberti* from the early Principate deserves mention: VI 5909: C. Iulius Augusti l. l. Priamus; 20002: C. Iulius Caesar l. l. Felix; XIV 2302 = D 7462: C. Iulius Aug. liberti libertus Eros (AD 11); VI 5294: Telete Augustaes libertae liberta; 3879 = 32450: M. Livius Divae Aug. l. l. Severus; *AE* 1953, 24: M. Livius Augustae liberti libertus Tanais. All are from Rome or nearby. They all suppress the name of their immediate patron leaving only his status indication. Accidental omission of the patron's name cannot be the explanation. Nor lack of space: the unabbreviated forms 'liberti libertus' and 'libertae liberta' are used in 3/6 cases. The facts of status are indicated clearly and unambiguously. But the personal connection with the immediate patron is blurred, presumably because it was immaterial for expressing the simple fact of being associated with the emperor's Familia, which is all the dedication is concerned with here.[4] The only occupation mentioned – XIV 2302 = D 7462: *pistor candidarius* – is that of specialist baker, which suggests business enterprise or even a post in the Imperial palace, rather than service formerly as a slave's personal slave. The two latest examples are from the reign of Claudius – VI 3879 = 32450 cannot be earlier than the deification of Livia in 41, and *AE* 1953, 24 records the decurions of an association of Imperial household personnel (*collegium Augustianum maius castrense*) dated very probably to the year 45.[5] Both these have the *nomen* 'Livius' which derives from their patrons who were freedmen of Livia, manumitted before AD 14. Their own manumission could, of course,

---

[1] There are twenty-four age figures for *lib. liberti*, ranging from 50 to 5 years, and eleven figures for *lib. servi*, ranging from 32 (a *dispensator*) to 1 year.

[2] On the manumission of slaves of Imperial slaves 'per interpositam personam', a device whereby slaves might attempt to obviate their own incapacity to perform the act of manumission directly, see Erman, *Servus Vicarius*, pp. 458 f.; Weaver, *JRS* 54 (1964), 121.

[3] On age at manumission, see Part II, chapters 5 and 11.

[4] But see Chantraine, p. 393 with n. 35.

[5] Gordon, *Alb.* I, No. 90; cf. No. 91 (pp. 90 f.).

Liberti servus and liberti libertus

be much nearer the reign of Claudius. The period of the Julian emperors, especially Augustus, exhibits considerable variation in the status nomenclature of Imperial freedmen, e.g. the forms 'Divi Aug. l.', 'Caesaris Aug. l.', 'Caesaris l.', which are common under Augustus but rare under Claudius and Nero, and disappear completely from the time of Vespasian, when 'Aug. lib.' becomes standard. The suppression of the immediate patron's name by some *Aug. lib. liberti* and *Augustae lib. liberti* was one of the forms of this early period which disappeared along with the other variant forms during this process of regularisation.

The occupations of the slaves and freedmen of Imperial freedmen show that they are mostly personal slaves, e.g. *aedituus, a cubiculo, rogator, paedagogus, a manu*. The few that could have any clerical or administrative significance are probably personal to the freedman-patron, as in the case of the slaves of Musicus Scurranus discussed above.[1] Instances of a group of *lib. liberti* dedicating an inscription to their freedman-patron are frequent.[2] Again these groups correspond to the personal slaves of, e.g., Musicus Scurranus. Whether manumitted individually or as a group on some particular occasion after the manumission of their *ordinarius* or at his death, these freedmen are for the most part the former personal slaves acquired by their patron both when a slave himself and later after his manumission. The proportion of inscriptions of *lib. liberti* and *lib. servi* that come from Rome – 77% and 76% of the respective totals – is just above the average for the Familia Caesaris as a whole. This is to be contrasted with the unusually small proportion of *vicarii* found in Rome – only 37%. The personal slaves were mostly employed in the household of their freedman-patron or master in the metropolis, not, as were the *vicarii*, as his deputy in the emperor's service in the provinces.

In another respect the *lib. liberti* differ significantly from the *vicarii* (and 'vicariani'). Almost half of them are in fact women – *lib. libertae*. Such phrases as 'viro et patrono', 'patronus et contubernalis', 'patrono idem coniugi', 'lib. et coniugi', etc. are very common among their inscriptions and indicate what was the most important role of the female slaves of Imperial slaves and freedmen. There was always a strong tendency for slaves, especially *vilici*, to find their marriage partner within the same *familia*.[3] This could be due to inclination induced by proximity, but could also be because the

---

[1] The occupational titles in VI 8410, for example, show this. Fortunatus, the freedman and personal accountant of the important Atticus Aug. lib., *a rationibus*, is simply called *tabularius*, whereas Fructus Atticianus, a former slave of Atticus but now belonging to the emperor Domitian, has a post in the Imperial administration as *tabular(ius) a rationib(us)*.

[2] VI 8498 = D 1738, 8547, 8581, 9059, 33738 = D 9027; *AE* 1950, 170; III 14180; V 42, 7751 = D 1822; VIII 12883; XII 4490.

[3] Plautus, *Casina* iii. 3.36; Cato, *RR* 143; Varro, *RR* i. 17.5; ii. 10.6; Columella, *RR* i. 8.5.

The emperor's service

master, strictly exercising his rights of ownership, refused to allow them to marry outside his *familia*.[1] But for the slave-husband it was often preferable not to be assigned his partner by his master but to marry his own female slave, if he could afford one. The master's respect for his slave's *peculium* was obligatory in the domestic law of the *familia*, but ordinary *contubernium* was protected only by ties of sentiment and humanity. *Contubernales* might be separated at the will of the master whenever he thought it in his interest to do so. As slave-owning Imperial slaves were normally manumitted fairly early, the freedman-husband would also normally manumit his slave-wife at the earliest possible moment in the interests of the status of the children.[2] Cases of *libertae* in the Familia Caesaris manumitting their slave-husbands are rare – there are three examples, against seventy-seven cases of *liberti* manumitting *servae*, most of whom are their wives. These latter, before manumission, are the missing *vicariae* of the Familia Caesaris.

From the social point of view the wives' names provide a positive indication of the difference in status between the freedmen and slaves of Imperial freedmen, on the one hand, and the *vicarii* (and 'vicariani') on the other. As we have seen, the *vicarii*, who are still of slave status, are in nearly all cases already married to women who have *nomina*, and are therefore either freedwomen or freeborn. The prevalence of non-Imperial *nomina* amongst these allows the probability that most of them are in fact freeborn. By contrast, the *lib. libertae* mostly marry their own freedman-patrons, and the *lib. liberti* normally marry slave women or freedwomen with status indication. Moreover where the wives have a *nomen*, indicating that they are either *ingenuae* or *libertae*, this is mostly one of the Imperial *nomina*, which suggests that most of them are from the Familia Caesaris itself. Few wives of *lib. liberti* have a non-Imperial *nomen*. In chronological order they are: Iulia Glaphyra (colliberta), Baebia Ɔ. l. Parhalia, Iulia Thyrsi l. Iole, Tertia, Iulia Sperata, Iulia Coetonis, Dionysia, Carithe, Moschis (contub.), Domitia Nereis, Primigenia (contub.), Geminia Syntyche, Flavia Acte, and Ucena Victoria (?).[3] The wives of the *lib. servi*, who should follow the same pattern, are: Felicula, Claudia Prima, Flavia Avita, Atreia L. f. Procula (the exception, she is freeborn; her husband is the *dispensator* of a procurator, Halotus Aug. l.), Terpusa (conserva), Iulia Pyrallis, and Ampliata (conserva).[4] Remembering

---

[1] Tertullian, *ad uxor*. ii. 8: 'nonne...severissimi quique domini et disciplinae tenacissimi servis suis foras nubere interdicunt? scilicet ne in lasciviam excedant, officia deserant, dominica extraneis promant.'

[2] On manumission 'matrimonii causa', cf. Gaius, i. 19; see Part II, chapters 5 and 11.

[3] XIV 2302 = D 7462; VI 5909, 19060; *AE* 1913, 216; V 1251; III 2097; VI 13659, 8761 = D 1736; XIV 2780; VI 8598, 18112, 14646, 8762; XIV 3718.

[4] VI 11242, 8759, 18296 cf. 25429, 8833, 8605, 20649; X 695.

Liberti servus and liberti libertus

that single names without status indication refer to *servae*, we can see here a marriage pattern for the *lib. liberti* similar to that of the Imperial slaves in the provinces, whose wives are in general of lower social status than the corresponding wives in Rome.

The conclusion to this section of the argument is that personal slaves of Imperial slaves and freedmen existed in considerable numbers. Except in a very few cases, such as that of Musicus Scurranus who comes from early in the first century, in the reign of Tiberius, these personal slaves avoid using the term 'vicarius'. They are either called 'vernae' if young, or are found in the inscriptions as *servi* and especially, because of their high rate of manumission, as *liberti* of the *Augusti liberti*. Female slaves who would all belong to the category of personal slaves and who had the legal status of *vicariae* do not use that title either. They are mostly found manumitted as *libertae* of *Augusti liberti* to whom they are usually married.

CHAPTER 14

'VICARIANI'

Higher in legal and occupational status than either of the two preceding groups are what I have called the 'vicariani'. The use of the term 'vicarianus' in the early Empire requires explanation.

Imperial freedmen and slaves in the period from Augustus to Trajan frequently exhibit in their inscriptions second names (*agnomina*) ending usually in *-ianus*, sometimes in *-anus*, and occasionally in *-inus*.[1] These names are derived from the *nomen* or *cognomen* of a former master from whose *familia* they have passed either by gift, purchase or inheritance into the Familia Caesaris. Such *agnomina* are found in only a comparatively small minority of the total inscriptions of each class and period – not more than 6% of all Imperial freedmen with or without *nomen* from the Iulii to the Ulpii, and about the same proportion of all Imperial slaves from Augustus to Hadrian.[2]

If every slave of a Roman master on being transferred to the ownership of the emperor regularly took a second name derived from his former owner, we would possess valuable information on the sources of recruitment of the Familia Caesaris for the first century and a half of its existence. Unfortunately this is not so. Even allowing for the incomplete nature of the inscriptional evidence, it is difficult to believe that under 10% of the Familia Caesaris – although the figure is nearer 12% for the Iulii and Claudii – was recruited from such sources in the first century AD. Slaves deriving from the client kings and princes of the Julian period also appear, as the following names

[1] (*a*) *-anus*: Acteanus (VI 15027), Augustanus (VI 8772, VIII 13092, *AE* 1937, 72), Popp(a)eanus (VI 99, 8954 = D 1782), Priscillanus (*IRT* 302 = *AE* 1926, 164), Scapulanus (VI 10302 = D 7352), Scurranus (VI 5197 = D 1514), Hyperephanus (VI 18205).
(*b*) *-inus*: Amphioninus (VI 12797), Rufioninus (VI 20201).

[2] Hülsen, *Röm. Mitt.* 3 (1888), 222–32, compiled the list as it stood at that time, including several without status indication. His remarks are mostly in the nature of annotations rather than a full discussion of the implication of the second names. The basic list is now that of Chantraine, pp. 295–350, and has been increased to well over three hundred items. Chantraine's work is very thorough and accurate. He includes in his catalogue full references, with a discussion of the possible alternative derivations of each *agnomen*. While his main concern is with the nomenclature, he also discusses its implications (pp. 350–88) without, however, analysing the *agnomina* in groups according to social origin, or discussing the question of the 'vicariani' with which I am primarily concerned here. In my discussion I have not included those without specific status indication, which are from the early first century or earlier (see esp. VI 10395 and X 6638), because of their uncertain status and the likelihood that some at least are *servi publici* (e.g. VI 4431 = D 1971: Hymnus Aurelianus a bybliothece Latina porticus Octaviae; 4435: Montanus Iulianus vilic. a byblioth. Octaviae Lat.).

'Vicariani'

attest – Amyntianus, Archelaianus, Herodianus, Iubatianus, Pylaemenianus.[1] These names are also one important source of evidence for the growth of the emperor's *patrimonium* in this period. Slaves may be regarded as one form of property, and imply the acquisition of other forms such as villas, estates, mines, etc. by the *patrimonium* as well.[2] Slaves born and bred within the Familia (*vernae*) are unlikely to have supplied anything like 90% of the *servi Caesaris*, especially in the early part of the period, as this was a time of expansion in numbers. It follows that the *agnomen* does not occur in all cases of transference into the Familia Caesaris, and is even the exception rather than the rule. Moreover, as each succeeding emperor inherited the slaves of his predecessor, the examples of Neronianus, Galbianus, Othonianus, Domitianianus, and others would be incredibly few if the second name was regularly assumed.[3] The *agnomen* is not, therefore, an obligatory expression of a change in legal status. In seeking to account for these names it is first necessary to discuss briefly their occurrence outside the Familia Caesaris.[4]

Agnomina in *-ianus* are commonly found from the second century BC among senatorial families in cases of adoption when the *nomen* of the adoptive father was taken but that of the real father retained, with the suffix *-ianus* added, as a second *cognomen* (or *agnomen*), e.g. P. Cornelius Scipio Aemilianus, C. Iulius Caesar Octavianus. This nomenclature expresses the transference of *patria potestas* by adoption. In slave and freedman nomenclature *agnomina* in *-ianus* express the transference of *dominica potestas* from one master to another and they thus originate among those of slave status and were retained on manumission. For slaves and freedmen such second names are not personal names and are quite distinct from ordinary personal names in *-ianus*, e.g. Philetianus, Trophimianus, etc., which are themselves of frequent occurrence. They are also distinct from the double *cognomen* occasionally borne by some freedmen under the Republic, e.g. P. Dindius P. l. Davos Calidus, Eros Merula, etc.[5] Among the slave classes of society second names are commonly found, apart from the Familia Caesaris, among the *servi publici* where they are regular.[6] Among slaves of *municipia* individual examples

---

[1] Amyntianus: VI 8894; 4035 (M. Livius Aug. l.); 8738 = D 7866 (I BC); 10395 (three: I BC, AD I) without status indication. Archelaianus: VI 4776, 5872. Herodianus: VI 9005 = D 1795. Iubatianus: VI 5754, 9046. Pylaemenianus: VI 5188 = D 1589.

[2] See Hirschfeld, 'Der Grundbesitz der römischen Kaiser in den ersten drei Jahrhunderten', *Klio* 2 (1902), 46 f. = *Kleine Schriften* (1913), 516 f.

[3] See below, p. 216 n. 4 and n. 6.

[4] See now Chantraine, pp. 293 f., 360 f.

[5] Mommsen, *Staatsr.* III, 426 n. 3; Vitucci, *Diz. Epig.* IV, 916.

[6] But with exceptions, e.g. VI 2344 = D 1974, 2345 = D 1975. See L. Halkin, *Les esclaves publics chez les romains* (1897), p. 35; Buckland, *Roman Law of Slavery*, p. 320 n. 7; Mommsen, *Staatsr.* I, 323 n. 3.

The emperor's service

occur but as the exception rather than the rule.[1] Occasional examples are also found among noble families of high position and pretension such as the Vipsanii and Statilii.[2]

With the *servi publici* the *agnomen* is placed sometimes before, sometimes after the status indication 'publicus',[3] e.g. VI 2320: Herodes Volusianus publicus, septemvir; 2327: Fortunatus publicus Sulpicianus, curionalis. The same is true in the Familia Caesaris. In the nomenclature of Imperial freedmen the *agnomen* regularly follows the *cognomen* when *praenomen* and *nomen* are present. Where *praenomen* and *nomen* are omitted, and in slave nomenclature, the second name regularly comes after the status indication. These usages are all illustrated by the case of *Atticianus* from the Flavian period: VI 18049: T. Flavius Aug. l. Epaenus Atticianus; 8451: Epaphra Aug l. Atticianus; 8410: Fructus Imp. Caesaris Domitiani Aug. Germanic(i) Atticianus; 11390: Alexander Caesar. ser. Atticianus; 8408: Abascantus Aug. a rat(ionibus) Attic(ianus). In a number of cases, particularly examples of the Julio-Claudian period, the *agnomen* follows the word indicating occupation or official position, as sometimes, though much less frequently, happens with the status indication proper of Imperial slaves.[4]

With *servi publici*, again, the second name is derived from the *nomen*, or, less frequently, the *cognomen* of senatorial families – the most common are Aemilianus, Annianus, Cornelianus.[5] Mommsen connects these names with the high social status which the *servi publici* enjoyed among the slave section of the population (although *servi publici* who do not have a second name are not necessarily of lower status), and appears to give them quasi-legal significance.[6] But the apparently optional nature of these names makes this doubtful. As Mommsen himself points out,[7] whereas *servi publici* enjoyed several formal legal privileges, e.g. *ius testamenti*, which other slaves did not, slaves of the Familia Caesaris were not so privileged. The *agnomen* can have no legal significance.

[1] Cf. Halkin, *Les esclaves publics*, pp. 145 f. Among these one case is interesting as indicating explicitly the means of acquisition by the new owner: II 2229: 'Trophimus c(olonorum) c(oloniae) ser. emptu Germanianus'.

[2] VI 6228, 6356 = D 5256, 18269. For the *Germani corporis custodes* of the Statilii cf. Mommsen, *Staatsr.* II, 824 n. 6. For other examples, all from the early Principate, see Hülsen, *Röm. Mitt.* 3 (1888), 222 n. 2; cf. Chantraine, pp. 293 f.

[3] *Servi publici*: VI 2307–2374. For the frequent omission of 'servus' from the status indication of *servi publici* compare the similar omission in the nomenclature of the Imperial slaves. 'Caesaris' is the predominant form for *Caesaris servi* in the Julio-Claudian period.

[4] Examples of this form of nomenclature with 'vicariani' are: VI 8727; III 12289; V 2386; XIV 2259; post-Claudian: VI 8408, 8754, 8831 = D 1657, 9059; X 6666.

[5] Halkin, *Les esclaves publics*, p. 34.

[6] *Staatsr.* I, 323 n. 3, 'man darf sie wohl als den Ausdruck einer Zwitterstellung zwischen den wirklichen Freien und den wirklichen Sclaven auffassen'.

[7] *Staatsr.* II, 836.

'Vicariani'

The use of *agnomina* by *servi publici* indicates social rather than a legal position among the upper ranks of the slave hierarchy. There are other indications, both legal and social: their salary, right of *peculium* and of making a valid will,[1] and above all their marriage unions usually with freeborn women, occasionally with freedwomen, but not with slave women,[2] and the freeborn status of their children. The use of *agnomina* by freedmen and slaves is part of the same process whereby freedman nomenclature was assimilated to that of the freeborn classes, which in its turn kept changing.[3] Trimalchio, the caricature of an upstart, took an *agnomen* and had the name 'C. Pompeius Trimalchio Maecenatianus' engraved on his monument.[4]

From the earliest Principate the slaves of the emperor, conscious of their own place in the social hierarchy and under the influence of the nomenclature of the *servi publici*, took second names which they retained as *agnomina* on manumission. A chronological analysis of the names gives interesting results.[5] Freedmen and slaves of the Iulii and Livia show a high proportion of *agnomina* derived, as are those of the *servi publici*, from noble families, e.g. Antonianus, Cornelianus, Cornificianus, Lollianus, etc.,[6] not to mention those derived from members of the Imperial family itself, e.g. Agrippianus, Drusianus, Germanicianus, Livianus, etc.[7] Others are derived from the names of client princes[8] and equestrians, notably Maecenas.[9] Less than a quarter are from other sources and most of them later than the reign of Augustus – Agathoclianus, Alypianus, Anterotianus, Celadianus, Faustianus, Rufioninus.[10]

Under Claudius and Nero the proportion of *agnomina* derived from the Imperial family, noble or equestrian names is considerably smaller – less than half, with Iulianus accounting for 6/20 instances. There are fewer from

---

[1] Salary: Frontinus, *De Aqu.* 100; Pliny, *Ep.* x. 31; *peculium*: *Dig.* xvi. 2.19; will: Ulpian, *Frag.* xx. 16; *CIL* vi 2354.

[2] Mommsen, *Staatsr.* I, 324; Halkin, *Les esclaves publics*, pp. 118 f.; but cf. Buckland's reservations, *Roman Law of Slavery*, pp. 319 f.

[3] H. Thylander, *Étude*, pp. 128 f.; I. Kajanto, *Onomastic Studies*, pp. 4 f.

[4] Petronius, *Cen. Tr.* 71.

[5] As the time of taking the second name is the important point, rather than the date at which the inscription was put up, inscriptions of Imperial freedmen with *nomen* are relevant to the reign of the emperor concerned or *earlier*, as the second name in *-ianus* was taken by a slave before manumission.

[6] VI 4018, 4124, 4173, 5180 = D 1948, 5194, 5245, 5858, 8753, 8893, 8911, 16658, 20112, etc.

[7] VI 4180, 4351 = D 1802, 4357, 4398, 4409, 4435, 5202 = D 1778, 5203, 5223, 5299, 5540 = D 1789, 5849, 8012 = D 8436, 8820, etc. See Chantraine's lists arranged alphabetically under the individual *agnomina*. On Germ(anici) or Germ(anicianus), see Gordon, *Alb.* I, 98.

[8] See above, p. 213 n. 1.

[9] Maecenatianus: VI 4016, 4032, 4095, 19926, 22970; *AE* 1921, 69.

[10] Agathoclianus: VI 20706a, cf. 10245; Alypianus: VI 33788 = D 1821; Anterotianus: VI 12652 (a *lib. libertus*), 25033; *PIR*², A 738; Celadianus: VI 8909; *PIR*², C 616; Suet. *Aug.* 67; Faustianus: VI 14828; Rufioninus: VI 20201. For Demosthenianus, VI 4173; cf. *PIR*², D 47; and for slaves of Livia: VI 3927, 4245, 8727.

The emperor's service

outside the Imperial family circle itself – Fabianus, Tadianus, Vestinianus, Vinicianus[1] – and none from the client princes who have by this time been largely eliminated. On the other hand, names derived from well-known Imperial freedmen (and freedwomen) appear – Acteanus, Acteniana, Pallantianus[2] – and many others clearly of slave or freedman origin – Diodorianus, Epagathianus, Epaphroditianus, Pamphilianus, Primigenianus, etc.[3]

In the Flavian period the proportion in the first category declines still further to less than one-third, mostly names derived from past emperors and *Augustae* – Agrippinianus, Antonianus, Galbianus, Neronianus, Octavianus, Othonianus, Poppaeanus[4] – and the two remaining names probably date back to the Neronian period – Crispinillianus, Volusianus.[5] Under Trajan only Arminianus, Augustanus and Domitianianus appear in this category.[6] All the others, as for the Flavians, are of servile origin with the names of the important freedmen and freedwomen again figuring prominently – Atticianus, Caenidianus, Parthenianus, Epaphroditianus.[7]

Thus it is clear that *agnomina* of Imperial, senatorial, equestrian or client prince origin decline steadily, and in some cases rapidly, in importance from Augustus to Trajan, while those of servile and particularly Greek derivation show an equally steady proportional increase in the same period.[8] There is no need to doubt that most if not all in the group classed as of servile origin are derived from Imperial slaves and freedmen themselves. Many of their names can be illustrated from the lists and in several cases from the same inscription, e.g. VI 10245: Gamus Caesaris Agathoclianus – Priscus Aug. l. Gamianus; VI 8410: Atticus Aug. lib. a rationib. – Fructus Imp. Caesaris

---

[1] Iulianus: VI 5751, 5837, 22679; AE 1953, 24; IGR I 39; IV 1477. Fabianus: VI 23569; XIV 3920; PIR², F 13; Seneca, *Apoc.* 13. Tadianus: VI 15062. Vestinianus: XI 3173; PIR¹, V 410. Vinicianus: VI 8938 = D 1690; PIR¹, V 445.

[2] Acteanus, Acteniana: VI 15027; X 7980. Pallantianus: VI 143 = D 3896a, 8470 = D 1535.

[3] Daphnidianus: V 6638. Diodorianus: AE 1902, 78. Epagathianus: III 12289. Epaphroditianus: VI 15082. Gamianus: VI 10245, 15350. Gratianus: VI 8933 = D 1689, 8934. Lentianus: V 2386. Pamphilianus: VI 4226 = D 1620. Primigenianus: IX 4977 = D 6558. Regillianus: XI 7745. Thamyrianus: III 12289; VI 8486 = D 1600. Thyamidianus: XI 3199 = D 3481. Vitalianus: X 1732.

[4] Agrippinianus: VI 15616, 24164, 33737. Antonianus: VI 18203. Galbianus: VI 8819 = D 1656, 18048, 37759, 38003. Neronianus: VI 10172 = D 5152, 10173, 15347. Octavianus: VI 15551 = D 7933. Othonianus: XIV 2060. Popp(a)eanus: VI 8954 = D 1782.

[5] Crispinillianus (VI 8726 = D 7733a) is probably derived from Calvia Crispinilla, Nero's former 'magistra libidinum' (Tacitus, *Hist.* i. 73). Volusianus (VI 10267) is assigned by Hirschfeld to L. Volusius Saturninus (PIR¹, V 660) who is probably too early. Cf. Chantraine, p. 341.

[6] Arminianus: VI 12348, perhaps C. Arminius Gallus (PIR², A 1065). Augustanus: VI 8772; VIII 13092; AE 1937, 72. Domitianianus: VI 8532 = D 1747; AE 1922, 122.

[7] Atticianus: VI 8408, 8410, 8451, 11390, 16616, 18049. Caenidianus: VI 15110, 18358; X 6666. Epaphroditianus: VI 239 = D 1633 (Epaphroditus, however, is a common name in these inscriptions, cf. from this period VI 8439 = D 1527, 8865, 15615, 33468). Parthenianus: V 2156.

[8] Those without status indication are mostly dated to the reigns of Augustus and Claudius. They are listed by Chantraine (cf. esp. pp. 299 f., 342 f.). Their *agnomina* belong predominantly to the senatorial or non-servile group.

'*Vicariani*'

Domitiani Aug. Atticianus tabular(ius) a rationib(us); VI 29960: Diogenes Caesaris – Ilissus Caesaris Aug. Diogenia(nus); VI 9035: T. Flavius Aug. lib. Narcissus – T. Flavius Aug. lib. Firmus Narcissianus; VI 1884 = D 1792: M. Ulpius Aug. lib. Phaedimus – Valens Aug. lib. Phaedimianus; III 12289: Thamyrus Aug. disp. Alexandrianus – Hymenaeus Aug. lib. Thamyrianus. Other pairs in different inscriptions are numerous.[1] In all these cases the *agnomen* and the personal connection make it obvious that the second member of each pair is a former slave of the first member, and has been transferred to direct ownership of the emperor, in some cases even before the manumission of the slave owner.

On the question of the chronological range of these *agnomina*, Hülsen[2] argued that there is no example of an Imperial freedman or slave with second name in *-ianus* definitely from the period after Trajan. But Valens Aug. lib. Phaedimianus, although deriving his second name from M. Ulpius Aug. lib. Phaedimus who died in 117, was still using it in 130.[3] Ἐπαφρόδιτος Καίσαρος Σειγηριανός,[4] P. Aelius Aug. lib. Ep[...] Polybianus,[5] and Callistianus Aug. lib. Sabinianus[6] are later than Trajan. Also, against Hülsen,[7] there are two examples from the Imperial *sepulcreta* in Carthage, in fact from the later one belonging to the mid-second century: VIII 13045: Fortunatus Aug. Corinthianus; 13092: Philomusus Aug. ser. Augustanus. But these examples are few compared with those extant from the reign of Trajan. We must conclude that *agnomina* ceased to be used in the Familia Caesaris under Hadrian and probably from early in the reign.

Thus in the early Principate *agnomina* in *-ianus*, hitherto among slaves used mostly by the *servi publici*, were adopted by the slaves of the Familia Caesaris who had been bequeathed or presented to Augustus, Livia and Tiberius by other members of the Imperial family, prominent *nobiles* and equestrians, and client princes. Under Claudius – perhaps as early as Augustus with Licinus[8] – when the freedman magnates rose to similar

[1] E.g. Amphion (V 1067), Amphioninus (VI 12797). Atimetus (XIV 4793), Atimetianus (VI 656 = D 3536; XV 7289, 7818 = D 8681); etc.
[2] *Röm. Mitt.* 3 (1888), 231 f.
[3] VI 1884 = D 1792. Cf. H. Bloch, *Bolli laterizi*, pp. 17 f. = *Bull. Com.* 64 (1936), 157 f.; where also see his brilliant chronological argument for the dating of brick-stamps, based on the nomenclature of Anteros Severi(anus) Caesaris n. (XV 811).
[4] *IGR* I 1256 = *SEG* XIII 601, cf. XIV p. 206; *IGR* I 1255 = *OGIS* II 678 (both dated to 118).
[5] VI 33760. In line 2 Hülsen proposed to read 'P. Aeli Aug. liber[...]' against the reading, the standard abbreviation 'Aug. lib.' for the freedmen of Trajan and Hadrian, and the spacing of the line which must have contained the personal name. Cf. now Chantraine, p. 366.
[6] VI 28789: 'L. Vibio Charixeno alumno Callistianus Aug. lib. Sabinianus'. It is almost certain that here we have a former slave of Vibia Sabina Augusta (but cf. *CIL* ad loc.).
[7] *Röm. Mitt.* 3 (1888), 232. Cf. Mommsen, *CIL* VIII p. 1335 and n. 14.
[8] Licinianus: VI 244, 3968. Cf. Chantraine, pp. 321 f., Nos. 206–8.

The emperor's service

positions of influence with the emperor, their slaves also assumed *agnomina* on becoming *Caesaris servi* in keeping with the social status which they accorded themselves. The *agnomen* thereby acquired an added significance for these holders. As slaves of Imperial freedmen and slaves they had been in the inferior legal position of *vicarii*. But the rise in status to become direct slaves of the emperor was of great importance to them. Their legal status improved. They did not exchange one master for another of the same legal status but they achieved the actual status of their previous master. But in addition their social status and, as will be seen, their occupational status improved also. They were selected for promotion to the status of *Caesaris servi* because of their personal qualities and training. This change of status they marked in their nomenclature, where appropriate, by dropping the signification 'vicarius' and by taking a second name in *-ianus* in its place. Thus from at least the middle of the first century former *vicarii* would quite naturally have acquired *agnomina* which, being derived from slave names in all cases, would have made up an important section of *agnomina* in that category. Hence the term 'vicariani' to characterise bearers of slave-derived *agnomina*. These *agnomina* need not have belonged exclusively to administrative officials, any more than the term 'vicarius' is exclusively an administrative one in the Familia Caesaris. It would be strictly possible for a personal slave to exchange one slave master for another who would finally manumit him in the same way that the emperor manumitted other 'vicariani'. There is only one such instance: VI 12652: Atimetus Pamphili Ti. Caesaris Aug. l. l. Anterotianus.[1]

The occupational data on both main groups with *agnomina* tend to confirm this administrative orientation of the 'vicariani'. Of thirty-six who are employed in domestic posts – excluding those belonging to the *familia* of Livia – two-thirds are from the Julio-Claudian period, and only ten from all periods are or could be 'vicariani'.[2] On the other hand, the forty who are employed in the financial offices in Rome and the provinces as *dispensatores, tabularii*, etc. are distributed chronologically as follows, in terms of the 'vicariani':[3] Julian, 3/6; Claudian, 6/9; Flavian, 15/17; Ulpian, 3/3; un-

---

[1] Similarly there is one example of a *vic(arii) vicarius* – Bull. Com. 1925, p. 218: 'Eleuther Tharsi Charitonis Aug. se(r). dis(pensatoris) vic(arii) arc(arii) vicarius', where the occupational title of Tharsus, *arcarius*, makes it probable that Eleuther is his deputy in the administrative sense, not his personal slave.

[2] All are from Rome: VI 252 = D 1824, 602, 1884 = D 1792, 8504 = D 1845, 8886, 8909, 8920, 8933 = D 1689, 8934, 33788 = D 1821.

[3] VI 3968, 4037, 5197 = D 1514; Claudian: V 2386; VI 9060 = D 1641; IX 4977 = D 6558; X 1732; XIII 5092 = D 15192; XIV 2259; Flavian: V 2156; VI 239 = D 1633, 301, 8408, 8410, 8438, 8439 = D 1527, 8451, 8475 = D 1542, 8575 = D 1502, 8831 = D 1657, 9059, 33468; X 6977 = D 1558; XIV 2431 = D 1586; Trajan: VI 634 = D 1540a, 8865; IRT 302; *incerti*: VI 594, 8723, 8836; XII 117.

'Vicariani'

certain date, 5/5. Total, 32/40. Of all administrative posts held by Imperial slaves or freedmen who also have *agnomina*, over 80% are 'vicariani' from the time of Claudius, and for the period Vespasian to Trajan the proportion is 90%. This more than reflects the overall proportion of 'vicariani' in each of these periods. For example they account for less than 70% of all *agnomina* in the Flavian period. Thus not only does the overall proportion of 'vicariani' steadily increase from Claudius to Trajan but also the proportion of them occupying posts in the administration, mostly financial ones, increases at an even higher rate. There is as positive a correlation between holders of these posts and 'vicariani', as between *vicarii* and the posts held by their *ordinarii*. It seems to me that this can hardly be accidental. Of the eight with second name in *-ianus* whose former masters were not Imperial slaves, six are from the Julio-Claudian period when numbers of slaves of all kinds entered the Familia from outside by inheritance or gift.[1] Another point to be noted is that the *agnomina* of those freedmen who reached procuratorial rank are Antonianus, Caenidianus, Domitianianus, and that of the slave who rose to be a *trierarchus* is Livianus,[2] all former slaves of an *Augustus* or *Augusta*, except Caenis whose position and influence was nevertheless equivalent to that of an *Augusta*. Thus special patronage may have eased the way to the procuratorial grade for these members of the Familia. The 'vicariani' may have simply dropped their *agnomen* on rising to senior rank, but as the others did not do so this is unlikely. Perhaps they were normally manumitted later than other *dispensatores* who had reached that rank by a different route at an earlier age. The 'vicarianus', who usually served in the provinces, may not have completed his slave service until his mid- or late forties and thus have been behind in the promotion race for the limited number of senior posts open to him. Thus his original lowly legal status and the fact that his patron was merely an ordinary freedman may in the end have prevented him from reaching the top.[3]

[1] Julian: VI 4358, 8820, 9066; Claudian: VI 8822 = D 1655, 8823-4; XI 5756; XIV 3920; Flavian: VI 8819 = D 1656, 33737.

[2] *EE* VIII 335; X 6666; *AE* 1922, 122; XII 257 = D 2822: 'Anthus Caesaris trierarchus Livianus'. The slave status of Anthus is clear, in my opinion, from his personal nomenclature, as it is in the cases of 'Malchio Caesaris trierarchus de triere Triptolemo' (IX 41 = D 2819), 'Helios Caesaris trierarchus' (VI 8929 = D 2820), and 'Caspius trierarchus Ti. Caesaris' (VI 8928 = D 2821), despite the arguments of Starr, *Roman Imperial Navy*, pp. 44, 69 f., and now of Boulvert, *EAI*, pp. 62-3. These are cases where the occupational titles cannot outweigh the personal nomenclature, which is here unambiguous. If these are indeed Imperial freedmen without status indication, their occupational titles are perilously misleading. All the instances of Imperial freedmen *trierarchi* with status indication find the simple title 'trierarchus' sufficient. E.g. X 3357 = D 2817, 3358 = D 2818; VIII 21025; XIII 3542; *IGR* I 781. See above, p. 52; Chantraine, pp. 155, 177.

[3] T. Flavius Epaphroditus Ephebianus Aug. lib., *a rationibus* (VI 33468), a 'vicarianus', was almost certainly not in charge of the *a rationibus* bureau, nor even of senior status. On the terminology of the bureau officials, see chaps. 17 and 20 below.

The emperor's service

Nevertheless the 'vicariani' achieved a high rate of mobility, much above the average for the Familia Caesaris as a whole. This is indicated partly by the substantial number who rose one step further to freedman status. Although they probably remained slaves into their forties, those of a greater age in the inscriptions are invariably freedmen. But further evidence of their social mobility is to be found in their marriages. I estimate that there are forty-seven names of wives recorded, twenty-nine for 'vicariani' who are still slaves, and eighteen for those now freedmen. In all these cases there is, remarkably, not one instance of a 'vicarianus' marrying a slave or at least a wife who is still a slave, even though the 'vicarianus' husband in the majority of cases is still himself of slave status at the time the inscription was erected.[1] Specifically *ingenuae* are only Lucilia C. f. Pira and Antonia M. f. Dionysia, whose husbands are in both cases slaves. Freedwomen are found as wives, once of a freedman (VI 18358: Callistus Aug. lib. Hyginianus = Fl(avia) Aug. lib. Helpis Caenidiana), and four times of slave 'vicariani' (VI 15350: Actius Aug. Gamianus = Claudia Aug. l. Amanda; *AE* 1912, 183: Secundus Caesaris Aug. Erotianus = Attia Sex. l. Daphne; VI 4903: Anthus Caesar. Aug. ser. Sebosianus = Nonia Nymphe A. Noni. l.; 18456: Onesimus Imp. Caesaris Nervae Traiani Aug. Germ. ser. Phoebianus = Flavia Aug. lib. Tyche. All except the last are Julio-Claudian in date). The marriage pattern for slave and freed 'vicariani' should, of course, be similar as marriage would have taken place in almost all cases before the manumission of the husband. Interesting are two cases of *vicarii* of 'vicariani' one of whom, Secundus Secundi Aug. l. Vitaliani dispensator(is?), marries an *ingenua*, Titacia C. f. Procula and the other, Ursio Thalami Caesar. Aug. Xanthiani vic(arius), marries a Caecilia Primig(enia).[2] In the majority of cases the status of the wife is not explicitly stated, but for all the slave 'vicariani' their upward

---

[1] *Wives of liberti: Julio-Claudian:* Claudia Homonoea (VI 12652), Antonia Mystiche (VI 4037), Claudia Emma (*AE* 1902, 78), Pompeia Secunda (III 12289; VI 8486 = D 1600), Claudia Aphrodisia (VI 15357), Perellia Gemella (amico) (X 2857), Antonia Laeta (VI 17901); *Vespasian-Trajan:* Laitonia Festa (VI 8504 = D 1845), Flavia Idusa (VI 8920), Herennia Secunda (VI 8451), Fl(avia) Aug. lib. Helpis Caenidiana (VI 18358), Mulleia Tertulla (VI 18242), Flavia Nice (VI 8438), Sextia Chrysis (VI 9035), Ulpia Camilla (VI 29138), Vibia Fortunata (VI 29194), Ulpia Alypia (VI 29154); *undated:* Cornelia Gemella (VI 16397).

Wives of servi: Julio-Claudian: Iulia Constans (VI 8901), Claudia Aug. l. Amanda (VI 15350), Iulia Procula (XI 7745), Lucilia C. f. Pira (XIV 2259), Attia Sex. l. Daphne (*AE* 1912, 183), Claudia Psamathe (VI 15570), Nonia Nymphe A. Noni l. (VI 4903). *Vespasian-Trajan:* Sextilia Prisca (VI 11390), Flavia Faustina (III 4894), Caelia Marcella (VI 13910), Flavia Aug. lib. Tyche (VI 18456), Claudia P[...] (VI 31099), Ulpia Bassa (VI 8865), Volusia Comice (XIV 3396), Antonia Auge (VI 27388), Iulia Iusta (VI 8575 = D 1502), Memmia Panthera (VI 28593), Claudia Prisca (XIV 2431 = D 1586), Antonia M. f. Dionysia (VI 38010); *undated:* Maia Fortunata (VI 33553), Iulia Restituta (X 4225), Plautia Ianuaria (VI 8723), Claudia Thelge (VI 15615), Annia Cypris (VI 11782), Sextilia Prima (VI 18553), Scantia Priscilla (VI 25997), Iulia Elate (VI 20433), Claudia Arescusa (VI 19456), Cornelia Regilla (VI 34014).

[2] X 1732; VI 13850.

'Vicariani'

mobility through marriage is still remarkably constant whether their wives are freed or freeborn women. *Cognomina* such as Amanda, Daphne, Nymphe, Tyche, etc. cannot be used to distinguish between freed and freeborn status. The age of the wife at marriage or death, where it is known, is very often in the early twenties, somewhat early for manumission if the wife is a freedwoman.[1] The children are nowhere stated to be Imperial slaves (in most cases they bear Imperial *nomina*) and in status are similar to the children of *servi publici*. The use of such terms as 'testamentum', 'heres', etc. shows that they probably have the same right of testamentary disposition, at least in practice.

Another telling point is the *kind* of *nomina* of the wives of 'vicariani'. In 25/47 (53%) of the instances they have non-Imperial *nomina*, and in 22/47 (47%) Imperial *nomina*. In some cases where husband and wife have *different* Imperial *nomina* the wife is likely to be freeborn, but in very few of the cases where she has a non-Imperial *nomen* is she likely to be a freedwoman, as women normally married at an early age, well before the normal age of manumission, and children born to *servae* of non-Imperial masters were legally the property of those masters and not of the emperor. Marriage of Imperial slaves with non-Imperial slave women was in any case rare in the Familia Caesaris.[2] Marriage with freeborn women is therefore probable for a high proportion of 'vicariani' as it is for *vicarii* and *servi publici*. Indeed if 'vicariani' are for the most part merely *vicarii* at a later stage of their career, and if they had normally already married while still *vicarii*, one would expect the marriage patterns of the two groups to correspond significantly.

On the other hand, the marriage pattern of the other group with *agnomina* (the former slaves of other members of the Imperial family and of senatorial and equestrian families), who belong for the most part to the earlier half of the first century, many being found in the Imperial *columbaria*, not unnaturally conforms more closely to that of the Familia Caesaris as a whole in the pre-Claudian period. In this group marriages with slave partners are common, e.g. V 1067: Prima cont(ubernalis); VI 8822 = D 1655: Secunda (Drusilliana); 4776 (mother a freedwoman, child born a slave); 244 = D 7358, cf. 4395 etc.; and there is one case of a freedman, Eutychus Aug. lib. Neronianus, marrying his own freedwoman, VI 10172-3: Irene lib. The marriages of the female slaves and freedwomen with *agnomina* (the *-ianae*) conform to this pattern of downward mobility or none at all: VI 18358: Flavia Aug. lib. Helpis Caenidiana = Callistus Aug. lib. Hyginianus; VI 4402: Thetis Antoniae Drusi l. Scapliana = Marius cons(ervus); VI 3952: Asia Liviae Cascelliana =

---

[1] Servilia Primilla (d. 25), Iulia Constans (d. 22), Claudia Psamathe (d. 23), Caelia Marcella (d. 32), Claudia Thelge (d. 45, married 22 years), etc.

[2] See Part II, chapter 7, above, pp. 125, 133 f.

The emperor's service

Eutactus Liviae capsar(ius); cf. VI 8822 = D 1655: Secunda (Drusilliana) above.

In another important respect the parallel with the *vicarii* and the *servi publici* is close – the absence of women from their ranks. Of those with second name in *-iana*[1] the only two that could be classed as 'vicarianae' are Claudia Aug. l. Pythias Acteniana and Flavia Aug. lib. Helpis Caenidiana. But these are former slaves of freedwomen who were Imperial concubines rather than ordinary Imperial freedwomen; Acte and Caenis were *Augustae* in all but name, and they may fairly be considered exceptional. Female slaves born outside the Familia Caesaris had small chance of entering it – their services were not required for official posts in the administration; but also inside the Familia female slaves of slaves had no chance of rising to be 'vicarianae' in the administrative sense; such posts – as regular counterparts of the 'vicariani' – did not exist. Thus, although women are found as often as men among the *lib. liberti* and the *lib. servi*, where the balance between the sexes is what one would expect to find in a normal social group, among the 'vicariani', as among the *vicarii* and *servi publici*, females do not occur at all. The explanation for this is similar in all cases, namely that 'vicariani', *vicarii* and *servi publici* were recruited for occupations in which male slaves held a virtual monopoly. 'Vicariani' were not ordinary personal slaves of Imperial slaves who had simply accrued to the emperor's Familia, i.e. *patrimonium*, on the death of their Imperial slave or freedman owner.

The conclusion is that the recruitment of 'vicariani' is connected with the need for trained personnel as the Imperial administration expanded, particularly in the latter half of the first century. They are in fact, with rare exceptions, former *vicarii* in the administrative sense in which that term was used in the Familia Caesaris. The 'vicariani' are by and large the career grade above that of the *vicarii*. Promotion would not be automatic between the two grades, as the instance of a former *vicarius* who was not a 'vicarianus' shows.[2] Recruitment of 'vicariani' for financial posts would be to a considerable extent selective. This might occur either during the lifetime of the *ordinarius* upon his promotion and manumission, or by selection after his death to fill his vacant position.[3] Selection was in fact promotion and would account for the evident pride taken by 'vicariani' in their second name.

[1] Cascelliana: VI 3952; Maecenatiana: VI 4095; Scapliana: VI 4402; Drusilliana: VI 8824; Acteniana: X 7980; Caenidiana: VI 18358.
[2] III 7853 = D 1860: Felix Caes. n. ser. ex vi(k). Cf. III 5121 = D 1857, 5691.
[3] That such recruitment did in fact take place during the lifetime of the *ordinarius* is shown by VI 8410, where one slave of Atticus Aug. lib., *a rationibus* under Domitian, passed into the emperor's Familia as 'Fructus Imp. Caesaris Domitiani Aug. Germanici Atticianus tabular(ius) a rationibus', while another remained to be manumitted by Atticus as 'Fortunatus Attici Aug. lib. a rationib(us) lib. tabular(ius)'. Cf. III 12289.

'*Vicariani*'

After the Julian, and certainly from the Claudian period, this method of recruitment became common; until the time of Hadrian. One of the casualties of Hadrian's reorganisation of the Familia Caesaris was the use of *agnomina* in *-ianus*, probably as the result of an Imperial decision to which all Imperial slaves had to conform. The limitations on their privileges were now well-defined, and included nomenclature.[1] It is not likely that the administrative need for 'vicariani' disappeared completely after Hadrian despite the influx of *vernae*, who are increasingly evident in the emperor's service. The grade of *vikarius* continued into the third century but, in the absence of their distinctive second name, those *vikarii* who became 'vikariani' in the period after Hadrian cannot be traced.

[1] SHA *Hadr.* 21: 'libertos suos nec sciri voluit in publico'.

CHAPTER 15

THE OCCUPATIONAL HIERARCHY: SOME POINTS OF METHOD

It is now necessary to consider more closely the hierarchy and the system of promotion in the sub-equestrian regions of the Imperial administration. No bureaucracy can function efficiently without order and opportunity in its lower as well as its higher ranks. It is necessary to affirm this of the lower ranks of the Roman bureaucracy in the early Empire precisely because it has so often been denied or ignored. The impression gained from reading many works on the Imperial administration is that of fervid equestrian movement from post to post and province to province at the top, with a static substratum of Imperial slaves and freedmen providing stability and continuity below.[1] Such an account is to some extent true. But that it is not true enough emerges from a detailed consideration of the inscriptional evidence.

To begin with, two general points of method in the use of the inscriptions need to be made, as they are fundamental to any reconstruction of the slave and freedman hierarchy.

In the first place, there is a difference between the manner of recording an equestrian career, where all the posts from that of, say, *praefectus cohortis*, held in the twenties, are recorded, and a freedman career, where in the clerical and sub-clerical grades only the highest post actually reached by the end of a career (e.g. *tabularius, a commentariis, dispensator*) is recorded. This is not to be interpreted as meaning that the slaves and freedmen spent their lives in a single post on a single grade. The first point on the promotion ladder which was normally mentioned as the beginning of a *cursus* in the equestrian sense was that of *proximus* or even *procurator*. But as these grades, at least in the administrative service proper, were not normally reached till about the age of 40, those who did gain senior posts must have previously

[1] For this, the accepted view, it is sufficient to mention among many others: Hirschfeld, *Verwalt.* pp. 429, 459; W. Liebenam, *Verwaltungsgeschichte des römischen Kaiserreichs*, I (Jena, 1886), p. 14; Rostovtzeff, *Diz. Epig.* III, 137; Vaglieri, *Diz. Epig.* I, 80. The view outlined below was first presented in a paper to the Cambridge Philological Society and published in *Proc. Camb. Philol. Soc.* 10 (1964), 74–92. Boulvert is in substantial and welcome agreement; cf. esp. *EAI*, pp. 374 f.; and II, 585 f. He is particularly concerned with the procuratorial grades, and treats the hierarchy in descending order. Our accounts prove to be largely complementary. In what follows I have adopted an ascending approach, concentrating on the lower and middle grades of the 'cursus'.

The occupational hierarchy

served as *Caesaris servi* in their twenties, and as *Augusti liberti* in their thirties, in at least two of the junior and intermediate clerical or other posts. There is little evidence of short-circuiting in freedman careers, and not much of early manumission for those in administrative positions. It was in the emperor's interest to extract good service from his slaves during their early working life, and in the interest of the *fiscus libertatis et peculiorum* to have manumission purchased by Imperial slaves from their *peculia*, which, presumably, could not have been done before the legal age. The normal age of manumission for an Imperial slave was 30 or soon after – in fact the minimum age prescribed by the lex Aelia Sentia.[1] For those in the administration this implies at least ten years' service in a junior slave grade or grades.

The second general point concerns the use of age figures in the inscriptions, especially the figures recording age at death but also on occasion the figures recording years of married life, and the ages of children. If a given post is regularly one of senior standing, it should be exceptional, and in fact it is, to find an occupant of it who died in his twenties or even thirties and had therefore been appointed to it at an even earlier age. Thus eight *procuratores* whose age at death is known died aged 72, 98, 62, 55, 86, 96, 65 and 71 respectively.[2] The youngest is 55, and the average is just over 75. A further four died having been married for 44, 10, 21 and 36 years respectively.[3] High figures for years of married life, i.e. 20 years and over, indicate middle or old age, as a minimum of 18–20 years needs to be added for males to get the approximate age at death. On the other hand, low figures sometimes represent late or second marriages.

More significant still are the age-at-death figures for *dispensatores*. Of seven known from Rome and Italy six died between the ages of 30 and 37; the other, *dispensator* at the Imperial villa at Formiae where his son was already *procurator*, died aged 66.[4] Others died after having been married for 11 years or with daughters aged 16 and 7 years, which could easily also mean a

---

[1] Jones, *JRS* 39 (1949), 43 f. = *Studies*, pp. 159 f. For the references on early manumission, see Part II, chap. 5, pp. 101 f.

[2] VI 8512, 9019, 33136; III 1312; VIII 12880; X 1740, 6785; XIV 176. In X 6785, the age of Metrobius, who governed Pandateria 'longum per aevom', is described as 'ann(o)s ter decies quinos', i.e. thirteen *lustra*, or 65 years. Cf. Statius, *Silv.* iii. 3.146, who describes the age of Claudius Etruscus' father as 'bis octonis lustris', i.e. 80 years, and Martial, vii. 40.6: ter senas vixit Olympiadas, for the same person's age. In X 6093 = D 1583, Amazonicus Augg. lib., *procurat(or)* of the Imperial villa at Formiae, dedicates the inscription to his father 'Laeonas vern(a) disp(ensator)' who died at the age of 66. Amazonicus can therefore hardly be much over 40–45 years old. He is the youngest of the procurators, but is in charge only of an estate in the patrimonial service. Note also the *subprocurator domus Augustianae* (VI 8640 = D 1630), M. Ulpius Aerasmus Augusti lib., who died aged 35.

[3] VI 8432 = D 1526; III 287 = 6776; X 6571; XIII 1800.

[4] VI 8687, 8839, 33775; *Epigr.* 4 (1942), p. 51 n. 23; X 1731, 6093 = D 1583, 7588.

The emperor's service

reasonably early death in the thirties.[1] From the provinces the ages are 37, 54, 57 and one with the *legio III Augusta* who died allegedly 110 years old.[2] The consistency of the figures from Rome and Italy is striking, and seems to me more than coincidence. The eccentricity of the age data from Africa is well known. Nevertheless, 7/11 of *dispensatores* whose age figures are known died in their thirties. Their mortality rate was not predictably higher than that of other officials, although they handled and disbursed large sums of money. They all had to remain slaves beyond the normal age for manumission because of their special financial responsibilities – both a lucrative and a desirable sacrifice of freedom for which there was considerable competition. But they did not remain either slaves or *dispensatores* indefinitely. In the central offices in Rome their manumission was mainly a means of promotion, opening the way to the higher freedman posts, and the age figures show that in Rome this had normally taken place by their fortieth year.[3] At the other end, the fact that none died in their twenties is significant, as it is likely that this would have been noticed on the tombstone of one who had been appointed *dispensator* at such an early age. This creates the presumption that none were appointed at that age, and that about 30 was the normal age at appointment.

The age-at-death figures of other grades, e.g. *tabularii, a commentariis, adiutores*, etc. will be dealt with in the appropriate sections below. It must be stressed that they do not provide an instrument of excessive refinement but one which can be used with varying effectiveness for different grades and different localities. But it is clear that the age and the promotion structure must correspond. A further point emerges. The age figures for Rome and the provinces, particularly Carthage, are sometimes at variance. Those who were still slaves and still of junior grade at the age of 40 or over – in other words, the unsuccessful – are in almost all cases found in Carthage. This reflects the higher status of the capital. In the provincial administrative centres there is evidence of a comparative lack of opportunity for advancement, especially from the lowest grades. To offset this, however, there is evidence of considerable mobility from one centre to another for the senior clerical and especially the higher grades.

[1] *EE* VIII 720; VI 8825a; XIV 3639 (Tibur).
[2] III 7102; VIII 1028 = D 1512, 3289, 12892 = D 1510. On the *dispensatores legionis III Augustae*, see Boulvert, *EAI*, pp. 121 f.
[3] The restorations in III 7130 (cf. Pflaum, *CP*, pp. 170–3; *AE* 1966, p. 134): 'M. Ulpius [Aug. lib.]/Repenti[nus qui dis]/pensavi[t in provin]/cia Asia [annis trigin]/ta[. . .]/h. [c.]', especially the number 'triginta' in full, are highly conjectural. This cannot be taken as evidence of long tenure of office by *dispensatores*. Repentinus must have relinquished his post on manumission, in any case. I would suggest reading in the final lines: '[in provin]/cia Asia, [ob meri]ta [eius]/h(onoris) [c(ausa)]', to avoid the difficulties inherent in the accepted restorations, including filling out the missing half of the penultimate line. See *Epigr. Studien* (1972).

CHAPTER 16

SUB-CLERICAL GRADES

What were the posts which gave access to the promotion scale, and how were they recruited? In the first place one can rule out the sub-clerical workers – the non-clerical, non-financial, non-professional; for example, the *pedisequi*, *custodes*, *nomenclatores*, *tabellarii*, and most of the often-quoted specialists who served on the purely domestic staff of the Palace. A gap, or occupational discontinuity, opened between the sub-clerical and the clerical staff of the administration and it was rare indeed for anyone to jump it.[1]

The age figures suggest this. Typical are those for the *pedisequi* (attendants), a dozen of whom died at ages evenly spread from 20 to 70. They are all slaves, and the high proportion – more than half – who were aged over 40 indicates an occupation unskilled and unremunerative, without prospects but perhaps not excessively strenuous, and congenial to the unambitious. One exception to the rule is instructive. A certain Eutychus, as a slave, was *pedisequus a vinis* – sub-clerical. He is found later as T. Aelius Aug. lib. Eutychus, still in the same department, as *adiutor a vinis*.[2] That is to say, after some years as attendant in the department of the Imperial wine supply, in his thirties probably, and after manumission, he rose to the bottom rung on the clerical ladder, a grade usually occupied at the beginning of their careers while still slaves by those fortunate enough to be professional civil servants all their lives from their initial appointment in their late teens.[3]

Similarly sub-clerical are the *tabellarii*. They began as slaves and remained so during their service from the age of 20 to that of 40, as the strikingly consistent age figures show. Apart from two *optiones*, freedmen who died aged 61 and 55, all the *tabellarii* for whom we have age data are slaves. Their ages at death are: 45 (*ex tabellaris*), 40, 35, 30, 28, 28, 25, 25, 25, 20, and one Florus Aug. ser. *tabellarius* from Carthage (VIII 12908), who must surely have retired some time before he died at the age of 82.[4] However, unless one sup-

---
[1] For the junior personnel of the Imperial civil service the best discussion is that of Jones, 'The Roman Civil Service (Clerical and Sub-clerical Grades)', *JRS* 39 (1949), 38 f., reprinted in *Studies*, pp. 151 f. But see now also Boulvert, *EAI*, pp. 23–48; 178–87; 237–48.
[2] VI 9091, 8527; cf. Hirschfeld, *Verwalt.* p. 459 n. 4.
[3] E.g. VI 5062 = 9092 = D 1794: Erasinus Caes. n. ser. adiutor a vinis.
[4] *Optiones*: *AE* 1930, 93 (Gerasa, Palest.); VI 8424a = D 1706. *Ex tabellaris*: VIII 12625 = D 1711. Epictetus (Aug.) lib. tabellarius = tabularius (III 3 = D 4395); Dessau, *CIL* III p. 967; Chantraine, p. 44 n. 13.

The emperor's service

poses the mortality rate of Imperial postmen to have been extraordinarily high, especially during the first fifteen years of service on the Roman roads, those who survived to the age of 40/45 must have gone to other occupations. Their new jobs would not have been clerical. A few were manumitted and promoted to supervisory rank – that of *praepositus* or *optio tabellariorum*, e.g. VI 8445 = D 1553: M. Aur. Aug. lib. Alexander p(rae)p(ositus) tabell(ariorum) st(ationis) XX her(editatium); VI 8424a = D 1706: Titus Aelius Montanus Aug. lib. optio tabellariorum offici ratio(num). Rank and file *tabellarii* changed to a less strenuous occupation and became, e.g., *pedisequi*, as one inscription suggests: X 1741: 'Suc(c)es(s)us Augustorum tabellarius... pedisecus in [d]ie vitae suae'. Socially, if the status of their wives is any indication, *tabellarii* were of lower standing than the holders of clerical posts – more of their wives are slaves. But, surprisingly, the difference is not as easily discernible as we might expect.[1]

There is no question of recognised grades of promotion at this level of competence in the sub-clerical and domestic Palace service, except for the *praepositi*. The title 'praepositus' is rarely found in the clerical and administrative service and never constituted a regular grade there in the early Empire.[2] 'Praepositus', with its strong military associations, like 'optio', rather illustrates the military lines along which the great slave *familiae* were normally organised in Rome. The most highly supervised among these was the *familia* of the Imperial Palace with its middle-aged freedman *praepositi*, e.g. VI 9045: Aelius Anthus Aug. lib., married for twenty years; VI 8642: M. Ulpius Augusti lib. Graphicus, praepositus balneariorum domus Aug(ustianae), and many others.[3] Nor is the military flavour of the subordinates of the *praepositi* surprising – we find, besides the *optiones tabellariorum* (died aged 61, 55), a *decurio unctorum* who died aged 71 (VI 9093 = D 1791), a *decurio lecticariorum* who died aged 60 (VI 8873 = D 1750), etc., all freedmen, somewhat elderly at death and probably not appointed much before the age of 40.

The lives of the slaves and freedmen in the Palace service would be basically similar to those of countless other slaves and freedmen of noble houses familiar from the literary sources of the first and second centuries AD. Their importance depended on the particular posts they held, especially the *a*

---

[1] See Part II, chapter 7, pp. 119 f.
[2] An exception is VI 8528 = D 1650: 'Hermeros Aug. lib. praepositus tabular. rationis castrensis'. Other examples are from the late second or early third centuries, and in all cases except one (*AE* 1935, 20) refer to officials in charge of *stationes* for the collection of the *portoria*: V 5090, 7643; XIII 5244; *AE* 1919, 21; 1934, 234. Under the Severi it became increasingly common for Imperial freedmen and slaves in the provinces to use this term of their equestrian procurator, e.g. II 1085; III 251; X 7584; *IGR* I 623.
[3] On the *praepositi*, see now Boulvert, *EAI*, pp. 237–40, where the evidence is cited in detail.

Sub-clerical grades

cubiculo, tricliniarchi, praegustatores, and others.[1] Their personal contact with, and influence over, particular emperors was crucial to their success – particularly the *a cubiculo* – and in the early Empire several emperors were susceptible to such influence.[2]

I shall not dwell longer on this personnel. The *tabellarii* were without doubt a necessary cog in the administrative machine, but most of the others in the jungle that was the Palace service seem to have been somewhat less than indispensable to the efficient running of the Roman Empire. The burden of this fell on the civil servants from the junior clerical slave officers, through the freedmen *a commentariis* and *tabularii*, the senior freedmen *proximi*, *procuratores* and heads of departments, up to the equestrian procurators themselves.

The equestrians had an established salary and promotion structure. This reached downwards to the freedmen and slaves. HS 40,000 is attested as the salary for *proximi* in the early third century,[3] but for the rest salary as a source of income is scarcely mentioned. For this reason a detailed examination of the pay structure of the Familia Caesaris is not attempted here.[4] The number of equestrian posts was economically few, although adequate for the purpose until considerably expanded at top and bottom by Septimius Severus.[5] The substructure, too, must have borne some relation to the superstructure – no extravagant crowds of slaves and freedmen pullulating on the Palatine, and not understaffed to to the point of inefficiency. Thus we are considering a service where opportunities for promotion were dependent on influence, patronage, merit and service – no doubt in that order – and where the element of competition for available places was not unduly wasteful of talent and was stimulating for the ambitious.

It is not easy to reduce a whole bureaucratic system, or even part of one,

[1] E. Fairon, 'L'organisation du palais impérial à Rome', *Musée Belge* 4 (1900), 5-25; and esp. Boulvert, *EAI*, pp. 23 f., 237 f.

[2] On the lists of *cubicularii* and *a cubiculo*, see J. Michiels, 'Les *Cubicularii* des empereurs romains d'Auguste à Dioclétien', *Musée Belge* 6 (1902), 364-87. For discussion, see Boulvert, *EAI*, esp. pp. 241-7 (where he establishes a distinction in status and function between the *a cubiculo* and the *cubicularii*), and pp. 438-43 (for their unofficial influence).

[3] VI 8619.

[4] Hirschfeld, *Verwalt.* p. 464, considered it unlikely that fixed grades according to pay, as were regular for the equestrian procurators, existed in the Familia Caesaris before Diocletian; in the early period salary was determined by merit and length of service. This is virtually denying the existence of a 'cursus' in the bureaucratic sense, a view which is untenable according to the whole evidence. On the other hand, Boulvert (II, 608 f.) goes too far in deducing elaborate grades and divisions of grades for salary purposes, on the model of Pflaum's scheme for the equestrian procurators. I believe that the slave-freedman system was less rigidly formalised than Boulvert believes. On salary scales at least, the state of the evidence compels us to suspend judgement.

[5] See Pflaum, *Proc. Equest.* pp. 29 f. and passim.

The emperor's service

to one or two patterns; there is always the risk of dangerous over-simplification. It is possible to discern, however, two main sequences of posts which led up to the senior freedman *cursus*, the procuratorships. The one leads through posts held entirely by slaves and almost exclusively financial. The other is a mixed slave–freedman sequence leading to senior clerical and administrative posts.

The first begins with the *vicarii* and leads by way of 'vicariani' to the post of *dispensator*, and then after manumission, at the age of 40 or shortly after, to the grade of *tabularius* in more or less important departments such as the central financial bureaux in Rome. Some *dispensatores*, but perhaps not the 'vicariani', rose to become *procuratores*. I have discussed this sequence fully in chapters 12 and 14 above.

CHAPTER 17

ADIUTORES: JUNIOR CLERICAL GRADES

The starting point for the second regular sequence – the clerical posts – is the grade of *adiutor*. 'Adiutor' is basically a generic term meaning 'assistant', and is used for a wide variety of posts in the civil and military administration.[1] It is always further defined, sometimes by a noun in the genitive (e.g. *tabulariorum, praefecti, principis, procuratoris*, etc.), sometimes by the name of an administrative or domestic office (e.g. *a rationibus, a cognitionibus, ab admissione, a vinis, a lagona*, etc.). The problem is to sort these out according to rank in the administrative hierarchy. But before we can make any progress we must examine critically the seniority and regular status of the *adiutores procuratoris* because of their disturbing effect on the status of the rest. The examples are as follows:

(1) VI 8470 = D 1535; cf. 143 = D 3896 a: Carpus Aug. lib. Pallantianus, adiutor Claudi Athenodori praef(ecti) annonae. (Nero.)

(2) III 431 = 7116 = 13674 = D 1449 (Ephesus): Hermes Aug. lib., adiut(or) eius (sc. [Valerii Eudaemonis]... proc. heredit(atium) et proc. pro[vin]ciae Asiae, proc. Syriae). (Pflaum, *CP* No. 110, pp. 264–71; late Hadrian.)

(3) *CIG* II 1813b = LBW II 1076 = D 8849 (Nicopolis, Epirus): Μνηστὴρ Σεβαστοῦ ἀπελ[εύθε]ρος, βοηθὸς αὐτοῦ (sc. A. Ofellii Maioris Macedonis, proc. prov. Epiri, proc. prov. Ponti et Bithyniae, a voluptatibus). (Pflaum, *CP* No. 112, pp. 272–4; Hadrian.)

(4) VI 10234 = D 7213: (M. Ulpius) Capito Aug. l., adiutor eius (sc. Fl(avii) Apolloni, proc. Aug. qui fuit a pinacothecis). (Dated 153.)

(5) VI 4228: M. Ulpius Aug. lib. Menophilus, adiutor proc(uratoris) ab ornamentis. (Died aged 35; dated 126; father P. Aelius Aug. lib. Menophilus.)

(6) VI 8950 = D 1771: Fortunatus, Pompeianus, Optatus Aug. lib., adiutores proc(uratoris) rationis ornamentorum.

(7) VI 10083 = D 1768: Marcus [....], adiut(or) proc(uratoris) summi chor[agi].

(8) XIV 1877 (Ostia): [...]tianus Aug. lib., adiutor proc(uratoris) sum[mi choragi]. (Father Callidromus ex disp[...] signo Leucadi; sister Seia Helpis. Date: probably 3rd c., cf. 'Leucadi', a detached *signum*.)

(9) III 14192.15 = *IGR* IV 1317 (Tyanollus, Lydia): Parthenius Aug. lib., a(diutor) p(rocuratoris) = βο[η]θ(ὸς) ἐπιτρόπ(ου). (A bilingual dedication to his brother, M. Ulpius Horimus.)

(10) VI 738 = Vermas. 626: Nicephorus Augg. lib., adiut(oris) procc. [...]. (A Mithraic dedication to Septimius Severus and Caracalla; line 5: 'procurantibus Hermete et Euphrata Aug. lib...'.)

[1] A good collection of material is still Vaglieri, *Diz. Epig.* I, 81 f. s.v. 'adiutor'.

The emperor's service

(11) VII 62 = *RIB* 179 (Bath, Brit.): Naevius Aug. lib., adiut(or) procc. (Dedication to Caracalla or Elagabalus; lines 4 f.: 'principia ruina op(p)ressa a solo restituit'.)

(12) *IGR* IV 1651 (Philadelphia, Asia): Σεουῆρος Σεβαστο[ῦ] ἀπελεύθερος, βοηθὸς ἐπιτρόπων ῥεγιῶνος Φιλαδελφηνῆς. (A dedication to his wife, Αὐρηλ(ία) Ποία.)[1]

The pattern of usages here is complex but, I suggest, falls into three main forms: (i) 'adiutor eius' (Nos. 1, 2, 3, 4); (ii) 'adiutor proc(uratoris)' (Nos. 5, 6, 7, 8, 9); (iii) 'adiutor procc. (procuratorum)' (Nos. 10, 11, 12).

(i) The first group is distinguished from the other two by the fact that the superior official, the *procurator* (*praefectus* in No. 1) is mentioned by name in all four cases, whereas he (or they) are not even alluded to in any of the others. Carpus (No. 1) alone incorporates the name of his superior into his actual occupational title, *adiutor Claudi Athenodori praef. annonae*. The only parallel to this nomenclature is to be found in those equestrian *adiutores* who, at the beginning of their procuratorial careers, serve as personal assistants of senior equestrian or even senatorial officials; e.g. II 1180 = D 1403: Sex. Iulius Possessor, *adiutor Ulpii Saturnini praef(ecti) annon(ae)*, who was appointed for the special task of checking supplies and provisions in Hispalis, Baetica. These are personal appointments, the result of patronage exercised on the initiative of the senior official concerned. Carpus was a former slave of Pallas, who was no stranger to the use of patronage; hence perhaps a previous connection with Claudius Athenodorus. Hermes (No. 2) dedicates the acephalous inscription from Ephesus 'honoris causa' to his superior who is certainly Valerius Eudaemon. Pflaum has conjectured that Eudaemon held his unusual cumulation of posts as *proc. hereditatium* and provincial procurator while accompanying Hadrian on his eastern travels in 129 and later also in Syria.[2] If Hermes did not accompany Eudaemon to Syria, he is less likely to have been a personal appointment on the staff of the latter than the freedman assistant procurator of the province of Asia. The fact that he does not use the official title 'proc. provinciae' is either because that title did not come into general use for freedmen till after Hadrian's reign, or because in a personal dedication Hermes prefers to use less formal, unofficial language. The personal tone is clearer in the case of Mnester (No. 3) who actually uses the expression 'τὸν ἴδιον εὐεργέτην' in his dedication to Ofellius Maior, a former equestrian procurator of Epirus. In No. 4 Salvia C. f. Marcellina, the freeborn wife of M. Ulpius Capito Aug. l., in making a gift to the *Collegium Aesculapi et Hygiae*, dedicates it jointly to the memory of Flavius Apollonius, former procurator of the Imperial art galleries, and to his *adiutor*, her

---

[1] Boulvert, *EAI*, p. 113 n. 126, adds the following, who are, however, without status indication: *BGU* IV 1047; *IGR* I 1310; and VI 37110 (dated to 242): 'Hermes et Gelasinus adiut(ores) proc(uratoris) et Crescens adiut(or) tabul[....].'

[2] Boulvert, ib.

Adiutores: junior clerical grades

husband. This double dedication is an unusual touch where two officials are involved and indicates again a personal rather than an official relationship between the two.

In each of these cases we have a freedman official described as 'adiutor' of an equestrian procurator or prefect in terms that suggest some degree of personal familiarity between the two. Carpus Pallantianus (No. 1)[1] looks like a personal appointment of the *praefectus annonae*, Claudius Athenodorus, and probably held his position only during the latter's term of office. He is exceptional for a freedman and does not fit into the regular slave–freedman 'cursus'. He is therefore comparable with those equestrians who are found at the beginning of their careers serving as personal *adiutores* of some *curatores* and provincial governors of senatorial and perhaps consular rank. The range of these posts is restricted, the style in which the name of the superior appears in the inscription linked with that of the *adiutor* is exceptional and indicates that these are personal appointments due in the first instance to the initiative of the superior. This privilege was curtailed by the time of the Severi. The following equestrian careers belong to this group and together are an interesting commentary on the exercise of patronage in the non-Imperial sphere during the late first and second centuries:[2]

M. Te[....] (*CP* No. 52); Sex. Attius Suburanus Aemilianus (*CP* No. 56); L. Vibius Lentulus (*CP* No. 66); L. Dudistius Novanus (*CP* No. 82); L. Volusius Maecianus (*CP* No. 141); L. Vibius Apronianus (*CP* No. 160 bis); Sex. Iulius Possessor (*CP* No. 185); Q. Petronius Melior (*CP* No. 201); Ti. Claudius Zeno Ulpianus (*CP* No. 228); Herennius Ser[...] (*CP* No. 267); M. Aemilianus [....] (*CP* No. 282 bis).

The cases of Hermes, Mnester and Capito (Nos. 2, 3 and 4) do not belong to this pattern. They are assistant procurators, themselves of procuratorial rank, senior in status, and officially entitled 'procurator'. They are in each case the freedman member of the equestrian–freedman pair of procurators working together in what has been called the system of 'unequal collegiality'.[3]

[1] *PIR*[2], C 794. Carpus could not have been Pallas' *freedman* (as M. T. Griffin, *JRS* 52 (1962), 105), but was probably manumitted by Nero. He could have passed into the Familia Caesaris before or after the manumission of Pallas, but as Pallas was manumitted by Antonia Minor between AD 31 and 37 (see Oost, *AJPh* 79 (1958), 114), a date between his retirement in 55 and his death in 62 is more likely. See also Hirschfeld, *Verwalt.* p. 241 n. 3. Chantraine (p. 326) hesitates over the *nomen* of Carpus. Unnecessarily, I think, especially if, as it is natural to assume from the wording of VI 8470 = D 1535, Ti. Claudius Romanus is a former slave of Carpus and not of his wife Claudia Cale. This does not exclude a date later than 68 for the *praefectura annonae* of Claudius Athenodorus.

[2] For details and discussion, see Pflaum's *Carrières Procuratoriennes* – e.g. p. 1264: Index, s.v. 'adiutor' – where, however, frequent references are made to his long unpublished *Mémoire sur les sous-procurateurs*. The conclusions of this indubitably important work are now most conveniently available in the work of Boulvert, *EAI passim*.

[3] The phrase 'collégialité inégale' is Pflaum's, 'Principes de l'administration romaine impériale', *Bulletin de la Faculté des Lettres de Strasbourg* (1958), n. 3, 1–17 at p. 16; see also Boulvert, *EAI*, p. 375.

The emperor's service

This system is examined in detail in chapter 21 below. A group of letters from Pliny, Book x, illustrate and confirm all these usages. They concern the equestrian procurator of Pontus and Bithynia, Virdius Gemellinus, who served under Pliny there in 111, and the freedmen Maximus and Epimachus, who served in succession as the provincial assistant procurators with Gemellinus. In Pliny, *Epist.* x. 27 (to Trajan) Maximus is referred to as 'libertus et procurator tuus'; cf. 85: 'Maximum, libertum et procuratorem tuum, domine...', where Pliny uses the official title 'procurator'. Trajan in his reply (*Epist.* 28) refers to Gemellinus as 'procurator meus quem *adiuvat* (Maximus libertus meus)', indicating the function of Maximus as 'adiutor', not his official title as 'procurator'. These passages show that the relationship between the equestrian and freedman in the system of procuratorial pairs is that of principal and assistant, so that the freedman might in unofficial language refer to himself as *adiutor* of his equestrian principal. Other passages show that these freedman procurators are not personal appointments of their equestrian principals, thus differing from Carpus Pallantianus (No. 1 above). In *Epist.* 85 Pliny addresses to Trajan a testimonial on behalf of Maximus, who has now been moved elsewhere ('Maximum libertum et procuratorem tuum, domine, *per omne tempus quo fuimus una*, probum et industrium...'). In *Epist.* 84 we already find his successor as assistant procurator, Epimachus, on the job working with Gemellinus: 'adhibitis Virdio Gemellino et Epimacho, liberto meo, *procuratoribus*', where Trajan suggests that the two procurators, equestrian and freedman, be called in by Pliny to advise on a matter concerning the *fiscus*. It is interesting that Mnester (No. 3) was procurator in Epirus with Ofellius Maior, who then himself went to become equestrian procurator of Pontus and Bithynia not long after Virdius Gemellinus. So the complex dual procuratorial system continued, both in the provincial administration and in Rome.

(ii) The next group (Nos. 5–9) all have the title 'adiutor procuratoris', variously abbreviated as 'adiut(or) proc(uratoris)' (or even as 'a(diutor) p(rocuratoris)' in the bilingual III 14192.15 = *IGR* IV 1317, from Lydia). These are all private sepulchral inscriptions (not honorific career dedications, as in Nos. 2 and 3). The title 'adiutor procuratoris' is an official one. In no case is the name of the superior mentioned, nor is any personal relationship even hinted at. The very title this time shows that these *adiutores* cannot be of procuratorial rank, as they cannot be called both 'procurator' and 'adiutor procuratoris'. They are not part of the equestrian–freedman dual procuratorial system; VI 8950 = D 1771 (No. 6) names two, probably three[1] freedmen who

---

[1] VI 8950 = D 1771; the text runs (6 f.) 'fecerunt Fortunatus Pompeianus Optatus Aug. lib. adiutores...'. We have here either two *Augusti liberti*, Fortunatus Pompeianus and Optatus, or

Adiutores: junior clerical grades

simultaneously are '*adiutores proc(uratoris) rationis ornamentorum*'. Nor are they of junior rank. All have already been manumitted; the only one for whom we have an age figure, M. Ulpius Aug. lib. Menophilus (No. 5) died aged 35. He must have been manumitted earlier, perhaps at least nine years earlier, by 117, i.e. at the age of 26 or under, if he died in 126, the date of his inscription (VI 4228). In any case he was manumitted by Trajan, before his father, P. Aelius Aug. lib. Menophilus, who had to wait till Hadrian's reign for his freedom. The age figure and the multiple *adiutores proc(uratoris)* Fortunatus, Pompeianus and Optatus (No. 6) incline me to suppose that these *adiutores* are of intermediate clerical status, comparable with *tabularii, a commentariis*, and *dispensatores*, but with duties which gave them a special place apart from the regular staff of the departmental bureau and under the direct control of the procuratorial head, whether equestrian or freedman. It is noteworthy that four of the five inscriptions in this group refer to two very closely related departments in Rome both concerned with administration of the public theatrical performances, the *ratio ornamentorum* (*ab ornamentis*) and the *ratio summi choragii*. This can hardly be coincidental. These departments also have a full range of clerical staff besides the *adiutores proc*.[1] From these points of view, VI 8950 = D 1771 (No. 6) is particularly instructive. It was erected to Servatus Caes. n. ser., *contrascriptor rationis summi choragi* who died aged 34, by several friends with posts in the *ratio ornamentorum* – Fortunatus, Pompeianus and Optatus Aug lib. *adiutores proc(uratoris)*, Irenaeus Caesaris verna, *adiutor tabulariorum*, and Isidorus, *vicarius* of Primitivus, *dispensator* in the same department, as well as by Helius, who is *vicarius* of Servatus himself. The post of *contrascriptor* is of intermediate status, but less important than that of *dispensator*, but both slave posts involving delayed manumission; Servatus' age at death, 34, is thus regular for the grade. The friends of Servatus are all of similar or lower standing and are arranged in order of seniority, first the three freedmen, *adiutores proc.* of intermediate status, and then the three slaves of junior clerical status, headed by the *adiutor tabulariorum*, a *Caesaris verna* and last the two *vicarii*. We have a glimpse here of the clerical hierarchy at its lower levels.

(iii) The remaining group have the title 'adiut(or) proc(uratorum)' (Nos. 10, 11) or the Greek 'βοηθὸς ἐπιτρόπων' (No. 12). The first two are dedications to Severan emperors, and the last is perhaps also of Severan date –

preferably three: Fortunatus, Pompeianus, and Optatus. The absence of 'et' is in favour of three. 'Pompeianus' as an *agnomen* in the early second century (cf. slave indications: 'Caesaris n. ser.', 'Caesaris verna') is not impossible. It would, however, be derived from 'Pompeius', and would thus be unlikely for a 'vicarianus' in the Flavian or Trajanic period. See above, p. 216.

[1] Including *tabularii, a commentariis, dispensatores, contrascriptores, adiutores a commentariis*, even a *medicus*. See Boulvert, *EAI*, pp. 250 f.

The emperor's service

Severus Aug. lib. in a dedication to his wife Aurel(ia) Poia. In status they are comparable to the *adiutores proc.* of the previous group, i.e. of intermediate clerical status. The plural 'procuratorum' refers to the two procurators of the equestrian-freedman pair, and rules out senior or procuratorial status for these *adiutores*. This form of the official title would seem to belong to the third century. The only department that can be identified is the domanial district of Philadelphia in Asia Minor. One comes from Britain – a rare occurrence in the Familia Caesaris – and the other is a Mithraic dedication from Rome. Another inscription with comparable terminology is also Severan, from the first decade of the third century – *AE* 1930, 152 (Tarragona, Spain): 'L. Sep(timius) Augg. nn. lib. Polybius, *comm(entariensis) procc. p(rovinciae) H(ispaniae) C(iterioris)*'. The status and functions of this official would be similar to those of the undifferentiated *adiutores procuratorum* and, indeed, of the *adiutores procuratoris*.

We now come to those *adiutores* with titles such as *adiutor a rationibus, adiutor ab epistulis*, etc. Are these *first* assistants of the *head* of the department in question, the *a rationibus*, etc., or do they play a much more junior role in the Palatine bureaux? Here one well-known example and the authority of Mommsen have had a disproportionate influence. This is Septimianus, *alias* Septumanus, *adiutor* of Cosmus Aug. lib. who was *a rationibus* under M. Aurelius and L. Verus. Septimianus is mentioned in two documents which clearly show his role as the intermediary through whom requests, or at least some requests, made to the *a rationibus* are passed and decisions communicated to the petitioners. In IX 2438 (iii), a letter from Septimianus to Cosmus, Septimianus explains the trouble which he has been having with the magistrates of Saepinum and Bovianum, who have been interfering with the rights of passage for the emperor's flocks; he specifies the complaints of the *conductores*, indicates what steps he has taken ('necesse habuimus etiam atque etiam scribere, quietius agerent, ne res dominica detrimentum pateretur'), the response of the magistrates ('et cum in eadem contumacia perseverent, dicentes non curaturos se, neque si tu eis scripseris haut fieri rem'), and suggests to Cosmus that he secure the intervention of the *praefecti praetorio*, Bassaeus Rufus and Macrinius Vindex. This Cosmus does in a letter in which he refers to Septimianus as 'collibertus et adiutor meus' (ib. ii). The date is thus *c.* 168–72, the years within which fell the period of office of these prefects. The second inscription, VI 455, dated to 168, concerns worship of the *Lares* by a *collegium* in Rome. The relevant passage, as restored by Mommsen, runs: 'Cosmus a rationibus Augg. [ob curam sacrarum] imaginu[m litter]is ad Septumanum adiutorem s[uum datis probavit].' Septimianus is clearly not of very junior status; his affinities are

Adiutores: junior clerical grades

much closer with the miscellaneous group of *adiutores procuratoris* discussed above than with those who have the title of 'adiutor a rationibus'. But, despite the personal mode of reference, 'collibertus et adiutor meus', he cannot be of procuratorial or senior status, as he is not the freedman member of an equestrian–freedman pair. His superior, Cosmus, is himself a freedman. Moreover, the position of Cosmus himself needs some consideration.[1] He is not *the a rationibus*. The magistrates of Saepinum and Bovianum are contumacious and show a lack of respect for the authority of Cosmus that would be as surprising, if he were the *head* of the Imperial financial administration, as the matter in question appears to be unimportant. It is hard to believe that in 168 a *freedman* could occupy the highest and apparently only trecenarian equestrian post in the administration. This is especially the case if we believe the bureaucracy had rules, grades and a momentum and tradition of its own, relatively independent of the whims of particular emperors.[2] Cosmus' reference to his own freedman status ('collibertus') is as surprising as it would seem inappropriate, despite the laconic statement in the *Historia Augusta* (SHA *Marc.* 15), 'multum sane potuerunt liberti sub Marco et Vero' – an undeservedly overworked eight words. Moreover, it was precisely at this time – between October 166 and February 169 – that L. Aurelius Nicomedes was chosen as the first occupant of the post of *procurator summarum rationum*, the second senior equestrian official in the financial administration, a *ducenarius*.[3] A former freedman of L. Aelius Caesar and of L. Verus, he had been raised to equestrian status before assuming high office in the administration. If Cosmus were really the head of the *a rationibus*, he would surely have been similarly honoured, if only for the sake of consistency, as the father of Claudius Etruscus had, indeed, been honoured while *a rationibus* by Vespasian. M. Bassaeus Rufus, *praefectus praetorio* in 168, is himself found as *procurator a rationibus* just two or three years before, in 165.[4] Cosmus is, in fact, likely to be the senior *freedman* in the central finance department, the subordinate of its equestrian head, in the same way as equestrian procurators were placed above the senior freedman procurators in each of the provincial financial departments. Freedmen, as a rule, remained in a given post longer than did the equestrians; Cosmus had probably only recently served under Bassaeus Rufus as his deputy in the *a rationibus*, which

---

[1] *PIR*², C 1535.
[2] The other freedman *a rationibus* after Hadrian is T. Aurelius Aug. lib. Aphrodisius (XIV 2104 = D 1475), manumitted by Antoninus Pius before the latter's adoption by Hadrian. He has the title – exceptional for a freedman – 'proc. Aug. a rationibus'. Cf. Friedländer, *Sittengeschichte*¹⁰, IV, 28. Another possible case is T. Aelius Aug. lib. Proculus *a rat(ionibus)* (XIV 5309.23, 28).
[3] Pflaum, *CP*, p. 395; cf. Hirschfeld, *Verwalt.* pp. 32 f., 35.
[4] Pflaum, *CP*, pp. 391, 1019.

may help to explain his readiness to approach the praetorian prefects directly for assistance.

The case of Septimianus might seem good *prima facie* evidence that these *adiutores a rationibus*, etc., are quite senior in status. But the age figures are decisive against this. They are as follows: *adiutor a rationibus* (died aged 19), *adiutor rationalium* (d. 23), *adiutor a cognitionibus* (d. 18), all slaves; T. Aelius Crispinus Aug. lib. *adiutor a rationibus* (d. 22), Faustus Aug. lib. *adiutor ab epist. Lat.* (d. 19), P. Aelius Aug. lib. Agathemerus *adiutor ab epist. Lat.* who is described as 'iuvenis', T. Aelius Felix Aug. lib. *adiutor ab annona* (d. 32).[1] There are other examples of slave *adiutores* in this group, for example, Hilarus Aug. vern. *adiutor a rationibus*, Astylus Caesaris ser. *a rationibus adiutor*, Flavianus Caesaris n. ser. *qui fuit adiutor a rationib(us)*, Pallans Caes. n. ser. *adiutor a rationibus*, who are likely to be under thirty.[2] In fact 6/12 *adiutores a rationibus* are *servi* (whereas 9/9 *tabularii a rationibus* are *liberti*).[3] But apart from the fact that slaves are found at all with these titles it is significant that only 1/6 of those for whom we have age figures is over 30 – and that one only 32 – and 3/6 are under 20, including, surprisingly, one freedman. These cannot be administrative or senior clerical positions. There are several freedman *adiutores* from Rome for whom age data are lacking.[4] There is no reason to suppose that any of these had been manumitted under the age of 30, but in view of the fact that 5/6 age figures of freedmen and slaves with these titles are under 30, it cannot be assumed without further evidence that the freedmen are all or any of them senior officials, second or third in command of the various departments from which they come. It should also be noted that no equestrian held any of the posts of *adiutor* with the titles included in this group.[5]

It is probable, therefore, that the *adiutores* of the group discussed above, both slaves and freedmen, are of junior rank in the administration. The words 'a rationibus', 'ab epistulis', etc. in their titles refer not to the head of the department in question but to the department itself in general. This nomenclature is characteristic of the *adiutores* of the central administration in Rome. All the thirty-five examples are from Rome, except for three, two of whom are

---

[1] VI 8424, 9033 = D 1480, 8635 = D 1681, 8417, 8613, 8612, 33730.
[2] VI 5305, 8419 = D 1479, 8421, 8423 = D 4997.
[3] See below, p. 242; cf. Rostovtzeff, *Diz. Epig.* III, 134 f.
[4] E.g. VI 8577 = D 1507 (adiutor fisci Asiatici), 8442 = D 1531 (adiutor a codicillis), 8634 = D 1697 (adiutor a cognit.), VIII 12613 = D 1680 (adiutor a cognitionibus), VI 8695 = D 1688 (adiutor ab actis); cf. III 6107 = D 1692 (adiutor ab admissione).
[5] Duff, *Freedmen*, p. 225, quotes Dessau, VI 1564 = D 1452: '[...]ilius...ab epistulis [Latinis adiutor]', but Mommsen's restoration had already been rejected by Hirschfeld (*Verwalt*. p. 32 n. 4), Domaszewski (*Rangordnung*, p. 220), and more recently by Pflaum (*CP*, pp. 445 f.) and Townend (*Historia* 10 (1961), 378).

Adiutores: junior clerical grades

for some reason in Greece.[1] The third, VIII 12613 = D 1680, from Carthage, is instructive. It reads: 'd. m. s./Victori et Urbicae/Aug. ser. parentibus/ piissimis, Iucundus/Aug. lib. adiut. a co/gnitionibus, *quo/usque spatium per/misit*, renovavit'. Iucundus, who was resident in Rome, arranged for the restoration of his parents' tomb in Carthage. His parents had remained slaves, but Iucundus had bettered himself by leaving Carthage for Rome and is unable or unwilling to make a journey back.[2] These positions in Rome are held in the first place by slaves at the beginning of their civil service career at about the age of 20, and lead after manumission (rarely before it, and often not coinciding with it) to the rank of *tabularius* or *a commentariis*, usually in the same department. Thereafter their mobility greatly increased. Some may have preferred a slightly earlier promotion – to the rank of *dispensator*. But this probably meant transfer to a different department, and to the provinces, and would be at the cost of deferring manumission.

A third group of *adiutores* are the *adiutores tabulariorum* and their indistinguishable equivalents, the *adiutores a commentariis*. Note that there are no 'adiutores dispensatoris'.[3] This nomenclature is characteristic of the provincial centres, especially Carthage, but a few are found in minor departments in Rome.[4] The age figures here show more variation than in the previous groups. Of twenty-nine cases, eleven died under 30, a further nine between 30 and 40, and the remaining nine were aged over 40 at death. The significant fact is the proportion who died while still in their twenties (38%). This and the fact that 23/29 are slaves point to about 20 as the normal age for taking up these posts. They are initially slave posts. But in Carthage, and presumably in the other provincial centres, those beginning at the bottom of the clerical scale seem to be at a disadvantage compared with their equivalents in the high-prestige central bureaux in Rome. In Carthage manumission and promotion tended to come later. It may be that the senior clerical posts of *tabularii* were often filled by transfer from Rome, as one who died in Africa testifies, 'indignans hic data morte',[5] or maybe there lurks here undetected a further provincial refinement in the *adiutor* grade. It is hard to tell. The use of 'provincia' in the titles of two *adiutores tabul(ariorum)* from Poetovio in Pannonia Superior may indicate such a grade. These are: III 4020 cf. p. 1746 = Hoffiller–Saria 272: 'Iunianus (Aug.) lib. adiut(or) tabul(ariorum)

---

[1] III 6107 = D 1692; *AE* 1950, 171.

[2] Mommsen, *CIL* VIII p. 1336 n. 5. Iucundus may have been more unable than unwilling. If his parents died at the African age of 102 and 80 respectively, and he was *restoring* their tomb, Iucundus must have been about 60 or more at the time and still *adiutor*. Perhaps he had not bettered himself much after all.   [3] See above, pp. 205 f.

[4] For the Imperial *columbaria* at Carthage, Mommsen, *CIL* VIII pp. 1335 f. Full references are given in Boulvert, *EAI*, p. 189 n. 674, p. 194 nn. 704 f.

[5] VIII 21008.

p(rovinciae) P(annoniae) S(uperioris)' (dedication to Septimius Severus); 4023: 'Fortunatus Aug. lib adi[ut(or)] tabul(ariorum) p(rovinciae) P(annoniae) S(uperioris)'; cf. 4062 (Poetovio): 'Fortunatus Aug. lib. adiut(or) tabular(iorum)'.[1] The term 'provincia' is otherwise reserved for senior clerical officials.[2] Perhaps we have here an assistant to the chief provincial *tabularius*, i.e. *adiutor tabularii provinciae*, rather than an undifferentiated junior assistant in the provincial *tabularium* (*adiutor tabulariorum*) for which the term 'provincia' does not appear to be used.[3] One other variation in this terminology deserves mention: VI 603 = XIV 49 = *IPO* B 305: T. Flavius Aug. lib. Primigenius *tabularius adiutor*, who is of junior (*adiutor*) rather than intermediate clerical (*tabularius*) grade.

It must be concluded that the rank of *adiutor* was junior clerical. This applies to both the *adiutores tabulariorum* and *adiutores a commentariis* as well as to the *adiutores a rationibus*, *adiutores ab epistulis*, etc. Status variations within this basic grade depended on the location of the office where the position was held (especially Rome), and on the prestige of the particular department (especially the *a rationibus*). The important central departments in Rome tended to develop a distinctive nomenclature of their own. After manumission, with or without further service in the junior position, the *adiutor* proceeded to the freedman grades of *tabularius* and *a commentariis*. A notable omission from the ranking nomenclature is the grade of 'adiutor dispensatoris'. Assistants were needed for *dispensatores* as much as for *tabularii* or *a commentariis*. The explanation is that in the Familia Caesaris the assistant *dispensatores* are in fact called *vicarii*.

[1] For a possible third case, III 6075 = D 1366; but cf. restorations proposed in *JRS* 58 (1968), 120 n. 40.
[2] See Weaver, *JRS* 58 (1968), 118 f.
[3] Boulvert, however, frequently reads 'adiutor tabul(arii)' or 'adiutor tabul(ariorum)' without distinction. (See above, p. 239 n. 4).

CHAPTER 18

INTERMEDIATE CLERICAL GRADES

The intermediate grades in the mixed slave–freedman clerical sequence are the freedman posts of *tabularius* and *a commentariis*.[1] From within these grades there arose a range of higher posts, such as *proximus tabulariorum* and *proximus commentariorum*, which must also be considered.

The *tabularius* was the basic clerical post in a departmental office or *tabularium*. His functions were essentially those of accountant, involving the recording of payments made and those due, balancing the accounts of the department and communicating the results to the central bureau in Rome, whether the *a rationibus* itself or the *ratio patrimonii*. Much would depend on the sphere of operations of the particular department outside Rome, i.e. whether it was concerned with the revenue from a particular tax, overseeing the operations of *conductores* or direct supervision of patrimonial interests in a particular province or region. In the larger bureaux there must have been several officials assigned to these duties; hence further refinements in these clerical grades would have developed. Other duties were also involved, especially the drafting of documents, including receipts. A good example is in VI 10233 (dated 211) where Martialis Augg. lib. *prox*(*imus*) *tab*(*ulariorum*) records having received from P. Aelius Chrestus the proceeds of the sale of Imperial property negotiated by the equestrian procurator Agathonicus on behalf of the *fiscus*.[2] The actual physical control of funds is the function of the *dispensator*, who sometimes is aided by an *arcarius*. As cashier the *dispensator* is distinct from the *tabularius*, and as part of the slave-only financial sequence he is also a control over him.

The *a commentariis* (sometimes called *commentariensis* by the third century) was essentially an archivist or registrar in charge of the departmental records. He was responsible for the safe custody of original documents, for making them available for authorised copying and for certifying the authenticity of such copies. While not as numerous as *tabularii* the *a commentariis* were nevertheless an essential complement to the staff of any moderately sized bureau and are found with the same hierarchy of titles as the *tabularii*.

The age figures of thirteen *tabularii* show a minimum age at death of 29

[1] On *tabularii*, see Hirschfeld, *Verwalt.* pp. 58 f., 460 f; Sachers, P-W IV A, 1969 f.; Boulvert, *EAI*, pp. 420 f. On *a commentariis*, see *Diz. Epig.* II, 540 f.; von Premerstein, P-W IV, 726 f., 759 f.; Boulvert, *EAI*, pp. 425 f.   [2] Further examples and discussion in Boulvert, *EAI*, pp. 421

The emperor's service

(and one of the three who died at that age was a slave).[1] Appointment normally followed soon after manumission at the age of thirty. This shows their intermediate clerical status. Only 16/145 attested *tabularii* in the Familia Caesaris, apart from those of the *Augustae*, are or could be still slaves and of these 9/16 are to be dated to the Julio-Claudian period.[2] Only three can be dated later than the early second century.[3] The improvement in status of *tabularii* from the early first century is concurrent with the expansion in the number of clerical posts in the administration, first in Rome and later in the provinces. The *tabularii* remained the intermediate clerical grade, while the new grade of *adiutor*, which was added in individual departments when the need arose, came in beneath them at the junior clerical level.[4]

With the growth in the numbers of clerical staff, especially in all large financial departments, and with the increasing complexity of the departmental organisation, the need arose for more differentiation among the grades of clerical posts. Hence from Rome, in the early second century, come M. Ulpius Cadmus Aug. lib. 'qui fuit princeps tabularius in statione XX hereditatium' (VI 8446 = D 1551), and Hermeros Aug. lib. 'praepositus tabular(iorum) rationis castrensis' (VI 8528 = D 1650) which is unlikely to be earlier.[5]

These titles do not occur again, but those of *proximus tabular(iorum)* and *proximus comm(entariorum)* are found from at least the same period. The examples are:

(1) M. Ulpius Nicephorus Aug. lib. (x 1729; Puteoli), prox(imus) comm(entariorum) ann(onae). (Wife Ulpia Profutura.)[6]

(2) Soter Augg. lib. (VI 8508 = D 1646), proximus tabular(iorum) rationis patrim(onii). (Wife Aurelia Vitalis.)

(3) Martialis Augg. lib. (VI 10233), prox(imus) tab(ulariorum). (Dated to 211.)[7]

(4) Menander (VI 8544), prox(imus) comm(entariorum). ('Pater et collibert(us)' of Menander Aug. lib. adiut(or) tabul(ariorum) rat(ionis) ves[t(iariae)].)

---

[1] VI 8466 = D 1606 (40), 8467 (48), 8476 = D 1544 (29), 8484 (37), 8488 = D 1607 (29 y. 10 m.), 37744 (33); XIV 4482–3 (29 y. 10 m.); II 3235 = D 1555 (45); VIII 12595 (70), 12596 (70), 12882 (57), 24702 (30); XI 3885 = D 1643 (59). Add: VI 9072 (married 15 years).

[2] VI 4038, 4358, 5822, 9066, 10090, 33797, 37768; IX 4977 = D 6558 (a freedman, in Dessau's restoration); III 7047.

[3] VI 776 = D 3727 (Severan); 8476 = D 1544 (Donatus Augustorum (ser.), father P. Aelius Aug. lib. Donatus); *AE* 1938, 154 (Aug. nostrorum (ser.)). The others are: VI 301, 9058, 9063; IX 5064.

[4] On the dating of the extant *adiutores* in the central bureaux, see below, pp. 262 f.

[5] P-W IV A, 1972 and 1968, wrongly quotes VI 1135 and III 251 = D 1373 on this point. In the first, Flav(ius) Pistius, from the mid-*fourth* century, is a *praepositus* but not an Imperial freedman; in the second, Zeno Augg. lib. is an Imperial freedman but not a *praepositus* (even if, with Sachers, we consider 'Zeno' to be in the dative case!).

[6] This inscription has been generally misunderstood. The correct relationship of the persons recorded is that M. Ulpius Nicephorus Aug. lib. (= Nicephorus), *prox(imus) comm. ann.*, is the husband of Ulpia Profutura and the father of Gregorius who died aged 18. 'Gregorius' is not a detached *signum*, but the earliest instance of its use as a *cognomen*. See *Antichthon* 5 (1971).

[7] See above, p. 241.

Intermediate clerical grades

To these should be added:

(5) Marullus Aug. lib. (VI 8503), subseque(n)s a comm(entariis) ration(is) patrim(onii). (Wife Coelia Septi[mi]na.)

All but one of these are from Rome, two belonging to the *ratio patrimonii*, two others from unspecified departments there, and one from the administration of the corn supply in Puteoli. None are from the provinces. All have been manumitted; hence their posts are not of junior grade. Martialis (No. 3) is found playing the part of a responsible official of some standing, and his name is recorded with that of the procuratorial head of department himself. Menander (No. 4), who is called 'sen(ior)' and has presumably about twenty years more experience in the administrative service, has reached a grade appropriately higher than that of his son who is still at the junior level of *adiutor*. They are of higher clerical status and would not have gained these posts till well after manumission at the normal age of thirty, perhaps as much as ten years later. On the other hand, these *proximi tabulariorum* and *commentariorum* do not proceed to more senior appointments or to procuratorial rank; nor, indeed, is any other appointment mentioned in their inscriptions, which thus conform with those of the Imperial slaves and freedmen who never advanced beyond the junior and intermediate grades of the administrative *cursus*.

Despite some prolonged careers outside Rome without change or promotion, in Rome itself the chance of further promotion about the age of 40 to 45 appears to have been fairly good for those with patronage and ability – again assuming that *tabularii* and *a commentariis* did not regularly die from occupational or other hazards before that age. In terms of opportunities for advancement in their careers the grades of *tabularius* and *a commentariis* are roughly equivalent, allowing for local variations and positions of special responsibility. But overall the *tabularii* do have the edge. In the large bureaux in Rome the *a commentariis* do not figure so prominently and do not appear to have proceeded as easily to the procuratorial grade – at least no *procurator* states that he has formerly been an *a commentariis*, whereas several do say that they have held posts as *tabularii*. In the provinces also the *a commentariis* seem to have followed the pattern of the *tabularii*, but on a slightly lower level. In terms of social status of wives there is little to distinguish the two grades, but the higher proportion of slaves found in the ranks of the *a commentariis*, both in the first and second centuries, shows that they did not have full parity of status with the *tabularii*.[1] In the running for senior posts and higher salaries the *tabularii* must be considered the better placed. To illustrate these points we must consider the senior clerical grades in some detail.

[1] III 1997 = D 1595; V 475; VI 8572 = D 1516, 8624, 8625; *AE* 1908, 194.

CHAPTER 19

SENIOR CLERICAL GRADES

TABULARIUS A RATIONIBUS

In the career-type inscriptions of the Imperial freedmen, senior clerical status is very rarely mentioned in the sequence of posts held, although it can be assumed that the vast majority of all freedmen who reached the senior rank of *procurator* in the administrative service must have held at least one post in the clerical grades, probably of senior clerical status, before rising to procuratorial status. But here mention should be made of one type of exception which is significant – the careers of those who held the post of *tabularius a rationibus*. The examples are:

(1) T. Flavius Aug. lib. Delphicus, tabularius a ratio[nibus, p]roc. ration(is)͵thesaurorum, hereditatium, fisci Alexandrini (*AE* 1888, 130 = D 1518).

(2) Martialis A[ug. lib. ...], tabulariu[s a rationibus?], proc. fiscorum [transmarinorum e]t fisci castr[ensis, pr]oc. h[ereditatium et fisc]i libe[rtatis et peculiorum] (VI 8515, with the restorations of Sanders, *Mem. Amer. Acad. Rome* 10 (1932), 81).

(3) T. Aelius Augg. lib. Saturnin(us), pr[oc. provinc.] Belgicae [...], proc. fisci libertatis et peculior(um), tabul(arius) a rationibus, tabul(arius) Ostis ad annona(m) (VI 8450 = D 1521).[1]

The prestige of a post held in the central department of the *a rationibus* was always high. This is confirmed by the fact that only in the *a rationibus* is the clerical grade of *tabularius* recorded as giving access to the procuratorial grade.[2] But it is the chronological distribution of the *tabularii a rationibus* that is significant here. Considering that the post of *tabularius* would be first held in the years soon after manumission, i.e. between the ages of thirty and forty, T. Flavius Aug. lib. Delphicus (No. 1) would have reached this grade by the end of the first century. T. Aelius Augg. lib. Saturninus (No. 3), who

---

[1] There are several other 'T. Aelii Aug. lib. Saturnini', who are not to be identified with the above or with each other. Cf. *JRS* 58 (1968), 117 n. 29.

[2] Two special posts of *tabularius* outside Rome, one from Egypt, the other from Africa, and both unique, which precede the holding of a procuratorial post, are mentioned in late second-century inscriptions:

(1) Fortunatus Augg. lib., ἀρχιταβλάριος Αἰγύπτου καὶ ἐπίτροπος προσόδων ᾿Αλεξανδρ[είας] (*IGR* III 1103).

(2) M. Aurellius Aug. lib. Inventus, proc. dioecesis Leptitanae (*AE* 1908, 158), tabul(arius) leg(ionis) III Aug(ustae) (*AE* 1956, 123 = Pflaum, *Libyca* 3 (1955), 123 f.). However, if the form 'Aurellius' is considered as an indubitable indication of a third-century date for *AE* 1908, 158 = D 9026, the identification becomes unlikely as the second inscription is dated *c.* 170 (see Pflaum, loc. cit.).

Senior clerical grades

had the post of *tabul(arius) Ostis ad annona(m)* during the time between his manumission and his appointment as *tabularius a rationibus*, would have reached the latter grade by the end of the reign of Antoninus Pius, or at the latest in the early 160s.[1] The date as well as the precise career of Martialis is more problematical. Sanders' restorations are bold but fit well with the surviving letters and the posts held by Delphicus and Saturninus.[2] Both of these advance to financial procuratorships in Rome involving supervision of one or more of the separate Imperial *fisci* located there. If the restoration 'proc. fiscorum [transmarinorum]' is correct, Martialis could be the predecessor of the separate procurators of the *fiscus Alexandrinus* (as Delphicus above) and the *fiscus Asiaticus* (cf. VI 8570), both of which date from the Flavian period.[3] Likewise the restoration 'proc. h[ereditatium]', if correct, would indicate a Flavian date, or at least a date not later than the end of Trajan's reign, for Martialis.[4]

Thus, the evidence that the post of *tabularius a rationibus* gave access to the freedman procuratorial grades, i.e. the senior freedman career, belongs to the period *up to* the reign of M. Aurelius. On the other hand, the evidence that the post of *proximus* in the *Palatine* bureaux likewise gave access to the freedman procuratorial grades dates from the reign of M. Aurelius or *later*.[5] This, together with the fact that no instance of a *tabularius* is found in the *a rationibus* (or in the other Palatine bureaux) from the reign of M. Aurelius or later, shows what role these prestige posts played in the freedman career in the later first and second centuries up till the reforms of M. Aurelius.

TABULARIUS PROVINCIAE, A COMMENTARIIS PROVINCIAE, ETC.

Another item of chronological interest in the inscriptions of senior clerical officials is the use of the term 'provincia'. I include the slave posts of *arcarius* and *dispensator*, as well as the freedman posts of *tabularius* and *a commentariis*.

First, the status significance of the term 'provincia'. *Tabularii* and *dispensatores* are found in most provinces in most periods of the early Empire, except the early first century. *Arcarii* and *a commentariis* are also found in the provincial administrative centres, but less commonly.[6] However, only in a

---

[1] On the *Augustorum liberti* in this period, see Part I, pp. 66 f.
[2] For the restoration 'tabularius a rationibus', see Rostovtzeff, *Diz. Epig.* III, 137; Hirschfeld, *Verwalt.* p. 429 n. 6.   [3] See Jones, *Studies*, pp. 110 f.
[4] Cf. Pflaum, *Proc. Equest.* pp. 55 f.; and (on Domitius Lemnus) Weaver, *Historia* 14 (1965), 511 f.   [5] See below, pp. 252 f.
[6] Vulič, *Diz. Epig.* II, 1922 f.; and esp. Boulvert, *EAI*, pp. 429 f.; see also above, p.205. *Arcarii*: Habel, P-W II, 429 f.; Fuchs, *Diz. Epig.* I, 632 f.

The emperor's service

minority of such cases do the titles *tabularius provinciae, dispensator provinciae, arcarius provinciae* and *a commentariis provinciae* appear. On the other hand, the simple titles *tabularius, dispensator*, etc., are frequent and, in the second century, the titles *ex tabulariis, ex dispensatoribus* also appear: the earliest is M. Ulpius Martinus Aug. lib. ex tabulariis (VI 9074). There is no reason to doubt that the status of a *tabularius provinciae* was that of the senior official of clerical grade in charge of the central *tabularium* in his particular province, just as the freedman *procurator provinciae* was the senior freedman procurator in the province, and as the *princeps tabularius* was the senior freedman of his grade in his department in Rome. The larger provincial administrative centres would certainly have a number of officials of each kind in the clerical grades, and some title to distinguish the senior posts would be necessary. 'Provincia' was used for this purpose.

For dating purposes it should be borne in mind that a senior clerical post was unlikely to be obtained till at least the age of 35, that is a minimum of some five years after manumission at the normal age. Thus, the Imperial *gentilicium* of a freedman holding such a post is a fairly good indication that the post was held during the reign of the manumitting emperor or very shortly afterwards; this is in contrast with the freedman procurators, who as a rule gained senior rank in the reign *following* that of the manumitting emperor or even later.[1] The chronological distribution of the *tabularii provinciae* is as follows:

TRAJAN/HADRIAN

(1) M. Ulpius Aug. lib. Gresianus (II 3235 = D 1555; Mentesa Orentanorum, Tarrac.), tabularius XX hereditatium, item tabularius provinciae Lugudunensis et Aquitanicae, item tabularius provinciae Lusitaniae. (Died aged 45.)

(2) M. Ulpius Fortun[atus Au]g. lib. (XIII 1826; Lugudunum), tabula[rius ...]cia [(?)...].

HADRIAN/ANTONINUS

(3) P. Aelius Aug. lib. Onesimus (VI 8579 = D 1494), tabul(arius) prov(inciae) Iudiae.

(4) P. Aelius Vitalis Aug. lib. (II 485 = D 1493; Emerita, Lusit.), tabul(arius) provinc(iae) Lusitaniae.

(5) P. Aelius Aug. lib. Alexander (II 486 = D 1492; Emerita, Lusit.), tab(ularius) provinciae Lusit(aniae). (Wife: Iulia Optata.)

ANTONINUS

(6) Atimetus (Aug.) lib. (II 4089; Tarraco), tabul(arius) p(rovinciae) H(ispaniae) C(iterioris). (Dedicated to Antoninus Pius.)

(7) Aelius Aug. lib....(III 14689; Salonae, Dalm.), [tabul(arius)?] provinc(iae) Dalm(atiae).

---

[1] See below, pp. 269 f.

Senior clerical grades

M. AURELIUS or SEVERAN

(8) Aurelius Augg. lib. Aphrodisius (v 7253 = D 1495; Segusio, Alp. Cott.), tabularius Alpium Cottiarum.

(9) Fortunatus Augg. lib. (*IGR* III 1103 = D 8846) (AD 161–9), ἀρχιταβλάριος Αἰγύπτου καὶ ἐπίτροπος προσόδων 'Αλεξανδρ[είας].

(10) Augustinus Augg. nn. libertus (III 3964; Siscia, Pann. Sup.), tabul(arius) prov(inciae Pannoniae Superioris).

(11) Zeno Augg. lib. (III 251 = D 1373; Ancyra, Galat.) (AD 198–211), tabular(ius) prov(inciae) eiusd(em) (i.e. Galatiae).

(12) Lucretius Augg. (lib.) (x 7584 = D 1359; Carales, Sard.) (AD 198–211), tabul(arius) prov(inciae) Sard(iniae).

(13) Primitivus Aug. lib. (III 7955: Sarmizegetusa, Dac.) (AD 222–35), tabularius prov(inciae) Dac(iae) Apulens(is).

(14) Hilarus Aug. lib. (III 4800 = D 4198; Virunum, Noric.) (AD 239), tab(ularius) p(atrimonii?) r(egni) N(orici).

(15) M. Aurelius Augg. lib. Euemer(us) (D 1496; Livorno, Etrur.) (3rd c.), tabul(arius) sacrarum pecuniarum provinciae Cretae.

UNDATED

(16) Successus Aug. lib. (II 4181; Tarraco), tabul(arius) p(rovinciae) H(ispaniae) C(iterioris). (Son P. Aelius Aelianus, wife Plaetoria Annia.)

(17) Favor Aug. lib. (*AE* 1956, 23; Tarraco), tabul(arius) p(rovinciae) H(ispaniae) C(iterioris). (Children C. Iulius Aquilinus, Iulia Favorina.)

(18) Diogenes Aug. lib. (III 1993; Salonae, Dalm.), tabul(arius) prov(inciae) Dalm(atiae).

(19) Eucarpus Aug. lib. (III 4043; Poetovio, Pann. Sup.), tab(ularius) p(rovinciae) P(annoniae) S(uperioris).

(20) [...Aug. lib.?] (III 4066; Poetovio, Pann. Sup.), tabul(arius) p(rovinciae) P(annoniae) S(uperioris).

(21) Carpion Aug(us)ti lib. (III 980; Apulum, Dac.), tabularius provinc⟨c⟩iae (Daciae) Apulensis. (Cf. Carpion Aug. lib. (III 1467, 7939; Sarmizegetusa, Dac.), tabul(arius); son M. Aurelius Onesimus.)

(22) Carcophorus Aug. lib. (*AE* 1933, 263; Pergamum), tabular(ius) provinc(iae) Asiae.

(23) Earinus Aug. lib. (III 6081 = 7121; Ephesus), tabula[r(ius)] provinc(iae) Asia[e].[1]

All of the instances that can be firmly dated (15/23), either by their Imperial *nomen* or by reference to particular emperors or to equestrians of known date (Nos. 1–15), are from the second or early third century. Of the remaining eight undated examples (Nos. 16–23) none can be assigned to the first century; indeed, one suspects that most of these are late second- or early third-century. It is to be noted that the only wife with Imperial *nomen*, Iulia Optata, is married to P. Aelius Aug. lib. Alexander (No. 5), a freedman of Hadrian. Her *nomen*, Iulia, therefore, is valueless as a dating criterion. The two earliest

[1] Note also: II 4184 = D 1556 (Tarraco, Spain): Felix Aug. lib., a comment(ariis) XX her(editatium) H(ispaniae) C(iterioris); Hilarus collib(ertus), tabul(arius) XX her(editatium) prov(inciae) Lusitaniae. *EE* VIII 26: Aurelius Rufus, tabul(arius) provinc(iae) Lusit(aniae) rat(ionis) pat(rimonii).

The emperor's service

instances are freedmen of Trajan; but of these, one (No. 2) rests on a very uncertain reading, the other (No. 1) had already filled the post of *tabularius XX hereditatium* after his manumission by Trajan, and, as he died aged 45 still as a *tabularius provinciae*, his first appointment to this post (in the provinces of Galliae Lugdunensis et Aquitanica) could well date from the reign of Hadrian. In view of the several examples from the time of Hadrian (Nos. 3, 4, 5 and probably 1) it is tempting to connect the new style of nomenclature for senior *tabularii* in the provinces with Hadrian as part of his regrading of freedmen in the administration. This development would appear to have preceded the use of the title 'procurator provinciae', also by freedmen, from early in the reign of M. Aurelius.[1]

At the very time when senior *tabularii* were acquiring a distinctive nomenclature both in Rome (*princeps tabulariorum*) and in provincial administration (*tabularius provinciae*), another title also appears – 'ex tabularis or 'ex tabulario'. Of twelve instances, eight are certainly Aurelian or later in date (VI 9071, 9072, 9073, 9075; III 348 = D 1477 (Tricomia, Phryg.); VIII 3290 (Lambaesis, Numid.); *AE* 1908, 30 (Cherchel, Afr.); *AE* 1924, 83 (Ephesus)) and a further three are from the mid-second century or later (III 4063 (Poetovio, Pann. Sup.); 6082 = D 8245 (Ephesus); VIII 12882 (Carthage)). The remaining instance is also the earliest – M. Ulpius Martinus Aug. lib. (VI 9074).[2] In only one case is the *tabularium* specified – Felicianus Aug. n. lib. ex tabulario vect(igalis) Illyr(ici) (III 4063; Poetovio, Pann. Sup.) – and this not the central *tabularium* of the province. The plural form of the designation, 'ex tabulari(i)s', can be taken to be regular: 'ex tabularis' occurs six times (VI 9071, 9074, 9075; VIII 12882; *AE* 1924, 83; III 6082 – restored ἀπὸ ταβλαρί[ων] in D 8245, cf. line 13 'ab iis qui sunt in tabulario Ephes[i]'); 'ex tabulario' twice (III 4063; VI 9073); the remaining instances are variously abbreviated, most frequently as 'ex tabular.' (III 348 = D 1477; VI 9072; VIII 3290; *AE* 1908, 30). This makes it improbable that these terms (which are clearly equivalent) mean '*former* tabularius', as in the case of 'ex procuratore' and 'ex vicario'. Nor does the plural indicate mobility of the holder of this title from one *tabularium* to another. Mobility of this kind for *tabularii* was uncommon or at least not often recorded, despite the fact that promotions within the overall grade of *tabularius* must have been frequent, especially after the development of senior clerical posts; the only clear cases are M. Ulpius Aug. lib. Gresianus (No. 1), who held posts as *tabularius provinciae* in both Gaul and Spain; T. Aelius Augg. lib. Saturninus (VI

---

[1] See below, pp. 276f.
[2] There are also two instances of 'a tabulario castrensi' which cannot be dated: VI 8529; *AE* 1948, 76 (Rome). In XIV 205 = *IPO* B 188 the restoration is uncertain.

Senior clerical grades

8450 = D 1521) who moved from *tabularius ad annonam* at Ostia to become *tabularius a rationibus* at Rome. The plural is also used, and in the same way, for those on the junior-clerical grade, the *adiutores tabulariorum* who had even less reason than the *tabularii* to move from one centre of administration to another. The term 'ex tabulariis' is a late second-century and early third-century equivalent of 'tabularius', and in this period simply denotes an undifferentiated holder of a post in this general grade (i.e. not a senior *tabularius*). It thus forms part of the changing pattern of nomenclature in the expanding clerical grades of the administration during the middle and late second century.[1]

The second group, the *a commentariis provinciae*, are also all of freedman status. There are seven examples, as follows:

(1) T. Aelius Aug. lib. Tyrannus (*AE* 1945, 134; Trèves, Gall. Belg.), qui fuit a comm(entariis) prov(inciae) Belgicae. (Wife: Aelia Andria.)

(2) Aurel(ius) Rhodismianus Aug. lib. (v 7882; Cemenelum, Alp. Marit.), comm(entariensis) Alp(ium) Marit(imarum). (Wife: Flavia Bassilla.)

(3) [Aur(elius) Fa]ustinus Augusto[rum liber]tus (II 6085 = D 1560; Tarraco, Hisp. Cit.), commentar[i]ensis XXXX Gall(iarum), item urbis al(b)ei Tiberis, item provinciae Baetic(a)e, item Alpium Cotti(arum). (Died aged 41. Wife: Statia Felicissima.)

(4) Tertiolus Aug. lib. (x 6092 = D 1500; Formiae), proxim(us) rational(ium), et a commentari(i)s provinc(iae) Belgicae. (Wife: Flavia Irene.)[2]

(5) Callistus Aug. lib. (III 12298 = 14203.31; cf. *Historia* 3 (1955), 247; Paramythia, Epirus), ab commentari(i)s Epiri et Achaiae. (Wife: Claudia Primigenia.)]

(6) Victor Au[g. l]ib. (III 258; Ancyra, Galat.), a co[mm(entariis)?] prov(inciae) [G]a[lat(iae)]. (Wife: Apuleia Laudice.)

(7) Verus [Aug. lib.] (*AE* 1903, 245; Philippopolis, Thrac.), a commen[tariis] provinc(iae) [Thraciae?]. (Wife: Coelia [...].)[3]

---

[1] Not included in the discussion above is: Aurelius Saturion (XII 4254) 'ex tabul(ariis) provinc(iarum) III Mauret(aniae), Narb(onensis), Syriae Palaestinae' (quoted by Sachers, P–W IV A, 1968). He is without status indication and need not be an Imperial freedman. He can hardly be from a single *tabularium* for provinces as far apart as Mauretania, Gallia Narbonensis and Syria Palaestina (as Sachers appears to assume). If the explanation of the title 'ex tabulari(i)s' given above is correct, that it signifies not a senior *tabularius* (i.e. *tabularius provinciae*) but an ordinary undifferentiated holder of the post of *tabularius*, the transfer of a freedman official to three such clerical posts so far apart would call for comment. Nor would the order of posts appear to be in chronological order, if the inscription, from Baeterra in Narbonese Gaul, was put up by Saturion's wife and children after his death. It is possible (but unlikely) that he was a former *tabularius provinciae* of *three* provinces in succession – but in this case the nomenclature would be unique.

[2] Weaver, *JRS* 58 (1968), 111 f.

[3] Note also: P. Ael(ius) Aug. l. Victor (*AE* 1932, 85; Tarraco, Hisp. Cit.), a comm(entariis) XX h(ereditatium) p(rovinciae) H(ispaniae) C(iterioris); and II 4184 = D 1556 (Tarraco): Felix Aug. lib. a'comment. XX her. H. C. Very difficult and exceptional is III 12130 (Patara, Lycia) which reads: 'Felici Caesaris ser/vi[k.] a commentar(iis)/pr(ovinciae) Lyc(iae)/Hermes optimo/ cogn(ato) ob merita/eius fecit'. The date is probably Antoninus Pius or later (cf. Boulvert, *EAI*, p. 299 n. 235). In this period a *vicarius* = *Caesaris servus* = *a commentariis provinciae* seems to me not only exceptional but impossible. I would suggest: 'Hermes (Aug. lib.) a commentarii(s) pr. Lyc.... Felici Caesaris serv(o)...'.

The emperor's service

Here, again, the pattern is the same. Those instances (Nos. 1, 2, 3) which can be dated by Imperial *nomen* and status indication are all mid-second-century or later. A fourth instance (No. 4) is possibly Severan in date on other grounds (the title *proximus rationalium*). The remaining three (Nos. 5, 6, 7) are undated. The same conclusion follows, that the occurrence of 'provincia' in the occupational title is an indication of mid-second-century date or later. If this is so, it is noteworthy that in only one case does the Imperial *nomen* of wife and husband correspond: T. Aelius Aug. lib. Tyrannus (No. 1) = Aelia Andria; but in three cases the Imperial *nomen* of the wife does not provide a dating criterion:

Aurelius Rhodismianus Aug. lib. (No. 2) = Flavia Bassilla; Tertiolus Aug. lib. (No. 4) = Flavia Irene; Callistus Aug. lib. (No. 5) = Claudia Primigenia.

There is also an instance of the title 'ex comm(entariensibus)' from the late second or early third century: M. Aur(elius) Augg. lib. Aurelianus (VI 8519), 'ex comm(entariensibus) rat(ionis) kastr(ensis)'.

The clerical grades of *tabularius* and *a commentariis* are of roughly equivalent status, and were both normally filled by freedmen. The other two grades of comparable status, *dispensator* and *arcarius*, were filled by officials who remained slaves, even though they were usually over the age of 30 and thus eligible for manumission. However, the dating of the inscriptions of slave officials is much more difficult than for the freedmen because of the absence of Imperial *nomen*. Here, for want of a more precise criterion, we have to fall back on the Imperial slave status indication, especially the use of 'Aug(usti)' and 'n(ostri)' in combination.[1]

There are four instances of *arcarius provinciae*:

(1) Apollonius Aug. n. verna, arcarius provinciae Asiae (III 6077 = D 1505; Ephesus);
(2) Alcimus Aug. ser. verna, arcarius provinc(iae) Achaiae (III 556 = D 1504; Athens). Cf. V 8818 = III 7268 = D 1503 (Corinth), where Alcimus is styled simply 'arcarius');
(3) Coenus August(i), arcar(ius) provinciae Belgicae (VI 8574 = D 1501);[2]
(4) Antiochus Aug. n. Lucconianus, ark(arius) provinciae Africae (VI 8575 = D 1502).

Only the first instance, where mention is made of a 'collegium Faustinianum commentaresium', can be certainly dated to the period of Antoninus Pius or later. Antiochus Aug. n. Lucconianus (No. 4), from his status indication, would appear to be second-century in date (cf. Apollonius Aug. n. verna (No. 1), and the spelling 'ark(arius)'), but as he is also a 'vicarianus' with *agnomen* (Lucconianus) he cannot be later than Hadrian, and should probably be assigned to the reign of Trajan. Note that his wife is Iulia Iusta. Similarly, the status indication of Alcimus Aug. ser. verna ('Aug. vern.' in III 7268 = V

---

[1] See Part I above, pp. 54 f. [2] Discussed in *JRS* 58 (1968), 110 f.

Senior clerical grades

8818 = D 1503), indicates a second- rather than a first-century date. In the remaining case, Coenus, neither his status indication, 'August(i)', nor the name of his son, C. Iulius Proculus, is decisive for a first-century date; the occupational title *arcar(ius) provinciae Belgicae* is here the best criterion and can be taken to indicate a date in the second century.

With the *dispensatores provinciae* the position is not quite so clear. Disregarding three patrimonial *dispensatores regionis*, at least two of whom are late second-century,[1] there remain eleven instances. Of these seven belong to the mid-second century or later:

(1) [...] disp(ensator) Divi Marci provinciae Ciliciae (VI 8577 = D 1507);

(2) Fronto Augg. nn., dispens(ator) Moes(iae) Inf(erioris) (III 754 add. = 7436; Nicopolis, Moes. Inf.);

(3) Iucundus Aug. n., disp(ensator) p(rovinciae) P(annoniae) S(uperioris) (III 3960; Siscia, Pann. Sup.);

(4) [...]omo.. Aug. n., d[isp(ensator)] rationis p(rovinciae) P(annoniae) (III 4049; Poetovio, Pann. Sup.);

(5) Nicolaus Aug., disp(ensator)...regn(i) Noric(i) (III 4797 = D 1506; Virunum, Noric.);

(6) Eutyches Aug. n., disp(ensator) p(atrimonii?) r(egni) N(orici) (III 4828; Virunum, Noric.) (cf. III 4800 = D 4198 (Noricum): tab(ularius) p(atrimonii?) r(egni) N(orici) dated to AD 239);

(7) Salvianus Aug. n. vern., dispensator rationis extraord(inariae) provinc(iae) Asiae (III 6575 = 7127 = D 1421; Ephesus) dated by the procurator Claudius Xenophon (Pflaum, *CP* No. 222) to the reign of Septimius Severus.

One gives no reliable indication of date:

(8) Diadumenus Aug. ser., disp(ensator) p(rovinciae) S(ardiniae) (X 7588; Carales, Sard.).

The remaining three could possibly be from the late first century but could also be Trajanic or later – these all omit the term 'provincia' from their title, which may indicate an earlier date than for the rest:

(9) Menophilus Aug. n., dispensator Ciliciae (VI 6639), from the first-century *Monumentum Statiliorum* (cf. *CIL* VI p. 1011), but whose status indication would indicate a later date;

(10) Lochus Aug., disp(ensator) Delmatiae, and (11) his son Himer Aug. disp(ensator) Moesiae (III 1994 = 8575 = D 1508; Salonae, Dalm.), whose inscription Hirschfeld (*CIL* III, ad loc.) thought to belong to the first century.[2]

One well-known inscription remains – that of Musicus Ti. Caesaris Augusti Scurranus, dispensator ad fiscum Gallicum provinciae Lugdunensis (VI 5197 = D 1514), from the reign of Tiberius.[3] The title does not conform

---

[1] Herma Augg. verna (V 2385 = D 1509; Ferrara); Epictetus Augustorum ver(na) (VIII 12892; Carthage); Primus Aug. vern(a) (*AE* 1915, 20; Thuburbo Maius).
[2] V 2156 has been excluded; cf. Chantraine, p. 348, No. 376.
[3] Cf. the undated Ligorian inscription VI 8578 = D 1511: 'Protoctetus Aug., dispensator ad census provinciae Lugdunensis'.

The emperor's service

to the pattern of any other period and can only be regarded as early and exceptional.[1]

In the case of No. 10, however, omission of 'provincia' from the title, and the unlikelihood of both father and son holding posts of senior clerical grade at the same time, posts normally held between the ages of 35 and 45, cause one to suspect here either an inscription put up by the son years after the father's death, or two ordinary *dispensatores* whose careers, less spectacular and less likely to include manumission and promotion to the administrative grades, could possibly overlap.[2]

In the provincial administrative centres, first the grade of 'adiutor' was introduced for the junior slave and freedman *tabularii, a commentariis*, and that of 'vicarius' for the junior slave *dispensatores, arcarii* and *vilici*. Later, in the second century, the term 'provincia' was gradually introduced into the titles of senior officials as the distinction between senior and intermediate clerical grades developed. Then the titles *ex tabulariis, ex commentariensibus*, and *ex dispensatoribus* were introduced for subordinate posts. Such a differentiation in nomenclature was likely to arise first where the largest number of officials of the same category was found.

Thus the *tabularii, a commentariis, dispensatores*, and *arcarii* had adopted the new style by the time of Hadrian or at least Antoninus Pius. The highest officials of the freedman service, the procurators, were fewer in number – the title 'procurator provinciae' as distinct from other freedman procurators with lesser responsibilities and, presumably, lower salary, including those in the purely domestic service, did not come into general use till somewhat later, in the early years of M. Aurelius' reign, as part of his wide-ranging reforms of the senior levels of the administration.[3] But first we must consider again the senior clerical grades in Rome, especially in the central Palatine bureaux.

PROXIMUS A RATIONIBUS, PROXIMUS AB EPISTULIS, ETC.

To make clear the chronological distribution of these freedmen *proximi*, we must list the extant examples:[4]

(1) M. Ulpius Aug. lib. Zopyrus (VI 8701 = D 1693), prox(imus) ab admissione.

(2) T. Aelius Aug. lib. Titianus (VI 8878 = D 1685), prox(imus) a libr(is) sacerdotal(ibus). (Died aged 42.)

---

[1] On the use of 'vicarius', and on Scurranus' personal slaves, see above pp. 201 f.

[2] For the wealth of these *dispensatores*, see Suetonius, *Otho* 5; *Vesp.* 23. Cf. Mommsen, *Staatsr.* II, 839 n. 2; P. A. Brunt, *Historia* 10 (1961), 222. [3] See chapter 21 below.

[4] Equestrians with the title *proximus* are not found in the early empire; the earliest is Iulius Achilleus, *ex prox. memoriae*, who held this post before 275, according to Pflaum, possibly under Gallienus (*AE* 1951, 101; Pflaum, *Proc. Equest.* pp. 317 f.; *CP*, p. 624 n. 10).

Senior clerical grades

(3) M. Aurelius Aug. lib. Isidorus (VI 8425 = D 1478), melloproximus a rationibus.

(4) Aurelius Alexander (XIV 2815 = XV 7832 = D 1669), prox(imus) ab epistul(is) Lat(inis); cf. M. Aur(elius) Alexander Aug. lib. (VI 8606 = D 1668), ab epistulis Graecis.

(5) M. Aurelius Aug. liber. Marcio (III 348 = D 1477; *IGR* IV 676, 704), proximus rationum, proc(urator) marmorum, pro(curator) prov(inciae) Britanniae, proc(urator) summi chorag(ii), proc(urator) prov(inciae) Fryg(iae).

(6) M. Aurelius Aug. lib. [...] (XIII 1800), proximus a memoria itaco[...], proc(urator) fisci Asiatici, proc(urator) h[ereditat(ium), proc(urator)] provinciarum Lugudune[ns(is) et Aquitan(icae)].

(7) (L. Septimius) Antonius (Aug.) lib. (VI 180 = D 3703), proximus a libellis.

(8) (M. Aurelius?) Ianuarius (Aug.) lib. (VI 8619), proximus officii memoriae, (procurator?) voluptatum ('ad splendidam voluptatum statio[nem promotus]').

(9) Bassus Aug. lib. (VI 8608 = D 1485), prox(imus) ab epistulis Graecis, proc(urator) tractus Carthaginiensis.

(10) Terpsilaus Aug. lib. (VI 8637 = D 1683), prox(imus) a studiis.

(11) Hilarianus Aug. l. (*AE* 1954, 65), prox(imus) a rat(ionibus).

(12) Tertiolus Aug. lib. (X 6092 = D 1500), proxim(us) rational(ium), et a commentari(i)s provinc(iae) Belgicae.

We must date T. Aelius Titianus (No. 2) to the reign of M. Aurelius. He died aged 42, and presumably in office, at Carnuntum where that emperor spent a three-year period during the Marcomannic War (*c.* 170–2?). To this long absence of the emperor from Rome can be attributed the unusual nature of Titianus' post and the fact that he alone of the senior *proximi* had duties away from the capital.[1] Of the others who can be securely dated from their *nomen* (Nos. 1, 3, 4, 5, 6), or other internal criteria (Nos. 7, 8), only one, M. Ulpius Zopyrus (No. 1), is earlier than the reign of M. Aurelius. Though a freedman of Trajan, Zopyrus would not have held his post till about the age of 40 or later, that is, some ten years after manumission; thus, he would very likely have served as *proximus* under Hadrian. Zopyrus is not only much the earliest *proximus*, but also his post is the only one in this group which was held in a domestic department of the Palatine service. Freedman officials were responsible for controlling admission to the emperor's presence for an audience. The *officium admissionis* had a large staff ranging from its freedman head and deputy (*proximus*), to its freedman *adiutores* and *nomenclatores*.[2] The influence and demeanour of these officials is illustrated by the story of one who was rude to Vespasian at Nero's court (Suetonius, *Vesp.* 14: 'trepidum eum (Vespasian) interdicta aula sub Nerone quaerentemque, quidnam ageret aut

---

[1] On the date, Titianus' status indication 'Aug. lib.' (not 'Augg. lib.') perhaps indicates a period of sole rule; see above, p. 67. On *proximi* in the early empire, see especially Ensslin, P-W XXIII, 1034 f.; Hirschfeld, *Verwalt.* pp. 335, 441, 460; and now Boulvert, II, 599 f.

[2] *Ab admissione*: VI 8698, 8699 = D 1691, 8702; *AE* 1907, 125; *proximus ab admiss.*: VI 8701 = D 1693; *adiutor ab admiss.*: III 6107 = D 1692; VI 8700; *nomenclator ab admiss.*: VI 8930, 8931. For a *proximus* in the fourth century, Amm. Marc. xxii. 7.2: '...inductis per admissionum proximum'. On the *officium admissionis* and the *admissionales*, see P-W I, 381; D-S I, 71; *Diz. Epig.* I 92; Boulvert, *EAI*, pp. 181 f.

The emperor's service

quo abiret, quidam ex officio admissionis simul expellens abire Morboviam iusserat') and, for the Flavian period, by the remarks of Pliny in his *Panegyricus* (47 f.) on the ready accessibility of Trajan. The new senior grade of *proximus* arose first in the hierarchy of the numerous Palatine officials.

Four undated examples remain. Of these, two, Terpsilaus (No. 10) and Hilarianus (No. 11), provide no clue as to date. But in the case of the remaining two, Bassus (No. 9) and Tertiolus (No. 12), there are definite indications, which have been obscured by the family nomenclature, that they should be placed with the other dated *proximi* belonging to the central departments, that is, in the period of M. Aurelius or later. Bassus and Tertiolus have been assigned to the reign of Claudius and the Flavian period respectively solely on grounds of family nomenclature.[1] Tertiolus' son is Flavius Fuscianus, and Bassus' son is Claudius Comon. But the *nomina* of children are of no independent value as dating criteria for these inscriptions.[2] The mother of Fuscianus, Flavia Irene, has the same *nomen* as her son – a name that readily occurs from the first century to the third. Besides the possibility that she had already been married to Hermeros Aug. lib.[3] there are very many examples of children of *Augusti liberti* deriving their *nomen* from their mother and not their father.[4]

The other inscription is VI 8608 = D 1485: 'Basso Aug. lib. prox(imo) ab epistulis Graecis, proc(uratori) tractus Carthaginiensis, Fabia Q. f. Priscilla marito piissimo, item Claudius Comon patri bene merenti fecerunt.' Again it is hazardous to assume – as has always been done to my knowledge[5] – the *nomen* of the father, and hence the date of the inscription, solely from the *nomen* of the son (Claudius, and without *praenomen*), which in this case differs from that of the mother (Fabia). Adoption of the son into another family (or even a previous marriage of the mother with an *ingenuus* despite the use of the word 'pater') is possible as the explanation of the different *nomina* of mother and son.[6] It cannot be confidently assumed that the son was born after the manumission of the father and so took his father's *nomen* and not his mother's, and even less that he is actually an Imperial freedman without status indication.

[1] Hirschfeld, *Verwalt.* pp. 34 n. 2, 320 n. 1; Friedländer, IV, 39; Pflaum, *Proc. Equest.* p. 318; Ensslin, P–W XXIII, 1034; Boulvert, *EAI*, p. 93 n. 9; Chantraine, p. 116.
[2] See *JRS* 58 (1968), 110 f; and Part II, pp. 152 f. above.
[3] VI 8614 = D 1674; cf. X 6092 n.
[4] E.g. VI 15317, 20579, 23716; *AE* 1923, 76. See above, pp. 150 f.
[5] The consequences of this assumption are made fully explicit by Boulvert, *EAI*, p. 93 n. 9: 'L'existence à cette époque d'un tel *proximus* nous conduit à situer dès le règne de Claude la création de la fonction de *proximus* dans les grands bureaux...'. Cf. id. p. 98 n. 38. The assumed *nomen* of Bassus is the sole evidence for this important development.
[6] Cf. VI 8077, 10648, 15221; XIV 1386. See above, pp. 144 f.

Senior clerical grades

There are other features about these two allegedly first-century *proximi* which have been obscured by the family names. Tertiolus is *proximus rational(ium)*. The term 'rationalium' has distinctly late second- and third-century associations.[1] Tertiolus Aug. lib. is surely from that period. The other, Bassus, was *proximus ab epistulis Graecis*. The title 'ab epistulis Graecis' otherwise dates from Trajan–Hadrian[2] although the earlier division of the *ab epistulis* bureau is implied by two *ab epistulis Latinis* from the late Flavian or early Trajanic period.[3] The permanent appointment of a second equestrian head *ab epistulis* was later, and may not have been till the reign of M. Aurelius, when the second equestrian was appointed to the equally important bureau *a rationibus*.[4] The formal division of the department, and the division of functions within the new department which the titles 'ab epistulis Graecis' and 'proximus' imply, belong naturally to a more fully developed stage of administrative organisation than was likely under Claudius or Nero. Bassus is best placed with the other *proximus ab epistulis* (in this case *Latinis*), Aurelius Alexander (No. 4), under M. Aurelius or later.

Bassus advanced to the post of *procurator tractus Carthaginiensis*. This title is attested for the reign of Hadrian,[5] and an equestrian *procurator centenarius* was probably in Carthage as early as 69.[6] Pflaum puts the creation of this equestrian post under Nero if not earlier. This does not exclude a freedman in charge of the Imperial domains administered at that period from Carthage, but the title 'procurator tractus Carthaginiensis' for such a freedman post in the provinces suggests the second century when such freedman titles are definitely attested. The freedman *procuratores provinciae* are dated to the middle of the second century and later,[7] which is the period covered by the dated *proximi*. If Bassus' post as *proc. tractus Carthaginiensis* was the equivalent of that of a freedman *proc. provinciae* – freedman *proc. prov. Africae* are not attested, nor are equestrians with this title after Trajan[8] – then his

---

[1] On *rationalis*, see Hirschfeld, *Verwalt.* p. 34; Friedländer, IV, 27; Liebenam in P–W I A, 263 f., who, however, is forced to take the use of the term in x 6092 (Tertiolus, No. 12) as an (unexplained) early example, as he assumes a Flavian date for the inscription.

[2] VI 8607: M. Ulpius Aug. lib. Eros.

[3] The title 'ab epistulis Latinis' is found of Flavian date: VI 8610, 8611. For the equestrian *ducenarii ad legationes et responsa Graeca*, who were no doubt distinct from the *ab epistulis*, since Claudius, see Pflaum, *CP*, pp. 34 f. (Ti. Claudius Balbillus); pp. 41 f. (C. Stertinius Xenophon); pp. 111 f. (Dionysius Alexandrinus); *Proc. Equest.* p. 60.

[4] As argued by G. Townend, *Historia* 10 (1961), 375 f., but rejected by Boulvert, *EAI*, p. 284 n. 137.

[5] VIII 14763 = D 6781: T. Flavius Gallicus, *proc. Aug. prov. Afric. tract. Kart.* See Pflaum, *CP* No. 192, pp. 517 f.

[6] Tacitus, *Hist.* iv. 50 (Baebius Massa); cf. Pflaum, *CP*, p. 99; *Proc. Equest.* p. 44.

[7] Hirschfeld, *Verwalt.* p. 381 n. 4, 380; and see further below, pp. 276 f.

[8] See Pflaum, *CP* No. 150 bis (Claudius Paternus Clementianus), pp. 354 f. and esp. p. 978.

The emperor's service

career would fit naturally with that of M. Aurelius Aug. lib. Marcio (No. 5) who rose from *proximus rationum* to be *proc. prov. Phrygiae* under M. Aurelius or later.

At this point, however, it must be observed that the *proximi* have another feature in common. They not only (apart from Zopyrus) should be dated to the period from M. Aurelius to the early third century, but they also belong (with the exception of Titianus, mentioned above) to the large departments of the central administration in Rome. They do not belong to any of the provincial administrative centres nor to any of the smaller special financial or other administrative departments located in Rome. The one early Imperial instance of a *melloproximus*, i.e. next in rank to the *proximus*,[1] also occurs in the *a rationibus* bureau, and is from the Aurelian period: M. Aurelius Aug. lib. Isidorus (No. 3). The extant examples are representatively spread over the central bureaux – *a rationibus* (Nos. 3, 5, 11, 12); *ab epistulis* (Nos. 4, 9); *a memoria* (Nos. 6, 8); *a libellis* (No. 7); *a studiis* (No. 10).[2] The senior freedman status of these officials is not in doubt: a salary of HS 40,000 is mentioned in two rescripts of an emperor of the early third century to Ianuarius (Aug.) lib. VI 8619: '[quoniam functus es per annos... ministerio officii m]emoriae ...iustum arbitratus sum [adaequare te] ceteris proximis qui in aliis stationibus quadragena millia n. [accipiunt]'. Cf. ib. ll. 9f.: '[quoniam]...fides et modestia...[et commendatio] magistri tui hortantur ut te ad splendidam voluptatum statio[nem promoveam, defero tibi officium] colliberti tui...'. The salary is thus fixed below that of the lowest procuratorial grade, the *sexagenarii*, but undoubtedly above that of the *tabularii* and the other clerical grades. The position of *proximus* was always held by freedmen and, like that of *tabularius a rationibus*, was in fact the first point on the promotion ladder which was normally mentioned in the *cursus* of those freedmen who reached the highest grades. Thus, while the *proximi* before they reached the age of 40 or thereabouts must have filled the intermediate and junior posts below that of *proximus*, these are not mentioned. This is not to be taken to mean that *tabularii, a commentariis* and *dispensatores* did not ever reach the senior ranks. What is surprising is the small number of freedman *procuratores* who seem to have served as *proximi*, and the fact that those who did were regularly transferred to another department for their first procuratorship. The number

---

[1] *Melloproximus*: P-W XV, 558; Hirschfield, *Verwalt.* p. 460 n. 2.

[2] In XIII 1800, line 2, the reading 'ITACO...' perhaps represents: 'it(em) a co[mm(entariis) prov(inciae)...]' (cf. X 6092, lines 6–7). The suggestion given in *CIL* ad loc., 'it(em) a co[mmentariis]' is distinctly unlikely as the simple post of *a commentariis* without further qualification is an undistinguished one of intermediate clerical status, and does not occur in the career-type inscriptions of the senior freedmen. Another possible restoration: 'it(em) a co[gnit(ionibus)]' is unlikely unless it represents the accumulation of two posts of the rank of *proximus* held at the same time. For the restorations in lines 3–4, see Boulvert, *EAI*, p. 108 n. 91.

Senior clerical grades

of posts of the rank of *proximus* must have been small, as would be the case if they were largely confined to the central bureaux in Rome.

It would appear, therefore, that from the period of M. Aurelius to the Severans, the rank of *proximus* in the central bureaux in Rome was created and regarded as giving access to the freedman procuratorships.

What were the functions of the *proximi*? Their title implies that they had the role of deputies. But deputies to whom? Not to the equestrian head of the central bureau to which they belonged. There is evidence that other freedmen occupied these senior posts in the central bureaux up till and after the reign of M. Aurelius. But if these *proximi* date from the period of M. Aurelius and later, are they in fact the Aurelian and Severan equivalents of these senior freedmen? This cannot be so. Although the grade of *proximus* gave regular access to the freedman procuratorships, including the highest provincial posts of freedman *procurator provinciae*, there is little indication that these *proximi* of the Palatine bureaux proceeded regularly to the senior freedman posts (such as that of Cosmus) in the same or even a different Palatine bureau.[1] The *proximi* regularly proceed to freedman procuratorships which are of lower standing than the headships of these central bureaux. Thus: M. Aurelius Aug. liber. Marcio (No. 5), *proximus rationum*, becomes *proc. marmorum*; M. Aurelius Aug. lib. [...] (No. 6), *prox. a memoria*, becomes *proc. fisci Asiatici*; (M. Aurelius?) Ianuarius (Aug.) lib. (No. 8), *proximus officii memoriae*, is promoted to (*proc.*) *voluptatum*; and Bassus Aug. lib. (No. 9), *prox. ab epistulis Graecis*, to *proc. tractus Carthaginiensis*.

They are rather the late second- and third-century equivalents of the *tabularii a rationibus*. They are the senior freedmen of the *clerical* staff in the most important of all departments, the central bureaux in Rome. It so happens that the senior freedman auxiliary heads of these bureaux appear to have been replaced by equestrian auxiliaries during this same period. Thus, by the early third century the rank of *proximus* is left as the highest grade, albeit clerical, to which Imperial freedmen could aspire in the Palatine central bureaux. Promotion beyond this grade led to procuratorships either in the provinces or in the subsidiary financial departments in Rome.

The *proximi* are found in the Palatine offices of the *sacra scrinia* under the *magistri memoriae, epistularum,* and *libellorum,* who are themselves, from the time of Constantine, under the general supervision of the *magister officiorum*. But the status of the *proximi* is not that of deputy to the respective *magistri*,

---

[1] There is perhaps one instance to the contrary: if the identification of Aurelius Alexander (No. 4) *proximus ab epistulis Latinis* with M. Aurelius Alexander Aug. lib. *ab epistulis Graecis* (VI 8606 = D 1668) is accepted, it would be natural to assume that he moved up from being *proximus* in the *ab epistulis Latinis* to the freedman headship in the *ab epistulis Graecis*.

The emperor's service

but that of headship of the clerical staff in each *scrinium*. Each *proximus* had his own deputy, a *melloproximus*, and his retirement was controlled by strict rules which progressively reduced the maximum period of service from three years to one year in both East and West by the early fifth century. On retirement these posts were saleable by this period. The clerks of the *sacra scrinia* were of high official and social status – many were from curial families – and they were accorded high honorary rank on retirement (*Cod. Th.* vi. 26.1 f.; *Cod. Iust.* xii. 19). But the rank of *proximus* (despite its designation) is the highest open to these clerks, as it was also for freedmen in these same bureaux by the time of Septimius Severus.[1]

[1] On the *proximi* of the late empire, see Jones, *LRE*, pp. 576 f. and, for full sourc eferences, Vol. III (Notes), 166 f. Also Ensslin, P–W XXIII, 1035 f.

CHAPTER 20

SENIOR ADMINISTRATIVE GRADES: A RATIONIBUS, AB EPISTULIS, ETC.

We must now consider perhaps the best-known of all Imperial freedman positions, the senior administrative grades in Rome, the headships of the great Palatine bureaux *a rationibus, ab epistulis, a libellis, a studiis, a cognitionibus, a codicillis, a memoria* and *a diplomatibus*. The roll-call of slave and freedman dignitaries with the first two of these titles in the inscriptions is a surprisingly long one. There are eighteen, possibly twenty, *a rationibus*, not counting M. Antonius Pallas and the father of Claudius Etruscus, all but three of whom are from the period before Hadrian. There are no fewer than seventeen *ab epistulis*, all probably before Hadrian, not counting a further four *ab epistulis Latinis* and two *ab epistulis Graecis*. It is obvious from the instances of slaves with these titles that *a rationibus, ab epistulis*, etc. cannot refer exclusively to the head of a department. The problem is how to distinguish between, e.g., an *a rationibus* and *the a rationibus*.

The lists given in Friedländer, as revised by Hirschfeld and later by Bang, are accompanied by no explicit formulation of the principles for distinguishing between the 'oberste Dirigenten' and the 'Unterbeamten'.[1] It is clear from their age and status that the slaves cannot be senior: Libanus Caesaris vern. ab epistulis (died aged 16), Victor Caes. vern. a cognit(ionibus) (d. 18), Abascantus Aug. a rat(ionibus) Attic(ianus), Apolaustus Caesaris a rationibus, Ianuarius Caesaris Aug. ab epistulis, Aphnius Caesaris Aug. ab epistulis.[2] It is unlikely that all these are pre-Claudian, as Hirschfeld suggests for the *ab epistulis*.[3]

As for the freedmen, it is difficult, if not impossible, to fit them all in between the retirements of Pallas and Narcissus at the beginning of Nero's reign, on the one hand, and the 'superposition' of equestrians in these posts under Domitian, Trajan and Hadrian, on the other. If Pallas began his work as the *a rationibus* early in the reign of Claudius, and if he was succeeded in 55 by Phaon[4] and in 70/1 by the father of Claudius Etruscus, who occupied the

---

[1] Friedländer, IV, 26 f.
[2] VI 8597, 8631, 8408, 33467, 8596; Gordon, *Album* I, No. 122.
[3] *Verwalt.* p. 319. Libanus and Victor are *Caesaris vernae*.
[4] On Phaon as the probable successor of Pallas, see below, p. 289; also Boulvert, *EAI*, p. 97 n. 37.

The emperor's service

post till the reign of Domitian,[1] and if, after the appointment of Vibius Lentulus[2] in the reign of Trajan, the head of the *a rationibus* was thenceforth an equestrian,[3] where can one possibly fit in Claudius Abascantus (died aged 45; VI 8411 = D 1473), Claudius Actiacus (VI 8412), Claudius Eros, Claudius Felix (the last two perhaps brothers; VI 8413 = D 7859), the two unnamed Claudii of XI 4360, Atticus (who was *a rationibus* by AD 85),[4] Crescens[5] and Diadumenus[6] (both possibly freedmen of Nero), and Flavius Epaphroditus Ephebianus,[7] not to mention the more uncertain cases?[8] Note that there is only one certain *Flavius* and no *Ulpius*.

Similarly with the *ab epistulis*. Narcissus died in 54. From Statius, *Silvae* v. 1, we know of Abascantus under Domitian (cf. VI 8598–9). There is also the equestrian friend of Pliny, Cn. Octavius Titinius Capito,[9] who was *ab epistulis* from the reign of Domitian to early in the reign of Trajan. We still have to account for the following freedman *ab epistulis* before Hadrian: Claudius Eudaemon (VI 8600), Claudius [Phil]ologus (VI 8601), Claudius Primio (VI 8603 = D 1670), Flavius Epictetus (XIV 2840 = D 1571), Flavius Euschemon (VI 8604 = D 1519), (Flavius) Fortunatus and his brother Epaphroditus (VI 1887 = D 1944), Flavius Protogenes (XI 3886), and Glyptus, Ionius, Pistus, and perhaps Clem[ens], of uncertain date.[10] Once again there are no *Ulpii*, although Glyptus, whose wife is Ulpia Athenais, is probably from the reign of Trajan.[11] But this time there is a multiplicity of *Flavii*, who have to be fitted into the early Flavian period when a rapid turnover was least likely.

[1] For a full discussion of the career of Claudius Etruscus' father, see chapter 22 below, pp. 284f.
[2] Pflaum, *CP* No. 66.
[3] R. H. Lacey, *Equestrian Officials of Trajan and Hadrian* (Princeton, 1917), p. 40; Pflaum, *CP*, p. 157; Boulvert, *EAI*, p. 271. No freedman is known to have held the post under Trajan; and the passage in SHA *Hadr.* 22.8 does not mention the *a rationibus* in connection with Hadrian.
[4] X 6640 = D 3338; cf. VI 8410; *PIR*², A 1336.
[5] *PIR*², C 1576; VI 8414 is of Flavian date. Crescens' sister is Flavia Aug. l. Daphne. Tacitus, *Hist.* i. 76, records the activities of a 'Crescens Neronis libertus', a freedman of procuratorial standing, at Carthage in 69.
[6] VI 8415 = D 1474. Cf. X 3347; VI 33903. There were several senior freedmen called Diadumenus in this period: the *a rationibus*, the *a libellis* (XV 7444), the *procurator* at Pausilypum (*EE* VIII 335–6, 337 = D 5798), and another procurator (VI 9017). Cf. *PIR*², D 64–6. It is not clear that any two of these are the same person.
[7] VI 33468, a 'vicarianus'. Cf. Chantraine, p. 312, No. 133.   [8] VI 8416, 33724, 37742.
[9] Pliny, *Epist* i. 17; v. 8; viii. 12. Pflaum, *CP* No. 60. Cf. Sex. Caesius Propertianus, already under Vitellius (*CP* No. 37).
[10] XIV 3909 = D 3892, XV 7837a; VI 8605, 37747. This list does not include four freedman *ab epistulis Latinis* (VI 8610, 8611; XI 1434 = D 1667; VI 8609), and two freedman *ab epistulis Graecis* (VI 8607, 8606 = D 1668).
[11] If, as is not unlikely, the 'Glyptus Aug. lib. proc.' of VI 37763b = D 9025 is the same person, Glyptus may well have been of senior standing, presumably an early freedman auxiliary head *ab epistulis*. Glyptus' predecessor (or, less likely, successor) as *procurator praetori Fidenatium*, etc. in VI 37763a = D 9024 was a freedman of Trajan, M. Ulpius Aug. [li]b. Diadumenus.

Senior administrative grades

The inscriptions are less forthcoming about the freedman heads of other Palatine bureaux in this period. Only two out of seven *a libellis* are found there: Diadumenus Aug. l., on a lead pipe of Claudian date (XV 7444), and Hermeros Aug. lib. (VI 8614 = D 1674). Diadumenus belongs to the period *c.* 50–4, following Polybius, who died 47/8, and Callistus, *c.* 48–50, and preceding Doryphorus *c.* 54 till his death in 62,[1] and Epaphroditus 62–8(?).[2] Hermeros is to be fitted in either under the Flavians, before Entellus,[3] one of the participants in Domitian's assassination in 96, or under Trajan before T. Haterius Nepos, Hadrian's equestrian *a libellis*.[4] There are also two freedman *a cognitionibus* from the late first or early second centuries: T. Flavius Aug. lib. Abascantus (VI 8628 = D 1679)[5] and Astectus Aug. lib (VI 8629 – dedicated to his freedwoman, Flavia Nysa).[6]

It is characteristic of the freedman posts that they were normally held for longer periods than equestrian posts. Ten years or so in a single post was common. In fact, the only two freedmen who were certainly in charge of the *a rationibus*, Pallas and the father of Claudius Etruscus, both held office for longer than ten years each, as did Narcissus as *ab epistulis*.

Moreover, there are aspects of the careers and family relationships of some of the above freedmen that make it unlikely that they held high office. This is the case when two brothers or two persons are mentioned in the same inscription both holding the same office, apparently concurrently: Ti. Ti. Claudi Eros et Felix (VI 8413 = D 7859); the two unknown *a rationibus* under Nero (XI 4360); the brothers Epaphroditus and Fortunatus, *ab epistulis* in the Flavian period (VI 1887 = D 1944); also the fact that M. Ulpius Aug. l. Eros, *ab epistulis Graecis*, has two brothers Epaphroditus and Stachys, who are both still *Caesaris n. servi* (VI 8607), must cast doubt on the senior status of Eros himself. Among the *ab epistulis*, Flavius Epictetus had previously held the position of *lictor curiatius* as well as that of *a copiis militaribus* (XIV 2840 = D 1571); Flavius Euschemon may have been senior *ab epistulis* if he advanced from the procuratorship *ad capitularia Iudaeorum* to be *ab epistulis*, but not if the other way round, as is perhaps implied by the words 'qui fuit ab epistulis' (VI 8604 = D 1519); Fortunatus, *ab epistulis*, had been *accensus*

---

[1] Claudius Doryphorus: *PIR*[2], D 194; Dio, lxi. 5.4; Tacitus, *Ann.* xiv. 65; Suetonius, *Nero* 29. On the order of Polybius and Callistus, see Boulvert, *EAI*, p. 94 n. 16.

[2] Epaphroditus: *PIR*[2], E 69; Suetonius, *Nero* 49. On the length of his tenure of the post, F. Millar (*JRS* 55 (1965), 141) thinks that it is likely that he did not continue under the Flavians. See also Boulvert, *EAI*, p. 94 n. 17, who gives further opinions.

[3] *PIR*[2], E 66.

[4] XI 5213 = D 1338; *PIR*[2], H 29; Pflaum, *CP* No. 95.

[5] Abascantus' wife is Flavia Hesperis; he is thus different from Abascantus, *ab epistulis* under Domitian, whose wife was Priscilla (Statius, *Silv.* v. 1).

[6] A third is probably T. Flavius Epagathus (VI 8630), who is without status indication. His wife is Flavia Cale.

The emperor's service

to Vespasian, *lictor curiatius*, and *viat(or) honor(atus) dec(uriae) co(n)s(ularis) et pr(aetoriae)* (VI 1887 = D 1944).[1]

For an explanation of the nomenclature of the *a rationibus, ab epistulis*, etc. we must refer back to the *adiutores*. In the first place, with the *adiutores a rationibus, adiutores ab epistulis*, etc., as has been seen,[2] the terms 'a rationibus', 'ab epistulis', etc. clearly refer to the department in question and do not refer to its head. This conforms to the normal administrative terminology and can be seen in a host of cases in the domestic services, e.g. *ab argento, a veste*, etc., where a special title such as 'praepositus' is commonly used from the second century to indicate senior status. The use of the name of the function or department, e.g. *a rationibus*, to indicate the chief such functionary or head of department no doubt goes back to the domestic terminology of small *familiae* where there was only one slave or freedman for each function. With the growth of the Imperial administration, grades within a department were expressed by such terms as 'procurator', 'tabularius', 'adiutor', and so on, but the distinction between the various grades was only made when the need arose, and was a function of developing organisation and complexity. Thus, a *tabularius* was required to supervise the accounts and the clerical side generally, an *a commentariis* to keep the records, and a *dispensator* to be responsible for the cash in his particular *fiscus* – all specific and obvious duties, and attested from the Claudian period. *Adiutores*, however, apart from some, e.g. *adiutores procuratoris*, who are attached to particular senior officials, are general assistants, the juniors in a department. But *adiutores* – and this is the second point – are not certainly found before the Flavian period for the *a rationibus*, nor before the Trajanic period for the *a libellis* and the *a codicillis*, the Hadrianic period for the *ab epistulis*, and that of Antoninus Pius for the *a cognitionibus*.[3]

Everyone employed in an undifferentiated capacity without special ranking in a given department, whether freedman or slave, was simply labelled with the name of the department, e.g. *a rationibus, ab epistulis*. But this applied to the rapidly growing central bureau of finance only in the Claudian and perhaps early Flavian period. Thereafter the title was reserved for seniors. In the central secretariat, on the other hand, the practice lasted at least during the whole of the first century. The reason for the late appearance of *adiutores* in the large department of the *ab epistulis* is the subdivision or specialisation within the department into Latin and Greek sections, which is attested from

---

[1] On the status of *lictores, accensi* and the other *apparitores* see Mommsen, *Staatsr.* I, 332 f. and esp. 355 f.; Jones, *JRS* 39 (1949), 38 f. = *Studies*, pp. 154 f.   [2] See above, p. 238.
[3] *Adiutores* (in chronological order): *a rationibus*: VI 8422, 8417; *AE* 1950, 171; VI 8420, 37743, 8418; slaves: VI 8423, 8419, 8421, 8424, 5305, 9033; *ab epistulis*: VI 8612, 8613; *a libellis*: VI 33741, 8615; *a cognitionibus*: VI 8634; VIII 12613; VI 8635 (slave, died aged 18); *a codicillis*: VI 8442.

Senior administrative grades

the end of the first century by Flavius Alexander Aug. lib. *ab epistulis Latinis* (VI 8610), and T. Flavius Aug. l. Thallus, likewise *ab epistulis Latinis* (VI 8611). This delayed the need for the further rank of *adiutor*, which, when it appears in the second century with P. Ael(ius) Aug. lib. Agathemerus, who is described as 'iuvenis' (VI 8612), is found only within the subsections – also an indication of its later rather than early appearance. In general in these central departments, *adiutor* can be taken to imply a second-century date or later rather than a first-century one.

The head of department, one supposes, would naturally be distinguished from those beneath him. In the *senatusconsultum* referring to his honours Pallas is called 'custos principalium opum'.[1] The title 'procurator' would normally suffice. But this is not found for the freedman *a rationibus*, etc., at least not before Hadrian,[2] and sometimes not for the equestrians either. The earliest literary evidence for the use of the titles 'a rationibus', 'ab epistulis' and 'a libellis' in the sense of head of department is Tacitus, *Ann.* xv. 35: 'qui immo libertos habere quos ab epistulis et libellis et rationibus appellet, nomina summae curae et meditamenta', and xvi. 8: 'tamquam disponeret iam imperii curas, praeficeretque rationibus et libellis et epistulis libertos', referring to charges made against Torquatus Silanus and his nephew of the same name in 64–5; cf. Suetonius, *Claud.* 28. That this is good contemporary evidence for the titles of Narcissus and the other heads of departments under Claudius and Nero is confirmed by the inscriptional evidence – if the 'Narcissus Aug. l. ab epistulis' on three lead pipes (XV 7500 = D 1666), and the 'Abascantus Aug. lib. ab epistulis' in two epitaphs of his freedmen (VI 8598–9), refer to the well-known persons we think they do.

We must suppose, therefore, that the titles 'a rationibus', etc., which were no doubt in frequent use in private households of the wealthier sort, were originally extended to all officials within the one department in the Imperial household, from the head down to the lowest slave assistant. It was only later, as the official nomenclature developed in response to the administrative expansion, and especially after the introduction of the term 'adiutor' for the lower clerical grades, that the titles 'a rationibus', 'ab epistulis', 'a libellis', etc. were exclusively and specifically attached to the head of department and became what Tacitus describes as 'nomina summae curae'. We may assume that most, if not all, the Imperial freedmen who did achieve real eminence in the *officia Palatina* before Trajan and Hadrian also achieved a mention in

---

[1] Pliny, *Epist.* viii. 6. Hirschfeld (*Verwalt.* p. 30 n. 4) says the title 'a rationibus' was avoided here as being too plain; the same may be said, no doubt, for Statius, *Silv.* iii. 3.87, 'sanctarum digestus opum'.

[2] T. Aurelius Aug. lib. Aphrodisius, *proc. Aug. a rationibus* (XIV 2104 = D 1475). See further below, p. 268.

The emperor's service

the sensitive literary sources of the period. A single epitaph with the simple name of a department, unless confirmed by other evidence, in the first century does not constitute proof that the bearer rose to the responsibilities of a Narcissus or the father of Claudius Etruscus.

What of the period after Trajan and Hadrian? There is evidence that freedmen continued to occupy senior posts in the Palatine bureaux right up to the reign of Septimius Severus. This is especially true of the largest bureau, the *a rationibus*, with three instances from the reigns of Antoninus Pius and M. Aurelius:

(1) T. Aurelius Aug. lib. Aphrodisius (XIV 2104 = D 1475), proc. Aug. a rationibus.
(2) T. Aelius Aug. lib. Proculus (XIV 5309.23, 28), a rat(ionibus).
(3) Cosmus Aug. lib. (VI 455 – dated to Sept. 168; IX 2438; XV 7443 = D 1476), a rationibus.

Instances also occur in this period for the *ab epistulis Graecis* (VI 8606 = D 1668: M. Aur(elius) Alexander Aug. lib.), the *a codicillis* (VI 8440 = D 1529: T. Aurelius Egatheus Imp. Antonini Aug. lib.; cf. *IGR* I 113; Fronto, *Epist. ad M. Caes.* ii. 16), and perhaps the *a cognitionibus* (V 179: T. Aelius [...]r[...]us Aug. lib. a cog[....]).[1]

In this period these freedmen can scarcely be the official *heads* of their departments, displacing the equestrians who were by now long established in these Palatine secretariates. The best known case is that of Cosmus Aug. lib. (No. 3); if he were *the* secretary *a rationibus* in 168, he would have had a status (and salary) higher than that of any equestrian procurator. These freedmen are in fact the auxiliary heads of their bureaux according to the dual equestrian–freedman procuratorial system. Confirmation of their status is to be found in an inscription (VI 1585 b = D 5920) which records the correspondence of the *rationales* with various officials in Rome in August 193 over the construction of a small building for the procurator of M. Aurelius' column. The *rationales* are named as 'Aelius Achilles, Cl(audius) Perpetuus, Flavianus, Eutychus'. Accepting Pflaum's convincing interpretation,[2] the first two, with *nomen*, are the equestrian *procurator a rationibus* and *procurator summarum rationum*, and the second pair, with *cognomen* only, Flavianus and Eutychus, are respectively the freedman auxiliary procurators of the two equestrian procurators. This form of nomenclature – equestrians with *nomen* and *cognomen*, freedmen with *cognomen* only – is common in documents

---

[1] The bureau *a memoria* and its adjunct *a diplomatibus* appear from the period of Hadrian with a freedman head: VI 8618 = D 1672: Aelius Cladeus; VI 8622 = D 1677: T. Aelius Aug. lib. Saturninus; X 1727 = D 1678: Aurelius Symphorus Aug. lib. Equestrian heads did not take over till the Severan period. Cf. Boulvert, *EAI*, pp. 284 f.

[2] Pflaum, *CP*, pp. 516 f., 758–9; P–W XXIII, 1271; Chantraine, p. 271; and esp. Boulvert, *EAI*, pp. 303 f. nn. 263–8 (with further remarks of Pflaum), 396 f.

Senior administrative grades

jointly issued by equestrian–freedman pairs of procurators.[1] This example of bureaucracy in action reveals that the bureau called *summae rationes*, established c. 170 with the appointment of L. Aurelius Nicomedes (*CP* No. 163) by M. Aurelius, functioned in close coordination with the *a rationibus* bureau, although staffed with head, auxiliary head and subordinate personnel of its own.[2] It also shows that when the appointment of a second equestrian procurator is accompanied by the formal division of a bureau, as was also the case earlier with the *ab epistulis*, a freedman auxiliary head is also appointed for each division. Further, the dual equestrian–freedman procuratorial system was still in operation in the great central bureaux at the beginning of the Severan period.

How long did this system continue there? The implications of appointing *equestrian* auxiliary procurators instead of proceeding with further subdivision of the bureaux in which each had their separate establishment should be considered. Under M. Aurelius considerable impetus was given to the appointment of equestrian auxiliaries to assist and control superior officials, particularly those of senatorial status (e.g. the *procurator regionum sacrae urbis* alongside the *praefectus urbi*, the *subcurator operum publicorum*, the *procuratores ad alimenta*), but also equestrian *praefecti* (e.g. the *subpraefectus annonae*, the earlier *subpraefectus vigilum*, and the later auxiliary of the *procurator ludi magni*).[3] Under the early Severans the system of equestrian auxiliaries *within* departments was extended to the Palatine bureaux themselves. About 193 an auxiliary *procurator a studiis* of sexagenarian and later centenarian rank is found, P. Messius Saturninus (*AE* 1932, 34; *CP* No. 231), and another about 208, M. Herennius Victor (VIII 18909 = D 9017; *CP* No. 272). Septimius Severus also created the auxiliary equestrian post of *procurator sacrarum cognitionum* with centenarian rank – Aurelius Augg. lib. Alexander, v(ir) e(gregius), *praep(ositus) sacr(arum) cogn(itionum)* (*AE* 1935, 20); M. Aurel(ius) Thallus *signo* Brecetius, v. e., *proc. sacrar. cognit.*[4] Other

---

[1] As in the African patrimonial documents from the second century; e.g. Verridius Bassus et Ianuarius (VIII 25943 iv 5 = *FIRA²*, I p. 492); Tussanius Aristo et Chrysanthus (VIII 14464 iv 11 = *FIRA²*, I p. 498); cf. Licinius [Ma]ximus et Felicior Aug. lib. procc. (VIII 25902 = *FIRA²*, I p. 485). Cf. Boulvert, *EAI*, pp. 394 f.

[2] VI 37743: [Aug.] lib. adiut(or) summ(arum) rat(ionum) tab(ulariorum?) *or* tab(ularius?); *AE* 1933, 273: a Greek inscription from Pergamum (of the Severan period?), perhaps recording a freedman (? status indication missing) *procurator summarum rationum;* cf. Boulvert, *EAI*, p. 304 n. 269.   [3] Pflaum, *Proc. Equest.* pp. 73 f., 79 f.

[4] The inscription of Thallus is very probably late third-century (VI 37099 ad loc.; Pflaum, *CP*, p. 1024; against Hirschfeld, *Verwalt.* p. 330 n. 2, who thought it could not be later than Caracalla). On the other hand, Pflaum (*CP*, p. 1024) dates that of Alexander to between 161 and 169. This is possible. But for the *Aurelii Augg. lib.* the status indication 'Augg. lib.' can occur well into the third century; 161 is only a *terminus post quem*. Moreover, both the title 'v(ir) e(gregius)' indicating *equestrian* procuratorial status (which is quite exceptional in the nomenclature of Imperial freed-

The emperor's service

signs of a dual equestrian system are found in the *ratio privata* and in the patrimonial administration of this period.[1] Evidence of auxiliary equestrian procuratorships is lacking for the bureaux *a libellis* and *ab epistulis*.[2] But it is not unreasonable to expect to find among the numerous new equestrian posts created by Septimius Severus and his successors examples of auxiliary *ab epistulis Latinis* and *ab epistulis Graecis*.

For the freedmen who had hitherto been the auxiliary heads of these bureaux, and in other departments of the administration in Rome or the provinces where this occurred, this fact means, I believe, their elimination from these senior posts. A system of freedman auxiliary heads and equestrian auxiliary procurators in the same department would be incompatible unless the freedman was demoted to a rank below that of the equestrian auxiliary. Under the Severans freedmen do not appear to have been appointed to such positions unless they had been raised to equestrian status first – as with Aurelius Alexander (*AE* 1935, 20). The elimination of these senior freedmen would be an important and irreversible breach in the dual equestrian–freedman procuratorial system. It would also be a significant illustration of the fact that the progressive militarisation of the administration was a matter of Imperial policy from the time of Septimius.

men), and the rank-title of 'praepositus' for Imperial freedmen outside the Palace domestic service, as well as the departmental designation 'sacrarum cognitionum', all alike seem to indicate a Severan or third-century date. We can only suppose that Aurelius Alexander (who is not to be identified with the *ab epistulis Graecis* of the same name, but of different status indication: 'Aug. lib.') was a former freedman who was raised to equestrian status by Caracalla, Elagabalus or Severus Alexander and appointed to the auxiliary equestrian procuratorship in the *a cognitionibus*. On his dedicatory inscription, however, the decurions of Minternum for some reason mentioned both his former Imperial freedman status *and* his subsequent elevation to equestrian rank.

[1] Pflaum, *Proc. Equest.* pp. 85 f.
[2] Ib. p. 93.

CHAPTER 21

FREEDMAN PROCURATORS

The senior administrative career of the Imperial freedmen has a second and perhaps more important aspect, that of the freedman procurators. They are much more numerous, less notorious, but longer lasting than their Palatine counterparts. Their numbers and responsibilities increase rather than decrease with the expansion of the bureaucracy in the second century, although they fill the same roles as the Palatine heads, both as sole heads of departments and also as auxiliary heads in conjunction with a superior colleague of equestrian rank. The freedman procurators are found not only in the administration of the emperor's estates, villas and other property in Italy and elsewhere throughout the empire, but also in the smaller departments in Rome as well as in all the main administrative centres in the provinces. The number of senior posts in the Palatine bureaux was relatively few and their holders were somewhat exceptional. The procuratorial posts on the other hand, whether carrying the responsibilities of sole or auxiliary head of a department, or whether exercised in a minor Imperial villa or a major province, make up the normal senior freedman career. The range of these freedman posts and the extent to which they were formally organised into a system of grades on the model of the equestrian procuratorships must now be considered.

'Procurator' in the late Republic was a term of private law meaning a personal agent or manager of another's affairs and under the Empire it continued to be used in this sense.[1] For private citizens such procurators were usually their freedmen.[2] The emperor's procurators were both equestrians and freedmen.[3] As they managed his household, his patrimonial properties both in Italy and the provinces, and were increasingly employed in the financial departments of the administration, they rapidly took on a public, official character. When equestrians actually became governors of some provinces this development was inevitable. For equestrians this is indicated by the title 'procurator Augusti' which becomes normal from the

---

[1] *Dig.* iii. 3.1 pr.; Kaser, I, 227 f., esp. 230–1; Berger, *Encyc. Dict.* s.v. 'procurator' p. 654 (with bibliography); Boulvert, *EAI*, pp. 388 f.
[2] E.g. VI 7370 = D 7406a, 9830 = D 7388, 9834 = D 7387, etc.
[3] On the Imperial procurators the works of Hirschfeld and Pflaum are especially important. To these should now be added that of Boulvert on the freedmen, esp. *EAI*, pp. 387 f.

The emperor's service

reign of Claudius, with or without the inclusion of the personal nomenclature of the emperor in the title, e.g. *procurator Ti. Claudi Caesaris Augusti Germanici* (V 1838 = D 1349; *AE* 1914, 27; etc.).[1]

For Imperial freedmen the use of the title 'procurator' differs from that for equestrians in two respects. Firstly, the title 'proc. Augusti' is used only exceptionally and in only one instance by a freedman official of the highest rank – T. Aurelius Aug. lib. Aphrodisius proc. Aug. a rationibus (XIV 2104 = D 1475, under Antoninus).[2] Secondly, the personal nomenclature of the emperor is not found in the title of freedman procurators of reigning emperors, apart from a single, late instance under Severus Alexander – Theoprepes Aug. lib., *proc. domini n. M. Aur. Severi Alexandri Pii Fel. Aug.* (III 536 = D 1575). On the other hand, the use of the personal or other *cognomen* of their patron is regular among freedmen of other members of the Imperial family as the commonest means of distinguishing them from freedmen of the emperor. This applies both to their status indication and with the title 'procurator', e.g. Cn. Domitius Chrysanthus *proc. Domitiae Domitiani* (X 1738).[3] For the private procurators, both freedman and freeborn, of members of the Imperial family except the emperor this is the normal nomenclature.[4] But for the freedman procurators of the emperor the simple title 'proc(urator)' was regular and sufficient for whatever official position they occupied.

The existence of a procuratorial freedman *cursus* cannot be doubted. Apart from the extant career inscriptions of freedman procurators, the most explicit *literary* evidence is from the second century. Fronto, in a letter of

[1] See Jones, 'Procurators and Prefects in the Early Principate' in *Studies*, pp. 117 f., against Pflaum, *Proc. Equest.* pp. 10 f., esp. 14–15, who argues for an earlier date for the official use of the term 'procurator'; cf. Hirschfeld, *Verwalt.* pp. 411 f. esp. 411 n. 4; Mommsen, *Staatsr.* III, 557 f.; Sherwin-White, 'Procurator Augusti', *PBSR* 15 (1939), 11 f.

[2] The others are: T. Fl(avius) Aug. lib. Martialis, proc. Aug. ad Castor(em) (VI 8689 = X 8058. 168); T. Flavius Aug. lib. Symphorus, proc. Aug. IIII P. A. (*AE* 1949, 30); Auximus Aug. lib. proc. Aug. (VIII 21010); Ael(ius) Priscianus lib. et proc. Augg. (VI 9008). Ti. Claudius Aug. lib. Eutychus proc. Augustor(um) (VI 9015 = 29847a = D 8120), is probably a procurator of the joint property of Nero and Agrippina; cf. Hirschfeld, *Verwalt.* p. 28 n. 1; Boulvert, *EAI*, p. 38 n. 154; but see Chantraine, pp. 238 f., and esp. 243 f. T. Aelius Eutychus, proc. Aug. n. villae Alsiensi(s) (XI 3720 = D 1580) would be the only instance of 'proc. Aug. n.' in this group; he is also without status indication and is just possibly not an Imperial freedman at all. Ti. Claudius Marcellinus (VI 8501a = D 1487) is almost certainly not a freedman, but an equestrian. See *Historia* 14 (1965), 511 n. 21; Pflaum, *CP*, p. 1025; Boulvert, *EAI*, p. 105 n. 70.

[3] See Hirschfeld, *Verwalt.* pp. 27 f. For the status indication of non-reigning members of the Imperial family, see Part I above, p. 47.

[4] In VI 8500 = XI 1753 = D 1490, Domitius Lemnus *procur. Germanici Caesaris* cannot be an official procurator of the reigning Domitian or, indeed, of Domitian at all as he did not take the title 'Germanicus' until 83. For a full discussion of the career of Domitius Lemnus, which is to be placed in the reigns of Claudius and Nero, see *Historia* 14 (1965), 509 f., and now Chantraine, p. 65 n. 15.

Freedman procurators

recommendation on behalf of the Imperial freedman Aridelus who is seeking a procuratorial post, says 'petit nunc procurationem ex forma suo loco ac iusto tempore' (Fronto, *ad M. Caes.* v. 37; p. 87 Nab.).[1] The phrase 'ex forma suo loco ac iusto tempore' is significant; it means: 'in accordance with the regulation (governing the appointment of Imperial procurators), having reached the appropriate grade and being of sufficient seniority within that grade for such promotion' or perhaps just 'according to his grade and seniority and at the appropriate time'.[2] This passage explicitly attests the existence of a well-established hierarchy among the Imperial freedmen in the administration, not merely within the ranks of those already of procuratorial grade but, as there is no indication that Aridelus is or should be already a *procurator*,[3] throughout all the other slave and freedman grades as well, from junior clerical upwards to senior procuratorial. Letters of recommendation were, of course, common for those freedmen seeking to advance from one procuratorship to another, as Pliny's testimonial to Trajan on behalf of Maximus 'libertus et procurator tuus' shows (Pliny, *Epist.* x. 85; cf. ib. 86–7, and the standard formulae used therein).[4]

While the phrase 'ex forma' should not be pressed for freedman careers as hard as it is by Pflaum for equestrians, and strict adherence to 'rule' is not always to be looked for, nevertheless the seniority of the procurators among the Imperial freedmen in general is also clear. The age data for the freedman procurators has been quoted above.[5] These figures give an average age at death of nearly 75, which is senior by any standard. More significant perhaps is that the youngest was 55 years old when he died.[6] It is reasonable to conclude from this and from the age data on the other clerical and managerial grades that these procurators are regularly of senior status and that the 'iustum tempus' for promotion to these posts is probably not before the age of about 40–45. There is the further implication that the first appointment to one of these positions would not normally be won until at least ten or fifteen years after manumission. Further still, as even in the Antonine period the average length of reign was only about twenty years, it is reasonable for us

---

[1] Pflaum, *Proc. Equest.* pp. 198 f., 210; Boulvert, II, 579.

[2] Professor Jones pointed out to me that in the fourth and fifth centuries the term 'forma' is used to indicate the grades (*prima, secunda, tertia*) into which the *largitionales* and the *castrensiani* were divided. Promotion was normally from grade to grade (*Cod. Theod.* vi. 30.7; 32.2; cf. Jones, *LRE*, pp. 571, 584). As these posts correspond with those formerly held in the administrative and domestic Palace services by freedmen and slaves, he suggested that 'ex forma' in this passage of Fronto may mean 'according to his grade'.

[3] Pflaum and Boulvert (locc. citt.) follow the reading 'procurabit vobis industrie', not '*procuravit*'.

[4] On letters of recommendation: Pflaum, *Proc. Equest.* pp. 198 f.; Sherwin-White, *Letters of Pliny*, pp. 681 f.   [5] Pp. 225 f.

[6] III 1312 = D 1593: M. Ulpius Aug. lib. Hermias, proc. aurariarum (Ampelum, Dacia).

The emperor's service

to assume as a rule for dating purposes that, unless there is evidence to the contrary, the inscriptions and also appointments of freedman procurators relate to the reign *subsequent* to that in which they were manumitted. There are many examples of freedmen serving under later emperors than their manumittor. For the Imperial procurators, these are: C. Iulius Aug. l. Samius (XIV 3644 = D 1942), manumitted at the latest by Gaius, and *accensus* to both the emperors Claudius and Nero before he became procurator; Ti. Claudius Aug. lib. Bucolas (XI 3612 = D 1567, XV 7279–80 = D 8679), manumitted at the latest by Nero, *proc. aquarum* under Domitian and subsequently *proc. castrensis*, presumably at the age of 60 or older; T. Flavius Aug. lib. Nereus (VI 9019), who died aged 98, was certainly a procurator well into the second century; M. Ulpius Chresimus Aug. lib. (*IGR* I 1255–6; *SEG* IV 531) was *proc. metallorum* in Egypt at Mons Claudianus in 118. The only instance of a freedman procurator to be dated to the reign in which he obtained manumission is Trophimus Aug. l., *proc. prov(inciae) Cretae* (XIV 51), whose freedman, P. Aelius Syneros, participated in dedicating an altar on 1 October 124. The chronological significance of these age figures and dated inscriptions should be borne in mind in any consideration of the careers of the freedman procurators as a whole.

Just as the equestrian procurators occupy a wide range of posts differing greatly in importance and in salary, so too the freedman procurators vary considerably in the range of their functions and, presumably, salary. These functions can be gauged both from specific indications in their titles, e.g. 'proc. villarum Tusculanarum', 'proc. aquarum', 'proc. provinciae Pannoniae Superioris', etc., and from the particular location of the inscription with the simple title 'procurator'. Thus, on *fistulae* found in and near Rome, 'proc. (aquarum)' is to be understood, 'proc. (metallorum)' on inscriptions from the mining centre Ajustrel in Portugal, 'proc. (marmorum)' on quarry marks, and so on.

Broadly speaking, the careers of freedman procurators fall into two main categories, domestic and administrative, corresponding to the basic division of the Familia Caesaris itself into the domestic and administrative services.[1] The domestic career, involving duties in the Palace itself, including the top post of *procurator castrensis*, and those of managers on individual villas and estates belonging to the emperor, corresponds to that of procurators of wealthy private citizens. The senior posts in the administrative service were basically financial, and as the emperor's *patrimonium* more and more acquired a public character, the patrimonial procurators who were engaged in major revenue-producing domains came to be assimilated to the administrative

---

[1] Introduction, pp. 5 f.

Freedman procurators

service proper. In fact we might go so far as to see in the rapidly expanding patrimonial administration of the first century many of the essential features of the second-century administrative service, including, I believe, the origin of the dual equestrian–freedman procuratorial system itself. However that may be, as compared with the administrative posts the proportion of domestic and unassigned procurators in fact declines steadily throughout the period from the early first to the early third century, from 100% domestic among the 'Iulii Aug. lib.' to less than one-third among those from the late second and early third century.[1]

While it is clear that the procurators in general had the highest status rankings among the *Augusti liberti*, considerable variations in status nevertheless existed between the procurators themselves. For example, the *procurator* of a single estate – e.g. T. Flavius Aug. l. Epaphra, *proc. villarum Tusculanarum* (XIV 2608 = D 1579); M. Ulpius Aug. lib. Diadumenus, *proc. praetori Fidenatium* etc. (VI 37763 = D 9024–5) – necessarily holds a lesser post than the *procurator* of an entire patrimonial district – e.g. Asiaticus Aug. lib., *proc. regionis Assuritanae* (VIII 12879 = D 1486); Bassus Aug. lib., *proc. tractus Carthaginiensis* (VI 8608 = D 1485); cf. Felicior Aug. lib., *proc. (tractus Carthaginiensis)* (VIII 25902). The *procurator* of the provincial office of a single financial department – e.g. Ti. Claudius Aug. lib. Saturninius, *proc. XX here(d). provinciae Achaiae* (VI 8443 = D 1546); Graphicus Aug. lib. Domitianianus, *proc. hered. tractus Campaniae* (*AE* 1922, 122) – is undoubtedly lower in rank than one with the title 'proc. provinciae' – e.g. M. Ulp. Augg. lib. Probus, *proc. provinc. Pannoniae Super(ioris)* (XIV 176 = D 1484); P. Aelius Aug. lib. Trophimus, *proc. prov. Cretae* (XIV 51).

It would be impracticable to attempt to construct any precise framework of regular grades of promotion within the procuratorial offices held by freedmen, such as Pflaum has succeeded in elaborating for the equestrian careers. The number of examples is too small and most of these are just names and titles of single procuratorships. The instances of a sequence of two or more posts, even including sub-procuratorial posts, are even fewer – barely fifty in all – and are spread over too long a period for the development of any freedman procuratorial *cursus* to be traced. In several cases only one instance exists of a particular procuratorship in a career sequence. This is scarcely sufficient to establish a firm grading for some posts and also invites circular argument when the example and the grade of the post must justify each other. Moreover, by the very nature of these freedman appointments and the status of the personnel involved, the emperor must have felt much less

---

[1] For the detailed breakdown into domestic (and unassigned) and administrative procurators, see *Historia* 14 (1965), 461.

The emperor's service

obliged to follow any rules of promotion. If the freedmen did not reach procuratorial rank until they were into their forties, they had little opportunity to hold more than one or two procuratorships for any length of time before the end of their career. And we must assume that length of tenure was as much a characteristic of the procuratorships as of all other grades in the slave and freedman *cursus*. Thus a freedman procuratorial *cursus* comparable with the equestrian *cursus*, which occupied a whole life's career and in which individual posts were held for a shorter period of time, could scarcely have come into existence.[1] However, some broad distinctions can be drawn from a consideration of the freedman careers which we do possess.

Access to the procuratorial grades of the administrative type has already been discussed. The posts of access were, in the period before M. Aurelius, those of the *tabularii*, especially that of *tabularius a rationibus* in Rome. In the period beginning with M. Aurelius and L. Verus the main posts of access were those of the *proximi* who also, as has been shown above, belonged to the large central bureaux in Rome. However, whatever the nature of the 'forma' was which Fronto alludes to in his testimonial on behalf of Aridelus (and there is danger in pressing its meaning too hard, for freedmen at least), the emperor permitted himself considerable discretion in the making or confirming of procuratorial appointments, as the concluding section of Fronto's letter (*ad M. Caes.* v. 37) suggests: 'Faveto ei, Domine, quod poteris. Si formam non cognosces hominis, ubi ad nomen Aridelı ventum fuerit, memento a me tibi Aridelum commendatum.' The role of Imperial impulse and patronage should not be underestimated, as with the procedure for the appointment of *dispensatores* in the time of Otho and Vespasian mentioned in Suetonius.[2]

Procuratorial careers approached from these posts, which were very largely financial in nature, usually continued with the holding of exclusively financial posts. These were sometimes held exclusively in Rome, as with T. Flavius Aug. lib. Delphicus (*AE* 1888, 130 = D 1518) who was *tabularius a rationibus* and advanced to the posts of *proc. rationum thesaurorum, proc. hereditatium, proc. fisci Alexandrini* (in inverse order), and Martialis Aug. lib.

---

[1] The first and perhaps definitive attempt to establish a freedman procuratorial *cursus* has been made by Boulvert (II, 577–638). Modelled on Pflaum's schema for the equestrian procurators, Boulvert establishes criteria for no fewer than six freedman procuratorial grades, including both chief and auxiliary procurators. He estimates the salaries for the two highest grades at HS 200,000, for the next two highest grades at HS 100,000 and for the remaining two at HS 60,000 and HS 40,000 respectively. These figures seem too high when compared with the equestrian salaries. The danger here, as with other aspects of the scheme, is that the admirable reasoning by analogy sometimes overstrains what the actual evidence can bear.

[2] *Otho* 5; *Vesp.* 23. See above, p. 252 n. 2. The technical term was 'ordinare'; cf. Hirschfeld, *Verwalt.* p. 443 n. 1, and the passages there quoted.

Freedman procurators

(VI 8515), another who began as *tabularius a rationibus*; or they moved from Rome to a provincial post, e.g. T. Aelius Augg. lib. Saturninus (VI 8450 = D 1521) who from being *tabularius a rationibus* became *proc. fisci libertatis et peculiorum* in Rome and then *proc. prov. Belgicae*; M. Aurelius Aug. lib. [..] (XIII 1800) may have repeated this process twice.[1] In the career of M. Aurelius Aug. lib. Marcio (III 348 = D 1477) the post of *proc. marmorum*, a patrimonial post of sole responsibility away from Rome, intrudes between the financial ones of *proximus rationum* and auxiliary *proc. provinciae Britanniae*. This is an unusual career as Marcio was later *proc. summi choragii* and then *proc. provinciae Frygiae*; thus he moved from Rome to take charge of the Imperial quarries, perhaps in Africa or more probably, in view of his final appointment to Phrygia, in Asia Minor, then to Britain, back to Rome, and finally to Asia Minor again; the mobility both in location and type of post is unusual (but cf. XIII 1800 above). Bassus Aug. lib. (VI 8608 = D 1485) also changed from the non-financial post of *proximus ab epistulis* to that of *proc. tractus Carthaginiensis*, a financial post in the later second century equivalent in status to that of *proc. provinciae*. Several other examples of procuratorial careers where the post of access is not known also show a continuation of a career in purely financial supervisory posts to be normal in most periods. M. Ulpius Augg. lib. Probus (XIV 176 = D 1484) was presumably *proc. Africae regionis Thevestinae* before becoming *proc. provinciae Pannoniae Superioris*; M. Aurelius Aug. lib. Crescens (D 8856 = *IGR* IV 749) was successively auxiliary provincial procurator in Gallia Lugdunensis and in Phrygia, and then appointed to the highest chief procuratorship in that period, *proc. rationis castrensis* in sole charge of the Palace domestic establishment; Tyrrhenus (Aug.) lib. (VI 790 = D 391) was *proc. regionis Thevestinae* and then *proc. Pannoniae Superioris* under Commodus; M. Aurelius Faustus Aug. lib. (*AE* 1930, 96) was *proc. rationis urbicae vobultarensis* (= voluptarensis?) (clearly financial),[2] *proc. provinciae Arabiae*, and then *proc. provinciae Ciliciae*; cf. Priscus Aug. l. (X 6668 = D 1549) *proc. IIII Publicorum Africae*, previously *proc. XXXX Galliarum*; Acastus Aug. lib. (X 6081 = D 1483) *proc. provinciae Mauretaniae*, previously *proc. (hereditatium?) tractus Campaniae*; [...Aug. l]ib. (III 14158) *proc. prov. Ciliciae*, previously *proc. prov. Arabiae*; Optatus Aug. lib. (unpublished, cf. *Diz. Epig.* IV, 943) 'qui pr(ocuravit) ad anabolicum Alex(andriae), item in provincia Cilicia'.

Two types of sequence appear in two careers each: (1) *proc. prov. Arabiae – proc. prov. Ciliciae* (*AE* 1930, 96; III 14158), which is confined to the eastern portion of the empire and presumably made use of local origin or knowledge;

---

[1] On the career of this 'M. Aurelius Aug. lib.', see above, p. 256 n. 2.
[2] Boulvert, *EAI*, p. 183 n. 643.

The emperor's service

(2) *proc. regionis Thevestinae – proc. prov. Pannoniae Superioris* (XIV 176 = D 1484; VI 790 = D 391), in which the connection is obscure.

There are a number of careers of mixed type in which the holder of a purely domestic post proceeded to a procuratorship normally held as part of the administrative *cursus*. The earliest example is Ti. Claudius Aug. lib. Bucolas (XI 3612 = D 1567; XV 7279 = D 8679, 7280) who began his recorded career in the Palace as *praegustator* and then *tricliniarchus*, proceeded to the post of *proc. a muneribus* which involved supervision of the Imperial gladiatorial games, then became *proc. aquarum* under Domitian and lastly *proc. castrensis*, a post which brought him back to the Palace as financial supervisor. The last two posts are among the most important and senior in the freedman procuratorial hierarchy.[1] During the whole of this mixed career, which is non-financial and most of which dates from the Flavian period, Bucolas, it should be noted, does not leave the capital. Another mixed career that begins with domestic posts and proceeds through those of *proc. munerum, proc. patrimonii*, back to the Palace, all without leaving Rome, is that of M. Aurelius Augg. lib. Prosenes (VI 8498 = D 1738);[2] and the mixed descending career of Theoprepes Aug. lib. which took him twice outside Rome as manager of patrimonial estates and finally to Achaia as *proc. provinciae Achaiae et Epiri et Thessaliae rationis purpurarum* under Severus Alexander (III 536 = D 1575).[3] Also to be mentioned is the undated mixed descending career of Paean Aug. lib. (XIV 2932 = D 1569), *proc. castrensis, proc. hereditatium, proc. voluptatum, proc. (fisci) Alexandr(ini)*, which again did not take him outside Rome. These mixed domestic–administrative careers are relatively few in number and probably exhibit the emperor's favour both in the number and location of the posts held. Normally only a single domestic post was held without change once the procuratorial level had been reached.

Domestic careers are prominent in the earliest inscriptions of the freedman procurators. In fact they account for all four of the 'Iulii Aug. lib.' Two from Rome and one from Tibur, C. Iulius Epagathus (VI 1934), C. Iulius Nymphodotus (*AE* 1945, 113), C. Iulius Aug. l. Samius (XIV 3644 = D 1942), had all served as *apparitores* to one or more of the Julio-Claudian emperors ('accensus Caesaris patroni'; 'accensus Div. Claudi et Neronis Augusti patronorum' in the case of Samius) before rising to a domestic procuratorship. Epagathus had also been *viator trib(unicius)* before becoming *accensus*. The only other example of this kind of procuratorial career is under the Flavians – Eutactus Aug. lib. (VI 1962 = D 1943) who was *procurator*, after having been 'accensus delatus Divo Vespasiano'; (cf. also under the Flavians, Fortunatus Aug. l. (VI 1887)

---

[1] *Ratio castrensis*: Boulvert, *EAI*, pp. 164 f.   [2] Friedländer, IV, 51.
[3] Cf. Friedländer, IV, 53 f.

Freedman procurators

'verna paternus, ab epistulis, accensus patron(o) Divo Aug. Vespasiano, lictor curiatius, viator honoratus...'). These early procurators who had risen from being *apparitores* cannot have been of comparable status with the administrative procurators of the same period who, with the exception of the *procuratores aquarum* in their stamps on *fistulae*, tended to include in their title the name of the department for which they were responsible – e.g. among the 'Claudi Aug. lib.': Claudius Optatus Aug. l. (XIV 163 = XV 7146 = D 1533) *proc. portus Ostiensis*; Ti. Claudius Aug. l. Scirtus (X 1739 = D 1587) *proc. bybl(iothecarum)*; Ti. Claudius Aug. libertus Saturninus (VI 8443 = D 1546) *proc. XX here(d). provinciae Achaiae.*

The fourth freedman procurator of the Julian emperors is Ti. Iulius Aug. l. Mellon (*AE* 1948, 141) with the simple title 'proc(urator)'. He was procurator of the Imperial estate at Jamnia in Palestine. This was clearly a post of some responsibility as the equestrian, C. Herennius Capito (*CP* No. 9), is also found as procurator under Tiberius and Gaius (Josephus, *AJ* xviii. 6.3). Mellon was not necessarily the subordinate of Capito at Jamnia as he could easily have succeeded him in the reign of Claudius, nor need we assume here the first example of an equestrian and freedman procurator, both with the same title, working as a pair, as Pflaum assumes.[1] Such equestrian–freedman pairs are not apparent on individual estates owned by the emperor, but are reserved for important patrimonial districts such as those in Asia Minor and Africa.

The status of the freedman procurators who have been classed as domestic, i.e. concerned with duties in the Imperial Palace or on individual estates belonging to the emperor, or of otherwise undetermined function, is lower than that of the freedman procurators, both chief and auxiliary, in the Imperial administration itself, except in the infrequent cases of mixed careers mentioned above where Imperial favour secured the transfer from the domestic to the administrative post at procuratorial level and sometimes back again to important Palace posts such as that of *procurator castrensis*. An example from the early period of a private procurator of the young Nero being advanced, after Nero's accession to the throne, to the important administrative post of *procurator patrimonii et hereditatium* is that of (Domitius) Lemnus Aug. l.[2] It is also not unlikely that many of the early holders of procuratorships in the provinces limited to particular items of Imperial property such as mines, quarries, etc., which were rarely if at all held by equestrians in the first century, made their way up to these senior posts through the domestic service by having been procurator-bailiff at one or

---

[1] *Proc. Equest.* p. 34 n. 11. Against Pflaum, see also Boulvert, *EAI*, p. 79 n. 443.
[2] See above, p. 268 n. 4.

The emperor's service

more Imperial villas or estates rather than through the clerical grades of *tabularius, dispensator,* etc.

Of particular importance are the status and function of the freedman *procuratores provinciae*.[1] The examples, in chronological order, are as follows:

(1) *AE* 1930, 86 (Ephesus): Eutactus lib., proc(urator) provinciarum Asiae et Lyciae. (Dated AD 80.)[2]

(2) XIV 176 = D 1484 (Ostia): M. Ulp(ius) Augg. lib. Probus, proc(urator) provinc(iae) Pannoniae Super(ioris) et Africae reg(ionis) Thevest(inae). (Died aged 71.)

(3) XIV 51 (Ostia): (P. Aelius) Trophimus Aug. l., proc(urator) prov(inciae) Cretae. (Dated 1 Oct. 124.)

(4) VI 8568 = D 1482: T. Ael(ius) Augg. lib. Restitutus, proc(urator) [S]yriae Palaest(inae).

(5) VI 8450 = D 1521: T. Ael(ius) Augg. lib. Saturnin(us), pr[oc(urator) provinc(iae)] Belgicae [....], proc(urator) fisci libertatis et peculior(um), tabul(arius) a rationibus, tabul(arius) Ostis ad annona(m).

(6) VI 8569 = D 1481: T. Ael(ius) Aug. lib. Saturus, proc(urator) pr[ovinc(iae)....].

(7) ibid.: [.....] Aug. lib. Lucianus, proc(urator) provin(ciae) Narbonensis. (Son of Saturus, No. 6?)

(8) III 14179 = *IGR* III 675 (Patara, Lycia): T. Aelius Aug. lib. Carpus, proc(urator) provinc(iae) Lyciae.

(9) *CIG* 3888 = *IGR* IV 749 = D 8856 (Stectorium, Phrygia): M. Aur(elius) Augg. lib. Crescens, ἐπίτροπος Λυγδούνου Γαλλίας καὶ ἐπίτροπος Φρυγίας καὶ ἐπίτροπος καστρῆσις.

(10) VI 790 = D 391: Tyrrhenus lib., proc(urator) reg(ionis) Thevestinae item Pannoniae Superioris. (Dedic. to Commodus, 185-92.)

(11) III 348 = D 1477 (Tricomia, Phrygia): M. Aur(elius) Aug. liber. Marcio, proximus rationum, proc(urator) marmorum, proc(urator) prov(inciae) Britanniae, proc(urator) summi chorag(ii), proc(urator) prov(inciae) Fryg(iae).

(12) X 6571 (Velitrae): M. Aurelius Philippus Aug. lib., proc(urator) Asia[e]. (Married 21 years.)

(13) *AE* 1930, 97 (Gerasa, Palaest.): M. Aurel(ius) Dom[...Aug. lib.? proc.?] provinc(iae) Arabia[e...].

(14) *AE* 1930, 96 (Gerasa, Palaest.): M. Aur(elius) Faustus Aug. lib., proc(urator) rationis urbicae vobultarensis (!), item [p]rovinciae [Ar]abiae, i[tem] pro[vinciae C]il[iciae...].

(15) XIII 1800 (Lugdunum): M. Aurelius Aug. lib. [.....], proximus a memoria it(em) a co[.....], proc(urator) fisci Asiatici, proc(urator) h[ereditat(ium), proc(urator)] provinciarum Lugdune[ns(is) et Aquitan(icae)].[3]

Undated:

(16) X 6081 = D 1483 (Formiae): Acastus Aug. lib., procurator provinciae Mauretaniae et tractu(s) Campan(iae).

---

[1] See *Historia* 14 (1965), 460 f. for a criticism of F. Millar's view on these freedman procurators, which he expresses in *JRS* 53 (1963), 196 (in the course of a review of Pflaum's *Carrières procuratoriennes*), and also in *Historia* 13 (1964), 187. [2] *PIR*², E 128; Pflaum, *Proc. Equest.* p. 39.
[3] Accepting the restorations proposed for lines 3-4 by Boulvert *EAI*, p. 108 n. 91; see also his article, 'La Procuratèle de Lyonnaise et Aquitaine dans la carrière des affranchis impériaux' [to appear].

Freedman procurators

(17) *AE* 1927, 150 (Gerasa, Palaest.): Amandus Aug. lib., proc(urator) provinc(iae Ar[abiae...].

(18) III 14158 (Gerasa, Palaest.): [....Aug. l]ib., proc(urator) prov(inciae) Cilic(iae), proc(urator) prov(inciae) Arabia[e].

(19) *AE* 1910, 169 = D 9470 (Laodicea Combusta, Galat.): [...]ενος Σε[β]αστοῦ ἀπελεύθερος, ἐπίτροπος καλενδαρίου Οὐηλιανοῦ, ἐπίτροπος χαρτηρᾶς 'Αλεξανδρείας, ἐπίτροπος Καππαδοκίας.

(20) unpublished; cf. *Diz. Epig.* IV, 943: Optatus Aug. lib., qui pr[ocuravit.....] in provincia Cilicia.[1]

Apart from Eutactus (No. 1), the two earliest by their *nomina* are M. Ulpius Augg. lib. Probus (No. 2) and (P. Aelius) Trophimus Aug. l. (No. 3). The latter is dated to 124; the former, who died aged 71, could well have been appointed procurator under Hadrian, served under Antoninus Pius as well and even survived into the reign of M. Aurelius. Next in date are the 'T. Aelii Aug. lib.' (Nos. 4, 5, 6, 8) whose procuratorships could all date from the reign of M. Aurelius. Significantly, two of these four (Nos. 4, 5) are *Augustorum liberti* which in this period indicates a date within 161-9. From the reign of M. Aurelius or later come as many as nine more (Nos. 9-15, 19, 20).

The dating of these instances of *proc. provinciae* among freedmen is so heavily late second-century (at least 14/20), and only one instance is certainly pre-Hadrianic, that an explanation for their occurrence has to be sought in the circumstances of the period or the stage of development which the Imperial administration had reached by that period. Eutactus (No. 1) is the earliest by nearly half a century. With his nomenclature, I would hesitate to accept him as the auxiliary procurator of an equestrian in charge of this accumulation of provinces, for which Eutactus lib. would be the only evidence at this time.[2] If he is the same as Eutactus Aug. lib. (an uncommon enough name), who was 'pro(curator), accensus delatus a Divo Vespasiano' (VI 1962 = D 1943), his rise from the ranks of the *apparitores* to senior administrative status would be remarkable in this or any other period. It is possible that he is a procurator in charge of a *vectigal*, e.g. the *XX hereditatium*, for which a circumscription such as Asia *and* Lycia would be appropriate, and for a freedman at this date. Cf. VI 8443 = D 1546.

Two Imperial freedmen, possibly in the first century, held powers that were similar to those of procuratorial governors of equestrian provinces. One,

---

[1] Note also: VI 8608 = D 1485: Bassus Aug. lib., proc. tractus Carthaginiensis; *AE* 1908, 158 = D 9026 (Sufetula, Afr.): M. Aurellius Aug. lib. Inventus, proc. di[oe]coesis Leptitanae; VIII 12879 = D 1486 (Carthage): Asiaticus Aug. lib., proc. regionis Assuritanae; *AE* 1903, 117 (Berytus, Syr.): Phrasis Aug. lib., proc. reg(ionis) Paphlag(oniae); and VI 8443 = D 1546: Ti. Claudius Aug. libertus Saturninus, proc. XX here(ditatium) provinciae Achaiae.

[2] The equestrian procurator C. Bienus Longus (*PIR*², B 127), found in Lycia in AD 80/81 (*IGR* III 690 = D 8796), is assigned to the province of *Lycia-Pamphylia* by Pflaum (*CP*, p. 1075). See further B. Levick, *Roman Colonies in Southern Asia Minor* (Oxford, 1967), pp. 112, 164.

The emperor's service

Metrobius Aug. lib., 'praefuit longum Pandotira per aevum' (x 6785); he was put in charge of Pandateria, a small island in the Tyrrhenian Sea used as a place of confinement for exiles, and died there (under the Flavians?) after a long tenure. The other, Chrestion Aug. lib. (x 7494 = D 3975, Malta), *procurator insularum Melit(ae) et Gaul(i)*, may also have belonged to the first century. Both places were unimportant in the administrative scheme of things and are not to be compared with the *provinciae*, both Senatorial and Imperial, in which the equestrian procurators were the chief financial officers and sometimes the equal in importance of the governors themselves.

Freedman *procuratores provinciae* cannot be of equal status with their equestrian homonyms, but are the senior *freedmen* in the administration of each province. The emergence of their new title is to be connected with the reform and expansion of the administration carried out in the early years of the reign of M. Aurelius and L. Verus.[1] The distinction between the equestrian and the freedman *cursus* is made more rigid, if anything, in the second century, and indeed after Hadrian this is what one would expect. Nor do the freedmen take the equestrian title of 'procurator Augusti', which illustrates a distinction of principle between equestrian and freedman procurators.[2]

The explanation of the titles of the freedman *procuratores provinciae* given above implies acceptance of the view that senior freedman procurators in the administration regularly became the *assistants* of the corresponding equestrian procurators.[3] The whole history of the development of the Imperial administration from the Flavian period onwards, and particularly from the reigns of Trajan and Hadrian, shows a progressive superseding of freedman heads of departments by equestrian procurators of various grades in all important branches of the administration.[4] This does not mean, however, the elimination of the senior freedman posts. It is apparent from the greater numbers of freedman procurators in the latter half of the second century, and these more concentrated in administrative than domestic posts, that the need for senior freedmen in the administration did not diminish with Hadrian but in fact

[1] Cf. the dating of the title 'proximus' to this same period. See above, pp. 253 f.
[2] Cf. *Historia* 14 (1965), 465 n. 29.
[3] When I wrote my article 'Freedmen Procurators in the Imperial Administration' published in *Historia* 14 (1965), 460-9, I was not able to take into account Pflaum's *Mémoire sur les sous-procurateurs* which was then, and still is, unpublished. Boulvert, *EAI*, pp. 392 f., has now given an admirable and detailed treatment of the whole dual equestrian-freedman procuratorial system, which now must be considered standard. Not the least of its merits is that it makes available at last the results reached by Pflaum in his *Mémoire*, which must surely hold the record for the most referred to and most eagerly awaited unpublished work in this field. Cf. also Pflaum's article 'Principes de l'administration romaine impériale', *Bulletin de la Faculté des Lettres de Strasbourg* (1958), No. 3, pp. 1-17, where (at p. 16 = 194) he characterised this dual system as 'collégialité inégale'.
[4] For the full treatment of this process of what he calls 'superposition', see Boulvert, *EAI*, pp. 270 f., 283 f., 303 f., 324 f.

Freedman procurators

substantially increased throughout the second century. These senior freedmen, however, cannot have enjoyed the status of the senior equestrians with whom they were associated.

The origin of the senior freedman procurators in an assistant capacity is to be found in the patrimonial administration in the first century.[1] Ti. Iulius Aug. l. Mellon at Jamnia is probably not the first, as the estate concerned was not important enough and he is not linked in any text with Herennius Capito.[2] Antonius Felix, brother of Pallas, governor of Judaea 52–60, was almost certainly of equestrian status at that time as he had command of troops, and probably also in the period prior to 52 when he shared control of the province with Ventidius Cumanus who governed Galilaea while Felix governed Samaria.[3] The earliest equestrian–freedman *pair* is mentioned in Tacitus, *Ann.* xiii. 1, referring to AD 54: 'Ministri fuere P. Celer eques Romanus et Helius, rei familiari principis in Asia impositi.' Celer was tried for extortion in 57.[4] Helius achieved further notoriety in 67 when he was in charge in Rome during Nero's absence in Greece.[5] These two might seem an unsuitable pair on which to base an administrative principle, but Helius was certainly of procuratorial rank and Celer's duties were concerned with the Imperial *patrimonium* ('rei familiari principis in Asia impositi') as were the duties of the earlier equestrian *procurator Asiae*, Lucilius Capito, who was likewise prosecuted on a charge of extortion in 23, with the assertion by Tiberius 'non se ius nisi in servitia et pecunias familiaris dedisse' (Tacitus, *Ann.* iv. 15).

That the relationship between equestrian and freedman in such a pair is that of principal and assistant is shown clearly by the cases of Virdius Gemellinus and the Imperial freedmen Maximus and Epimachus in Bithynia during Pliny's term as governor.[6]

Beside suggesting that the duties of patrimonial procurators in provinces where Imperial estates were numerous gradually extended from purely patrimonial interests to those of provincial procurators, these passages throw some light on the working of the dual procuratorial arrangement. It may not have been so important to have a freedman who could keep a check on the equestrian procurator in a province of special financial interest to the emperor as that there should be continuity at the top administrative level. Freedmen

---

[1] Boulvert, on the other hand, attributes the full-scale implementation of the dual system in most spheres of the administration to Claudius; see *EAI*, pp. 111 f.   [2] See above, p. 275.
[3] Suetonius, *Claud.* 28; Josephus, *BJ* ii. 247, *AJ* xx. 137; Tacitus, *Ann.* xii. 54; *PIR*², A 828. His equestrian status is unavoidable, despite Tacitus' scathing comment in *Hist.* v. 9: 'Claudius ...Iudaeam provinciam equitibus Romanis aut libertis permisit, e quibus Antonius Felix per omnem saevitiam ac libidinem ius regium servili ingenio exercuit...'; cf. Stein, *Ritterstand*, p. 114; Sherwin-White, *PBSR* 15 (1939), 24 n. 89; against, Millar, *Historia* 13 (1964), 182.
[4] Tacitus, ib. 33.1; *PIR*², C 625.   [5] *PIR*², H 55; Cassius Dio, lxiii. 12.
[6] The relevant letters of Pliny (x. 27, 28, 84, 85) have been discussed above, pp. 234 f.

The emperor's service

would generally remain in such posts for longer periods than equestrians – the changeover of Maximus and Epimachus in the midst of Gemellinus' term as equestrian procurator is not evidence to the contrary as freedman procurators must have come and gone during someone's term of office. The passages from Pliny show that *both* procurators, equestrian and freedman, did not leave at the same time. Hermes Aug. lib., who described himself as 'adiutor eius' in an inscription put up at Ephesus in the time of Hadrian to an equestrian *procurator provinciae Asiae* on the occasion of the latter's promotion to the post of *proc. Syriae* (III 431 = D 1449), was another such auxiliary procurator; he remained behind in Ephesus when his former superior moved on to his next appointment. The title of 'procurator provinciae' did not come into general use for freedmen until after Hadrian (see above). Further examples of freedman auxiliary procurators are to be found in two third-century inscriptions from Pergamum: 'Didius Marinus et Aur. Takitus (Aug.) lib. procc.' (*AE* 1933, 282), and '[...]taenetus [et ...]is (Aug.) lib. procc.' (*AE* 1933, 281).

All the examples of freedman assistant procurators discussed above relate to Asia Minor where the patrimonial estates were particularly numerous. All the other examples from the provinces come from Africa, the other area where, since the large-scale confiscations of Nero, the greatest concentration of Imperial estates was to be found. An equestrian *procurator tractus Carthaginiensis* was probably in Carthage as early as the reign of Nero.[1] After the time of Trajan the administration of Africa was organised in terms of patrimonial districts rather than on a provincial basis – at least equestrians with the title 'proc. prov. Africae' are not attested after that date.[2] In correspondence and injunctions concerning the Imperial estates in the *tractus Carthaginiensis* from the time of Trajan the names of *two* procurators, one equestrian and one freedman, always appear at the head of official documents. Thus, in the *Lex colonis villae Magnae data* (VIII 25902 = *FIRA*² I, p. 485) of 116/17, 'data a Licinio [Ma]ximo et Feliciore Aug. lib. procc.'; in the inscription of Aïn-el-Dschemala (VIII 25943 = *FIRA*² I, pp. 491 f.) from the reign of Hadrian, 'procurato[res, per pro]videntiam vestram, quam [nomine Ca]esaris praestatis' (I. 1), 'Sermo procurato[rum im]p. [C]aes. Hadriani Aug.' (II. 2), 'Verridius Bassus et Ianuarius Martiali suo salut[em]' (IV. 5); in the Aïn Ouassel inscription (VIII 26416 = *FIRA*² I, p. 493) of the Severan period, 'aram legis Divi Hadriani Patroclus Auggg. lib. instituit et legem infra scriptam intulit. ...Sermo proc[u]ratorum' (l. 7 f.); in the inscription from the Saltus Burunitanus (VIII 14464 = *FIRA*²

---

[1] Tac. *Hist.* iv. 50; cf. Pflaum, *CP*, p. 99; *Proc. Equest.* p. 44.
[2] See Pflaum, *CP*, p. 978 on Claudius Paternus Clementianus.

Freedman procurators

I, pp. 495 f.) under Commodus (AD 180/3), '...ut se habent litter[a]e procc., quae sunt in ta[b]ulario tuo tractus Carthag.' (III. 10), cf. 'procc. litteris' (ib. 17, 26), 'Procc. contemplatione discipulinae et instituti mei...curabunt...' (IV. 4), 'Tussanius Aristo et Chrysanthus Andronico suo salutem' (IV. 11). The freedman auxiliary procurator in each of these examples is placed in the secondary position after the equestrian *procurator tractus Carthaginiensis*. With the dual procurators in Africa may be compared the single (freedman) procurator in the inscription concerning the mines in Portugal, the *Lex metallis dicta* (*FIRA*² I, pp. 499 f.) from the reign of Hadrian, where single mines or groups of mines are involved and are not important enough to warrant both an equestrian and a freedman procurator.

The evidence thus suggests that the system of dual procuratorships had its origin in the patrimonial administration in Asia Minor and Africa in the later first century, and was well established there under Trajan. Other freedmen whose activities in the provinces in the first century are mentioned in the literary sources were probably of procuratorial standing, but there is no indication that they were auxiliary procurators; for example, Iberus who was temporarily in charge of Egypt in 32 (Cassius Dio, lviii. 19.6);[1] Crescens, the freedman of Nero, who gave a public banquet in Carthage on the news of Otho's accession without waiting for the proconsul Vipstanus Apronianus (Tacitus, *Hist.* i. 76); Hilarus the Imperial freedman who usurped authority in Spain and was punished by Vitellius (Tacitus, *Hist.* ii. 65); and perhaps Halotus[2] whom Galba saved from popular resentment and 'procuratione amplissima ornavit', presumably away from Rome (Suetonius, *Galba* 15). To these might be added Polyclitus, Nero's freedman, who was sent to Britain in 61 to mediate in the celebrated dispute between the legate and the equestrian procurator there (Tac. *Ann.* xiv. 39).[3]

Following the rapid replacement or rather 'superposition' of senior freedmen by equestrians not only in the *officia Palatina* but also in other important branches of the administration from the beginning of the second century, an alternative senior *cursus* in addition to the remaining posts of sole responsibility gradually emerged for the highest grade of freedmen. The patrimonial system of auxiliary procuratorships was extended to include assistantships to many of the senior posts in the equestrian *cursus*, both in Rome and the provinces. This process reached its culmination under M. Aurelius, both in the Palatine bureaux and in the provincial administrative centres where the title 'procurator provinciae' came to mark one of the peaks of the freedman procuratorial career.

---

[1] For Imperial freedmen in Egypt, cf. Strabo, xvii. 1.12.   [2] *PIR*², H 11.
[3] Cf. Weaver, *Past & Present* No. 37 (1967), 16 f.

CHAPTER 22

IMPERIAL FREEDMEN AND EQUESTRIAN STATUS: THE FATHER OF CLAUDIUS ETRUSCUS

While the freedman procurators and heads of departments from early in the second century were systematically denied equality of status with their equestrian replacements or counterparts, it occasionally happened that individual freedmen were advanced to membership of the equestrian order itself and full parity of status with the equestrians. In even rarer cases senatorial honours, the *ornamenta praetoria* and *quaestoria*, were granted. The main legal barrier which the freedman aspiring to equestrian status had to overcome was that of free birth. Freeborn status (*ingenuitas*) was conferred by the grant of the *anuli aurei*, which was in the hands of the emperor, and emperors, both good and bad, in the first and second centuries were very sparing in conferring such free birth on their own freedmen and in admitting them formally to the *ordo equester*. The very paucity of such instances emphasises the difference in status between the Imperial freedmen in general and the *equites*, and in particular is an argument against any intermingling of the freedman and the equestrian procuratorial *cursus*.

Augustus (Cassius Dio, liii. 30.3) granted the *anuli aurei* to his successful physician Antonius Musa,[1] but there is no need to suppose that he did the same for his notorious procurator in Gaul, Licinus.[2] On the other hand, Antonius Felix was almost certainly an *eques* when he was appointed procurator of Judaea in 52 and given command of troops there.[3] His brother, Antonius Pallas,[4] was even more highly honoured under Claudius by the *ornamenta praetoria* decreed him by the Senate in 52. Narcissus had already received *ornamenta quaestoria* in 48.[5] The next case is that of Icelus[6] 'quem anulis donatum equestri nomine Marcianum vocitabant' (Tacitus, *Hist.* i. 13) under Galba. Then Asiaticus under Vitellius (Tacitus, *Hist.* ii. 47; Suet. *Vitell.* 12).[7] Vespasian advanced two freedmen to the equestrian order,

---

[1] *PIR²*, A 853.
[2] *PIR¹*, L 193; cf. Hirschfeld, *Verwalt.* p. 468 n. 1; against Stein, *Ritterstand*, p. 112, and Mommsen, *Staatsr.* II, 837 n. 1, on the grounds that he had a 'cognomen equestre'. On *cognomina equestria*, see *CQ* 14 (1964), 311 f. [3] See above, p. 279 with n. 3.
[4] *PIR²*, A 858; cf. Oost, *AJPh* 79 (1958), 113 f. [5] *PIR¹*, N 18.
[6] *PIR¹*, I 14; *CQ* 14 (1964), 311 f. [7] *PIR²*, A 1216.

Imperial freedmen and equestrian status

Hormus,[1] who was one of the leaders of the Flavian party ('is quoque inter duces habebatur', Tac. *Hist.* iii. 12), in 70, and the father of Claudius Etruscus, the well-known secretary *a rationibus* under the Flavians, probably in 73/4.[2]

In the second century the examples are even fewer, three only. L. Aurelius Nicomedes, the 'educator' of L. Verus who had a distinguished, if favoured, equestrian career;[3] M. Aurelius Cleander who was praetorian prefect under Commodus with the title 'a pugione';[4] and Saoterus, *cubicularius* of Commodus who may have become *clarissimus vir*.[5]

In the third century there are the doubtful cases of Theocritus[6] and Epagathus[7] who were powerful under Caracalla, and Aurelius Zoticus[8] under Elagabalus. During the reign of Elagabalus, according to two rhetorical passages in the *Historia Augusta* and Herodian,[9] all barriers between classes were broken, and freedmen filled the highest offices. The reaction came with Severus Alexander who, according to the *Historia Augusta* (*Sev. Alex.* 19.4) never advanced freedmen to equestrian status. To these we should add Aurelius Augg. lib. Alexander, who was made *vir egregius*, probably under the Severans.[10]

These examples are extraordinarily few and well spread over two and a half centuries. No particular freedman post secured advancement to the ranks of the *equites*, with the exception perhaps of the *a rationibus* in the first century and the *cubicularii* in the late second and early third centuries. Nor does origin or homeland play any particular part. There are exceptional and personal favours conferred by the emperor on particular favourites. Hormus and the father of Claudius Etruscus were no doubt rewarded for particular services to the Flavian cause during the Civil War, but most of the others after that date seem to have been unworthy recipients of unworthy Imperial favour. The true reward of the successful Imperial freedman from the early second century was a senior auxiliary procuratorship in one of the important departments of the administration in Rome or in one of the important provinces abroad.

Two of these figures are subject to detailed scrutiny. They are M. Antonius Pallas and the father of Claudius Etruscus. Their careers invite comparison and contrast. Both were freedman holders of the premier post of

---

[1] *PIR*², H 204; cf. Tac. *Hist.* iv. 39.
[2] On the father of Claudius Etruscus, see below, pp. 288f.
[3] See Pflaum, *CP* No. 163   [4] See Pflaum, *CP* No. 180 bis and pp. 1007 f.
[5] *PIR*¹, S 137, but see *PIR*², A 247 and Heer, *Philol.* Suppl. IX, 42 f., 46 f.
[6] *PIR*¹, T 117; cf. Stein, *Ritterstand*, pp. 120 f.
[7] *PIR*², E 67; cf. Stein, *Ritterstand*, p. 124.   [8] *PIR*², A 1641.
[9] SHA *Elagab.* 11.1: 'Fecit libertos praesides legatos consules duces omnesque dignitates polluit ignobilitate hominum perditorum'; cf. Herodian, v. 7.7.
[10] See above, p. 265 with n. 4.

The emperor's service

a rationibus in the first century, the one under the Julio-Claudians, the other under the Flavians. The one was given honorary senatorial status at praetorian rank, the other was raised to equestrian status. Pallas, who is perhaps too well known and whose name has been synonymous with the vices of Imperial freedmen, has been the subject of an admirable recent study.[1] The father of Claudius Etruscus, on the other hand, whose name we do not even know, but who appears in the literary sources as almost uniquely virtuous among freedmen, has not received his fair measure of attention. Yet from the social point of view he is particularly interesting. I conclude this part of the work, therefore, with a case study of the father of Claudius Etruscus.[2]

THE FATHER OF CLAUDIUS ETRUSCUS

The career of the father of Claudius Etruscus is of special importance in the history of the Imperial administration in the first century AD. In the course of a long life he rose from slave status under Tiberius to be head of the Imperial financial administration and to equestrian status under Vespasian. He was one of the most important, wealthy and influential of the Imperial freedmen in the first century when their influence was at its peak; he is one of the best documented of their number outside the pages of Tacitus; yet we do not know his personal name – he has to remain simply 'the father of Claudius Etruscus' – and even his *nomen gentilicium* and the date of his appointment to be the secretary *a rationibus* are subject to dispute. The reason for this lies in the allusive nature of the sources bearing on his life and career – especially Statius, *Silvae* iii. 3.[3] However, I believe that a closer analysis of the poem will yield further information both on the stages of his career and on his family.

First, as to his date of birth. He was exiled at the age of 80 during the reign of Domitian (*Silv*. iii. 3.146, 'dextra bis octonis fluxerunt saecula lustris'); at his death he was approaching the end of his ninetieth year (Martial, vii. 40. 6, 'hic prope ter senas vixit Olympiadas').[4] Statius' *consolatio* cannot be before January 93, the date of Domitian's return from the Sarmatian war against the Iazyges, over whom he did not celebrate a triumph (lines 170-1).[5] The poem was probably written at no great interval after the death of Etuscus' father, who therefore died in the second half of 92, or shortly before

---
[1] Oost, *AJPh* 79 (1958), 113-39.
[2] This study first appeared in substantially the same form in *CQ* 15 (1965), 145-54.
[3] The sources are: Statius, *Silvae* i. 5.65; iii. 3; Martial, vi. 83; vii. 40. See *PIR²*, c 763; *PIR¹*, c 691; P-W III, 2670 (Claudius, 31). For Claudius Etruscus, see: Statius, *Silvae* i. pr.; *PIR²*, c 860; P-W III, 2719 (Claudius, 143).
[4] For Olympiad = *lustrum* in Martial, cf. Friedländer's Martial ad loc.
[5] Cf. Martial, viii. 2; ix. 31; *CAH* XI, 177.

284

Imperial freedmen and equestrian status

the publication of Martial's Seventh Book in December 92. He was born, therefore, in late AD 2 or early AD 3. His exile occurred in 82/3.[1]

After the conventional opening (1-42), Statius devotes the central place in his *consolatio* to the career of Etruscus' father. His servile origin in Smyrna is alluded to (43 f. 'non tibi clara quidem, senior placidissime, gentis / linea nec proavis demissum stemma'; 60, 'Smyrna tibi gentile solum'). After his arrival in Rome at an early age, as a *Caesaris servus* under Tiberius he filled a number of regular ('ex ordine') slave posts either in the domestic Palace service or in junior clerical posts in Rome which, at this comparatively early stage in the development of the administration, could be said to involve close contact with the emperor (63 f. 'laeta dehinc series variisque ex ordine curis / auctus honos'). It was during this service under Tiberius that Etruscus' father was manumitted:

> Tibereia primum
> aula tibi vixdum ora nova mutante iuventa
> panditur. hic annis multa super indole victis
> libertas oblata venit.   (66-9)

This suggests that his manumission came before the age of 30, the regular age for formal manumission laid down by the lex Aelia Sentia. Early manumission before 30 years of age was rare enough in the Familia Caesaris, especially for those in the clerical grades. Yet even if not manumitted before the regular age, Etruscus' father was shown a mark of favour by not having to purchase his freedom. The existence of the *fiscus libertatis et peculiorum*, attested from the Claudian or Flavian period,[2] implies that the purchasing of freedom was the common, if not the regular, practice in the Familia Caesaris, and it is unlikely that the frugal Tiberius had not already adopted it. Etruscus' father was granted his freedom without payment ('oblata') at the age of 30 or shortly before, about AD 30-3, in the latter part of Tiberius' reign. His name would therefore have been 'Ti. Iulius Aug. l....'.[3]

As an *Augusti libertus*, he next accompanied Gaius to Gaul on his pretended

---

[1] On the dates, cf. F. Vollmer's edition of the *Silvae* (Leipzig, 1898), p. 408.

[2] VI 8450a, 8451. Cf. Hirschfeld, *Verwalt*. p. 109 n. 1; Jones, *JRS* 39 (1949), 43 f. = *Studies*, pp. 159 f.; Boulvert, *EAI*, pp. 137 f.

[3] For prosopographical purposes he is always (wrongly) entered as 'Claudius', e.g. *PIR*², C 763 (Ti. Claudius); P-W III, 2670 (Claudius, 31); *OCD*¹, p. 198 (Claudius, 13); but cf. now Chantraine, pp. 89, 92, 94; *OCD*², p. 111. Duff, *Freedmen*, p. 184, is overcautious in stating that he was manumitted either by Tiberius or by Claudius. There is no evidence that his *nomen* was ever 'Claudius'. In the Familia Caesaris the *nomen* of a freedman father cannot be inferred from that of a son; in this case there is evidence to the contrary. The conjecture of Hirschfeld (*Kleine Schriften* (1913), p. 840 = *Wien. Stud.* 3 (1881), 273 f.) that Tiberius' freedmen may sometimes have taken his original *nomen* 'Claudius' *after* his adoption into the Julian gens by Augustus in AD 4 is very unlikely. Tiberius' freedmen who had been manumitted before his adoption (and change of *nomen*) may possibly have changed their *nomen* to accord with that of their patron (i.e. '*Iulius*' instead of 'Claudius'). See Part I above, pp. 26 f.

The emperor's service

invasion of Britain (71, 'huic et in Arctoas tendis comes usque pruinas'). His function could not have been that of *dispensator* connected with the paying of the troops or other disbursements for which slaves only were employed, and as yet he was too young to have risen to procuratorial rank, for which 40–45 was the minimum age – at least there is little evidence of freedman procurators under that age; it is likely that he served Gaius in some personal capacity in a post of intermediate status, perhaps as *tabularius* or one of his secretarial staff.

In this position he remained under Claudius until he had proved by his service to that emperor ('merito') his claims to promotion to senior rank:

> praecipuos sed enim merito surrexit in actus
> nondum stelligerum senior dimissus in axem
> Claudius...   (76–8)

This probably occurred in the latter part of Claudius' reign ('senior'), at the appropriate age for entering on senior status, i.e. about the age of 45, *c.* AD 48. He would not have been Pallas' deputy *a rationibus*. Such a post at this period must have been very much the creation of Pallas. He did not succeed Pallas as *a rationibus* upon the latter's retirement in 55, but neither does he appear to have been implicated in his eclipse. Pallas and Etruscus' father were almost exact contemporaries and their careers were strangely parallel. Pallas was born *c.* AD 1; he was still a slave in 31,[1] and was manumitted between AD 31 and 37, at the regular age. Pallas was also of eastern origin – of Greek rather than Hellenised oriental descent. Of both it could be said that Claudius 'praecipuos sed enim merito surrexit in actus'. Both became *a rationibus*, became very wealthy, and were forced to retire early in the reign of a new emperor, perhaps because of their associations with the court of the previous emperor. It is difficult to see Etruscus' father as the subordinate of Pallas under Claudius – his 'curarum socius' (cf. l. 161). The words 'praecipuos actus' rather suit the independent position which the title 'procurator' or the headship of another department, not necessarily as important as the *a rationibus*, would give. His absence from the pages of Tacitus suggests a financial procuratorship away from Rome, probably in the East, where he later would have become known to Vespasian and Titus, and would have acquired some first-hand acquaintance with the sources of revenue alluded to in lines 89–105.

The next few lines are important in the interpretation of his career:

> ...et longo transmittit habere nepoti.
> quis superos metuens pariter tot templa, tot aras
> promeruisse datur? summi Iovis aliger Arcas

[1] Josephus, *AJ* xviii. 182. Cf. Oost, *AJPh* 59 (1958), 113 f.

Imperial freedmen and equestrian status

nuntius; imbrifera potitur Thaumantide Iuno;
stat celer obsequio iussa ad Neptunia Triton:
tu totiens mutata ducum iuga rite tulisti
integer, inque omni felix tua cumba profundo.
(78–84)

Line 78 is difficult as the text stands, especially the epithet 'longo', so curiously used of Nero.[1] The sense is temporal, and its emphatic predicative position is best explained if it is taken in sense with 'habere' (as by Gronovius); thus 'nepos habet longus' is a Graecism for 'nepos habet longum, i.e. 'diu'. 'Longo' = 'longum', then, refers to the particular situation of Etruscus' father, i.e. his fifteen years away from Rome, from the accession of Nero to the outbreak of the Civil War. He was lucky. Many of the senior freedmen of Claudius did not survive at all until the end of Nero's reign, and were in any case early replaced by Nero's own favourites. Hence the curt reference to Nero and to a period of long duration that helps to explain why Etruscus' father did not become *a rationibus* till so late in his career, in 70 or 71 at the age of 67.

On the assumption (which is almost universally accepted)[2] that he had already been given that appointment under Nero on the retirement of Pallas in 55 (lines 86 f.), the passage (79 f.) 'quis superos... profundo' must refer to the reign of Nero and those of his predecessors, Claudius, Gaius and Tiberius ('tu totiens mutata ducum iuga rite tulisti').[3] Three examples are given of gods or goddesses and their attendant ministers – Jupiter and Mercury, Juno and Iris, Neptune and Triton. But in the chronological sequence characteristic of the *laudatio* this surely refers to what *followed* the reign of Nero rather than what preceded it. The rapid and frequent change of leaders ('tot...tot...totiens mutata', contrasted with the preceding 'longo'), whose yoke ('iuga') Etruscus' father duly bore without shipwreck (a difficult

---

[1] Emendations have not won general acceptance. On this difficult passage, see *CQ* 15 (1965), 147 n. 3.
[2] E.g. Stein, *PIR*², c 763; P-W III, 2670; Klebs, *PIR*¹, c 691; Momigliano, *OCD*¹, p. 198; Friedländer, IV, 28; Vollmer, *Silvae*, p. 413; Rostovtzeff, *Diz. Epig.* III, 136; Charlesworth, *CAH* XI, 30 n. 2; Mozeley, Loeb ed. p. 167; Frère, Budé ed. I, 115 n. 4. Hirschfeld, *Kl. Schr.* p. 839, hesitates. Gsell, *Essai sur le règne de l'empereur Domitien* (1894), p. 70, even thinks that he was already *a rationibus* under Claudius. Duff, *Freedmen*, pp. 153, 184, judiciously says that he was *a rationibus* under the Flavians, but without discussing the period 55–70. Pflaum, *Proc. Equest.* p. 208, states without comment that Phaon was *a rationibus* from 55 to 68. But for Phaon, see now Boulvert, *EAI*, p. 97 n. 37.
[3] Following his interpretation of line 78, Vollmer takes the passage 79–84 to be a 'declamatory parenthesis' referring to the father's career from Claudius to Domitian; 85 f. then marks a return to the period Claudius–Nero. But the times of trouble ('iuga rite tulisti integer; inque omni... profundo') more naturally precede the happy success of 'iamque piam lux alta domum praecelsaque ...intravit Fortuna' than follow it. The whole section 59 to 105 is in chronological sequence; line 84 marks the end of the first stage of the father's career – up to the end of the Civil War; the second stage, under the Flavians, opens with 85 f.

The emperor's service

feat as well as a mixed metaphor), must have been Galba, Otho and Vitellius. 'Inque omni felix tua cumba profundo' describes much more appropriately the fortunes of individuals and the state in the years 68–9, than those of one who was promoted to senior rank by Claudius and is supposed to have become *a rationibus* under Nero. Otherwise there would be, surprisingly, no reference at all in the poem to the period of the Civil War, nor to the three emperors whom an *a rationibus* from Nero to Vespasian would seem (also surprisingly) to have served. The treatment of Nero's freedmen by Galba, for one, was not sympathetic, and one so prominent as the *a rationibus* in Rome can scarcely have escaped his attentions. The not inconsiderable sources for the period 68–70 have failed to notice him. He acquired his wealth while *a rationibus*, and if he had done so under Nero, Galba would have stripped him of it. It is not necessary to equate Galba with Jupiter, Otho with Juno, and Vitellius with Neptune; but the number three is not accidental or merely a stock, thrice repeated literary allusion. 'Tu totiens mutata ducum iuga rite tulisti' refers to the career of Etruscus' father from the end of Nero's reign to the accession of Vespasian. He remained at his procuratorial post in an eastern province, and did not return to Rome till 70 with Vespasian, or 71 with Titus.

The next three lines refer to the house of Etruscus' father in the year 70 or 71 under the Flavian dynasty, and not to the year 55 under Nero:

> iamque piam lux alta domum praecelsaque toto
> intravit Fortuna gradu; iam creditur uni
> sanctarum digestus opum... (85–7)

Appointment to the post of *a rationibus* was the long-delayed reward (hence the repeated 'iam...iam') for the father's merit and service, as well as for his loyalty, recently displayed, to the Flavian house. He saw both his sons made *equites* by Vespasian; then he himself was granted the *anuli aurei*; later, under Domitian, his brother-in-law won a consulship and a high military command. 'Piam lux alta domum... intravit' was written under a Flavian emperor, Domitian, and refers to honours bestowed by another Flavian emperor, Vespasian. The main difficulty here lies in the age of Etruscus' father at the date of his appointment as *a rationibus*. In AD 70 he would have been 67. However, as he certainly held the post till 82/3, the date of his banishment by Domitian, when his colleague (161, 'curarum socius') in the *a rationibus* department suffered relegation overseas (160 f.), he was still considered fit to hold that office up to the age of 80.[1] Vespasian called on him because of his experience and reliability.

[1] Stein, P-W III, 2670, curiously says that he could not have been *a rationibus* under Domitian *because* he had already been given equestrian status by Vespasian.

Imperial freedmen and equestrian status

The question of who filled the post of *a rationibus* during 55–70 cannot be answered with any certainty. There is an ample supply of freedmen who had the title *a rationibus*, or could have had it, in the reign of Nero.[1] Phaon, who is attested both in the literary and epigraphical sources, is perhaps the most likely candidate for at least the latter part of Nero's reign.[2]

There follows in Statius the well-known and frequently discussed description of the duties of the secretary *a rationibus* under the Flavians (86–105).[3] Then comes the passage on the father's marriage to Etrusca and on her family (106–37).

Lastly, the final stages of the father's career under the Flavians. Vespasian honoured him twice, once by allowing him despite his freedman status (142, 'tenuesque nihil minuere parentes') to participate honourably in the Jewish triumph in 71:

> illum et qui nutu superas nunc temperat arces
> progeniem claram terris partitus et astris,
> laetus Idymaei donavit honore triumphi;
> dignatusque loco victricis et ordine pompae
> non vetuit, tenuesque nihil minuere parentes.
>
> (138–42)

This has a double significance. Vespasian's special grant of this privilege to a freedman (cf. 'donavit', 'dignatus', 'non vetuit', 'nihil minuere') is not without reason, and is best explained as due to the father's contribution to or participation in the organisation of the Jewish campaign while in the eastern Mediterranean. Secondly, a connection between Titus and Etruscus' father is established. This is the only reference in the poem to Titus, under whom the father must have served as *a rationibus*. The suppression of any mention of Titus as emperor may in fact be due to the fact that Etruscus' father was a special protégé of Titus. Domitian's relations with his brother are well known.[4]

Vespasian also honoured Etruscus' father, probably during his censorship held together with Titus in 73/4, with the grant of the *ius anulorum aureorum* and raised him to equestrian status. The father was now over 70 years old. His sons had reached the ranks of the *equites* before him, presumably during service in the Civil or Jewish wars under Vespasian or Titus (143 f., esp. 145, 'et celso natorum aequavit honorem'). Admission of freedmen to the *ordo equester* was a rare honour, accorded only to special favourites or for special

---

[1] On the possible candidates, see chapter 20, above, pp. 259 f.
[2] III 14112.2; cf. Suetonius, *Ner.* 48.1, 49.2; Dio, lxiii. 27.3.
[3] E.g. Mommsen, *Staatsr.* II, 1003 n. 1; Rostovtzeff, *Diz. Epig.* III, 136; Hirschfeld, *Verwalt.* p. 30 n. 4; Boulvert, *EAI*, pp. 383 f.
[4] Suetonius, *Titus* 9; *Domit.* 2; cf. *CAH* XI, 19 f.; Garzetti, *L'Impero*, p. 269.

The emperor's service

services.[1] Vespasian was not over-liberal with such honours. Moreover, as Etruscus' father remained the *a rationibus* for another nine years after his elevation, he was the first equestrian *a rationibus*, a recognition of the preeminence of the financial secretaryship. He was probably succeeded as *a rationibus* by a freedman, Atticus Aug. lib., who was holding the post by 85. But from Vibius Lentulus under Trajan the post was again held by equestrians.[2]

In 82 or 83 came the thunderbolt from Domitian (146 f.). The causes of disgrace are not unnaturally left obscure in the poem (156 f.); but the downfall and banishment of the *a rationibus* so soon after the accession of Domitian may be compared with that of Pallas himself. Both were too closely involved with the policies and personalities of the previous reign to have the full confidence of the new regime. Domitian also banished another senior official in the *a rationibus* (160 f.). What is clear is that the banishment lasted for at least seven years, despite Statius' blurring of the interval (164 f., 'nec longa moratus / Romuleum reseras iterum, Germanice, limen'). Etruscus' father probably returned from exile in 90, after the opening of the son's baths (*Silvae* i. 5.65, 'et tua iam melius discat fortuna renasci'; Martial, vi. 42); but he died not long after, in 92 (182 f.).

Apart from the career of Etruscus' father, his family life is of considerable social interest. He married a lady of freeborn status and, indeed, of high birth and connections, a fact on which Statius lays much emphasis (114 f. 'nec vulgare genus', 'sic quicquid patrio cessatum a sanguine, mater / reddidit'). But neither her *nomen* nor the date of marriage is indicated directly. Her personal name was *Etrusca* (111, 207), from which that of her son was derived.

The passage describing the marriage and the birth of the children and the early death of the mother (106–37) follows directly on the description of the duties of the *a rationibus* (86–105), and is immediately followed by the passage describing the honours bestowed by Vespasian, and the exile and recall by Domitian (138 f.). However, the events described in this section (106–37) cannot be said to be in chronological sequence with the stages of the father's career. If he did not take up the post of *a rationibus* till AD 70, his marriage at this point is clearly out of the question. On the other hand, if he assumed the duties of *a rationibus* at the earliest date possible after the retirement of Pallas in 55, and married *subsequently*, his two sons could not have been born before 57 at the earliest. As they were members of the equestrian order by 73, and probably earlier (145) – the minimum age for which was normally at least 17 years[3] – AD 55 is still too late as a *terminus ante quem* for the

---
[1] See Stein, *Ritterstand*, pp. 109 f., and above, pp. 282 f.   [2] See above, pp. 259 f.
[3] Cf. Mommsen, *Staatsr*. III, 496 n. 2; Stein, *Ritterstand*, p. 56 n. 4, where exceptional cases found in the inscriptions are quoted.

Imperial freedmen and equestrian status

marriage. As sons of a freedman father, however eminent, Etruscus and his brother were not likely to have been admitted to the *ordo* at an even earlier age than that reserved for Imperial princes. It is more likely that they were already of full military age by the time of the Civil War and that they were admitted to the *ordo* either then or following Vespasian's victory. Another indication that the marriage *preceded* the appointment as *a rationibus* may be found in line 85, 'iamque piam lux alta domum... intravit'. 'Piam domum' suits a home with wife and children better than it does a bachelor establishment. Apart from the reasons given above for rejecting 55 as the date of the father's accession to the post of *a rationibus* – 52 years of age would in any case seem somewhat late for a first marriage – it is difficult to place his marriage at this point, and therefore the position in the poem of the passage 106–37 cannot be used to date the marriage.

As for the *terminus post quem*, there are good reasons for supposing that the father did not marry Etrusca while he was still of slave status. The only indications to the contrary are a somewhat literal interpretation of line 110, 'et fidos domino genuisse clientes' – where the word 'domino' would specify the slave status of the father, and 'clientes' indicate the relationship of children born of an *ingenua* mother and a slave father to the father's master; and the fact that as Etruscus appears not to have derived his *nomen* from his father but from his mother or someone else, this would indicate that he was born *in contubernio*. But under Domitian 'dominus' clearly refers to the emperor, and, while one would not expect Statius to hint at the illegitimate status of Etruscus at birth, even if this were the case, legitimisation by adoption was open to the father after his manumission.

But the fact that Statius has not given the *nomen* of the father, but left us to imply that it was different from that of the son, need not be taken as implying illegitimacy. In the Familia Caesaris, while the status and other nomenclature of *servi* and *liberti*, particularly those with posts in the administration, was fairly strictly observed, that of the children born to Imperial slaves and freedmen shows considerable variation.[1] It is much more likely that Claudius Etruscus took a *nomen* which was different from that of his father than that his father changed his name from 'Ti. Iulius Aug. lib....' to 'Ti. Claudius Aug. lib....'. On the other hand, it is probable that the reason why the personal name of Etruscus' father (and perhaps that of his brother) is nowhere mentioned in the poem, although it must have been a household name because of his eminence, is because of its servile connotation in the first century.

Etruscus' father married after manumission. His marriage was a *iustum*

---
[1] Cf. Part II above, pp. 137 f.

The emperor's service

matrimonium.[1] A further indication of the date of the marriage is that Statius clearly regards Etruscus and his brother as his juniors. While 'puer' in *Silvae* i. 5.64, 'macte, oro, nitenti / ingenio curaque puer', is merely a Vergilian adaptation and cannot be interpreted literally – in 90 Etruscus would have been at least 35 years old, even if born in 55 – it does imply that Statius was the senior. Some indication of the age of the brothers in 90 can be got from lines 154–5:

> quas tibi devoti *iuvenes* pro patre renato,
> summe ducum, gratis, aut quae pia vota rependunt!

Statius, who was born c. AD 40 and was thus nearly 50 years old at the date to which this passage refers, could scarcely have called the brothers 'iuvenes' if they were older than himself. This reduces the limits of the marriage date to between c. 45 and c. 50. The father's socially successful marriage – which was in any case much later than the average age of marriage for men in the Familia Caesaris – is much more likely to have taken place at or after the time he was promoted to senior rank. This occurred in the latter half of Claudius' reign. The marriage is therefore to be dated to c. 48–50.

The passage (106 f.) which connects the description of the duties of the *a rationibus* with the section on the father's domestic life is as follows:

> hinc tibi rara quies animoque exclusa voluptas,
> exiguaeque dapes et numquam laesa profundo
> cura mero; sed iura tamen genialia cordi
> et mentem vincire toris ac iungere festa
> conubia et fidos domino genuisse clientes.
>
> (106–10)

But if the whole section 106–37 is not in chronological sequence with the preceding and following sections dealing with the father's public career, 'hinc' cannot refer only to the duties of the *a rationibus* in the lines immediately preceding, but must refer to the whole preceding account of the father's career. 'Exiguae dapes...' does not characterise his table as that of the *a rationibus* alone, whether under Vespasian, or Nero,[2] but the father's mode of life during his whole career as a civil servant. A fresh section of the poem begins at this point.

The hypothesis of a long sojourn in the provinces would help to explain a remark of Statius at this point. In line 112 he says of Etrusca, 'haudquaquam

---

[1] This much may be inferred from the phrases 'ac iungere festa conubia' (109–10), and 'conubio gavisa domus' (121); cf. 'plenis venient conubia taedis' (*Silv.* iii. 5.62) of Statius' step-daughter.

[2] Cf. the discussion on luxury and 'domestica parsimonia' in Tacitus, *Ann.* iii. 52 f., esp. 55.

Imperial freedmen and equestrian status

proprio mihi cognita visu'. If Etruscus' father had been in Rome throughout the reign of Nero and Statius had not seen Etrusca, either Etrusca died very early or Statius arrived in Rome late, not till *c*. 60 at the age of about 20. Etrusca did in fact die before middle age, but apparently not in childbirth (121 f.).[1] The children were born soon after the marriage, about 50 (121, 'nec pignora longe'), but Etrusca did not live to see them grow up. She probably died before AD 60, and her date of birth may be conjectured as *c*. 30. If she did not marry till AD 55 or later, the remark of Statius is more difficult to explain.

Finally, the brother of Etrusca:

> nec vulgare genus; fascis summamque curulem
> frater et Ausonios ensis mandataque fidus
> signa tulit, cum prima truces amentia Dacos
> impulit et magno gens est damnata triumpho.
>
> (115–18)

The clues here are explicit. He was a *consularis*, and commanded legions in the campaign that led to Domitian's triumph over the Dacians in 89 (probably not the indecisive campaign of 85). This brother, being of senatorial rank, has understandably been the starting point for the study of Etruscus and his parents. His *nomen* and *cognomen* are not given, but attempts have been made to identify him from the limited number of possibilities open. But whether or not Gsell[2] is right in identifying him with L. Tettius Iulianus (*cos. suff.* 83), it does not necessarily follow that his sister was called Tettia Etrusca and that Claudius Etruscus must derive his *nomen* from his father. Iulianus could well have been adopted from the Claudian *gens*, perhaps from a family of not very noble origin, into a family where a senatorial career was open to him. The lex Iulia of 18 BC prohibited marriages between freedmen and women of senatorial rank,[3] and although the emperor could grant dispensations from this law, these were no doubt rare and one cannot be assumed for Etruscus' father who was at most an ordinary procurator at the time of his marriage. The law was made more severe in the second century.[4] The one certain point in the nomenclature of the family of Etruscus is that he derived his personal name from his mother; another point hardly less certain is that he did *not* derive his *nomen* from his father.

Etruscus and his brother would have been about 18–20 years old when the Civil War broke out. They rose to equestrian status soon after. But they do

---

[1] Cf. Martial, vii. 40.5.
[2] *Mél. d'Arch. et d'Hist.* 8 (1888), 74 f. and *Domitien*, p. 219. For Tettius Iulianus, see *PIR*[1], T 102; P-W V A, 1107 f. (Tettius, 10); cf. Syme, *JRS* 52 (1962), 96.
[3] *Dig.* xxiii. 2.44.
[4] Cf. Duff, *Freedmen*, pp. 62 f.

The emperor's service

not appear to have taken advantage of the position and influence of their father or their maternal uncle by entering on a regular equestrian career. Rather, under Domitian, on the exile of their father when they were about 35 years of age, they chose a safe retirement and the enjoyment of their father's wealth (147 f.). Statius on the baths of Claudius Etruscus bears witness (*Silvae* i. 5). These were the fruits of their father's professional and social success.

CONCLUSION

The literary sources show clearly that the Familia Caesaris in general was an élite among the slave and freedman classes of Imperial society. But it is also clear that this was not equally true for all its members, nor for all periods. A detailed examination of the voluminous inscriptional material reveals a considerable degree of social differentiation *within* the Familia Caesaris.

In nomenclature, apart from the legal differentiation between *vicarius*, *servus*, *libertus*, etc., the use of status indication, *agnomen* and occupational title are all significant for status and, with some exceptions (e.g. *aquarii*) and some regional variations (e.g. Africa), are rarely used by those of low status. The occupational élite are the professional civil servants of the clerical and senior administrative grades who could rise to auxiliary procuratorships or to sole headships of departments, always distinct from, but within measuring distance of, the equestrian procurators themselves. Those in the clerical-administrative service, whether through background or connections within the Familia Caesaris, patronage, training or ability, began their professional careers early and were distinctly superior to those who spent their lives in sub-clerical or domestic occupations. With the exception of posts of special opportunity or responsibility within the Palace, there was little chance of crossing the occupational dividing line upwards into the administrative service. In terms of location, Rome held the advantage over the provincial centres for most administrative grades, with the exception of those higher freedman careers where movement from one centre to another was more frequent, and among the slave *dispensatores*.

Social differentiation between the Imperial freedmen and slaves and freedmen and slaves outside the Familia Caesaris is confirmed by the marriage patterns that can be broadly established for these two separate categories. There is a striking contrast between the high proportion of wives of freeborn status found in the Familia Caesaris and the low proportion of such wives found in the rest of slave-born society. The marriage pattern and the status of children also, but to a more limited extent, confirm the social differentiation within the main groups and areas into which the Familia Caesaris can be divided. Social mobility occurs at widely different rates for the different

Conclusion

elements of slave-born society in Rome under the early Empire. But easily the most mobile and 'unstable' of these elements and the most important socially as well as professionally are to be found in the Familia Caesaris, especially among the holders of posts involving financial responsibility in the Imperial administration.

APPENDIXES
BIBLIOGRAPHY
INDEX

APPENDIX I

'FAMILIA CAESARIS'

'Familia' appears as early as the Twelve Tables (v. 4-5) in the sense of 'household' or all those persons under the *potestas* of the *pater familias*, including a wife *in manu* and a *filius familias*, as well as slaves.[1] But in a narrower sense it referred specifically to slaves (*famuli*) in relation to their *dominus*. The *potestas* of the *pater familias* over his *servus* was the same as that which he exercised over his *filius familias* or wife *in manu*, and a qualitative distinction between *patria potestas* and *dominica potestas* should not be pressed.[2] A *pater familias* is correctly so called even when he has no *filius* under his *potestas* (*Dig.* l. 16. 195.2). The original household cult of the *Lares* presided over by the *pater familias* came to have a specifically slave connotation by the second century BC, and the slave *vilicus* came to represent the head of the household in the celebration of the cult.[3]

By a natural extension of this meaning 'familia' also included manumitted slaves (*liberti*) in relation to their patron, e.g. *Dig.* l. 16. 195.1 (Ulpian): 'ad personas autem refertur "familiae" significatio ita cum de patrono et liberto loquitur lex'. Cf. *Pauli Sent.* v. 1.3: 'ex officio fisci inter fiscalem familiam'. In inscriptions *liberti* are commonly assumed to be part of a given *familia*, especially in the *collegium familiae* and in *columbaria* for purposes of worship or burial, e.g. VI 479 = XIV 32 = D 6152: 'corpori familiae public(a)e libertorum et servorum'; cf. VI 10107 = D 5212, 10257, 10258, etc. For Imperial freedmen: VI 8456: 'libertis libertabusque utriusque sexus qui ex familia mei erunt'; cf. VI 43-4 = D 1634-5 with VI 298 = D 1636, 8533, 10170 = D 5129.[4] However, the formula 'liberti (libertae) et familia' is also common on sepulchral inscriptions, e.g. VI 5931 = D 7851, 6068, 7397 = D 7852, 9268, 9320, 9321 = D 7853, 9322, 9323, 11998 = D 7858, 20646, 26197 = D 7854, 26258 = D 7856, 35199 = D 7857, 36474, etc.[5] Examples from the Familia Caesaris are: VI 8413 = D 7859: 'libertis et familiae Ti. Ti. Claudiorum Erotis et Felicis Aug. l. a rationibus posterisque eorum...'; *ILAlg.* 3992 (Hippo): 'collegium larum Caesaris et liberti et familia item conductores qui in regione Hipponi[ens]i consistent (!)'.

'Familia Caesaris', in the general collective sense in which it is used throughout this study, does not occur in the ancient sources. Where the phrase does occur without further determination in the inscriptions and literary texts, the reference is to a particular 'familia' or branch of the administration, and has a purely local significance; e.g. III 7380 = D 5682

---

[1] Festus, p. 87: 'famuli origo ab Oscis dependet, apud quos servus *famel* nominabatur, unde et familia vocata'. The derivation from I-E *dhǝ-mo* = 'house' is generally accepted, see Kaser, *Röm. Privatrecht*, I, 44 f. But for a different view: R. Henrion, 'Des Origines du mot *Familia*', *L'Ant. Class.* 10 (1941), 37 f. On 'familia' see *Dig.* l. 16. 195, and *TLL* VI, 238 f.; P-W VI, 1981 f.; *Diz. Epig.* III, 30 f., and especially Bömer, I, 431 f. A detailed semantic study of the work 'familia' is lacking and, as Bömer (p. 439 n. 1) justly points out, it would yield interesting sociological results.
[2] As by Westermann, *Slave Systems*, p. 59, quoting (n. 26) Just. *Inst.* 1.8. pr.: 'aliae [personae] in potestate parentum, aliae in potestate dominorum sunt'; cf. ib. 1. The phrase 'dominica potestas' occurs only once, in *Dig.* xxi. 1. 17. 10 (Ulpian). On *patria potestas*: J. A. Crook, *CQ* 17 (1967), 113-22.   [3] Bömer, I, 406 f.   [4] Ib. 441 f.
[5] Cf. Dessau, *ILS* III, p. 950; *Diz. Epig.* III, 31; and esp. Bömer, I, 433 f.

Appendixes

(Thracian Chersonese; AD 55): 'numini domus Augustae/T. Claudius Faustus Regi[n.] et/Claudia Nais Fausti/balneum populo et familiai/Caesaris n(ostri) d(e) [s(ua)] p(ecunia) f(ecerunt)'.[1] The phrase 'familia Caesaris' occurs in Frontinus, also in reference to a *familia* of slave workers, the *aquarii* inherited by Augustus from Agrippa; Frontinus, *de aq.* 116: 'Familiae sunt duae, altera publica, altera Caesaris', 'Caesaris familiae numerus est quadringentorum sexaginta'; 118: 'Caesaris familia ex fisco accipit commoda' (cf. 98, 117). Lactantius, *de mort. pers.* 14.5: 'Nihil usquam reperiebatur; quippe cum familiam Caesaris nemo torqueret', refers specifically to the slaves of Galerius before he became *Augustus*. References to a particular *familia* of Imperial slaves are not uncommon; e.g.

X 1685 = D 1397: 'L. Bovius L. f. L. n. Fal. Celer...procur(ator) ludi famil(iae) glad(iatoriae) Caesaris Alexandreae ad Aegyptum'.

XIII 1550 (Villefranche de Rovergue): 'Zmaragdo vilico quaest(ori) magistro ex decurion-(um) decr(et)o familiae Ti. Cae[sa]ris quae est in me[tal]lis'.

XII 4449 (Narbo): '[Collegium sa]lutare [f]amilia[e] tabellario[rum] Caesaris n. quae Narbone in domu...'.

X 1750 = D 7368 (Puteoli): 'Mystis Caesaris vilic. et familia quae sub eo est'.

VIII 22670a (Leptis Magna): 'C[e]ler proc. lib. [e]t [f]amilia sp[l]endidissim. vectig. IIII P. A.'

Cf. also *familia castrensis*   VI 8532 = D 1747, 8533, 30911, 33469 = D 9028; VIII 2702 = 18250 = *AE* 1914, 38 (Lambaesis), 5234.
familia monetalis   VI 239 = D 1633, 298 = D 1636, 8456.
familia XX libertatis   V 3351 = D 1870.
familia gladiatoria   V 8659 = D 1412; VI 10170 = D 5129; X 1685 = D 1397 (above); cf. VI 632 = D 5084a.
familia l(udi) m(agni)   VI 10168 = D 5126.

Compare the use of the term *familia publica* for particular groups of public or municipal slaves: Frontinus, *de aq.* 116, 117 (above); *Dig.* l. 15. 1 (Paulus); VI 2342 = D 1964; XIV 32 = VI 479 = D 6152 (Ostia), XIV 255 = D 6153 (Ostia); IX 32 (Brundisium); X 4856 (Venafrum); XI 4391 (Ameria); II 2229 (Corduba), etc.[2]

'Familia Caesaris' is preferred to, e.g., 'Familia Principis', 'Familia domus Augustae', etc.; the determinative 'Caesaris' is particularly associated with slavery in the nomenclature of the Imperial household (cf. 'Caesaris servus' but 'Augusti libertus'), and together with 'familia' stresses the slave origin of the individuals under discussion. 'Familia imperatoria' does not occur in the inscriptions, and in the literary sources is quite exceptional; it is found only in SHA, *Aelius* 3.7 and 7.3, and there has the sense of *domus Augusta*, the Imperial family itself. Compare, for this latter use of *familia*, Suetonius, *Aug.* 4.1: 'Balbus, paterna stirpe Aricinus, multis in familia senatoriis imaginibus'. Throughout this study I have regularly used such phrases as 'Imperial slaves', 'Imperial freedmen' as alternatives to 'Familia Caesaris', in the sense of the slaves and freedmen of the emperor.

[1] Cf. Boulvert, *EAI*, p. 79. It is difficult to accept Bömer's suggestion (I, 439 n. 1) that the phrase 'familia Caesaris' here refers to the Imperial family itself (*'familia Caesaris* gleichbedeutend mit *domus Augusta*'). The phrase 'domus Augusta' itself already appears in the dedication of the inscription. If 'populo' (l. 4) refers to the local *populus Coelanus* (as Dessau, note 1, ad loc.; cf. Boulvert, loc. cit.), 'familiai Caesaris' also should have a local signification (cf. its position after 'populo') and refer to the *familia* of slaves inherited as part of the estate of Agrippa by Augustus and forming part of the *res privata* of the emperor (Dio, liv. 29).   [2] Bömer, I, 433 f.

APPENDIX II

INSCRIPTIONS OF IMPERIAL FREEDMEN AND SLAVES DATED TO A PARTICULAR YEAR OR REIGN

Period	A Year	B *Fistula*	C Dedication	D Imp. Name	E Equestrian	Total
Augustus	21	—	1	1	—	23
Tiberius	6	—	—	122	—	128
Gaius	4	—	1	18	—	23
Claudius	5	—	2	38	—	45
Nero	6	1	1	39	1	48
Galba	—	—	—	1	—	1
Vespasian	7	2	1	6	—	16
Titus	2	—	—	11	—	13
Domitian	4	14	2	17	—	37
Nerva	1	—	1	—	—	2
Trajan	17	6	12	8	1	44
Hadrian	15	3	8	3	4	33
Antoninus Pius	15	6	9	6	2	38
M. Aurelius (161–80)	11	3	8	1	4	27
Commodus	9	2	5	2	7	25
Pertinax	—	—	1	—	—	1
Septimius Severus	21	3	18	2	9	53
Caracalla	4	2	11	2	—	19
Caracalla/Elagabalus	3	4	4	—	1	12
Severus Alexander	4	3	4	1	—	12
Maximinus–Philip (235–49)	4	—	1	1	1	7
Total	159	49	90	279	30	607

The same inscription is listed only once under a given reign, although it is possible to date several under more than one heading. Categories A, B, C, D and E are listed in that order of precedence. Some miscellaneous items are included, with brief annotations where they occur. As more than one freedman and/or slave often appear in a single inscription, the combined total of individual freedmen and slaves is larger than the total number of inscriptions. For complete lists of freedmen and slaves of non-reigning members of the Imperial family (not including those of the *Augustae*, however), see Chantraine, pp. 35–41.

AUGUSTUS

A: XI 3200 = D 89; *EE* VIII 316 = D 6387; XIV 2302 = D 7462; VI 10395; *BGU* 1118, 1152, 1177, 1166, 1129, 1171, 1137 = *Chrest.* 112, 1110, 1175, 1130; *P. Oxy.* 743; VI 8738 = D 7866, 10377, 34013 = D 7868, 33768; IX 1456 = D 3806; VI 9050 = D 1787.

Appendixes

B: —
C: XI 3083 = D 5373.
D: Unpublished, Aphrodisias, Caria (see above, p. 22 n. 3).
E: —

TIBERIUS

A: *P. Lond.* II 256 = *Chrest.* 443; VI 34005, 1963 = 5180 = D 1948, 29681; XI 3805 = D 6579; VI 244 = D 7358.
B: —
C: —

D: *Freedmen:* VI 4312 = D 1733, 8409, 10383, 10449 = D 7909, 12652 = *IG* XIV 1892, 17900, 20497, 33130; *AE* 1923, 72 (cf. Chantraine, p. 18 n. 13); 1930, 66.

Slaves: VI 3935, 3951, 3972, 4014, 4036, 4278, 4339, 4341 = D 1717, 4351 = D 1802, 4353, 4354, 4398, 4409, 4472, 4733-4, 4886 = D 5225, 4950, 5189 = D 1588, 5193 = D 1757, 5197 = D 1514, 5200, 5358 = D 1772, 5381, 5540 = D 1789, 5746 = D 1817, 6040, 6088, 6152, 8655a = XIV 4120.3 = XV 7142 = D 1702, 8849, 8880, 8909, cf. p. 3463, 8928 = D 2821, 8956a, 8967, 9061a, 10368 = 34009, 12697, 13628, 14828, 14843, 17869, 19623, 21203, 22396, 33099, 33104, 33121, 33777, 33788 = D 1821, 33799; *Bull. Com.* 1941, p. 187, No. 132; XIV 2420 = XI 2916; V 1067, 1304, 6884 = D 4850b = *I. It.* XI 1.83; X 1735 (?); XIII 1550, 1820 = D 1639.

Tiberius and Livia

Freedmen: VI 4173, 4352, 4470, 5223, 5248, 8656, 8913, 14843, 19857, 26674; X 3358 = D 2818.

Slaves: VI 4358, 4776, 5181 = D 1676, 5215, 5226, 5316, 5745 = D 5001, 8989 = 24079 = D 1827 (cf. Chantraine, p. 218 n. 8), 9066, 33275, 37661.

Divus Augustus

Freedmen: VI 5202 = D 1778, 5203, 5254, 5289, 5747 = D 1743, 5870 = 33081, 8012 = D 8436, 8893, 8980, 10410, 11377, 11381, 12595, 16586, 19060, 19926 = Gordon, *Alb.* I p. 59, No. 50; 24223, 29069, 35612, 38419b; Gordon, *Alb.* I p. 60, No. 51; XIV 3539 = *I. It.* IV 1.41; V 236 = *I. It.* X 1.53; 1251, 1319; *EE* VIII p. 164, No. 671.

Slaves: VI 8887 = 14399 = 33754.

Freedmen/Slaves: VI 8764, 21748, cf. 30556.146, 26608 (?).

E: —

GAIUS

A: X 6638 = I² pp. 247 f. No. xvii = *I. It.* XIII I pp. 320 f. No. 31; *AE* 1935, 47 (cf. Chantraine, p. 15 n. 4); VI 9005 = D 1795, 20141.
B: —
C: V 6641 = D 191.
D: *Freedmen:* VI 19785.

Slaves: VI 3991, 3996, 4094, 4119, 4331, 4357, 5188 = D 1589, 5196 (?), 5822, 8823, 9061, 17177, 20706a, 21162, 29569 (?), 33767; XIV 2519.

E: —

CLAUDIUS

A: X 6638c; VI 10399 = XI 3806; *AE* 1953, 24 = Gordon, *Alb.* I p. 90, No. 90; *IGR* I 1262 = *SEG* VIII 794; X 769 = XVI 1 = D 1986.

Inscriptions dated to a particular year or reign

B: —
c: *IGR* III 578 = *TAM* II 178; *IGR* III 579 = *TAM* II 184.
D: *Freedmen:* VI 15455; *NS* 1922, p. 413, No. 25; V 2931.
   Slaves: VI 64 = D 3502, 138 = D 3969, 3964, 4226 = D 1620, 4226a, 4236, 5011, 5239, 8662 = D 1631, 8665, 8708 = D 5000, 8719, 8740, 8810 = D 1724, 8822 = D 1655, 8839, 8843, 10090, 12167, 15884, 16707, 37754a; XIV 489, 1830, 3920; III 2097, 4808; V 2386, 6638; VIII 5384 = 17500 = *ILAlg.* I 323; IX 321; X 696, 7536; XI 3199 = D 3481, 7745.
E: —

NERO

A: III 7380 = D 5682; X 1549; Bruzza Nos. 138–9; *EE* VIII 335–7 = D 5798; Bruzza Nos. 140, 191, Add: *AE* 1968, 35 = *Epigr.* 29 (1967), p. 93.
B: XV 7271.
C: VI 927 = D 236.
D: *Freedmen:* VI 194 = XIV 2861; 8783 = D 1735, 14647 = 34085, 37752; *AE* 1946, 99; XIV 2780, 3644 = D 1942 = *I. It.* IV 1.179; X 6324 = D 1734; XI 4360.
   Slaves: VI 8712, 8864, 8889, 22977; *AE* 1959, 299, 300; XIV 2832 = D 1760; III 7047 = *IGR* IV 710 = *MAMA* IV 53; 12131 = *TAM* II 486; VIII 5383.
   Corporis Custodes: VI 8802 = D 1729, 8803 = D 1730, 8806 = D 1727, 8808 = D 1728, 37754; *NS* 1950, p. 87, p. 88 (three), p. 89; IX 4977 = D 6558.

Divus Claudius
   Freedmen: VI 1921, 4305 = D 1732, 8554 = D 1765, 8636 = D 1682, 9060 = D 1641, 15314, 32775 = 33131 = D 2816, 34909; X 527 = D 1671.
E: VI 8470 = D 1535, cf. VI 143 = D 3896a.

GALBA

D: *Slave:* VI 14356.

VESPASIAN

A: VI 10350; X 4734 = D 3868; V 7239; Bruzza Nos. 147, 151, 153–4; *AE* 1905, 188 = *IG* V I 1431, 40 f.
B: *AE* 1951, 198 = *NS* 1949, 71; *AE* 1954, 61.
C: *IGR* IV 228 (?).
D: *Slaves:* VI 301, cf. 30731, 346, 15551 = D 7933, 28637a; *AE* 1923, 79 = *NS* 1923, p. 32; XI 1315.
E: —

TITUS

A: *AE* 1930, 86; Bruzza No. 159.
B: —
C: —
D: *Slaves:* VI 276, 8780, 8819 = D 1656, 8867, 8971, cf. 33755, 14428, 15616; XIV 50; *ILTun.* 461.

Divus Vespasianus
   Freedmen: VI 1887 = D 1944, 1962 = D 1943.
E: —

Appendixes

DOMITIAN

A: X 6640 = D 3338; Bruzza No. 168; *IGR* I 781; Bruzza Nos. 198–9.

B: XV 7279 = D 8679, 7280, 7283, 7284, 7285, 7286, 7287, 7288, 7289, 7791, 7818 = XIV 2657 = D 8681, XV 7819 = XIV 2304 = D 8680; Bruzza Nos. 277, 278 = D 8713.

C: VI 31295a; III 14192.10 = *IGR* IV 847 = *MAMA* VI 2.

D: *Freedmen:* VI 8768. Add: *AE* 1968, 489 = *JÖAI* 47 (1964–5), col. 25–8.

Slaves: VI 5405, 8410, 8558, 8726 = D 7733a, 8831 = D 1657, 8892, 8921 = D 1804, 9052 = D 1703, 15368, 18290 = 34114, 23454, 33470 = D 9033, 34246; *AE* 1959, 42; VIII 5415; *IGR* IV 1297.

E: —

NERVA

A: II 956 = D 276.

C: III 7146.

TRAJAN

A: VI 32429; *IGR* IV 690; VI 2184 = 32445 = D 4971; Bruzza Nos. 200–1; VI 8826 = D 7276; III 14195.2 = D 4046; VIII 14560; VI 630 = D 1699 = D 3541; Bruzza Nos. 205, 207, 209; VI 8821; *IGR* IV 1738; VI 542; Bruzza No. 294; VI 43 = D 1634, 44 = D 1635, cf. VI 791.

B: XV 440, 7295, 7296–7, cf. *AE* 1940, 40; 7893–4; XI 3548a–b = XV 7770–1; XI 4415, cf. XV 7279.

C: VI 252 = D 1824, 634 = 30804 = D 1540a, 780, 8844; XIV 2161 (Plotina); III 3, cf. p. 967 = D 4395, 8684; VIII 25902. i. 5 = *ILAlg.* I 440; X 106 = D 4039 (Marciana); XI 3614 = D 5918a; *SEG* XI 1124; *IGR* IV 333 = *AE* 1933, 266.

D: *Slaves:* VI 8865, 9090, 18456, 26515, 31099, 36911; X 3346 = D 2906; *IRT* 302 = *AE* 1926, 164.

E: III 7130, cf. *AE* 1966, p. 134.

HADRIAN

A: *SEG* XIII 601 = *IGR* I 1255 = *OGI* II 678; VI 9100 = D 1850; XV 464–5, 810; *P. Tebt.* II 296 = *Chrest.* 79; XIV 51; VI 4228, 8744, 30901 = D 1622, 1884 = D 1792; Bruzza No. 4 = D 8718; XV 461; VI 975 = D 6073; Bruzza Nos. 258–9 = D 8716a–b; *IGR* III 1056 = *OGI* II 629.90.

B: XV 7738 = XIV 1976; XIV 5309.11; XV 7896 = XIV 3698.

C: VI 978; *AE* 1915, 9 = D 3563; II 2780; III 6998 = D 7196; *SEG* I 441, cf. IV 417; IV 531 = *AE* 1927, 97; 1922, 18 = *ILAlg.* I 3991; 1942/3, 35 (iussu Hadriani).

D: VI 619; *SEG* II 529 = *AE* 1924, 103.

Divus Traianus

Slave: VI 10194 = D 5088.

E: III 431 = 7116 = 13674 = D 1449; LBW II 1076 = D 8849; VIII 25943. iv. 5–6; *AE* 1922, 19 = *ILAlg.* I 3992.

ANTONINUS PIUS

A: XIV 2795 (domus Domitiae Augustae); VIII 14551, 14571–7; X 6000; VI 658 (?); VIII 2339; VI 644 = D 3537; 10235 = D 8364; XV 466–70; XIV 250 = D 6174; VI 10234 = D

Inscriptions dated to a particular year or reign

7213, 2120 = D 8380 (Arriae Fadillae lib.); 376 = D 3670; *IGR* III 1103 = *OGI* 707 = D 8846; *P. Ross. Georg.* II 26.

B: XV 7314 = D 8685; 7740 = XIV 2008a = *IPO* B 381 = D 8686; 7743 = XIV 1980 = 5309. 19.

Brick-stamps: XV 225 = *IPO* A 352.3 (Aurel. Caes. n.); 622, cf. 620-1, 2515 (Aurel. Caes. et Faustinae Aug.).

C: VI 3756 = 31317 = D 5160 (Diva Faustina); *AE* 1956, 19 (Diva Faustina); XIV 100 = *IPO* B 317; II 4089; III 6070a = 7123 = D 327 (Matidia II); *MAMA* IV 55; X 1562 = D 344; 4746-7 (Matidia II); *AE* 1957, 231 = *IRT Supp.* 4 (Aurel. Caes.).

D: VI 8440 = *IGR* I 1113 = D 1529; 33784 = D 9034 (Rufina n. et T. Aug., cf. Chantraine, p. 23 n. 32); 166 = D 3862 (M. Aurel. Caes.); 8941 (Diva Faustina); 10909 = XIV 3721 (Divus Hadrianus); VIII 21122 (Aelii Augusti).

E: VIII 7039 = *ILAlg.* II 665 = D 1437; XIII 1808 = D 1454.

M. AURELIUS (161-80)

A: *BGU* 102.1; II 2552 = *AE* 1910, 3 = D 9125; VI 552 = D 3861; *AE* 1967, 444; II 2556 = *AE* 1910, 6 = D 9129; 2553 = *AE* 1910, 4 = D 9127; X 6706 = D 8217; VI 455, 1013, cf. p. 3777; 631 = D 5084; XIV 2856 = D 376.

B: XV 7741 = XIV 1979, 7742, 7823 = XIV 2307.

C: VI 1586 (exornatus ab Imp. Antonino et Vero Aug.), 31053 = D 3272; II 2555 = D 9128; *EE* VIII 307-8; VIII 587 = D 5567, 10827 = 17050 = *ILAlg.* I 863; 16525, cf. p. 2731 = *ILAlg.* I 3009; *IGR* IV 679.

D: VI 8972 = D 1836 (Divus Pius).

E: VI 1598 = D 1740; IX 2438; *AE* 1956, 123 = *Libyca* 3 (1955), p. 123 f.; III 6574 = 7126 = D 1344.

COMMODUS

A: *AE* 1967, 230; III 752 = 7435 = D 1856; VI 8420; 723 = D 4203; II 2554 = *AE* 1910, 5 = D 9126; *MAMA* I 23; VI 8775 = D 1745; XIV 2113 = D 5193; *AE* 1910, 2.

B: XV 7744, 7745.

C: VI 790 = D 391; XIV 109; *EE* VIII 369 = D 5186 (ex indulgentia Commodi); III 349, cf. p. 1265 = *MAMA* V 197, 8256.

D: XI 4427; VI 8577 = D 1507 (Divus Marcus).

E: VI 623 = D 5084a; III 8042; VIII 10570. iv. 10; *AE* 1965, 1-2; VI 8541 = D 1573 (prima et secunda expeditio Germ. fel.); V 2155 = D 1574 (exped. fel. II et III Germ.).

PERTINAX

C: XIII 4323 = D 410.

SEPTIMIUS SEVERUS

A: VI 1585b = D 5920; 724 = D 4204; *AE* 1922, 102; *Chrest.* 81; VI 1052; V 27 = *I. It.* X 1.41; VI 2270 = D 4331; XIV 4254 = D 5191; 4322 = *AE* 1921, 78; *BGU* 156 = *Chrest.* 175; VI 218 = D 2107; 716; XIV 4570 = *AE* 1922, 93; *P. Oxy.* 735; Bruzza No. 279 = D 8720; *AE* 1952, 192; III 4035 = D 1499; *IGR* IV 889; III 8185; VI 10233; *AE* 1903, 287, cf. 1933, 160.

B: XV 7327, 7746 = XIV 1981 = D 8688a; *AE* 1954, 172.

C: VI 180 = D 3703, 410, cf. 30760 = D 1707, 738, 1038 = 30955 (?); *AE* 1926, 116; XIV 2977 = D 5194; *AE* 1914, 217; III 427 = D 430, 978 (?), 4020, cf. p. 1746, 15184.4; *AE*

Appendixes

1933, 160; 1938, 154 (?); 1944, 100 = 1959, 310; VIII 26416, 27550; *AE* 1932, 15 = *ILTun.* 1534; VI 1020 = D 387 (Vibia Aurelia Sabina Marci Aug. f.).
D: VI 19365; *AE* 1930, 152 (Plautia Divi Veri soror).
E: II 1085 = D 1406; III 249 = 6753 = D 1396, 251 = D 1373, 4024, 6075 = D 1366, 6575 = 7127 = D 1421; *IGR* III 168; VIII 7053 = *ILAlg.* II 668 = D 1438; X 7584 = D 1359.

CARACALLA

A: *AE* 1959, 308; III 1697 = 8243; VI 8498 = D 1738; V 5090 = D 1561.
B: XV 7747 = XIV 1982 = D 8688b; *AE* 1954, 64.
C: VI 619, 1071+36883, 36935; Gordon, *Alb.* III p. 27, No. 269; III 1565, 3269, 3327 = 10301; *AE* 1903, 265; 1933, 282 (Iulia Domna); V 7643; *AE* 1934, 234.
D: *AE* 1953, 188 = *IRT* 606; VIII 10630 = *ILAlg.* I 3132 (?).
E: —

CARACALLA/ELAGABALUS

A: *IGR* IV 891; VI 2106, 1529 = 31671.
B: XV 7321, 7322, 7330; XIV 5309.21 = *AE* 1913, 82.
C: VII 62; VIII 22670a; *MAMA* VII 107; *AE* 1954, 28 (?).
D: —
E: VIII 11175.

SEVERUS ALEXANDER

A: XIV 125 = *IPO* B 324 = D 2223; XIV 3553 = *I. It.* IV 1.57; *AE* 1903, 286; III 8112, cf. 12656.
B: XV 7332, 7336 (Iulia Mamaea); XIV 5309.22.
C: III 7955, 13722 = 14207.41 = D 9274; *AE* 1933, 281; *MAMA* I 24 (Iulia Mamaea).
D: III 536 = D 1575.
E: —

MAXIMINUS–PHILIP (235–49)

A: *P. Oxy.* 1114; VI 816 = D 1928; III 4800 = D 4198; V 5090 = D 1561 (?).
B: —
C: *I. It.* X 2.216.
D: *IGR* I 623 = D 8851.
E: *AE* 1908, 30.

APPENDIX III

WIVES OF IMPERIAL FREEDMEN AND SLAVES

The following lists are arranged in chronological order where possible, firstly in terms of the status and name of the husband (freedmen: §§ 1–12; slaves: §§ 13–14); and secondly in order of the wives' *nomina*, where available, within each section. Wives of *vicarii*, and of slaves and freedmen of Imperial freedmen have not been included. For these, see Part III, pp. 204, 210 Also excluded are inscriptions of patron and freedwoman, where the husband–wife relationship is not specified. On the other hand cases have been included where the name of a woman appears on the same inscription with an Imperial freedman or slave and where the husband–wife relationship, though not specified, can reasonably be inferred. Doubtful cases are specially indicated.

1. *Iulius Aug. l.* =
   Iulia: VI 1963 = 5180 = D 1948, 4222–3 = D 4995, 4770, 4777, 5202 = D 1778, 5203, 5254, 5263, 8912 (?), 9044 = D 7355, 19785, 19870, 19919, 20335, 20497, 20666, 35594, 38489, 38494; II 4185 (?); *AE* 1923, 72; 1951, 156.
   Claudia: VI 8927 = D 2823, 37752.
   Non-Imperial: VI 4230, 5436, 6520, 8409, 16663, 19872, 24223, 32775 = 33131 = D 2816; V 3404; X 3358 = D 2818.
   Serva: VI 1957.

2. *Claudius Aug. l.* =
   Iulia: VI 1921, 5318, 8506–7, 8538, 8782, 9016, 14950, 15131, 15194, 20389, 32468; XIV 3743; *IPO* A 60.
   Claudia: VI 4741 (?), 8411 = D 1473, 8470 = D 1535, 8554 = D 1765, 8600, 8685, 8907 = D 1846, 9003 = D 1796, 15027 (?), 15207, 15228, 15302 (?), 15598, 15648, 16810, 33194 = D 7297, 34888, 37745, 37900 = 34886; *AE* 1949, 191 = 1946, 213; III 456 = *IGR* IV 957; X 1971 = D 8193, 6144, 6640 = D 3338; XIII 2969.
   Sulpicia: XI 3612 = D 1567.
   Flavia: VI 1859–60, 10089 = D 1766, 15110, 15235.
   Ulpia: VI 8898.
   Non-Imperial: VI 5654, 6189, 8426 = D 1642, 8450a, 8451, 8583 = D 1578, 8601–2, 8603 = D 1670, 8811, 8872, 9183 = D 7501, 10223 = D 6071, 11824, 12776–7, 14897, 14913, 14945, 14978, 15002, 15082, 15135, 15153, 15180, 15243, 15862, 22423, 23398, 25028, 28269, 29012, 29045, 34401; XIV 815, 3647 = D 4979; VIII 21008; X 527 = D 1671, 582, 1739 = D 1587; XI 1371, 3885 = D 1643.
   Serva: VI 8443 = D 1546, 8711 = D 7803, 15015; XIV 2780 (?).

3. *Sulpicius Aug. lib.* =
   Sulpicia: VI 27008.
   Non-Imperial: VI 8707 = D 4421, 26955.

Appendixes

4. *Flavius Aug. lib.* =
Iulia: VI 8431, 8610, 8768, 9051, 17992, 20548; V 987; VIII 12639.
Claudia: VI 8709 = D 4996, 15605, 15634, 38366 = XI 3835, 38367 (?); *IPO* A 104; III 2093 = 2325; V 7209.
Flavia: VI 5764, 6191, 8438, 8449 = D 1552, 8543, 8604 = D 1519, 8628 = D 1679, 8902, 8920, 8978 = D 1834, 10172 = D 5152, 12565 (?), 17645 (?), 18048, 18185, 18212, 18235–7, 18238, 18254, 18294, 18314, 18366, 18407, 18455; XIV 2840 = D 1571, 4482–3 = *IPO* B 67–8; X 4142; XI 3932 = D 5770, 4462.
Ulpia: VI 8970 = D 1831; *EE* VII 1263 = D 1518.
Aelia: VI 8467, 18094.
Non-Imperial: VI 2249 = D 4407, 8504 = D 1845, 8549 = D 1761, 8611, 8623, 8673, 8676, 8695 = D 1688, 8704 = D 4994, 8935, 9035, 9035a, 9590 = D 9434, 10162, 10238 = D 8353, 10518, 12623, 18028, 18057, 18083, 18095, 18111, 18122, 18166, 18211, 18242, 18305–6, 29603, 33731 = X 1743 = D 1608, VI 35272 (?), 37993; XIV 2608 = D 1579; *IPO* A 110, 196; III 2483, 14195.2 = D 4046; IX 4651; X 6609; XI 3886.
Serva: VI 8870, 22876; LBW 167.

5. *Cocceius Aug. lib.* =
Cocceia: VI 8546 = D 1763, 15929, 15936.
Aelia: X 3356.
Non-Imperial: VI 8681 = D 1627.

6. *Ulpius Aug. lib.* =
Iulia: VI 4228, 29132, 29147, 29234.
Claudia: VI 8463, 8607, 8794, 15406, 15592–4 = D 8063a–c, 29223; XI 3275.
Sulpicia: VI 8701 = D 1693.
Flavia: VI 8466 = D 1606, 8479 = D 1602, 8542, 8627, 10164 = D 5153, 18408 = 35306, 29191, 29219, 29225, 35310 (bis); XI 3206.
Cocceia: VI 8502, 15893, 29127.
Ulpia: VI 8456, 8533, 8553 = D 1764, 8626, 8640 = D 1630, 8642, 8737, 8770 = 33749 = D 1749, 8772, 8891 (?), 17398, 29138, 29154, 29174, 29203, 29222, 29272, 29289, 29294 (?), 29304, 29368, 29377, 29378, 33764 = D 1815, 36186, 37542, 37958, 39063; *AE* 1946, 140; II 3235 = D 1555; X 1729.
Aelia: VI 10992.
Non-Imperial: VI 3880 = 32464, 5303, 5737, 8490, 8550 = 27908 = D 1756, 10234 = D 7213, 12842, 13517–18, 23716, 26040, 28700, 29124, 29128, 29155, 29159, 29169, 29175, 29194, 29224, 29239, 29242, 29244, 29736–7, 33741, 35898, 38351; *AE* 1948, 57; XIV 5175 = *IPO* A 252; III 1312 = D 1593; X 2959; XI 1434 = D 1667; XIII 2308.
Serva: VI 8922, 9069, 29247.

7. *P. Aelius Aug. lib.* =
Iulia: VI 4857, 20579; II 486 = D 1492, 2646.
Claudia: VI 15317, 15413, 15612; *AE* 1954, 86.
Flavia: VI 10667 = XIV 3433, 10755, 12504 (?), 37744; III 14606.
Ulpia: VI 8432 = D 1526, 9056, 10626, 10752, 10958 = D 8065, 27348 (?), 29117 (?), 29358; XI 1222 = D 1554.
Aelia: VI 8448, 8476 = D 1544, 8857, 8930, 8997, 10085 = D 1770, 10711, 10730, 10740a, 10775, 10835, 10849, 10876; *AE* 1926, 48; *NS* 1928, p. 352; *Arch. Class.* 1953, p. 264 n. 2; XIV 524, 4767 = *IPO* A 4; X 7264; *AE* 1922, 132; 1940, 194.

Wives of Imperial freedmen and slaves

Non-Imperial: VI 8648, 9041, 10431, 10624, 10625, 10660, 10666, 10682 = D 8227, 10712 = XIV 4019, 10748, 10761, 10935, 11814, 17003, 23364, 27807, 34226, 37925; *AE* 1926, 48 (?); *Bull. Com.* 1940, p. 183 n. 18; III 8263; V 565; VIII 12667, 12951; *AE* 1908, 250.
Serva: VI 8981; X 7614; *AE* 1937, 111.

8. *T. Aelius Aug. lib.* =
Iulia: VI 20412, 20505; XIV 3720.
Claudia: VI 10779; XIV 508 = *IPO* A 1.
Sulpicia: VI 5554 = D 1547.
Flavia: VI 8569, 8878 = D 1685, 10648, 18385 = 34115, 18457 (L. Aelius Aug. lib.); XIV 3637.
Ulpia: VI 29396; XIV 1796 = *IPO* B 160.
Aelia: VI 5169, 5310, 7458 = D 1798, 8750, 8908 = D 7810, 8914 = D 1807, 10676, 10701 = D 8274, 10706, 10791 = D 8228, 10900, 10931, 12402, 33773, 34244; *AE* 1945, 134; XIV 3717; III 14179 = *IGR* III 675.
Aurelia: VI 10728, 13219 (T. Aurelius Aug. lib.), 13339; *AE* 1953, 64 (T. Aurelius Aug. lib.).
Non-Imperial: VI 5 (T. Aurelius Aug. lib.), 8429–30 = D 1647, 8518, 8731 = D 1816, 8774, 8778 (L. Aelius Aug. lib.), 9042, 10630, 10762 (L. Aelius Aug. lib.), 13025, 22987, 27233, 33785–6, 34227a; XIV 505, 3718; III 287 = 6776; XIII 2068.
Serva: VI 22789; XII 2254.

9. *Aelius Aug. lib.* =
Iulia: VI 8751.
Claudia: AE 1923, 76.
Flavia: VI 10934.
Aelia: VI 5308, 9008, 10620 = 10853, 10707a, 10718.
Aurelia: VI 13394.
Non-Imperial: III 14689; X 6614; XIII 2038; *AE* 1929, 24.
Serva: VI 9045.

10. *Aurelius Aug. lib.* =
Iulia: VI 13137, 13142.
Claudia: VI 8445 = D 1553, 8698, 15421, 34625; XIV 3967.
Sulpicia: XIV 3006.
Flavia: VI 13043, 13200, 34637; V 7882.
Cocceia: VI 9057.
Ulpia: VI 5339, 13010, 13063, 15860 = D 8304, 23481 = 29322, 37751; XII 2397; *IGR* III 18; *AE* 1928, 199.
Aelia: VI 8650 (?), 10823, 10840, 10860 = 34032, 13104; *AE* 1956, 199; III 348 = *IGR* IV 676; X 563 (Maestria Aelia); 6571; *AE* 1957, 182; Ramsay, *RP* 137.
Aurelia: VI 8403, 8505, 8735, 8931, 9029, 9071, 10860 = 34032 (?), 12994, 13040, 13225, 13293, 13312, 13337–8, 13369, 33136; *AE* 1946, 141; *AE* 1957, 128; XIV 642 (?), 660; X 6571 (Aelia Aurelia); *AE* 1940, 181 = *MAMA* VI 18; *JHS* 1914, p. 28 n. 37.
Incerta: VI 12989.
Non-Imperial: VI 1598 = D 1740, 5825, 8480 = D 1601, 8615, 8859–62, 8932, 9087 (?), 10209 = D 5159, 12405, 12988, 13004, 13025, 13029, 13060, 13070, 13071, 13085, 13086, 13151, 13159–60, 13181, 13193 = D 8326, 13215, 13226, 15981, 17920, 22559, 23555,

Appendixes

24040, 26477, 26598, 28283, 28875 = D 8024; *AE* 1937, 159; 1949, 68; XIV 3031; *Ant. Class.* 1955, p. 74 n. 26; II 6085 = D 1560; X 563, 2140, 4036; XI 7735; XII 2227, 4254; XIII 1800, 1816, 2189, 2238, 3688; *Bull. Inst. Arch.* 1884, p. 12 = D 1496.

Serva: VI 8582 = D 1576, 8745, 13089, 13256, 37770; II 4182; VIII 10531 = 13229.

11. *Septimius Aug. lib.* =
Ulpia: VI 26257.
Aurelia: Bull. Com. 1928, p. 314 n. 2.
Septimia: VI 8825b = 26277.
Non-Imperial: VI 2271 = D 4270, 9028; *AE* 1930, 152; 1940, 177; XIV 1597; *EE* IX 287.

12. *Aug. lib. (with cognomen only)* =
Iulia: VI 8734 = D 1814, 9016, 17345, 20373, 20388, 20542, 20679, 20711, 22937; X 607, 6668 = D 1549, 6785; XI 7542 (?).
Claudia: VI 778, 8567, 8591 = D 1564, 15357, 15424, 15574, 15642, 15647, 19069, 33229; III 12298 = 14203.31.
Flavia: VI 8474 = 33727 = D 1541, 8487 = D 1609, 8525, 8537, 8614 = D 1674, 8732 = D 1811, 11245, 18314, 18358, 18365, 18420, 18435, 33782-3, 36253, 38377; *AE* 1952, 31; XIV 2262 = D 1645, 2469; V 41 = D 1644; X 6092 = D 1500.
Ulpia: VI 7010, 10086 = D 1769, 16809, 23928, 26624, 29299, 29301, 29326; XIV 3909 = D 3892; III 1297 = D 1594, cf. 1313, 6107 = D 1692; VIII 21010; X 5046 = D 3149.
Aelia: VI 327, 8977, 10253, 10874, 10925, 10940, 10976, 10994, 19386, 21698a, 29658; *AE* 1949, 70; XIV 2527; *IPO* A 279; *AE* 1927, 136; II 487 = D 1548; VIII 8996, 12939; *ILTun.* 843 (?); X 1737, 7544; XII 4548; XIII 236 = 5244 = D 1562.
Aurelia: VI 574 = 30798 = D 4380, 5738, 8508 = D 1646, 13305, 17211, 30557.20; *Epigr.* V/VI (1943/44), no. 87; XIV 3440, 3640; III 1286, 1469, 2239 = 6372, 4035 = D 1499; VIII 3290 = *AE* 1951, 86; IX 5860 = D 8234; XIII 1817 = D 1563; *IGR* IV 245, 1651.
Septimia: VI 10246.
Incerta: VI 8477 = D 1543, 25444; III 2558.
Non-Imperial: VI 4025, 4037, 5750, 7506, 8420, 8499-500 = D 1489-90, 8503, 8530, 8573, 8608 = D 1485, 8694 = D 1687, 8715, 8729 = D 1813, 8769, 8855, 8862, 8937 = XIV 4010, 8998 = D 1801, 9018, 9081, 10087, 10170 = D 5129, 10278, 10453 = 14054, 10516, 11162, 11241, 11488, 11552, 11855, 12655, 14536, 14638, 16172, 16397, 16457, 16993 (cf. 11855), 17173, 17584, 17632, 17901, 18824, 19128 = D 8451, 19204, 19323, 19438, 19635, 21487, 21593, 22487, 22536, 23715, 24806, 24956, 25708, 26670, 26845, 27755, 28176, 28763, 33222, 33791, 33796, 34654, 34685, 35630, 37743, 37767, 38052; *AE* 1903, 245; 1913, 194; 1927, 104; 1931, 3; 1939, 149; *Bull. Com.* 1940, p. 196 n. 64; XIV 774 (?), 2860 = D 3687, 2938, 3818, 3968; II 4181; III 255, 258, 563 = 12289 (cf. VI 8486 = D 1600), 2184a, 4987, 14536 = *AE* 1902, 35; 1903, 245; V 157, 5921; VIII 12907; *ILAlg.* I 89; *IRT* 656 = *AE* 1931, 3; IX 1753; X 1736, 2799, 2810, 2857, 4120, 4734 = D 3868, 6081 = D 1483, 6371, 7144, 7951, 8293; XI 466, 3553; XII 720; *AE* 1930, 128 = *ILGall.* 151; *AE* 1959, 303.
Serva: VI 297 = D 1767, 4391, 7973, 9031, 9072, 11373; *AE* 1930, 95; XIV 3780 (?); VIII 19174 = D 8102, 24703; X 695, 1917.

13. *Caesaris servus* (Rome) =
Iulia: VI 4119, 4776, 5193 = D 1757, 5200, 5359, 5872 = 876*, 5873, 6639, 8497 = D 1614, 8575 = D 1502, 8596, 8654 = D 1773, 8669 = D 1617, 8687, 8703, 8785, 8790, 8839,

310

Wives of Imperial freedmen and slaves
8894, 11288, 13609, 13628 (?), 14843, 19745, 20433, 20551, 20564, 20572, 20617, 20706a, 38514; *NS* 1923, 67 = *Epigr.* v/vi (1943/44), no. 98; *AE* 1925, 20; XIV 3920.
Claudia: VI 4236, 5062 = 9092 = D 1794, 8419 = D 1479, 8494 = D 1613, 8495 = D 1612, 8560, 8668, 8759, 8829, 8921 = D 1804, 8924 = D 1808, 8957, 10163 = D 5155, 15114, 15347, 15396, 15479, 15528, 15551 = D 7933, 15570, 15585, 15604, 15615, 15616, 16544, 19387, 19456, 20564, 25458, 26145, 26846, 31099, 34901, 37769; XIV 2431 = D 1586, 2832 = D 1760; *IPO* A 77, 251.
Sulpicia: VI 5884, 27007; XIV 662.
Flavia: VI 8473 = D 1705, 8539, 8835, 8853 = D 1536, 8868–9 = D 1780, 8892, 16879, 17413, 18042, 18290 = 34114, 18312, 18325, 18369, 18398, cf. 8580 = D 1497, 18414, 18424, 18456, 19407, 19699, 23927, 25437, 33129, 33798, 35491; XIV 2469.
Ulpia: VI 6716, 8658, 8821, 8865, 8897, 9058, 20150, 23758, 23830, 29296, 29308, 29329, 29353, 29405.
Aelia: VI 7666, 8521, 8522, 8625, 8828, 8984, 10166 = D 5154, 10836, 10877, 10883, 10898, 10908, 10988, 11186, 12311, 16829, 23920, 27274, 29645.
Aurelia: VI 8841, 13297, 13350, 13354, 25069, 36038; XIV 2856 = D 376.
Incerta: VI 16811.
Non-Imperial: VI 74 = D 3507, 776 = D 3727, 4019, 4086, 4094, 4154, 4274, 4370, 4903, 5011, 5226, 5299, 5349+5486 = 33077, 5488, 8436a, 8444, 8454, 8465, 8489, 8491 = D 1610, 8495 = D 1612, 8552 = D 1759, 8574 = D 1501, 8592–3 = D 1566, 8641, 8644, 8655 = D 1629, 8674, 8682 (?), 8723, 8740, 8793, 8818, 8819 = D 1656, 8837 = 33752, 8887 = 14399 = 33754, 8923, 8939, 8963, 8973a = D 1830, 8984, 8996, 9049 = 33758, 9050 = D 1787, 9052 = D 1703, 9077, 10267, 10540, 11002, 11390, 11555, 11782, 11833 = 34047a, 11931, 12053, 12167, 12697, 12854, 13850, 13910, 14356, 14663, 14857, 16454 = 34102, 16595, 16674, 16707, 17015, 17250–1, 17453 (?), 18315, 18816 = 27772, 18553, 19172, 19412 (?), 19775, 21142, 21492, 21604, 22284, 22679, 23044 = 37881, 23049, 23569, 23729, 24196, 24337, 24572, 24578, 24666, 25283, 25926, 25997, 26079, 26258 = D 7856, 26515, 26586, 26796, 26845, 27032, 27388, 28398, 28593, 28637a, 28872, 29025, 29047 (?), 29513, 29552, 29569, 29573, 30855 = D 1621, 33204, 33553, 33724, 33733 = D 1611, 33746, 33763, 33775–6, 33780 = D 1806, 33781, 33789, 34014, 35188, 36507, 37749 = 8994, 37762, 38003, 38010; *AE* 1912, 183; 1912, 263; 1928, 7; XIV 198, 598, 1727, 1877, 2259, 2465, 3396, 3816, 4793 = *IPO* B 19; *IPO* A 96.
Serva: VI 1876, 3951, 4185, 4278, 4354, 4398 (?), 5745 = D 5001 (?), 7563, 8472 = XIV 2834 = D 1537, 8524, 8548, 8558, 8645, 8653, 8657, 8717 = D 1686, 8788, 8822–4, 8864, 8926, 9040, 9058 (?), 9099, 9114, 10141 = D 5261, 11244, 11859, 12305, 12603, 13456, 14047, 14427, 14732, 14776, 16572, 17159, 17190, 17244, 17328, 17432, 17836, 19459, 19734, 21162, 22472 = IX 5926, 22960, 22975 (?), 24070, 25738, 27073, 27469, 29116, 33235, 33772, 34195, 37546; *AE* 1930, 64; 1959, 299; XIV 196 = D 1590, 485, 3763, 3817; *IG* XIV 2008.

14. *Caesaris servus* (Italy and Provinces) =
Iulia: III 1554 = 7998, 1995, 1996 = D 1557; 4712, cf. V 706; VIII 12637, 12785; IX 41 = D 2819; X 1750 = D 7368, 4225; XI 3173, 7745; XIII 1820 = D 1639; *AE* 1923, 73; *NS* 1928, p. 208 n. 9.
Claudia: III 422, 4828; V 2411; VIII 12657 = D 1744, 24821; IX 5481; X 7536; XI 1358; *IGR* IV 1477.
Flavia: III 333 = *IGR* III 25 = D 1539, 4894, 12143; VIII 1027 = D 1710, cf. 12468, 12620, 12641, 12642, 12656; X 2514, 3346 = D 2906; XI 688; *AE* 1937, 72 = *ILTun.* 868a.

Appendixes

Ulpia: V 1159; X 1990; XI 2706.

Aelia: II 1197, 2644–5; III 754 = 7436, 1839; VIII 12892 = D 1510, 12918, 24695; IX 4782; X 1730; XIII 3089, 5697.

Aurelia: III 1303 = D 3382, 1468; V 368, 7752 = D 1658; X 1731; XII 4471; *EE* VIII 720; *IGR* IV 529; *MAMA* I 25.

Incerta: VIII 12602, 12757.

Non-Imperial: III 1085 = 1301 = D 3014, 1470 = 7074 = D 1513, 2082, 4065 (? Venuleia), 6077 = D 1505, 7047 = *IGR* IV 710 = *MAMA* IV 53; V 2385 = D 1509; VIII 12611, 12792, 12836, 13090, 13189, 24688, 24717, 24719, 24740; X 529 = D 1605, 1751; XI 3738, 6379a; XII 717 = D 1565, 1926; XIII 1824, 5386 = D 8143; *IGR* IV 1297; *Hesperia* 10 (1941), 243 n. 43 = 32 (1963), 87.

Serva: II 373, 2128, 2336, 4065; III 1532, 7802 = 1222 (?), 11099 = 4526; V 222, 237, 369, 370, 1067; VIII 1129, 10628, 12597, 12629, 12630, 12635, 12675, 12687, 12699, 12715, 12755, 12818, 12903, 12909, 12919, 13104, 17051 = *ILAlg.* I 758, 18327 (?), 24704, 24711, 24770, 24792, 24815; IX 3721, 5926 = VI 22472; X 713, 1734, 1749, 6181, 7308, 7653, 7831; XI 3745, 4427; XII 648; XIII 2973; *AE* 1897, 4 = D 9035; *AE* 1913, 210; 1914, 230; 1935, 57; *IGR* III 265; IV 235, 531, 538 (Plotia), 753 = *MAMA* IV 114; *SEG* VI 380 = *MAMA* I 29.

BIBLIOGRAPHY

This bibliography does not include articles in standard works of reference (e.g. *CAH*, P–W, etc.) or general treatments of the Imperial period. I have attempted to draw up a working bibliography on the Familia Caesaris from those works which I have found most useful, including those dealing with the wider fields of early Imperial social and administrative history. For the standard collections of inscriptions see the list of abbreviations.

Ashby, T. *The Aqueducts of Ancient Rome.* Oxford, 1935.
Bang, M. 'Die Herkunft der römischen Sklaven', *Röm. Mitt.* 25 (1910), 223–51; 27 (1912), 189–221.
  'Caesaris Servus', *Hermes* 54 (1919), 174–86.
  'Das gewöhnliche Alter der Mädchen bei der Verlobung und Verheiratung' in Friedländer, *Sitteng.*[10], IV, 133–41.
Barrow, R. H. *Slavery in the Roman Empire.* London, 1928.
Baumgart, J. *Die römischen Sklavennamen.* Diss. Breslau, 1936.
Benveniste, E. 'Le nom de l'esclave à Rome', *REL* 10 (1932), 429–40.
Berchem, D. van, *Les Distributions de Blé et d'Argent à la Plèbe romaine sous l'Empire.* Geneva, 1939.
Besnier, R. 'Les Procurateurs provinciaux pendant le règne de Claude', *RBPh.* 28 (1950), 439–59.
Bloch, H. *I bolli laterizi e la storia edilizia romana* (Rome, 1947) = *Bull. Comm.* 64 (1936), 141–225; 65 (1937), 83–187; 66 (1938), 61–221.
  The Roman Brick-Stamps not published in Vol. XV 1 of the Corpus Inscriptionum Latinarum, including Indices to the Roman Brick-Stamps. Cambridge, Mass. 1947–8.
Bömer, F. *Untersuchungen über die Religion der Sklaven in Griechenland und Rom.* I. *Die wichtigsten Kulte und Religionen in Rom und im lateinischen Westen* (Abhandl. Akad. d. Wissensch. u. Lit. Mainz, 1957, No. 7).
Boulvert, G. *Les Esclaves et les Affranchis Impériaux sous le Haut-Empire romain*, Vols. I–II. Diss. Aix-en-Provence, 1965.
  'Servi et Liberti du Prince', *Labeo* 12 (1966), 94–103.
  Esclaves et Affranchis Impériaux sous le Haut-Empire romain: rôle politique et administratif. Naples, 1970. [Revised edition of Vol. I above.]
  'Tacite et le Fiscus', *Rev. Hist. de Droit franç. et étrang.* (1970), 430–8.
  'Le Gentilice de L. Aurelius Augg. lib. Apolaustus Memphius', *Mélanges L. Falletti* 2 (1971), 29–36.
  'La Procuratèle de Lyonnaise et Aquitaine dans la carrière des affranchis impériaux', *Études...Jean Macqueron* (1971), 153–8.
Brunt, P. A. 'Charges of Provincial Maladministration under the Early Principate', *Historia* 10 (1961), 189–227.

Bibliography

'The "Fiscus" and its Development', *JRS* 56 (1966), 75–91.
Bruzza, L. 'Iscrizioni dei Marmi Grezzi', *Ann. dell'Instit. di Corrisp. Archeol.* 42 (1870), 106–204.
Buckland, W. W. *The Roman Law of Slavery*. Cambridge, 1908.
Burn, A. R. 'Hic Breve Vivitur: a Study of the Expectation of Life in the Roman Empire', *Past & Present* 4 (1953), 2–31.
Calza, G. *La necropoli del Porto di Roma dell'Isola Sacra*. Rome, 1940.
Castello, C. 'La condizione del conceptio da libero e schiava e da libera e schiavo in diritto romano', *Studi Solazzi* (1955), 232–50.
Chantraine, H. *Freigelassene und Sklaven im Dienst der römischen Kaiser: Studien zu ihrer Nomenklatur*. Wiesbaden, 1967.
Cichorius, C. *Römische Studien*. Leipzig–Berlin, 1922.
Corbett, P. E. *The Roman Law of Marriage*. Oxford, 1930; repr. 1969.
Crook, J. A. *Consilium Principis*. Cambridge, 1955.
Law and Life of Rome. London, 1967.
Davies, G. R. C. *Imperial Administrative Officers*. Diss. Oxford, 1946.
Degrassi, A. 'Epigrafia Romana I, Roma (1937–46)', *Doxa* 2 (1949), 102 f.
'L'indicazione dell'età nelle iscrizioni sepolcrali latine', *Akte d. IV Internat. Kongr. f. griech. u. latein. Epigraphik, 1962* (Vienna, 1964), 72–98.
De Laet, S. J. *Portorium, Étude sur l'Organisation douanière chez les Romains, surtout à l'époque du Haut-Empire*. Brugge, 1949.
Dill, S. *Roman Society from Nero to Marcus Aurelius*. London, 1905; repr. 1956.
Doer, B. *Die römische Namengebung: Ein historischer Versuch*. Stuttgart, 1937.
Duff, A. M. *Freedmen in the Early Roman Empire*. Oxford, 1928; repr. 1958.
Durry, M. 'Réhabilitation des "Funerariae"', *Rev. Arch.* (1961), 11–21.
'Le Mariage des filles impubères à Rome', *CRAI* (1955), 84–91.
'Le Mariage des filles impubères dans la Rome antique', *RIDA* 2 (1955), 263–73.
'Le Mariage des filles impubères chez les anciens Romains', *Anthropos* 50 (1955), 432–4.
'Sur le mariage romain', *RIDA* 3 (1956), 227–43.
Duthoy, R. 'Notes Onomastiques sur les *Augustales*: *Cognomina* et Indication de Statut', *Ant. Class.* 39 (1970), 88–98 (+ XI Tables).
Erman, H. *Servus Vicarius, l'esclave de l'esclave romain*. Université de Lausanne – Recueil publié par la Faculté de Droit; Lausanne, 1896, 391–535.
Étienne, R. and Fabre, G. 'Démographie et Classe Sociale: l'exemple du cimetière des *officiales* à Carthage', *Recherches sur les structures sociales dans l'Antiquité classique: Colloque C.N.R.S. Caen 1969* (Paris, 1970), pp. 81–97.
Fairon, E. 'L'organisation du palais impérial à Rome', *Musée Belge* 4 (1900), 5–25.
Finley, M. I. (ed.). *Slavery in Classical Antiquity: Views and Controversies*. Cambridge, 1960.
'The Black Sea and Danubian Regions and the Slave Trade in Antiquity', *Klio* 40 (1962), 51–9.
'Between Slavery and Freedom', *Compar. Stud. in Soc. and Hist.* 6 (1964), 233–49.
Fishwick, D. 'The Equestrian Cursus in CIL 2, 3271', *Historia* 19 (1970), 96–112.
Forbes, C. A. 'The Education and Training of Slaves in Antiquity', *TAPA* 86 (1955), 321–60.
Frank, T. 'Race Mixture in the Roman Empire', *Am. Hist. Rev.* 21 (1916), 689–708.
(ed.) *An Economic Survey of Ancient Rome*. 5 vols. Baltimore, 1933–40.
Friedländer, L. and Wissowa, G. *Darstellungen aus der Sittengeschichte Roms in der Zeit von Augustus bis zum Ausgang der Antonine*. 4 vols. (9th–10th ed.) Leipzig, 1920–2.

Bibliography

Gagé, J. *Les classes sociales dans l'Empire romain.* Paris, 1964.
Garnsey, P. *Social Status and Legal Privilege in the Roman Empire.* Oxford, 1970.
Gordon, A. E. and J. S. *Album of Dated Latin Inscriptions, Rome and the Neighborhood.* Vols. I–IV. Berkeley and Los Angeles, 1958–65.
J. S. and A. E. *Contributions to the Palaeography of Latin Inscriptions.* Berkeley and Los Angeles, 1957.
Gordon, M. L. 'The Nationality of Slaves under the Early Roman Empire', *JRS* 14 (1924), 93–111.
'The Ordo of Pompeii', *JRS* 17 (1927), 165–83.
'The Freedman's Son in Municipal Life', *JRS* 21 (1931), 65–77.
Gsell, S. 'Esclaves ruraux dans l'Afrique romaine', *Mélanges Gustave Glotz* I (Paris, 1932), 397–415.
Guey, J. 'Lepcitana Septimiana VI' (Seconde partie), *Rev. Africaine* 93 (1952), 25–63.
Gummerus, H. *Der römische Gutsbetrieb.* Leipzig, 1906.
Halkin, L. *Les Esclaves publics chez les Romains.* Brussels, 1897; repr. 1965.
Harkness, A. G. 'Age at Marriage and at Death in the Roman Empire', *TAPA* 27 (1896), 35–72.
Henrion, R. 'Des origines du mot *Familia*', *Ant. Class.* 10 (1941), 37 f.; 11 (1942), 253 f.
Hirschfeld, O. 'Die Getraideverwaltung in der römischen Kaiserzeit', *Philologus* 29 (1870), 1–96.
Die Kaiserlichen Verwaltungsbeamten bis auf Diocletian. (2nd ed.) Berlin, 1905.
'Der Grundbesitz der römischen Kaiser in den ersten drei Jahrhunderten', *Klio* 2 (1902), 45–72 = *Kleine Schriften* (1913), 516 f.
Hoetink, H. R. 'Autour du S. C. Claudien', in *Droits de l'Antiquité et Sociologie juridique. Mélanges Henri Lévy-Bruhl* (1959), 153–62.
Hopkins, M. K. 'Eunuchs in Politics in the Later Roman Empire', *Proc. Camb. Philol. Soc.* N.S. 9 (1963), 162–80.
'Elite Mobility in the Roman Empire', *Past & Present* 32 (Dec. 1965), 12–26.
'The Age of Roman Girls at Marriage', *Population Studies* 18 (1965), 309–27.
'On the Probable Age Structure of the Roman Population', *Population Studies* 20 (1966), 245–64.
Hülsen, C. 'Nota...sopra i nomi doppi di servi e liberti della casa imperiale', *Röm. Mitt.* 3 (1888), 222–31.
Instinsky, H. U. *Marcus Aurelius Prosenes – Freigelassener und Christ am Kaiserhof* (Abh. Akad. d. Wissensch. Mainz, 1964, No. 3).
Jones, A. H. M. 'The Roman Civil Service (Clerical and Sub-Clerical Grades)', *JRS* 39 (1949), 38–55 = *Studies in Roman Government and Law* (Oxford, 1960), 153–75.
'Procurators and Prefects in the Early Principate', in *Studies in Roman Government and Law* (Oxford, 1960), 117–25.
The Later Roman Empire 284–602. 3 vols. Oxford, 1964.
Kajanto, I. *Onomastic Studies in the Early Christian Inscriptions of Rome and Carthage* (Acta Instit. Rom. Finland II. 1). Helsinki, 1963.
The Latin Cognomina (Soc. Scient. Fenn.; Comm. Hum. Lit. 26.2). Helsinki, 1965.
Supernomina: a Study in Latin Epigraphy (Soc. Scient. Fenn.; Comm. Hum. Lit. 40.1). Helsinki, 1966.
'The Significance of Non-Latin Cognomina', *Latomus* 27 (1968), 517–34.
Kaser, M. *Das römische Privatrecht.* 2 vols. Munich, 1955–9.

Bibliography

Kolendo, J. 'Sur la Législation relative aux grands Domaines de l'Afrique romaine', *REA* 65 (1963), 80–103.
Review of Chantraine, in *Rev. Hist. de Droit franç. et étrang.* 46 (1968), 298–302.
Lacey, R. H. *Equestrian Officials of Trajan and Hadrian.* Princeton, 1917.
Lanciani, R. 'I Comentarii di Frontino intorno le acque e gli aquedotti. Silloge epigraphica aquaria', *Atti della R. Accad. dei Lincei* 277 (1879–80), serie terza, Memorie Vol. IV, 215–616.
La Piana, G. 'Foreign Groups in Rome during the First Centuries of the Empire', *Harv. Theol. Rev.* 20 (1927), 183–403.
Lemonnier, H. *Étude historique sur la condition privée des affranchis aux trois premiers siècles de l'empire romain.* Paris, 1887.
Liebenam, W. *Zur Geschichte und Organisation des römischen Vereinswesens.* Leipzig, 1890.
Beiträge zur Verwaltungsgeschichte des römischen Kaiserreichs, Vol. 1. *Die Laufbahn der Procuratoren bis auf die Zeit Diocletians.* Jena, 1896.
Städteverwaltung im römischen Kaiserreiche. Leipzig, 1900.
Loane, H. J. *Industry and Commerce of the City of Rome (50 B.C.–A.D. 200).* Baltimore, 1938.
Macdonell, W. R. 'On the Expectation of Life in Ancient Rome, and in the Provinces of Hispania and Lusitania, and Africa', *Biometrika* 9 (1913), 366–80.
Magie, D. *Roman Rule in Asia Minor.* 2 vols. Princeton, 1950.
Maier, F. G. 'Römische Bevölkerungsgeschichte und Inschriftenstatistik', *Historia* 2 (1953/4), 318–35.
Marquardt, J. *Privatleben der Römer.* Vol. 1 (2nd ed.). Leipzig, 1879.
Mattingly, H. *The Imperial Civil Service of Rome.* Cambridge, 1910.
Meiggs, R. *Roman Ostia.* Oxford, 1960.
Meyer, P. M. *Der römische Konkubinat.* Leipzig, 1895; repr. 1966.
Michiels, J. 'Les *Cubicularii* des empereurs romains d'Auguste à Dioclétien', *Musée Belge* 6 (1902), 364–87.
Millar, F. 'The Fiscus in the first two centuries', *JRS* 53 (1963), 29–42.
Review of Pflaum, *CP* (q.v.), *JRS* 53 (1963), 194–200.
'The Aerarium and its officials under the Empire', *JRS* 54 (1964), 33–40.
'Some Evidence on the Meaning of Tacitus Annals XII. 60', *Historia* 13 (1964), 180–7.
'The Development of Jurisdiction by Imperial Procurators; further Evidence,' *Historia* 14 (1965), 362–7.
'Epictetus and the Imperial Court', *JRS* 55 (1965), 141–8.
'Emperors at Work', *JRS* 57 (1967), 9–19.
Mócsy, A. 'Die Entwicklung der Sklavenwirtschaft in Pannonien zur Zeit des Prinzipates', *Acta Antiqua* 4 (1956), 221–47.
Mohler, S. L. 'Slave Education in the Roman Empire', *TAPA* 71 (1940), 262–80.
Mommsen, Th. *Römische Forschungen.* Vol. 1. Berlin, 1864.
'Officialium et Militum Romanorum sepulcreta duo Carthaginiensia', *EE* v (1884), 105–20 = *CIL* VIII, pp. 1335–8.
Römisches Staatsrecht (3rd ed.). Leipzig, 1887–8; repr. Basle, 1952.
Römisches Strafrecht. Leipzig, 1899; repr. Graz, 1955.
Gesammelte Schriften. 8 vols. Berlin, 1905–13; repr. 1965.
Moretti, L. 'Statistica Demografica ed Epigrafica: Durata media della Vita in Roma Imperiale', *Epigraphica* 21 (1959), 60–78.
'Due Iscrizioni Latine inedite di Roma', *Riv. di Fil. Class.* N.S. 38 (1960), 68–76.

Bibliography

Nesselhauf, H. 'Patrimonium und res privata des römischen Kaisers', *Historia Augusta Colloquium 1963* = *Antiquitas* 4 (1964), 73-93.
Oost, S. I. 'The Career of M. Antonius Pallas', *AJPh* 79 (1958), 113-39.
Oxé, A. 'Zur älteren Nomenklatur der römischen Sklaven', *Rhein. Mus.* 59 (1904), 108-40.
Pergreffi, O. 'Ricerche Epigrafiche sui Liberti', *Epigraphica* 2 (1940), 314-36; 3 (1941), 110-31.
Pflaum, H.-G. *Les Procurateurs équestres sous le Haut-Empire romain.* Paris, 1950.
Les Carrières procuratoriennes équestres sous le Haut-Empire romain. 3 vols. Paris, 1960-1.
'Principes de l'Administration romaine impériale', *Bull. Fac. d. Lettres, Strasbourg*, 1958, No. 3, 1-17.
'Deux Carrières équestres de Lambèse et de Zana', *Libyca* 3 (1955), 123-54.
Plassard, J. *Le Concubinat romain.* Paris, 1921.
Ramsay, W. M. *The Social Basis of Roman Power in Asia Minor.* Aberdeen, 1941.
Rawson, Beryl, 'Family Life among the Lower Classes at Rome in the first two centuries of the Empire', *Class Phil.* 61 (1966), 71-83.
Review of I. Kajanto: 'The Latin Cognomina', in *Class. Phil.* 63 (1968), 153-9.
[See also under Wilkinson, B. M.]
Rogers, R. S. 'The Roman Emperors as Heirs and Legatees', *TAPA* 78 (1947), 140-58.
Rostovtzeff, M. *Geschichte der Staatspacht in der römischen Kaiserzeit, von Augustus bis Diocletian, Philologus* Supplementb. 9 (1902), 331-511.
Studien zur Geschichte des römischen Kolonates (Archiv f. Papyrusforschung, Beih. 1). Berlin, 1910.
The Social and Economic History of the Roman Empire. 2 vols. 2nd ed. Oxford, 1957.
Sanders, H. A. 'Some Inscriptions in Rome', *MAAR* 10 (1932), 69-83.
Schulten, A. *Die römischen Grundherrschaften.* Weimar, 1896.
Schulze, W. *Zur Geschichte lateinischer Eigennamen* (Abhand. Gesell. Wissensch. z. Göttingen. Phil.-Hist. Kl. N.F. v. 5). Berlin, 1904; repr. 1966.
Sherwin-White, A. N. 'Procurator Augusti', *PBSR* 15 (1939), 11-26.
Sotgiu, G. 'La Sardegna e il Patrimonio Imperiale nell'alto Impero', *Epigraphica* 19 (1957), 25-48.
Starr, C. G. *The Roman Imperial Navy, 31 B.C.-A.D. 324.* New York, 1941.
'Verna', *Class. Phil.* 37 (1942), 314.
Stein, A. *Der römische Ritterstand.* Munich, 1927.
Stockton, D. 'Tacitus Annals XII. 60: A Note', *Historia* 10 (1961), 116-20.
Strack, M. L. 'Die Freigelassenen in ihrer Bedeutung für die Gesellschaft der Alten', *Hist. Zeit.* 112 (1914), 1-28.
Taylor, L. R. 'Augustales, Seviri Augustales, and Seviri: a Chronological Study', *TAPA* 45 (1914), 231-53.
'Freedmen and Freeborn in the Epitaphs of Imperial Rome', *AJPh* 82 (1961), 113-32.
Thylander, H. *Inscriptions du Port d'Ostie.* 2 vols. Lund, 1951-2.
Étude sur l'Épigraphie latine. Lund, 1952.
Toynbee, J. and Ward Perkins, J. *The Shrine of St. Peter and the Vatican Excavations.* London, 1956.
Treggiari, S. *Roman Freedmen during the Late Republic.* Oxford, 1969.
Van Nostrand, J. J. 'The Imperial Domains of Africa Proconsularis', *Univ. Calif. Publ. Hist.* XIV, No. 1 (1925).

Bibliography

Veyne, P. 'Vie de Trimalcion', *Annales* 16 (1961), 213–47.
'Trimalchio Maecenatianus', *Hommages à Albert Grenier – Coll. Latomus* 58 (1962), 1617–24.
Vitucci, G. 'Libertus', *Diz. Epigr.* IV (1958), 905–46.
Vogt, J. *Sklaverei und Humanität: Studien zur antiken Sklaverei und ihrer Erforschung* (*Historia Einzelschriften*, Heft 8). Wiesbaden, 1965.
Wachtel, K. 'Sklaven und Freigelassene in der staatlichen Finanzverwaltung des römischen Kaiserreiches', *Acta Antiqua* 15 (1967), 341–6.
Wallon, H. *Histoire de l'Esclavage dans l'Antiquité.* 3 vols. Paris, 1879.
Waltzing, J. P. *Étude historique sur les Corporations professionnelles chez les Romains.* 4 vols. Louvain, 1895–1900.
Weaver, P. R. C. 'The Status Nomenclature of the Imperial Freedmen', *CQ* 13 (1963), 272–8.
'The Status Nomenclature of the Imperial Slaves', *CQ* 14 (1964), 134–9.
'Cognomina Ingenua: a Note', *CQ* 14 (1964), 311–15.
'Augustorum libertus', *Historia* 13 (1964), 188–98.
'The Slave and Freedman "Cursus" in the Imperial Administration', *Proc. Camb. Phil. Soc.* N.S. 10 (1964), 74–92.
'*Vicarius* and *Vicarianus* in the Familia Caesaris', *JRS* 54 (1964), 117–28.
'Gaius i. 84 and the S.C. Claudianum', *CR* 14 (1964), 137–9.
'The Father of Claudius Etruscus: Statius, *Silvae* 3.3', *CQ* 15 (1965), 145–54.
'Irregular Nomina of Imperial Freedmen', *CQ* 15 (1965), 323–6.
'Freedmen Procurators in the Imperial Administration', *Historia* 14 (1965), 460–9.
'*ILS* 1489, 1490 and Domitius Lemnus', *Historia* 14 (1965), 509–12.
'An Administrative Official from Trèves', *Latomus* 25 (1966), 910–11.
'Social Mobility in the Early Roman Empire: the evidence of the Imperial Freedmen and Slaves', *Past & Present* 37 (1967), 3–20.
'Family Dating Criteria, *Proximi* and '*Provincia*' in the Familia Caesaris', *JRS* 58 (1968), 110–23.
'Cognomina, Supernomina and *CIL* X 1729', *Antichthon* 5 (1971).
Review of Boulvert, 'Esclaves et Affranchis Impériaux', *Labeo* 17 (1971).
'Notes on Dated Inscriptions of Imperial Freedmen and Slaves', *Epigraphische Studien* (1972) [to appear].
Westermann, W. L. *The Slave Systems of Greek and Roman Antiquity.* Philadelphia, 1955.
Wickert, L. 'Die Flotte der römischen Kaiserzeit', *Würzb. Jahrb. f. d. Altertumsw.* 4 (1949/50), 100–25.
Wilkinson, B. M. *The Names of Children in Roman Imperial Epitaphs. A Study of Social Conditions in the Lower Classes.* Diss. Bryn Mawr, 1961.
'A wider concept of the term *parens*', *Class. Journal* 59 (May 1964), 358–61.
[See also under Rawson, Beryl.]
Wolf, M. *Untersuchungen zur Stellung der kaiserlichen Freigelassenen und Sklaven in Italien und den Westprovinzen.* Diss. Münster, 1965.
Wuilleumier, H. *Étude historique sur l'emploi et la signification des signa.* Acad. des Inscr. et Belles-Lettres. Mémoires, vol. 13 (1932), 559–696.

INDEX

I. SOURCES

A. AUTHORS

Cassius Dio
  liii. 30. 3 282
  lviii. 19. 6 281
  lxiii. 12 279
Cicero
  ad Att. iv. 15. 1 24n.
  Phil. viii. 11 97
Cod. Iust.
  v. 4. 3 185
  xi. 37. 1 205
Cod. Theod.
  iv. 8. 7 205
  iv. 12. 3 11, 98, 165–6, 168
  x. 20. 10 166
Cyprian
  Epist. 80. 2 26
Digesta
  xxiii. 2. 44 293
  xl. 2. 9 97, 184
  xl. 2. 14. 1 185
  l. 16. 195. 1 299
Epictetus
  Enchir. 40 107n.
Frag. de iure fisci
  6 168
  7 203
  12 166, 167
  13 168n.
  16 166
Frontinus
  De Aq. 100 215
  116–18 300, 301
Fronto
  ad M. Caes. ii. 16 26, 264
    v. 37 268–9, 272
  ad Ver. i. 2 27
Gaius
  i. 18 97, 183
  i. 19 97, 184
  i. 30–4 98
  i. 80–5 162–3
  i. 91, 160 163–4
  ii. 95 205
Herodian
  v. 7. 7 283

Josephus
  AJ xviii. 182 286
Martial
  i. 101 98
  ii. 18 201n.
  vii. 40 225n., 284, 293
  ix. 79. 1 10
Pauli Sent.
  ii. 21. 6 166
  ii. 21. 14 165
  iv. 10. 2 164
  v. 1. 3 299
Petronius
  Cen. Tr. 71 215
Pliny
  Ep. viii. 6 263
    x. 27–8 234, 279–80
    x. 31 215
    x. 84–5 234, 269, 279–80
  Panegyr. 88 10
Pliny, Eld.
  NH xii. 12 36
Plutarch
  Galba 7 88
SHA
  Hadr. 21 223
  Marc. 15 237
  Verus 8. 10 27
  Comm. 7. 2 27
  Elagab. 11. 1 283
  Sev. Alex. 19. 4 283
Statius
  Silvae i. 5 290, 292, 294
    iii. 3 2, 171, 225n., 263n., 284–94
    v. 1 171, 260
Suetonius
  Calig. 56 10n.
  Claud. 25 88
    28 263, 279
  Galba 12 200
    14 88
    15 281
  Otho 5 252n., 272
  Vitell. 12 282
  Vesp. 3 170

Index

Suetonius (*cont.*)
    14 253–4
    23 89, 101, 252n., 272
Tacitus
  Ann. iv. 15 279
    vi. 15 183
    xii. 53 162–5
    xii. 54 279n.
    xiii 1 279
    xiii. 27 85
    xiii. 45 144–5
    xiii. 47 2
    xiv. 39 281
    xv. 35 263
    xv. 71 89n.
    xvi. 8 263
  Hist. i. 13 88, 282
    i. 49 10
    i. 76 260, 281
    ii. 47 282
    ii. 65 281
    ii. 92 36
    iii. 12 283
    iv. 39 283
    v. 9 279n.
Tertullian
  ad uxor. ii. 8 163, 210
Ulpian
  i. 12 97n.
  iii. 1 98
  iii. 2 166

B. INSCRIPTIONS

AE **1888**, 130: 244–5, 272; **1897**, 4: 117;
1903, 117: 277n.; 245: 249–50;
1908, 158: 244n., 277n.; **1910**, 169: 277;
1912, 183: 220; **1915**, 9: 55n., 57, 66;
20: 251; **1922**, 122: 271;
1923, 76: 159, 254n.;
1927, 2: 64; 136: 69, 101; 150: 277;
1930, 86: 276–7; 96: 273, 276–7;
152: 107, 109, 236; **1932**, 85: 249n.;
1933, 273: 265n.; 281–2: 280;
1935, 20: 265–6, 283; **1937**, 159: 158;
1939, 145–6: 203n.; **1940**, 177: 57;
1945, 112: 146; 113: 274; 123: 200n.;
134: 249–50; **1946**, 140: 34;
1948, 141: 275, 279; **1949**, 30: 268n.;
68: 106, 109; **1951**, 198: 55;
1952, 192: 54, 58, 59n.; **1953**, 24: 38,
208–9; **1954**, 65: 253–4, 256; 86: 66n., 69;
1956, 23: 247; 123: 244n.;
1959, 300: 175; 307: 141;
1964, 96: 204
Arch. Class. **1953**, p. 264: 106
Bruzza, Nos. 200–1: 55
Bull. Com. **1925**, p. 218: 201n., 218n.
CIL II
485–6: 246–8; 1197: 116–17;
1198: 201, 205; 2229: 214n., 300;
2644: 116–17; 3235: 242, 246–8;
4089: 246–7; 4181: 247;
4184: 247n., 249n.; 6085: 106, 249–50
CIL III
3: 227n.; 249: 57; 251: 242n., 247;
258: 249–50; 333: 118;
348: 253, 256–7, 273, 276–7;
431: 231–3, 280; 536: 268, 274; 556: 250;
704: 118; 754: 117, 251; 980: 247;
1085: 113, 117–18; 1222: 204n., 205;
1312: 225, 269; 1470: 118, 145, 147;
1839: 117; 1993: 247; 1994: 251–2;
1995: 118, 145; 1996: 118; 2082: 118;
3960: 251; 3964: 247; 4020: 239;
4023: 240; 4034: 58; 4043: 247;
4049: 251; 4063: 248;
4065: 118, 139n., 143; 4066: 247;
4797: 251; 4800: 247, 251;
4828: 117–18, 205, 251; 6075: 240n.;
6077: 118, 250; 6081: 247; 6082: 248;
6574: 56; 6575: 251; 7130: 226n.;
7268: 250–1; 7380: 54, 299–300;
7853: 222; 7955: 247; 8914: 101n.;
12130: 249n.; 12143: 118;
12289: 217, 220, 222n.; 12298: 249–50;
14112. 2: 289; 14158: 273, 277;
14179: 276–7; 14689: 246–7
CIL V
179: 264; 706: 122; 1067: 221;
1801: 204; 2385: 251; 2931: 101n.;
3510: 57; 7209: 130n.; 7253: 247;
7753: 60; 7882: 249–50; 8386: 143;
8818: 250–1
CIL VI
42–3: 75, 299; 180: 253, 256;
376: 30n., 31n., 35–6;
455: 60, 236–7, 264; 544: 81;
552: 59n.; 604: 38; 619: 47; 630: 38;
634: 81; 644: 31n.; 682: 75, 81;
723–4: 75; 738: 231, 235–6; 746: 82n.;
776: 59n., 242; 790: 273–4, 276–7;
816: 26, 58; 975: 75; 1261: 49n.;
1564: 238; 1585b: 25n., 60, 264–5;
1598: 27; 1884: 34, 38, 75, 103n., 217;
1887: 260–2, 274–5; 1934: 274;
1962: 274, 277; 2997: 158; 3952: 221–2;
4049: 158; 4053: 159; 4095: 222;
4228: 34, 40, 157, 231, 234–5; 4281: 20 7;
4402: 221–2; 4448: 24n.; 4566: 82; 4636:

320

Index

CIL VI (*cont.*)
146; 4776: 143, 221; 4884: 51; 4887: 82n.;
4903: 220; 4923: 176; 4951: 98;
5189: 142; 5197: 52, 201, 212, 251–2;
5248: 63; 5294: 38, 208; 5436: 127;
5822: 203, 242; 5873: 160; 5884: 122;
5909: 38, 208; 6189: 37, 156;
6639: 122, 251; 7778: 101;
8077: 101n., 151, 254n.; 8408: 214, 259;
8410: 201n., 209n., 214, 216–17, 222, 260;
8411: 33, 260; 8412: 260; 8413: 260–1, 299;
8414: 260; 8415: 260;
8417: 69, 101, 103n., 238, 262;
8424: 238, 262; 8425: 253, 256;
8432: 28n., 130n., 225; 8434: 65;
8438: 34, 220; 8440: 26, 44, 264;
8443: 271, 275, 277n.; 8444: 141;
8445: 154, 159, 228; 8446: 242;
8449: 34, 103n.;
8450: 67, 244–5, 248–9, 273, 276–7;
8451: 149–50, 151, 214, 220, 285;
8456: 299; 8463: 56–7; 8470: 231–3;
8476: 153–4, 242; 8486: 220;
8488: 103n., 242; 8494: 122;
8495: 76, 122, 144n.; 8498: 274;
8499, 8500: 29n., 38–9, 64, 81, 268n., 275;
8501: 82n., 268n.; 8502: 130n.;
8503: 243; 8508: 242–3;
8515: 38, 244–5, 272–3; 8518: 156;
8519: 250; 8527: 227; 8528: 228, 242;
8542: 130n., 153; 8544: 242–3;
8546: 153–4; 8568: 67, 276–7; 8569: 276–7;
8570: 66n., 245; 8574: 39, 250–1;
8575: 55, 122, 220, 250; 8577: 251;
8578: 251; 8579: 246–8;
8580: 143–4n., 158, 160; 8596: 259;
8597: 259; 8598–9: 260, 263; 8600: 260;
8601: 260;
8603: 260; 8604: 260–1; 8605: 260;
8606: 253, 257n., 260n., 264;
8607: 255, 260n., 261;
8608: 38, 39, 149–50, 253–7, 271, 273, 277n.; 8609: 260n.;
8610: 33, 255n., 260n., 262–3;
8611: 260n., 262–3; 8612: 238, 262–3;
8613: 69, 101, 103n., 238, 262;
8614: 254, 261; 8618: 82, 264;
8619: 229, 253, 256–7; 8622: 264n.;
8628–9: 261; 8631: 259; 8633: 50;
8634: 25, 35–6, 157, 238, 262;
8637: 254–5, 256; 8640: 225n.;
8644: 143n.; 8655: 145; 8656: 69, 101;
8668: 142–3; 8687: 122, 225;
8689: 268n.; 8701: 252–3, 256;
8732: 154–5; 8737: 105;
8740: 107, 109; 8754: 146–7; 8764: 22n.;

8790: 122; 8792: 143; 8793: 121;
8796: 157; 8806: 46, 83; 8816: 145–7;
8818: 121; 8822–4: 221–2;
8825b: 24n.; 8832: 201; 8865: 145, 220;
8866: 100; 8873: 228;
8878: 34, 106, 252–3; 8885: 145–6;
8887: 22n., 45n., 46, 121; 8898: 39, 56n.;
8921: 122; 8931: 101, 154–5, 253n.;
8933: 50n.; 8934a: 50n.;
8950: 231, 234–5; 8951: 103n.;
8957: 102n., 130–1n.; 8963: 121;
8965: 52; 8972: 170; 8978: 54, 66n.;
8992: 59n.; 8997: 34; 9005: 31, 213;
9008: 268n.; 9015: 64, 65n., 268n.;
9017: 260n.; 9019: 225, 270;
9033: 238, 262; 9035: 217, 220; 9041: 151;
9042: 156, 160; 9045: 228;
9047: 61, 64n., 68, 101, 159; 9050: 121;
9052: 121; 9072: 106, 109, 242, 248;
9074: 246, 248; 9077: 143; 9091: 227;
9093: 228; 9100: 75; 9857: 142;
10083: 231, 234; 10089: 151–2;
10172–3: 221; 10233: 241, 242–3;
10234: 75, 231–3; 10245: 216;
10449: 44, 158–60, 176; 10547: 207n.;
10648: 40, 151, 254n.; 10666: 69, 157;
10682: 157; 10685: 69, 101n.;
10728: 154n.; 10778: 69, 101n.;
10860: 57; 10988: 102n.;
11002: 145; 11186: 142–3; 11242–3: 54;
11801: 194; 12348: 158; 12533: 36–7;
12652: 218, 220; 12948: 207;
13017: 106, 109; 13060: 106; 13084: 157;
13151: 101n., 157, 160; 13200: 159;
13328: 145–7; 13850: 204, 220;
14047: 139n.; 14452: 138n., 159;
14897: 159; 15041: 150; 15110: 130n.;
15131: 149–50; 15235: 25, 130;
15317: 25, 35–6, 159, 254n.; 15350: 220;
15406: 159; 15489: 176; 15492: 204;
15592–5: 149–50; 15598: 106, 109;
15615: 107, 109, 220; 15860: 159;
16658: 158; 16663: 150; 16741: 146–7;
16787: 204; 16823: 145–7; 17159: 143n.;
17301: 158; 18122: 151; 18142: 69, 101n.;
18290: 141; 18315: 145;
18358: 130n., 220, 221; 18398: 143–4n.;
18428: 57; 18456: 25, 220; 18824: 156;
19015: 76n.; 19172: 106; 19365: 47;
19710: 157; 19785: 44; 20002: 38, 208;
20237: 24n.; 20268: 194;
21748: 46; 22044: 158; 22284: 145, 147;
22423: 34; 22789: 76n.; 23044: 107, 109;
23549: 146–7; 24108: 158, 160; 24316: 36–7;
24337: 107, 109; 24806: 56;
25033: 145–6; 25444: 107, 109;

321

Index

CIL VI (*cont.*)
25556: 46; 25721: 101n.; 26608: 22n.;
26732: 51; 27749: 157; 28699: 157;
28789: 217; 29069: 102n.; 29116: 106;
29133: 68, 101n.; 29152: 69;
29194: 91n., 220; 29234: 149–50;
29244: 149–50; 29272: 34; 29299: 56–7;
29378: 100; 29396: 25, 130n.;
29960: 217; 30556. 146: 46;
32429: 55; 32450: 38, 208–9;
32775: 31, 34, 71; 33468: 219, 260;
33730: 238; 33731: 36n.; 33760: 217;
33781: 141–2; 33788: 202;
33966: 69, 101; 34320: 107, 109;
34805: 27; 35188: 145; 35308: 176;
35612: 159; 36507: 146–7; 37099: 265;
37743: 265n.; 37752: 130–1n.;
37759: 50n.; 37763: 271;
37763a–b: 260n.; 38010: 220;
38351: 156; 38366: 151, 160

CIL VII
62: 232, 235–6

CIL VIII
7075: 26n.; 9434: 69, 101n.; 12314: 202;
12620: 115–16; 12631: 202n., 203, 238,
239, 262; 12637: 115–16; 12641: 115–16;
12642: 115–16; 12657: 115; 12667: 67;
12857: 56–7; 12879: 271, 277n.;
12892: 115–16, 226, 251; 12918: 115–16;
12922: 36, 37n.; 12951: 106, 109;
13045: 217; 13092: 217; 13130: 50;
14464: 38, 265, 280–1; 14560: 55, 76n.;
17335: 204, 205; 21008: 239;
21010: 268n.; 22670a: 300;
24695: 115–16; 25902: 38, 265, 271, 280–1;
25943: 38, 265, 280–1; 26416: 38, 280–1

CIL IX
41: 52, 219; 321: 204; 344: 27, 60n.;
888: 138n.; 2438: 60, 236, 264;
3640: 146–7; 4782: 141

CIL X
527: 45n.; 654: 69, 101n.; 1685: 300;
1727: 264; 1729: 69n., 101n., 242–3;
1732: 201n., 220; 1738: 29n., 66, 268;
1739: 275; 1741: 228; 1743: 36n.;
1750: 300; 3356: 82n.; 3357: 159, 219;
3716: 27n.; 4734: 49;
6081: 38, 273, 276;
6092: 39, 249–50, 253–6; 6093: 225n.;
6571: 276–7; 6668: 273; 6773: 75;
6785: 38, 225, 277–8; 7489: 63;
7494: 277–8; 7584: 247; 7588: 251;
7653: 53n., 58; 7819: 146–7

CIL XI
1222: 130n.; 1358: 122; 1434: 260n.;
2706: 143; 3612: 38, 40, 151, 270, 274;
3614: 38, 75, 81; 3720: 268n.;
3886: 260; 4360: 260–1; 6712.7–8: 76

CIL XII
257: 219; 717: 117; 1926: 117;
4254: 249n.; 4449: 300; 4471: 117

CIL XIII
1550: 300; 1800: 225, 253, 256n., 257, 273,
276–7; 1818: 203, 205;
1820, 2177: 40, 116–17, 143;
1824: 117, 145; 1826: 246–8;
2068: 106, 109; 2189: 106, 109; 2308: 105;
3089: 116–17; 5697: 116–17, 143

CIL XIV
51: 75, 270–1, 276–7; 163: 275;
176: 61, 67, 225, 271, 273–4, 276–7;
250: 26; 331: 158; 508: 151;
524: 100; 662: 145; 821: 61;
1386: 158, 254n.; 1877: 231;
2104: 26, 237n., 263–4, 268; 2113: 60;
2161: 67; 2259: 220; 2302: 38, 208;
2504: 67; 2608: 271; 2690: 101n., 157;
2795: 29n., 66n.; 2815: 253, 255–6, 257n.;
2840: 260–1; 2932: 38, 274; 2977: 60;
3393: 157, 160; 3637: 149;
3644: 2, 31, 71, 270, 274;
3718: 101n., 106n.; 3909: 260;
3935: 61, 65; 4062: 69, 101, 157;
4254: 28, 60n.; 4482–3: 103n., 242;
4570: 59; 5309. 23, 28: 237n., 264

CIL XV
466–70: 75; 810–11: 91n., 217n.;
814: 50; 7279–80: 38, 270, 274;
7285–6: 55, 76; 7327: 26n.;
7444: 260n., 261; 7500: 263;
7740, 7743: 29n., 264; 7744: 75

D 1496: 247
EE VIII 26: 247n.; 335–7: 260n.
Gordon, *Alb.* I, No. 122: 259
Hesperia 10 (1941), 243f. = 32 (1963), 87: 56, 76
IGR I 623: 22n., 25–6, 44, 228n.; 1255–6: 217, 270
  III 1086: 72n.; 1103: 244n., 247
  IV 235: 118; 544: 26n., 28n.;
  749: 273, 276–7; 754–5: 81n.;
  1297: 113, 118; 1317: 231, 234;
  1477: 144n.; 1651: 232, 235–6;
  1699: 146–7
ILAlg. 3992: 299
IPO A 251: 141; A 261: 107, 109
IRT 606: 28, 44
LBW II 1076: 231–3, 234
NS **1917**, p. 291, Nos. 6–7: 25, 35–6
SEG XIII 623: 26n.
Unpublished, Aphrodisias, Caria: 22n., 72
  Diz. Epig. IV, 943: 273, 277

Index

C. PAPYRI

BGU 102. 1: 202n., 203n.; 1110f. : 20n.   *P.Oxy.* 735: 59, 201n.   *P.Ryl.* II 255: 8

II. PERSONS

A. EMPERORS AND IMPERIAL FAMILY

L. Aelius Caesar, 27, 237
Agrippina Augusta, 29, 46n., 47n., 64–5, 73n., 182, 216
Agrippina Germanici (uxor), 47n.
Antonia Minor, 23, 29, 47n., 63–4, 73n., 91, 126n., 159, 170, 216, 219, 221, 233n.
Antoninus Pius, 6n., 24, 26, 31n., 32, 44, 50n., 67–8, 75, 76n., 116, 130–1n., 170, 231, 245, 246, 250, 252, 264, 301, 304–5; as *privatus*, 26, 28, 237n.
Arria Fadilla, mother of Antoninus Pius, 54, 304–5
Augustus 5n., 17, 20, 21n., 24–5, 32–3, 45, 46, 49, 50, 63, 83 97, 98, 159, 171, 199, 208–9, 216–17, 282, 293, 300, 301–2; Divus Augustus, 22, 30, 37, 44–5, 46, 72, 102n., 121, 159, 209, 302
M. Aurelius, 6, 17, 21, 24, 245, 248, 252, 253, 255–7, 264, 265, 277, 281, 301, 305
M. Aurelius Caesar, 29n., 63, 269, 272, 305
M. Aurelius with L. Verus, 53, 55, 58–60, 67, 71, 78, 81n., 236, 272, 278, 301, 305

Britannicus, 29

Caracalla, 24, 28, 44, 53–4, 58–60, 203, 231–2, 266n., 283, 301, 306
Claudia Antonia, 47n.
Claudius, 21n., 22, 24–5, 44–5, 46, 70, 72, 83, 88, 98, 107, 121, 122, 133, 162–3, 164–5, 167, 171n., 177, 185, 192, 201, 208–9, 216–17, 254n., 255, 259, 263, 268, 275, 279n., 282, 286–8, 292, 301, 302–3; as *privatus*, 29; Divus Claudius, 22, 33, 44–5, 66n., 71, 303
Clodius Albinus, 25
Commodus, 24–5, 27, 53, 58–60, 75, 171, 273, 281, 283, 301, 305

Didius Iulianus, 25
Domitia Augusta, 29n., 47n., 54, 65–6, 126n., 140, 146, 304
Domitia Lucilla, mother of M. Aurelius, 6
Domitian, 21n., 22, 25, 31n., 40, 46, 55, 76, 81n., 91, 118, 121, 122, 141, 146, 171, 209n., 213, 214, 216, 219, 259–60, 261, 274, 284, 288–9, 290–1, 293–4, 301, 304
Drusilla, 23, 51n., 183, 221–2
Drusus, 91, 215

Elagabalus, 24, 88, 232, 266n., 283, 301, 306

Faustina I Augusta, 29, 47n., 66, 68, 100, 170, 250
Faustina II Augusta, 63, 66, 126n., 145, 305

Gaius, 21n., 22, 25, 44n., 46, 51, 64, 133, 146, 203, 275, 285–6, 301, 302
Galba, 24, 83, 88, 91, 129, 142, 213, 216, 281, 282, 287–8, 301, 303
Germanicus, 23, 29, 47n., 91, 215
Geta, 25, 53–4, 58–60
(M. Antonius) Gordianus III, 22, 25–6, 44, 301, 306

Hadrian, 17, 24, 28n., 31n., 32, 44, 47, 51, 53, 55n., 57n., 67, 75, 91–2, 98, 154–5, 162, 164, 168, 199, 217, 223, 231, 232, 235, 247–8, 252–3, 255, 259–60, 263, 264, 277–8, 280–1, 301, 304

Iulia, Titi f., 29, 47n., 65
Iulia Domna, 29, 59n., 81n., 203, 306
Iulia Mamaea, 29, 306
Divus Iulius, 22n.

Livia, Iulia Augusta, 24, 28–9, 31, 44, 51, 62–3, 64, 72n., 73, 121, 127, 143, 159, 208–9, 213n., 215, 217, 218–19, 221–2, 302
Lucilla Augusta, 29

Marcella Minor, 29
Marciana Augusta, 37n., 47n., 66, 304
Matidia I Augusta, 28, 66, 107
Matidia II Augusta, 305
(C. Iulius) Maximinus, 25, 301, 306
Messalina, 29, 46n., 47n., 64, 126n.

Nero, 21n., 22, 25, 29n., 38–9, 44, 46, 64–5, 71, 83, 89n., 91, 98, 122, 170, 175, 213, 216, 221, 231, 233n., 253, 255, 259, 263, 275, 279, 280–1, 287–8, 289, 292–3, 301, 303
Nerva, 24, 70, 129, 130–1n., 153, 173, 301, 304
Octavia, 30, 65n., 182, 216
Octavia, Aug. soror, 47n.
Otho, 25, 213, 216, 272, 281, 287–8

323

Index

Pescennius Niger, 25
Pertinax, 25, 301, 305
(M. Iulius) Philippus, 25, 301, 306
Plotina Augusta, 29, 37n., 47n., 66, 147, 304
Poppaea Augusta, 29, 47n., 64–5, 144–5, 212n., 216

Sabina Augusta, 29, 47n., 55n., 57n., 66, 217
Scribonia, 29
Septimius Severus, 17, 24, 28, 33, 47n., 53–4, 58–60, 75, 138, 185, 229, 231, 236, 239–40, 251, 258, 264, 265–6, 301, 305–6
Severus Alexander, 24, 266n., 268, 283, 301, 306

Tiberius, 22, 24, 32–3, 37, 40, 44–5, 46, 49, 51, 62–3, 68, 71, 72n., 98, 116–17, 121, 122, 142, 143, 146, 199, 211, 217, 218, 219n., 251, 275, 279, 284–5, 300, 301, 302
Titus, 21n., 22, 25, 46, 75, 277, 289–90, 301, 303
Trajan, 21, 22, 24, 25, 31n., 32, 46, 50n., 55, 56–7, 67, 75, 81n., 91, 98, 99, 101, 131, 145, 160, 217, 219, 220, 234–5, 245, 248, 250, 253–4, 255, 259–60, 261, 269, 280–1, 290, 301, 304

L. Verus, 24–5, 26–7, 237, 283
Vespasian, 17, 21, 22, 24–5, 33, 44–5, 46, 55–6, 78, 87, 89, 98, 101, 163, 170, 209, 253, 262, 272, 274–5, 282–3, 284, 288–90, 291, 292, 301, 303
Vibia Aurelia Sabina, daughter of M. Aurelius, 306
Vitellius, 25, 36, 281, 282, 287–8

B. IMPERIAL FREEDMEN AND SLAVES

Abascantus, 171, 260, 261n., 263
Acastus Aug. lib., 38, 273, 276
Acte, 54, 91, 170, 212n., 216, 222
Adrastus Aug. (Augg. nn.) lib., 60, 264
P. Aelius Alcibiades, 82
P. Aelius Aug. lib. Secundus, 34
T. Ael(ius) Augg. lib. Restitutus, 67, 276
T. Ael(ius) Augg. lib. Saturnin(us), 67, 244–5, 248–9, 273, 276
T. Aelius Aug. lib. Titianus, 34, 106, 252–3, 256
L. Aelius Aug. lib. Aurelius Apolaustus, 27–8, 60n.
Agathyrsus Aug(ustae?) lib., 8, 66, 75
Anteros Severi(anus) Caesaris n., 91n., 217n.
Antiochus Aug. n. Lucconianus, 55, 250.
M. Antonius Felix, 111, 279, 282
Antonius Musa, 282
M. Antonius Pallas, 8, 10, 23, 88, 111, 133, 163, 164–5, 167, 216, 231–2, 233, 234, 259, 261, 263, 282, 283–4, 286, 290
Aridelus, 269, 272
Ascanius [Ca]esaris Au[g. l. Ant]iochianus, 50n.
Asiaticus, 282
C. Asinius Aug. lib. Paramythius Festianus, 36, 37n.
T. Aurelius Aug. lib. Aphrodisius, 26, 237n., 263n., 264, 268
T. Aurelius Egatheus Aug. lib., 26, 44, 264
L. Aelius Aug. lib. Aurelius Apolaustus, 27–8 60n.
L. Aurelius Augg. lib. Apolaustus Memphius, 27–8, 60n.
L. Aurelius (Aug. lib.) Nicomedes qui et

Ceionius et Aelius vocitatus est, 27, 237, 265, 283
L. Aurelius Aug. (Augg.) lib. Pylades, 60
M. Aurelius Aug. (Augg.) lib. Agilius Septentrio, 60
Aurelius Alexander (Aug. lib.), 253, 255, 257n.
Aurelius Augg. lib. Alexander v.e., 265–6n.
M. Aurelius Cleander, 82, 171, 283
M. Aurelius Aug. lib. Crescens, 273, 276
M. Aur(elius) Faustus Aug. lib., 273, 276
(M. Aurelius?) Ianuarius (Aug.) lib., 229, 253, 256–7
M. Aurellius Aug. lib. Inventus, 244n., 277n.
M. Aurelius Aug. liber. Marcio, 253, 256, 257, 273, 276
M. Aurelius Augg. lib. Prosenes, 274
Aurelius Saturion, 249n.
Aurelius Zoticus, 88, 283
M. Aurelius Aug. lib. [. . .], 253, 256n., 257, 273, 276

Bassus Aug. lib., 38, 149–50, 253–7, 271, 273, 277n.

Caenis, 130n., 131, 170, 216, 219, 220–1, 222
Callistus, 10, 88, 133, 261
Cerulus, 89
Chrestion Aug. lib., 277–8
Ti. Claudius Aug. lib. Abascantus, 33
(Ti. Claudius) Atticus Aug. lib., 32, 91, 149, 209n., 214, 216, 217, 222n., 260, 290
Ti. Claudius Aug. lib. Avitus, 35–6, 157
Ti. Claudius Aug. lib. Bucolas, 31–2, 38, 40, 151, 270, 274
Ti. Claudius Aug. l. Censorinus, 35–6, 159

324

Index

Ti. Claudius Aug. lib. Diomedes, 34
Claudius Etruscus, father of, 2, 31–2, 34, 40, 88, 98, 111, 171, 225n., 237, 259, 261, 264, 283, 284–94
Ti. Claudius (Aug. lib.) Eutrapelus, 35–6
Ti. Claudius Aug. lib. Saturninus, 271, 275, 277
Ti. Claudius Aug. lib. Zena, 32
Coenus August(i), 250–1
Coetus Herodianus, 31, 213n.
Cosmus Aug. lib., 60, 236–8, 264

Diadumenus Aug. l., 260n., 261
(Domitius) Lemnus Aug. l., 38–9, 64, 81, 268n., 275
Doryphorus, 261

Eclectus, 171
Entellus, 261
Epaphroditus, 88, 91, 216, 261
Epimachus, 234, 279–80
Eutactus (Aug.) lib., 274, 276–7

Flavius Alexander Aug. lib., 33, 263
T. Flavius Aug. lib. Cerialis, 143–4n., 158
T. Flavius Aug. lib. Chrysogonus Lesbianus, 34, 154
T. Flavius Aug. lib. Delphicus, 244–5, 272
T. Flavius Aug. lib. Euschemon, 260–1
T. Flavius Aug. l. Ianuarius, 34, 103n.
Fortunatus Augg. lib., 244n., 247

Glyptus Aug. lib., 260n.
Graptus Aug. lib., 2

Halotus, 281
Helius, 279
Hermes Aug. lib., 231–3, 280
Hilarus, 281
Hormus, 282–3

Iberus, 281
Icelus (Marcianus), 87–8, 282
(C. Iulius) Aesc(h)inus Caes. l., 49n.
C. Iulius Aug. l. Samius, 2, 31, 71, 270, 274
C. Iulius Aug. lib. Satyrus, 30n., 35–6
Ti. Iulius Aug. l. Mellon, 275, 279
Ti. Iulius Aug. lib. Optatus, 8
Ti. Iulius Aug. l. Secundus, 31
Ti. Iulius Aug. lib. Xanthus, 31, 34, 71

Ti. Iulius Aug. l. . . . ., see Claudius Etruscus, father of
Iulia Ti. Caesar. Aug. l. Iconio, 44, 158–60, 176

Licinus, 217, 282
Lysistrata, 170
M. Macrius Trophimus Aug. lib., 36, 37n.
Malchio Caesaris, 52, 219n.
Martialis A[ug. lib.], 38, 244–5, 272–3
Maximus, 234, 279–80
Metrobius Aug. lib., 38, 225n., 277–8
Musicus Ti. Caesaris Augusti Scurranus, 52, 201–2, 204, 209, 211, 212n., 251–2

Narcissus, 10, 88, 111, 217, 259, 260, 261, 263–4, 282

Optatus Aug. lib., 273, 277

Paean Aug. lib., 38, 274
Pallas, see M. Antonius Pallas
Parthenius, 216
Phaon, 259, 287n., 289
C. Plotius Aug. lib. Gemellus, 36, 37n.
Polybius, 133, 261
Polyclitus, 281
C. Pompeius Trimalchio Maecenatianus, 215
Priscus Aug. l., 273

Saoterus, 283
Septimianus, 236–8

Tertiolus Aug. lib., 249–50, 253–5
Theoprepes Aug. lib., 268, 274
Tyrrhenus (Aug.) lib., 273, 276

M. Ulpius Aug. lib. Cerdo, 34
M. Ulpius Augg. lib. Chariton, 69
M. Ulpius Chresimus Aug. lib., 270
M. Ulpius Aug. lib. Gresianus, 246, 247–8
M. Ulpius Aug. lib. Menophilus, 34, 235
M. Ulpius Nicephorus Aug. lib., 242
M. Ulpius Aug. lib. Phaedimus, 34, 75, 103n., 217
M. Ulpius Aug. lib. Philetus Arminianus, 158
M. Ulp(ius) Augg. lib. Probus, 67, 271, 273, 276
M. Ulpius [Aug. lib.] Repenti[nus], 226n.
M. Ulpius Aug. l. Thallus, 34
M. Ulpius Aug. lib. Zopyrus, 252–4, 256

Index

III. SUBJECTS

ab admissione: head, 7; department 101n., 154–5, 238n., 252–4
ad anabolicum Alex(andriae), 273
ab annona, ad annonam, annonae, 238, 242, 244–5, 249, 276
ab argento, 262
a bybliotheca Latina, bibl(iothecarum), 122, 142, 212n., 275
ad capitularia Iudaeorum, 261
ad caput Africae, 121
ad Castorem, 268n.
accensus, 31, 71, 261–2, 270, 274–5, 277
a codicillis: head, 26, 207, 259, 262; department, 238n.
a cognitionibus: head, 259, 261, 264–5; department, 35, 157, 238, 256n., 259, 262
a commentariis, 7, 50n., 103n., 206, 224, 226, 229, 239, 241–3, 245–6, 247n., 249–50, 252, 253, 256, 262; *commentariensis,* 236, 241, 249, 250;
ex commentariensibus, 250, 252
a copiis militaribus, 261
a cura amicorum, 140, 157
a cyato, 145
a diplomatibus, 259, 264n.
adiutor, 7, 35, 69, 101n., 103n., 119–21, 156, 157, 226, 227, 231–40, 242–3, 252, 253, 262–3
 tabulariorum, 103n., 140–1, 143, 153, 156, 206, 232n., 235, 239–40, 242, 249
 tabularius, 240
 tabul(arii), 240n.
 a commentariis, 103n., 140, 156, 206, 235n., 239–40
 procuratoris, 34, 231–6, 237, 262
adlectus, 69, 100, 101n., 157
adoption, 143–5, 153, 158–9, 171, 176, 254
aedituus, 6, 209
ab epistulis: head, 7, 259–66; department, 101n., 238, 255–6, 259, 262, 273
 ab epistulis Graecis: head, 253, 257n., 259–60, 264, 266; department, 150, 253, 254–5, 257
 ab epistulis Latinis: head, 33, 259–60, 262, 266; department, 69, 103n., 238, 253, 255, 257n.
aequator monetae, 116, 143
age at death, 30–4, 67–70, 99–100, 103–4, 105–7, 109, 115, 139, 141, 145, 149, 183–6, 190, 203, 208, 221, 225–6, 227, 235, 238–9, 241–2, 259, 269; years of married life, 105–7, 110, 225

 at manumission, 30, 33, 35, 68–9, 70, 86, 97–104, 123, 130–1, 136, 138, 184–6, 206, 219, 225–6, 285; early manumission, 68–9, 70, 97–104, 185, 193, 208, 285
 at marriage, 34, 86, 100, 105–11, 123, 182–4, 186, 190, 290–1; of husbands, 105–6, 108, 110, 183; of wives, 106–7, 108–9, 110, 182–3
agnomina, 23, 37n., 50n., 51, 71, 90–2, 109, 146, 158, 160, 199, 205, 212–23, 233, 234n., 250, 260
ab instrumentis, 118, 145
a iuvencis, 145
a libellis: head, 7, 259, 260n., 261, 263, 266; department, 253, 256, 262
a libris sacerdotalibus, 252–3
alumnus, 97, 144
a manu, 22n., 24n., 45n., 46, 120–1, 145–6, 209
a memoria: head, 82, 259, 264n., 276; department, 69, 100, 101n., 157, 252n., 253, 256–7
a muneribus, munerum, 274
ancilla, 97, 163, 168n., 175, 204n.
anuli aurei, 282, 288–9
ab ornamentis, ornamentorum, 34, 103n., 157, 231, 235
a pinacothecis, 231
a potione, 34
apparitor, 82n., 262n., 274–5, 277
aquarius, 5, 295, 300
a rationibus: head, 7, 26, 32, 33, 60, 167, 209n., 216, 222n., 236–8, 240, 259–66, 283–4, 286, 287–92; department, 7, 69, 101n., 103n., 209n., 216, 219n., 222n., 228, 238, 241, 244–5, 249, 253, 255–6, 257, 259, 262, 273, 276; *rationalium,* 249–50, 253, 255–6; *rationalis,* 264
arcarius, 55, 118–20, 122, 141, 145, 201–2, 218n., 241, 245–6, 250–2
archimagirus, 6, 158
archimimus, 82n.
architectus, 8, 82n.
argentarius, 7
a studiis, department, 253, 256
atriensis, 121, 174
Augustae libertus/servus, 63–6, 68, 70, 104, 113–14, 124, 126n., 147, 159, 172, 192, 208, 219
Augustorum libertus, 13, 58–72, 231, 236, 242, 244, 247, 249, 265, 271, 273–4, 276
Augustorum servus/verna, 58–72, 228, 242, 251
aurifex, 121

326

Index

a veste, vestiariae, 242, 262
a vinis, 227
a voluptatibus, voluptatum, 231, 253, 256–7, 273–4, 276

balnearius, 228
brick-stamps, 20, 29n., 41n.,55, 66, 75, 81, 91n., 218n.
brothers/sisters, 139–40, 145–7, 151, 157–9, 160, 176

caelator, 7
Caesariani, 26
capsarius, 222
Carthage, 18, 56, 80, 103–4, 114, 122, 172, 174, 217, 239
castellarius, 122
castrensis, 6, 32, 156, 228n., 242, 248n., 250, 270, 273, 274, 276, 300
children
   of Imperial freedmen, 101n., 137, 148–61; freeborn, 24n., 28n., 125, 149–51; slave-born, 34, 150–61; omission of status indication by, 148–53, 154, 159–60, 168
   of Imperial slaves, 80, 101n., 137–48; freeborn, 141, 143, 168; slave-born, 138–40, 141–3, 145–7, 168; omission of status indication by, 138–40, 142–3, 168; modification of status, see *Senatusconsultum Claudianum*
cocus, 146
cognomina, 84–6, 87–90; single name, as indication of slave status, 83, 113–14, 123, 138–40, 147, 180–1; *cognomina* in *-ianus*, 89–90, 213; *nomina* as *cognomina*, 89, 113, 118; second *cognomina*, 27, 213; of Greek derivation, 84–5, 88–90; of Latin derivation, 84–5, 89; *ingenua*, 87, 88–9, 194; *equestria*, 87–8, 282n.; change of *cognomen*, 87–8, 89
   of children: derived from father's, 122, 138–9, 142–3, 144, 145–6, 149–51, 153–4, 156–7; derived from mother's, 142–3, 144, 146, 149, 151, 156–7
coin legend, 49n.
collegia, 20, 55, 83, 208, 232, 236, 250, 299
'collégialité inégale', 233, 278n.; *see also* procurator, auxiliary
collibertus, 82, 84, 113, 159, 179, 181, 185, 187–8, 236–7
columbaria, 18, 22, 32, 46, 49, 50n., 63, 79–80, 103, 114, 122, 172, 174, 180, 221, 239n., 299
concubinage, 170–1, 194–5
conservus, 82, 116, 185
contrascriptor, 202, 235

contubernalis, 84, 100, 139, 171, 180, 210, 221
contubernium, 105, 108, 137, 144, 152, 153, 162, 171, 179, 210
conubium, 105, 162, 171, 179, 291–2
corporis custos, 44, 46, 52n., 83, 214n.
cubicularius, 7, 115, 121, 122, 229n., 283; *a cubiculo* 22n., 27n., 55, 66n., 82, 209, 229
curator, 83
'cursus', *see* promotion
custos, 6, 7, 115–16, 227

dated inscriptions, 20–3, 30–1, 32–4, 37, 43–5, 58–9, 75, 91n., 301–6
dating criteria: Imperial *nomina*, 3, 24–41, 51n., 55n., 56n., 58, 61, 122f., 150, 247, 250, 253–5; status indication, 43, 49–50, 51, 54–5, 58–60, 73–6, 77; *agnomina*, 90–2, 217
decurio, 228
dediticii, 1, 98
diaetarchus, dietarcha, 119–21
diaetarius, 101n.
dispensator, 7, 10, 22, 28, 52, 65n., 104, 115–22, 131, 141, 143, 146, 201–6, 210, 217, 218–19, 220, 224, 225–6, 230, 235, 239, 241, 245–6, 250, 251–2, 256, 262, 272, 276, 286, 295; *ex dispensatoribus*, 117, 145, 203n., 246, 252
dissignator, 82n.
duumvir, 49n.

equestrian officials, 23n., 231–4, 236–7, 251, 260–1, 264–6, 267–8, 277n., 279–81
equestrian status for Imperial freedmen, 171n., 282–4, 289–90
eunuchs, 7n., 111n.
exactor, 65, 202, 203n.

familia, 4–5, 54, 84, 95, 167, 172, 182–4, 191–2, 210, 212, 228, 299–300; *publica*, 300; *rustica*, 4–5; *urbana*, 4–5
Familia Caesaris, *passim*, esp. 2–10, 95–6, 299–300
family, 95, 300
figlinae, 6, 8
filiation, 42, 74, 195
fiscus, 6, 11, 89, 101, 165, 167–8, 178, 234, 262, 300
fiscus: Alexandrinus, 244–5, 272, 274; *Asiaticus* 245, 253, 257; *frumenti*, 153; *Gallicus*, 52, 201, 251–2; *libertatis et peculiorum*, 67, 99–100, 225, 244, 273, 276, 285; *fisci transmarini*, 244–5
fistulae, 8, 21, 26n., 38, 55, 75, 81, 263, 270, 275, 301f.
forma, 269, 272

327

Index

freedmen: general, 4; of *privati*, 36, 88, 124; see also status indication

geographical factors, including provincial centres, 7, 9, 18, 26n., 55, 57, 66, 78–80, 103–4, 112, 114–15, 118–19, 121, 133–6, 140–1, 173, 204–5, 226, 238–40, 243, 246, 267, 280–1
Germanus, see *corporis custos*
Greek inscriptions, 44, 53n., 54, 56, 72, 231–2, 244n., 247–8, 276–7

horrearius, 122
horti, 6

interpretes, 82n.
invitator, 35, 157

lapidarius, 8
Latini Iuniani, 1, 97–9, 165, 168, 185
lecticarius, 6, 228
legio III Augusta, 226, 244n.
legitimisation, 111, 144, 149, 151–3, 154n., 171, 176, 194–5
lex: Aelia Sentia, 86, 97–8, 104, 149, 163, 183–4, 186, 225; *Fufia Caninia*, 97; *Iulia*, 171, 293; *Iunia*, 97
libertus liberti, 31n., 35–6, 38, 99, 104, 207–11
librarius, 22n., 118
lictor, 66, 82n., 261–2

magister: officiorum, 257; *vicorum urbis*, 75
manumission, *passim*; joint manumission, 28, 44, 58–72; 'matrimonii causa', 97, 99, 100, 109, 176, 183, 185, 193, 210; 'pathetic' manumission, 98–9, 104; 'per interpositam personam', 208n.; 'vicario relicto', 205
marmorarius, 8
marriage, *passim*; second marriage, 102n., 110–11, 130–1n., 144, 145, 151, 153, 159, 254; widowhood, 110–11, 125; divorce, 111, 125
medicus, 82, 101n., 235n.; *auricularius*, 31
mensor agrarius, 115–16
ministrator, 119–20, 121, 122, 141, 160
mulio, 140, 146
municipal slaves, 165, 213–14

nomenclator, 7, 50n., 66, 82n., 101n., 154–5, 227, 253
nomina
Imperial freedmen, 3, 11, 24–41, 81–3, 85; irregular *nomina*, 30n., 35–7, 169; alternative *nomina*, 27, 28n.; double *nomina*, 27–8n., 44; abbreviation of, 24n., 40–1, 77–8; omission of, 3, 37–40, 73n., 113
freedmen of *Augustae*, 28–30, 126
of *privati*, omission of, 83
of wives, 39, 51n., 115, 123, 125–36; Imperial, 39–40, 109, 115–16, 117–18, 119–22, 125–33, 135, 141–3, 153–6; same *nomen* as husband, 129–30, 132; earlier *nomen*, 129, 130–3, 150, 154, 159; later *nomen*, 129, 130, 132; non-Imperial: 39, 86, 109, 115, 117–18, 119–22, 126, 128, 133–5, 142, 145–8, 153–7; omission of, 113, 139n.
of children, 39, 40, 141f.; same as father's, 148–9, 152–3, 172; same as mother's, 141, 143, 148, 150, 152–3; different from both father's and mother's, 40, 144, 151–2; omission of *nomen*, 143, 147
noster, n(ostri), see status indication
notarius, 115–16, 118
nummularius, 56n.

occupational nomenclature, 52–3, 61–2, 71–2, 76–7, 82, 150, 169
officinator, 8, 21, 56n.
οἰκονόμος, 53n., 59n., 72n., 202n.
optio, 227, 228
ordinarius, 200–5, 209, 219, 222
ordinatus, 75, 272
origins of Imperial slaves, 90n., 285, 286
ornamenta praetoria, quaestoria, 282
ornatrix, 102n.
Ostia, 18, 21, 61n., 245, 249
ostiarius, 121

paedagogus, 97, 119–20, 122, 209; *ex paedagogio*, 52
palaeography of inscriptions, 11, 26n.
Palatine bureaux, see *a rationibus, ab epistulis*, etc.; also 236–40, 242–5, 248, 252–7, 259–66, 272–3, 281
pantomimus, 27–8, 72, 101
papyri, 10, 20n.
parens, 117, 144–5
paternus, 63
patrimonium, 3–6, 46, 199, 202, 213, 270, 275, 279–81
patronage, 17, 219, 229, 232–3, 234, 269, 272, 282–3, 289, 293
patronus, 4, 98, 113, 163–4, 167–8, 179, 183–5, 187, 209; successive *patroni*, 61, 65n., 66–7, 68–72
peculiaris, 200n.
peculium, 95, 98–9, 104, 182, 200–1, 205, 210, 215
pedisequus, -a, 7, 59n., 115–16, 119–21, 202, 227–8

Index

peregrini, 43, 52n., 85
pistor candidarius, 208
pistrinus, 98
 potentia', 10, 36, 229
potestas, 43, 95, 205, 213, 299
praeceptor, 54, 82n.
praeco, 82n., 174n.
praefectus, 8, 38, 47; 'praefuit', 202, 225n., 278
praegustator, 6, 31, 229, 274
praenomen, see *nomina*; also 24n., 25, 41, 44, 47, 62, 143; omission of, 61, 76–8; 'Imp(eratoris)', 46–7
praepositus, 7n., 47, 82n., 153, 154, 228, 242, 262, 265–6n.
princeps tabularius, 242, 246, 248; ἀρχιταβλάριος, 244n., 247
procurator, 6, 7, 10, 26, 28, 31, 38, 61, 63, 64, 65n., 66, 67, 71, 72, 97, 99, 101, 157, 206, 210, 219, 224, 225, 229, 231–2, 243, 244, 256, 257, 260, 262, 264, 267–81, 282, 286; auxiliary procurators, 38, 75, 150, 231–4, 237n., 246, 248, 252, 253, 255–6, 257, 260n., 263–6, 267–81, 295; *ex procuratore*, 248; *procurator Augusti*, 264, 267–8n., 278; *procurator aquarum*, 21, 31–2, 270, 274–5; *procurator castrensis*, 6, 32, 270, 273, 274–5, 276
promotion, 205, 222, 224–30, 233, 235, 237, 239, 241–3, 244–58, 259–66, 267–81
'provincia' in occupational titles of Imperial freedmen and slaves, 55n., 232, 239–40, 245–52, 271, 273, 276–81
proximus, 7, 150, 224, 229, 245, 249–50, 252–8, 272–3, 276; *melloproximus*, 253, 256, 258; *proximus tabulariorum*, 241–3; *proximus commentariorum*, 241–3

quarry-marks, 20–1, 270, 303f.

ratio, 202, 251
 aquarum, aquariorum, 36n., 103n.
 beneficiorum, 103n.
 castrensis, see *castrensis*
 fisci frumenti, 153
 hereditatium, 50n., 231–2, 244, 253, 271–2, 273(?), 274–5, 276
 marmorum, 253, 257, 270, 273, 276
 patrimonii, 67, 118(?), 201, 241, 242–3, 247, 274–5
 purpurarum, 274
 XL Galliarum, 117, 249, 273
 IIII P(ublicorum) A(fricae), 268n., 273, 300
 sacrarum pecuniarum, 247
 summi choragii, 59n., 231, 235, 253, 273, 276
 thesaurorum, 244, 272

vectigalis Illyrici, 248
 XX hereditatium, 103n., 117–18, 141, 143, 228, 242, 246–8, 249n., 271, 275, 277n.
recruitment, 177–8, 199, 212–13, 215–23
res privata, 6n., 266
rogator, 209

sacra scrinia, 257–8
salary, 215, 229, 256, 272n.
sale of slaves, 138n., 144n., 146–7, 158, 183, 194
scriba unctorum, 82n.
Senatusconsultum Claudianum, 30n., 36–7, 61, 113, 147, 162–9, 177, 185, 188, 199
sepulcrales, 8, 17–18, 20, 22, 110–11, 114, 137, 172, 179–95
sevir Augustalis, 66, 158–9
signacula, 76
slaves, general, 4, 43n.; of *privati*, 90–2; *servi communes*, 51, 58–9, 62–72; *servi fiscales*, 10, 165, 299; *servi publici*, 125, 133, 165, 177, 213–15, 221–2; *servus liberti*, 200–2, 207–11; *servus servi*, see *vicarius*
speclariarius, 7
spurii, 165–6
statio, 202, 228n., 242, 253
statistical method, 3n., 106–7, 195
status indication
 Imperial freedmen, 2, 42–86; abbreviation of, 60, 72–5; position of, 24n., 76–8; omission of, 77, 80–3; extended forms of, 21–2, 38, 43–8; *Caesaris/Augusti*, 48–50, 56–7, 72–3; 'n(ostri)', 51, 56–7; *Augustorum/Augg.*, 57, 61, 68; *Auggg.*, 58–9; *eorum, eorundem*, 77; *lib/l(ib).*, 56, 73–5; different forms for individual freedmen, 25n., 50n., 60, 68, 72; irregular use of, 36
 Imperial slaves, 2, 42–86; abbreviation of, 72, 75–6, 78; position of, 52–3, 76; omission of, 81–3, 138–40, 142; extended forms of, 46, 48; *Caesaris/Augusti*, 50–4, 55–6, 72–3, 79–80; 'n(ostri)', 51, 54–6, 57, 71; *verna*, see *verna*; omission of 'ser./vern.', 52–3, 55, 76; *Augustorum/Caesarum*, 53, 55, 58–9; *Auggg.*, 60
 freedmen of *Augustae*, 47–8, 57, 77; freedmen of *privati*, 43, 59, 72, 74, 76, 81, 83; omission of status indication by *privati*, 83–6
 slaves of *Augustae*, 48; *servi publici*, 214; slaves of *privati*, 83
step-children, 139n., 144, 151, 158
structor, 8, 68, 101n., 140
subpraefectus, 31, 34, 71
subprocurator, 6, 225n.

329

Index

subsequens, 243
subvil(l)icus, 203n.
supernomina, 107, 118, 145, 231, 242n.
'superposition', 259, 278n., 281
sutor, 121

tabellarius, 7, 49, 82n., 115, 121, 142, 174n., 202, 227–9, 300; *ex tabellaris*, 227
tabularius, 7, 10, 36, 50n., 52n., 59n., 66, 67, 102, 103, 118(?), 140, 143–4n., 146, 153, 158, 201n., 202n., 206, 209, 216, 218, 222n., 224, 226, 227, 228n., 229, 230, 235n., 238, 239, 241–3, 244–5, 246–9, 250, 252, 256, 262, 276, 286; *a rationibus*, 7, 67, 244–5, 257, 272–3, 276; *ex tabulariis, ex tabulario*, 246, 248–9, 252; see also *princeps tabularius*
topiarius, 6
tractator, 71
tricliniarchus, 6, 229, 274
trierarchus, 32, 52, 82n., 83, 219n.

unctor, 228

veneria, 72, 175
verna, 49, 51–3, 54, 56, 71, 76, 78–80, 85, 130, 168, 177–8, 183, 199, 202n., 203, 204n., 207, 211, 213, 223, 274
viator, 262, 274–5
'vicarianus', 91, 104, 131, 199, 204, 206, 210, 212–23, 230, 235n., 250; 'vicariana', 220, 221–2
vicarius, 1, 7, 10, 117–18, 141, 144n., 146, 177, 199, 200–6, 207, 209, 211, 218–19, 220–2, 223, 230, 235, 240, 249n., 252, 295, 307; *vicaria*, 203–4, 210–11; *vicarii vicarius*, 201n., 218n.; οὐικάριος, 203n.; *vices agens*, 200; *ex vicario*, 222n., 248

victimarius, 141
vilicus, 5, 52n., 117–20, 122, 143, 144n., 145, 201–2, 205, 210n., 252, 299, 300
v(ir) e(gregius), 265, 283

wives
  of Imperial freedmen, 109, 112, 122–36, 307–12; freeborn, 24n., 123–4, 128, 130–6, 148–53, 156–7, 162, 173–4, 232, 290f.; slave-born, 108–9, 113, 123–4, 130, 132, 134, 148–56; *incertae*, 112, 123–4, 155
  of Imperial slaves, 80, 109, 112–22, 128, 204, 228, 307–12; freeborn, 36–7, 113–18, 122, 128, 133–5, 140–8, 162–9, 199, 204; slave-born, 108–9, 113–14, 115–18, 119, 122, 128, 133, 138–40, 141–3, 146–7, 204; *incertae*, 112, 114
  of *vicarii*, 204; of '*vicariani*', 220–2; of *lib. liberti*, 210; of *servi publici*, 215
women, *passim*; see esp. 170–8
  servae Caesaris, 70, 123, 125, 130, 134, 138f., 163, 166, 168n., 173, 204; marriage pattern, 174–6; children of, 176–7; occupations, 177
  libertae Augusti, 39, 70, 101n., 102, 128, 131, 159–60, 166–7, 170, 172, 204; marriage pattern, 174–6; omission of status indication, 160, 173, 177; children of, 176–7; occupations, 177
  outside Fam. Caes., 179–95; *servae*, 175–6, 180–2, 183–6, 187–94; *libertae*, 121, 123–4, 125, 128, 130, 159, 163–5, 170, 175–6, 180–2, 183–4, 187–94; *ingenuae*, 162–9, 182, 185, 187–92, 194, 215, 220–1; *incertae*, 187–92; *lib. libertae*, 70, 99–100, 170, 172, 208, 209–11, 222; see also *vicaria*, 'vicariana'
  proportion in population, 172, 177, 203